350

c6676

D0296430

331.11

331.024

MANPOWER RESEARCH

MANPOWER RESEARCH

The proceedings of a conference held under the aegis of the
NATO Scientific Affairs Committee in London from 14th–18th August, 1967

Edited by: N. A. B. Wilson

THE ENGLISH UNIVERSITIES PRESS LTD
ST. PAUL'S HOUSE   WARWICK LANE
LONDON E.C.4

138

First printed 1969

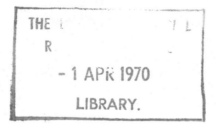

SBN 340 05263 5

*Printed in Great Britain for The English Universities Press Limited
at the Pitman Press, Bath*

CONTENTS

FOREWORD

In planning the 1967 NATO conference on manpower research, we aimed at a systematic and comprehensive account of research into the structure and working of manpower systems. We wanted to deal with as many as possible of the interactions which make such systems complex. Not least, we sought to consider their dynamics, so that improvements might become possible in forecasting, planning, changing course, and achieving desired objectives. Everything was designed, implicitly, to lead up to the ultimate problem of social science, the problem of social preference and social choice.

A defence context was used, partly because NATO is a defensive alliance, but mainly because some of the best authorities had been working partly or even wholly in that context. But it will be evident to the reader that, so far as research is concerned, there are no essential differences between military and civilian industrial manpower problems; there are only differences of level at which resources have to be allocated, forecasts made, humans energised and satisfied, environmental pressures dealt with and desirable changes attempted. One of the more basic problems concerns allocation *between* military and civilian effort: how much will an affluent society decide to "afford" for defence and other expenditures respectively? Not every element in such a problem is researchable, but research can solve some parts and clarify others, so that final decisions are likely to be more informed and satisfying.

As conference director, I was able to invite experts from a dozen of the fifteen NATO nations: demographers, econometricians, applied mathematicians, operational researchers, occupational and other social psychologists, psychiatrists, sociologists, business men, officers of the armed forces, and others. The contributions they made have been put together with an absolute minimum of editing. This means a long and diverse book but one which seems to me to go a substantial way towards achieving the aims with which we started.

I have many debts of gratitude and can only acknowledge the most prominent of them here: first of all to my contributors who have given so freely of their skills and experience; to the Science Committee and Scientific Affairs Division of NATO who provided a basic budget; to Dr. Richard Trumbull of the Office of Naval Research, Washington, to Mr. A. R. Smith now of the Civil Service Department, London, and to Professor Roger W. Little of the University of Chicago, for mobilising most of the contributors to the conference and to this volume; to the United Kingdom government through the office and staff of the Permanent Under Secretary of State for Defence for official facilities and entertainment; not least to the British Petroleum Company Limited for both papers and entertainment.

I conclude with an important disclaimer. None of the papers has any official status; all the authors write in a purely personal capacity and in no wise commit the organisations with which they are or have been connected.

N. A. B. WILSON
Conference Director, and lately
Chairman, NATO Advisory Group
on Human Factors.

PART I MANPOWER PLANNING

An Introduction

A.R. SMITH

MINISTRY OF DEFENCE, LONDON

INTRODUCTION

This Conference has been given a compact label, Manpower Research in the Defence Context, which is intended to cover a vast range of concepts and aspects of manpower, all inter-connected one with another in a large multi-dimensional system. The aim in this introductory paper is to draw attention to one or two aspects in such a way as to identify the relevance of papers which follow. Putting it in terms of a picturesque and convenient jargon, I am going to make one or two quick slices through the multi-dimensional space which is our system of ideas, and describe some essential characteristics of certain sub-systems which lie on different but inter-connecting planes.

I. THE RELATIONSHIP BETWEEN MANPOWER RESEARCH, PLANNING AND MANAGEMENT

Manpower planning, whether it is applied on the broad scale of national or macro-economic plans, or on a micro-scale as in the meticulous attention to detail which is given to the planning of the careers of a small number of people, is inseparable from, and in some respects indistinguishable from, research. The planning process needs to be at every stage an application of scientific methods. It involves the empirical deriva-tion of relationships; the formulation, testing and modification of hypotheses; the constant search for explanations of phenomena and measures of their importance in terms of quantitative functional relationships which can be used as the basis of forecasting – and so on. The planning process, meaningfully carried out, is in fact research and applied science. If planning is not so regarded – if, for example, it is regarded merely as the routine application of a rule-book – then it may very quickly degenerate into an uncomprehended and useless ritual. Manpower planning must involve a very substantial element of research, and constant modification to meet changing circumstances and new knowledge.

Planning is of course to a very considerable extent a matter of forecasting or attempted prediction. But unlike forecasting in the natural sciences, manpower fore-casting is dealing with a raw material whose statistical behaviour is determined by an immensely large range of complex factors, not least amongst which are the social and economic policies of Governments and employers. It follows that planning cannot sensibly be divorced from policy formulation. Planning helps to determine policies, and the policies adopted by Government or management are essential factors in planning.

Looked at from a slightly different viewpoint the purpose of planning, put most briefly in trite and generalized form, is to obtain the best-possible utilization of human resources. But virtually all the variables and parameters which go into the equation of manpower supply and demand are potentially capable of being modified by research or policy-variation. For example, people who would otherwise be outside the labour force because of advanced age might be brought within it by a change in

Government or management policy in respect of retirement; or by medical research which
" prolongs active life "; or by technical advances which make work more suitable for
elderly people. To take another example, either changes in education policy, or
advances in socio-medical research designed to help handicapped people, or advances in
the application of training research might change the quality of manpower and hence the
supply. In short, both policies and research can influence the validity of planning; and
planning processes, by locating potential trouble-spots in the supply-demand relationships, can in turn point to the targets on which research effort needs to be concentrated,
or management attitudes modified. Policies, planning and research cannot be separated
one from another without serious risk of sub-optimization. This is our first hypothesis
or contention.

2. DEFENCE MANPOWER AS A SUB-SYSTEM OF THE NATIONAL ECONOMY

I turn now to my second slice through space. My purpose in this second section is to
emphasize the relationship between manpower planning for the very large socio-economic
system which is usually the nation, and manpower planning for the small sub-system which
may be an industry, or a large firm, or a region, or in the case with which we are
primarily concerned, the Armed Forces.

The Armed Forces draw their intakes of manpower from the national manpower system
(if we exclude from consideration mercenary or dependency forces), and they do so
usually by taking a very substantial proportion from a particular and not very extensive
age-group. They retain them on average for comparatively few years, and return them to
the civil sector of the economy often with qualities or qualifications different from
those which they had at entry to the Forces. Where these circumstances apply, any
significant variation in the quantitative or qualitative demand for manpower which the
defence sub-system imposes on the national system can have important consequences for
the rest of the economy. Equally, any significant variation in the flow of manpower into
the age-band for recruitment to the Forces may have important consequences both for the
economy and for the manning of the Forces. Further, any considerable change in the
methods and the extent of technical training in the Forces may have important consequences for the supply of technically-trained manpower to industry.

The conclusions which I suggest we should draw from this reasoning are that manpower
planning in the defence context cannot be adequately carried out without fairly detailed
reference to the national circumstances, and equally that national manpower planning is
most unlikely to be valid unless it takes account of likely developments in the various
relevant aspects of defence manpower policies. Similar arguments may be applied in
respect of each of the many other logical sub-systems of the economy. I include here not
only the employed manpower in industry and the public services, but also the large sub-
system which is often over-looked, that is, the sub-system made up of the young people
in various stages of education and pre-employment training.

3. A COMPARISON BETWEEN THE ARMED FORCES AND INDUSTRY

There are important differences between the characteristics of the Armed Forces
manpower structures and those found in industry in countries which have political
systems not too dissimiliar from those of the United Kingdom. For example, men in the
Armed Forces of most countries cannot exert pressure by association on management to
have their pay and prospects improved. Hence defence manpower management might be said
to have a moral responsibility to inject into the planning procedures considerations
which substitute for the missing trades-union pressures. Taking another example, an
accelerating rate of technological change may have a devastating effect on training
costs in both Armed Forces and industry, but the effect may be quite different in kind.
In high-turnover Armed Forces the effect may be primarily to change the nature and
timing of recruit and normal career training, but in Industry it may create serious

4

problems of mobility between trades, firms, industries and locations with all the consequent problems of redundancy, re-training and re-housing. Government intervention may well be needed to identify and provide the social and economic wherewithal to induce the necessary mobility without either coercion or vast waste of resources.

Despite these differences, however, there is a large area of common ground between the Armed Forces and Industry so far as manpower planning and research are concerned. For example, the forecasting techniques are in most cases essentially similar. And to return to an earlier point, both depend for success upon adequate information about national trends and policies. There is probably a great deal to be gained in Armed Forces' management, in Industry, and indeed in all agencies engaged in manpower planning and research, from a continuing exchange of ideas, methods, and information generally.

CONCLUSIONS

To sum up, my belief is that:-

First: manpower planning, manpower research, manpower management and manpower policy-formulation are best regarded as inter-dependent aspects of one process.

Second: national manpower planning and planning of the manpower sub-systems of the economy, of which defence is one, are also best regarded as inter-dependent aspects of one process.

Third: Armed Forces' manpower planning and Industrial manpower planning, despite differences between the structures, have a great deal of common ground and should learn from each other.

La Prévision de L' Emploi en France

JEAN FOURASTIÉ

(INTRODUCTION PAR V. BRIJATOFF)

INTRODUCTION

C'est un redoutable honneur pour moi que de remplacer le Pr. Fourastié, qui regrette vivement de ne pouvoir être aujourd'hui dans cette salle. Avant de parler de la prévision de l'emploi en France, je pense qu'il n'est pas inutile de rappeler très brièvement les données et les objectifs du 5è Plan Français en cours d'application et qui doit s'achever en 1970.

I. LES DONNÉES DU 5è PLAN

(i) La population active

De l'ordre de 49 millions la population totale de la France doit dépasser les 51 millions en 1970. Mais la population active ne suivra pas cette augmentation. De 20.1 millions en 1965, elle ne doit passer qu'à 20.7 millions en 1970 soit une croissance de 0.6% par an pour la période considérée. Ceci peut sembler très faible mais représente un progrès par rapport à la période couverte par les deux derniers recensements (1954 et 1962) où la population active totale n'a pas varié. La stabilité relative de la population active et la croissance de la population totale implique donc la nécessité d'accroître la productivité.

(ii) L'urbanisation

La croissance des villes sera plus rapide que celle de la population totale. En gros on prévoit que la population urbaine va doubler dans les 20 ans à venir ce qui implique un vaste programme pour modifier les structures actuelles et s'adapter progressivement a la nouvelle situation.

(iii) L'ouverture des frontières

Le Plan part de l'hypothèse de la réalisation complète de Marché Commun mais souligne plus les difficultés qui nous attendent encore que les bénéfices que nous pourrons en retirer. C'est ainsi que le taux général de 5% d'expansion retenu tient plus compte des limites économiques d'expansion que des limites physiques des possibilités françaises. De toute façon le Plan insiste sur la libéralisation des échanges et sur les problèmes de la concurrence que cela impliquera.

C'est dans cette optique concurrentielle qu'il faut juger les options prises pour réaliser l'expansion.

2. LES OBJECTIFS DU 5è PLAN

Il ne faut pas oublier que le Plan n'est pas seulement un instrument de prévision, mais qu'il permet aussi d'orienter le développement économique suivant certaines priorités. Au probable il ajoute également le souhaitable. Dans quoi s'exprime ce souhaitable?

(i) Développer l'innovation scientifique et technique

Pour cela le 5è Plan vise à préparer des "actions concertées" entre administrations, universités et entreprises. Il insiste sur le développement nécessaire de la recherche de tous ordres: fondamentale, appliquée et recherche-développement, ce qui conduira la France à y consacrer en 1970, 2.5% de son Produit National Brut contre 1.7% en 1963.

(ii) Développer la formation des hommes et pratiquer une politique active de l'emploi

On assiste actuellement à des efforts de "déspecialisation" de l'enseignement technique, à des actions de formation assurées par l'Education Nationale et d'autres, d'adaptation et de perfectionnement à la charge des entreprises et professions. La promotion sociale reste au centre des préoccupations du Plan étant donné que l'appareil scolaire et universitaire sera insuffisant pour satisfaire aux besoins de personnels qualifiés de 1970. Si l'on ajoute à cela les transformations importantes de la structure de l'emploi qui accompagnent la croissance économique on comprend que l'un des objectifs d'une politique active de l'emploi soit d'augmenter d'une part la "transparence" du marché du travail (c'est a dire la capacité de bien s'orienter dans le choix d'un métier ou d'un poste de travail) et d'autre part sa fluidité.

(iii) Promouvoir une politique d'exportation plus efficace

Ici les objectifs sont assez ambitieux puisqu'ils fixent un accroissement de 10% par an, mais s'expliquent par le désir de la France d'avoir une balance des paiements équilibrée et de passer d'une position importatrice à celle, exportatrice, de capitaux.

(iv) Investir d'avantage et developper l'épargne

On constate que l'industrie française est comparativement moins developpée que celle des grands pays industriels. Elle n'est pas assez spécialisée au niveau des branches ni assez polyvalente au niveau des firmes. Il devient donc primordial d'accroître les investissements productifs qui devraient s'élever à 53 milliards de Francs pour la période 1965–1970.

(v) Les problemes de Défense Nationale

Il convient de souligner qu'une loi-programme militaire a été votée avant l'élaboration du 5è Plan et qu'elle a été fournie comme dounée obligatoire aux experts travaillant pour le Plan. Cela signifie que du point de vue d'articulation une modification en hausse ou en baisse des dépenses de la Défense risque d'avoir de sérieuses repercussions sur la réalisation du plan. En fait il est prévu que les dépenses militaires varieront grosso modo comme l'indice de la production. Au point de vue des effectifs il a été prévu que le contingent passerait (en milliers) de 310 en 1954; 510 en 1962 et 290 en 1965 à 245 en 1970. (Pour les mêmes dates les chiffres des militaires de carrière hors métropole sont de 125, 120, 45 et 25.

C'est dans ce contexte, fortement teinté sur le plan économique par le fait que la France soit entrée sans possibilité de retour dans la competition internationale, que doit être replacé l'exposé du Prof. Fourastie.

LA PROVISION DE L'EMPLOI EN FRANCE

Dès la création du Commissariat du Plan, en janvier 1946, une Commission fut constituée pour l'étude des problèmes de main-d'oeuvre; elle fut renouvelée par décret, lors des trois plans suivants. Son rôle fut avant tout de déterminer les besoins de main-d'oeuvre nécessaires à la réalisation des objectifs de production fixés par le

Plan, et de suggérer les moyens capables de satisfaire ces besoins. Mais, à mesure que les travaux de la Commission se sont déroulés, celle-ci prit conscience d'une tâche beaucoup plus vaste. Aujourd'hui, tout en conservant son premier objectif, la Commission de la main-d'œuvre a pour mission de veiller au plein emploi dans la Nation ; elle a mis sur pied des techniques de prévision de l'emploi qui font partie intégrante des calculs économiques de la planification économique française.

Cette Commission, appelée "Commission de la main-d'œuvre", mais qui serait mieux nommée "Commission de la population active et de l'emploi", groupe des représentants des ministères (Travail – Santé publique et population – Affaires économiques – Agriculture – Industrie et commerce – Education nationale), des membres des syndicats de salariés et de chefs d'entreprises, des services statistiques officiels (Institut national de statistique (I.N.S.E.E.) – Institut national d'études démographiques – bureau universitaire de statistique).

Lors du premier Plan (1946–1950), les travaux de prévision de l'emploi, d'un caractère tout à fait nouveau et pour lesquels, par conséquent, aucune méthode n'avait été mise au point, étaient rendus plus difficiles encore par l'absence à peu près totale de données numériques récentes. En outre, un délai de six mois seulement était fixé pour l'exécution de ces travaux et la présentation des conclusions. Ces raisons expliquent le caractère succinct du premier rapport de la Commission de la main-d'oeuvre, fixant les objectifs de l'emploi pour 1950. On doit toutefois signaler que c'est dans le sein de cette première Commission que fut étudié, pour la première fois en France, le problème de la productivité du travail et des moyens propres à développer cette productivité.

Le travail exécuté par la deuxième Commission (créée en avril 1953) a été beaucoup plus vaste et plus détaillé. La Commission s'est basée principalement, pour dresser ses prévisions, sur les évaluations faites par les diverses Commissions verticales spécialisées dans l'étude d'un secteur déterminé. Mais c'est surtout lors du IIIe Plan (1956–1961) que la Commission de la main-d'œuvre a précisé et perfectionné ses méthodes. La prévision comporte maintenant deux processus : une méthode globale qui détermine des objectifs généraux et une méthode analytique permettant des prévisions plus détaillées.

La Commission de la main-d'œuvre a donc deux tâches essentielles : collecter les prévisions d'emploi faites par les Commissions verticales et veiller à ce qu'elles soient homogènes au point de vue des méthodes et ne présentent ni double emploi, ni lacune ; vérifier que le total des prévisions ainsi faites coincide avec la population active globale, afin d'éviter aussi bien le sous-emploi que le manque de main-d'oeuvre.

Parallèlement, en 1953, une procédure de prévision à court terme et de révision permanente fut établie afin de combler les intervalles des prévisions à moyen terme et de conserver un contact annuel entre toutes les personnes ayant un rôle à jouer dans ce domaine. Ainsi fut constitué un groupe de travail chargé de mettre en commun, chaque année, les prévisions économiques élaborées par les différents services compétents, et d'en examiner, industrie par industrie, les conséquences sur l'emploi.

I. LES PRINCIPES DE LA PRÉVISION DE L'EMPLOI

La prévision de l'emploi ne saurait se faire en dehors d'un cadre plus vaste de prévision économique. En effet équilibre économique est pratiquement synonyme d'équilibre entre production et consommation. Il s'agit non de consommer ce que l'on a produit, mais de produire ce que la population désire consommer. Il faut donc adapter la production à la demande de la consommation et cette adaptation ne peut se faire que par la population active qui, en se déplaçant d'une activité vers une autre, permet de modifier la structure de la production. Finalement, pour déterminer l'orientation souhaitable de la main-d'œuvre, il faut connaître la structure souhaitée de la production, connaissance qui suppose une prévision de la consommation.

Or, ces grandeurs (production et consommation) sont toutes deux soumises – mais plus ou moins directement et indépendamment l'une de l'autre – à l'influence du progrès technique. Il n'est pas nécessaire de développer ici les effets directs du progrès technique sur la production. Ils sont assez évidents : découverte de nouvelles matières premières, de nouvelles formes d'énergie, de nouvelles machines ou de nouvelles techniques de travail, permettant d'accroître la *productivité*, c'est-à-dire le volume de la production par travailleur et par unité de temps. Sur la consommation, les effets du progrès technique sont non moins certains. En effet, l'augmentation du volume et de la valeur de la production par travailleur permet une augmentation des salaires et des revenus. Or, toute variation des revenus se traduit par une modification de la consommation.

Par ailleurs, une forte augmentation de productivité peut entraîner une réduction relative des coûts de production et, par conséquent, des prix de vente d'un produit déterminé, et modifier ainsi le comportement des consommateurs à l'égard de ce produit.

La productivité n'agit pas de la même façon, ni selon le même rythme, sur chacun des secteurs de la production et, de même, l'élévation du pouvoir d'achat ne favorise ou ne défavorise pas de la même manière, ni selon le même rythme, chacun des secteurs de la consommation. Il en résulte normalement des *distorsions* importantes, pour un produit déterminé, *entre les tendances de la production modifiée par le progrès technique et les tendances de la consommation modifiée par l'élévation du niveau de vie*. Il faut donc sans cesse réorienter la production en fonction des demandes de la consommation et cela ne peut se faire que si la main-d'oeuvre se déplace.

Les composantes fondamentales de la prévision de l'emploi sont donc : 1°) La prévision de la population qui détermine le volume et la structure de la main-d'oeuvre disponible ; 2°) Le progrès technique et 3°) La consommation. Le commerce extérieur, les investissements, les prix, interviennent également, mais en seconde ligne, afin de modifier ou de préciser les perspectives faites à partir de la consommation et de la productivité. Cependant il est clair que, pour un espace économique de faible dimension géographique, comme la Belgique, les Pays-Bas, le commerce extérieur peut, pour certains secteurs prendre un poids prépondérant ; ce facteur peut alors non seulement rendre plus incertaine la prévision de l'emploi, mais encore, à la limite, la rendre illusoire.

2. LES TECHNIQUES FRANCAISES DE PRÉVISION D'EMPLOI

La prévision de l'emploi comporte quatre phases:

- une prévision globale permettant de déterminer les *disponibilités* totales de main-d'oeuvre ;
- une prévision *par secteur*, recherchant la répartition souhaitable de la population active, selon les secteurs d'activité (agriculture, mines, métallurgie, textile, etc, etc...) afin d'adapter la production à la consommation et de susciter le plus fort accroissement possible du revenu national;
- une prévision *par qualification*, la plus difficile, mais sans doute la plus utile, puisqu'elle permet d'orienter utilement l'enseignement et la formation professionnelle en fonction des besoins futurs;
- enfin, une prévision *par région géographique* qui conduit souvent à une action volontairement différenciée des pouvoirs publics pour implanter les entreprises, ou au contraire, freiner les accumulations urbaines.

2.1. Prévision de la population active totale

Elle est relativement simple. La population qui sera en âge de travailler dans 5, 10 ou 15 ans est déjà née ; les prévisions démographiques des personnes en âge d'activité sont donc assez sûres ; il suffit de faire des hypothèses sur l'évolution de la mortalité, et il est difficile de faire de graves erreurs en ce domaine, car la mortalité varie assez lentement. Il suffit ensuite d'appliquer un taux d'activité à ces perspectives de population par âge. Ces taux sont pratiquement constants entre 25 et 60 ans ; on suppose donc qu'ils se maintiendront ainsi. En ce qui concerne les moins de 25 ans, et les plus

de 60 ans, certaines hypothèses sont nécessaires pour tenir compte de l'allongement de
la scolarité d'une part ; de la possibilité d'une mise à la retraite plus précoce ou au
contraire d'une prolongation spontanée de la vie active, d'autre part.

De même, il est généralement nécessaire de faire des hypothèses sur l'évolution de
l'activité féminine, moins stable que l'activité masculine, car dépendant plus directement de facteurs économiques, culturels, sociaux, familiaux. Les hypothèses en ce
domaine sont plus délicates, l'évolution de chacun de ces facteurs étant plus difficile
à prévoir.

Enfin, la détermination des disponibilités globales de main-d'oeuvre fait aussi
intervenir des hypothèses sur les mouvements migratoires. Ces hypothèses sont fonction
des tendances observées dans les années passées, de l'importance du déséquilibre qui
peut apparaître entre les besoins et les disponibilités de main-d'oeuvre ; enfin des
possibilités réelles d'immigration.

Finalement, l'ordre de grandeur des erreurs faites sur ces évaluations de main-
d'oeuvre globale est faible et reste certainement inférieur à celui que l'on est bien
obligé d'accepter sur l'évaluation des phénomènes économiques, ainsi que le feront
apparaître les prévisions analytiques.

2.2. Prévisions par secteur

C'est ici que l'on distingue les deux méthodes reconnues plus haut.

(i) Méthode globale déterminant le sens général de l'évolution

Cette prévision est faite par le Commissariat du Plan et de la Productivité, en
collaboration avec l'Institut National de la statistique et avec la Direction de la
Prévision du Ministère des finances. Il s'agit en effet d'abord d'un travail de
comptabilité nationale ayant pour but de déterminer le revenu national, la production
nationale et la demande finale dans le cadre de la détermination de la population totale et de la population active définie dans le premier paragraphe.

La population active est alors répartie en sept grands secteurs d'activité :
Agriculture – Industrie – Transports – Commerce – Services – Services domestiques –
Administration. Cette estimation est faite globalement par la prolongation des tendances
observées dans le passé ou selon les tendances de pays techniquement plus avancés. La
contribution de chacun des secteurs au produit intérieur brut est ensuite estimée en
multipliant les effectifs au travail par leur productivité étant ici comprise dans le
sens de valeur ajoutée par travailleur et par an, compte tenu de l'augmentation moyenne
de productivité observée les années précédentes en France ou dans divers autres pays et
de la mise en place de nouvelles techniques. Plusieurs hypothèses se sont avancées pour
les années à venir.

Ces hypothèses permettent d'évaluer la production par secteur d'où l'on déduit, par
sommation, la valeur du produit national. Il faut ensuite rechercher quelle sera
l'utilisation de ce produit national et, en particulier, ce que seront la valeur et la
structure de la consommation des ménages, afin de vérifier que la répartition de la
population active estimée en début d'étude permet de satisfaire cette demande des
consommateurs.

La valeur de la consommation des ménages, est obtenue par différence entre le produit
intérieur et les autre "consommations" : administrations, investissements et solde du
commerce extérieur. L'évaluation de chacune de ces grandeurs nécessite, bien entendu,
un certain nombre d'hypothèses.

La demande finale des ménages ainsi estimée est ensuite décomposée par nature du
produit – en 10 postes. Cette décomposition est obtenue en appliquant des coefficients
d'élasticité, exprimant la variation relative de la demande des divers biens et services
en fonction de celle de la dépense globale de consommation. Ces élasticités sont
d'ailleurs variables selon le groupe socio-professionnel des consommateurs, dont il faut
donc tenir compte (exploitants et ouvriers agricoles ; travailleurs indépendants ; cadres
supérieurs, autres salariés non actifs.)

Les tableaux d'échange inter-industriels permettent de passer de la demande finale par produit à la production nécessaire dans chaque secteur. Enfin, il faut vérifier que l'évolution des productions ainsi évaluées est cohérente avec celle des valeurs ajoutées (ou produit intérieur brut) par secteur. S'il n'y a pas cohérence, il y a lieu de revenir sur les hypothèses de départ, relatives à la répartition de la population active selon les secteurs. Ainsi, par approximations successives, on parvient à une certaine évaluation de la main-d'oeuvre et de la production par secteur.

Ces perspectives globales par secteur servent ensuite d'objectif aux études analytiques des Commissions du Plan spécialisées dans l'étude de chacun des secteurs.

(ii) Méthode analytique

Le principe de la méthode analytique est d'étudier séparément l'évolution de chacun des facteurs influant sur la production : productivité, consommation, commerce extérieur, etc. ; la combinaison de tous ces facteurs permet ensuite de déterminer l'emploi souhaitable dans chaque secteur d'activité.

Chacune des Commissions du Plan, spécialisées dans l'étude d'un secteur particulier doit, dans le cadre des perspectives générales d'expansion de l'économie précédemment évaluée, déterminer l'objectif de production et d'accroissement de productivité, dans son propre secteur, et les moyens nécessaires pour atteindre cet objectif : main-d'oeuvre, investissements, moyens de financement, etc. Collaborent à ce travail, dans des "groupes de travail" créés, au sein des Commissions, des agriculteurs, des industriels, des commerçants, des artisans, des ouvriers, des cadres, des syndicalistes, des économistes, des financiers, toutes personnes choisies par le président de chaque Commission, en raison de leur compétence dans le secteur étudié.

Il ne s'agit pas d'extrapoler les tendances de l'emploi, mais d'étudier les besoins de main-d'oeuvre en fonction du progrès technique et d'un accroissement donné de la production. Les documents dont disposent les Commissions pour effectuer ce travail sont assez restreints ; ils concernent l'évolution de la production et de l'emploi depuis quelques années ; la durée du travail et l'utilisation des capacités actuelles de production ; l'essentiel de la documentation est constitué par les connaissances concrètes que les membres des groupes de travail ont personnellement acquises dans l'exercice de leur profession. A partir de ces connaissances des réalités, les Commissions doivent élaborer des programmes englobant l'accroissement de la capacité de production, la productivité, l'emploi, les moyens de financement, etc. Elles sont invitées à répondre à des questions sans cesse plus précises, relatives à la qualification, à la fonction, au niveau culturel de la main-d'oeuvre.

Pour certains secteurs, tels que l'agriculture et le commerce, où les mouvements de main-d'oeuvre sont liés d'une façon moins étroite aux fluctuations de la production, les méthodes employées sont différentes. En ce qui concerne l'agriculture, par exemple, les chiffres résultant de la prolongation des tendances antérieurement observées sont modifiés pour tenir compte d'éléments nouveaux, tels que la prolongation de la scolarité, la mise en place de systèmes de retraite agricole. On a ainsi été amené à donner un chiffre annuel moyen de diminution de la population active agricole (80.000 personnes par an entre 1966 et 1971).

La Commission de la main-d'oeuvre rassemble ensuite les prévisions en matière d'emploi effectuées par chacune des Commissions verticales et fait, en outre, des hypothèses sur l'évolution des secteurs qui ne sont étudiés par aucune commission spécialisée (Services – administrations). Enfin, la Commission de la main-d'oeuvre doit vérifier que l'ensemble des prévisions ainsi faites coïncide bien avec les objectifs généraux fixés en début d'étude. S'il y a des écarts entre le total des besoins de main-d'oeuvre exprimés par les commissions et les disponibilités définies par les perspectives démographiques, le Commissaire général au Plan est saisi du problème et les Commissions sont priées de réviser leurs objectifs ou leurs hypothèses, afin d'utiliser une main-d'oeuvre plus importante, ou moins importante, selon des disponibilités.

2.3. Prévisions par qualification

C'est une phase importante de la prévision de l'emploi car elle permet d'orienter utilement l'enseignement et la formation professionnelle des jeunes. Mais c'est également la plus délicate. C'est pourquoi elle ne fut abordée pour la première fois qu'en 1960, une sous-commission ayant alors été chargée d'étudier les perspectives d'évolution des qualifications pour l'ensemble de la population active française.

L'échéance d'un plan (4 ou 5 ans) est trop courte pour de telles prévisions. En effet la formation des cadres nécessaires à l'économie ou des professeurs susceptibles d'enseigner ces cadres requiert largement plus de 5 ans. La sous-Commission des qualifications doit donc délibérément dépasser les délais du Plan et prolonger ses prévisions jusqu'à 10 ou 15 années.

La principale difficulté de ce travail réside en la rareté des statistiques dans ce domaine. Les seuls renseignements utilisables, bien que partiels sont ceux obtenus par des enquêtes effectuées juridiquement par le Ministère du travail. Ces enquêtes donnent pour quinze branches industrielles et six branches du secteur tertiaire la répartition des salariés selon les catégories suivantes :

Cadres et techniciens

- Cadres administratifs et commerciaux
- Ingénieurs
- Techniciens et dessinateurs
- Contremaîtres

Employés

Ouvriers

- Ouvriers qualifiés
- Ouvriers spécialisés
- Manoeuvres.

Mais ces résultats ne concernent que les établissements occupant plus de 10 salariés. Ils sont donc plus ou moins représentatifs suivant chaque branche, en particulier dans le domaine des services.

La sous-Commission doit ensuite traduire en terme de durée d'enseignement et autant que possible de catégorie d'enseignement (littéraire, scientifique, technique, commercial) les perspectives de qualifications. Une bonne étude sur les méthodes françaises de prévision des besoins en personnel qualifié, a été effectuée à la demande de l'OCDE, en juillet 1966, par M.A. Page [1], on se reportera utilement à ce document.

Les prévisions sont sans cesse révisées. On trouvera en annexe l'état actuel des prévisions 1975.

2.4. Prévisions régionales

Le but essentiel de ces prévisions est de mettre en évidence les zones de la dépression économique requérant une politique particulière. Ces prévisions ont été mises en oeuvre seulement à partier de 1960. On trouvera des renseignements sur ces prévisions dans le rapport de la Commission de la main-d'oeuvre pour le 5eme Plan.

Les pages qui suivent, extraites du *Rapport général de la Commission de la main-d'oeuvre pour le 5eme Plan* [2] donnent un aperçu des prévisions d'emploi par qualification pour 1978 et des méthodes de réflexion que ces ces réflexions impliquent.

---

[1] "L'Adaptation de l'offre de personnel scientifique et technique de haute qualification aux besoins de l'économie : l'experience française et les progrès possibles de l'information", Organisation de coopération et de développement économique, Paris, Juillet 1966, DAS/EID/66.50, 95 pages.

[2] Commissariat Général au Plan, *Rapport général de la Commission de la main-d'oeuvre,* 5è Plan, (Edité par la revue française du travail), mars 1966, 423 pages.

12

Les prévisions finales de la répartition de l'emploi par professions en 1970 et 1978 peuvent s'apprécier à la fois par rapport à la période passée et par rapport à l'évolution récente de l'emploi dans un pays techniquement plus avancé.

(i) Comparaison avec la période 1954-1962

A. Les prévisions impliquent les modifications rapides de la structure de l'emploi : la méthode de prévision utilisée, et notamment l'inflexion des projections linéaires à l'aide des travaux des commissions de modernisation, a eu tendance à accélérer le rythme de ces transformations par rapport à la période de référence (Tableau I).

TABLEAU I

MODIFICATION DE LA STRUCTURE DE L'EMPLOI
PREVUES POUR QUELQUES PROFESSIONS EN NOTABLE EXPANSION

	Evolution de la part de chaque profession dans l'emploi total				Taux de variation annuels moyens des pourcentages		
	1954 %	1962 %	1970 %	1978 %	1954/ 1962 %	1962/ 1970 %	1970/ 1978 %
Personnel de recherche (051)	0,02	0,06	0,12	0,29	+12	+ 8,3	+5,2
Techniciens (054)	1,32	1,79	2,64	3,53	+ 3,9	+ 5	+3,7
Médecins, chirurgiens, dentistes, pharmaciens, vétérinaires (091)	0,42	0,50	0,60	0,72	+ 3,2	+ 2,2	+2,8
Infirmiers diplômés et specialisés (092)	0,42	0,50	0,72	1,07	+ 2,1	+ 4,7	+4,7
Professeurs et assistants de l'enseignement supérieur (104)	0,03	0,05	0,17	0,32	+ 8,6	+15	+8,4

La diminution des métiers en régression s'accentue généralement par rapport à la période de référence s'agissant des métiers d'agriculteurs, de marins et pêcheurs. La prévision n'accélère pas, en revanche, la diminution des emplois d'industriels non salariés, dont le rythme se poursuit à peu près également jusqu'en 1978.

Les plus fortes progressions prévues d'ici 1970 et 1978 n'apparaissent pas démesurées par rapport à la période passée. Les variations de la part relative de chaque profession dans l'emploi total prévues de 1962 à 1970 et 1978 sont parfois inférieures aux mouvements observés entre 1954 et 1962 et dépassent rarement le double du rythme d'accroissement 1954-1962.

B. Les prévisions supposent une élévation de la qualification de la population active supérieure à celle qui a été observée entre 1954 et 1962.

L'élévation de la qualification impliquée par les prévisions est conforme au sens de l'évolution passée, à l'évolution qui a été observée dans certains pays étrangers et au sens des prévisions qui ont pu être établies[1].

La progression des métiers qualifiés est cependant plus importante de 1962 à 1970 et 1978 que durant la période 1954-1962. Un calcul attribuant à chaque profession un

---

[1] voir p.16) Cf. en particulier les prévisions faites sous les auspices de l'OCDE pour divers pays méditérranéens.

13

niveau déterminé de formation jugé souhaitable pour son exercice[1] permet d'évaluer la
qualification théorique de la population employée en 1954, 1962, 1970 et 1978.
L'évolution de la part de chaque niveau de formation traduit le seul accroissement de
qualification imputable à la progression des métiers qualifiés.

D'après ce calcul, les métiers exigeant un niveau équivalent à celui du doctorat et
de la licence augmentent beaucoup plus rapidement par rapport à l'emploi total de 1962
à 1970 et 1978 que de 1954 à 1962. Au contraire, la diminution des métiers ne
nécessitant aucune formation particulière au-delà de la fin de la scolarité obligatoire
s'accentue très sensiblement par rapport à la période de référence (Tableau II).

TABLEAU II

	1954	1962	1970	1978
Professions du niveau doctorat ou licence	4,6	5,3	6,3	7,5
Professions du niveau technicien supérieur ou propédeutique	7,3	7,8	8,3	9,0
Profession du niveau baccalauréat ou brevet de technicien	13,7	12,6	11,9	11,8
Profession du niveau CAP ou BEPC	40,6	41,4	42,1	42,2
Profession n'exigeant pas de formation particulière au-delà de la scolarité obligatoire	33,8	32,9	31,4	29,5
	100	100	100	100

Les progressions les plus notables prévues d'ici 1978 concernent toutes des
catégories de personnel qualifié et hautement qualifié ; techniciens et agent techniques,
dessinateurs, ingénieurs, personnel de recherche, cadres administratifs supérieurs,
fonctionnaires supérieurs, métiers du secteur sanitaire et social, professeurs et
assistants de l'enseignement supérieur, sont appelés à une progression nettement
supérieure à la moyenne.

Malgré l'accélération que lui ont imprimée les prévisions, le rythme de progression
de la qualification de la population active est vraisemblablement encore sous-estimé.
Les prévisions reposent en effet, pour environ 50% de la population active, sur le
résultat d'extrapolations linéaires. Or il semble que la pénurie de main-d'oeuvre
qualifiée s'est aggravée de 1954 à 1962, période de base de la projection.

(ii) Comparaison des prévisions avec l'évolution récente de l'emploi aux Etats-Unis

L'observation des tendances récentes de l'évolution de l'emploi dans les pays
étrangers devrait fournir un facteur d'appréciation intéressant sur la rapidité du
rythme de transformation et d'élévation de la qualification prévue en France à moyen et
long terme.

Les comparaisons internationales en la matière se heurtent malheuresement à de très
grandes difficultés. Ainsi les personnes actives rangées dans la catégorie "ingénieurs"
lors du recensement de 1962 en France représentent 0,9% de l'emploi non agricole total.
Aux Etats-Unis, lors du recensement de 1950, le pourcentage correspondant était de 1,07%

---

[1] Cf. En troisième partie, les développements relatifs au tableau de correspondance entre
professions et niveau de formation.

pour la catégorie "engineers". Une interprétation rigoureuse de cet écart
nécessiterait une recherche difficile sur les contenus respectifs des deux catégories.

Il a cependant paru interessant à titre d'élément d'appréciation de comparer les
prévisions faites pour la France avec l'évolution qu'a connue dans le passé récent un
pays sensiblement plus avancé que le nôtre. Le Tableau III présente les résultats d'une
comparaison des prévisions faites pour la France de 1962 à 1970 avec l'évolution
observée aux Etats-Unis entre les deux recensements de 1950 et de 1960.

Ce tableau ne couvre pas la totalité de la population active, mais seulement des
professions (ou groupes de professions) dont le contenu paraît relativement proche
sinon identique — dans les deux groupes.

Les groupes retenus correspondent à environ 60% de l'emploi total en France, en 1962
et à 59% aux Etats-Unis en 1950.

Ce tableau fait apparaître non pas des effectifs en nombres absolus par catégories
professionnelles, mais la part respective en pourcentages que l'effectif de chaque
catégorie représente par rapport à l'emploi total.

Les colonnes 3 à 6 indiquent respectivement, pour la France (1954–1962, 1962–1970,
1970–1978) et les Etats-Unis, le taux annuel de variation, en pourcentage, de la part
de l'effectif de chaque catégorie dans l'emploi total.

Dans l'ensemble, on constate un certain parallélisme entre les deux séries de taux
qui figurent dans les colonnes 5 et 6 ; les métiers pour lesquels on prévoit en France
un accroissement rapide de l'importance relative de leurs effectifs ont été, pour la
plupart, en accroissement rapide aux Etats-Unis entre 1950 et 1960 ; quant aux métiers
moins nombreux parmi ceux qui sont examinés ici, dont les effectifs baisseraient
relativement à l'emploi total d'après les prévisions faites pour la France, on note
qu'ils ont tous vu leur importance relative diminuer aux Etats-Unis.

L'examen de ce tableau révèle cependant des différences qui méritent quelques
réflexions:

Les principales divergences concernent les métiers suivants

(i) Personnel enseignant

Pour le personnel de l'enseignement supérieur, on prévoit, de 1962 à 1970, une
croissance beaucoup plus rapide que pendant les autres périodes en France et que de 1950
à 1960 aux Etats-Unis : cette croissance exceptionnelle correspond à l'arrivée au niveau
de l'enseignement supérieur de classes d'âge nombreuses nées à partir de 1946.

On note que l'accroissement prévu pour l'ensemble du personnel enseignant est
légèrement inférieur à ce que l'on a observé aux Etats-Unis et plus inférieur encore à
ce que l'on a enregistré en France au cours de la période 1954–1962. C'est en effet,
pendant cette dernière période que la relèvement de la natalité après la guerre a eu la
plus forte incidence sur l'évolution des effectifs scolaires totaux.

(ii) Hommes de science, personnel de recherche

Le personnel recensé dans cette catégorie en 1962 comprend essentiellement les hommes
de sciences de diverses spécialités (économistes, sociologues, géologues, biologistes,
chimistes, astronomes, physiciens, mathématiciens, etc.), à l'exclusion de ceux qui se
déclarent enseignants. Des techniciens de laboratoire ont pu sans doute également se
déclarer "personnel de recherche". L'effectif ainsi recensé paraît sensiblement
équivalent à l'effectif global en 1962 de chercheurs des grands organismes de recherche
publics (CNRS, CEA, INSERM, INRA, etc.) et privés (Centres de recherche des entreprises,
Institut Pasteur, etc.) à l'exclusion du personnel enseignant de l'enseignement
supérieur et des ingénieurs employés dans des activités de recherche. En effet, ces
derniers, qui constituent une très forte proportion du personnel de recherche des
entreprises et de certains grands organismes tels que le CEA, se sont vraisemblablement
déclarés "ingénieurs", au recensement de 1962.

Professions	Effectif de la profession en % de la population totale ayant un emploi en 1962	Variation annuelle moyenne du pourcentage que représente l'effectif de la profession par rapport à l'emploi total en %		
F R A N C E				
		de 1954 à 1962 observé	de 1962 à 1970 prévu	de 1970 à 1978 prévu
Agriculteurs	20,170	− 3,6	− 4,2	− 4,4
Mineurs et carriers	1,168	− 2,9	− 4,4	− 4,0
Couvreurs et plombiers	0,821	+ 3,6	+ 3,3	+ 1,1
Peintres	0,915	+ 2,5	+ 1,6	+ 0,6
Electriciens	0,977	+ 3,1	+ 3,0	+ 1,7
Métiers de la photographie et photogravure	0,153	+ 1,8	+ 0,4	− 0,2
Métiers de la composition et de l'impression	0,423	− 1,2	+ 0,2	+ 0,1
Métiers de la boulangerie et de la patisserie	0,776	− 1,1	− 1,9	− 1,5
Charpentiers et menuisiers	1,584	− 0,4	− 1,2	− 1,6
Conducteurs d'engins de transport sur route	2,012	+ 3,7	+ 2,7	+ 1,9
Personnel scientifique	0,065	+12,0	+ 8,3	+ 5,2
Ingénieurs	0,743	+ 2,9	+ 2,6	+ 2,2
Architectes	0,046	− 0,3	+ 0,8	+ 0,3
Dessinateurs	0,617	+ 4,3	+ 4,9	+ 3,9
Entrepreneurs, industriels et commerçants	5,600	− 2,0	− 2,0	− 2,0
Personnel administratif autre que de direction	11,298	+ 2,5	+ 2,0	+ 1,1
Employés de commerce	3,335	+ 2,2	+ 1,8	+ 1,4
Fonctionnaires supérieurs	0,518	+ 2,3	+ 1,6	+ 2,2
Médecins, chirurgiens	0,280	+ 2,6	+ 2,4	+ 2,4
Dentistes	0,084	+ 2,1	+ 1,5	+ 2,5
Vétérinaires	0,023	+ 3,1	+ 2,5	+ 2,5
Infirmières, sages femmes	0,496	+ 2,1	+ 4,7	+ 4,7
Aides infirmières	0,509	+11,3	+ 5,0	+ 5,0
Assistantes sociales	0,107	+ 0,7	+ 2,4	+ 3,3
Instituteurs et professeurs du 2eme degré	2,347	+ 4,7	+ 1,6	+ 1,9
Assistants et professeurs d'enseignement supérieur	0,056	+ 8,6	+15	+ 8,4
Professeurs d éducation physique et moniteurs de sportifs	0,087	+ 5,2	+ 3,2	+ 5,3
Personnel qualifié des services juridiques	0,297	+ 1,3	+ 0,3	+ 0,7
Métiers des soins personnels	0,680	+ 2,4	+ 1,5	+ 2,5
Personnel de service	5,773	+ 0,5	+ 0,1	+ 0,6
Ensemble des professions ci-dessus	59,980			

Variation annuelle moyenne etc.	Effectif de la profession en% de la population	Professions
de 1950 à 1960 observé	totale ayant un emploi en 1950	

E T A T S — U N I S

Variation annuelle moyenne etc. de 1950 à 1960 observé	Effectif de la profession en% de la population totale ayant un emploi en 1950	Professions
— 6,1	12,080	Farmers and farm managers. Farm labourers and foremen
— 9,8	0,836	Mine operatives and labourers (except oil, natural gas)
— 0,2	0,582	Plumbers and pipefitters, roofers and slaters
— 1,1	0,913	Painters
— 0,2	0,559	Electricians
— 0,2	0,197	Photographers, compositors, etc.
+ 0,2	0,404	Pressmen and plateprinters, compositors, etc.
— 2,0	0,216	Bakers
— 2,2	1,782	Cabinet makers, carpenters
+ 0,2	3,030	Bus, taxicab, truck and tractor drivers
+ 2,1	0,273	Natural scientists, social scientists
+ 4,0	0,995	Engineers
+ 1,5	0,043	Architects
+ 4,6	0,289	Designers, draughtsmen
— 3,5	4,657	Self employed managers (except farm)
+ 2,0	(12,487)	Clerical and kindred workers
+ 0,7	7,015	Sales workers
+ 1,6	0,381	Public administration officials and inspectors
+ 0,8	0,346	Physicians and surgeons
=	0,135	Dentists
=	0,024	Veterinarians
+ 2,2	1,104	Nurses, midwives
+ 5,6	0,369	Attendants (hospitals and other institutions)
+ 1,5	0,136	Social and welfare workers
+ 3,0	2,022	Teachers
+ 2,6	0,224	College presidents, professors and instructors
+ 4,5	0,081	Sports instructors and officials
+ 0,2	0,322	Lawyers and judges
+ 1,3	0,690	Barbers, hairdressers and cosmetologists
+ 0,9	6,895	Service workers (domestic, recreational, custodial)
	59,087	

Le programme de développement de la recherche défini par le 5è Plan implique un accroissement très rapide des effectifs de cette catégorie, accroissement plus rapide qu'aux Etats-Unis entre 1950 et 1960, qui n'empêcherait pas que l'importance relative de cette catégorie resterait très inférieure en France en 1970 à ce qu'elle était aux Etats-Unis en 1950.

Il convient cependant de souligner que les indications chiffrées présentées pour cette catégorie assez difficile à définir sont particulièrement sujettes à caution. Une comparaison sérieuse entre pays concernant l'effectif du personnel consacré à la recherche impliquerait une étude approfondie et le recours à des sources d'informations autres que les recensements généraux de la population.

(iii) *Médecins, dentistes, infirmières*

Les prévisions pour la France d'ici 1970, et 1978 impliquent une croissance plus rapide qu'aux Etats-Unis. Le nombre de médecins et d'infirmières par rapport à la population active totale ou par rapport au nombre d'habitants serait cependant inférieur en France en 1970 à ce qu'il était en 1960 aux Etats-Unis ; les travaux faits en la matière par la Commission de l'équipement sanitaire et social confirment d'ailleurs clairement qu'il n'y a pas à craindre d'ici longtemps en France d'excédent de personnel sanitaire.

(iv) *Ingénieurs*

Les prévisions retenus correspondent à une croissance du pourcentage d'ingénieurs dans l'emploi total moins rapide qu'aux Etats-Unis, et légèrement moins rapide qu'en France même au cours de la période 1954–1962. Il est possible que certaines commissions verticales, d'abord préoccupées par l'indéniable nécessité d'accroître de façon très notable le nombre des techniciens, aient eu tendance à sous-estimer les besoins d'ingénieurs.

Manpower Planning for the National Economy

COLIN LEICESTER

DEPARTMENT OF APPLIED ECONOMICS
UNIVERSITY OF CAMBRIDGE

I. INTRODUCTION

Like other management problems, manpower planning at the level of the economy requires the analysis of information. In this paper, we are concerned with the different types of information that seem to be required, the various frameworks which may be used to collect and arrange it, and the kinds of analysis that may have to be performed. We are less concerned with the decisions that follow from such analysis, or the actions that may follow from the decisions.

For obvious reasons, our starting point has to be the specific nature of the task set for such analysis of information. Accordingly, a simplified account of the manpower planning problems is given in the next section. These have certain obvious implications for the concepts and methods to be used in manpower analysis, and a discussion of the most important of these occupies the succeeding sections.

Broadly speaking, these appear to be the following. We need a framework of economic accounts within which all the economic variables can be found a place; and a framework of demographic accounts to enable us to take an inventory of the population: these topics occupy sections 3 and 4. We need to describe how the magnitudes of some economic variables influence other parts of the economic system, and how demographic variables may be said to determine each other. Some of these functional relationships within each account form the subject of section 5. Finally, there are further relationships, this time between economic variables and demographic variables, and these links between the two accounts are discussed in a brief manner in section 6.

In our work on *A Programme for Growth* at Cambridge, we have proceeded some distance along the road towards establishing economic accounts and relationships which yield the kind of information it seems desirable to have. It seemed apparent early on [7] that the social framework was not only linked to the economic framework, and linked in a rather complex manner, but that we, at any rate, felt that it could be better understood.

Of all the important links that might deserve attention, the way in which economic activity utilised manpower seemed the most crucial. The nature of such job-creating activity forms the subject of sections 7 and 8; and in a sense the earlier parts of the paper provide a context for it. That such a context would be useful can be deduced from the manpower planning so far attempted by business firms, in which personnel managers appear to take little heed of the long-term sales plans of the marketing department; and that it is important can be learnt, though in a converse manner, from the well-advanced experience of other micro-economic institutions [9] who through *force majeure* have had to grasp this nettle in a firm hand years ago.

The steps taken by the manpower analyst of the national economy which are analogous to those of the institutional planner will be obvious to the reader. The extent to which this paper mirrors what consensus of agreement exists over the macro-economic problems will be equally obvious. While indications of the steps we intend to take in the future at Cambridge are given here, it is clear that a number of matters are paid insufficient attention and a number of problems remain to be solved. Rome, after all, took more than 24 hours.

19

2. A SIMPLIFIED VIEW OF THE PROBLEMS

The central consideration from which it is generally agreed manpower analysis starts is the possibility that imbalance between the demand and supply of labour may exist; it may also continue to occur in the future.

If boundaries are drawn between jobs in the sense that each requires some difference in the input of skills and talents, then a heterogeneous demand for labour pertains. If distinctions occur between groups of workers, in the sense that each possesses a different bundle of skills and talents, then a heterogeneous supply of labour has to be acknowledged. The phenomena of imbalance and heterogeneity are illustrated in Diagram 1.

Diagram 1

The demand for and supply of a type of labour

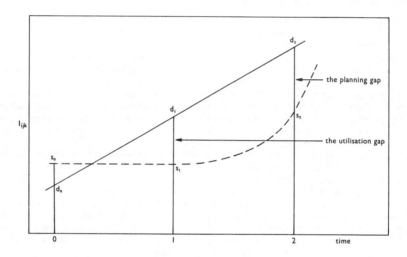

The graph shows the hypothetical course of the demand for and supply of a specific type of labour, with the characteristics i, j and k. There may be more ways of distinguishing the skill of labour (natural ability, experience, formal education and informal training) but here we consider labour as distributed in three dimensional skill space. The continuous line describes the growth in demand, and the broken line how supply has adapted to such growth. The period from 0 to 1 may be taken as the past under analysis, and the period from 1 to 2 as the future up to a stated horizon.

In the example shown, there is a present short-fall of labour, denoted by $d_1 - s_1$. A deficit may also be expected in the future, indicated by $d_2 - s_2$, if the developments proceed as shown. The first may be called the utilisation gap, and would be the only matter that concerned the manpower analyst if there was no expected difference between current and future demand (i.e. if $d_2 = d_1$). His chief concern, in this case, would be that supply grew to match the current deficit (i.e. that $s_2 = d_1$).

Demand is, however, expected to grow in the future. A deficit at the target year may be called the planning gap, and may have come about in various ways. If supply in the future will merely grow to match the current deficit, then the planning gap is equal to the change between current and future demand $(d_2 - d_1)$. If, alternatively, supply will increase to meet the change in demand, then the planning gap and the utilisation gap are identical in size. In the extreme position (not shown) where supply remained constant at the current level (i.e. if $s_2 = s_1$) then the planning gap would be the sum of demand changes and present misutilisation. Of whatever magnitude, or however resulting, alleviating this future gap may be attempted through planned action.

It is implicit in the description given of these divergences so far, that the demand and supply patterns shown are generated by systems which have a dynamic momentum of their own, and that external intervention is only needed when their paths fail to coincide. The analysis for manpower planning is precisely an anticipation of whether this has occurred, and is likely to occur, for all labour types (all i, j, k).

Such analysis must consist of the following as a minimum. First, it should include an understanding of the processes determining the changes in demand. Since labour obtains employment in economic activity, then a monitoring of how the environment of the economic system alters through time is called for.

Second, it must include a corresponding understanding of the processes causing the alterations in supply. Since both the quantity and the quality of labour alter as a result of demographic forces and the influence of the education and training system, the likely trends produced by these if left to themselves need to be anticipated.

Our first need, in other words, is a way of understanding why the levels of the economic variables are what they are, and this would emerge from viewing the relationships between them. These relationships are of two kinds. On the one hand, there must be accounting identities which are implied by the levels of transactions that occur in various forms of economic activity, in the sense that the total money incomings into any one such activity must equal its total outgoings. On the other hand, there must also be functional relationships between specific variables, in the sense that the levels of some are causes of the levels of others. The tools coping with these phenomena are: a system of economic accounts and a system of behavioural and technological relationships.

It must become apparent that similar requirements are seen when we consider the demographic variables. In this case, we are not concerned with transactions but with units of the human population, not with economic activities but states within which the population is to be found. These states are mutually exclusive, and may for example distinguish being employed or unemployed, economically active or inactive. Any person in any one such state at an earlier date must either still be there or in some other state. If we have a well articulated system of demographic accounts, then every individual may be monitored; we may be able to keep an inventory of manpower resources. If we also have a set of relationships explaining why transitions may have occurred, then, as with the use of economic functions, we may be able to anticipate future changes in the demographic variables.

In the next two sections, we consider the system of economic accounts and the system of demographic accounts in turn. Certain similarities exist between them. But attention is drawn to those points where they differ radically. In the section after that, we consider functional relationships that may be described between economic variables only; and between demographic variables taken in isolation. These are relationships, that is, which operate within each set of accounts.

This leads to the third requirement of manpower analysis. Links must exist between the two sets of accounts. One such connection occurs in the work-place where the levels of economic activity impose demands for the economically active population. We accordingly need to know how the demand for labour is derived from the demand for industrial output. If, as the levels of these economic outputs grow over time, the accompanying growth rates of forms of employment are dissimilar, then we must consider the implications they may have for the variables of the demographic framework. For example, if there is a tendency for labour with higher qualifications to become increasingly employed at the expense of labour with lower qualifications, then there should be a corresponding tendency for the education and training system to keep in step with these trends. This may be called the manpower link between economic growth and education [3].

In addition to this, we know that systems of education and training need to be paid for, and when these have a changing structure the total costs to the nation will themselves vary. The more expensive parts of the system may be those which cater for students obtaining the higher qualifications; then, if these grow relatively faster than the others, educational expenditures will increase for this reason alone. Whether these can be met may depend on whether the income of the nation also grows to provide the necessary finance. The wealthier a nation, the more students it can support. This may be called the financial link between education and economic growth [6].

In any investigation of these links between the economic and the demographic systems, we should not assume them to be rigid at the outset; nor, of course, can we imagine them to be extremely flexible. The real world is somewhere in between. These characteristics may be illustrated in terms of the manpower link, and reference may be made to Diagram 1 again.

We might, as suggested, see an imbalance between demand and supply in the current period. As shown, the current imbalance is a deficit ($d_1 > s_1$) but it had earlier been of the opposite kind, a surplus ($s_0 > d_0$). Whichever its nature, we should be aware of the effects arising from either kind of imbalance under conditions of extreme rigidity.

If the demand system was completely rigid, then in a deficit situation some loss of production would occur. If the output of a certain commodity only increased proportionately with the level of skill (i, j, k) available, then a limit is set to the supply of commodities by the supply of this labour type. As long as employers describe some such limits as being crucial to their operations, then to that extent rigidities must exist.

There may on the other hand be rigidities in the supply system, and in a situation of surplus some manpower becomes unused, if not unusable. For if the only forms of employment which labour skill (i, j, k) can enter have vacancies for less than the total in that category, then some unfortunate members of that group will become unemployed. As long as we continue to view certain kinds of structural unemployment, we must entertain the notion that rigidities exist for that reason too.

It would be foolish, however, to accept this as being the whole story. It is clear that both the employers of labour and the suppliers of labour may react to a situation of imbalance by adopting, on the part of the former, flexible hiring standards; on the part of the latter, flexible vocational choice.

How flexible hiring standards may be practised can be illustrated as follows. To meet a deficit in supply, the employer might choose to recruit an additional number of workers with something less than the optimum mix of skills. In doing so, he might have to take on more than the number actually denoted by the absolute imbalance. A lower level of productivity might be achieved if the actual numbers recruited are underqualified.

Different types of labour, too, might adopt flexibility in the matter of vocational choice. It is always possible for an individual to take a job requiring less than the actual mix of skills he possesses. If income differentials are set in line with the skill differentials required for different jobs, then this individual's income is less than a true reflection of his qualifications: he would earn more elsewhere. Once again, there is a loss of total productivity, but here it results from labour being overqualified where it is.

The possibility that flexibility in both hiring standards and vocational choice may operate in the labour market makes the identification of an imbalance more difficult. As indicated here, it implies that to some extent employers may be able to find someone to fill the vacancies, and labour may be able to find some job. This may be satisfactory only to the extent that manpower is somehow employed in the economic system; it means however that it is less than optimally utilised. It further means that any labour market possessing such characteristics yields no immediate indication of what the optimum pattern of deployment should be. The actual statistical records of past patterns of employment do not, in other words, lie on either the demand or supply graphs in Diagram 1. Not all those in a certain occupation will possess the right mix of skills; not all those with certain qualifications will work where their mix of skills are required. The conditions of demand and of supply interact in such a way to yield these observed patterns of employment; they create an identification problem for the manpower analyst.

Accordingly, in estimating the manpower link between the economic and demographic systems, we must acknowledge that the demand and supply conditions they create are not independent of each other. We might, as in section 7, assume temporarily that they are; but we should, as in section 8, consider what results when they interact.

We turn first, however, to a description of the accounting frameworks for each system.

3. THE SYSTEM OF ECONOMIC ACCOUNTS

The nature of an accounting framework may be described in terms of its units of measurement, the different accounts shown and how they are connected to one another.

If it is economic activity that is being represented then we are concerned with various transactions measured in their money values; some of these will be associated with commodities and services flowing in the opposite direction (e.g. private consumption) while some of these may not (e.g. taxes). For each of these transactions, there must be a payer and a recipient of money, and any one transaction represents an outgoing from the account of the former, and an incoming into the account of the latter. It follows from this, that the different accounts identified must be mutually exclusive. Since we are concerned with all transactions involving all accounts, then, for example, we must document not only the payments between members of an economic system, but also those between them and the members of other economic systems. The characteristic of comprehensiveness has to be added to the requirement of consistency.

An example of a set of economic accounts is given in Diagram 2. It is expressed in symbolic terms, and is highly aggregated compared to some that have been constructed statistically for the United Kingdom [2].

Diagram 2

The symbolic economic accounts

	Activities	Institu- tions	Govern- ment	Capital Accumulation	Rest of the world	
	1	2	3	4	5	
1. Activities	X	c	b	v	z	
2. Institutions	y'				ρ	
3. Government		τ				
4. Capital Accumulation	d'	σ	γ			time (t)
5. Rest of the world	u'			κ		

time (t)

It will be noted that the matrix is square, and that each pair of a row and a column bear the same name. It will also be noted that both dimensions of the matrix relate to the same date. The row for an account represents its incomings, while its column represents all its outgoings. Any cell in the matrix, accordingly, is the transaction between two accounts at a certain point in time.

The conventions used here apply throughout the paper. The algebraic symbols have the following meaning: a capital letter is a matrix; primed and unprimed small letters are row and column vectors respectively; and Greek letters are scalars. The economic nature of the various parts of the framework may now be described.

The first account relates to activities: most of these will be industries producing goods and services, and it will be assumed that each one produces only its principal product; that is to say, that the categories of industries and commodities produced by them are co-terminous. The total incomings into activities are obtained as shown in the first row. These are: what they sell to one another as intermediate products (X); plus private consumers' expenditure (c); plus public expenditure (b); plus investment in fixed assets and stocks (v); and plus exports of goods and services (z). Their outgoings consist of: their purchases of intermediate products; plus net value added i.e. the payments of wages and net profits earned (y'); plus the value of depreciation allowed for (d'); plus imports (u'). Since both sides of an economic account must balance, total incomings must be equal to total outgoings, that is

$$Xi + c + b + v + z = X'i + y + d + u \qquad (3.1)$$

where i denotes the unit column vector, and X' is the transpose of X.

The second row collects together the income payments in the economy. These are value added (y') plus net income from abroad (ρ) giving the Net National Income at Market Prices. This is divided, as shown, between private consumption (c), indirect taxes (τ) and net saving (σ). Once again we observe the accounting identity:

$$i'y + \rho = i'c + \tau + \sigma \qquad (3.2)$$

where i' denotes the unit row vector.

The account for government shown here indicates that the total of indirect taxes (τ) may be spent on those commodities needed for public activities (b) or may go as a financial surplus (γ) into capital accumulation. This last item, together with depreciation (d') and savings (σ) constitute in the fourth row the total of capital finance available; and this total capital, as shown in column 4, provides for investment in fixed assets and stocks (v) or else is lent abroad (κ). The identities for these accounts are

$$\tau = i'b + \gamma \qquad (3.3)$$

$$i'd + \sigma + \gamma = i'v + \kappa \qquad (3.4)$$

All the items in the account for the rest of the world have been referred to already, and from its accounting identity

$$i'u + \kappa = i'z + \rho \qquad (3.5)$$

we see that κ is in fact the balance of payments, being positive if there is a surplus, negative if a deficit, on this account.

Such matrices of economic accounts might be drawn up in like manner or in more detail for any number of years. If we have two of these n years apart (T_0 and T_n, say) valued at a common set of prices, then any simple operation may be performed on them which preserves the accounting identities e.g.

$$T^* \equiv T_n - T_0 \qquad (3.6)$$

T^* then represents the changes in the levels of economic activity represented by the accounts from which it was derived, and is as comprehensive and consistent as they are.

For example it is useful to calculate the gross outputs of activities (q) as the sum of what they sell to each other as well as final customers, namely

$$q_t = X_t i + f_t \qquad (3.7)$$

where

$$f_t = c_t + b_t + v_t + z_t - u_t \qquad (3.8)$$

The corresponding incremental change is

$$\Delta q = \Delta X i + \Delta f \qquad (3.9)$$

where

$$\Delta f = \Delta c + \Delta b + \Delta v + \Delta z - \Delta u \qquad (3.10)$$

Δ representing increments of the corresponding levels of flows. Later we may describe the functional relationships these lead to.

4. THE SYSTEM OF DEMOGRAPHIC ACCOUNTS

We now turn to consider how a set of demographic accounts might be constructed.

In this case, we are concerned with members of the human population, and the units of the system are various counts of heads. Each account represents one state in which the members of this population might be found. If these states are defined in a mutually exclusive manner, and if they cover the whole population, then both consistency and comprehensiveness are possessed by this accounting system too. Finally, it follows from what has been said that the system of accounts is designed to show possible transitions from one demographic state to another.

Diagram 3

The symbolic demographic accounts

	In Employment	Unemployed	In Education and Training	At Home	Elsewhere	
	1	2	3	4	5	
1. In Employment	$\hat{o}$	f	N	r	m	
2. Unemployed	h'	μ				
3. In Education and Training	G		E	w		time (t)
4. At Home	j'		s'	φ	δ	
5. Elsewhere	a'			β		

time ($t + n$)

Diagram 3 represents a possible framework for a system of demographic accounts. This too is highly aggregated and expressed in the form of symbols. At the time of writing, no attempt to statistically represent in full such a framework appears to exist, though the mechanics of it are known [10] and documentation of parts of it already achieved [11].

Once again, the matrix of accounts is square. However, it will be noticed that its two dimensions belong to different dates, the rows relating to an earlier point in time than the columns. Accordingly, the totals of the rows denote numbers in those states at the first date, and the column totals the numbers in them at the second date. It must be emphasised at this stage, that any row total would generally differ from the corresponding column total, although in certain exceptional circumstances they could be the same. However that may be, a cell in the matrix is the number of people who moved from the state denoted by the row to that denoted by the column, between the two dates.

The nature of the matrix may be illustrated by a description of its component accounts. The first relates to the employed labour force, which for the time being is imagined to be sub-classified by education and training qualifications. The row of the first account indicates how it may have changed its demographic status: some remain in employment ($\hat{o}$) where o is a vector spread out to form a diagonal matrix and implying that people do not change qualifications while staying in employment; some have been fired, or otherwise become unemployed (f); some have gone for further qualifications in the various branches of education and training (N); some have retired or otherwise gone home (r); and some have emigrated abroad (m). The column of the first account describes the sources of employed labour at the later date: some had previously been at work ($\hat{o}$); some were hired from the pool of unemployed (h'); some graduated from the branches of the education and training system with various qualifications (G); some joined from households, perhaps participating in economic activity for a second time (j'); and some were immigrants (a').

The second row and column indicate that the total unemployed at the first date were either given jobs (h') or were not (μ); and that the latter plus those discharged (f) constituted the unemployed at the later date. Unemployment would decline if those hired exceeded those fired.

The third account is sub-classified by branches of education and training. Those in these institutions at the first date would either join the labour force (G), continue their courses (E) or constitute wastage by choosing not to employ their recently received qualifications (w). To those still in courses at the second date (E) must be added adults entering from the labour force (N) and children from households (s') to give the new total in education and training.

The fourth account relates to those both economically and educationally inactive. Of those in this state at the beginning of the period, some have joined the labour force (j'), some have gone to school (s'), some have remained at home (φ), and some have died (δ). Those staying there (φ) are augmented by those retiring (r), the wastage from education (w) and births (β).

The items in the fifth account have been already mentioned in passing, and need not be referred to again.

From the way in which accounts have been distinguished in this illustrative system, it can be seen that the sum of the first two are the economically active, and the sum of the next two the economically inactive. Together, all four refer to the total population. The grand total of the matrix accordingly is the members of the population at either of the two dates, or at both. With a static population, constant proportions of it economically inactive in schools or at home, and a constant percentage of unemployment, the row totals might indeed be the same as the column totals. If furthermore, the numbers in the leading diagonal were the same as the equal row and column totals, then we have a stable demographic system. As long as we do not, then it must pay us to document the changes for which such a framework caters.

Let us now denote the matrix of demographic accounts by P. It is useful to observe that we might form

$$P^* = P - P' \tag{4.1}$$

		$f - h$	$N - G'$	$r - j$	$m - a$
$=$	o				
	$h' - f'$	o	o	o	o
	$G - N'$	o	$E - E'$	$w - s$	o
	$j' - r'$	o	$s' - w'$	o	$\delta - \beta$
	$a' - m'$	o	o	$\beta - \delta$	o

which says much the same thing, though more familiar identities may be seen by looking at the first and third columns of the partitioned matrix.

In the first column, we see that the increase in the labour force, sub-classified by qualification, is the sum of the following changes: the net reduction in unemployed, plus those graduating minus those leaving to re-train, plus participation from house-holds minus retirement, plus net immigration. The identity,

$$\Delta l \equiv l_n - l_o$$
$$= h - f + (G' - N) i + j - r + a - m \qquad (4.2)$$

where l is total employment and Δl its incremental change, is of course neutral as to the source of any major change in employment. It is, however, apparent that if all items on the right are pre-determined then so is Δl, the change in labour supplied for employment. Alternatively, if a certain change in employment was required, then fixing every single item on the right except one also determines the desirable level of that one too. If the change in both unemployment $(h - f)$ and participation $(j - r)$ were zero, then a desired stepping up of manpower resources can only be obtained from the domestic training system, or be imported. If the domestic system is well developed and there is adequate time for action, then more reliance could be placed on the former. If the converse is true, then greater emphasis would be placed on imports. This is valid as a way of describing the behaviour of different micro-economic systems (e.g. business organisations) but is just as true for macro-economic ones; as becomes apparent when we view the present diverse policies of developed as opposed to developing economies.

The third column of P^* tells us how, if we measure it in terms of students, the size of the various branches of education and training grow. If there were no re-training ($i'N\ i = 0$) and we could discount wastage ($i'w = 0$) then the total numbers to be catered for would be the excess of those entering school over those graduating $= i'\ (s - G'i)$. However, the change in the capacity of individual branches represented would be influenced by the net result documented by $E - E'$. If more people enter a certain part of further education than leave it, its capacity would need to be corres-pondingly increased.

Such changes in the student population may be represented by functional relation-ships. Those relationships that may operate within both the economic and demographic accounts are now described.

5. THE RELATIONSHIPS WITHIN THE ACCOUNTS

In the economic system, part of the explanation of how changes in the levels of activity are determined might be expressed as follows.

$$\Delta q = \Delta X i + \Delta f$$
$$= A^* \Delta q + \Delta f \qquad (5.1)$$
$$= (I - A^*)^{-1} \Delta f$$

I is the unit matrix, and A^* is a set of marginal input-output coefficients, and the other variables are as defined in section 3.

The essence of the relationships is the notion that each activity has a technology which, at each point in time, denotes the amounts of input per unit of its own output which would have to be purchased from other activities. At a point in time, input-output coefficients have average values (A_t); but as technology changes over time, these coefficients tend to alter, and the marginal coefficients (A^*) would be greater than the average for intermediate inputs that become increasingly used, less for the opposite kind of technological change.

Knowing A^* and Δf, and solving simultaneous equations, yields a consistent set of output changes, Δq, which are required to satisfy the changes in final demand, Δf. Other functions might describe how these changes in final demand were previously determined [4]. But these other economic relationships will not be considered here.

In the demographic system, part of the way in which people become prepared for employment should consist of how the education and training system expands and how supplies of qualified labour emerge from it. For the sake of simplicity, we here assume that the branches of the system are so defined (e.g. primary and secondary schools, sub-university institutions, universities) that there are as many qualifications as branches, and they are co-terminus with one another.

The capacity of this system may be denoted by the numbers to be catered for. Let us define this as the vector d_t denoting the stocks of students in various branches of education and training at the end of period t. This will be the sum of adults and children entering during the period $(n_t + s_t)$ plus those who were also in the stock of students at the end of the previous period (e_t). Hence

$$d_0 = e_0 + n_0 + s_0 \tag{5.2}$$

$$d_1 = e_1 + n_1 + s_1 \tag{5.3}$$

Only certain proportions of those in the stock at the end of the first period were still students at the end of the second, and they may have switched branches meanwhile. These transitions may be described by

$$e_1 = E^* d_0 \tag{5.4}$$

where E^* is a matrix of transition ratios each of whose columns represents the proportions of those who start in the branch represented by the column and end up in the branches represented by the rows. The coefficients in the leading diagonal indicate those staying in the same course. Typically, these coefficients in any column will sum to 1 only if the branches they represent give courses requiring more time than the period for which the transition ratios are calculated or if they only prepare students for further education and training. That is

$$E^{*\prime} i \neq i \tag{5.5}$$

If we substitute equation (5.4) in equation (5.3) for a succession of years, then the stock of students at the end of time t will be given by

$$d_t = E^{*t} d_0 + \sum_{\theta=1}^{t} E^{*t-\theta}(n_\theta + s_\theta) \tag{5.6}$$

which indicates that we should know the numbers in education and training at some date in the future if we know the numbers now, the entrants into the system between now and then, and if the nature of the courses they undertake and their choice of succession of courses may be described by a set of stable transition coefficients.

Their emergence from these courses into the labour force and into households might also be denoted by transition ratios.

$$g_1 = \hat{g}^* d_0 \tag{5.7}$$

$$w_1 = \hat{w}^* d_0 \tag{5.8}$$

where g^* and w^* represent coefficients of the rates of graduation into employment and of wastage, respectively. Since all students at the earlier period, who did not continue education and training, must be accounted for in this way, then

$$g_1 + w_1 + e_1 = d_0 \tag{5.9}$$

and

$$g^* + w^* + E^{*\prime} i = i \tag{5.10}$$

Accordingly, the augmentation of the labour force that we might expect from these processes follows from equations (5.3), (5.4) and (5.7).

$$g_t = \hat{g}^* \{ E^{*\,t-1} d_0 + \sum_{\theta=1}^{t-1} E^{*\,t-\theta-1}(n_\theta + s_\theta) \}$$

(5.11)

To these must be added the other items in the accounting identity of section 4 to give the change in the levels of employment, classified by types of qualifications. This change in levels of employment should match the change in economic activities requiring labour, and a description of this is one link between the economic and demographic accounts.

6. THE RELATIONSHIPS BETWEEN THE ACCOUNTS

Consider first this manpower link. We might imagine, for the sake of simplicity, that all net changes in qualifications get allocated among economic activities in fixed proportions; and that in whatever economic activity he is employed each additional qualified man has the same incremental productivity even though the contributions to output may differ between qualifications, the higher ones being more productive than the lower. These two assumptions might be represented by a matrix Q^* which has as many rows as economic activities and as many columns as qualifications. Each cell of this matrix is the multiplicative product of the proportion of the net increase in a certain kind of qualified labour that finds employment in a particular industry, and the incremental output/labour input coefficient of that type of labour.

At the moment, we ask no questions about the nature of this allocative process, nor of what determines such incremental productivities. These will be examined later. For the time being we simply assume that the gap may be bridged between economic output, classified by activities, and manpower resources, classified by qualifications, as described in Q^*.

Accordingly, we write

$$\Delta q_1 = Q^* \Delta l_1$$
$$= Q^* g_1 + Q^*(h_1 - f_1 - n_1 + j_1 - r_1 + a_1 - m_1)$$

(6.1)

which says that increases and decreases in the levels of economic activity are pre-determined by changes in available supplies of labour qualifications. These in turn, as shown by equation (4.2) from section 4, consist of a number of items which together go to make up the net change in manpower resources. It can be seen that g is a gross supply of extra labour which not only off-sets any net tendency for labour to retire out of useful activity, the sum of the items in the brackets, but also provides the extensions to the manpower stock.

Consider that the financial link between economic activity and education might be described in the following way over two periods. In the previous period indirect taxes had been obtained by a levy at a proportional rate (τ^*) on all outputs from these activities.

$$t_0 = \tau^* q_0$$

(6.2)

where t is a vector of educational finance obtained from activities. This total finance is allocated among branches of education and training in a manner which takes into account not only the numbers of students in each, but also the nature of their educational experience and the costs of each part of this experience. Clearly, this is a complex matter: the educational experience of a class might change to more costly forms or the size of class might alter though the curriculum stays the same. Either way we might imagine that, no matter how approximate a way of describing the matter, the education and training supported by this finance may be, in terms of students,

$$d_0 = D^* t_0$$

$$= \tau^* D^* q_0 \tag{6.3}$$

D^* has as many rows as branches of education, and as many columns as economic activities; so that each cell of D^* represents the inverse of a £'s worth of taxes needed to support one student in that branch multiplied by the proportion of finance allocated to it by that activity. Equation (6.3) might be interpreted in a number of ways. Each industry might do its own training, and its training costs might come entirely out of the levy it pays; in which case $D^* = \hat{d}^*$ the elements of which are the reciprocal of the costs per student in each industry only. On the other hand, if some education and training takes place outside industries, then each finances the branches of this system in various proportions, because the allocative nature of D^* indicates the actual source of finance.

In the next period, as we assumed before, the numbers graduating into employment are determined by the stock of students.

$$g_1 = \hat{g}^* d_0$$

$$= \tau^* \hat{g}^* D^* q_0 \tag{6.4}$$

Combining equations (6.1) and (6.4) and dividing through by the output levels of the earlier period, we obtain an expression for the rates at which the different levels of economic activity grow.

$$\Delta \hat{q}_1 q_0^{-1} = \tau^* \hat{Q}^* \hat{g}^* D^* i + \hat{q}_0^{-1} \hat{Q}^* (h_1 - f_1 - n_1 + j_1 - r_1 + a_1 - m_1) \tag{6.5}$$

The growth rates we observe on the left are a compound of two effects: first, those due to changes in the manpower stock produced by the education and training system by itself; and second, those due to other changes in the stock. In manpower analysis we cannot realistically afford to ignore either.

On the one hand, various depletions of labour resources might take place, and the full result implied by the terms in the bracket might be a reduction in specific types of labour available. It may be there is no change in unemployment ($h_1 = f_1$) and that households supply enough people to offset the loss of adults who re-train and retire ($j_1 = n_1 + r_1$) for all types of qualifications. But the brain drain could mean that the skills of the immigrants do not compensate for the loss of those emigrating, i.e. $a' - m' \neq \{0, 0, 0, \ldots 0\}$. Multiplying such non-zero cells as may be recorded by the corresponding incremental productivities, and dividing by output levels in the base period, gives the negative (or positive) percentage change in output due to these losses (or gains).

On the other hand, there may be no overall scrapping of labour, and the vector sum of all the terms in the right-hand brackets has zeros in all its cells. In this case, those graduating into employment from the education and training system contribute exactly the required extensions to employment. Under this assumption, it can be seen that the growth in economic activity will be determined by the first four sets of coefficients on the right of the equals sign. It will overall be higher, the higher the levy for education and training, the higher the rate at which all students graduate, the lower overall the costs per student, and the higher the combined incremental productivities of the qualifications in each of the economic activities. The first three denote the rate at which manpower resources may be augmented, given the level of economic activity; and the last describes how such activity might increase, given the augmentation of resources. For any one economic system, the coefficients determine the rate of growth to be expected. It is clear that it describes for human capital exactly what the Harrod-Domar statement says for physical capital, except that instead of a rate of saving we have a financial provision for students in education and training who become employed; and instead of incremental capital-output ratios for fixed assets, we have the same for men. Like it, the equation provides a certain amount of insight; but like it, it possesses certain limitations.

The major limitation rests in the description of how different kinds of labour are used in different forms of economic activity, a matter which we shall now have to consider in greater depth. The financing of education and training might equally well provide meat for a more detailed discussion; but those ramifications will no longer be referred to in this paper.

7. THE NATURE OF ECONOMIC ACTIVITY

From the global view taken of manpower analysis so far, it becomes clear that a priority for investigation is the way in which changing economic activities alter the composition of jobs that have to be done; that certain jobs tend to require specific qualifications; and that these may or may not be supplied by the skill mix of the labour force. This link between the two accounts is complex, and if we break it up into its component parts this is simply to aid analysis. We could, for example, isolate the following three problems.

First, to provide the output of goods and services the various economic activities require that, in each, certain occupations need to be filled. Such occupational structures may be said to be determined at a point in time by the nature of the technology and form of organisation used by the economic activity; as these change over time, so will the occupational structure. Second, there are norms of qualification for each such occupation, but employers adopt flexible hiring standards around such a norm to cope with the bonus of recruiting labour more qualified than average, or the drawback of taking on labour less qualified than average. Third, the labour force itself has a tendency to make a vocational choice in line with the qualifications each individual possesses. Such choices might not overall lead to a meeting of the requirements of employers, and the way in which labour bends before such restrictions has to be considered.

The first matter may be described as structural, involving as it does the nature of economic activity. The second and third may be described as adaptive, and refer to the way requirements and availabilities interact in the labour market in situations of disequilibrium. In this section, we consider the first, and leave discussion of the others till later.

Any description of how economic activity works, which also takes into account the possibility that labour may be heterogeneous, draws upon at least two sources of inspiration. The first is the discussion by economists on the nature of the production function [1]. The second is the experience of statisticians in processing manpower data [17]. Both yield certain insights; but both possess limited frames of reference, and in adopting their ideas we might have to adapt them. Accordingly, what follows should be treated as a speculative attempt to develop the description of occupational employment that may be applied to manpower data with meaningful results.

Such manpower data might be collected in the form of matrices (L, say) in which the columns represent different activities and the rows different occupations. The first question to be dealt with is that of classification. The disaggregation of activities might already be pre-determined by the establishment of the economic accounts and relationships described earlier, and we need say no more about them.

It seems wise, however, to use explicit principles in deciding on the occupational classification, otherwise arbitrary groupings may lead to ambiguous results. As a first step, we consider the possibility of not making the disaggregation of occupations independent of the economic activities. This is because there are jobs traditionally associated with each sector; and examples of these are transport workers in transport, doctors in health services, sales workers in distribution. If these were the only employees in each sector, or alternatively if none of them were employed elsewhere, then each sector would put out a homogeneous demand for labour, and the total demands for an occupation would be determined by the level of the corresponding activity.

Since this is not the case, we shall define L as a square matrix with as many occupations as economic activities, the leading diagonal of which contains those employed in such mainstay occupations. This term, or one like it, may be used to describe that type of labour fundamental to a sector and without which it would cease to exist [8]. We may now separate the components of L.

$$L \equiv \hat{l}^* + L^{**} \tag{7.1}$$

The labour documented in L^{**} is accordingly the employees ancillary to the sector in which they work. It is observed in the statistics that such a matrix, L, is heavily diagonal; and both the row and column totals of L^{**} are usually less than the corresponding cells of l^*. The evidence of the data suggests that this diagonal becomes less dense as time passes: hence such a principle for the occupational classification may be worthwhile, and allows us to represent later such an extension of the division of labour.

The demand functions for the two kinds of labour may be represented by the following hypotheses. Since the mainstay occupations are fundamental to the productive activity of the economic sectors, we should expect to see them grow in step with output, though not necessarily as fast.

$$l_1^* l_0^{*-1} = \hat{p}_{01}^b i$$

$$= \begin{bmatrix} {}_1p_{01}^{b1} \\ {}_2p_{01}^{b2} \\ \cdot \\ \cdot \\ \cdot \\ {}_kp_{01}^{bk} \end{bmatrix} \tag{7.2}$$

This says that over time, from period 0 to period 1, these occupations are a logarithmic function of the change in their sectors' output levels (q) where

$$p_{01} \equiv \hat{q}_1 q_0^{-1} \tag{7.3}$$

The cells of the vector of coefficients, b, may be different for each sector, and may take any value greater than 0; and if less than, equal to, or greater than 1 denote that there are economies, constant returns, or diseconomies due to output growth for that sector. In the case, that is, when a particular b is small, the requirements of that labour per unit of output will decline as output grows, i.e. the elemment of $b - i$ is negative in

$$\hat{l}_1^* \hat{l}_0^{*-1} p_{01}^{-1} = \hat{p}_{01}^{b-i} i \tag{7.4}$$

It is not altogether obvious that a single interpretation could be given to these functions. It is usual to attempt a distinction between, say, labour saving due to economies of scale and due alternatively to technological change. The former would require an expression denoting that a percentage change in output was associated with a less than proportionate change in labour input. The latter would need a statement of how input-output coefficients altered over time. But if over time, output also grew, and so did profits, then investment in labour-saving machinery could be stepped up. The alternative versions of this function (7.2) and (7.4), we hope, beg no questions on this score.

In line with them, however, we would expect a relation describing the changing demand for capital.

$$\hat{k}_1 k_0^{-1} = \hat{p}_{01}^\varepsilon i \tag{7.5}$$

The vector, k, denotes levels of the stock of capital working with this mainstay labour. If the only plant and machinery used was of this type, then k represents all capital.

This is clearly not so; and capital is practically as heterogeneous as labour. But for the time being we shall ignore this complication. Instead we should note that the cells in the vector of coefficients, c, may be different for each sector; and if any one is greater than the corresponding cell of b, then the technology of that industry is becoming more capital-intensive; if the converse, more labour-intensive.

We now turn to the ancillary occupations. Changes in the matrix, L^{**}, over time may be considered as a compound of column and row effects, the former acting on all ancillary occupations in a certain sector, the latter acting on a certain ancillary occupation in all sectors, as follows.

$$L_1^{**} = \hat{r}_{01} L_0^{**} \hat{s}_{01} \tag{7.6}$$

$\hat{r}$ and $\hat{s}$ are row and column multipliers spread out to form a diagonal matrix. The elements of r indicate that there is a general tendency for an ancillary occupation to grow throughout the economy, relative to all others. The elements of s indicate the rate at which any sector will step up its requirements of such occupations compared to all other sectors. These coefficients might be determined, up to a scalar ε which divides one vector and multiplies the other, by a method described in [3].

We have so far considered the coefficients, b, to be independent of c, and even independent of r and s. We now attempt to describe their connection.

For a reason mentioned before, we should expect a sector which has a relatively high b to have a corresponding low c, and vice versa. In sectors which are labour-intensive (e.g. hairdressing) we would expect the labour economies of output growth to be slight; in those which are capital-intensive (e.g. oil refining), employees might grow considerably more slowly than production.

Over and above this, there might be another factor influencing the elements of b. This would be any tendency for increasing specialisation. If a unit of labour wears a number of hats (e.g. a working proprietor selling in his shop) it is reasonable to suppose that his marginal productivity is less that that of the corresponding special-ist (e.g. a salesman). In the old days, when a cobbler making shoes at home was manager, salesman, technologist, and production worker all rolled into one, the efficiency of the shoe industry was rather less than it is now. Any increase in specialisation in any sector may accordingly be described as a lowering of b associated with a corresponding increase of s: the higher productivity of the mainstay occupation can only be obtained by taking on ancillary workers who now perform the tasks and duties he once did.

This increasing specialisation of mainstay occupations should, however, also have effects outside their own sector. Such specialisation might be interpreted as involving an increased standardisation of the goods and services they offer. If the transport sector required that all freight carried had to satisfy certain standard specifications, for it to achieve economies, then it would cater less for goods that required special treatment. If the transport network could only link up major sites for on-loading and off-loading, then connections to these terminals would not be their concern. As a re-sult of either, we might see that other industries tend increasingly to do their own transporting. The general implications of such thoughts would lead one to suppose, finally, that since the L matrix is square the elements of b are connected to the elements of r. When the former was lower, because of increased standardisation of out-put and specialisation of mainstay workers in their own sector, so the latter would be higher, resulting in a spread of such occupations elsewhere.

We now imagine that estimates of b, c and the reasonable estimates of the row and column multipliers ($\varepsilon^{-1} r_{01}$ and εs_{01}, say) are restrained by scalars, π and ψ, for all sectors and for all occupations, thus.

$$\pi i = \varepsilon s_{01} + b + c \tag{7.7}$$

$$\psi i = \varepsilon^{-1} r_{01} + b + c \tag{7.8}$$

From these equations, we obtain

$$r_{01} = \varepsilon^2 s_{01} + \varepsilon(\psi - \pi) i \tag{7.9}$$

33

where ε^2 and the other group of constants might be calculated by multiple regression analysis. $\psi = \pi$, if the latter term is equivalent to zero. Within these two restraints, the elements of b can only fall if there are corresponding increases in c, other coefficients remaining constant; alternatively, a decline in the elements of b would lead to an increase in the corresponding parts of r and s, c remaining constant. ε would be estimated by equation (7.9). The simplest estimates of π and ψ separately would be the average value of the cells in the vector which summed the values of b, c, $\varepsilon^{-1}r$ and εs obtained from equation (7.2), (7.5), (7.6) and (7.9). Alternative estimation procedures could of course be applied.

The features of the manpower model described in this section may now be summarised. We implicitly retain the notion that the capital-intensity of an industry's technology might alter over time and implicitly avoid the notion that economies of scale might be neutral in this respect. There are, after all, too many case studies from real life which substantiate the former but contradict the latter [5]. Furthermore, we assume complementarity between capital and labour for the sake of time series analysis: the discussion by economists of the impossibility of quick substitution between factors and the well-known statistical problem of multi-collinearity seem to us overwhelming. We have chosen to stipulate demand functions for factors, as opposed to the supply relationships usually found in the production function literature, though as will be obvious, each of equations (7.2) and (7.5) indicates necessary, if not sufficient, conditions for supply.

To cope with the problem of heterogeneity, we have avoided the temptation of generalising from two to n kinds of inputs. Usually with the kinds of production functions documented, such generalising, if not actually difficult, leads to absurd economic results: the notion of substitution between inputs across n-dimensional factor space implies, for example, that if the number of typists in a steel-mill were increased to infinity, other employees remaining constant, then the output of steel would continue increasing indefinitely also. We ought to avoid building such a feature into any manpower model.

Instead, our treatment of the different types of labour, crude though it may be at this stage, seems to have the following advantages. Over a short period, the organisational characteristics of sectors, denoted by their ancillary employment would be relatively stable if both the r's and s's were found to be low, and near 1. Variations in output would accordingly create greater variations in mainstay employment than in them. Furthermore, the lower are those row and column multipliers, the greater might be the tendency for the b's to express diseconomies due to rapidly increasing output in the short-run. On the other hand, in the long run, if the r's and s's might become substantially greater than 1, the ability of a sector to enjoy increasing returns would itself increase over time. Finally, although ancillary workers are not described as influencing the level of production directly, they help to shape the nature of the technology function. This gives them an important organisational role, even if not a productive one.

No results of applying this model will be presented here: our purpose has been to illustrate the nature of economic activity in terms of the quantitative modelling of it in statistical data. However, the results of applying similar estimation procedures to future needs for manpower are referred to in the next section. At the same time, we consider the extent to which the qualifications of those in certain occupations have satisfied some norm in the past and, whether given likely supplies in the future, disequilibrium will tend to improve or worsen.

8. THE NATURE OF MANPOWER IMBALANCES

There are three aspects of the planning gap we should need to consider, and all of them cannot be ignored if we attempt to match an estimation of needs with availabilities at a future date. The first is that the economy should not require more total manpower than the demographic trends indicate will be seeking work: this is a statement in which each man is counted as equivalent to any other. The second is that a further disaggregation into vectors of qualifications should on the demand and supply side match, cell for cell; the same statement could be rephrased in terms of occupations. Both these are measures of absolute imbalances, and would need to be accompanied by a description of how adopting flexible hiring standards on the part of employers and flexible vocational choice on the part of employees lead to relative imbalances; that is, departures from the norm of skill mixes required in each job. This is the third aspect of the planning gap.

That the first might exist was indicated by the application of a method similar to that described in the preceding section, to estimate the occupational needs of industrial sectors in Great Britain in 1970 [12]. The model used was

$$\bar{L}_2 = \alpha \hat{r}_{01} L_1 \hat{p}_{12}^{1-\beta} \qquad (8.1)$$

$\bar{L}_2$ was an estimated occupation by industry matrix for that future date, and L_1 an actual for 1961. Such matrices were rectangular. Estimates of row and column multipliers were obtained with the aid of the latter and a corresponding matrix for 1951, L_0,

$$\bar{L}_1 = \hat{r}_{01} L_0 \hat{s}_{01} \qquad (8.2)$$

and in projection the s-multipliers were substituted for by an expression in the growth of outputs, p, the coefficients of which were obtained from past data.

$$\cdot \hat{s}_{01} p_{01}^{-1} = \alpha \hat{p}_{01}^{-\beta} i \qquad (8.3)$$

This implies that the column effects were the results of the economies of output growth; and furthermore assumes that such economies were the same (β) for all industries; and that such potentialities for labour-saving would continue during the future as in the past. All that remained was to project the growth rates of industrial outputs, and this had been done by an extension of the techniques described in section 5, to a situation in which the economy grew at an overall rate of 4 per cent per annum up to 1970 [4].

The assumption $r_{12} = r_{01}$, which imagines the impact of technological change on occupational structure to remain constant in the future also, was modified when it was found that $i'L_2 i > \lambda$. λ was a single figure denoting total labour available for industrial employment in 1970 after the requirements of public sectors and unemployment had been subtracted from the economically active total indicated by demographic trends. Accordingly, we used

$$r_{12} = \hat{r}_{01}^{\theta} i \qquad (8.4)$$

where θ (greater than 1) was set by an iterative programming procedure at a level such that the total labour required exactly equalled the numbers likely to be available, λ. That such additional labour-saving was possible by accelerating the impact of technological change on occupational structure, and presumably the rate of innovation itself, was due to occupations in which few were employed having r-multipliers greater than 1, and those with many, less than 1. The application of θ expressed an inelastic substitution between types of labour.

Such a method yielded estimates of the change in demand for specific occupations. Two of these were scientists and technologists, and how these occupations were defined is given in [12]. If we gross these up by using the reciprocal of the proportion of total scientific and technological occupations to be found in industries, we obtain future needs for these two types of labour in all economic activities in 1970. These and the actual totals of occupations in 1961 are given in table 1.

The skill norm for these may be defined as the possession of the appropriate scientific and technological qualifications, being a university degree or its diploma equivalent for either. Such a norm is expressed both in terms of level and type of education. Projections of the available stock of manpower so qualified were made in [13] for 1968, by the use of what amounted to demographic accounting; and corresponding projections for 1970 were added by assuming that the stock would continue to grow at the underlying percentage rates right up to the end of the decade. These estimates of availabilities, and the corresponding 1961 levels, are also shown in Table 1.

Table 1

Actual and projected needs and availabilities
for two specific types of manpower

thousands, G.B.	1961	1970
SCIENTISTS		
Occupations	52.1	65.1
Qualifications	109.8	179.0
TECHNOLOGISTS		
Occupations	209.5	547.9
Qualifications	140.0	213.5

The first observation that could be made is that scientific qualifications are expected to grow faster than corresponding occupations; but that technological skills would become in relative short supply if technological jobs up to 1970 are seen to grow at the projected rate. Such a comparison might indicate absolute imbalances for specific occupations, and possibly describe the magnitude of the planning gap.

We know nothing at this stage of the existence of any utilisation gap. We might attempt to document it as in Table 2. This shows how, in G.B. in 1961, the total of these qualifications were distributed among occupations: those possessing them might not all work as scientists and technologists, and in particular they might be teachers. It also shows how those who did work as scientists and technologists were qualified.

Table 2

The matching of qualifications and
occupations for two specific types of labour

| thousands, G.B., 1961 | QUALIFICATIONS | | | Totals |
	Scientific	Techno-logical	Others	
OCCUPATIONS				
Scientists	27.9	3.8	20.4	52.1
Technologists	6.0	69.8	133.7	209.5
Teachers	41.7	8.5	*	*
Others	34.2	58.0	*	*
Totals	109.8	140.0	*	*

*These figures are considerably larger than the ones shown.

The items in the first two columns and their totals were obtained from [15], The totals of the first two rows were found in [14, 16]; the third items in these rows were obtained as a residual.

One notes immediately from the tabulation that, in 1961, only a half of scientists and a third of technologists possessed what were described as their appropriate qualifications. Errors in the data processing and definition of this norm aside, this must imply the following. First, that even a satisfactory overall balance (e.g. for scientists) tell us insufficient about how well each job receives the right mix of skills. We need to know the distribution of qualifications among occupations, and skill mix of each occupation, to identify possible utilization gaps.

Second, we need to know how any such misutilization occurred. If employers, adopting flexible hiring standards, somehow satisfied their recruitment needs when there was insufficient of the appropriately qualified labour available, and if these occupations remained so occupied even when later the right supplies come forward, then immobility of labour during its working-life would ensure those jobs remained under-qualified.

Third, we need to know the result of having labour under-qualified. If this is recruiting more than the numbers which otherwise would be taken on with the norm of skills, then some kind of over-employment exists. More manpower than the minimum implied by the norms would be needed to run an economy not in perfect balance. The wastage implied cannot be ignored.

Fourth, if this is the result, then the actual numbers employed in a certain occupation, being disequilibrium values, cannot, unadjusted, be used in projections of needs. If labour is under-qualified and over-employed, then projecting levels of employment into the future will overstate the equilibrium demand. Conversely, if qualifications are not used in the right occupations, and have been under-employed, projecting them into the future will understate their equilibrium values.

The first statement describes the data that would need to be processed, and the second and third the functional relationships that should be estimated from them. The fourth implies that future estimates of needs must use such functions and should not, realistically, be independent of but be made conditional on likely future availabilities. All of these points might be ignored at both the macro and micro-economic level. Certainly, the national model, as formulated in this section, does not escape this charge. Equally, statements by employers of their changing demands for qualifications might be at fault for the same reasons; if they furthermore failed to take account of changing economic conditions, they would in addition lack the advantage of a technique that did.

Unable to monitor changing economic demands, employers might adopt one of two courses of action. They might measure their future needs as identical to the present utilization gap. If supply is expected to grow correspondingly, if might be thought that their future needs would be met. (Tables 1 and 2 show that supplies of technological qualifications might grow between 1961–70 to match 1961 technological occupations, and [13] shows that employers' total stated needs grow in step with such supplies). Alternatively, employers might project their past and present use of qualifications, ignoring misutilization. If these uses have been limited by past supplies available, and if future supplies grow at the same rates seen in the past, then such statements of needs might indeed match future availabilities. Far from everything being rosy in the garden, any unanalysed utilization gap that exists might become more serious. In so far as they say something meaningful, tables 1 and 2 indicate this might happen with technologists in Great Britain.

Estimating the impact of deviations from the norms of qualified jobs, and for occupations that do not have a norm as obvious as those discussed here, forms a complex identification problem. The matter is taken up again in [8] but for the time being we shall bring our discussion of the problems of manpower analysis to a close.

9. CONCLUDING REMARKS

Certain major points are implicit in the discussion of methods and concepts throughout this paper, and attention may be drawn to them here.

The first is that, whether manpower planning takes place at the macro- or the

micro-economic level, the techniques of analysis to be used must be rather similar.
Whether we are dealing, on the one hand, with the national economy or, on the other,
with an industry or public sector, such as Defence, it is clear that forecasts of needs
have to be made and an inventory of manpower resources available has to be taken; that
these are done against the background of the levels of economic activity which generate
patterns of employment. Our discussion of functional relationships is given momentum by
the fact that such forecasts of demands and supplies of labour should be reasonably
realistic: the livelihood, even if not the lives, of human beings are at stake. Our
discussion of the accounting frameworks for economic and demographic variables is necessitated by the consideration that, whatever else it does, a manpower plan should at
least add up. Though such similarities might exist between the calculations carried out
at different levels, it is also clear that differences of emphasis will be seen. The
psychological characteristics of individuals, their preferences and career histories will
only appear in macro-economic data in a highly aggregated form: average behaviour, and
not distribution around the mean, will occupy our attention at the level of the economy.
Furthermore, the concepts and variables to be used for it must be applicable all the way
across the board, so that, for example, the specific features of the technology of
individual micro-economic institutions may not be adequately described in general statements applicable to all.

Second, however, despite the loss of some detail, each sector of the economy is
given a place somewhere in the comprehensive frameworks presented. It is clear, for
example, that a disaggregation of the economic accounts is always possible within the
limitations of data available, so that the demands for commodities placed on industries
by Defence expenditure, as well as all its other outgoings, may be documented simply by
adding a row and column to the square matrix used. Equally, the possibilities for
disaggregation in the demographic accounts described are in principle unlimited. The
account for employment might be given a set of multiple classifications, the first
categories denoting different activities such as Defence, within each of which we would
identify different occupations, which in turn would be subdivided among qualifications.
The junction of the first demographic account with itself would then be a full matrix,
0, instead of one with the non-zero diagonal $\hat{\delta}$. Within this matrix we might observe
many forms of labour mobility: the movement of labour from military to civil employment,
without changing either occupations or qualifications; the transfer or promotion from
one occupation to the other, while still remaining in the Armed Forces or in a certain
industry; if we imagine experience to be a skill category represented, the movement from
one qualification to another, without changing either sectors or types of work; or
mobility in all three directions. In practice, it may be impossible to set out such a
matrix at the moment, but this does not mean that attempts to collect the necessary data
should not be given urgent consideration. Within such disaggregated and fully documented
economic and demographic accounts we can identify the extent to which the use of manpower, both in Defence and elsewhere, are inter-dependent. This could be illustrated by
either imagining defence expenditure to be increased; or reduced to zero. In the latter
situation of total disarmament, the levels of activity in the industries manufacturing
weapon systems, as well as others selling them intermediate inputs such as fuel, would
be lowered with a corresponding unemployment of some labour in them. At the same time,
the manpower pool of the economy would be augmented by those previously in uniform,
and now seeking civilian employment. The result that would be seen in unemployment would
depend on the economic performance of other sectors, and individual abilities to obtain
jobs. In the former case, when defence expenditures rise, to the direct increase in
employment due to the expansion of the armed forces must be added the indirect pressure
on manpower resources felt via the industries making weapons. For such and similar
reasons, the manpower planning by individual institutions needs to be placed in a much
wider context.

Third, there must be some division of labour. If the manpower models of individual
institutions cope somewhat unsatisfactorily with changes some distance away in the
economy, then it may be thought they should be linked to a global model. If the global

model is unable to represent details specific and secret to the individual institutions, then the story that it tells may be improved by its being linked to sector models. In the Cambridge Growth Project, the views of local experts on the calculations of the global model have always been sought as a matter of course; and the resulting interchange of information appears useful to both parties. The chief condition necessary is a common currency of concepts in both types of models; which in the context of manpower is agreed classifications of occupations and qualifications, applied not only to Defence but to other identifiable government purposes and industrial sectors. Whether that is possible, we shall soon see.

REFERENCES

1. Brown, Murray. *On the Theory and Measurement of Technological Change*. Cambridge University Press, London, 1966.
2. Cambridge, Department of Applied Economics. *A Social Accounting Matrix for 1960*. No.2 in *A Programme for Growth*. Chapman and Hall, London, 1962.
3. Cambridge, Department of Applied Economics. *Input-Output Relationships 1954–1966*. No.3 in *A Programme for Growth*. Chapman and Hall, London, 1963.
4. Cambridge, Department of Applied Economics. *Exploring 1970*. No.6 in *A Programme for Growth*. Chapman and Hall, London, 1965.
5. Edwards, R.S. and H. Townsend. *Business Enterprise: Its Growth and Organisation*. Macmillan, London, 1958.
6. Harbison, F.H. and C.A. Myers. *Education, Manpower and Economic Growth*. McGraw-Hill, New York, 1965.
7. Leicester, Colin. " The composition of manpower requirements " in *Economic Growth and Manpower*. British Association for Commercial and Industrial Education, London, 1963.
8. Leicester, Colin. " The manpower link between economic growth and education: an analysis of 10 O.E.C.D. countries ". Mimeographed, O.E.C.D., 1965. Revised, 1967. To be published.
9. Smith, A.R. "Manpower planning in management of the Royal Navy ". *Journal of Management Studies*, May 1967.
10. Stone, Richard, "Input-output and demographic accounting: a tool for educational planning ". *Minerva*, Vol.IV, No.3, Spring 1966.
11. Stone, Richard and Giovanna, and Jane Gunton. "An example of demographic accounting." *International Association for Research in Income and Wealth*, Tenth General Conference, Maynooth, Ireland, August, 1967. To be published.
12. Stone, Richard and Colin Leicester. "An exercise in projecting industrial needs for labour ". Mimeographed, Cambridge, 1966.
13. U.K., Committee on Manpower Resources for Science and Technology. *Report on the 1965 Triennial Manpower Survey of Engineers, Technologists, Scientists and Technical Supporting Staff*. Cmnd. 3103. H.M.S.O., London, 1966.
14. U.K., General Register Office. *Census 1961, England and Wales: Occupation and Industry, National Summary Tables*. H.M.S.O., London, 1965.
15. U.K., General Register Office and General Registry Office, Scotland. *Census 1961, Great Britain: Scientific and Technological Qualifications*. H.M.S.O., London, 1962.
16. U.K., General Registry Office, Edinburgh. *Census 1961, Scotland: Occupation and Industry, National Summary Tables*. H.M.S.O., Edinburgh, 1965.
17. U.K., Ministry of Labour, *Occupational Changes in the United Kingdom from 1951 to 1961*. H.M.S.O., London, to be published.

Manpower Planning in Major Organisations
I. Chairman's Introduction

B.D. MISSELBROOK
DEPUTY CHAIRMAN
BRITISH AMERICAN TOBACCO CO. LTD.

As I understand this session, it is a slight digression from the main plan of the programme. Its general purpose is to direct your attention to the potential value of exploring the similarities and differences between military manpower planning and research on the one hand, and civilian – and for this occasion it means business organisations – on the other. I would regard this as an imaginative notion, and those of us who come from business or the fringes of business warmly welcome it. But we have to bear in mind the limitations which are inevitably imposed by the short time available. In their presentations speakers can only present certain selected aspects of their work in manpower planning, and we must all remember that this work has been done in a particular company or a particular industry under particular circumstances. Had the industries been different, had the geographical, social and economic areas been different, perhaps the selection of facts and emphases would have been varied. In my judgment, nevertheless, the selection of topics which are going to be put before you today is a very happy one; and it may well be that out of this session, in addition to the intrinsic interest of the material which is presented, there may be a further benefit namely, a sense of urgency to continue on a broader and particularly realistic basis these interchanges of experience, information and research between governmental, business and military organisations.

2. Manpower Planning in the British Petroleum Company

2.1 Introduction

H.S. MULLALY
STAFF MANAGER,
THE BRITISH PETROLEUM CO. LTD.

Since the War, my Organisation has been studying the development of planning techniques and at present focuses on the preparation of Seven-year general forecasts, Seven-year Supply forecasts, and Three-year Plans: the former are prepared centrally for the whole Group and the latter by each individual operating Company. Special long-term studies are handled by a Central Planning Department.

In addition, research and development into forecasting techniques is carried out by a highly specialised research Unit, working under the name of Dynamar, whose services are made available to industry and any other interested organisations on an agency basis: a description of their investigation into the practicabilities of long-range forecasting — The 1980 Study — will be given later.

One result of the 1980 Study was the recognition of the urgency of the need to understand and develop manpower plans at a performance level much higher than that so far achieved. This generated a detailed examination of ways and means, leading into what we now call the European Staff Planning Project (ESPP). Preliminary discussions to define the problem and design a work programme were held in July, 1964 and a directive was sent to the management of the BP Companies in October, 1964 seeking their support for the setting up of a special study of forward manpower requirements, on a Company by Company basis. This support was given.

After further planning work, with which a number of operating Companies were associated, thirteen Companies have been participating directly in the European project, while Canada, Australia and New Zealand have organised their manpower planning study independently of the European scheme but have been kept informed of developments. A project team was established in Paris to define the factors likely to influence manpower needs over the period 1965 — 1980, to lead research into the impact of those factors in quantitative and qualitative terms, to seek out other organisations working in this field, and to disseminate information to the rest of the BP Group.

Research, development and co-ordination is carried out by a small group working in London with the assistance of a Steering Committee consisting of the senior Personnel men from Germany, Italy, Sweden and Switzerland.

Following a Group Conference held in May, 1965, an outline Planning Guide was sent to all Companies who were invited to prepare their first Manpower Plans and to study a number of special aspects of planning.

The main results of this work will be outlined later, but one was the holding of top Management Seminars in a number of European Companies during the latter half of 1965 and in 1966. These were designed to discuss the feasibility of manpower forecasting and planning, and the part that each function of the operating Company should play in the preparation of this part of the management task, to examine their own Manpower Plan as co-ordinated by their Personnel Department and to decide any immediate action to be taken to implement the Plan. The interplay between the planning of trading, financial, technical and manpower needs could not have been demonstrated more clearly.

To provide the background of the environment in which the Group would be operating and to seek and test means whereby long-range forecasting may be done, a Project was established in 1960 by Dynamar.

2.2 The Socio-Economic Environment in the Nineteen Eighties

V. BRIJATOFF

DYNAMAR, FRANCE

2.2.1. INTRODUCTION

The aim of the "1980 Study" was to define the consumer and the consumption environment as it emerged from an analysis of 28 countries in Europe: 19 western and 9 eastern.

Dynamar started as an organisation specialising in Marketing and Market Research but very quickly it became clear that in order to optimize these two functions it was necessary to look into the future. We found that there were clear indications of an evolution from a producer market to a consumer market. In such a consumer market the producing companies would be more and more obliged to adjust their products and services to consumer needs. These consumer needs and reactions would reflect the way of life of families, socio-economic groups, professional groups, regions and nations. It was therefore important for a producing company not only to be as fully informed as possible about consumer attitudes, needs and reactions of today — a function fulfilled by Market Research — but also to be able to forecast consumer behaviour and needs in the future. For this reason the "nineteen eighties" study was started with what we have called a "prospective marketing" approach. What do we mean by this? Simply that we tried to collect, to complete and to integrate all available data in order to obtain an overall socio-economic picture. In this way we hoped to avoid both an exercise in wishful thinking and also the mere stringing together of opinions from experts in various fields and their extrapolation.

2.2.2. THE METHODOLOGY USED

The general approach:

Why nineteen eighties?

For our calculations we had to choose a point in time. But for the general analysis we prefer to speak about the "nineteen eighties" which means sometime from the year 1980 onwards. This was only 16 years ahead of us when the first results of the study came out. We were not really diving entirely into the dark, since 3/4 of the consumers of 1980 were already alive. In addition the working population of 1980 is already alive and it is this working population which will have the purchasing power and in many cases the purchasing decision. Finally the technological means of 1980 are either in existence or else at the research or development stage. Thus, if we exclude unforeseeable changes due to wars, radical political changes and revolutionary discoveries, it seems that it should be possible to detect the other important developments in time providing an appropriate forecasting instrument is developed.

The consumer of 1980 will find himself in a new environment produced by a set of inter-related factors.

  (i) demographic factors: importance and structure of the population,

 (ii) production factors: output by branches, inner structure of each branch, investment and labour,

(iii) consumption factors: population needs and habits, available income, priority of expenses and so on.

Our approach consisted of forecasting the development of economic structures by taking into account the pressures which are exerted upon them by current needs and by trying to assess to what extent new structures were going to satisfy only former needs or to give rise to new needs.[1] (For references see p.48).

For example:

– the desire for a car is a current social phenomenon; the development of structures will make it possible to achieve car-ownership but not to satisfy the need fully – particularly when it is a question of its use in built-up areas. The desire for a car will therefore be modified by the possibilities of using it.

– because of the movement away from the land the need for mechanisation in agriculture has to be met. The development of economic structures will make this possible but will create new needs: more extensive regrouping of holdings, better education, etc..

– the socio-economic trend is pushing women to take up employment which means a reduction in her time spent in the house. This leads to a need for more functional equipment (machines and labour-saving devices) and for relaxation (comfort, better furnishings, simple heating system, etc.). This satisfaction of current needs by new structures will create new needs, (facilities for looking after children, preparation of meals, rest).

The technical approach:

The available techniques

The concept of studying the future is not new and much work has already been done, employing a large number of different approaches.[2] If basically it is more or less always an extrapolation from the present to the future it can range from the use of graph paper and a ruler to that of input/output matrixes.[3][4]

From a mathematical point of view the methods available could be divided in two groups:[5]

– time series analysis,
– model building techniques.

Unfortunately when one looks over a period of time of more than 10 years the purely mechanized techniques tend to be less and less efficient and the results obtained have to be corrected by a combination of the subjective judgement of the forecaster and the advice of experts.

The general method of forecasting[6] is to make a hypothesis on the growth of a main variable such as a Gross Domestic or National Product or Private Consumption and to see what implications this growth would have on the other components such as the evolution of branches of production or functions of consumption, taking into account as far as possible the present knowledge of the impact of technical progress, disposable manpower, possibilities of investment and so on.

Because of our objectives our own approach was slightly different.

The technique used

We had to work, as I said before, on 28 different countries. This meant that we had to find a standard framework, and such a framework was provided by the statistics of National Accounts published by U.N.O.[7] and O.E.C.D.[8]

As a first stage we wanted only a general framework or backcloth of the economic evolution in Europe. This meant using a method more sophisticated than a simple extrapolation, requiring limited technical equipment however, (only a small computer was used) and permitting the modification of the results as time goes by.

It was also essential to be able to cross-check the results obtained and to ensure the coherence and consistency of the whole.

The possible Gross Domestic Products (G.D.P's)

We wanted to take into account the structural relationships between the growth of each sector of production and then by adding together the possible added values of each sector to obtain the possible Gross Domestic Products.

    (i) Population trends were predicted according to standard procedures or taken, after cross-checking, from published forecasts for each country. The working population was predicted for 1980 using corrected occupation rates for each five year group of total population, and then broken down by branches.

    (ii) The average growth of each branch of the production over the base period (1950–1962) was calculated by regression and projected up to 1980.

    (iii) To allow for relative growth between branches the ratio of each branch's performance to all the others was calculated and also projected by more or less sophisticated regression up to 1980.

    (iv) The results obtained in (ii) were then multiplied by the calculated coefficients which gave us a number of possible G.D.P.'s equal to the number of branches studied. These values were examined and the unlikely ones rejected.

    (v) The remaining results were then studied in relation to the available manpower and the possible amount of investments thus enabling us to assess the likelihood of the figures obtained.

The possible private consumption

    (i) Quite independently a procedure similar to that for branches of production was used for the functions of consumption (e.g. food – housing – clothing and so on).

    (ii) Using international comparisons and taking into account known sociological trends the values obtained were examined and unlikely ones rejected.

Comparison between production and consumption

    (i) Because of the type of variable on which we had worked we were able to apply the classical relationship of National Accounting which states that: G.D.P. equals Public Consumption plus Private Consumption plus Investment plus the end result of balance of payments.[9]

    (ii) We calculated the Public Consumption by correlation with the growth of G.D.P. and then obtained the *disposable sum* for Private Consumption which equals: G.D.P. less Public Consumption less Investments.

    (iii) We compared then the obtained results with the remaining possible private consumptions and have systematically chosen the three maximum possible figures allowing for a " normal " balance of payments.

At the conclusion of this process, which I tried for sake of explanation to simplify as much as possible, an overall framework of the economy of each country has been derived for 1980 with a bracket of high, medium and low hypotheses of evolution.

2.2.3. THE MAIN FINDINGS

It is quite impossible to present all the results we got during our study. I think it best to give some findings which either derive directly from the obtained results or were established during the whole research.

Changes in Population

(i) The general increase of the population in Europe will be of about 23 per cent from 1960 to 1980. The total population will rise from 668 million to 822 million, which means an increase of 154 million in twenty years. But there will be a difference between Western and Eastern Europe: plus 66 million for the former, plus 88 million for the latter.

(ii) Increase in number and percentage of old people, particularly women. It can be said that there will be twice as many people aged seventy five and over as there are now. This leads to a retirement and pension scheme problem and the possible "political " significance of old people. There will also be a slight decrease in the proportion of the working population in spite of a slight increase in the number of women at work. In 1960 the "active " or working population represented 46.6 per cent of the total population (European average figure) and in 1970 it will represent only 45.5 per cent.

(iii) This decrease will derive from the present structure of the population and as far as the active population is concerned from the higher school-leaving age, and from the increase in the number of old people.[10] From the socio-economic point of view this will lead to a modification in working conditions and family life, greater need for efficiency and mechanisation, more intense concentration of production factors, which will mean a more concentrated and urbanised population structure. The increased number of women who will be working will give a new economic significance to the female population.

(iv) Professional qualifications will be more and more required with more and more equality between men and women. This will come from the needs of more and more complex industrial procedures and from the extensive use of all kinds of technology.

Gross Domestic Product

There will be a general increase in the income both in absolute terms and per capita, but the rates of growth will depend on the starting level (more important for less industrialised countries) and the general economic structure of each country, as shown in the following table:

Table 1

The increase of G.D.P. - Indices

	1960	1970	1980
Belgium	100	175	296
F.R. of Germany	100	160	250
Italy	100	238	460
Spain	100	282	620

Current prices

The average income will double during these 16 years but the nature of private or personal consumption will be quite different from what it is now. The fact to stress is that only 50 per cent of the family budget will be spent on vital needs (i.e. food, housing and domestic equipment). The rest naturally differs from country to country and will be used as "Discretionary Income". This means that the pressure of the consumer on the market will be greater and greater with the rise in income and confirms our first marketing hypothesis. It also means that the production will be determined by the totality of consumer demands over the next twenty years, and it stresses the need to be as aware as possible of consumer behaviour.

Table 2

Discretionary Income

	1960	1980
Sweden		
Millions of crowns	14,560	31,930
Index number	100	220
Portugal		
Millions of escudos	20,130	53,120
Index number	100	260

Industrial Consumption

The industrial population will represent 30 to 40 per cent of the active population. In fact, this represents an increase but the output (volume and value) per person employed will increase more quickly.

One of the important results of the passage from a production market to a consumption market will be the need for the Industrial Consumer to adopt a new attitude in order to develop his market or even to keep his traditional one. Industries will have to be:

(i) more concentrated and of bigger size because of the growing complexity of technological processes and of the amount of investments involved to enlarge production, to risk money in innovation and to accelerate output.

Table 3

Total Investments — Indices

	1960	1970	1980
Belgium	100	220	400
F.R. of Germany	100	240	350
Italy	100	250	570

Current prices

(ii) more organised and specialised in order to reduce unitary cost prices or increase the quality or output of the products for the same price, search for the highest possible efficiency and be able to produce more and more elaborate and complex products. This leads to the necessity of skilful production control and the multiplication of the intermediate and final goods necessary to meet the consumer's requirements.

(iii) better informed in order to satisfy the real needs of the consumer and often try to forecast them, to keep up with competition and anticipate the technological changes and to reduce as much as possible all the financial risks.

The industrial consumer will buy and sell more according to the technical quality of the products than to their price. He will often be a Government. That means that the needs of the Industrial Consumer will apply to:

(i) investments in order to expand or even only survive. The necessity to maintain, increase and renew production will lead to great physical investments but even greater intellectual ones.

(ii) new equipment and greater variety of intermediate products necessary for the creation of new products or the improvement of the quantity or quality of output.

(iii) automation[11] and mechanisation in order to create mass production or to free manpower from manual tasks. They will be applied to the industrial process from work feeding and assembly to packaging and distribution as well as to intellectual activities from output control to helping with decision making. One can find beneath an illustration of the past development in the installation of computers:

Table 4

Growth in the use of computers

	1957	1958	1959	1960	1961
France	15	35	60	125	260
F.R. of Germany	20	45	85	170	390
United Kingdom	75	130	170	240	340

Source: " l'Automatisation dans le secteur des travaux administratifs E.E.C. 1963 "

Since the O.E.C.D. seminar was held in Zurich in 1966 it has been estimated that the total number of computers in Western Europe was 5,520 in 1966, of which 4,620 were used for administrative purposes and 900 for scientific calculations. The number of computers in the first category will probably be 10,500 in the year 1971.

2.2.4. A PROVISIONAL CONCLUSION: SOME IMPLICATIONS FOR MANPOWER PLANNING

Our forecasting exercise led us to a series of questions on manpower.

On the National Level

The demographic factors (age – fertility rate – sex ...) have direct[12] influence on the structure of the working population and it was essential to see what were the long term trends in this field. The structural changes observed led us to stress the necessity of appraisals of the prospective demand and supply of such categories as scientists or engineers. These figures of quantitative and qualitative nature are needed by the Government as a basis for planning research, development and other tasks and also by Industry for planning future capital investment, recruitment, training and salaries. [13]

If we take a sector, let us say banking, one can forecast a limited rise in the number of accounting clerks or tabulating-machine operators because of the increasing use of computer equipment. But the demand for systems analysts and programmers, relative newcomers in this branch, will increase sharply. That means that the competition, not only between firms but also between the different sectors of Government and academic bodies, for high talent manpower is great and growing.

The economic growth implies manpower mobility in order to adapt the production to the consumers needs; it also means a parallel adaptability of the working population in order to maintain the equilibrium necessary for growth, and the reduction of possible conflicts between man and technical evolution. This means that not only forecasts by industry are necessary but also — and it was not done in our study, but we felt the need of it — by occupation.

This concept is the link between economics and education, and forecasts in this field are essential for individuals in making their career plans and for firms or officials for planning their programmes of education or training.

On the Firm Level

Until recent years businessmen felt no need for manpower planning since they had the possibility of recruiting the numbers and the kinds of employees they required. They very often considered the manpower as a cost rather than an economic resource. Now that this optic has changed and if we consider the future, manpower planning could have three main functions: [14]

(i) to give managers more flexibility to conduct their business,

(ii) to obtain and keep better people,

(iii) to give employees themselves a greater sense of accomplishment and stability.

The analysis of possible economic evolution in all the countries studied gives the same feed-back: acceleration, complexity. This many-faceted challenge can only be met if people start today. The social, scientific and technological ideas and processes might become so interlocked that only a minority will direct or even understand them. If the only pay-off of our study is to open a discussion on the implications of the future environment on manpower needs, it has already been worthwhile doing it.

REFERENCES

1. Katona George. *The mass consumption society* — McGraw-Hill Book Company — New York — 1960.
2. Asepelt — *Europe's future consumption* — North-Holland Publishing Company — Amsterdam — 1964.
3. Stone R. — *A programme for growth* — The Department of Applied Economics, University of Cambridge, Chapman and Hall — Cambridge — 1963.
4. Chenery H.G. — Clark P.G. — *Interindustry economics* — John Wiley & Sons, Inc. — New York — 1965.
5. Kendall M.G. — Stuart A. — *The advanced theory of statistics* — Charles Griffin & Company Ltd. — London — 1963.
6. Wolff J. — *La Prévision* — Berger Levrault — Paris — 1963.
7. U.N.O. — *Yearbook of National Accounts Statistics* — United Nations — New York.
8. O.E.C.D. — *Statistics of National Accounts* — Organisation for Economic Co-Operation and Development — Paris.
9. Piatier A. — *Statistique et Observation Economique* — Presses Universitaires de France — Paris — 1961.
10. Fourastié J. — *Les 40.000 heures* — Laffont-Gonthier — Genève — 1965.
11. O.E.C.D. — Automation progrès technique et main d'oeuvre — *Conférence Européenne Zurich 1er-4 Février 1966, Supplément au Rapport final* — Organisation de Coopération et de développement économiques Direction de la Main-d'oeuvre et des affaires sociales division des affaires sociales — Paris — 1966.
12. U.N.O. — Aspects démographiques de la main-d'oeuvre — *Premier rapport: La participation à l'activité économique selon le sexe et l'âge* — Nations Unies, New York — 1962.
13. National Science Foundation — *The Long-range demand for scientific and technical personnel* — The National Science Foundation — Department of Labour — Washington — 1961.
14. General Electric — *Manpower in General Electric Planning for the future* — General Electric — New York — 1964.

2.3 Manpower Planning in the British Petroleum Company

E.S.M. CHADWICK

MANAGER, STAFF PLANNING & RESEARCH,
THE BRITISH PETROLEUM COMPANY LIMITED

2.3.1. INTRODUCTION

The implications of the Dynamar 1980 Study are consistent with the many studies that have been made on future manpower needs and supply, all of which indicate a general European-wide shortage of skilled manpower in the next 5–10 years. The oil industry is particularly sensitive to such a situation in that the people who go to make up its manpower form a group that at all levels and in all areas is heavily weighted with skill in the broadest sense. An industry that handles liquids and gases in vast quantities does not need thousands of unskilled men to carry the product around; instead it needs comparatively large numbers of good engineers and good operators who can make the best of the expensive equipment that replaces unskilled manpower in a modern "capital intensive" industry.

In contrast to more traditional industry, the oil industry employs relatively few people but a high proportion of qualified manpower. Indeed the Ministry of Labour, at the end of 1966, calculated that of 22,700 men employed in oil (excluding distribution) some 38% were administrative, technical and clerical; by contrast the motor vehicle manufacturing industry employed 431,550 men of whom only 18.3% were in these categories.

This emphasis on formal "quality" is not the only characteristic of the manpower employed by BP. The Company does not employ very large numbers of people concentrated in one immediate area; even our largest installations are comparatively modest in employment terms. Instead the Company has a considerable number of people scattered around the globe in quite small groups, whether they be running a refinery, working in an exploration or production area or helping to man a marketing company. However, not everyone agrees that there is a shortage of quality staff; some take the view that what exists is a considerable under-use of existing talents and abilities. Certainly studies in the U.K. have indicated that there is a large, as yet untapped, potential for the exercise of higher skills if only adequate training and education can be made available. This, in itself, is a very large subject. Suffice to say that manpower planning must go hand-in-hand with activities directed towards the optimum effective use of manpower.

It is against this background, that manpower planning in BP has been developed. Our original objectives were twofold:

(i) To establish our requirements of manpower both quantitatively and qualitatively over the years 1965–70, and to consider requirements up to 1980.

(ii) To establish how those needs may be met.

2.3.2. COMPANY MANPOWER PLANS

It was soon obvious that a grand manpower plan for BP was neither practical nor, in our view, desirable. While there is a global Company plan in terms of production, shipping and refining, this must be translated into the contribution which each Associate or Subsidiary Company makes to the total and, since there is no significant inter-changeability of staffs of different nationalities, each company in manpower terms stands on its own.

Our first task was to produce a planning guide which would be equally applicable to the small Marketing Company employing less than 500 people and to the large integrated Company employing 5,000/6,000. We started by defining the factors which appeared most likely to affect manpower requirements. These are many and varied but to fall into three main groups which are nevertheless closely inter-related.

Trading and Production patterns

The first group, trading and production patterns, includes gross tonnages (e.g. production, throughput, sales) range of products handled, distribution methods, organisation and company policy, and any changes which can be foreseen such as expansion, contraction, diversification and the introduction of new products. Preliminary studies showed that there was very little direct correlation between gross figures of sales, tonnages and throughputs with gross manpower needs. It was more realistic to study individual sections (production, manufacturing, distribution and sales) and individual categories (e.g. chemists and engineers).

Technological change

The second group, technological change, includes the impact of automation and of data processing; the application of operational research techniques and the application of computers to the overall company operations; the effect of technological evolution on operating methods; market demand; the development of new products and the improvement of existing products. These are the factors which have been shown to be most likely to affect our requirements of men and skills.

Social and economic change

The third group, social and economic change, is concerned with factors such as fiscal policy; education; prices and incomes; which, although entirely outside the control of the company are becoming more and more influential as Governments enter the field of national economic planning. Economic factors can only be studied in the short term because Government regulation of the economy is conditioned by political considerations. On the other hand, the development of national plans may at least indicate the desired future of the economy towards which stimuli or regulators may be applied.

Apart from economic developments, there is also the impact of social advance in the fields of education, hours of work and holidays, retirement pensions, retirement and school leaving ages, all of which can affect manpower either in terms of availability or cost.

Conclusions

Consideration of these factors led to a number of conclusions on manpower planning:-

(i) attempts to forecast 15 years ahead are unlikely to produce results which would justify the tremendous amount of work involved. At best they could produce warning signs and indications of trends but little which would dictate present action.

(ii) it is only necessary to plan manpower sufficiently far ahead to allow time to take remedial action. The period will depend on the category of employee and the particular local circumstances.

(iii) manpower plans are an integral part of company plans. Planning is too often applied to money and materials whereas a plan should be concerned with money, materials and men.

Outcomes – The Five-year Manpower Plan

As a result of our preliminary work we were able, in September, 1965, to circulate a guide to manpower planning incorporating the many considerations which I have touched upon and on which each company could proceed to the preparation of a Five-year Manpower Plan. Since that date, work has proceeded in three directions.

    (i) the preparation, company by company, of Five-year Manpower Plans linked with company plans and forming an integral part of them. A five year forward look was chosen because, on the one hand, it appeared to be the maximum which, in the state of our knowledge and experience, we could forecast with any reasonable accuracy, and, on the other, it was the minimum realistic period in relation to quality staff. A high proportion of such staff enter through company training schemes – craft and process apprenticeships, commercial and industrial student apprenticeships and university apprenticeships – in all of which the period from initial recruitment to effective work is about five years. In the light of experience we would not tie ourselves to any specific planning period since there are some sections of our employees for whom a shorter forecasting period may be adequate, whereas for others, particularly the graduate/professional staff with management potential, one must look much further ahead.

    (ii) a study of the impact on manpower of such matters as automation, automatic data processing and other specific technological developments within our industry, drawing upon the fund of experience existing within the group and outside.

    (iii) the investigation of mathematically based prediction techniques in order to discover whether it is possible to assist in policy decisions on recruitment patterns, retraining, staff movements and retirement.

The Three Phases of Manpower Planning

As our work progressed it became increasingly clear that it was convenient to think of manpower planning as comprising three phases:-

Phase 1   Overall Planning
                Planning for total numbers, skilled groups, organisational groups, costs, etc.

Phase 2   Individual Planning
                Planning in the context of Phase 1 for management succession, career planning, recruitment, training, etc.

Phase 3   Review and Audit
                Continual amending and auditing of plans as circumstances change.

Phase 2 of this progression is familiar in many areas of industry and is often taken to be synonymous with "manpower planning." Phase 1 on the other hand, though familiar enough on the broad national level in the planning of educational facilities, is comparatively uncharted territory at the level of the firm even though it attempts to explore the context in which phase 2 must work. Any manpower planning activity must embrace all three phases. To do one without the others is unlikely to achieve any worthwhile results. At the end, one has not one plan but a series of plans. First, the overall (or strategic plan) concerned with total activities and total numbers and, second, a series of individual (or tactical) plans embracing recruitment planning, career planning, management succession, training plans, etc.

I shall concentrate on phase 1, the overall planning, because I think it is this aspect that will be of most interest to you.

2.3.3. THE PREPARATION OF COMPANY MANPOWER PLANS

Since Company Manpower Plans form an integral part of Company Planning, the starting point must be the overall Company Plan. The first stage is to establish the present position in all its aspects – total tonnages, sales, throughputs, product mix, organisation, manning schedules, etc., and the present manpower position in terms of categories and skill levels. From this base it is necessary to look backwards in time to detect trends. This will include changes in production and distribution patterns, sales tonnages, etc. and their impact upon manpower and such specifically manpower aspects as wastage by category and group.

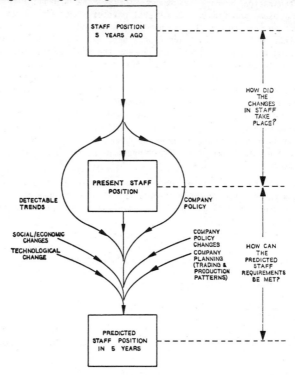

FACTORS AFFECTING MANPOWER PLANNING

Fig. 1

What this involves may perhaps best be illustrated by describing briefly how our German Company prepare their Five-year Plan. The distinction is made between two areas of manpower requirements:

(i) Increased and decreased in requirements.

(ii) Replacement.

BP
Germany   ESTIMATES OF STAFF NUMBERS 1967-1972   Functional Sector _____ Division _____ Branch _____

		Actual Number 30.6.1966	Estimates of increases + decreases in requirements + year end balances																								Code
			1966		Actual 30.6.1967	1967			1968			1969			1970			1971			1972			
			+	-	=		+	-	=	+	-	=	+	-	=	+	-	=	+	-	=	+	-	=	
1	a																									
	b																									
2	a																									
	b																									
3	a																									
	b																									
4	a																									
	b																									
5	a																									
	b																									
6	a																									
	b																									
7 Total holders of established posts																										
8 Number of approved established posts																										
9 Staff reserve																										
10 Transitional staff																										

a) Estimates of previous planning 1966 – 1971
b) Estimates of current planning 1967 – 1972

Date/Signature of Functional Sector Manager | Date/Signature of Managing Director

Please explain briefly increases and decreases in requirements and reasons of alteration to previous planning

Fig. 2

53

The first is produced by functional managers who are required to forecast the different activities and changes within their fields of responsibility. The second by Staff Department, since they have wastage and recruitment information, which is evaluated for planning purposes.

Forecast of Requirements

(a) A schedule is prepared centrally (Fig. 2) which shows the previous planning in numbers and with an attachment giving the reasons for changes planned during the previous period.

(b) The actual position as at 30th June, 1967 divided by categories of staff.

Functional managers are required to:

(a) Prove the actual position as at 30th June, 1967 both as regards numbers and categories.

(b) Plan the activities within the different branches and departments with respect to changes of jobs either numerically or by qualification, involving consideration of the following areas:-

> Organisational changes
> Changes in work patterns, e.g. Contracting out
> Mechanisation and automation
> Changes of quantities procured, produced, distributed and sold.
> Reasons for Plan changes must be stated.

The functional sector managers are required to discuss this with their superiors and the Plan must ultimately be approved by the Managing Director.

Five-year Manpower Plans have been integrated into the annual budgeting system and approval of additional established posts is very difficult to obtain unless they have been included in the Plan. Even so Board approval must be obtained.

All Sector Plans are finally co-ordinated and analysed by Staff Department to arrive at the total increase and decrease in requirements by numbers and categories. To these are added changes in requirements in numbers of staff due to external factors. For example, it is estimated that between 1968 and 1970 the present working week of 42½ hours will be reduced gradually to 40 hours. Considerations such as these are brought to the attention of the functional managers to enable them to plan organisational changes which may be required and to consider alternatives to avoid additional manpower costs. To the figures so obtained Staff Department applies its forecast of wastage in order to arrive at an estimate of the replacement requirement by numbers and categories. (Table 5).

Finally, manpower requirements are costed for inclusion in the financial budget.

The system of flow of information in producing the final Plan is illustrated at Fig. 3.

Concurrently the social/economic environment is studied in order to establish the manpower supply situation which is conditioned by the school leaving age, the educational output, the level of employment and total national demand.

2.3.4. PREDICTION

Up to this point I have been discussing forecasting, i.e. the assessment of manpower needs to meet task objectives, the supply of manpower of various categories and skills, and environmental influences and constraints.

The third direction of our work is the use of mathematically based prediction techniques to assist in policy decisions, to detect trends, to indicate the futurity in present courses of action, to assess the probable future consequences of alternative possibilities. The basic concepts and information requirements for studies of this kind are extremely simple. Nevertheless, in an analysis of the heterogeneous society which

Table 5

	1966	1967	1968	1969	1970	1971
No. of jobs at beginning of period under review	5,129	5,222	5,482	5,554	5,593	5,650
Functional sectors' anticipated changes in numbers of jobs +	346	426	138	139	63	21
−	253	166	105	100	47	6
Increased requirements due to shorter working hours +	−	−	39	−	41	−
No of holders of established posts at end of period under review	5,225	5,482	5,554	5,593	5,650	5,665
Anticipated requirements (+ in numbers of jobs (−	93 −	260 −	72 −	39 −	57 −	15 −
Replacements due to wastage +	264	552	566	568	576	578
Reduced replacement due to labour market −	89	94	98	106	112	119
Recruits required during period under review	268	718	540	501	521	474

exists in BP, even with the simplest of information, prediction calculations can become extremely complicated. Yet it is vital in planning the manpower of a company the size of BP in the United Kingdom to "quantify " certain of our basic individual characteristics.

Employees of BP in the United Kingdom have been divided, for the purposes of planning, into three sections. The first is senior staff, defined as those employees filling or potentially capable of filling a managerial position at some stage in their working life. The second section includes craftsmen, clerks and skilled operators; and the third, female clerks and typists. The section for which planning has proved most difficult both at the national level and in most companies is the first one, senior staff; it is this section to which we have devoted most of our attention up to the present.

For each individual who fits the definition of senior staff, a career card has been punched with the simplest and least equivocal information, which includes movements between grades and departments. From this store of information it is possible to extract such essential factors as wastage rates in whatever category is required or probability of promotion between grades as related to age, length of service and qualifications. By establishing this picture of movement within the senior staff of the company, it becomes possible to consider forecasts of movements within the next five years.

The first approach has been to use the trends of the past five years to forecast the position within the next five years. This, of course, can only be done with the full realisation of the assumptions involved. Just because there has been a certain promotion pattern over the last five years, it will not necessarily be the same for the next five years. The aim indeed is to examine the effect of a variety of trends and see whether the projected position achieved by these trends is satisfactory or not. The executive decision lies in deciding what position is desirable, what trend produces this position and what action, if any, is necessary to produce this trend. There is no method of

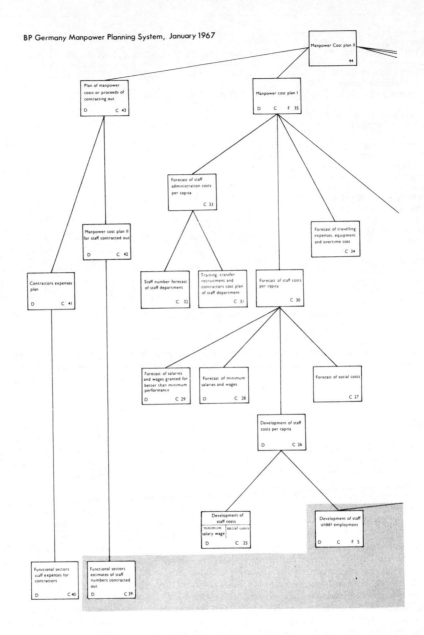

BP Germany Manpower Planning System, January 1967

Fig. 3

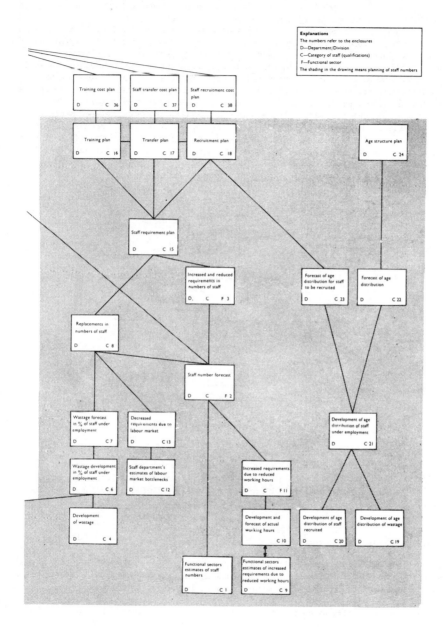

Fig. 3

establishing a staff position which, in five years time, will _inevitably_ be achieved;
but decisions can be made which in all probability will approximate to this position –
the accuracy of the approximation depending not only on the accuracy of the prediction
method, but also on the unpredictable effect of outside influences.

With the aid of a computer to do the vast number of trivial calculations involved,
it has been possible to investigate a number of hypotheses. One approach which may be of
particular interest is based on work described by Professor Young of Liverpool
University. A group of people, in this instance senior staff, is divided into a series
of statuses which can best be understood as the grading system in BP. The status, or
grade, is effectively a measure of seniority. Any number of statuses can be defined and,
in fact, it is convenient to subdivide grades by considering the number of years spent
within a grade. The aim is to calculate the probability of moving between statuses and
then, using these probabilities, to predict the number of people in each status in five
(or more) years time. This can best be understood diagramatically. (Fig. 4) Each of the
movements shown can be expressed in terms of probability. It is easily seen that the

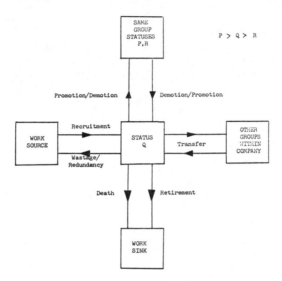

Fig. 4 MANPOWER MOVEMENT

situation, although essentially simple, can become complex as a result of the amount
of detail involved. Such an analysis can, however, lead to a more complete understanding
of the factors involved in producing a particular staff position and possible remedial
action for undesirable forecasted situations can be more carefully assessed.

2.3.5. SOME RESULTS AND CONCLUSIONS

As I said earlier, our first attempts at making five year company manpower plans
were intended to develop and test methodology and procedures, to assess the effects of
the various factors on demand and supply, and to isolate problem areas.

The apparent stability of manpower

One remarkable result has been the great similarities which have been found in all
the companies of Europe, despite some marked differences in the state of development of
the economy, level of employment etc. This applies to all the examples which I will give.

Although total sales and refinery throughputs are estimated to increase by some 8%-9% annually over the next 5 years, total numbers of manpower will remain almost constant and in some instances will show a slight reduction. In the U.K., for example, it is estimated that sales will increase by 10% per annum and refinery throughput by 16% per annum yet manpower will increase by only 1%.

Yet within this apparent stability of manpower, some very significant factors have been noted. The advent of full employment in most countries of Western Europe has affected the demand for manpower at every level. New industries and activities have developed that need a high proportion of highly trained manpower: the electronics industry, the chemical industry, the expanding universities. These alternative opportunities have greatly increased the mobility of manpower particularly in the highly skilled categories up to 35 years of age, the consequence of demand for quality exceeding supply. This situation, by all available information, is likely to worsen. It is estimated that in the U.K. the demand for graduates will increase by 7.4% annually over the next 5 years while the output from universities will increase by only 4.6%. Even in countries such as Turkey or Portugal with comparatively high total unemployment there is nevertheless a shortage of skilled manpower.

All companies report high wastage rates up to 35 years of age but their mobility factor from 35 years of age is insignificant until 55/60 when retirement begins to have an impact. Unlike the Services, there are no fixed terms of engagement or established drop out points so that a man who has reached the age of 35 in our employment wants and expects to continue until about 60 years of age. The achievement and maintainance of a stable age structure so avoiding major problems and upheavals in the future is a matter of considerable importance particularly for career staff. Mathematically based prediction techniques are proving very helpful in this area. If I may quote some figures to illustrate the scale of this, in our German company, it is forecast that the total number of employees will increase from 5,129 to 5,665 between 1966 and 1971, but this increase of 546 is almost wholly accounted for by the manning of a new refinery and an increase in the research activity, yet during that same time 2,324 people will need to be recruited in order to replace wastage. (See Table 5)

The changing pattern of skill requirements

The other conclusion that has emerged strongly within the apparent stability of numbers is the changing pattern of skill requirements. In our Turkish company, for example, whereas in 1960, 20.4% of employees were graduates, by 1965 this proportion had risen to 27.4%. This is a common pattern and a trend which, by all indications, is likely to increase over the next 5–10 years. This increased demand for skills, and it is not confined to the factory or works, but applies equally in offices, springs from the great technological advances of the past decade. When this is linked with a completely new organisational structure in line with technological capabilities, some very dramatic changes can be seen. Whereas a refinery built only 15 years ago, with a throughput of 5 million tons a year, required a total of 2,500 employees, refineries of similar throughput are being built today requiring less than 200. Men in these modern refineries must be of a new type – multi-skilled rather than uni-skilled and very flexible in their approach. Men with this type of skill and outlook are not easy to find; to man a modern refinery means a search for men of high potential and rigorous and complex training programmes to fit them for their responsibilities.

But it is not just a matter of recruiting and training the right sort of men. Our calculations have shown that more than 50% of the people on our payroll today will still be there 15 years from now. A major effort must be mounted to train and develop these men to fit them for the world of 1975 if we are not to face a situation with a serious shortage of skilled manpower on the one hand and a surplus of men unfit for the task required on the other.

The cost of manpower

Finally, may I touch upon another aspect that has been brought to the fore by our studies, namely the cost of manpower. While manpower costs have been rising steadily over the past 5 years, all our forecasts indicate a very much steeper rise in the cost per man over the next five years, particularly of the higher skilled men which we are going to need in ever-increasing numbers. It has been demonstrated to our satisfaction that the per capita cost of men is not something within our control, except very marginally. In Italy taking the 1960 level as 100, this had risen to 185 by 1965 and is expected to rise to 300 by 1970. A very similar pattern is shown in Turkey.

This, coupled with the expectation that skilled manpower will become even more difficult to obtain and the fact that even in a capital intensive industry such as ours manpower represents, on average, 35% of our operating costs, emphasises the need to achieve optimum utilisation of manpower, and it is towards this end that manpower planning should be directed.

Specifically we must

(a) Plan to balance recruitment to needs in numbers and skills.

(b) Have a planned programme of re-training and development of existing manpower.

(c) Improve manpower utilisation by

    (i) Rationalisation incorporating all technological capabilities

    (ii) Developing organisation structures in keeping with modern needs

    (iii) Applying the findings of social science research to achieve maximum individual motivation.

2.4 Summary and Conclusions

H.S. MULLALY
STAFF MANAGER,
THE BRITISH PETROLEUM CO. LTD.

Major conclusions we draw from the European Staff Planning Project are:- A Project of this sort, requiring the full play of local circumstances, laws, customs, and habits, and calling, in the end, for action at local, National level is likely to run effectively and quickly if full freedom to design, develop and apply know-how and experience is deliberately placed at local, National level.

A central, co-ordinating Unit is equally necessary if duplication is to be avoided and new developments are to be shared through a commonly accepted and respected central "clearing house".

The marriage between decentralisation and co-ordination/control seems to be presenting satisfactory results.

Manpower forecasts and plans are an essential part of the total operation. However, major factors influencing manpower – quality, cost, supply – spring from the social and economic environment and from technological change outside the direct control of the organisation. Long range forecasts of the "1980 Study" type provide the essential signposts to the factors which need sophisticated examination in depth before plans can be developed to a stage where sensible action may be taken.

The demand for quality manpower is growing at an increasing rate, but supply is not growing at an equal rate. In our view special action is required from industry if the reality of the situation is to be demonstrated to education – the supply area. BP's endeavours in this field have, for example, led to the establishment of some twelve joint education and industry mathematics projects in this country, one in Italy, and others now being planned in most European countries. A very close association also exists between BP and the Nuffield Foundation in the encouragement of liaison between education and industry in chemistry as well as in mathematics. A number of you may be familiar with the Esso Education Foundation in the States.

The demand for quality staff is urgent and is increasing: quality costs money. This factor, together with the factor of growth in the size of industrial organisations, points to the need to understand those actions likely to lead to the profitable, effective employment of manpower. Research into and application of social technology is now being developed.

There is much criticism of the social and behavioural sciences, it being alleged that they are neither scientific nor of good behaviour. I must admit that many of us in industry have no time to indulge in this fascinating argument and must leave this pleasure to others: it is the knowledge that we are after and we have to exercise judgment as to how to apply this knowledge, even at risk, in the existing and exacting tasks before us. In the end, we have to manage, and this through and with the power of our personnel.

A closer study of the longer range implications of activity currently before us is being instituted. I hope we are not dazzled by the long range look and thus fail to see what is going on under our noses. For example, the increase in school leaving age and the information to young employees through television and other mass media, generates a well-informed curiosity of mind better equipped to understand – and to challenge if not satisfied – the basis of management decisions. The mode and perhaps the authority of management requires review.

The main solutions to the problem of shortage of quality in manpower appears to lie in developing quality in existing staff – some 50% of the present payroll is expected to be working in the organisation in 15 years' time. The increase in education and training facilities, the definition of training needs through the skills definition of jobs and individuals, and the continuing application of modern training methods has resulted from our planning conclusions. Project "100,000" in the States and the U.K. Industrial Training Boards on the wider scene have the same intent.

Despite the national, social, legislative and economic differences between the Companies concerned with the E.S.P.P., a great measure of similarity exists in the critical factors and the conclusions reached in each separate Plan.

There is, we suspect, a strong mutual concern in the matter of manpower planning as expressed in the Armed Services and in large industrial organisations. The high capital cost of equipment and competition – and I stress the word competition – for skilled, intelligent manpower suggests, for example, that combined research may provide a substantial economy in effort and money.

During this Conference many pieces of the large, intricate jig-saw displayed before the various BP companies in their manpower plans are clearly familiar to many here: I quote –

> Data Banks;
> Computers for manipulation of larger numbers;
> Definition of the skills of the individual and of his needs and attitudes;
> Definition of the skills required of the job in order to achieve the goals;
> The effective utilisation of manpower;
> Action starts and finishes with the individual;
> Make the job fit for the man and the man fit for the job;
> Costs of alternative mixes of men and machines;
> Skills first learnt are not necessarily adequate for a total working life which
>   may call for two or three major career learning changes;

and so on and so on.

I am sure we all recognise these and other similar elements as essential in any manpower task: I hope very much that the means by which they may be handled will develop even more effectively as a result of the deliberations of this Conference.

2.5 Comment on Manpower Planning in the British Petroleum Company

J.A.A. VAN DOORN

PROFESSOR OF SOCIOLOGY,
NETHERLANDS SCHOOL OF ECONOMICS

It is a pleasure for me to have been invited to give some comment on the impressive work of the BP planning and research group. Their report presented this afternoon is evidently a summarised result of a very elaborate piece of highly qualified work and it will be clear that my remarks can only cover some minor aspects of the many topics mentioned here. My point of view is that of a sociologist and my intention is to trace some comparisons between manpower problems, indicated in the BP report – and generally typical for big business firms – and like problems in the armed forces.

Let me say first that it has struck me that at a conference like this such comparisons have only been made by exception, systematic comparisons that is, although there are obviously many opportunities for fruitful comparative studies in this field. Nearly every paper, presented here, is to be considered a challenge to analyse the implications for both military and industrial policy. This is easy to acknowledge in the case of research techniques and construction of models, but it is rather neglected, I am afraid, in the analysis of concrete themes, in the field of economics, especially labour economics, industrial psychology, etc. A topic like marginal manpower is most interesting for industrial firms which have to cope with the challenge of an over full employment economy, being confronted day after day with marginal manpower in the labour market and in the plant.

In the report of BP we are also confronted with a lot of opportunities to detect parallel tendencies and policies especially in the field of technological progress, social and economic change and, as a consequence, with the increasing shortage in skilled and higher qualified personnel; furthor, the problem of the rising cost of manpower, the need for more systematic analysis and planning and so on.

In addition, some convergence can be observed in military and industrial organisation. The big firm of today is a huge organisation with tens of thousands of people to manage; it has to tackle, therefore, a whole range of problems of management, organisation, and communication, problems which belong traditionally to the military field – since armies and navies were amongst the first large scale organisations in history.

On the other hand, the armed forces have for some decades been developing prowess in handling highly technical instruments and meeting as a consequence of this the essential problems of the technological changes since the Industrial Revolution in so far as this revolution was a replacement of labour by capital, of manpower by machines.

I should like to go on now more systematically by selecting three important structural problems, indicated in the BP papers. First, the interconnection between the organisational goals and the environmental influences, and its importance for manpower planning. Second, the relationship between manpower planning and organisational structure, both in industry and in the Services. Third, the problem of institutional identity in relation to the influx of large numbers of managerial and technical oriented personnel. I shall conclude my comment with some personal remarks.

(i) Organisational Goals and Environmental Structures

The BP report starts from the analysis of the socio-economic environment of the nineteen eighties, especially the changes in consumption and consumer behaviour, supporting other studies in the field, e.g. from the point of view of Unilever, a firm also very much interested in the consumer behaviour of the future.[1] One can say, that this part is the keynote of the report.

This is quite understandable, since the consumer's dollar and therefore the so-called "consumer environment" is the decisive element – and will be increasingly so – in the organisation of production. Market control can be considered the goal of the big business firm.

Looking at the paper of M. Brijatoff and at the relationship between his paper and that of Mr. Chadwick, I feel, nevertheless, some doubt about the evidence of the indicated connection between the future consumption pattern and the future manpower requirements. In any case, however, the development of a general view as to the necessary changes in the production system, as brought to the fore by M. Brijatoff, is, I think, an essential addition. It is this system which is the link, if I may say so, between the changing market and the change in required manpower.

This viewpoint can be generalised. Manpower planning cannot be understood from the goals of the organisation only (market control), but has to face the relative autonomy of the production system, built to tackle the market control problems. The production system is not the "expression" of the consumer's need only, but the concrete result of technological developments.

Let us turn now to the military establishment. If the main function of the business firm is the control of markets in competition with other firms, then the main function of the armed forces is the control of international relations in the case of conflict or potential conflict between the armed forces of other nation-states. The commercial goal of the business firm is also the political goal of the state when using military force.

Now it is my statement, that manpower planning should be considered not as a result of political (managerial) decisions as such but also as a combination more or less autonomous developments in the field of technology and organisation. Both factors, "management" decisions and "production" technology, have consequences for manpower planning.

This is not new, but what I want to suggest is this: manpower planning is only adequate planning if we are able to make some estimates in the fields of technology, organisational growth and complexity and in the fields of organisational goals, displacement of goals and succession of goals. In industry the managerial decisions reflect the consumption pattern and the competitive position; in the armed forces the decisions reflect the violence pattern and the international power situation. In both sectors the "productive" system reflects the technological development.

My question is how to measure the impact of both, interconnected but separate, developments. Is it possible to build up a manpower planning system on the knowledge of technical and organisational tendencies only? If not, how can the managerial or political decisions be brought into the forecasting?

The BP papers show an emphasis on market prospects but, if I see it correctly, pose the autonomy of production technology as a separate source of manpower requirements. Many military manpower plans, however, are restricted to technological and organisational presuppositions, neglecting the political and international developments.

I shall provide a concrete illustration, posed as a question: what are the consequences of the Defence White Paper of the British government presented last month to Parliament for the manpower planners in the military sphere?[2]

(ii) Manpower Planning and Organisational Structure

The second problem I should like to draw attention to is the connection between manpower planning and organisational structure.

As Mr. Smith has posed in a very recent article[3] the armed forces are highly institutionalised, with ranks, recruiting ages, training programmes, promotion systems, and other processes and procedures all codified. As a result of this institutionalisation or even "bureaucratisation" the military establishment lends itself more to manpower planning, career planning, systematic retention, and so on, than does any other organisation even the Civil Service. If other countries should follow the British way in turning to a volunteer army – and there are indications of just that – then the possibility for planning procedures would even increase.

The BP papers suggest, without explicitly saying so, that the military way is the best way, or, in any case, the better way. Manpower problems in industry have to be systematicised and planned as strictly as possible – and it can hardly be expected that most of the participants at this conference have a deviant opinion on the subject. Nevertheless, there are some doubts. The military organisation and planning model is partly a result of lack of real functions. In peace time, armies and navies are primarily training institutions – both for the professional soldier and the draftee – and their strict, rigid and formal way of doing things, planning operations and calculating risks is an expression of partly unreal or artificial working conditions. As we all know the only thing which makes an effective soldier or an effective army is battle experience.

An industrial organisation, however, is working in a full-fledged war-like situation, on a competitive market. Adopting the military system, e.g. of recruitment policy or career planning, could be ineffective since the flexibility of the business firm has to be far greater than that of the armed forces in peace situations.

The growth of the firm is of course a decisive step to formal organisation and bureaucratisation, but there are limits to accepting the bureaucratic model in industry. Comparative studies in career patterns in military and industrial settings do show enormous differences.[4]

A useful illustration, perhaps, is the problem of motivation. The armed forces, not able to offer high salaries, fringe payments, profit sharing, etc., stress training facilities and job security. This fact, however, is colouring the image of the armed forces as an occupational career – as indeed we learned from Dr. Wool, who presented most interesting information about the job characteristics of the services in comparison with those of civilian jobs.[5]

It is to be expected that the same organisation and planning systems could give rise to more or less the same motivational patterns and one has to be sure that the result will be in accordance with the intentions of the managers and with the requirements of the institution. My question is to ask how far manpower planning in industry can be developed without endangering the typical functional requirements of the business firm in a market economy. I do not suggest that manpower planning in industry is in fact developing too fast; the opposite is true. But there remains the danger of adopting already existing systems and solutions – e.g. from the services – without being aware of the different goals and functions of industry and the military establishment.

(iii) Institutional Identity

From this point I can jump to my third remark, concerning the influence of new categories of manpower on institutional identity – a subject on which I hope to touch in my paper elsewhere in this conference.

What is lacking in many manpower studies, also in the BP papers, is a differentiation of manpower along the lines of the traditional "hard core" personnel and the support and staff personnel; the professional men and the experts. The hard core may be defined as the category of manpower which has primarily the responsibility for the functioning of the organisation. This category is the expression, the reflection of the institutional identity of the organisation in question.

What I mean is this: every organisation is to be considered the instrument of an institutionally specified function in society: an army has to fight; a business firm has to sell products; a university has to produce and to transfer scientific knowledge; a court has to maintain law; etc.. The "hard core" is doing exactly these activities:

a soldier fights or is prepared to fight; a business man is selling goods; a professor teaches.

All organisations, especially the big ones and even more so the technically equipped ones, have an urgent need for personnel outside the hard core: employees, technicians, transport personnel, professional experts. The modern development shows an increasing percentage of these occupations in all sectors of society. I agree that the difference between hard core and the others is not absolute, it is gradual and the division lines are rather diffused. Yet I think that manpower policy has to make this division as exact as possible and has to measure the ever changing proportion between both categories. There is a growing need for higher trained manpower in all organisations, but above all a successful army needs first a hard core of soldiers with fighting spirit, a successful business firm needs primarily people with aggressive salesmanship.

From this point of view the hard core of every institution is more different, more institutionally specified, than the other personnel categories. A skilled technician is useful in the army, the plant, the hospital; a well-trained economist can make do in industry, in government, in medical services, in university, or where you will. The hard core shows a special professional identity, motivation and loyalty. His crucial position in his own institution correlates with his lower interchangeability among the diverse institutions – as can be seen from studies about the second career of military officers.[6]

From this part of my comment I come to a personal remark, concluding this contribution. Manpower policy is a task for experts. Being experts they believe in expertise, in the necessity of expert knowledge and therefore in the increase of highly qualified manpower. This is a fully legitimate belief and I think one highly relevant for the development of a more effectively managed society. However, to quote George Bernard Shaw, every profession is a conspiracy towards laymen. It seems to me that it is difficult for experts not to over-estimate the importance of expertise – in the same way as policy makers do over-emphasise the importance of experience and character, or whatever they call it. Both categories are making an ideology out of self-interest and self-justification.

Manpower research and planning, I should like to stress it, is necessary and useful, but it is only valid if there is an evident relationship to institutional function, social conditions and economic requirements. Research has no value, as such, except for the researcher. Manpower researchers therefore have to avoid the ideology of scientism, which can be done by adopting the pragmatic view of everyday life.

REFERENCES

1. A most fascinating essay from this side: Ernest Zahn – *Soziologie der Prosperität*. Köln/Berlin: Kiepenheuer & Witsch, 1960.
2. *Supplementary Statement on Defence Policy 1967*. London: H.M.S.O., 1967.
3. Smith, A.R. – Manpower planning in management of the Royal Navy. *The Journal of Management Studies, IV, 1967*, p.136.
4. Grusky, O. – The effects of succession: a comparative study of military and business organisation. In M. Janowitz (Ed.), *The New Military. Changing patterns of organisation.* New York: Russell Sage Foundation, 1964, pp.83–111.
5. Wool, H. – *Selected tables from surveys of the United States military age population, Oct.-Dec. 1964.* Elsewhere in these proceedings.
6. Biderman, A.D. – Sequels to a military career: the retired military professional. In M. Janowitz, *op. cit.*, 316 ff.

3. Approaches to Recruitment, Training and Redeployment Planning in an Industry

C.J. PURKISS

BRITISH IRON AND STEEL RESEARCH ASSOCIATION

I. INTRODUCTION

The British Iron and Steel Research Association (B.I.S.R.A.) is sponsored mainly by the steel industry and the government to undertake research relating to the Iron and Steel industry. The work described below is a part of the Operational Research Department's research programme. It is not yet complete, the results have not yet been implemented; some of the ideas have been tested and it is hoped that implementation of these will be effected within the next year. The research programme has the approval of the various sponsoring bodies of B.I.S.R.A., the results however have not yet been published. This paper, therefore, is representative only of the current viewpoint of the author.

Some aspects of two pieces of research work will be discussed. The first is concerned with the methodology of planning for the recruitment and redeployment of employees at Company level. The second concerns the formulation of approaches to forecasting the manpower requirements of the British steel industry and the consequential planning of the training programme.

2. THE COMPANY MODEL

2.1. Criteria Determining Choice of Model

Idealistically, in developing a model of a company we seek to incorporate all resources including that of labour, to assign costs to their use and to produce solutions which maximise some function of the value of these resources to the company. In practice, the committed investment in plant and the requirement to maintain as full utilisation of plant as the market will permit or to expand production to meet market demand, may mean that the requirement for labour is to a large extent predetermined. Alternatively, a programme for labour utilisation may be laid down for some period ahead with agreed variations to meet long term variances from an expected production level. The object of our work is to develop a method or model which can be used to help management to assess its recruitment and redeployment policies, to meet these requirements.

In the model being developed, we assume that desired manning levels have been set down. Our objective is to use the model to calculate the necessary recruitment to, training, redeployment and retraining of the work force, in order to meet these levels: where it is required, the permitted over or under-manning will also be calculated.

In general the management of any company will be considerably constrained in the possible policies they can follow. These constraints may be a result of union agreements. e.g. in respect of craftsmen-apprentices ratios or may reflect a community responsibility e.g. minimizing redundancies. From time to time such constraints will change. A practical model should have incorporated in it, all such constraints explicitly as they arise. For each change of constraint it should not be necessary to completely redevelop the model. A failing of many models of manpower planning is that changing circumstances or objectives cannot be readily incorporated.

All planning must reflect expectations or forecasts about the future. It is point-
less to develop complex methodology for decision taking, based on poor forecasts. Also
new, more accurate, information becomes available with time; plans should therefore be
sufficiently flexible to enable advantage to be taken of the new information.

A choice between alternatives should have some objective basis. To some extent the
costs of recruitment, training, redeployment etc. can be calculated and used to form
this basis; but the resultant effect of different policies on morale, and hence productivity, cannot be so easily quantified. Often the more desirable policy to pursue is
best based on objectives reflecting management intuition.

To summarise the above points we should incorporate the following features in order
to develop a useful model:

(i) The model must be based on reasonably accurate forecasts.

(ii) Plans produced from the model should be flexible, so that changes in policy
to accommodate likely new circumstances will be feasible so far as is
possible.

(iii) It should be possible to add new constraints to the model, some of which will
be explicit management policy, i.e. the model can be used as a simulation
procedure as well as a calculating device.

(iv) Decisions should be taken in accordance with the priorities of management,
the basis of these priorities will not necessarily be costs. This is to say
that management will not necessarily work from a single criterion – although
as Professor Kossack pointed out, we must have some quantifiable objective.
Some criteria will be considered to be more important than others. We should
be able to use our model to discover which of the priorities are being met –
and to what extent they are being met. For example, we might have as a
priority requirement – minimize redundancies, then we might try a second
criterion – minimize transfers, or undermanning and so on. Professor Fisher
in his excellent paper discusses the difficulties of being precise, when
using cost-effectiveness measures, this is particularly so in considering
redeployment, in which the effect on morale, of different policies, is
difficult to judge.

(v) Management should be able to "understand" how the model works and be able
to interpret the conclusions derived from using its procedures. In addition
they should be able to "play" with the model, trying out new ideas and
making improvements to reflect their own thinking. Sir James Dunnett has
spoken of the lack of quantitative manpower planning by British Industry. Dr.
Ferraro has emphasised the necessity for having procedures which can be made
sense of by administrators. This fifth requirement for a model tries to keep
this in mind.

2.2. Outline of Company Model

The steps involved in the model to calculate a manpower policy are given in outline
in Figure 1. Much of the detail of this has been developed, but emphasis has naturally
been on ensuring the incorporation of features peculiar to the present position of the
British Steel Industry. The following sections consider in turn how manning requirements
should be specified: methods of forecasting labour attrition; the relevance of labour
availability: how constraints on labour policy might be formulated, and some mathematical
descriptions of the model.

2.3. Manning Requirements

In a large steelworks there are several thousand separately identifiable jobs.
However, many of these jobs have similar characteristics and in order to facilitate the
manipulation of the model these can be grouped into larger "sets" of jobs. The

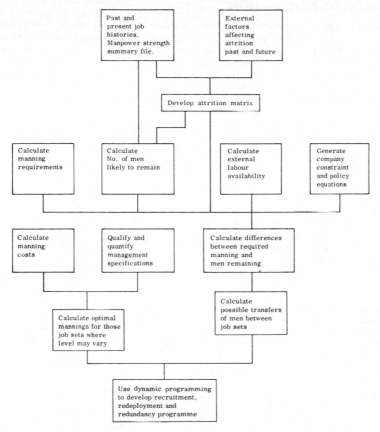

Fig. 1 COMPANY RECRUITMENT AND REDEVELOPMENT PLANNING

grouping should be by skill qualification, e.g. Turners, Blacksmiths, etc.; by job mobility
e.g. many jobs only require ability to do labouring; or by job function, e.g. certain
jobs are reached through a series of promotions, i.e. by seniority only, entry must consequently be to the lowest job and all subsequent jobs can be grouped together. In
general, calculations only involve movements into and out of these job sets, and
variations from the desired level of manning in the set.

Job sets are categorized in two ways; those for which the manning must be strictly
met and those in which some over or under-manning may be permitted — though at a cost.
Lengths of training periods at entry to each job set must be specified. Where it is
possible to recruit trained men, two entry groups for the set, trained and untrained,
must be identified.

Management are required to specify the manning level in each job set for each period
to be considered during the calculations. Permitted variations from these levels should
also be specified. Where levels will vary according to production level, these should
also be given.

Alternative manning levels, e.g. due to possible future productivity agreements
etc., can be considered, but each may require a recalculation of at least a part of the
policy to be followed. The way in which the model has been developed ensures that this
calculation is kept to a minimum.

2.4. Forecasting Labour Attrition Rates

The prime source of labour for the future is naturally the present work force of the company. Various methods of projecting attrition rates have been proposed. One of the most effective of these methods will be discussed and then the actual approach used in the model will be described. Lane and Andrew have described a method[1] in which the feature of attrition behaviour of a group of workers joining the company at the same point of time is approximated by a mathematical curve called the "log normal" (see also D. Bartholomew, elsewhere in these proceedings). The use of this curve would appear to have had remarkable success when used for short-term projections, particularly when the work force is fairly stable and unaffected by changing economic circumstances. The approach requires a division of the population into homogeneous groups, with similar behaviour and a further division by period of joining. The number of workers remaining at any point in time is then a projection of the early history of the group over time. Difficulties can arise when using this method if there is an interchange of personnel between groups. The idea of homogeneous work groups can usefully be covered by the use of job sets as described in section 2.3 above. This will also ensure that we are making separate predictions for the particular groups of men we are interested in. If we wish to allow for redeployment of men we may either have to make the assumption that redeployed men act as though they were new joiners – our research has shown this to be untrue in many situations – or it is necessary to retrace each prediction curve for the newly defined work group.

Factors in addition to length of service also appear to influence attrition rates, some of these relate to the men involved e.g. age, marital status, distance of home from company, etc. Normally in a fairly stable situation it is hoped that length of service would act as a sufficient indicator of different attrition rates due to these further factors, since men with a high likelihood of leaving will tend to leave after a short time. However, the company may well have to alter its policy of recruitment e.g. by recruiting from a greater distance than usual, and can expect differences in behaviour. One way of incorporating these factors would be to define finer groups; but the number of men contained in each of these groups may become statistically insignificant.

Additional factors affecting attrition rates are environmental e.g. local unemployment, trade conditions, earnings. Using a simple time curve for each group of workers would entail, after a change in such external influences, waiting for the curve to "settle down" before further forecasts can be made. It would be more desirable to accumulate evidence of how external circumstances influence turnover.

The approach to be used in our work is to calculate the probability of a man staying in the works as a function of his length of service in the works, length of service in his job, his age, and the economic circumstances pertaining at the time (see also E. Jones, elsewhere in these proceedings). The probability will apply only to men who are likely to leave voluntarily. Men retiring can be determined and those being made redundant or transferred to another group will be part of the decision process of the planning model.

These probabilities are derived at suitable intervals from the past behaviour of the work force. Predictions are made by applying the appropriate probabilities to each man in the work force and sampling from a distribution to determine whether or not the man is to stay – in a probabilistic sense. The future shape of the work force can then be derived. This approach is similar to that used by Orcutt in his socio-economic model of the U.S. economy[2].

A danger with this approach is the assumption of independent (Poisson) behaviour in applying the probabilities. Group effects are not explicitly accounted for. Nevertheless, the probabilities themselves have been derived from group behaviour, the planning procedure will only take account of values around the mean values of staying rates for the group and over this range the assumption is not likely to cause much trouble.

2.5. Labour Availability

The potential sources of recruits for skilled men or for trainees is of obvious importance in any planning model; they will exercise an upper bound constraint on the number of vacancies that can be filled. In the context of a single company, little work has been done on labour availability, other than on particular facets of the relative attractiveness of companies to the worker. What work has been done, has shown that it will be difficult to improve on the performance of company recruitment officers in assessing this availability. Many steelworks in Britain are in the position where recruitment is only a problem with a few of the more skilled jobs. These requirements will have to be satisfied by training young recruits; the number of these becoming available to the steel industry can only be estimated in association with local education authorities. We do not therefore intend to investigate in the near future any statistical approaches to labour availability in the context of the single company.

2.6. Constraints on Manning Policy

Each company will attach a predetermined priority to each of the aims of its manpower policy; those which it considers to be of greatest importance can be treated as constraints on the model. If the model indicates that no policy can be found which satisfies all the constraints, the less important constraints can be relaxed. The following is a non-exhaustive description of some of the conditions which may be limiting.

Each job can best be carried out by an agreed number of men, over or undermanning is usually permitted, but there will be a limit to the extent of this. Ratios between different job sets of men may have to be maintained, particularly where jobs interact, e.g. craftsmen and mates or craftsmen and apprentices. Limits may be set on the number of trainees by the maximum size of the training establishment or on the other hand, by a commitment to train some minimum number. A company may wish to minimise redundancies or even to avoid redundancies, hoping for long term gains in terms of stability, though in the short term this policy might appear to raise costs.

In describing the model it would be usual to include all the constraints, written as linear equations, and if no policy can be found to satisfy them all, some constraints would be altered.

2.7. Proposed Planning Procedures

This section discusses first the notation used in the planning procedures. Two approaches to the methodology are then described. The first is general in application but uses only the mean values of attrition values. The second approach incorporates the effect of uncertainty in the forecasts but is specific to the particular labour structure of the steel industry.

2.7.1. Notation and Equations Describing a Deterministic Equivalent System

A planning procedure must necessarily first isolate the "activities" which management use to achieve their objectives. Each activity can take place at a number of levels; we will represent the particular level of activity by a variable as follows; where i refers to the appropriate job set and t to the time period:

Trained men recruited	$X_A(i, t)$
Trainees recruited	$X_B(i, t)$
Redundancies	$X_R(i, t)$
Promotions from set i to set j	$X_P(i, j, t)$
Transfers from set i to set j	$X_T(i, j, t)$
Overmanning	$X_O(i, t)$
Undermanning	$X_U(i, t)$
Requirement for men	$b(i, t)$
Cost of recruitment, transfer etc.	$C_A(i, t)$.
	$C_T(i, j, t)$ etc.

We will indicate the proportion of men recruited in a particular year t^1, who are expected to stay to a subsequent year t, by the symbol $a_A(i, t^1, t)$. These proportions will have been calculated from the mean values of the attrition rates.

Using this notation, any particular policy can be described by a number of linear equations. Thus, writing $X(i)$ as the number of men at time zero in set i, the number of retirements in year t as $r(i, t)$ and considering the set $i = k$ and the present time period as zero, we can write the policy for time period 1 as follows:

$$a_A(k, 1, 1) \, X_A(k, 1) - a_R(k, 1, 1) \, X_R(k, 1)$$

$$+ \sum_{i \in I} a_T(i, k, 1, 1) \, X_T(i, k, 1)$$

$$- \sum_{j \in J_T} a_T(k, j, 1, 1) \, X_T(k, j, 1) + \sum_{i \in I_p} a_p(i, k, 1, 1)$$

$$X_p(i, k, 1)$$

$$- \sum_{j \in J_p} a_p(k, j, 1, 1) \, X_p(k, j, 1) - X_0(k, 1) + X_u(k, 1)$$

$$= b(k, 1)$$

$$- a(i, 1) \left(X(i) - r(i, 1) \right) - r(i, 1)$$

Where $\sum_{i \in I_T}$ etc., are the number of transfers from all sets I, from which transfer is permitted.

For the second period of the plan we will need to write two terms for each of the first six terms above:

e.g. $\qquad a_A(k, 1, 2) \, x_A(k, 1) + a_A(k, 2, 2) \, x_A(k, 2)$ etc.

After T time periods where T is the time taken to train a man, an extra term $X_B(i, 1)$ will appear in order to incorporate the trainees recruited in period 1 who will then be available for the work force. These identities, the coefficients of which represent staying rate, form a matrix similar to the resultant matrix derived from a succession of matrices in a Markov Chain as described in the paper by Professor Kossack.

Any further constraints may conveniently be written using the same notation, for instance the ranges of overmanning and undermanning may be written explicitly,

$$X_0(i, t) \leqslant 0(i, t)$$
$$X_U(i, t) \leqslant U(i, t)$$

where 0 and U are some agreed fixed range. Again if the number of trainees cannot exceed some fixed proportion K of the trained men, we can write:

$$X_B(i, t) - K \sum_{t^1=1}^{t^1=t} a_A(i, t^1, t) \, X_A(i, t^1) \leqslant Ka(i, t) \, X(i)$$

and so on.

2.7.2. Objectives of the System

If all the costs $C_A(i, t)$ etc., were known and suitably discounted over time, it would be simple to examine as our objective the function representing our total cost, namely ΣCX for all the X as defined above and to minimise this, subject to our requirements and constraints. In fact, we would have the classical form of a linear programme; a single linear objective to be achieved, subject to linear constraints, or written mathematically:

minimise $\qquad \Sigma CX$
subject to $\qquad AX \geqslant b, \; x \geqslant 0$

72

The method used to solve such a problem is trivial providing certain mathematical conditions hold, which would be the case here.

In practice, it is doubtful whether the costs will be known accurately, if at all. For instance, the cost of undermanning will be attributable not only to the extra cash involved by paying overtime but also to losses in productivity due to tiredness, overworking, increased accidents, etc., and these will be difficult to quantify.

The formulation as written above, while complete in an academic sense, is probably quite unrealistic because of our lack of cost information. We can however use this formulation of the constraints representing the bounds of our problem to study any of a number of sub-objectives which we may wish to consider.

One question of obvious importance is whether the equations and inequalities describe a feasible situation. This can be easily ascertained using standard linear programming techniques. If the problem is shown to be infeasible then further analysis will reveal which constraints are in discord. If the problem is feasible then simple sub-objectives such as minimizing redundancy, recruitment or the amount of retraining, etc., can be examined; alternatively, the various activities can be subjectively weighted by management and a number of alternative solutions examined. One further advantage of this formulation is that many of the constraints are only loosely linked through the transfer activities. Where men trained for one job set are unlikely to move to another, the problem can be readily decomposed on a job set basis. Techniques exist for examining the decomposed groups of constraints while maintaining any overall constraints. These techniques enable very large problems to be studied without any loss of accuracy and without involving extra costs.

2.7.3. An Approach Incorporating the Effect of Uncertainty

One of the more severe criticisms of using the linear programming formulation is that, as yet, no techniques have been developed which fully examine the effect of uncertainty in the relationships which are assumed to hold in the constraints (i.e. in the A matrix). In this case each of the $a(i, t)$ are forecasts of staying rates: the values incorporated into the constraints are expected or mean values of the true coefficients. A possible three stage approach which takes some account of the uncertainty will now be described.

In the steel industry it is generally found that, once in a well-defined promotion line, men tend to stay within the same job set. They continue to do so unless they leave the company or until their job ceases to exist and they are redeployed within the works. There is little transfer of men otherwise. Before qualifying for employment in an established promotion line (here called a primary job set), men usually do some service in a more general employment group (secondary job set). Men will be promoted by seniority from these secondary sets which may supply one or several primary sets. A second feature of this system is that the jobs on the promotion lines are in a sense essential. If a vacancy occurs, even though temporary, men must be promoted by seniority so that all such jobs remain filled. On the other hand, the number of men employed in the secondary set is somewhat flexible. The consequence is that any failure to exactly meet requirements will be met by adjustments in manning in the secondary set.

As a consequence of these features the effect of uncertainty will only be apparent in the secondary sets or in the very specialized trades where there is no secondary set to absorb the uncertainty effects. We make use of this differentiation by considering each type of set in turn.

The first stage of the calculation involves the primary sets. The only activities considered will be promotions or redundancies. By definition, for these there can be no under or overmanning. For each job set, in each time period, the calculations will indicate a number of vacancies or redundancies. Vacancies will be met either from redundancies in other job sets or by promotion from a secondary set. It can generally be assumed that there will be sufficient manpower in the secondary sets to supply all the needs of the primary sets. The purpose of this stage of the calculation is to reduce the number of sets which need to be taken account of by a stochastic model to cover uncertainty.

In the second stage of the calculation each of the secondary sets are considered in turn; the probability distribution of the likely required level of manning is calculated for each set, for each time period. The relative costs of under or overmanning from this level will be required and the costs of recruitment and redundancy. Most of these estimates will necessarily be subjective; it is sufficient to estimate the relative cost magnitude. As we shall be studying a range of policies and considering all possibilities this model is relatively insensitive and certainly less likely to produce infeasible solutions than the linear programming model under conditions of uncertainty. The probabilistic nature of the model is shown in Fig. 2. It can be shown that, providing it is possible to move from one state to another by a recruitment or redundancy programme, the best level of manning to aim at achieving in each period can be calculated to a first approximation independently of other periods, although it will be dependent on whether or not redundancies or recruitment will be necessary to achieve it. The dependence on other periods is due to variations in expected wastage rates if different policies of recruitment are followed. The static approach described above, i.e. considering each time period separately, will give an approximation to the manning levels to be aimed at.

The third stage of the calculation takes into account the dynamic aspects of the problem. Wastage rates for the secondary sets are the result of losses directly from the secondary sets and of promotions to the primary sets. The separate loss rates and their probability distributions can be compounded to give a single probability distribution for each secondary set. In practice, the smooth curves shown in Figure 2 for probability distributions will be discrete and cover a fairly narrow range. Operational Research techniques involving dynamic programming can be used to examine alternative criteria and make analyses over a continuing time range.

As in the linear programming approach, it is probably unrealistic to rely on costs as the sole criterion, although this is technically possible. The first application of this model would be to examine the feasibility of any plan and one objective could be to minimize the probability of a plan being infeasible. Various constraints limiting the range of policies can be specified by management, incorporated into the model and alternative objectives may be examined.

2.8. The Company Model - Some Conclusions

The above paragraphs sketch an attempt to provide a methodology which can be used to suggest and examine recruitment and redeployment policies. The necessity of complete

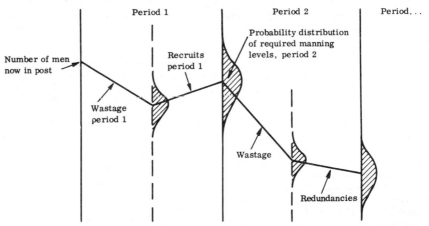

Fig. 2 PROBABILITY MODEL FOR RECRUITMENT PLANNING

involvement of management to formulate the specification of constraints and criteria is obvious. If an accurate specification of an objective can be made, the models can produce realistic solutions maximizing the value of the objectives. The models attempt to make a fair representation of a real situation and lend themselves to adjustment if new information becomes available. A solution to a new problem can usually be derived from a previous solution without complete recalculation when account has to be taken of new requirements.

The models may be used to derive a policy to meet a specified objective or to simulate some predetermined policy in order to assess its feasibility and practicability. In either case, after a decision has been taken, the system suggested can monitor events and indicate when new policies may have to be formulated.

Several pilot studies are being undertaken to validate the model for different situations, e.g. where part of a company is to be closed and the men re-absorbed into other parts of the work force; in another case where a general reduction in manpower across all parts of a company is to be made.

3. AN INDUSTRY MODEL

The British Iron and Steel Industry consists of some 700 establishments, of these some 70 account for 90% of the labour force. The areas where establishments congregate are fairly widely separated. No central body exists to control the whole of the industry; any planning that is to be done is therefore more advisory than statutory. As in company planning, manning and hence training problems cannot be easily separated from overall policy.

The work described here is that associated with isolating information which is pertinent to:

(i) establishing the likely level of manning in the industry by area,

(ii) the skill mix required in each area,

(iii) describing the flows of men into and out of the industry,

(iv) specifying the training programme necessary to achieve the desired manning levels.

Regionalism is emphasised above, not only because of the different work force characteristics exhibited in each area, but also because of lack of inter-regional mobility of labour. Nation-wide estimates of manpower requirements are insufficient. As an industry develops the balance of skills or numbers may change between areas; men however will often move to a similar occupation in another industry or even change their occupation rather than move to where there is a shortage. Even if mobility can be achieved, it can be only by exercising considerable social forces, providing housing etc., and these costs must be identified. Excellent work in this field has been done by the National Coal Board in carrying through the considerable run down of manpower in that industry.

If plans are to be of any use they must at least study, and if necessary, indicate alternative courses of action. Implementing such actions may result in a new state of the system seemingly unrelated to its previous states. In manpower terms this means it is not sufficient to simply study the development over a period of time of manpower levels or skill mixes. Manpower requirements must be related to the factors creating manpower need. Each of these factors and their inter-relationships must then be studied separately.

In considering an industry, it is not possible to impose a requirement that each company should develop a company model of the type discussed in section 2 and then to add the results together and call it an industry model. It is probably not even desirable; some companies may not do the work efficiently and in any case the considerable detail accumulated would not bear analysis. The alternative is to collect sufficient information in order to assess the particular position of each company and the general direction of development of the industry. Figure 3 shows in outline a possible linkage between manpower requirements and the basic demand, i.e. for the industry's products.

The first part of the model outlined in Figure 3 (Sections 1, 2 and 3) is concerned with determining the magnitude of demand for each of the industry's products and the establishments at which production will take place. Essentially this is a marketing exercise and it can be assumed that labour will not directly affect this, other than in so much as more efficient labour utilization may lead to an improvement in the industry's competitiveness. To incorporate feedback into the model directly would make it extremely cumbersome. From demand estimates and a knowledge of yields at each stage of the process, i.e. ironmaking, steelmaking, rolling, finishing (section 4) an estimate can be made of the process capacities likely to be utilized.

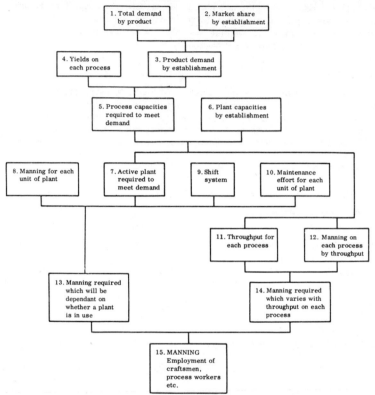

Fig. 3   OUTLINE OF AN INDUSTRY MANPOWER REQUIREMENTS MODEL

In section 6, plant configurations and capacities are incorporated. Projections will need to be made of future developments and innovations in plant. In general the time between making a decision to install and the actual installation of plant is considerable and usually sufficient to train new operatives for the plant. A large part of the projection may thus be reduced to incorporating a specification of decisions on capital investment, which at the time of the forecast have already been taken. In addition, mathematical models have been developed which describe the spread of innovations through an industry. Mathematically this behaviour is similar to that demonstrated during the spread of epidemics or the process of learning. Such mathematical projections can be checked for consistency with decisions which are already taken.

The actual manpower used will vary in two ways: first in steps depending on whether or not a piece of plant is in use and second in accord with the variation in throughput of the plant.

In the first case, the actual active plant needs to be calculated by marrying together demands and available capacities. The manning necessary to operate the plant, the maintenance manning and the particular shift system used, together with the estimate of active plant will give an estimate of actual manning required.

In the second case, similar information on manning will be required, but relating to throughput rather than active plant.

The above will require detailed job analysis in order to specify which class of manning is relevant and the skills to be developed by individuals through training. Forecasts will be concerned with likely future manning rather than with some ideal. A specification of an ideal manning level, though, would indicate a lower bound towards which companies might move. Inter-firm comparisons may indicate where savings in manpower are likely to develop, rather than to use a simple trend line indicator of manpower usage. An overall projection might however be useful to indicate the ongoing trends of skill mixes and manning levels and to ascertain whether or not the detailed analyses are sufficient to explain these.

It should be emphasised that as a prelude to any work on projecting manpower requirements a detailed analysis must be made of the component jobs. If this is not done any projections will be of very limited use in determining training loads. Obviously as many independent estimates as possible should be made of the constituent parts of the model. These can then be brought together statistically to give an improved estimate. In particular full discussions with the companies concerned should take place to ensure that all local and specialised knowledge is incorporated in the assessment.

In order to develop a programme for training, statistics must also be maintained on the existing manpower structure of the industry by age, skill, distribution etc., and mobility into and out of the industry. With respect to this, availability of labour and the demands of other industries must be taken into account. A model of manpower movement is being developed and an effort made to investigate the effects on this of wage rates, unemployment, output etc.

The estimates of manning requirements can be used in association with information on present manning and the likely future availability of manpower to develop a schedule of training etc., to meet specified objectives.

Much of the above model can be reduced to a series of two-way tables, one for each section of Figure 3. The specification of a particular requirement level can be derived by algebraic manipulation of these tables — by addition or multiplication. Alternative assumptions or estimates can be conveniently examined. The system is broken down into the essential elements involved and the effect of a change in an assumption affecting one element of a table can be readily calculated, as can changes due to new information becoming available. It is this feature, the ability to examine alternatives, which is felt to be of prime importance in developing models which incorporate the effects of unknown decisions.

4. CONCLUSIONS

The models described in sections 2 and 3 are still being developed. They have been described in the context of the steel industry, but most of the features are common to a number of industries.

The models have been developed to provide a system of describing personnel movement over time. Their use would help managers to plan deployment and to be better able to assure job security. The benefits to management should be those of increased labour stability.

The problem of recruitment and redeployment in the steel industry would not seem to justify more complex methodology at this stage. When better information on the consequences of poor planning is available a more refined system of analysis might be warranted.

As a research group we are indebted to a number of companies in the steel industry for their willing cooperation in this work and to the Iron and Steel Industry Training Board for their sponsorship of part of the research.

5. REFERENCES

1. Andrew, J.E. "Measuring Labour Stability and its Application to Employee Recruitment", Paper presented to *117th Annual Meeting of the American Statistical Association.*
2. Orcutt G.H. *et al. "Microanalysis of Socio-economic Systems: A Simulation Study "*, Harper & Row, N.Y. 1961.

4. Comment on Papers on Manpower Planning in Major Organisations

R.J. BALE

LONDON GRADUATE SCHOOL OF BUSINESS STUDIES

I think that in the short time I want to speak that it would not be profitable for me to pick up individual points of detail in the papers given by the speakers this afternoon. I would like first of all just to summarise where I think we've got to in discussing some of these problems and then to pose a very central question.

I suppose anybody starting with manpower planning inevitably starts with forecasts and both the papers this afternoon have had something to say about forecasting. I think it's worth making one or two observations about this. One is that people get very worried about the accuracy of forecasts and one questioner has already raised the issue of whether we could put any statistical margins on the sort of errors you make in forecasting or on the results that come out of models in general. I think the important thing to remember in forecasting in this area is, as Mr. Chadwick implied by talking about remedial action, that the point in the forecast is to make a decision now or to make a decision about something in the <u>very near future.</u> I have to, as it were, put my cards on the table and say that I'm a little less sanguine than I think Monsieur Brijatoff is about long term forecasting. From time to time I engage in the equally hazardous occupation of shorter term forecasting; being well aware of the problems that arise there, I think they may carry over very equally to the problems of 1980. But of course in many cases it may not matter. Mr. Purkiss I think said that if we don't have good forecasts and good data we can't get very far. Well I'm not sure about that insofar as the forecasting is, in part, to produce the next decision – the decisions that we have to make now, the decisions that we have to make in the next six months, year, or so on – the fact that we are wildly in error about what the forecast turn-out's going to be in 1980, well that may not matter. What matters is the extent to which the decision that we make now is sensitive to that sort of error. In other words, it could be that we, in fact, adopt a forecast which is out in 1980. The question is, if we are out by 10% or 15% in 1980, how does that affect the decision that we are now making? It may affect it comparatively little and there is also the point, again made by Mr. Chadwick, that in any case we try, if we're sensible, to adopt some form of sequential decision making; and the fact that we have a plan which is forecast doesn't commit us to an irretrievable set of actions between now and 1980. Therefore while the forecasts are an essential part of the planning process, I'm not sure that we should always be so worried, without at least conducting some sort of sensitivity analysis, about what the situation in 1980 is going to be. We can bet our bottom dollar that we will be substantially in error in our forecast. The question is how this affects the decision we make now.

It seems to me that anybody looking at the BP approach would agree that this is very sensible. This, if you like, is the first step in manpower planning as one generally sees it, namely the preparation of a set of forecasts which gives one some set of requirements in the future. Mr. Purkiss's paper, leaving the forecast on one side, then goes to the second stage of this, namely if you then have a whole set of requirements in the future based on your forecast, you need some programme in a sense to implement the decisions that you really want to make in terms of recruitment. You want to know to what extent your future requirements are going to be able to be met out of your existing labour force, you want to know the extent to which from your own labour force you're going to be able to produce something of a skill mix that is going to be required in the future. But this brings us to the third critical element which has not been emphasised so much – although I understand from what Mr. Mullaly said that it's very much in his mind – and this is of course the question of supply.

One thing that is very worrying to me, with my education hat on, is the fact that when we do manpower projections of one sort or another, we look at the requirements of the future, we also worry about supply in terms of whether we can get enough people out of our own labour force to meet some of the skilled requirements that we are going to face in the future. If not, we can go to Mr. Purkiss, i.e. we obtain a suitable recruitment plan that is produced from some model or other. But meanwhile, as all this is going on, of course, there are all sorts of people outside who are making decisions about what skills they will, in fact, adopt. You have what is described as a social demand for education and skill. Now there is nothing so far in what's been said that is going to match the social demands for skills, e.g. the willingness of young people to become engineers or to become chemists or to become social scientists or anything else, with the projections that are being made by companies as to what their requirements in 1980 are going to be. A very critical question here is what mechanism is going to be adopted or what mechanism, in the nature of things, is going in some extent to equate the demands that are being projected and the supply of the skills that are in part dependent on the decisions that are made by people who are nothing to do with the companies that are making these forecasts – or any other organisation for that matter.

Another question that arises is to what extent is the price mechanism able to, in fact, make this adaptation? Simple economics of this would be to think: well, if in fact there are shortages of skill in various areas, then the price paid for that skill will rise and in due course of time supply will adjust itself. Unfortunately I suspect that this is really by no means a complete answer to the problem. For one thing I think that the choices that people make in choosing their skills, in deciding what courses to follow in universities, other education institutions and so on, is very often only very incompletely governed by consideration of the market place. They may choose not to go into industry, but to go into some other occupation for reasons which have nothing to do with or are not closely related anyway to the price in fact paid. And yet if we look at it from a social point of view, we see the demands that are going to emerge in the future and we would like to match up demands and supply. Also in any case it's very difficult because, while many people in industry will, at one level, say that they have great belief in the price mechanism as an important factor in allocating the sources, very often when it comes to actually using it themselves, e.g. by deliberately raising the price of some form of labour to attract other kinds of labour, then there is a great deal of hesitation. This price solution can be very expensive because you don't only have to raise the price for the marginal people but, of course, you have to raise it also for the people that you already have, otherwise considerations of equity and so on intervene. Very often, particularly in this country, more so than in the United States, there is an extreme unwillingness to use the price mechanism. If I may say so I can see this very much in our universities, they are very unwilling to use the price mechanism to move resources around from one university to another. If that is so, generally speaking, then it seems that we have to consider some other mechanism that is going to adjust the supply skills to the sorts of demand for a skill that are being projected by companies like BP.

I think that the extent to which this is a major limiting factor, depends on the extent to which people are substitutable for each other. If everybody were perfectly substitutable with everybody else in every activity, then there would in some sense be no problems. There would be a problem of overall demand for labour or for people but, in fact, the critical problems that arise because of skill differences and the shortages in particular areas would not arise. This raises a very important strategic issue on the educational side. Namely – and I think this is mentioned by one of the BP speakers in referring to those people who are very much more multi-purpose and flexible – it raises a very interesting question of the extent to which various forms of education, particularly those that go on outside companies, should in fact be very specific. I'm very conscious of this in the field of management education, where I an now, because one is constantly under pressure from various companies to produce in some sense ready-made people. By ready-made they mean people they can wheel out of the education factory and put into another plant and the machine will work. Well, I think that if these are the sort of people we are turning out, we are taking an incredibly short run, both of the needs of these people and of their usefulness.

If we now look at 1980, we have heard many people say that it's very difficult to project to 1980, i.e. it's very difficult to project the technology; about all we can agree on is that there are going to be technological changes. The use of the computer, data processing and information systems are going to change organisations, we're going to move into a different sort of managerial world. Given this problem of substitutability, it seems to me that what is important is that our educational and training objectives should be changed so as to spend more time providing people with as basic a set of skills as we can; namely, concentrating very much more on the principles of activity, problem solving and decision making. These basic skills could then be supplemented by more specific training which would be relevant to the application of these skills in particular environments. I think this very much affects the issue of company decision making with regard to what I call educational gearing. We all know what financial gearing is, by educational gearing I mean roughly the ratio of the amount of education that is provided by the company within the company to the amount of education that is provided outside the company which, in fact, is required by the company if it is to get the skill mix and level of skills which are required. This is a problem which is perplexing a number of companies at the present time. Mr. Mullaly, I think, mentioned the BP Joint Committees which in a sense are projecting the company outside the company into the educational environment, in part as an equilibrating mechanism which is going to do something to help to produce the people required. Perhaps they can also persuade the people outside to adopt some of the skills that are going to be necessary in 1980.

I think that in today's session we concentrated, for the most part, on forecasting and on the estimation of requirements. We also concentrated through Mr. Purkiss's paper on, in some sense, implementation of recruitment policy but we've got to make sure that the right sort of people are there to be recruited and I think this is a fundamental problem which the price mechanism alone will not cope with. This raises very difficult questions for companies or any organisation with regard to the problems which I have called "educational gearing". What, in fact, is going to be the nature of in-company training and how much of the training is in some sense for education and to be done outside and what is the company policy about this and how do these things fit together?

Finally I think I would, as an economist, be somewhat hesitant in adopting too fixed a relationship between labour requirements and market projections for the future independently of broad considerations of possibility — there's an awful danger in this if you do manpower planning to some extent in a vacuum. It links also I think with the question raised by Dr. Wool about whether you should go to managers and ask them to project effectively what they want. This, too, I think can be a very dangerous thing to do because part of the time managers themselves may not be adopting an economic criterion for their requirements. I think that we have to introduce the broader aspects of profitability, cost and benefit into the whole process of manpower planning and this means we can't go on in a vacuum without considerations of what is the optimum relationship between labour and capital now and what it is going to be like in the future. We need also to give ourselves the opportunity of changing that mix as economic conditions change, as labour becomes more expensive or capital becomes more expensive, or whatever. I think that I would add to the general emphasis this afternoon on the problems of forecasting requirements and implementation the thought that the supply situation may not adjust itself. There may well be therefore a very serious decision problem for companies, governments and a variety of other people to intervene in this area to ensure that there is some sort of match between the projections that are being made by companies now and the people that are going to come along in 1980.

Manpower Planning in Major Organisations

B.D. MISSELBROOK

BRITISH AMERICAN TOBACCO CO.

5. CHAIRMAN'S CONCLUSION

I suggested at the beginning that we couldn't do more than get a sampling of the possibilities of comparison between manpower planning and research, between military organisations and, for this purpose, the business world. Having heard what has been said, it seems to me that, if we haven't got anything else, we've got one thing in common: manpower planning has the central role in any form of organisational company planning.

It's abundantly clear that the questions or problems concerning the attitudes of people to industry and commerce as a whole in a community; the attitudes of people to a particular industry; the attitudes of people to a particular company; the attitudes – as Professor Ball was indirectly touching on – of people to a particular type of occupation; the availability of and the ability of organisations to attract suitable people; the creation of organisational planning climates or cultures which foster individual and effective group development; the provision of the kinds of experience and training which assist development to meet the challenging and changing economy – these, I suggest, are the really and truly long term problems. Compared with them the erection of a building, the development of technological efforts, the development of machines, even possibly the development of weapon systems, these are just simple short term items which are capable of and susceptible to quite speedy solutions compared with those of manpower.

It has been said that business people have been a bit slow to get to grips with these manpower planning problems. I think that this is only partly true. To my mind what has happened is not that they haven't seen it as a problem but that they didn't know how to set about doing anything about it, even that it might be possible to do anything about it. They didn't know how to think about it, they didn't know how to analyse, they didn't know how to use the growing body of information that was being generated by the researches of the social and behavioural scientists. This I think is the reason why there is this growing interest in the contribution, as Mr. Mullaly was saying, of the social scientists.

But, to get that achieved, I suspect it's very much a two-sided problem. When business men came to make their approaches to find out the contributions that they could expect from social scientists, they got somewhat confused by the terminology they met. In fact, I think they sometimes wondered how the social scientists managed to communicate with each other! I say this as one who was once an industrial psychologist. But this was just the adolescent period of the social sciences; and maturity is coming. In the same way I think people in business are striving to get a better understanding. Now, if we can work constructively to get that understanding and, in parallel, to get better understanding between those who are working on manpower problems in military governmental organisations and those who are doing it in business, then I think we can get ahead very much faster than we might otherwise do.

Aspects of Cost-Benefit Analysis in Defence Manpower Planning

FRANKLIN M. FISHER[1]

MASSACHUSETTS INSTITUTE OF TECHNOLOGY

I. INTRODUCTION

Cost-benefit (or cost-effectiveness) analysis has become in recent years a rapidly developing and highly fashionable tool in defence and other governmental operations.[2] This is as it should be. Such analysis can be an invaluable aid to systematic and rational decision making in complex situations. Yet the proper application of cost-benefit analysis requires more than just the use of the appropriate words. Complicated questions are likely to require sophisticated analysis and proper use of the techniques of cost-benefit analysis requires detailed attention to the very hard problems that arise in particular cases. It may be all too easy to pass over such problems with a relatively perfunctory treatment, believing that one cost-benefit analysis is much the same as another.[3]

In the present paper, I shall discuss some of the hard problems that arise in cost-benefit analysis, particularly in defence manpower planning. Some of these problems have no easy solution in practice, and the analyst may have to get along with approximate or makeshift solutions. All these problems, however, must be faced as matters for conscious decision if a proper analysis with valid and useful answers is to be performed. While it may turn out in particular cases that some problems can be set aside, this cannot be assumed *ab initio* and careful attention rather than unconscious choice must be exercised.

The problems which I shall discuss do not form an exhaustive list of those which arise, nor can I give entirely satisfactory solutions to all of them. Indeed, in some cases I can do little more than call attention to the need for further analysis.

Many of the matters here discussed were suggested to me by my work as a consultant on a cost-effectiveness study of re-enlistment incentives in the United States Navy performed at the Institute of Naval Studies (INS) of the Center for Naval Analyses. This study is reported elsewhere[4] and is discussed in other papers presented to the present conference. I shall occasionally draw upon it for good and also bad examples of treatment of the problems discussed.

---

[1] This paper was begun during my tenure of a Ford Foundation Faculty Research Fellowship in Economics, while visiting the Hebrew University, Jerusalem. I am indebted to Anton S. Morton for discussion of an earlier draft.

[2] For a recent survey of the field, see Prest and Turvey [8].

[3] While engaged in the computer runs of the quite difficult nonlinear programming problem involved in Morton, Fisher, and Nitzberg [7], our programmer, C.R. Berndtson, encountered another programmer from a defence establishment organization. On being told that Berndtson was running a cost-effectiveness analysis program, the second programmer said that he was too and suggested that it was probably the same program. Cost-benefit analysis is not and probably never will be at that stage of development.

[4] The full study is given in Morton, Fisher, and Nitzberg [7]. The model and methodological results are given in Fisher and Morton [5] and substantive findings presented in Fisher and Morton [4].

2. COST-BENEFIT ANALYSIS: AN OVERVIEW

In this section and the next, we begin with a general outline of a cost-benefit analysis which will provide a background for the more specific discussion to follow. Several alternative policies involving the recruitment, training, and assignment of personnel are to be considered. Each of these policies involves expenditures on different items, typically spread out over several different time periods. Also, over several different time periods, each of these policies results in a pattern of effects, frequently quite complex, affecting several different dimensions of defence capability.

For example, different patterns of recruitment and training over time involve different patterns of expenditure on pay, training expenditures, fringe benefits, and capital equipment. They will result in different time patterns of size of forces, length of service distributions, amount of training in, and assignment to various tasks, and so forth.

The problem of cost-benefit analysis is to decide on a function which will reduce these variegated effects to a single criterion and then to choose the policy which is best according to that criterion. In principle, this is accomplished in the following way.

First, certain of the results of any program may relate to variables whose values are in some way constrained, in the sense that no program, however desirable on other criteria, will be considered at all if it does not satisfy such constraints. Thus programs requiring the sudden induction of abnormally large numbers of men may be simply ruled out. In a somewhat more complex circumstance, it may be required that the number of men on sea duty not exceed the number of berths and that the skill distribution of men on such duty be such as to allow the assignment of men with an appropriate mix of skills to each ship. Indeed, it may be specified what the number of men in each skill category is to be in a particular year and the program sought which most efficiently achieves this goal.

It is evident that the choice of such constraint can intimately affect the result of the whole analysis. Further, the nature of such choices is not generally so obvious as may appear. For example, is it really the number of men in each skill category that one wants to fix, or is it not rather what those men can achieve in terms of their work? Questions like these are not nearly so innocent as they may seem, and I shall have a good deal to say about this later on.

For the present, however, assume that the constraints have been chosen, wisely or not. The analysis now conventionally proceeds by combining the expenditure effects of any program into a single measure called "costs" and the non-expenditure effects into a single measure called "benefits."

In principle, the problem of how to combine different expenditure items into a single one has a more-or-less well-defined and well-known solution. Expenditure items are all in money terms and can apparently be combined in the obvious way. Indeed, the only difficulty typically arising stems from the fact that expenditures at different points in time are *not* in fact in the same money terms. An expenditure now and an expenditure equal in nominal amount ten years hence are not the same thing. This difficulty is overcome by the use of discounted present value of expenditures as the cost measure. Clearly, this raises the question of what discount rate should be used for discounting; this is by no means a trivial matter, although it is fairly clear what range of alternatives is involved.

The problem of the choice of a discount rate, moreover, may not be the only one above an accounting level involved in cost calculation. Just as expenditures at different times are not immediately comparable, so expenditures at different places are not. To take the simplest example, a program which involves a given expenditure abroad may be in fact more costly than one which involves the same expenditure at home if one's country has balance-of-payments difficulties and foreign exchange is in short supply. Of course, this sort of problem can be handled by constraining the amount of foreign exchange which may be used; alternatively, effects on the balance of payments may be treated as just another benefit (positive or negative), but the latter device renames rather than solves the problem of comparing foreign and domestic expenditures.

If the problem of combining expenditures into a single cost measure has its difficult aspects, however, the problem of combining non-monetary effects of policies into a single measure of benefits is the central and most difficult problem of cost-benefit analysis. I shall return to this problem below.

Now, it must be recognized that the division of policy effects into monetary effects (costs) and non-monetary effects (benefits) is an arbitrary one. Why should a deleterious non-monetary effect be counted as a negative benefit rather than as a positive cost? Similarly, if a program by expenditure in one time period reduces expenditure later on, there is no reason why that later saving should not be counted as an increase in benefits rather than as a decrease in costs. Since the decision as to what is a cost and what a benefit is thus an arbitrary one, we may immediately state the following conclusion:

Whatever decision procedure is used in combining benefits and costs into a single criterion to be optimized, the resulting criterion must not be affected by the arbitrary division of items into costs and benefits. That division may be a useful matter of convenience in analyzing the problem; it must not be allowed to affect the results. Another way of saying this is that the problem of combining non-monetary effects into a single benefit measure is but a part of the problem of combining all effects, monetary and non-monetary, into a single measure. The larger problem cannot be ducked.

This simple but important point has strong implications if we now assume that the problem of combining non-monetary effects into benefits has been solved and go on to the question of what decision criterion should be used. There are several possibilities.

3. WHAT SHOULD 3E MAXIMIZED?[1]

The first possibility is to take the total costs of the program as fixed, by higher governmental authority, for example, and given that fixed cost level to maximize the benefit measure so as to buy the most benefit for the given expenditure. If total cost really is fixed, this is an entirely appropriate thing to do, but are costs really fixed? To decide whether they are, we have to ask what increase in benefit would be obtained by a slight relaxation of the cost constraint. This can be discovered fairly readily by analysis; it is technically known as the *shadow price* of the cost constraint when benefits are maximized as described.[2] If this shadow price turns out to be high, as it may, then one must ask whether it is reasonable that costs will really remain fixed if whoever fixes them is presented with the fact that a slight increase in costs will result in a large increase in benefits. Here is one of many places in which the policy-maker and the analyst can usefully interact. How much benefit can be bought for an increase in costs can be found by the analyst. Whether the extra benefit makes the extra cost worth incurring is a problem for the policy-maker. It is, of course, part of the same problem just mentioned, namely, the decision as to how monetary and non-monetary effects are to be combined. By breaking up the larger problem as described, the cost-benefit analyst can lay out the alternatives that are open here, even if such a laying-out does not itself determine what alternative to take. Provided that the analyst does not forget to consider the question of the extra benefits resulting from a change in the cost constraint, the method of maximizing benefit for given cost can be a very useful one.

Similar remarks apply even more forcefully to the second possible decision

---

[1]   For an alternative discussion in the wider defence context of the problems treated in this section, see Hitch and McKean [6].
[2]   In general, the *shadow price* of a constraint measures the amount by which the objective to be maximized would increase if the constraint were made a little weaker. It is the price paid in terms of the objective for having the constraint as strong as it is.

criterion which stands the first one on its head. This is the fixing of the benefit measure at a pre-assigned level and the minimization of costs, so as to purchase the given benefit level most cheaply.[1] The difficulty here is that whereas it is reasonable to suppose that total costs can be given outside the problem, it is most unlikely that the level of a sophisticated benefit measure will be so given. We shall see that there are good ways of solving this, however, and this alternative is the one which we shall recommend in a somewhat more complex version. In any case here again it is a matter of considerable importance to consider the shadow price of the constraint – here the cost saving which would be obtained if the constrained level of benefits were changed. We shall have more to say about this below.

If neither of these first two alternatives is adopted, however, then the problem of combining costs and benefits into a single measure must be faced head on rather than usefully broken up. What form should such a measure take?

I shall consider two such forms. The first of these is often used but has absolutely nothing to recommend it. This is the use of the ratio of benefit to cost as the criterion to be maximized.

There are two crucial things wrong with this. In the first place, we saw in the preceding section that the division of effects into costs and benefits must not be allowed to affect the results. It is obvious, however, that maximizing a benefit-cost ratio does not meet this fundamental criterion. A policy which maximizes that ratio on a given division of effects into benefits and costs will in general not maximize it if some costs are treated as negative benefits and items moved from the denominator to the numerator and vice versa.[2]

This would be enough by itself to completely eliminate the benefit-cost ratio as a sensible decision criterion, but there are other, perhaps more subtle, reasons as well.

Even if one succeeds in combining all the dimensions of benefits into a single measure, that measure is almost certain to have only ordinal rather than cardinal properties. In other words, while meaning can be attached to the statement that in one situation benefit is higher than in another, no meaning can be given to statements as to how much higher. There is no natural unit for measuring increases in benefits. Two equivalent ways of expressing this are as follows: first, the most that can be done in combining different benefits into a single measure is to determine the marginal trade-offs between different benefits, that is, the amount by which a particular item would have to increase to just offset a small deterioration in another item. Second, any benefit measure which accurately reflects those trade-offs is as good as any other; it follows that if we have any measure of benefit which is adequate in this regard, any other measure derived from the given one by a monotonic transformation will do as well. Thus, all the information in a particular benefit measure will be preserved if we replace that measure by its square, or its logarithm, and so forth. This is just another way of saying that we can determine when benefits go up but not by how much they rise.

If the choice of a particular benefit measure is arbitrary to this degree, as in the case of the division between benefits and costs, we must be careful not to have a decision criterion which is affected by the arbitrary choice. In the present instance, this means that whether or not a particular decision is optimal must not depend on the particular choice of a benefit measure which we happen to use. Rather, such optimality must be preserved if that benefit measure is replaced by any monotonic transformation of itself,

---

[1] It is perhaps worth reminding the reader that these two approaches lead to the same result in the following sense. Suppose that costs are first fixed and benefits maximized. Take the maximized level of benefits and fix it and then minimize costs. The optimal policy in both cases will be the same and the minimized level of costs will be the same as the level which was fixed in the first place.

[2] There can be an exception to this if costs, treated as negative benefits, are combined with other benefits in the numerator in a nonlinear way; in this case, however, the crucial combination of costs and benefits is the one in the numerator and the numerator might as well be defined to include all costs and then maximized, eliminating the ratio form.

i.e., by any other benefit measure which also correctly reflects trade-offs among different benefit items.

Since if we maximize a given benefit measure, we also maximize its logarithm, its square, and so forth, it is easy to see that the invariance property just set forth is present if we choose to set costs and maximize benefits. Similarly, since if we fix the level of a benefit measure, we also fix the level of its logarithm, its square, and so forth, it is easy to see that the invariance property is present if we fix benefits and minimize costs. However, a policy which maximizes a benefit-cost ratio with a given choice of benefit measure will not in general maximize such a ratio if the given benefit measure in the numerator is replaced by its square, its logarithm, and so forth. Thus the benefit-cost ratio criterion fails on this point also.

Finally, even aside from the points just made, the use of a benefit-cost ratio ignores problems of scale. There is no guarantee that the policy which maximizes such a ratio does not do so at an unreasonably small or unreasonably large level of benefits and costs, requiring, for example, the induction of very small or very large numbers of men. While this can be guarded against in the constraints, the point remains that there is really no particular reason why one should want to maximize a benefit-cost ratio except in those cases in which such maximization happens to coincide with maximizing benefit at given cost or minimizing cost at given benefit. Thus, even aside from the crucial difficulties already raised, the basic rationale for maximizing a benefit-cost ratio is extremely weak. [1]

One final alternative remains to be considered. This is the maximization of the difference between benefits and costs. If all benefits were monetary or if they could be reduced to monetary equivalents by consideration of monetary versus non-monetary trade-offs, this difference would clearly be the natural thing to maximize. [2] In the present context, however, this is not a particularly useful conclusion. The comparison of monetary and non-monetary effects of a program is precisely the problem with which we are concerned. If one can already solve that problem, then costs can and should enter as a subtraction from benefits, but this is no help in solving the central problem of comparison itself.

We conclude then that reliance on simple formulae will not lead to appropriate results, this being true in particular of benefit-cost ratios. The problem of comparing monetary and non-monetary effects of programs must be faced in a reasonably explicit form. As outlined above, this can be usefully done by fixing costs and maximizing benefits or by fixing benefits and minimizing costs. We shall see below that the latter method, in a rather more general form, is quite flexible and can be used to advantage to help solve the problem of benefit measure itself.

This completes our general outline of cost-benefit analysis; we now turn to a more detailed discussion of the problems involved therein.

4. CONSTRAINTS: REAL OR IMAGINARY?

We saw above that cost-benefit analysis generally takes the form of a constrained optimization problem. The constraints involved can be relatively simple or quite complicated.

---

[1] Some of the problems in this paragraph can be avoided by the use of a *per man* (or per man-year) benefit-cost ratio. Doing this, however, requires the assumption (untrue in general) that the ratio is invariant to the number of men involved (constant returns to scale, even though items such as capital equipment are constant). In any case, there remains the question even on the per man level, as to why one should *want* to maximize the ratio of benefits to costs.

[2] The difference between benefits and cost is invariant to the treatment of costs as such or as negative benefits. It is not invariant to monotonic transformations of the benefit measure, but such monotonic transformations also destroy the reduction of non-monetary benefits to a monetary equivalent, hence are ruled out by the phrasing in the text.

4.1. Environmental Constraints

Some of these constraints are not really matters of policy choice at all; rather, they reflect the environment within which policy making must operate. Thus, for example, a real constraint in the INS study was the number of men estimated to reenlist for a given set of incentives. This is a parameter, different in value for each incentive package, and reflects underlying social and economic motivations of enlisted personnel. Policy can change the reenlistment rate by changing the incentives offered, but, at least within the range of policies considered in the study, policy cannot change the percentage of men who will reenlist for a given set of incentives.

This sort of constraint, of course, is frequently not stated formally as a constraint but, as in the example, enters by determining the parameters and forms of the functions involved in the problem. Clearly, the estimation of such parameter values is an essential and often difficult task in the course of a cost-benefit analysis. I shall not here dwell on the great importance of securing good reliable data and of the use of modern methods of statistical inference in the performance of that task.

4.2. Official Personnel Requirements: What Price?

There is another sort of constraint which is quite different and is a matter for policy choice. Indeed, such constraints are self-imposed by the policy-maker or the analyst and require far more conscious consideration than they sometimes get.

Official personnel requirements are frequently stated in terms of the number of men with particular skills or experience which it is required to have at particular moments in time. On the simplest level, this may be just the total number of men required; more generally it is a list of numbers of men in each of several classifications. Cost-benefit analysis is then required to find the policy which achieves such goals most efficiently, i.e., which minimizes the cost of achieving them.

There is nothing wrong with this if such personnel requirements can be taken at face value as immutable, but can this really be done? This question can be approached in two ways.

The first such way is to consider directly the consequences of imposing such a constraint. In principle, such imposition means that no amount of savings in costs, no matter how large, will compensate for the slightest deviation from the stated personnel requirements, no matter how small. The personnel requirements, in the precise form stated, become a *sine qua non* of policy making; they must be satisfied at any cost. This is a position which can, of course, be consistently held; it is not a very plausible position. Nevertheless, it is directly implied by the imposition of personnel requirements in their usual form as constraints on the analysis.

On the other hand, it may be objected that principle is all very well, but practice is likely to prove different. It is one thing to say that the imposition of rigid constraints involves being willing to pay any finite price rather than weaken such constraints at all, it is quite another to say that the price *actually* paid will in fact be indefinitely large. This is quite true. As in the case of fixing benefits and minimizing costs already briefly discussed in the preceding section, it is quite easy for the analyst to find the actual price involved. As in that case, the price involved is technically known as the shadow price of the constraint,[1] and is a useful thing to find. Naturally, that shadow price may turn out to be low. Indeed, if the constraint is not a binding one (i.e., if it is automatically satisfied when the optimization is carried out without it), the shadow price associated with it is zero, indicating that nothing is to be gained by weakening the constraint a little. More often, however, rigid personnel requirements are likely to have a very high shadow price. Whether that

---

[1] See footnote 1. p. 85. If constraints have more than one dimension (e.g., personnel requirements in different categories specified), there will, of course, be more than one shadow price. This makes no essential difference to the exposition in the text.

price is worth paying is a matter for conscious decision.

To put this slightly differently, the shadow price of a personnel constraint gives the actual trade-off between the personnel effects of the optimal program and the monetary effects. It gives the cost saving that will be achieved if the personnel requirements are relaxed just a little. The trade-off between these two effects from the viewpoint of the policy maker is another matter, however. This is the penalty (in monetary terms) which will be incurred, from his point of view, for falling short of the stated personnel requirements by just a little bit. Examination of the shadow price can aid in determining this penalty, but is not of course a substitute for it. Imposing a rigid personnel constraint implies that the penalty is infinite.

Moreover, such an imposition implies that the overfulfillment of a personnel requirement is worth nothing in itself, that the over-achieving of a minimum goal is not worth any additional expenditure, no matter how small. This is a more plausible position than the infinite penalty exacted for falling short of such a goal, but it too may often be unrealistic. Again, the policy maker must decide what the trade-offs between costs and personnel effects are for him. It is wrong to suppose that the simple statement of personnel requirements in rigid form avoids making a decision as to such trade-offs. Such a procedure merely makes that decision in a particularly extreme and implausible manner.

4.3. Substitution Possibilities

A second way of approaching the problem is to consider trade-offs among different personnel requirements and among personnel and non-personnel effects of a program instead of simply between personnel and costs. Typically, personnel requirements are not unidimensional; rather, requirements are stated in terms of the number of men required in each of several categories. Such categorization may be in terms of skill specialization, or experience, or of other variables.

It is not hard to see that imposing such multi-dimensional personnel requirements as constraints which must be satisfied by any program not only imposes a drastic assumption as to the trade-off between personnel and costs but also imposes such an assumption as to the possibility of substitution among men in different categories. If such requirements *must* be met (and thus, quite literally, met at all costs), then no addition of extra men in one category, however large, can compensate for falling short of the stated requirements in another category by even one man. Insistence on meeting such requirements imposes the assumption that there is no substitution possible among different categories of labour. Further, even in the unidimensional case, it also imposes the assumption that there is no substitution possible between labour of any category and capital equipment.

Are such assumptions valid? The answer is clearly no. Turn first to the simplest case, that of substitution between men and capital. Here it is easy to multiply examples of such substitution. Many, if not all tasks that can be performed by a military establishment with a large personnel complement can also be performed by an establishment with fewer personnel and more machines. The substitution of machines for men naturally has its limits and it may not be worth performing, but this is a matter for the analysis to determine. It is simply not true that such substitution possibilities are generally absent as a matter of principle.

On the other hand, rightly or wrongly, the analyst may decide that the available capital equipment must be taken as given and the analysis performed within that constraint. This may come about either because the constraint is a real one, or, more likely, because there is a limit to the size of problem which can be handled at one time. In this case, the analyst will ignore labour-capital substitution and hope that the consequences are not too severe.

Even when this is so, however, the analyst cannot afford to ignore substitution possibilities among different types of labour. This is all too easy to do, for such substitution many be more subtle than is generally realized.

In the first place, to assert that substitution among labour types is possible is not to assert that it must be on a man-for-man basis. What is at issue here is whether the loss of one man in a given category can be compensated for by the addition of *any* number of men in another category, not whether it can be so compensated by the addition of one such man. Indeed, if such substitution is possible, it is likely not even to be at a constant rate, with a fixed number of men of one type being worth a fixed number of men of another type, regardless of the total number of men of those and other types already employed. One-for-one substitution would be even more special than this. Rather the substitution possibilities are likely to depend on the number of men in each category to begin with and on the ways in which tasks can be reorganized to use men in different categories most efficiently.

Thus, let us consider what is involved in substituting raw recruits for experienced personnel. It is wrong to think that this must necessarily be a direct substitution with, say, two raw recruits taking over the tasks of one experienced man. In general, such direct substitution will not be possible if the effectiveness of the establishment is to remain unchanged. If such direct substitution were the only way in which substitution among labour categories could take place, then stating personnel requirements as constraints would be unobjectionable.

Effectiveness, however, is a matter of what the personnel of an establishment can do, rather than of who they are, and substitution takes place by reorganizing the tasks performed by the personnel so that the whole establishment runs most effectively. This may result in rather indirect substitution.

Consider first the loss of an experienced man in a relatively small part of the military establishment, a given ship or a given installation, for example. Suppose, first, that the installation is not so small that the man lost is the only man of his experience working on it. What happens if such a man is removed is, naturally, not the reassignment of his tasks to raw recruits. Rather the entire operating force of the installation is to a greater or lesser extent reorganized. If the experienced man was acting in a supervisory capacity, other supervisors are worked a bit harder, stretched a bit thinner to cover for his loss. This results in a loss of effectiveness as supervision becomes less close and less efficient, and as personnel with slightly less experience take over the less demanding tasks of experienced personnel. There is a similar adjustment all the way down the line, with a slight upgrading of the personnel assigned to the simpler tasks ordinarily assigned to those of more experience. Finally, raw recruits are required to take over or help with tasks ordinarily reserved for men with a very small amount of training. The loss of efficiency resulting from the loss of an experienced man is transmitted by redefining tasks and by less good supervision into a loss of efficiency in working parties. This is then compensated for by increasing the number of men available in such working parties.

To put it another way. If we agree that some number (perhaps more than one) of men with slightly less experience can compensate for the loss of a fully experienced man, then the loss of an experienced man can be translated into the loss of such a number of almost experienced men. If this can be done in general, then we can ultimately translate the loss of an experienced man into a loss of some number (perhaps quite large) of raw recruits and compensate for that loss directly. Direct substitution of raw recruits for experienced personnel need not be involved.

Note, further, that the numbers of men involved in the trade-offs described are likely to depend on the situation. If experienced personnel are very scarce, it may be impossible to compensate for the loss of even one by adding a reasonable number of relatively inexperienced men. If experienced men are relatively plentiful, then they may already be performing tasks that could just as well be performed by men with less experience, and substitution may be very easy. In any case, it is wrong to impose the assumption in advance that substitution is impossible. Even if experienced men are believed to be relatively scarce, a proper cost-benefit analysis will often involve recruitment and training programs changing such scarcities and thus changing the substitution possibilities. Such possibilities must not be implicitly assumed absent to begin with, particularly since scarcity of one or more types of personnel can be a subtler and more relative matter than may at first appear. [1]

Further, substitution between personnel types can be accomplished in ways even more indirect than those just exemplified. We restricted ourselves above to the discussion of personnel substitution in a relatively small unit. Substitution in the entire military establishment being analyzed is likely to take place in a wider variety of ways than in a small installation. For one thing, there is a wider latitude in the reassignment of personnel. When an experienced man is lost from one installation, he can be replaced by an experienced man from another; the other being chosen as one where experienced men are relatively more plentiful in order to minimize the effects of the loss. Further, a slight loss in efficiency in a given unit can often be compensated for by a slight re-defining of the missions of other units to cover the loss and an increase in personnel somewhere else in the establishment. These effects may be difficult to quantify, but they must not be assumed to be absent. Again, the imposition of official personnel requirements as constraints which must be satisfied rules out any substitution possibilities whatsoever.

4.4. Effectiveness Constraints

How should such substitution possibilities be handled then? How should official personnel requirements, which, after all, must reflect something of importance in terms of needs, be incorporated into a cost-benefit analysis in manpower planning?

The answers lie in a consideration of what official personnel requirements are pre-sumably designed to represent and here we enter the area of benefit measurement. Those requirements give the number of men in each category that, in the judgment of those producing the requirements, will be just sufficient to enable the military establishment to fulfill its mission. On the other hand, we have just seen that there are likely to be substitution possibilities among different personnel categories. It follows that the configuration of personnel given in official requirements is not the only one which will just enable the establishment to fulfill its mission (although, for various reasons, it may be the configuration which most naturally occurs to those producing the requirements). Surely, however, what is required is that the establishment be able to perform its mission, not that it be able to perform it in a particular way. The constraint which must be imposed on the cost-benefit analysis, therefore, is that of mission performance – of a given level of effectiveness – rather than that of satisfying official personnel requirements.

To impose such a general effectiveness constraint, however, seems at first glance to be practically impossible. Effectiveness has many dimensions, some readily quantifiable and some more elusive, and direct measurement of effectiveness is at best extraordinarily difficult. Fortunately, there is no need to measure effectiveness directly or even to decide in principle how it should be measured.

We have just seen that official personnel requirements provide one personnel con-figuration at which the requisite effectiveness level is achieved. To impose that level as a minimum constraint on our analysis, we need not worry about what that level is or how to measure it, we need only concern ourselves with the alternative ways in which it can be achieved. In other words, we only need to know the set of personnel con-figurations which will result in the same effectiveness as will the meeting of official personnel requirements (in technical parlance, the indifference surface passing through the point given by such requirements). This is, of course, not a particularly easy thing to find directly, but we can gain much information about it by starting with official requirements and considering substitution possibilities in a more than super-ficial fashion.

In other words, beginning with the personnel configuration given in official

---

[1] The results of the INS study show this very strongly. What appeared before analysis to be a shortage turned out to be an oversupply. See Morton, Fisher, and Nitzberg [7] and Fisher and Morton [4].

requirements, consider what trade-offs can be made among personnel in different categories while leaving effectiveness unchanged. Note that it is not necessary to say what the level of effectiveness objectively is in order to do this, merely to say if it goes up or down. Such effectiveness-preserving trade-offs obviously lead to alternative configurations just as good as official personnel requirements in terms of effectiveness.

4.5. Finding the Trade-offs

How can such trade-offs be found? There are ways, but there is no disguising that much more work needs to be done here.

In principle, the trade-offs required ought to be supplied by the policy maker for whom the cost-benefit analysis is being performed. It is his notions of effectiveness that must be satisfied. Unfortunately, one suspects that high-level decision makers are inclined to be a bit vague in replying to direct questions as to their marginal rates of substitution among various personnel categories. Nevertheless, it is seriously to be hoped that those who rely on personnel requirements, or at least those who produce them will give increasing thought to specifying what alternative personnel configurations will be equally satisfactory. The present situation implies that they believe effectiveness cannot be maintained in the presence of any deviation no matter how small from such requirements, and that such deviations must be avoided at any price. This is simply unrealistic.

If it is unlikely that the requisite trade-offs can be specified at a high policy-making level, the analyst must investigate such trade-offs much closer to the operational level itself. In the INS study, this was done by extensive interviewing of experienced officers in charge of relatively narrowly defined small units. These officers were asked directly for the number of men in one category which would just substitute for the loss of a single man in another category, leaving effectiveness unchanged (or for the number of men in one category they would just be willing to give up to get an additional man in another category). They were encouraged to think through the sort of task rearrangement required for efficient substitution. The responses were then adjusted in various ways (involving the size of the on-board complements with which the respondents worked) to estimate the indifference surface required for the analysis.

It cannot be claimed that this is an entirely satisfactory way to proceed. This is so for at least three reasons.

First, it is relatively clear from the experience of the INS interviews that it is not easy to get officers in such situations to give thoughtful responses really reflecting the substitution possibilities open to them. Possibly, this difficulty could be at least partially overcome by refined interviewing techniques.

Second, what one wants to elicit from such interviews frequently is the marginal trade-off involved – the rate at which substitution can take place if changes are relatively very small. This is so both for technical reasons involved in the estimation of the indifference surface from the responses and, more importantly, because small changes are more likely to be easy for the respondent to consider in an accurate manner. Yet at the organizational level at which the interviews had to be conducted, the loss of a single man in a particular category sometimes meant a loss of one hundred per cent and not at all a marginal loss. This can be overcome, in principle, by considering the loss of a small fraction of a man's time, but this may be hard for the respondent to do in practice.

Finally, as already discussed, substitution possibilities in a small installation are likely to be rather more restricted than in the entire military establishment for which the analysis is to be performed. Even if respondents in small installations give entirely accurate pictures of the substitution possibilities from their point of view, those pictures need not reflect the substitution possibilities in which we are basically interested. [1] This problem is one aspect of the general difficulty of performing

---

[1]   This difficulty can be overcome if certain assumptions are satisfied concerning the way in which men are assigned to installations, but the assumptions involved can be pretty strong. This is discussed in Section 6 below.

necessarily aggregative analyses, to which we shall return in a later section. It is, of course, an excellent reason to call for more serious interplay between the analyst and the relatively high-level manpower decision makers who wish to use the results of the analysis.

Such interplay can be facilitated by the analyst, as can the examination of marginal trade-offs in general, no matter whose the trade-offs to be examined, by once more considering the shadow prices of constraints. If costs are minimized, subject to official personnel requirements in their original form, then, as we have seen, one can obtain as a byproduct the cost saving that would occur if those requirements were slightly relaxed, or, alternatively, the cost increase that would have to be paid if those requirements were slightly tightened. Such a shadow price can in fact be obtained for each category of personnel in the requirements, so that we know the price in terms of costs of gaining or losing a man in each such category. It is then easy to see that the ratios of such prices net out the monetary effect and give the price of a man in category A in terms of men in category B. That is, such ratios give the number of men in category B which could be added to the official requirements for that category at no increase in costs, provided that requirements in category A are reduced by one man. This is the marginal trade-off between the two categories in terms of keeping cost constant. It serves as a useful benchmark from which to examine marginal trade-offs which keep *effectiveness* constant; one should ask whether such trades would aid or harm effectiveness. As with direct trade-offs between men and costs, judicious use of such information can aid in eliciting the true preferences of policy-makers.[1] As with the direct cost-personnel relationship, it must not simply be assumed that trade-offs are impossible. The space I have devoted to this issue perhaps underrates its importance, considering the present state of the art.

4.6. The Price of Effectiveness Constraints

Having successfully transformed official personnel requirements into an effectiveness indifference surface, an appropriate way to proceed is to insist that any policy have at least the effectiveness represented by that surface (and by official requirements). This substitutes for strictly stated and detailed personnel constraints a more reasonable effectiveness constraint. Subject to such an effectiveness constraint, cost is to be minimized.

There are, however, some problems involved in doing this. These problems turn out to be the same on a new level as those which led us to reject the imposition of detailed personnel requirements as constraints in the first place. Fortunately, they are not nearly so serious in the new context.

The principal such problem is that which arises with the imposition of any constraint. If an effectiveness constraint is imposed, the implied position is that no cost saving, however great, can compensate for any reduction in effectiveness below the constrained level, however small that reduction may be. Similarly, no credit is given for achieving an effectiveness level above that specified in the constraint. It may thus be more reasonable to specify the trade-off between effectiveness and cost, rather than specifying an effectiveness level.

There are three reasons for believing that this is not nearly so serious a problem as is the parallel one in the case of the imposition of a personnel requirements constraint.

In the first place, it may very well be that an effectiveness constraint correctly reflects the situation facing the military establishment. A certain state of readiness or effectiveness is to be achieved; this cannot be lowered without grave risk to national security, and there is no gain (or at least not much) from improving on it. In the strictest form, this is perhaps only approximately realistic, but it is far more

---

[1] On the general use of shadow prices in this way, see Dorfman [1].

realistic if such minimum goals are stated *in terms of what the establishment must be capable of doing* rather than in terms of the sorts of men it must employ.

Second, while, in principle, the imposition of any constraint implies that no cost saving will be worth any weakening of that constraint, the cost saving that will in fact be achieved by a slight weakening of a generally formulated effectiveness constraint, with substitution possibilities properly included, may not be at all great. Certainly, it is not hard to show that the cost saving involved in weakening an effectiveness constraint derived, as described, from personnel requirements is lower than the cost saving involved in a parallel weakening of those requirements themselves when they are directly imposed as constraints. Much of the cost savings involved are already taken up in the substitution possibilities. Nevertheless, the cost savings that would occur may be worth having, and this question ought not to be ignored.

Finally, and perhaps most importantly, the solution to the optimization problem of the cost-benefit analysis is far less likely to be affected by small adjustments in the level of the constraint if constraints are stated in the relatively free way involved in taking account of substitution possibilities rather than in the very rigid way involved in the imposition of official personnel requirements as direct constraints. In other words, the nature of the optimal policy is relatively more likely to be insensitive to the precise level of an effectiveness constraint than to the precise level of official personnel requirements stated directly as constraints.

The second problem involved in the use of effectiveness constraints is essentially that of substitution possibilities in a new form. It may not be possible to impose only a single effectiveness constraint, attractive though such imposition may be. The fact that a military establishment is made up of many different parts may mean that it is natural to impose constraints ensuring the achievement of minimum effectiveness levels *in each part*. If this is done, we are assuming no substitution among different parts of the establishment; that is, we assume that a reduction in the effectiveness of one part of the establishment cannot be compensated by an increase in the effectiveness of another part. This is quite possibly a valid assumption; it is far more likely to be valid than the similar assumption of no substitution among personnel of different types. Nevertheless, it deserves examination and this may not be easy.

A similar problem arises concerning effectiveness at different points in time. We shall show below that manpower planning is inevitably dynamic, that effectiveness cannot be considered at only a single time point, but that planning must take place for several years at once. As we shall see, the natural thing to do, therefore, is to insist on a minimum effectiveness level in each of those years.[1] To do this, however, is to assume that no substitution between years is possible, that no reduction in effectiveness in one year, however small, can be compensated for by an increase in effectiveness in a different year, however large. Again, this may be an entirely appropriate assumption, but it should be examined.[2]

---

[1] This was done in the INS study. See Morton, Fisher, and Nitzberg [7] and Fisher and Morton [5].

[2] In both these last two cases, the estimation of trade-offs — if trade-offs exist — is extremely difficult, but perhaps not quite so difficult as may at first appear. In the case of effectiveness at different points in time, for example, it is not necessary to pose the meaningless question: What increase in effectiveness in a given year would just compensate for a unit decrease in effectiveness in another year? One need only ask: How many additional men of a certain type in a particular year would just compensate for the loss of a single man of a certain type (not necessarily the same) in another year? The latter question may be almost impossible to answer, but is not meaningless. A similar statement holds for substitutes between small units.

5. COSTS AND BENEFITS OVER TIME

5.1. Why Time Effects Are Important

We have just observed that defence manpower planning is an essentially dynamic process. The costs incurred in and the benefits resulting from a particular program do not take place at a single point in time; rather they are spread out over perhaps fairly long intervals.

There are several reasons for this. In the first place, men inducted into the military typically undergo a period of training during which they acquire the skills which they need in the service. Such training continues on the job, even after the men begin to perform useful functions. This has two effects, however. First, there are direct costs of training – instructor salaries, provision of school and other training facilities, support of the trainees during the training period, and so forth. If training takes more than a negligible period, these costs are spread out over time and their level need not be constant. Second, a man in training is not the equivalent of a fully-trained man in terms of the benefits to be derived from his service. The extent to which his services approach those of a fully-trained man affects benefits at more than one point in time. Thus the existence of a non-negligible training period leads to consideration of costs and benefits at more than a single instant.

There is, however, a much more important reason than this for considering a whole time pattern of benefits and costs. Consider an effectiveness target stated for a particular year, say 1972. As we have seen, that target is probably best stated in terms not simply those of official personnel requirements, but this does not matter for the present argument. The burden of the preceding paragraph can be taken to be as follows. Since achievement of such a target depends, in part, on the skills possessed by the personnel in the service in 1972, and since those skills must be acquired through training, costs and also benefits associated with the achievement of the 1972 goal must begin before 1972.

A stronger point, however, is the following one. Since some, at least, of the men involved in meeting the 1972 target will remain in the service after that year, and since skills acquired in the course of training do not become obsolete overnight, the funds expended on training men to meet the 1972 target will result in benefits in later years as well. Another way of saying this is that the ease with which targets later than 1972 can be met is in part dependent on the carry-over of skilled personnel from 1972. Training provides an investment in human capital, the return on which, like that on any investment, is typically received over the lifetime of the equipment involved rather than in a single year. Naturally, if no skills, training, or experience were involved, then men already in the service would have no advantage over raw recruits. If that were the case, there would be no real need to consider costs and benefits over more than a single year. One of the things that makes defence manpower planning interesting and difficult, however, is precisely that such effects cannot be ignored.

Of course, it may just turn out that planning for a single year at a time leads to an optimal course of action. Unfortunately, this cannot be assumed in advance. Perhaps an example simplified from one of the results of the INS study will make this clear.

In that study, there is some substitution between relatively experienced and relatively inexperienced men. A given effectiveness goal can be achieved with a relatively large, relatively inexperienced navy or a relatively small, relatively experienced one. If one considers meeting just the next year's goal, the only way in which this can be done (for purposes of this example) is by varying the level of inductions, since the number of experienced personnel is a legacy from past decisions. Deciding on the level of induction for next year, however, influences or (given other factors) determines the number of experienced men who will be available to the navy in the year after next. It thus affects the number of men who will have to be inducted in that following year in order to meet that year's goals. Obviously, it may sometimes be cheaper to induct more men next year than are needed for next year's goals in order to produce trained men for later years.

As it turns out in the INS study, this is false as regards the analysis of the navy as a whole. Considering the entire enlisted navy, it just so happens that there is enough substitution between relatively experienced and relatively inexperienced men and enough loss of experienced men through failure to reenlist that just meeting each year's goal as it occurs is in fact the optimal policy.

On the other hand, this result is clearly not one that can be assumed beforehand. To drive this home, consider one result of the INS analysis of electronics maintenance and repair personnel. Here relatively untrained men are very bad substitutes for relatively trained ones. The result is that a myopic policy of inducting men as needed leads to a situation where goals in later years are very difficult to meet and expenditures on electronics personnel exceed the budget for the entire navy in those years. When one takes proper account of the carry-over between years, however, one finds that by slightly overachieving goals in some years, the costs of goal achievement in later years is dramatically reduced, and, indeed, the inductions and costs of the true optimal, non-myopic program are perfectly reasonable.

Clearly, results like these are not accidental. They reflect the fact, as stated, that manpower policies involve investment in human capital and that the costs and benefits of any investment program take place over time and not simply at a single instant. Pretending that planning is but for a single year can, and frequently will lead to results which are wrong and even ridiculous when considered from a longer-run point of view.

5.2. Discounting of Costs

Thus, cost-benefit analysis of manpower planning necessarily involves the combining of costs and benefits occurring at different moments of time. In the case of costs, such combination is relatively straightforward; what is involved is the calculation of the present discounted value of an expenditure stream.

Such discounting of future expenditures, so that future money is considered less valuable than present money is based on a number of considerations. Important among these, for a private firm, is the fact that in a perfect capital market, maximization of present discounted value can be shown to generate an income stream which in every period provides at least as much income as does any other policy. This occurs because the firm can lend a given amount of money now and receive a larger amount later. Alternatively, the firm can invest the money in its own operations now and reap a larger reward later. In a competitive capital market, the interest rates involved in these two transactions will be equalized at the margin, after allowance for risk.

It is important to realize that the same sort of principle applies to governmental operations. If policies are financed by present taxation, then resources are being taken from the private sector. Those resources, if put to use in that sector, would result in higher output later on; hence, just as for a private firm, the worth to society of a given value of resources now is greater than the worth of the same monetary value of resources later on.

This argument suggests that the appropriate interest rate to use in discounting is the rate of growth of the entire economy. However, this is only one of several possibilities.

Consider, for example, a different reason for discounting. For various reasons, individual consumers have time preference; they do discount future consumption. In deciding how to weight tax dollars now against tax dollars later, society ought to consider that a tax dollar saved now is worth more to individuals than a tax dollar saved later on, because of individuals' own preference for current over future consumption. Thus future money should be discounted relative to present money. What rate should be used in such discounting? A clear possibility is the rate at which individuals discount the future, as represented by the rate at which they are just willing to make risk-free loans. This latter rate, however, is the rate at which the government can borrow funds.

The government borrowing rate is also an attractive rate to use, of course, if one takes a purely accounting point of view and considers the government as an entity separate from the people and one whose operations must take into account the cost of capital to it.

Indeed, this discussion does not nearly exhaust what can be said on the subject of the appropriate discount rate. For example, both the above arguments have considered society's preferences as merely reflecting the preferences and opportunities of its members as expressed in the marketplace. Perhaps society's discounting of the future ought rather to reflect the collective preferences of its members as politically expressed; these two sets of preferences need not be the same, for individuals may well desire that society as a whole give heavier weight to the future of unborn generations than they themselves are willing to do in their individual capacities. If so, market rates of interest are higher than the rates which society should use in discounting expenditures on public projects.

There are many other facets to the problem of appropriate choice of interest rate. Indeed, there is a simply enormous literature on this subject,[1] and I shall not attempt to extend the relatively superficial remarks already given, as I wish to move on to a consideration of other topics. In practice, it seems clear that alternative discounting rates should be tried in a sensitivity analysis; if one is not too unlucky, all rates within a plausible range (which may be fairly narrow) may lead to roughly the same results. If not, close attention must be paid to this problem.

5.3. Comparison of Benefits at Different Points of Time

We come then to what is in some ways a similar and in others a very different problem, the comparison of benefits occurring at different points of time.

At first glance, there seems no reason to consider this a separate problem. Do not the arguments given for the discounting of costs equally apply to benefits? Moreover, is it not sensible to discount both costs and benefits at the same rate? It is easy to see that this would indeed be the case if benefits were strictly monetary or could be reduced to monetary equivalents by consideration of monetary-non-monetary trade-offs. Where this is not feasible, however, the solution is not so easy, and this is almost inevitably the case in problems of defence man-power planning.

Suppose that for each time period, we have constructed a benefit measure; we now wish to combine those measures into a single one covering all time periods. Alternatively (and this is not really any different), suppose that, as described in an earlier section, we have formulated effectiveness goals for each time period; we now wish to combine those goals into a single one by considering possible substitution between the goals of different time periods.

The difficulty in doing this arises for a reason already briefly discussed. Unlike costs, benefits have no natural unit of measurement. A benefit measure or an effectiveness target at a moment in time is constructed by somehow making comparable the different non-monetary effects of a program. This requires only information, potentially available, on trade-offs between different effects. Having formed such a measure, however, there is nothing specially privileged about it, in the sense that any other measure reflecting the same trade-offs will do as well.

Thus, for example, suppose that we require that effectiveness, measured in a particular way, reach the level implied by official personnel requirements. We can impose precisely the same substantive constraint by deciding to square the effectiveness measure used and requiring that any program achieve the squared effectiveness level that would be achieved by official personnel requirements. Once we have done this, however, there is no way to tell which is the "true" effectiveness measure. We could have begun with the second one and claimed that the first was derived as the square root of the second. Both measures code all the observable information on trade-offs; both are entirely equivalent. Moreover, it is obvious that the square is only an example. The

---

[1] Prest and Turvey [8, pp. 697-700] give a rather more complete survey than that given here (although still an abbreviated one), as well as references.

log, the cube, and indeed any increasing monotonic transformation will also serve. Which of these equivalent effectiveness or benefit measures one uses is purely a matter of convenience; the choice among them is a wholly arbitrary one.

The implication of this is clear, however. If the choice among equivalent represent-ations of a benefit measure is arbitrary, the problem must not be formulated in such a way that the results depend on which measure is chosen. We have already had occasion to consider this in dealing with the benefit-cost ratio as a criterion of optimality.

Now, unfortunately, it is easy to show that if one adopts a particular measure of benefits for each time period and maximizes the present discounted value of such benefits at given costs (or maximizes the present discounted value of benefits less costs), the result will *not* be the same if the benefit measure used is replaced by its square, its log, and so forth. Similarly, if we attempt to compare effectiveness goals in different years by requiring that effectiveness rise by, say, five per cent per year, we will not be making a comparison which is independent of the particular choice of one of a whole family of equivalent effectiveness measures. If an effectiveness measure rises by five per cent a year, its square will rise by 10.25 per cent, its square root by a bit less than 2.5 per cent, and its log by no constant percentage at all. Thus the discounting of a particular benefit or effectiveness measure imposes a wholly arbitrary condition on the results of a cost-benefit analysis. Hence such discounting is inadmissible in the kind of problem we are discussing.

How then ought effectiveness in different years to be compared? There are two possibilities, and, I think, only the second is likely to be practical.

The alternative which is in principle preferable but in practice likely to be infeasible is to consider seriously the question of substitution between effectiveness levels in different years. This need not be done directly. One need not ask the meaning-less question: "How much additional effectiveness in year A is required to just compensate for the loss of a unit of effectiveness in year B?" It should be apparent that such a question depends crucially on the definition of effectiveness units and is hence inadmissible if that definition is arbitrary. Rather, the question that must be asked concerns the trade-off that might be made between personnel of some type in year A and personnel of the same or different type in year B leaving effectiveness in both years unchanged. Since what is wanted is a summary measure of effectiveness which reflects the contributions of different men in different years, only such trade-offs need be considered.

Unfortunately, however, while such questions of trade-off between different personnel types in different years can perfectly well be asked in principle, it seems clear that to ask them in practice puts an unreasonable strain on what can legitimately be expected of those answering such questions. Obtaining accurate answers to trade-off questions is, as we have seen, a tricky matter even when the trade-offs involved are fairly directly within the experience of the officers responding; questions of the present sort are likely to be unanswerable in practice.

Fortunately, on the other hand, the answer to interyear comparisons of effectiveness may be very simple in the defence manpower context. As opposed to substitution among personnel categories or between labour and capital, it is entirely plausible to suppose. that substitution possibilities between years are extremely limited or altogether nil. Thus, within reasonable limits, the requirement that a country's forces always be at some minimum level of effectiveness implies that no decline from that level in one year can be compensated for by an increase in a different year. Since it is small consolation to a nation overwhelmed by enemy attack that its forces were more than prepared in another year, the assumption of no substitution among years seems a realistic one. If it is realistic, then the problem of obtaining answers to trade-off questions such as those just posed does not have to be solved; still, like all other points of this sort, the matter needs to be given more than cursory attention in performing cost-benefit analyses.

Suppose, then, that we accept the position that substitution between years is impossible. This immediately implies that there exists *no* single benefit or effectiveness measure subsuming all years. Instead, the analysis should proceed by imposing for each year considered an effectiveness constraint derived as already described and minimizing the present discounted value of costs while requiring that any program achieve in every year at least the level of effectiveness prescribed for that year by the constraints. This is the natural extension to many years of the fixing effectiveness – minimizing costs procedure outlined above. It is a flexible and powerful technique, and far superior to an incautious attempt to summarize benefits through discounting.

5.4. End Effects

Before closing this section on effects over time, it seems appropriate to add a few words concerning so-called end effects. As we have seen, it is necessary to consider costs and benefits over several time periods rather than only for a single moment in time. How does one know where to stop? Put differently, one wants to be careful to avoid terminating the consideration of future periods in such a way as to substantially influence the results.

Fortunately, this is not hard to do in the present context. In a more general context, such end effects arise for two reasons. First, if the problem is set up to maximize a single criterion function (for example, the present discounted value of benefits less costs), end effects tend to arise unless proper provision is made for the way in which the program is to terminate. Thus, for example, in considering investment problems, one cannot forget that the world (and the problem) will not really terminate at the end of the period considered and thus one must make some provision for the amount of capital that will be left over for the next planning period. If this is not done, one can obtain foolish results involving the eating up of capital toward the end of the planning period with no provision for the future.

In the present context, this problem is readily avoided if one adopts the approach outlined above and imposes effectiveness constraints for all periods of the program. By imposing such a constraint for the last period considered, one can easily ensure that the human capital acquired during the life of the program is not simply dissipated for no reason. An effectiveness constraint for the last year of the program here plays precisely the same role as a constraint on the terminal stock of capital in a more conventional context.

Now, the imposition of an effectiveness constraint for the terminal year of the planning period ensures that the manner in which consideration of future years is terminated will not affect the program in an outrageous way. This alone is not enough to avoid end effects, however, for we must also be sure that the very choice of which year is to be the last considered does not substantially affect the results.

This is where discounting of costs comes in again. We do not consider as costs, expenditures which arise after the end of the period for which we are planning. [1] Provided that we plan for a fairly long period however, it will usually turn out that the exact date at which we end is immaterial, because costs for years toward the end of that period are already discounted by so large a factor as to make their contribution to the present discounted value of all costs negligible. [2]

Moreover, such discounting is also likely to make the results relatively insensitive to the exact levels of the effectiveness constraints for periods in the relatively distant future. This is fortunate, since inability to predict the international situation and the effects of technical change on labour-capital and inter-personnel

---

[1] We may, however, choose to consider as costs all future expenditures committed by the end of the period by the induction of men then in the service. This was done in the INS study.

[2] This is not guaranteed *a priori*, however. If costs are likely to rise at five per cent a year in programs considered, discounting at five per cent or less will never make later costs negligible. This can happen if the effectiveness constraints tend to involve large growth in the military establishment. Such required growth for an indefinite period, however, is very unlikely. Note that the problem does not arise because of inflation. Proper calculation of costs is in terms of resources and thus in constant dollars.

category substitution is likely to make the formulation of constraints for such years a relatively uncertain business.[1]

6. AGGREGATE VS. DISAGGREGATE ANALYSIS

I turn now to another topic to which I already have had occasion to refer— the level of aggregation of the analysis. The difficulty here is as follows. On the one hand, the need to have a computationally feasible and analytically reasonably tractable analysis often dictates performing the work at a relatively high level of aggregation. If this is done, the results are likely also to be in broad overall terms: How many men should be inducted? What are efficient incentives for men in general? and so on. On the other hand, keeping the problem at a high level of aggregation may build in unwarranted assumptions as to matters which a more disaggregate analysis would treat more satisfactorily.

Thus, for example, one part of the INS study treated the U.S. Navy as a whole. For this purpose, a man of given length of service was treated as equivalent to any other man of the same experience in the Navy. This is clearly not very satisfactory. Aside from the evident fact that men enter the Navy with different aptitudes and acquired skills, a much more serious problem is raised by the training given in the Navy itself. A man with several years' experience in electronics is a different kind of human capital than a man with the same length of experience as a gunner's mate or a steward. Obviously, such men are not perfect substitutes for one another and it is wrong, in principle, to treat them as though they were perfectly interchangeable without considering the consequences for the results.

On the other hand, the problem treated in the INS study already involved a dynamic programming problem sufficiently large and complicated to strain the capacity even of the most modern computers then available. To have that problem expanded to include explicitly not only inductions and general levels of experience but also assignment and specific training of men would have produced a problem simply not computationally solvable.

Another aspect of the same problem has already been discussed. We saw above that the possibility of substitution among different personnel categories was unlikely to be the same for small units as for the entire military establishment being analyzed. Unless one is willing to specify something about the way in which different small units can substitute for each other, the rate at which men in one personnel category can be substituted for men in another will depend on where these men are assigned and what training they embody. Yet, again, explicitly to keep track of and decide on such assignments in the course of a general analysis can easily lead to an unmanageable problem.

Fortunately, it is possible to get around this difficulty in one or more ways. One such way is to regard the military establishment as made up of its smaller parts, and to neglect substitution possibilities among those parts, if such possibilities exist. This may not be an unreasonable thing to do, if the disaggregation is performed in such a way as to make substitution of men within an analyzed group fairly easy and substitution between groups relatively difficult. Thus, for example, it may be reasonable to say that electronics personnel (once trained) can be separately analyzed. Obviously, substitution between electronics technicians of varying experience is possible to a far greater degree than substitution between electronics personnel and stewards. It may thus be appropriate to analyze costs and benefits in electronics and in stewards separately, whereas, for example, it would be inappropriate to treat electronics personnel on destroyers as separate from and no substitute for electronics personnel on cruisers. (In fact, electronics personnel were separately analyzed in a separate part of the INS study).

---

[1] The subject of uncertainty in cost-benefit analysis of defence manpower planning is not treated in this paper. One can, of course, make some allowance for it by considering the expected values of different effects of programs and by using a higher rate of discount when risk is involved than when it isn't, but to say this is hardly even to get into the matter. The discussion in the present paper is relevant whether or not uncertainty is important, however. See the brief summary and references in Prest and Turvey [8, p.699].

If the overall problem can be broken up into *separate* subproblems in this way, those separate problems can be separately solved and a realistic level of disaggregation achieved at a manageable computational level.

On the other hand, close attention must be paid to the question of just how disjoint such subproblems really are. We have already pointed out that in breaking up an overall problem into such components, one ignores substitution possibilities which cut across such components. Further, one also ignores the possibility that the costs involved in one subproblem may not be independent of the solution of another. Thus, for example, the cost of providing berths and training facilities for one group may depend in part on whether existing facilities which may be used in common are already being used to capacity for some other group. If this is the case, the two problems cannot be separately analyzed. Nevertheless, the error involved in treating as separate two or more problems related in such a fashion may often be less that that involved in treating them together as a single undifferentiated unit.

Alternatively, analysis on an aggregate level may not be so bad as it at first appears, providing one is willing to make some assumptions about the relations among the units making up the establishment. Furthermore, these assumptions can sometimes be of a relatively general kind. Thus, for example, ignore for the moment difficulties caused by specialized training and consider only the problem raised above as to substitution possibilities for the entire establishment and for small units being different. To take this problem in its purest form, suppose that the mathematical form which such possibilities take is the same for each unit.[1] This means *not* that the trade-offs among different personnel categories are the same in each unit, but merely that such trade-offs would be the same if the number of men in each category assigned to one unit were the same as that assigned to another.

Suppose that we make two further relatively general assumptions. The first of these is that trade-offs depend only on relative numbers, so that trade-offs would be unchanged if all personnel assignments to a given unit were reduced or increased in the same proportion. Since it is likely to be the composition of the personnel in a unit rather than the absolute size thereof which determines substitution possibilities, this is by no means implausible.

Second, suppose we assume that effectiveness for the establishment as a whole is some increasing function of effectiveness in each unit. That is, we assume that if any unit becomes more effective, and no unit becomes less effective, the establishment as a whole becomes more effective. Were we to specify the form of this relationship, we could be specifying the way in which different units substitute for each other in the establishment as a whole; note, however, that it is not necessary to make such a specification to obtain the results which follow. Thus all that is required here is essentially the statement that such inter-unit substitution is possible; if it is not possible, then (provided that costs can also be broken up) each unit can be analyzed separately anyway and the problem we are now discussing does not arise.

In these circumstances, it can be shown that if the establishment acts in a rational way in its assignment of personnel to different units – that is, if it assigns personnel so as to make overall effectiveness as great as possible, given the available personnel, then whatever the relative importance of the separate units, substitution possibilities for the establishment as a whole take the same form as for the separate units. Analysis can then proceed on an aggregate level with substitution possibilities among personnel categories depending only on the composition of personnel in the establishment as a whole and neglecting the question of the units to which personnel are assigned.[2] The

---

[1]   Thus our discussion may be taken as relevant to the analysis of costs and benefits of men with a particular type of training when these men are assigned to different small units.

[2]   A demonstration for a specific case is given in Fisher and Morton [5] and in Morton, Fisher, and Nitzberg [7, Appendix G].

assignment problem can be handled separately, but there may be no need to handle it at all, for cost-benefit analysis at the aggregate level will in fact be appropriate in these circumstances, so far as the problem being considered is concerned.

Naturally, this strong-appearing result rests upon the assumptions made; nevertheless, similar results continue to hold if those assumptions are weakened somewhat. In particular, one can weaken the assumption that substitution possibilities in different units are in precisely the same mathematical form; under some circumstances, one can even weaken the assumption as to optimal assignment. [1]

On the other hand, this result takes care of the problem that substitution possibilities for the entire establishment may be different from substitution possibilities for individual units on the implicit assumption that men can be shifted between units with no loss of expertise. The problems raised for aggregate analysis by the embodiment of particular training in a particular man are not solved by the theorem under discussion. As already discussed, however, the extreme version of such problems, in which men in one group can at best be substituted for men of another group with great loss of the effectiveness, can often be handled by treating the costs and benefits of groups as entirely disjoint.

In general then, the level of aggregation of cost-benefit analysis in defence manpower planning deserves close attention. One wishes to preserve as much realism as possible while still obtaining a solvable problem, for the problem will be solved in practice, even if not by the cost-benefit analyst, through the adoption of a specific policy, optimal or otherwise. It is wrong to suppose that aggregation problems can be glossed over, but equally wrong to suppose that aggregate analyses must be mistaken, for, as the example just given shows, a high level of detail can be irrelevant to at least the broad outlines of the solution. [2, 3]

7. WHOSE COSTS? WHOSE BENEFITS?

In this concluding section, I wish briefly to raise an issue of rather a different kind from those so far discussed, although not unrelated to some of them.

What constitutes a cost and what a benefit, depends on the point of view from which the question is posed. Indeed, what effects of a policy are to be taken into account at all depends on that point of view. Because cost-benefit analysis is likely to be used to answer relatively specific questions, because the analysis is likely to relate to only a part of the full military establishment, and because even the full military establishment is only a part of governmental operations which in turn are only a part of the life and economy of society as a whole, it is very easy to ignore effects which extend beyond the relatively narrow confines within which the analysis takes place. Such overlooking of wider effects may or may not be justified, but it should always be a matter for conscious decision.

A few examples will make the issues clear. First, once more consider the INS study. That study was concerned with retention of enlisted personnel. Among the incentives offered for such retention was a program of rapid advancement to officer status. Since the study focussed on enlisted personnel, however, men advancing to officer status were treated as equivalent to men leaving the Navy; from the time of their promotion, costs and benefits later attributable to them were counted as zero.

Now, this procedure clearly requires some justification. It is perfectly true that, from the relatively parochial view of the enlisted Navy, such men cease both to incur costs and to perform useful services once they are promoted; from the point of view of

---

1   See Morton, Fisher, and Nitzberg [7, Appendix G].
2   In this connection, it is interesting to note that the substantive results of the analysis for electronics personnel of the INS study were not qualitatively different from those for the far more aggregative analysis for the Navy as a whole.
3   The aggregation problems involved in the treatment of human capital are, of course, not unique to that sort of capital. For a discussion of closely related problems raised for aggregation by the existence of different sorts of physical capital, see Fisher [2] and [3].

the entire Navy, however, this is not the case. If we agree that it ought to be the Navy and not just the enlisted Navy whose costs and effectiveness are analyzed, then at the very least, some analytic support must be given to such treatment of these men.

In fact, it is possible to justify that treatment, providing one is willing to accept one of two **alternative** (although perhaps not very plausible) assumptions. The first of these is that the training received by such men as enlistees does not improve their efficiency as officers beyond the level ordinarily possessed by men accepted from outside the Navy into officer's training. If the Navy can already easily acquire men from outside whose outside education and experience makes them just as fit for officer status as the men promoted under the incentive program considered, then such promotion does nothing to change the benefits and costs of naval officers. If, on the other hand, training as an enlisted man makes a man better qualified to be an officer than other men educated and trained outside the Navy, [1] or if there is a shortage of suitable officer material, then the benefits and costs of naval officers is affected by the rapid promotion program and this ought not to be ignored.

Alternatively, even if naval officers are in short supply, note that such officers not only contribute benefits but also incur costs. Thus, ignoring such promotions can be justified if the benefits and the costs are thought to just balance. This involves the assumption that such officers are just paid their marginal products, that they are just worth what they cost. This is an assumption that could be defended if the Navy were a profit-maximizing competitive firm, but I should not know how to begin rigorously to justify it in the actual situation, short of ceasing to ignore such benefits and costs and analyzing them as part of an overall cost-benefit analysis for the entire Navy, officers as well as enlisted men.

Just as the viewpoint of the enlisted Navy may be overly narrow when considered from that of the Navy as a whole, however, so may the viewpoint of the Navy as a whole be overly narrow if we consider program effects on the rest of society. Indeed, the example just given has a close parallel in the wider context.

A man taken into the Navy as an untrained man and given specialized training, often leaves the Navy a more valuable piece of human capital than he went into it. From the Navy's point of view, indeed, if such a man leaves relatively soon after training, such an increase in value represents an investment by the Navy which is not recouped in the form of services rendered. From society's point of view, however, the case is otherwise, at least in part. The fact that a trained electronics technician, for example, receives a higher civilian wage than does an untrained man, reflects the fact that he is performing more valuable services to the economy. This is the case whether or not he is performing them in the place where he was trained. I recognize, of course, that the military establishment is not and perhaps ought not to be in the business of deliberately providing training for men who will then perform their services to society outside that establishment; nevertheless, is it really appropriate to count such men as dead weight losses after they leave the service, as scrapped human capital? From society's point of view, we would not count them as lost had they received their training in a private firm, even if the firm itself properly so counted them. The military establishment is, of course, in a different position, but the question still seems worth raising. It is the same question to which the answer seemed clear when a man was trained in the enlisted Navy and performed his services as a naval officer. Ought the answer to be different here? [2]

---

[1] It is important to realize that what is involved is not whether the enlisted experience makes a particular man better suited to be an officer than he was before but rather whether that experience makes him better officer material than can be obtained from other sources.

[2] Note, incidentally, that this problem could not arise if the military establishment were a competitive private firm paying a market wage. In that case the marginal man would just be worth his cost and his leaving after training would have no effect on profits.

This example is one in which benefits from society's point of view are not the same as benefits from the point of view of all or part of the military establishment. Other examples in which costs to society and costs to the military establishment differ are also easy to find. Does a program greatly affect the economy and life of a particular locality or region, and are those effects adequately represented in the prices paid for resources by the military? Does a program require significant amount of foreign exchange? This may not increase costs from a purely military point of view, but it certainly does so from the point of view of the economy as a whole. In practice, large spillover effects of these sorts are recognized and, sometimes, adjustments are made for them. In performing a relatively abstract cost-benefit analysis, however, such problems are easy to overlook.

One might carry a list of such examples further. At a very different level, annual budgetary allotments are considered absolute constraints by those not responsible for budget making. Such constraints are hardly appropriate, however, as a basis for long-range or overall planning. In such a wider context, as already discussed, such constraints should be replaced by a consideration of the discounted cost of resources.

In all such circumstances – and they are very general – it is important that both analyst and decision-maker recognize that defence manpower planning is a large-scale affair, that planning for part of the establishment is but a part of planning for all of it, and that the wider economic and social effects of defence programs must at least be considered, where these are not entirely reflected in the costs and benefits of the military establishment. Here, as in the specification of trade-offs and measurement of effectiveness, and as in other aspects of cost-benefit analysis in defence manpower planning, frequent communication between policy maker and analyst is called for. Such analysis is too technical to be left to the policy maker and too important in its implications to be left to the technicians. Neither can afford a parochial viewpoint.

REFERENCES

[1] Dorfman, R. (1965), "Econometric Analysis for Assessing the Efficacy of Public Investment," Proceedings of the Study Week (October 1963) on *Le Rôle de l'Analyse Econométrique dans la Formulation de Plans de Developpement*, Pontifical Academy of Sciences, Vatican City, pp. 187–205.
[2] Fisher, F.M. (1965), "Embodied Technical Change and the Existence of an Aggregate Capital Stock," *Review of Economic Studies*, Vol. XXXII, No.4, pp. 263–288.
[3] Fisher, F.M. (forthcoming), "Embodied Technology and the Existence of Labor and Output Aggregates, " *Review of Economic Studies*.
[4] Fisher, F.M. and A.S. Morton (May 1967), "Reenlistments in the U.S. Navy: A Cost-Effectiveness Study," *American Economic Review*, Vol. LVII, No.2, pp. 32–38.
[5] Fisher, F.M. and A.S. Morton (May-June 1967), "The Costs and Effectiveness of Reenlistment Incentives in the Navy," *Operations Research*, Vol.15, No.3, pp. 373–381.
[6] Hitch, C.J. and R.N. McKean (1960), *The Economics of Defense in the Nuclear Age*, Harvard University Press, Cambridge, Mass.
[7] Morton, A.S., F.M. Fisher, and D.M. Nitzberg (Jan.–Feb. 1966), "Cost/Effectiveness of Reenlistment Incentives," *Navy Manpower Considerations 1970–1980 (U)*, Study 13, Institute of Naval Studies of the Center for Naval Analyses, FOR OFFICAL USE ONLY.
[8] Prest, A.R. and R. Turvey (Dec. 1965), "Cost-Benefit Analysis: A Survey," *Economic Journal*, Vol.LXXV, No,300, pp. 683–735.

On a System Analysis Approach to a Theory of Manpower Management[1]

CARL F. KOSSACK

UNIVERSITY OF GEORGIA

The problems associated with manpower systems policy decision making often elude scientific analysis due to the complexity found in large organizational patterns. This very complexity, however, often results in conflicting evaluations relative to the value of a particular policy since, from one point of view, the policy may appear to be near optimum while, when the policy is viewed from a different aspect, it shows up very poorly. For example, a policy may produce very satisfactory short range benefits only to produce highly undesirable long range effects. What is required if one is to be able to evolve a comprehensive policy evaluation procedure is to provide a "total-system" approach to such evaluations.

The modern approach to such total system investigation involves the development of a mathematical model of the system and, through the use of system analysis and/or simulation techniques, the examination of the effects that policy changes would evoke upon the operational characteristics of the system. Such policy changes normally are reflected by changing either the inputs of the system or some of the internal relationships which govern its operation. Since many systems of interest are large and complex, these studies must often be accomplished through an analysis that involves the use of high-speed computers, and often the complexity of variables involved in the systems and their interrelationships are such that the mathematical model employed can at best only approximate the actual system. However, it is generally recognized that even crude models, as long as they span the total system, provide an analytical vehicle that, if used properly, will increase one's appreciation of the system under study and will challenge one to examine carefully the more important aspects of the actual operational system.

In the study of manpower systems, interest centres around how the system utilizes its available manpower over time and thus the evaluation of the operational effectiveness of any such system is often complicated by the requirement of having to consider both the long term and the short term effect of any policy change proposed for the system. In addition, the analysis problem is complicated by the requirement of balancing the productivity of the system with the benefits that accrue to individuals as they are utilized within the system.

In this paper we will examine how systems analysis can be used to study problems associated with the role of manpower in an organization and will look at a theoretical approach to manpower management of a type that must be considered if one is to concern oneself with the more basic problems found in this area. An attempt will be made to consider not only methods of developing models to be used in such personnel utilization analyses but also, in connection with such models, several different types of evaluations. Emphasis will be placed upon the policy evaluation and planning function of manpower management rather than upon operational decision type problems since the state of the art of personnel utilization theory is not advanced enough to enable one to use it in a decision making role. However, even with this restriction, it is hoped that these considerations will eventually lead to the development of a general theory that is concerned with the role of personnel in an organization.

In the development of personnel utilization models, the approach most often utilized is that of considering a set of mutually exclusive states or conditions within which an individual can be found. Included as special types of states will be jobs, training programs or schools, and special assignments associated with the work being done by the organization. Now, if one attempts to differentiate between individuals assigned to the same job or training program using only this discrete state approach, each job must be broken down into sub-states with each sub-state carrying some additional distinguishing characteristic. Thus the state S_{27} may represent electrical technicians with less than three months' experience while state S_{28} may be used to represent electrical technicians with from 3 months to 6 months' experience, etc. From such a discrete state model we can develop what is called a Markovian model[2] since it may be assumed that there is no difference, as far as the system is concerned, between individuals in the same state during the same time period, and so we are only interested in describing the mechanism by which any individual is transferred from one state to another. The simplest type of stochastic mechanism that can be used to describe this transfer is to assume that there exists a transitional probability from each state to every other state including the given state, and that such transfers can occur only once during each given time period. That is, the time period selected must be of such a short duration that an individual may experience no more than one transfer per time period. Such a system is called Markovian and a simple personnel system is illustrated in Figure 1.

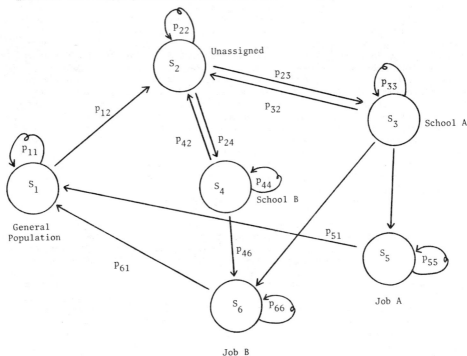

Figure 1: ILLUSTRATION OF A SIMPLE MARKOVIAN PERSONNEL MODEL

A second type of model begins with the same basic mutually exclusive "state" structure, but differentiates between individuals within the system by assigning to each individual a vector of descriptive variables which can be considered essentially as points within a Characteristic Space.[3] These descriptors can include aptitude measures, skills, physical characteristics, and even experience. This descriptive vector for the i th individual may be represented symbolically by $x_i(t)$, with the t

designation recognizing that the representation will vary over time. If one now desires to characterize the flow of individuals through the system, the existence of the descriptor variable X enables one to associate a probability *function* over the characteristic space and assign the transitional probability that an individual will be transferred from one state to another during a designated time period. This model has been called the Functional Markovian and provides additional flexibility since one can use the characteristic space concept to define other aspects associated with manpower utilization within an organization. For example, a man's job productivity can be represented by a numerical function defined over the characteristic space, as can be maintenance cost for any individual within any state. The experience which individuals obtained while in any state can be represented as a transformation of the characteristic space onto itself. In addition, such concepts as job or school quotas, availability and eligibility requirements for assignments etc. are all expressible in mathematical form through this general functional model.

We thus have available at least two mathematical models that can be used to represent manpower utilization systems: the Markovian, which is attractive because of its simplicity; and the Functional Markovian, which is noted for its flexibility. It should be recognized that in the Markovian model the representation is accomplished by the transitional matrix of probabilities

$$
T = \begin{bmatrix}
p_{11} & p_{12} & \text{---} & p_{1B} \\
p_{22} & p_{22} & \text{---} & p_{2B} \\
\text{---------} & & p_{jk} & \text{---} \\
p_{B1} & p_{B2} & \text{---} & p_{BB}
\end{bmatrix}
$$

where p_{jk} represents the probability that during any one time interval an individual who is in state S_j will be transferred to state S_k.

In the study of the operational characteristics of a personnel system, two different types of evaluations are possible. The first is the so-called steady state evaluation in which one is only interested in how a particular management system will operate in the long run assuming that there are no essential changes in the characteristics of the system. Since the interest is in the long run operational characteristics of the system, the initial conditions assumed for the system are of no real consequence and, in fact, for the Markovian Model we have the following relationships:

$$
\text{If} \qquad T^{(n)} = [T]^n = \begin{bmatrix}
p_{11} & \text{---} & p_{1B} \\
\text{-----------} & & \\
\text{-----------} & & \\
p_{B1} & \text{---} & p_{BB}
\end{bmatrix}^n = \begin{bmatrix}
p_{11}^{(n)} & \cdots & p_{1B}^{(n)} \\
\text{----------------} & & \\
\text{----------------} & & \\
p_{B1}^{(n)} & \cdots & p_{BB}^{(n)}
\end{bmatrix}
$$

represents the n – stage transitions probabilities,

$$
\text{and if} \quad U = \lim_{n \to \infty} T^{(n)} = \begin{pmatrix}
u_1 & u_2 & \text{--} & u_B \\
u_1 & u_2 & \text{--} & u_B \\
\text{-----------} & & & \\
u_1 & u_2 & \text{--} & u_B
\end{pmatrix},
$$

then, if there are N individuals in the system, the expected number of individuals who will be formed in state S_j approaches $u_j N$ as n approaches infinity. Thus one can obtain these steady-state expected numbers by simply squaring the transfer probability matrix repeatedly and, under most conditions, the convergence to the limit is most rapid. Steady-state evaluations using a Functional Markovian Model are more difficult and time-consuming in their application.

Since many personnel systems are subject to frequent changes in both basic inputs and in internal structure, steady-state evaluations are often not too meaningful and a more dynamic type of evaluation is required. Since dynamic evaluations are sensitive to initial conditions as well as to the conditions in each time period, such evaluation requires a large memory capacity along with rapid computational capabilities. Large variations in the operational characteristics of the system may be expected due to the probabilistic nature of most model inputs and thus the expected-value characteristics of any particular aspect of the system after a given number of time periods is often not too useful without some indication of the amount and type of variations that might be realized. Such detailed requirements are most often met through some type of Monte Carlo simulation procedure which imposes additional evaluation costs on any system study, whether one uses the simple Markovian or the Functional Markovian Model.

Any mathematical evaluation of an operational system must have associated with it some worth or cost consideration, and there are numerous approaches that can be utilized to meet such a requirement. One of the simplest approaches is most applicable to steady-state consideration as associated with the Markovian Model. If the system is describable by B states and, associated with each of these B states, there is a quota, say q_b, $b = 1, 2, \ldots, B$, and, as we have seen above, as for any transitional matrix T and for a given number of individuals, N, there will be an expected number of individuals to be found in each job-state, then one can define a discrepancy for the given system relative to the quota for each state as $\varepsilon_b = Nu_b - q_b$. In addition, if there is defined a cost function for each state, say $c_b(\varepsilon)$, then a measure of the operational effectiveness or worth of a given system, given an N and the matrix T, can be defined by

$$C = \sum_{b=1}^{B} c_b(\varepsilon).$$

From a mathematical point of view[4], it is convenient to take $c_b(\varepsilon)$ to be a quadratic function of the form $c_b(\varepsilon) = k_b \varepsilon^2$, but there is no justification available of this simple functional form from personnel systems considerations. However, once such a worth function has been established, one can not only compare the relative effectiveness of two or more possible systems ($T's$) in meeting a prescribed quota but one can also address oneself to the interesting mathematical problem of determining if an optimum system (minimum C) exists and how it might be determined.

In considering how a personnel system model may be evaluated beyond using the simple cost function consideration outlined above, there are numerous avenues through which one might approach such evaluations. As is the case in most systems evaluations that involve the time dimension, one does not long indulge in such considerations without appreciating the difficulty encountered when one attempts to combine short-term operational worth with long term operational advantages. This difficulty when applied to personnel systems evaluations can be interpreted as being associated with the problem of averaging the expected short term productivity of the system over the set of jobs that are presently defined against some long term operational characteristics of the system. Such a measure may be made in terms of some morale function defined over the set of individuals associated with the system.

To formalize this concept of a morale function one may consider a vector quantity that indicates the experience an individual has had while in the system. Thus we may introduce the experience vector for the i th individual as

$$E_i = (E_{1i}, E_{2i}, \ldots, E_{ti},)$$

where E_{ti} represents the state the individual was in during time period t. We then assume the existence of a numerical function, $M(E, x)$ defined over the vector space E and the characteristic space which reflects the "morale" of an individual after t time periods. Although such a functional representation of morale is of interest, one can easily defend the thesis that an individual's morale is a total system type function and thus to really attempt to quantize this type of psychological variable one must include some indication of the status of the entire system.

In spite of the obvious complexity of the problem, it is worthwhile, particularly from a more mathematical point of view, to attempt to reduce the dimension of the vector E since multivariate considerations introduce many mathematical complications. One such approach is to associate with each of the possible states a " zero-one " attribute type of variable, where the " zero " represents one type of experience and the " one " a complementary different type experience. For example, in naval personnel systems, unity may represent shore duty assignments and zero represent sea duty. Using this transformation, the experience vector can be converted to a zero-one vector which then can be plotted as a point on the unit interval. Thus the multi-variate morale functional representation problem can be reduced to that of defining such a function over the unit interval; but of course the critical problem now becomes that of how to plot the zero-one vector on the unit interval. One theory of morale would stress the existence of runs in the zero-one vector since, for many individuals, the rotation of assignments is important. For such a theory, the vectors that have alternating sequences of zeros and ones could be plotted close to unity while vectors with long runs of all ones or all zeros would be plotted near the origin. We now can see how personality factors may be introduced into such evaluations since one can identify at least two personality types. For the " any change is an improvement " type of personality the morale function should be monotonically increasing over the unit interval, while for the " I don't like to move or change " type the function should be decreasing.

With these considerations one can now identify more clearly the problem of balancing off the short range worth of a system with its long range advantages since, for the short range, we would have available for any system the operational effectiveness measure

$$C = \sum_{b=1}^{B} C_b(\varepsilon)$$

while for the long range advantage we would have some measure of average morale say

$$M = \frac{1}{N} \sum_{i=1}^{N} M_i [E, \ x]$$

Since, in general, systems whose operation is characterized with a large expected C will often have lower $M's$ and, conversely, systems which yield large $M's$ often have low $C's$, trade off between these two criteria must be considered. One possible way of accomplishing this is to borrow from the approach used in testing statistical hypotheses and to consider the existence of a budgeted or assigned value for C, say C_0. One can then introduce the concept of an admissible system as any system for which $C \leqslant C_0$, that is, an admissible system would be one that operates within the budgetary and task assignment constraints, which are usually of a short time nature. We would be interested then in determining from the class of admissible systems those that have large $M's$ and in fact, the " best " operational system could be defined as that system which is admissible and has maximum M relative to all other admissible systems.

A final personnel system consideration comes to mind in this context and is oriented around the problem of job structuring and assignment. In the previous considerations we have implicitly assumed that the various states (training programs, jobs, etc.) have been prescribed and that for a given group of individuals, represented by their distribution over the characterizing space, the system defining problem involved the determination of how this group of individuals might flow through the several states. The fundamental aspect of such an approach is the job assignment decision since the transfer of an individual from one state to another is essentially as assignment decision. However, if we look at the problem from the point of view of admissible systems one recognizes that there is no real constraint imposed relative to just what group of states or jobs are to be considered but simply that whatever the set of jobs used in the system the operational C must not exceed the budgeted C_0. Another way of saying the same thing is that the system must be able to get the "short range" job done within the budgetary limitations. Now we see that, when viewed from a long range evaluation point of view such as morale, one may "get the job done" by using different types of jobs or states with the expectation that some of these systems would have a better effect on the morale of the group of individuals involved in the system than would other possible systems. We are thus led to consider the job structuring type problem if we elect to evaluate the operational effectiveness of a personnel system with this type of depth.

Let me summarize our considerations up to the present before discussing certain total system considerations associated with such analyses. Two basic types of personnel utilization models have been introduced, the simple Markovian and the Functional Markovian. In utilizing system models for the evaluation of the operational characteristics of a personnel management system two approaches have been identified, the steady-state approach and the dynamic approach. In making system evaluations two criteria have been defined, the short range operational worth and the long range operational advantage. Finally, two basic orientations for personnel systems have been considered, the job assignment approach and the job structuring approach. These several considerations can be diagrammed as in Figure 2. It is challenging to recognize that even with this

MODEL

	Simple Markovian		Functional Markovian		
Approach:	Steady-State	Dynamic	Steady-State	Dynamic	Orientation
Criteria:					
					Assignment
Worth					
					Structuring
					Assignment
Advantage					
					Structuring

Figure 2: APPROACHES AVAILABLE FOR PERSONNEL SYSTEMS EVALUATION

preliminary type approach there exist at least sixteen different approaches to
personnel systems evaluation and that one should consider the problem of determining
the class of evaluation problems for which each approach is most appropriate.

Consider now the manner by which system considerations may be used to study
personnel policy evaluation problems within an organization. Rather than to discuss
this problem in the abstract it seems appropriate to introduce some degree of specificity
into the presentation. Let us therefore assume a very simple organization which we will
represent by using the simple Markovian Model. We will identify the following states:

O = State of being outside the organization
L = State of being in the first training program
S = State of being in the advanced training program
C = State of being in a clerical type job
M = State of being in a lower level professional job
H = State of being in a higher level professional job
A = State of being in a lower level administrative job
E = State of being in a higher level administrative job

We thus can represent the transitional matrix for the system by

$$
T = \begin{array}{c|cccccccc}
 & O & L & S & C & M & H & A & E \\
\hline
O & p_{oo} & p_{ol} & p_{os} & p_{oc} & p_{om} & p_{oh} & p_{oa} & p_{oe} \\
L & p_{lo} & p_{ll} & p_{ls} & p_{lc} & p_{lm} & p_{lh} & p_{la} & p_{le} \\
S & p_{so} & p_{sl} & p_{ss} & p_{sc} & p_{sm} & p_{sh} & p_{sa} & p_{se} \\
C & p_{co} & p_{cl} & p_{cs} & p_{cc} & p_{cm} & p_{ch} & p_{ca} & p_{ce} \\
M & p_{mo} & p_{ml} & p_{ms} & p_{mc} & p_{mm} & p_{mh} & p_{ma} & p_{me} \\
H & p_{ho} & p_{hl} & p_{hs} & p_{hc} & p_{hm} & p_{hh} & p_{ha} & p_{he} \\
A & p_{ao} & p_{al} & p_{as} & p_{ac} & p_{am} & p_{ah} & p_{aa} & p_{ae} \\
E & p_{eo} & p_{el} & p_{es} & p_{ec} & p_{em} & p_{eh} & p_{ea} & p_{ee} \\
\end{array}
$$

The relative values of the $p_{\alpha\beta}$'s in the T-matrix reflect the policy that is being
followed by the organization as far as manpower utilization or management is concerned.
Consider in a very preliminary way how certain well known approaches to certain manpower
management problems may be reflected in the above transitional matrix.

(a) The promotional $vs.$ the "new blood" outside hiring approach. The approach to
this problem is reflected in the manner by which H and E type vacancies are
filled within the organization. If an organization is following a promotional
policy the values of p_{mh}, p_{ae} and perhaps those of p_{mc} and p_{ch} would be large,
while organizations following the outside hiring policy would reflect a larger
p_{oh} and p_{oe}.

(b) The company training $vs.$ the hiring of trained personnel approach.

The differentiation between these two approaches will be reflected by the size of
the transitional probabilities p_{ol}, p_{os} and the probabilities of transferring from the
training programs to the various jobs as compared with the probabilities of transferring
directly from the outside to one of the jobs. Of course the differentiation would be
even more obvious if one were to separate the outside state into two states involving
untrained and trained individuals.

(c) The specialist $vs.$ the generalist in administration approach.

These two approaches are more difficult to distinguish between in our simplified
model since the first approach involves the use of individuals in administration who
also have a technical competence and experience while the latter policy favours the use of
individuals with broad and more general experience. However, even in our model one
should expect such divergent personnel utilizations patterns to be reflected in

differences in the p_{ma}, p_{me}, p_{ha}, p_{he} values with those of p_{Oa}, p_{Oe} and perhaps p_{ca}.

(d) The "hoarding" or release of trained personnel approach for short term reduction in level of activity.

In general when an organization is required to meet a reduction in overall activity this reduction would be reflected by a general increase in the transfer probabilities from any of the "within the organizational" states to the outside states. If an organization is following a "hoarding" policy the increase in the size of p_{mo} and p_{ho} would be small as compared with those of an organization facing a similar reduced activity situation but which elects to follow the general reduction policy.

Although additional illustrations could easily be developed it is felt that the above examples amply demonstrate how the transitional probability patterns in the T-matrix reflect the underlying manpower management approach of the organization. It does, however, appear to be pertinent to consider how such representations can be used to establish a theoretical basis upon which manpower management practices can be studied. In an initial response to such a challenge one realizes that, by restricting the approach to that of a simple Markovian, steady state, short term worth, job assignment type evaluation, the vector of quotas, q, along with vector of cost functions, $C_d(\varepsilon)$, completely describe the constraints under which a personnel management system is to operate. This means that any personnel management policy represented by a transitional matrix, T, can be evaluated through its steady-state characteristics and the resulting operational worth. The essential steps in such an evaluation are: (1) Approximate the steady-state matrix U by successive squaring of the transitional matrix T obtaining the vectors of probabilities u_b, $b = 1, 2, \ldots, B$, for each state of the system. (2) Evaluate the expected discrepancy, $\varepsilon_b = NU_b - q_b$, between the quota assigned to each state and the expected number of individuals that the policy would (on the long run) assign to the state. (3) Determine the penalty or cost associated with each discrepancy by using the available cost functions $c_b(\varepsilon)$. (4) Compute the operational worth of the proposed policy by $C = \sum_{b=1}^{B} C_b(\varepsilon)$. This procedure assigns to any personnel management policy a numerical value whose size indicates its worth, with the smaller C value indicating a better operational policy and with C having a minimum of zero.

Once this general procedure has been established one can start to study how different general policies such as those discussed earlier operated under different organizational constraints. To do this one must evolve a method of classifying such constraints into recognizable types. For illustration, one may look at the relative values of the quotas assigned to the different types of states in an attempt to describe how the organization is expected to operate. Thus, if the "training" states quotas are large relative to the "job" quotas, one might say that the organization is set up to operate using an inservice training approach to staffing requirements. If the "management" states quotas are low relative to the "job" quotas one may say that the organization is expected to operate with a minimum of supervision being given to operational personnel. Similarly, the characteristics of the set of cost functions can be studied as they are defined over the various types of states and thus hopefully describe broad or general categories for such cost functional constraints. Thus, one may, through a study of the derivatives of these functions, observe that small increments costs are imposed on say discrepancies involved in attempting to meet the quotas assigned to "clerical" jobs relative to those associated with the "administrative" jobs. This would indicate an organizational program in which administrators may find themselves frequently faced with the problem of having a shortage of clerical assistance. This type of penalty assignment indicates in some measure the importance of the role each type of position is expected to play in the organization or perhaps how flexible the work assignments may have to be relative to the several types of jobs. Other characterizations could undoubtedly be evolved from such considerations.

We can now see how these above concepts may be put together to form a body of theory relative to personnel management. One is interested in how certain policies will perform when applied to organizations operating under certain types of constraints and it would be expected that the theory would in time yield conclusions like the following: "Organizations required to operate under a flexible task assignment program coupled with a strong in-service training program should use a policy that stresses internal promotions and make use of technically qualified individuals as managers". Of course, the above statement is only indicative of the type of "theoretical" conclusions that may come out of such a study and any similarity between the above statement and the truth is purely coincidental.

Our present research activities are still at such a preliminary stage that one cannot at this time provide the reader with any concrete illustrations of how this above approach to developing a theory of personnel management based upon a mathematical model would actually evolve, but we have high hopes that some such considerations will provide a more substantial basis from which one can evolve personnel management policies and decisions and will in time provide a more scientific approach to general system problems in the personnel field.

The difficulties and complications that are present when one initiates such a fundamental approach in a field that is completely dominated by the personal factor is well recognized by the writer. One needs only to recall the multiplicity of models and associated evaluation techniques that were introduced earlier in the paper to appreciate the extent of these complications. Or one need only recognize that in the brief description of how a theory might be generated, that the simplest of all of these possible approaches was utilized and even here one encounters real conceptional problems. However the advancing state of the art of computer oriented mathematics and the ever-increasing analytical capabilities that are being brought about by the "computer era" makes it feasible to attempt to tackle such a program and the benefits that may evolve surely makes such an effort worthwhile.

REFERENCES

1. This work has been supported by Personnel Research Laboratory, Aerospace Medical Division, Air Force Systems Command, United States Air Force, under Contract AF41(609)-3145.
2. Feller, William (1966), *An Introduction to Probability Theory and Its Applications*, John Wiley, New York.
3. Kossack, Carl F., *The Mathematics of Personnel Utilization Models*, WADC-TR-59-359, November 1959.
4. Chernoff and Moses, (1959) *Elementary Decision Theory*, John Wiley, New York.

Mathematical Models in Manpower Planning

M.G. KENDALL

SCIENTIFIC CONTROL SYSTEMS LTD.

INTRODUCTION

By a "model" of a complex I mean a specification of the conditions which it obeys and the constraints under which it operates, given in sufficiently explicit form to enable us to study its structure and behaviour under a variety of circumstances.

Models are sometimes physical constructs which are built to imitate or to simulate the behaviour of the system under study. These are not the kind of model I shall discuss. In our present context the rules governing a system are specified in mathematical form, although I interpret the word "mathematical" in a rather wide sense to include, for example, tabular representation, and the chance behaviour of statistics as well as the deterministic behaviour of classical mathematics.

There are many ways of classifying models but for present purposes I need dwell on only one distinction. Some models are constructed merely to anatomize the system and to help us gain insight into its basic structure. They are part of the process of learning to understand what we are talking about. Other models (which also require structuring) are built in order to predict the behaviour of certain variables under specified assumptions, or to control by decision the future course of development. They are, so to speak, more quantified than models for understanding, in that they purport to yield numerical estimates of future behaviour of certain variables.

Model-building covers a very wide field; and, indeed, it may be argued that all science is model-building in so far as it helps us to construct economically a logical framework for the universe around us, or for selected parts of it. In studies of manpower there are some special features which are worth noting.

In the first place, we are dealing with human beings, who may not react to changing circumstances with the regularity which we find in physics or chemistry.

Secondly, the future course of the populations with which we are concerned is relatively easy to predict; or rather, if children do not enter the manpower orbit until, say, the age of 15, we have at least 15 years from birth to plan their future as a group; and this, notwithstanding that birth-rates since World War II have fluctuated in a most remarkable manner.

On the other hand, human beings take a long time to grow, and we cannot easily take measures to adjust supply and demand in the way, for example, that industry can adjust its output or consumption.

The organizational structure with which we are concerned is man-made and can, at least in theory, be altered very substantially at will. Admittedly there are many practical obstacles in the way of too sudden or too drastic a change, but at least we can design an optimal situation and work towards it, whereas in economics or business the structure of the system may be beyond our control.

In this connection it is worth while mentioning one feature of our current situation which is of relatively recent emergence in the history of mankind. Some time ago, in a sociological context, I was led to consider whether there were any natural constants in the economic or social field, analogous to the constants of physics: the velocity of light, the units of mass and electric charge, Planck's constant and so on. Such things are not easy to find, but there is one of great importance for our present discussions, namely the duration of human life, or perhaps preferably, the duration of the human working life, which we may put at about 45 years. Advances in medicine have extended the span of life by removing the causes of death, and perhaps living conditions are so much better than in the past that we are able to work rather longer. But broadly speaking there has been little alteration in the span of working life. It is, if you will permit the expression, an appoximate constant.

Now there are industries which develop within this period, for example television, electronic computers, air travel; and others which advance or change so much as to require a new technology: plastics, antibiotics and armaments. The days when a man might enter on a career and expect to spend his life doing much the same kind of thing, keeping apace with developments without refreshment of his expertise, are passing from us. Over the next century or so there is every likelihood that the speed of advance will increase. Thus we have a set of new problems in manpower planning, the production of new skills, the retraining of the middle-aged and, in general, the acceleration in the rate of obsolescence of knowledge and expertise. This is one of the reasons why systematic planning of resources is an increasingly important and urgent problem; and manpower is one of our major resources and will remain so in spite of the mechanization of the chores of life.

Against this kind of background I propose to review various types of model which have been proposed for the study of manpower systems. I cannot claim to have read, or even heard of, all the work which is proceeding at the present time. The cover may well be incomplete; but I hope that if anything important has been omitted contributors to the discussion will fill the gaps. I consider three broad classes: models concerning supply and demand; models concerning organization and utilization; models concerning industrial learning and education.

MODELS OF POPULATION GROWTH

Forecasts of total population are notoriously wide of the mark when attempted for twenty years or more ahead. It may therefore seem a rather poor recommendation for model-building in the manpower field to begin with any reference to them. But they demand attention on several grounds: the obvious ground that one must always have some regard to the total size of the population on which so many competitive claims will be made; the historical fact that early demographic models were the first in which more than trivial mathematics found an application; and as illustrations of another important fact which we shall have to notice in other contexts, that disaggregation does not necessarily improve a model.

One of the basic papers in this field is the Pearl-Reed essay of 1920, which fitted a logistic curve to the population of the U.S.A. Biologists had for some time been interested in this curve. If the rate of increase of a population is proportional to its size and also is limited by availability of living resources, it is natural to consider a population of size y obeying a differential equation

$$\frac{dy}{dt} = ky(a - y) \tag{1}$$

which leads to curves of the logistic type. However, such a model, though it gives a fair general account of population growth, has not been very successful for actual forecasts in recent years. (It did very well for the U.S.A. in 1920 and 1930). More recent attempts refine the process by attempting separate forecasts of birth rates, death rates and immigration, and proceed in many cases to considerable detail in discussing specific replacement rates in different age groups or social groups. Whether this can be described as model-building is arguable. It is not always true that these breakdowns of the population into separate sub-groups (disaggregation) improves forecasts for the total. In present circumstances forecasts of birthrates are particularly unreliable – Professor Wold recently remarked of the Swedish figures that it almost looked as if the actual birth-rate had gone out of its way to falsify the projections. However, techniques are improving. Anyone interested in the extent to which modern statistical and computational resources are brought into play in population models may like to consult the book by Orcutt *et al.* (1961).

Replacement tables

A very popular method of examining the manpower situation, either in a whole country or in individual groups such as a company, consists of a table showing the numbers of individuals in sub-groups which may be classifications by age, sex, salary, skills or other relevant characteristics. In some form or other, of course, every staff department has information of this kind. The point of putting it into tabular form (apart from the advantages of exhibiting the manpower inventory in summary) is that we can apply mathematical and computational methods to project its future. Some features of the situation are at our disposal, at least in part: retirements, recruitments and promotion. Others are unpredictable in detail, e.g. deaths and resignations. If we have enough past information we can assign probabilities to the losses and gains in the cells of the classification and hence make forecasts of the future course of the manpower.

There are many ways of using such tables. We shall probably hear something about them later in the conference, so I need notice only a few salient features:

    (i) By simulating the manpower flow through the system we can pinpoint the danger areas, i.e. those where shortages are likely to occur;

    (ii) If the probabilities of transition from one time-period to the next are constant we can forecast the stationary state of the system and tell how long it takes to get there (Young and Almond, 1961);

  (iii) The situation of constant transition probabilities is very dear to the heart of the modern probabilist, being one that has been extensively studied in physical contexts (as a multivariate Markoff process): but it has to be regarded with caution where a business is expanding or contracting;

  (iv) Sooner or later models such as this raise the problem of recruitment from already educated personnel versus internal training;

   (v) Too much disaggregation may ruin the model in that the numbers in the sub-classes are so small that the estimates of transition probabilities are very unreliable.

Hierarchic models

In this, as in nearly all model-building, it is essential that theory and practice go hand in hand. However, even where the basic data are unreliable, some genuine understanding of the problem of decision can often be gained by a study of the way in which hierarchical structures behave. I take a very simple illustration from a recent paper by Dill *et al.* (1966) who give a useful bibliography.

Suppose we have a simple hierarchy with one top job, one second job, one third job, and so on down to nth and last job; and suppose that when any job falls vacant the person immediately below is promoted and somebody recruited for the nth. Let us further suppose that the individuals in the top job hold it for times which are independent and distributed in the exponential form with mean λ^{-1}. This means that the man at the top vacates the position with probability λdt in any time interval dt. Suppose further that the probability that anybody in a subordinate position leaves the system (e.g. by death or resignation) with probability μdt. Then we may show that the average time taken to reach the top from job number k is approximately

$$\frac{1}{\mu} \log \left(1 + \frac{k\mu}{\lambda} \right) \tag{2}$$

In short, the rate of advances slows down as one approaches the top, and the time taken to reach it from entry varies as the logarithm of the number of ranks rather than linearly.

Such a model can be elaborated almost out of recognition: by considering a number of collateral converging lines of promotion; by considering different patterns of retirement or defection; by allowing for jumps up the promotional ladder, and so on. In this way one can study the behaviour of hierarchical systems in the light, for example, of such questions as whether an organization is too big to offer sufficient prospect of advancement, how long an individual may expect to wait at a given level before being promoted, or what are the effects of "sub-group" loyalties and patronage behaviour. The paper by Dill *et al.* under reference examines a number of these questions.

Division of labour

Population models and replacement tables are concerned with supply of labour at assigned levels of skill. The kind of hierarchic model I have just described is concerned with speeds of flow through the system and the structure of the hierarchies. We may also study, in the context of production lines, the extent to which an industrial process need be divided up among a number of workers. An example is given by Kilbridge and Webster (1966).

Suppose we have a production line divided into k parts, one worker for each part. If the division is inefficient, in the sense that one worker takes longer than the others to do his share, the cycle time is determined by that worker and the others are inadequately employed. We may then define the Imbalance of Work I (as a percentage) by the relation

$$I = \frac{\text{Max. Operator's Time-Average Operator's Time}}{\text{Max. Operator's Time}} \times 100 \qquad (3)$$

The authors studied I in a production line concerned with the soldering and assembly of radio sets and found an empirical relationship between I and the cycle time T

$$I = a/T^b \qquad (4)$$

where a, b are constants depending *inter alia* on the nature of the job. They also consider non-productive work (e.g. handling of tools, movement of the operator to and fro) and determine a curve expressing the productive work, as a percentage of total work, against the cycle time. (The curve has no simple algebraic expression.) Finally, they determine learning cost, the time taken by a new employee to learn to handle his job at the ultimate pace. All these factors can then be put together and graphical methods used to pick out the minimum cost cycle time.

For present purposes a point to note is that the relation (4) is an empirical one. The model is not constructed *a priori*, but by general reasoning plus observation. There are not many models of this kind in the literature of manpower planning. There should be more.

Utilization of Manpower Resources

A business which has a number of projects to fulfil over a period of time has problems additional to those of maintaining its staff at strength, and in particular that of deployment of resources. A building firm, for example, has requirements of different skills at various stages of the erection of a factory or a house and needs to plan ahead to make sure that idle time is minimized. Here we may notice two different types of approach among several possible cases, network analysis and linear decision rules.

Network analysis breaks down the whole operation into a number of activities, some of which may proceed concurrently and some of which must necessarily go in temporal sequence. These are represented on a network, each arc of which represents an activity and for which estimates of manpower requirements (by skill) and completion times are available. The computer then plans the operation from the network in order to make the

117

best use of resources. The problems of optimization become much more severe where Multiple Projects are concerned and have not yet been fully solved. But the network approach is a useful one and usually results in economies. From the model-building viewpoint it is, however, little more than a systematic anatomy of a constructional process and involves little mathematics. The article by Gorham (1966) may be referred to for an example.

A different approach is necessary when the business is producing a number of relatively small items. The input here is a fluctuating series of orders, and the problem is to schedule the production rate and work force in an optimal way, bearing in mind that inventories can be built up at a cost. Holt *et al.* (1955) discuss the problem as one of decision-making in the face of uncertainty and illustrate the theory on data from a paint factory. Information is required for labour costs (including recruitment and lay-off cost), inventory costs, handling, storage etc.; and restraints on the system. The model leads to certain decision rules (as to size of inventory, extent of overtime, and the extent of hire and fire where permitted) which, if not optimal, often turns out better than intuitive judgments.

Educational Models

Some aspects of the general problem of manpower planning, especially at the government level, bear a close resemblance to that of educational planning. In this connection reference may be made to a recent OECD technical report on a conference organized by the OECD Committee for Scientific and Technical Personnel (1967). Most of the models are sophisticated versions of the Replacement Table type, but some of them go beyond this to consider social and economic costs. The ideas may well find application in manpower problems, especially where there is a high rate of obsolescence of knowledge, as in industry with the development of new technology or the defence forces with the development of new weapons. I am not suggesting that ordinary manpower models should incorporate the educational models. One thing at a time. But in manpower planning for work requiring technical skill (and in this I include modern management) we have to remember that though an individual remains an individual, what he knows about the job he is required to do may not be constant. Quality is necessary, but so may be the refreshment of his expertise. Or to put it another way, a model which just ensures that the right number of people move into the right slots may be inadequate to represent the changing requirements of their skills.

Government and Private Models

We often find that model-building in the economic or social domains is rather a different exercise for Government than for private industry. Government is concerned with the allocation of the population among the various tasks which the community requires, but those tasks and the proportion of manpower assigned to them are to some extent at choice, albeit choice under some rather tight constraints. Apart from matters such as immigration and brain-drains, the manpower problem is one of allocating a basic resource. I am not saying that all Governments see it that way. A highly departmentalized central authority is quite capable of pressing a number of policies which are not, from the manpower point of view, consistent among themselves; for example different departmental estimates of requirements may add up to more than 100 per cent of the available labour.

Business, on the other hand, and especially small businesses, may regard themselves as drawing on an almost unlimited field. Their problem is more in the nature of decisions about when and where to set up the labour force, it being assumed that the persons required can either be trained or recruited from other organizations in the same line of business. So far as I know there have been no attempts to model the competitive bidding for labour in conditions of what is still rather quaintly called "free enterprise". Problems of wage structure, the determination of salaries and wages, the relationship between the salary of one man and that of his sub-ordinates, do not seem to have received much attention from the model builders.

Just as the "interface" between models of the economy and models of industries and firms is likely to become an increasingly important problem area, so the interface between national manpower models and private manpower models will become increasingly important. In both cases models at the national level provide in some sense the framework within which the more detailed limited models must be built, and in both cases we are already becoming aware of the problem of compatibility between the information systems used.

SUMMARY

To sum up what is already a brief summary, then, the present position seems to be as follows:

(i) For several reasons there is now, and will increasingly be in the future, a necessity for planning manpower resources as scientifically as possible.

(ii) Model building, as a scientific management tool, will probably have to contribute to manpower planning.

(iii) Model building itself, and the application of model building to manpower studies in particular, is as yet in the early stages of development.

(iv) Some models can be used for prediction or decision-taking and require a good deal of data input; but even where data are lacking the construction of a model may give real insight into the system under study.

(v) Studies of replacement tables and flows through an organization are already yielding useful results.

(vi) More ambitious models remain to be tested, but there have already been proposed by different authors a number of techniques which look promising and certainly merit a trial.

REFERENCES

Orcutt, G.H., Greenberger, M., Korbel, J., Rivlin, A.M. *Microanalysis of Socioeconomic Systems*, Harper and Row, New York, 1961.

Pearl, R., and Reed, L.J. On the rate of growth of the population of the United States since 1790 and its mathematical representation. *Proc. Nat. Acad. Sci.* 6, 275, 1920.

Dill, W.R., Gaver, D.P., and Weber, W.L. Models and Modelling for Manpower Planning. *Man. Sci.* 13, B-142, 1966.

Young, A. and Almond, G. Predicting distributions of staff. *Comp. Jour. 3*, 246.

Kilbridge, M. and Webster, L. An economic model for the division of labour. *Man. Sci.* 12, B-255, 1966.

Gorham, W. An application of a network flow model to personnel planning. *IEEE Trans.* EM10, 1963.

OECD. *Mathematical Models in Educational Planning*. O.E.C.D., Paris, 1967.

Renewal Theory Models for Manpower Systems

D.J. BARTHOLOMEW

UNIVERSITY OF KENT AT CANTERBURY,
UNITED KINGDOM.

I. INTRODUCTION

Renewal theory was originally devised to solve problems of industrial replacement and population mathematics. In recent years it has been developed extensively both for its mathematical and practical interest. A convenient and useful account of the theory is given in the monograph by Cox (1962). In the industrial application we have a collection of N items, the lifetime of each being a random variable with known distribution. When an item fails it is replaced at once by another having the same life distribution. Renewal theory provides methods for calculating such things as the number of replacements required in specified intervals of time and the age distribution of items at any given time.

There is an obvious similarity between such a system and the recruitment and wastage of manpower in a large organization. If the size of the organization is fixed and if its members can be assumed to have lengths of service which may be regarded as randomly drawn from a known distribution, then the system will be a renewal process in the sense described above. The object of this paper is to describe three applications of renewal theory to manpower planning problems.

The first application uses the simple renewal model for the prediction of recruitment needs in a newly established organization. Although the model is much simplified, the example serves to illustrate the limitations of a commonly used rule of thumb. In the second application we shall investigate the behaviour of a contracting organization. Our main interest centres upon finding the maximum rate of run-down which can be achieved without causing redundancies. Once again it will appear that the "obvious" answer can be misleading. Thirdly we shall describe some extensions of renewal theory which enable us to predict recruitment, wastage and promotion rates in simple hierarchical organizations. This will enable us to discuss the effect of the structure of an organization on the promotion prospects which it offers.

The use of renewal theory for predicting recruitment and wastage is not new. It was used in the United Kingdom to study labour turnover by the National Coal Board in the late nineteen fifties. Most of this work is contained in internal reports but it gave rise, indirectly, to the paper by Bartholomew (1959). A fuller discussion of the theory of contracting systems is contained in the book *Stochastic Models for Social Processes* (Bartholomew (1967)). The theory of multi-stage renewal processes was begun in Bartholomew (1963) and its application to hierarchical organizations is also described in the above-mentioned book. In the present paper we shall not derive the mathematical theory in detail but aim rather at pointing out its relevance to problems of manpower planning.

2. PREDICTION OF RECRUITMENT IN A NEW ORGANIZATION

Let us consider the following simplified model. An organization is established at time zero with N employees. We suppose that employees leave independently after length of service t where t is a random variable with known probability distribution $f(t)$. Each leaver is replaced immediately by a recruit having the same length of service distribution. The basic function required for predicting recruitment requirements is the expected number of replacements needed in $(0, T)$ which may be denoted by $NH(T)$. For our present purposes it will be more convenient to work with the *renewal density*, $h(T)$, which is the derivative of $H(T)$. Thus $h(T) \, \delta T$ is the expected number of renewals in $(T, T + \delta T)$. The renewal density may be thought of as the instantaneous recruitment rate at time T.

It is shown in renewal theory that $h(T)$ satisfies the integral equation

$$h(T) = f(T) + \int_0^T f(x) \, h(T - x) \, dx \tag{1}$$

and that, if T is large,

$$h(T) \sim \mu^{-1} \tag{2}$$

where μ is the mean length of service. It follows from (2) that the expected number of recruits needed in an interval (T_1, T_2), after the system has reached equilibrium, is $N(T_1 - T_2) \, \mu^{-1}$. Thus if $\mu = 2$ years an organization of size 1000 would expect to recruit 500 new employees per year. This conclusion seems almost self-evident and is, I imagine, the rule of thumb which most people would use if they had never heard of renewal theory. Perhaps the main value of our more formal treatment is that it exposes the limitations of this method. It only applies in general if a "steady state" has been reached or if the length of service distribution is exponential, that is if

$$f(t) = \lambda e^{-\lambda t} \quad (t \geqslant 0, \ \lambda > 0).$$

As we shall now see neither condition is likely to hold in practice.

There is a considerable body of data, reviewed in Bartholomew (1967), to show that the length of service distribution in civilian employment is much more skew than the exponential distribution. A quite different form of distribution occurs in organizations such as the armed services where a recruit is often engaged for a fixed period of time. Suppose, for illustration, that each new entrant signs on for 6 years. For various reasons some members may actually leave earlier or later but the distribution will have most of its frequency concentrated at 6 years. If re-engagement is allowed there will be subsidiary humps occurring after longer periods. There may also be a choice of period of service which will produce concentrations of frequency at other points but in no case will the distribution be even approximately exponential. In order to show how inaccurate the rule of thumb may be we have given some numerical values of $h(T)$ in Tables 1 and 2 for one distribution of each kind.

In civilian employment it has been found that length of service is approximately lognormally distributed. That is $\log_e t$ may be treated as normal with mean ω and variance σ^2. In practice typical parameter values are $\omega = 0$ and $\sigma = 2$ when time is measured in years. Approximate values of $h(T)$ are given below.

TABLE 1

Approximate values of $h(T)$ for a lognormal length
of service distribution with $\omega = 0$, $\sigma = 2$.
(Mean = 7.4 years)

T	1	2.71	7.39	20.1	54.6	∞
$h(T)$	0.574	0.424	0.318	0.244	0.194	0.135

Here we see that the renewal density is still almost twice its equilibrium value after 20 years. For any period of practical interest predictions based on the equilibrium value will grossly under-estimate actual requirements.

In order to illustrate the situation when length of service is fairly constant we have supposed that the distribution is normal with mean 6 years and standard deviation 1 year. This implies that 95% of all losses would occur between 4 and 8 years of service.

TABLE 2

Values of $h(T)$ for a normal length of service distribution
with mean = 6 years and standard deviation = 1 year.

T	0	3	4	5	6	7	8	9
$h(T)$	0	0.004	0.054	0.242	0.399	0.243	0.059	0.034
T	10	11	12	13	14	15	16	17
$h(T)$	0.104	0.220	0.283	0.224	0.120	0.081	0.123	0.196
T	18	21	24	27	30	33	36	∞
$h(T)$	0.233	0.116	0.205	0.138	0.189	0.150	0.179	0.167

In this case $h(T)$ approaches its equilibrium in a series of damped oscillations and even after 20 years there are considerable deviations from the equilibrium figure. The use of the limiting value for predicting recruitment needs say, on an annual basis, would be subject to large errors. On a longer time scale over 10 yearly intervals the predictions would be much better as errors in opposite directions would tend to cancel out.

The whole of the foregoing discussion is based on expected values. Renewal theory also enables us to calculate variances of the replacement numbers. Some calculations are given in Table 6.5 of Bartholomew (1967) and these suggest that prediction errors may be quite large in small organizations.

3. REDUNDANCY IN CONTRACTING ORGANIZATIONS

The theory upon which the last section is based can be extended to cover organizations whose size changes with time. In particular it can cope with contracting systems. We shall use the theory in this section to investigate the maximum rate of contraction which can take place without causing redundancies. It might be supposed that if an organization has reached a steady state with an annual wastage rate of 20% then it could be reduced in size by anything up to this amount by voluntary wastage alone. In fact this is true only in rather special circumstances which are unlikely to occur in practice. This remark is based on the following analysis.

Let $N(T)$ be the required size at time T where T is measured from the point in time at which contraction begins. Prior to this point we assume that the size has been constant and that a steady state has been reached. Let $R(T)$ be the recruitment density at time T then it may be shown that

$$\int_0^T R(x)\,dx = \int_0^T N(x)h(T-x)\,dx + N(0)\left\{\frac{T}{\mu} - \int_0^T h(x)\,dx\right\} \qquad (3)$$

where $h(x)$ is the renewal density defined in Section 2. The contraction required will be achieved without redundancies occurring if $R(T)$ as obtained from (3) is never negative. In the general case we may find the maximum rate of contraction without redundancy by finding a function $N(T)$ which makes $R(T)$ zero for all T. To pursue the matter further we shall consider a special case.

Suppose that we wish to achieve a constant rate of run-down; this implies that

$$N(T) = N(0) e^{-\alpha T} \tag{4}$$

for some positive α. It was shown in Bartholomew (1959) that observed length of service distributions could be successfully graduated, at least over the first two years, by the mixed exponential distribution with density function

$$f(t) = p\lambda_1 e^{-\lambda_1 t} + (1 - p)\lambda_2 e^{-\lambda_2 t} \quad (t \geqslant 0,\ 0 < p < 1,\ \lambda_1,\ \lambda_2,\ > 0) \tag{5}$$

This form happens to lead to a tractable mathematical solution to our present problem and so will be used in what follows. For this distribution the solution of (1) is

$$h(T) = \mu^{-1} + a e^{-bT} \tag{6}$$

where $a = p\lambda_1 + (1 - p)\lambda_2 - \mu^{-1}$ and $b = p\lambda_2 + (1 - p)\lambda_1$. Substitution in (3) and differentiation with respect to T then gives

$$R(T) = N(0) \left\{ \left(\mu^{-1} - \alpha - \frac{\alpha a}{a-b} \right) e^{-\alpha T} - \frac{\alpha a}{a-\beta} e^{-bT} \right\} \; . \tag{7}$$

The recruitment density will be non-negative for all T if the following two inequalities are satisfied:

$$\alpha \leqslant b \text{ and } \frac{1}{\mu} - \alpha + \frac{\alpha a}{a-\beta} \geqslant 0. \tag{8}$$

For the system we have described the equilibrium wastage density prior to contraction would be μ^{-1}. It is clear from (8) that both inequalities cannot be satisfied with $\alpha = \mu^{-1}$ if $\alpha > 0$; this means that if the run-down rate is equal to the wastage rate, redundancies are bound to occur. The exception to this rule occurs when $a = 0$ which happens only when (5) reduces to a simple exponential. We have already seen that the exponential distribution does not satisfactorily describe length of service distributions. Hence, in practice, we would not expect to achieve a rate of contraction as high as the equilibrium wastage rate. As an illustration of what this implies we take some parameter values obtained by fitting (5) to data from the Glacier Metal Company. These give $a = 1.0196$, $b = 1.6716$ and $\mu^{-1} = 0.3890$. The inequalities (8) are both satisfied in this example if $\alpha \leqslant 0.2280$. This means that the greatest annual rate of contraction without redundancies is $100 \left(1 - e^{-0.2280} \right) \% = 20.4\%$. On the other hand the annual equilibrium wastage rate is 32.2%. An intuitive explanation of this discrepancy is as follows. According to the assumed form for $f(t)$, recent joiners are more prone to leave than those who have been in the organizations for some time. Hence, as recruiting slows down, the proportion of long service employees increases and so the wastage rate decreases. In arriving at these conclusions we have ignored the psychological effect of being in a declining organization and the impact which it might have on the propensity to leave.

4. A MODEL FOR AN ORGANIZATION WITH HIERARCHICAL STRUCTURE

4.1. Description of the System

For many purposes it is not sufficient to treat an organization as a single homogeneous unit. Many organizations are divided into strata or grades and we may then be interested not only in overall recruitment and wastage but also in transfer rates between grades. We shall therefore consider a hierarchical system of the following kind. Members of the organization are divided into k grades of increasing seniority. The numbers in each grade are fixed and we shall denote them by N_1, N_2, ... N_k. Every movement is supposed to originate with a loss from the system. The vacancy thus created must be filled either by transfer from within the system or by recruitment from outside. To keep things simple we shall assume that vacancies are always filled by promotion from the next lower grade. Each loss thus sets in train a sequence of promotions which end with the recruitment of a new individual to grade 1.

Since leaving is, in some degree, unpredictable the model must be probabilistic and it is this feature which leads us to use renewal theory. In addition to the recruitment and wastage rates we shall wish to calculate the promotion rates between grades. These may be looked upon as indices of the promotion prospects at each level of the organization. The theory for doing this also enables us to study the relationship between the "shape" of the hierarchy and the promotion prospects available to its members.

The mathematical study of hierarchical organizations appears to have begun in the British Admiralty at the end of World War II. Some of the results of this work are contained in papers by Seal (1945) and Vajda (1947 and 1948). There are many similarities between their work and ours especially when the results are interpreted deterministically. The chief difference is that these authors treated the rates as fixed and the grade sizes as random variables. Since grade sizes are usually determined by the work available for their members to perform there seem to be advantages in choosing a model in which they are fixed. Other contributions have been made by Young and Almond (1961), Young (1965), Gani (1963) and Balderston (1966). Young and Almond developed a discrete time model and, like Seal and Vajda, they assumed fixed transfer and loss probabilities. Gani gave a similar model for predicting university enrolments; the grades in this case were the successive years of study. Balderston's report contained a preliminary discussion of how the development of models for hierarchical systems might proceed.

4.2. Some Basic Equations

It is possible to obtain certain results of value without specifying the model in any greater detail than set out in Section 4.1. Let the expected number of losses from grade i in $(T, T + \delta T)$ be denoted by $N_i \, w_i(T)$ and the expected number of promotions in the same interval by $N_i p_i(T)$. The functions $w_i(T)$ and $p_i(T)$ will be referred to respectively as the wastage and promotion densities. Since the grade sizes are fixed it follows that the total input to any grade in a specified time interval must equal the total output in the same interval. Hence

$$N_i p_i(T) = N_{i+1} \left\{ p_{i+1}(T) + w_{i+1}(T) \right\} , \tag{9}$$

$$(i = 1, 2, \ldots k - 1)$$

where $p_{k+1}(T) \equiv 0$. By repeated application of this result we obtain

$$N_i p_i(T) = \sum_{j=i+1}^{k} N_j w_j(T), \, (i = 1, 2, \ldots k - 1). \tag{10}$$

Equation (10) holds with $i = 0$ if we interpret $N_0 p_0(T)$ to mean the expected rate of input to the system (denoted by $R(T)$ in Section 2). These equations show that it is sufficient to determine either the $p_i(T)$'s or the $w_i(T)$'s. Assuming that the promotion and wastage densities approach equilibrium values we may suppress the T in the above notation. In these circumstances we may also deduce that

$$N_i p_i = N_{i+1}/\mu_{i+1} \quad (i = 1, 2, \ldots k - 1) \tag{11}$$

and

$$N_0 p_0 = N/\mu \tag{12}$$

where $N = \sum_{i=1}^{k} N_i$, μ is the average length of stay in the system and μ_i is the average length of stay in the ith grade.

An interesting question to which we shall return later is as follows: what structure is necessary in order to give equal promotion prospects at every level of the organization? Since the $p_i(T)$'s are functions of T this question can only be meaningfully asked about the equilibrium state. Then we find that (9) implies

$$w_i = (N_{i-1} - N_i) \ p/N_i \quad (i = 2, 3, \ldots k-1) \tag{13}$$

where p is the common value of the p_i's. (Again, we can include the case $i = 1$ if we define $N_0 = R/p$). The wastage rates must be non-negative and therefore

$$N_{i-1} \geqslant N_i \quad (i = 1, 2, \ldots k-1). \tag{14}$$

This means that the organization must "taper off" towards the top, each grade being smaller than the one below it. The case $i = k$ is not included in (14) and we shall find in Section 4.4 that N_k may have to be very large indeed if equal promotion chances are to be achieved.

4.3. A Renewal Theory Model

The system which we described in Section 4.1 is like k simple renewal processes arranged in series. The input to any grade is obtained from the next lower grade and the output is made up of losses to the system and losses, in the form of promotions, to the next higher grade. However, the description which we have given is incomplete in two respects. We have not specified the stochastic law governing losses and we have not said how members to be promoted are selected from among those eligible. In the simple model of Section 2 length of service was determined by a known probability distribution. This implied that propensity to leave was a function of length of service in the organization. In the present case we can either retain this feature or we can make propensity to leave a function of seniority *within the grade*. This amounts to assuming that an employee " begins again " on promotion. In practice it seems likely that seniority both within the grade and within the organization influence propensity to leave. It therefore seems worth investigating each case so we shall give the theory in a form applicable to both.

Two methods of selecting persons to be promoted have been investigated. One is to select the most senior member of the grade in question. The other is to select independently of seniority; for brevity this will be described as "selection at random ". Again it seems likely that the true situation will often lie between these extremes but only the seniority rule will be investigated here.

A full discussion of the models described above is contained in Bartholomew (1967). Here we shall use a simple deterministic argument which is sufficient to gain a worthwhile insight into the workings of the system. It depends on the assumption that the grade sizes are large and that the system has reached its equilibrium.

The first step in the argument is to find the average time spent in the ith grade. This can then be related to p_i by means of (11). Let $f_{i-1}(\tau)$ be the density function of length of service for a person on entry to grade i. This gives the distribution of time to leaving in the absence of promotion; it is *not* the distribution of sojourn time in that grade. If loss depends only on seniority in the grade these distributions will be given; if loss depends on total length of service the $f_{i-1}(\tau)$'s must first be found from $f(t)$, the overall length of service distribution. Let the average seniority at which promotions are made from grade i be τ_i. Then

$$\mu_i = \int_0^{\tau_i} \tau f_{i-1}(\tau) \, d\tau + \tau_i \int_{\tau_i}^{\infty} f_{i-1}(\tau) \, d\tau$$

$$= \int_0^{\tau_i} G_{i-1}(\tau) \, d\tau, \quad (i = 1, 2, \ldots k; \ \tau_k = \infty) \tag{15}$$

where $G(x) = \int_x^{\infty} f(\tau) \, d\tau$. The seniorities τ_i can now be found as follows. Of those who enter grade i a proportion $G_{i-1}(\tau_i)$ will survive to be promoted. This requires that

$$N_{i-1} p_{i-1} G_{i-1}(\tau_i) = N_i p_i, \quad (i = 1, 2, \ldots k-1). \tag{16}$$

On eliminating τ_i between (15) and (16) we obtain μ_i as a function of p_{i-1} and p_i. When μ_i is substituted into (11) a recurrence relation between p_{i-1} and p_i is obtained. If propensity to leave depends only upon seniority within the grade the solution is straightforward. The functions $G_{i-1}(\tau)$ are known. Hence we find p_{k-1} from

$$N_{k-1} p_{k-1} = N_k / \mu_k$$

and then the remaining p_i's follow recursively.

If propensity to leave depends only on length of service since entering the organization then all that is known is the distribution $f(t)$. Let t_i be the average length of service of those promoted from grade i then clearly

$$f_{i-1}(\tau) = f(t_i + \tau) / G(t_i). \tag{17}$$

Further, everyone in grades i to k must have longer service than any member of grades 1 to $i-1$ in consequence of the promotion rule. Hence the t_i must satisfy

$$\int_0^{t_i} a(t)\, dt = (N_1 + N_2 + \ldots + N_i)/N, \quad (i = 1, 2, \ldots k-1) \tag{18}$$

where $a(t)$ is the density function of length of service for members serving at any time. A standard result of renewal theory gives us that

$$a(t) = \frac{1}{\mu} G(t)$$

and so $f_{i-1}(\tau)$ can be expressed in terms of known quantities.

4.4. An Example

Suppose that the probability of a member of grade i leaving with seniority in that grade between τ and $\tau + d\tau$ is

$$\frac{\lambda_i}{1 - \tau/\nu_i}.$$

If ν_i is positive, propensity to leave increases with seniority and loss becomes certain at $\tau = \nu_i$. If ν_i is negative, propensity to leave is a decreasing function of τ. By allowing $\nu_i \to \infty$ we obtain a constant risk of leaving which is, in general, different for each grade. The above functional form is thus sufficiently flexible to accommodate a wide variety of possibilities. For this example we find

$$f_{i-1}(\tau) = \lambda_i (1 - \frac{\tau}{\nu_i})^{\lambda_i \nu_i - 1}, \quad G_{i-1}(\tau) = (1 - \frac{\tau}{\nu_i})^{\lambda_i \nu_i},$$

$$\int_0^{\tau} G_{i-1}(x)\, dx = \frac{\nu_i}{\lambda_i \nu_i + 1} \left\{ 1 - \left(1 - \frac{\tau}{\nu_i}\right)^{\lambda_i \nu_i + 1} \right\}. \tag{19}$$

If ν_i is positive the range of τ is $(0, \nu_i)$ and if ν_i is negative it is $(0, \infty)$. Substituting these results in (16, (15) and (11) it may be shown that

$$\left(\frac{\nu_i}{\lambda_i \nu_i + 1}\right) N_{i-1} p_{i-1} = N_i / \left\{ 1 - \left(\frac{N_i p_i}{N_{i-1} p_{i-1}}\right)^{1 + 1/\lambda_i \nu_i} \right\} \tag{20}$$

$$(i = 1, 2, \ldots k)$$

where $p_k = 0$. The successive p_i's can thus be calculated starting with

$$N_{k-1}\, p_{k-1} = \frac{N_k(\lambda_k \nu_k + 1)}{\nu_k} \tag{21}$$

In order to bring out some of the implications of these formulae let us find the structure necessary to give equal expected promotion rates. For simplicity let $\lambda_i = \lambda$ and $\nu_i = \nu$ for all i. The N_i's must then satisfy

$$\left(\frac{\nu}{\lambda\nu+1}\right)N_{i-1}p = N_i \left/ \left\{1 - \left(\frac{N_i}{N_{i-1}}\right)^{1+1/\lambda\nu}\right\}\right. \quad (i = 1,\ 2,\ \dots\ k-1). \tag{22}$$

Some values of the relative grade sizes are given in Table 3 for: $(a)\lambda\nu = \infty$ in which case $f_{i-1}(\tau)$ (and, incidentally, $f(t)$ is also exponential with parameter λ); (b) $\lambda\nu = -2$ which represents a decreasing propensity to leave; and (c) $\lambda\nu = 2$ which implies an increasing propensity to leave. Notice that the grade sizes, except the highest, will always form a geometric series as we move up the hierarchy.

TABLE 3

Relative grade sizes required to give equal promotion densities under various assumptions about the dependence of propensity to leave on seniority within the grade when $k = 5$ and $N_4 = 2N_5$.

Grade	$\lambda\nu$		
	-2	$\pm\infty$	$+2$
1	0.749	0.667	0.621
2	0.187	0.222	0.237
3	0.047	0.074	0.091
4	0.012	0.025	0.035
5	0.006	0.012	0.017

The relative sizes of the highest two grades are determined by the value we choose for $p\nu(\lambda\nu+1)$ by virtue of (21). Since $\nu/(\lambda\nu+1)$ is the average stay in any grade in the absence of promotion, we may think of this as the ratio of the chance of promotion to the average chance of loss. If we want to have promotion more likely than loss the highest grade would have to be larger than the one below it. This situation is typical in the case of some other variants of the model. It appears from the table that the hierarchy tapers more rapidly when propensity to leave is a decreasing function of length of service than when it is an increasing function.

The foregoing analysis is intended only as an illustration of the way in which the theory may be used. Empirical data are needed to guide us in the choice of assumptions and very little material is available at present. Nevertheless the theoretical investigation directs our attention to the kind of data that are needed. In particular we need to know how propensity to leave depends upon grade, length of service in the organization and seniority within the grade.

REFERENCES

Balderston, F. (1966), Private communication.
Bartholomew, D.J. (1959), Note on the measurement and prediction of labour turnover, *J.R. Statist. Soc.* 122, A, 232–239.
Bartholomew, D.J. (1963), A multi-stage renewal process, *J.R. Statist. Soc.* 26, B, 150–168.
Bartholomew, D.J. (1967), *Stochastic models for social processes*, John Wiley and Sons, London.
Cox, D.R. (1962); *Renewal Theory*, Methuen Monographs in Applied Probability and Statistics, London.
Gani, J. (1963), Formulae for projecting enrolments and degrees awarded in Universities. *J.R. Statist. Soc.*, 126, A 400–409.
Seal, H.L. (1945) The mathematics of a population composed of k stationary strata each recruited from the stratum below and supported at the lowest level by a uniform number of entrants. *Biometrika*,. 33, 226–230.

Vajda, S. (1947) The stratified semi-stationary population, *Biometrika*, 34, 245–254.

Vajda, S. (1948) Introduction to a mathematical theory of a graded stationary population. *Bull. del'Ass. Actuar. Suisses*. 48, 251–273.

Young, A. (1965) Models for planning recruitment and promotion of Staff, *Brit. J. Indust. Relations*, 3, 301–310.

Young, A. and Almond, G. (1961), Predicting distributions of staff. *Comp. J*. 3, 246–250.

Discussion

Dr. E. ANSTEY: We have heard some interesting and learned papers today and the Conference Director has asked me to initiate discussion, particularly on the contributions of Professors Kossack and Bartholomew.

Those of you who are either manpower administrators or social scientist advisers to the administrators will, I imagine, be concerned chiefly with three problems.

(i) Are there any aspects of manpower deployment and utilization on which performance has been unsatisfactory in the past or might be improved in the future?

(ii) If so, would systems analysis or renewal theory or any other mathematical technique be effective in improving performance?

(iii) If so, which techniques should be used or which expert advisers should you call on?

Let us consider first Professor Bartholomew's paper on renewal theory models for manpower systems. There can be little doubt that the practical problems which Professor Bartholomew had in mind are very real and that there will be plenty of room for improvement in tackling them. Every large organization is aware of the difficulties in maintaining policies with regard to recruitment, promotion, internal transfers and retirement in such a way as to meet two criteria: first, that the system be sufficiently stable to be understood and accepted by the personnel; secondly, that the system adapts readily to sudden changes and pressures from outside. As Professor Bartholomew points out, if the organization is fairly stable problems are relatively tractable. But consider for example a rapidly expanding industry, such as the British Atomic Energy Authority was in the immediate post-war years. There was rapid expansion, wonderful promotion prospects for all the staff – I remember when I first visited Harwell shortly after the war there seemed to be nobody there under the age of 30. But this doesn't last, you get a period when progress slows down to relative stagnation, all these young people in their 20s are now in their 40s. The need is to avoid excessive oscillations, first taking on too many people and promoting them too fast on the crest of the wave and later taking on too few with little promotion prospects in the trough. Similarly for a contracting industry, such as the British Coal Industry which Professor Bartholomew mentioned among the references in his own paper, there are problems such as the setting of the maximum rate of contraction without causing redundancies. It's for problems such as these I am sure Professor Bartholomew's mathematical models would be helpful. One detailed comment: I was amused at the suggestion that the alternative to selection/promotion on grounds of seniority was selection at random!

Now perhaps I could make a few comments on the use of machines in general and computers in particular for solving problems such as deployment of resources. It seems to me that the usefulness of the machines may depend critically on the extent to which the resources – units in question – can be described in objective quantitative terms.

At one extreme one might suppose that 1 cu. ft. of air at a given temperature, pressure and humidity, would behave very like any other such cu. ft. of air – though perhaps even this is an over-simplification. It does seem obvious that there is scope for increased use of computers in such a subject as meteorology, handling complicated masses of data about inanimate objects. At the other extreme there are questions requiring many imponderable human factors to be taken into account. Take for example the redeployment of miners in Britain during the past 10 years. This is generally acknowledged to have been one of the most successful large-scale redeployments ever carried out by a declining industry. Despite exceptionally severe difficulties, morale has been maintained and output per man has increased. There are seven computer centres used by the National Coal Board; one in each main coal region. They are used at the moment for all non-industrial staff salaries and full individual records. For industrial staff pay-roll data is done by the computers, but personnel records not yet, though they will be computerized by 1968. These computers have been found to help in redeployment but only up to a point. They can, for example, provide patterns of people staying and leaving, from which wastage can be classified and reasons for wastage can be deduced. But means have not yet been found of taking account of the individual miner's wishes, feelings and aspirations. For example, his willingness to move may be critically affected by local bus services, or desire to work for the same pit as his brother, or perhaps any pit rather than at the one where his brother is working. The present feeling at the National Coal Board is that decisions about any individual, whether he is to be moved and if so where, must be left to the local Manager. Moreover the chief success in redeployment is the human touch. The National Coal Board has a lengthy memorandum about the methods they use and they list, for example, 16 desirable reception features including the very obvious first one: meet a newcomer on arrival and welcome him. The more individual areas that use such practices, the more successful redeployment has been.

Manpower problems in the Armed Services are obviously different in one important respect. You are dealing with people subject to discipline everywhere and in many countries subject to conscription. Even so, I suspect individual feelings and treatment must be of major importance. This brings me back to my main point. Computers will improve on human decisions if one can be sure of feeding all relevant data into the computer. But can one be sure?

Finally, let us turn back to Professor Kossack's paper on a systems analysis approach to the theory of manpower management. There are two questions which I should like to put to Professor Kossack, namely:

(i) Have his models, Markovian or Functional Markovian, been applied to real life problems and, if so, with what results in terms of increased efficiency, lower wastage, or any other criterion?

(ii) Professor Kossack clearly recognized in his paper the need to feed into the model subjective data about the human beings concerned, such as, to give one example, preference for frequent changes of duty as contrasted to preference for persisting in one type of duty or one location. How can subjective data such as this be fed into the model?

PROFESSOR KOSSACK: I don't want to be the defender of the computer, but nor do I want to stand silent. May I only remark in passing, while this is just a friendly discussion, that in systems that have been studied in which human judgement has been used and in which evaluations have really been made, the humans usually do a little worse than chance in the decision making. You can take that or leave it. For example, have you ever looked at medical diagnosis — and that gets pretty personal — it isn't as if we were trying to replace a perfect system. And here we get into a real philosophical realm about whether we are even in a logical world! But let me go to the specific question in this regard. The experience that I have become familiar with in the field of job schedules and so on now indicates that some of the individuals that apply human judgement may do a very poor job. Even though their organization supports them and everything sounds great. In my lack of humility I would say that it seems to me that one of the characteristics needed to be a successful executive is to correct errors rapidly.

From the point of view of this particular system let me say that, yes, it is my understanding that the Air Force has utilized the Markovian model in policy evaluation and I believe with some success in aiding the decision-maker who has to evaluate policies relative to transfers of individuals. We've now moved from a steady state to a more dynamic type of analysis.

With regard to your second question, my current philosophy is that there is essentially no difference between subjective data and quantitative data — from the point of view of analysis. In fact the use of attribute-type variables allows this to be done in general. But I think there is more behind this, and I would like to comment that I feel that by even doing this on a pragmatic empirical testing approach if we only were to keep track of the response patterns for individuals with different characteristics as they go through the system carrying this data along we may thus find out how these factors really are effective. What bothers me now is the fact that we have these isolated areas of investigation which have no linkage with other aspects and thus no mechanism for ever utilizing it. So the individuals who are worrying about personalities don't really have a linkage with the people who are trying to fill jobs. I believe that in time, with experience and with the ability to store data and information and with models, we will find the data we'll need and will be able to do this type of thing.

Mr. COTTERILL: I would like to acknowledge my indebtedness to Professor Bartholomew — you will see it in my list of references. I think from a general point of view you might say taking an ideal organization shaped as you would wish, then Professor Bartholomew's theory tells you on certain assumptions what recruitment rates to plan for. I am afraid I almost took it for granted that the authorities had done this, and then the next question arose, given these recruitment rates, given a different set of loss conditions that would occur, what then happens? I think these are perhaps the two views of the two sides of the coin.

PROFESSOR BARTHOLOMEW: I wonder if I might add to Professor Kossack's answer to Dr. Anstey's question about the application of Markov models. The one which I am familiar with — and which is essentially the same model — is the application by Professor Young of Liverpool who in the first place projected the staff structure of Liverpool University and subsequently in his capacity as an official of the Association of University Teachers did it for Universities as a whole in this country. It does appear that the kind of assumptions which that model depends on are approximately satisfied for the University teaching profession over fairly short term periods. It is difficult to answer the second part of the question, with what results?, because the kind of things that the model forecasts for this particular thing are on the whole looked upon as rather undesirable and to be avoided. Therefore the success of the application will depend on the extent to which we can avoid the kind of situation which it forecasts, which is a big bottleneck in promotion. At the moment people like me are on the crest of the wave, expansion is going on very rapidly and we have risen to the top, but those who come after us have to wait 20 or 30 years until we retire. I think this work has highlighted or drawn attention to this feature of the present system and similar system.

Mr. JONES: Professor Bartholomew, in referring to the problem of equal promotion prospects at every level of an organization, you are saying that the very top rank might have to be very very large? I am not quite clear what deficiency there is in the model, because I don't think that's right. There is a really important problem here; you have the probability of promotion and you have the age of promotion and I think you must take both into account. Otherwise every entrant into the Ministry of Defence could become the Permanent Secretary for half an hour before he retired!

A second point is on redundancy. We want to keep redundancy within the wastage. You said here that, "... prior to this point we assume the size has been constant and that a steady state has been reached". That's not a very valuable model for everyday use is it? I feel you have to have two models. You have to have a steady state model to assess the long term career prospects and you must have a method of projecting such staff as you have, allowing for peculiar features and so on. I submit that the actuarial technique gives you both models. And works. And has done for many years.

PROFESSOR BARTHOLOMEW: I will answer the second one first. I dealt with a general case in my book and I took this one here because it was simpler. There is nothing that inheres in the method that prevents one from considering an organization starting up at an arbitrary time with an arbitrary age structure.

The first point you made does pick up a defect of this model. I mentioned that I was considering two in parallel as it were; one where a loss depended on seniority within the grade and one where it depended on total length of service, and neither is ever right. In effect you have, as you pointed out, a mixture of two and when you approach retirement, you are approaching a point at which you certainly leave. My answer then is, yes, the model ought to take this into account — and I hope it will. I haven't tended to concentrate on this because originally I was concerned with organizations where people stayed on average a very short time compared with, say, the Civil Service or the Forces, a matter of 2 or 3 years. Here the man's age was of very secondary importance.

Mr. PAYNE: I'd like to ask Professor Bartholomew if he has any thoughts on whether one can control the parameters of the model, for example promotion and recruitment rates, in order to give a specified desired structure to the organization at some future date?

PROFESSOR BARTHOLOMEW: Yes, though this is most easily done with the kind of Markov chain model that Professor Kossack talks about. But perhaps I should be more honest and say that I've done it with that kind of model and not with this one. The Markov chain models are easier to work with mathematically. You can find out much more, much more easily. I believe, though, they have a number of rather unrealistic features in the kind of context that I was speaking of, in particular that the numbers in the grades are randomly variable and can vary quite substantially to a degree that would never be tolerated, I think, in any organization where the people in a grade were there because they had a specific job to do. But to repeat a point I have made several times already, I think that in a way the more models and more assumptions the better. If we look at a situation from many points of view we are more likely to see the thing that matters than if we look at it from one point of view.

Mr. LEICESTER: Markov chain models have been used to a large extent by the educational planners. A very simple version of that kind of model is given in Section 5 of my paper and more extended versions are given in the last reference at the back of Dr. Kendall's paper. Broadly speaking the way the educational planners are moving at the moment is to stop thinking of these transition coefficients as determinants, but to start thinking of them as determinates. In other words to stop thinking of them as causal coefficients and to start thinking of them as things which could be influenced. The obvious example which arises from discussions so far is that of course the total number of people which might flow into a certain part of an organization or certain branch of education is limited by the number of vacancies that you have to offer to begin with. This is something which doesn't actually appear explicitly in any Markov chain model, but I should have thought that these factors of influencing the coefficients could very easily be built in. I am not really sure how one does this nor even, apart from some work that has actually been done in Nuffield College, Oxford, whether any of the experts have reached sensible solutions they could suggest to manpower planners like myself.

PROFESSOR KOSSACK: May I just say that you can obviously, at each time period, look at requirements and upgrade your transitional probabilities in order to accommodate this, but to do this in a functional systematic way we haven't got quite that far. I think the idea of thinking of these transitional probabilities as determinants that you can really work with is the way that will start to affect the system; it will teach us how to play with the system, how to respond.

A Model for Personnel Inventory Prediction

DEREK S. COTTERILL

DEFENCE OPERATIONAL RESEARCH ESTABLISHMENT,
OTTAWA

I. INTRODUCTION

I.I. Recruitment policies

Some organizations, such as the armed forces, fill all vacancies by promotion within the organization, and only recruit at the lowest rank. It is important that as each vacancy occurs, a qualified replacement shall be available. Such an organization must establish consistent standards for promotion, must institute training programmes and must enforce a compulsory retirement system so as to ensure a healthy flow of officers through the ranks with each having a fair opportunity of promotion. In particular it must manage its recruitment programme so that there shall be no shortages of qualified officers in any rank. There are three sources of difficulty:

(i) Officers leave the organization for a variety of reasons, in addition to compulsory retirement, and these unexpected losses may be as high as 6% per year.

(ii) If minimum standards of intelligence, education and character are set for new entrants, and if the salary to be paid is fixed by regulation, or by policy decisions, then the number of recruits during any period may be less than intended.

(iii) As many as 50% of new entrants may leave the organization during the first five years.

It may be impossible for a large complex organization to assess the effects of its recruitment and other policies except by using a digital computer to simulate the future. In order that a simulation programme may be accurate it must be based upon a mathematical model of the organization. This model may be simpler in structure than the organization, provided that it correctly accounts for the more important variables.

This paper presents a family of mathematical models, which may be applicable to various organizations.

I.2. Method

The method used is to consider the promotion of each officer as a stochastic process, influenced by the personal qualities of the individual, and to assume that the measures of these personal qualities are distributed over the population of officers according to some standard probability distribution.

To simplify these calculations a continuous variable A is defined, so that each rank of the organization corresponds to a range of values of A. A is termed the "level of achievement" of the officer. When an officer's level of achievement reaches some threshold A_i, he is assumed to be promoted to rank (i), and when he advances to level A_{i-1} he is assumed to be promoted out of rank (i) into rank $(i-1)$. This is an extension of the simple case when an officer's rank depends only upon his total length of service τ, and he is promoted into rank (i) when τ exceeds T_i, and into rank $(i-1)$ when τ exceeds T_{i-1}.

133

Then the mathematical model of promotion is completely specified by $F(A, \tau)$, the probability distribution of level of achievement, A, for officers with total length of service τ.

It is shown that each such model is characterized by a fundamental integral $G(\lambda, t)$,

$$G(\lambda, t) = \int_0^t e^{-\lambda\tau} F(A, \tau)\, d\tau \tag{1.1}$$

and that once $G(\lambda, t)$ has been solved, it is straightforward to calculate the more important parameters of the organization, for a wide variety of recruitment and attrition functions.

Since $G(\lambda, t)$ is a modified Laplace transform, the resources of Laplace transform theory are available to facilitate its solution.

To forecast the effect of assumed recruitment and attrition rates upon an existing organization:

(i) Simplify the form of the organization by lumping together distinct but similar categories of officer.

(ii) Compile the statistics of the organization, the number of officers in each rank, their average seniority in rank, and average total length of service, and the sample variances of seniority and total service.

(iii) Ascertain $n(\tau)$ as a function of τ, where $n(\tau)\, d\tau$ is the number of present officers who joined from τ to $\tau + d\tau$ years ago.

(iv) Postulate a mathematical model, characterized by $F(A, \tau)$ and $G(\lambda, \tau)$.

(v) Knowing $n(\tau)$ and the number of officers in each rank, calculate the threshold levels A_i.

(vi) Calculate the average seniority and total service for each rank.

(vii) Adjust the constants of the model until the calculated parameters provide a good fit to the observed statistics. Both the sample variances and the calculated variances permit a rough estimate of the goodness of fit.

(viii) If a good fit cannot be obtained, try another mathematical model.

(ix) Then the projected recruitment and attrition rates may be inserted into the model, to predict the future of the organization.

It has yet to be established that a mathematical model which is a good fit to an existing organization, can be relied upon to correctly forecast its future, even if the projected recruitment and attrition rates are correct. In the absence of such an existence theorem, it would be advisable to see if more than one mathematical model can be fitted to the organization, and, if so, this would give a range of possible forecasts.

The models treated in this paper are relatively simple, but very little ingenuity is required to design more complicated models. Even for the simple models, a digital computer is required to calculate numerical results.

2. FORMAL STATEMENT OF A GENERAL MODEL

2.1. Definitions

2.1.1. Model of Consistent Promotion

A model in which the level of achievement, A, of an individual officer is influenced by some parameter which has a different value for each officer.

2.1.2. Model of Haphazard Promotion

A model in which the promotion of individual officers is a matter of chance.

In the stochastic processes which account for promotion, the parameters have the same value for every officer.

Thus a model of haphazard promotion is always a special case of a more general model of consistent promotion. In this correspondence the model of haphazard promotion serves as a null hypothesis, against which to test the significance of any estimates of parameters.

2.2. Continuous Variables

2.2.1. Recruitment and Loss

Total number of officers = N
Rank of an officer = i, $i = 1, \ldots, 8$
Number of officers in rank (i) = N_i

$$N = \sum_{i=1}^{8} N_i \,. \tag{2.1}$$

Time for which forecast is made: $\tau = 0$ (= " now ").
Maximum length of service of any officer = T periods.
Number of officers now in service who joined between τ and $\tau + d\tau$ periods ago = $n(\tau)\,d\tau$, assumed, at this stage, to be an integrable variable.

Then

$$N = \int_{\tau=0}^{T} n(\tau)\,d\tau \tag{2.2}$$

Rate of recruitment τ periods ago = $Rr(\tau)$. (The constant R is separated for use as a scale factor.)

Proportion of officers who joined τ periods ago who have since left the service = $l(\tau)$.
Proportion who remain in service = $1 - l(\tau)$.

Then

$$n(\tau) = Rr(\tau)\left[1 - l(\tau)\right] \tag{2.3}$$

and

$$N = R \int_{t=0}^{T} r(\tau)\left[1 - l(\tau)\right]d\tau. \tag{2.4}$$

In general $\left[1 - l(\tau)\right]$ may have some such form as:

$$\left[1 - l(\tau)\right] = \int_{t=0}^{\tau} L(t,\,\tau)\,dt \tag{2.5}$$

2.2.2. Level of Achievement

Define a continuous variable A, the "level of achievement" of an officer, so that each rank (i) corresponds uniquely to an interval $[A_i,\,A_{i-1})$ on A.

Then assume that there exists a stochastic process relating A to the total length of service of an officer, so that when his level of achievement reaches a threshold value A_i he is immediately promoted into rank (i), and when he reaches level A_{i-1} he is at once promoted out of rank (i) into rank $(i - 1)$.

(Evidently, one of the first tasks is to evaluate the A_i, to within a scale factor, in terms of known quantities).

Assume that at time τ, the rate of achievement of the jth officer is $h(\tau, a_j)$ where

$$Pr\{a_j < a\} = \int_{-\infty}^{a} g(x)\,dx .$$ (2.6)

Assume that the probability that, after τ periods of service, the level of achievement of the individual officer is less than A, is

$$Pr\{\text{level of achievement} < A \mid \tau\} = F(A, \tau) = \int_{-\infty}^{A} f(z, \tau)\,dz$$ (2.7)

Then these are the basic assumptions for a particular model. The stochastic process assumed defines $g(x)$ and $h(\tau, a_j)$ and their relationship with $f(z, \tau)$ and/or $F(A, \tau)$.

2.3. Fitting the Model

The number of officers whose level of achievement is less than A, is $X(A)$.

$$X(A) = \int_{\tau=0}^{T} n(\tau) F(A, \tau)\,d\tau = \int_{\tau=0}^{T} n(\tau) \int_{z=-\infty}^{A} f(z, \tau)\,dz\,d\tau .$$ (2.8)

From this relationship it is possible to locate the threshold values A_i corresponding to promotion from rank $(i + 1)$ to rank (i). It may be possible to express A as an explicit function of X, either in a closed form or in a form suitable for computation, such as a series. Number in rank (i) = $N_i = X(A_{i-1}) - X(A_i)$

$$N_i = \int_{\tau=0}^{T} n(\tau) \int_{z=A_i}^{A_{i-1}} f(z, \tau)\,dz\,d\tau. \quad i = 1, \dots, 8$$ (2.9)

or

$$N_i = \left[\int_{\tau=0}^{T} n(\tau)\ F(A, \tau)\,d\tau \right]_{A=A_i}^{A_{i-1}}$$ (2.10)

or

$$N_i = R \int_{\tau=0}^{T} r(\tau) \left[1 - l(\tau)\right] \int_{z=A_i}^{A_{i-1}} f(z, \tau)\,dz\,d\tau$$ (2.11)

$$i = 1, \dots, 8$$
$$A_8 = 0.$$

That is:

the N_i are known
R, $r(\tau)$, $l(\tau)$, $f(z, \tau)$ have been assumed
then the set of equations (2.9) must be solved, if
only approximately, to find the values of the A_i.
(But see section 2.10).

2.4. Total Length of Service

The total length of service of an officer now in rank (i) is denoted by τ_i. For comparison with the statistics of real systems we need the expected values and the variances of the τ_i.

136

Denote   Mean $(\tau_i) = E(\tau_i) = \bar{\tau}_i$.

Variance $(\tau_i) = \text{Var}(\tau_i) = E(\tau_i{}^2) - \bar{\tau}_i^2$.

Then
$$\bar{\tau}_i = \frac{1}{N_i} \int_{\tau=0}^{T} \tau n(\tau) \int_{z=A_i}^{A_{i-1}} f(z,\ \tau)\,dz\,d\tau \qquad (2.12)$$

$$\text{Var}(\tau_i) \geqslant -\bar{\tau}_i^2 + \frac{1}{N_i} \int_{\tau=0}^{T} \tau^2 n(\tau) \int_{z=A_i}^{A_{i-1}} f(z,\ \tau)\,dz\,d\tau \qquad (2.13)$$

Since there are 8 ranks, there are 8 values of $\bar{\tau}_i$ and of $\text{Var}(\tau_i)$ to be calculated. $n(\tau)$ can always be expressed as $n(\tau) = e^{-\lambda\tau} q(\tau)$ where $q(\tau)$ is independent of λ, but λ may be zero.

Then
$$\bar{\tau}_i = \frac{-1}{N_i} \frac{\partial N_i}{\partial \lambda} = -\frac{\partial}{\partial \lambda}\ \ln(N_i) \qquad (2.14)$$

and
$$\text{Var}(\tau_i) \geqslant -\bar{\tau}_i^2 + \frac{1}{N_i}\ \frac{\partial^2 N_i}{\partial \lambda^2} \qquad (2.15)$$

that is,
$$\text{Var}(\tau_i) \geqslant \frac{\partial^2}{\partial \lambda^2}\ \ln(N_i) \ . \qquad (2.16)$$

2.5. Seniority in Rank

The Seniority s_i of an officer now in rank (i) is the length of time since he was promoted to rank (i). We require the expected value and the variance of s_i for each of the seven senior ranks.

Let $m(A_i)\,dA$ denote the number of officers with levels of achievement between A_i and $A_i + dA$

then
$$m(A_i)\,dA = \int_{\tau=0}^{T} n(\tau) \int_{z=A_i}^{A_i+dA} f(z,\ \tau)\,dz\,d\tau \ .$$

Let dA tend to zero

then
$$m(A_i) = \int_{\tau=0}^{T} n(\tau) f(A_i,\ \tau)\,d\tau \qquad (2.17)$$

Define
$$P(t) = \frac{1}{m(A_i)} \int_{\tau=0}^{t} n(\tau) f(A_i,\ \tau)\,d\tau \quad 0 \leqslant t \leqslant T \qquad (2.18)$$

then $P(t)$ is the probability that $t(A_i)$, the total length of service of an officer now at level A_i will be less than t, that is, $P(t)$ is a cumulative probability distribution function, and so

$$E[t(A_i)] = \int_{0}^{T} t\,dP(t) \qquad (2.19)$$

137

$$E[t^2(A_i)] = \int_0^T t^2 dP(t) \tag{2.20}$$

and
$$\text{Var}[t(A_i)] \geqslant E[t^2(A_i)] - [E[t(A_i)]]^2$$

then
$$E[t(A_i)] = \bar{t}(A_i) = \frac{1}{m(A_i)} \int_{\tau=0}^T \tau n(\tau) f(A_i, \tau) d\tau \tag{2.21}$$

$$\text{Var}[t(A_i)] \geqslant \frac{1}{m(A_i)} \int_{\tau=0}^T \tau^2 n(\tau) f(A_i, \tau) d\tau - [\bar{t}(A_i)]^2. \tag{2.22}$$

Assume that an officer now in rank (i) with seniority s_i and total length of service τ_i, attained level of achievement A_i and was thus promoted to rank (i) after a total length of service $\tau(A_i)$, where $\tau(A_i)$ is defined as

$$\tau(A_i) \underset{\Delta}{=} \tau_i - s_i \tag{2.23}$$

and, in every case
$$\bar{s}_i = \bar{\tau}_i - E[\tau(A_i)] \tag{2.24}$$

$$\text{Var}(\tau_i) = \text{Var}(s_i) + \text{Var}[\tau(A_i)] + 2 \text{ Cov}[\tau(A_i), s_i] \tag{2.25}$$

$$\text{Var}(s_i) = \text{Var}(\tau_i) + \text{Var}[\tau(A_i)] - 2 \text{ Cov}[\tau_i, \tau(A_i)] \tag{2.26}$$

where
$$\text{Cov}(x, y) = E(xy) - E(x)E(y). \tag{2.27}$$

There are three sufficient conditions for calculating $\text{Var}(s_i)$ in this way:

(a) If s_i and $\tau(A_i)$ are statistically independent, then from (2.25),

$$\text{Var}(s_i) = \text{Var}(\tau_i) - \text{Var}[\tau(A_i)] \tag{2.28}$$

(b) If the model is a stationary stochastic system,

(c) If the effects of losses can be neglected,

then
$$\tau(A_i) = t(A_i) \tag{2.29}$$

then
$$\bar{s}_i = \tau_i - E[t(A_i)]$$

$$\bar{s}_i = \bar{\tau}_i - \frac{1}{m(A_i)} \int_{\tau=0}^T \tau n(\tau) f(A_i, \tau) d\tau \tag{2.30}$$

$$\text{Var}(s_i) \geqslant \text{Var}(\tau_i) - E[t^2(A_i)] + (E[t(A_i)])^2$$

$$\text{Var}(s_i) \geqslant \text{Var}(\tau_i) + (\bar{\tau}_i - \bar{s}_i)^2 - \frac{1}{m(A_i)} \int_{\tau=0}^T \tau^2 n(\tau) f(A_i, \tau) d\tau \tag{2.31}$$

However conditions (a), (b) and (c) will only rarely be valid, and it will be necessary to study each specific example separately.

(i) Condition (a) will only be true for models of haphazard promotion. If the promotion of an officer is influenced by his personal qualities, then $\text{Cov}(\tau(A_i), s_i)$ is unlikely to be zero.

(ii) If $Rr(\tau)$ is not constant, or if $[1 - l(\tau)]$ is a function of the date of the forecast, then the system will not be stationary and $\tau(A_i) \neq t(A_i)$. Since the reason for constructing a mathematical model is to use it to forecast the effects of changes in recruitment and loss rates, condition (b) excludes all the interesting cases.

(iii) Condition (c). In most cases studied in this paper it seems valid to neglect the effects of losses. However, in general, it is to be expected that the officers who have left the organization during the time intervals s_i, will have different rates of advancement than those who remain in the organization. Then $\tau(A_i) \neq t(A_i)$ even if the system is stationary.

2.6. Approximate Values of Seniority

by 2.17

$$m(A_i) = \int_0^T n(\tau)f(A_i, \tau)d\tau \qquad (2.17)$$

then

$$m(A_i) = -\frac{\partial N_i}{\partial A_i} \qquad (2.32)$$

Define $\bar{s}_i^*$ and $\text{Var}^*(s_i)$ by

$$\bar{s}_i^* \underline{\Delta} \bar{\tau}_i - \frac{1}{m(A_i)} \int_{\tau=0}^T \tau n(\tau)f(A_i, \tau)d\tau \qquad (2.33)$$

$$\text{Var}^*(s_i) \underline{\Delta} \text{Var}(\tau_i) + (\bar{\tau}_i - s_i^*)^2 - \frac{1}{m(A_i)} \int_{\tau=0}^T \tau^2 n(\tau)f(A_i, \tau)d\tau \qquad (2.34)$$

Then $\bar{s}_i^*$ will often be a close approximation to $\bar{s}_i$, and $\text{Var}^*(s_i)$ may be a rough approximation to $\text{Var}(s_i)$.

$$\text{Express } n(\tau) \text{ as } n(\tau) = e^{-\lambda \tau}q(\tau) \qquad (2.35)$$

where $q(\tau)$ is independent of λ, but λ may be zero.

then

$$\bar{s}_i^* = \bar{\tau}_i + \frac{1}{m(A_i)} \frac{\partial}{\partial \lambda}m(A_i). \qquad (2.36)$$

by 2.34

$$\text{Var}^*(s_i) = \text{Var}(\tau_i) + (\bar{\tau}_i - \bar{s}_i^*)^2 - \frac{1}{m(A_i)} \frac{\partial^2}{\partial \lambda^2}m(A_i). \qquad (2.37)$$

By using (2.14) and (2.15)

$$\bar{s}_i^* = -\frac{1}{N_i} \frac{\partial N_i}{\partial \lambda} + \frac{1}{m(A_i)} \frac{\partial m}{\partial \lambda}(A_i)$$

$$= \frac{\partial}{\partial \lambda}(\ln[m(A_i)] - \ln(N_i))$$

$$= \frac{\partial}{\partial \lambda}[\ln(\frac{1}{N_i}(\frac{\partial N_i}{\partial A_i})) + \ln(-1)]$$

$$\therefore \qquad \bar{s}_i^* = \frac{\partial}{\partial \lambda}\ln[\frac{\partial}{\partial A_i}\ln(N_i)] \qquad (2.38)$$

$$\text{Var}^*(s_i) = \frac{\partial^2}{\partial \lambda^2} \, ln(N_i) + \left[\frac{1}{m(A_i)} \, \frac{\partial m(A_i)}{\partial \lambda} \right]^2 - \frac{1}{m(A_i)} \frac{\partial^2}{\partial \lambda^2} \, m(A_i)$$

$$= \frac{\partial^2}{\partial \lambda^2} \, [ln(N_i) - ln \, m(A_i)]$$

$$= -\frac{\partial^2}{\partial \lambda^2} \, [ln[\frac{1}{N_i} \, (\frac{\partial N_i}{\partial A_i})] + ln \, (-1)]$$

$$\text{Var}^*(s_i) = -\frac{\partial^2}{\partial \lambda^2} \, ln[\frac{\partial}{\partial A_i} \, ln \, N_i] \qquad (2.39)$$

2.7. Fundamental Integral

It is seen, from the above equations, that once N_i has been expressed as function of A_i, A_{i-1} and λ, where λ may be set to zero, the values of $\bar{\tau}_i$, $\bar{s}_i$, and $\text{Var}^*(s_i)$, and the minimum value of $\text{Var}(\tau_i)$ are very easily obtained.

There is a fundamental integral $G(\lambda, A, T)$ defined by

$$G(\lambda, A, T) \underline{\Delta} \int_{\tau=0}^{T} e^{-\lambda \tau} F(A, \tau) d\tau . \qquad (2.40)$$

Although it may be difficult to evaluate $G(\lambda, A, T)$ as a function of λ, A and T, it is a modified Laplace transform, and so the resources of Laplace transform theory are available. Once $G(\lambda, A, T)$ has been evaluated, N_i is usually very easy to calculate.

In the general case, where $n(\tau)$ is any function subject to certain conditions, there exists a functional relationship, such that

$$N_i = [\varphi(G(\lambda, A, T))]_{A=A_i}^{A_{i-1}} \qquad (2.41)$$

given that

$$N_i = [\int_{\tau=0}^{T} n(\tau) F(A, \tau) d\tau]_{A=A_i}^{A_{i-1}} \qquad (2.10)$$

and there are standard methods of deriving $\varphi(G(\lambda, A, T))$ from $n(\tau)$.

In most of the cases which are likely to be encounted in this application, this functional relationship is very simple. There are three forms of $n(\tau)$ that are most likely to be useful:

2.7.1. Case 1.

If all that is known are the average values of $n(\tau)$ over certain intervals, and if it is not considered to be worthwhile representing $n(\tau)$ by some continuous function, then $n(\tau)$ can be represented by a sequence of step functions:

$$n(\tau) = n_0 + n_1 u(T_1 - \tau) + n_2 u(T_2 - \tau) +++ n_p u(T_p - \tau) \quad T_j \leqslant T \text{ for all } j \qquad (2.42)$$

where $u(T_j - \tau)$ is the step function defined by

$$u(T_j - \tau) = 1 \quad \text{for} \quad T_j \geqslant \tau \qquad (2.43)$$

$$= 0 \quad \text{for} \quad T_j < \tau$$

then

$$N_i = [n_0 G(\lambda, A, T) + n_1 G(\lambda, A, T_1) +++ n_p G(\lambda, A, T_p)]_{\substack{A=A_i \\ \lambda=0}}^{A_{i-1}} \qquad (2.44)$$

140

Usually there will be some reason to attribute an average rate of attrition, λ, to the process and then

$$n(\tau) = e^{-\lambda\tau}[q_0 + q_1 u(T_1 - \tau) + q_2 u(T_2 - \tau) +++ q_p u(T_p - \tau)] \qquad (2.45)$$

$$T_j \leqslant T \text{ for all } j$$

where the q_j are not functions of λ

then $\quad N_i = [q_0 G(\lambda, A, T) + q_1 G(\lambda, A, T_1) + q_2 G(\lambda, A, T_2) +++ q_p G(\lambda, A, T_p)]_{A=A_i}^{A_{i-1}} \quad (2.46)$

2.7.2. Case 2.

If

$$n(\tau) = e^{-\lambda\tau}(n_0 + n_1 \cos w\tau) \qquad (2.47)$$

then

$$n(\tau) = n_0 e^{-\lambda\tau} + n_1 \text{Re}\{ \exp(iw - \lambda)\tau \} \qquad (2.48)$$

then

$$N_i = [n_0 G(\lambda, \tau) + n_1 Re\{G(\lambda - iw, T)\}]_{A=A_i}^{A_{i-1}} \qquad (2.49)$$

2.7.3. Case 3.

If

$$n(\tau) = e^{-\lambda\tau}(a_0 + a_1\tau +++ a_j\tau^j) \qquad (2.50)$$

then $\quad N_i = \{(a_0 - a_1 \frac{\partial}{\partial\lambda} + a_2 \frac{\partial^2}{\partial\lambda^2} ++ a_j(\frac{-\partial}{\partial\lambda})^j)G(\lambda, A, T)]_{A=A_i}^{A_{i-1}} \quad (2.51)$

There are other simple cases, which may be found in the texts on Laplace transform theory.

2.8. Characteristic Function

Since $F(A, \tau)$ is a cumulative probability distribution function, it has a unique characteristic function, $\varphi(u, \tau)$ defined by

$$\varphi(u, \tau)\underline{\Delta}E(e^{iuz}) = \int_{z=-\infty}^{\infty} e^{iuz}dF(z, \tau) \qquad (2.52)$$

$\varphi(u, \tau)$ is a Fourier transform of $F(A, \tau)$.
Then $\psi(\lambda, u, T)$ is the Fourier transform of $G(\lambda, A, T)$

where

$$\psi(\lambda, u, T) \underline{\Delta} \int_{\tau=0}^{T} e^{-\lambda\tau}\varphi(u, \tau)d\tau \qquad (2.53)$$

and there is a unique inverse transform

$$\frac{d}{dA}G(\lambda, A, T) = \frac{1}{2\pi} \int_{u=-\infty}^{\infty} e^{-iua}\psi(\lambda, u, T)du \qquad (2.54)$$

provided that $\psi(\lambda, u, T)$ is absolutely integrable with respect to u. The integrals of (2.52) and (2.54) may be found in standard tables of Fourier transforms.
It is often easier to evaluate $G(\lambda, A, T)$ in this way than by direct integration.

2.9. Recruitment and Attrition Functions

There are two steps to be taken:

(i) To fit a model of promotion to an existing organization whose statistics are known. For this purpose consider several alternative mathematical models, use the known values of $n(\tau)$ to calculate the N_i in terms of the A_i and of the other parameters of the model, adjust the values of the A_i and the other parameters of the model, to calculate values of N_i and the other population parameters which are a good fit to the observed statistics, and then select the best of these fitted models for use in forecasting.

(ii) Having fitted one or more mathematical models to an existing organization, various assumptions are made concerning future entry and release rates, and the model is used to forecast the future of the organization. (The conditions under which such forecasts are valid are not known to the author of this paper.)

Step 1

For fitting the model to the organization, it is probably best to express $n(\tau)$ in the form of equation (2.45)

$$n(\tau) = e^{-\lambda \tau} [q_0 + q_1 u(T_1 - \tau) + q_2 u(T_2 - \tau) ++ q_p u(T_p - \tau)] \qquad (2.45)$$

where

$$u(T_j - \tau) = 1 \quad \text{for} \quad T_j \geqslant \tau$$
$$= 0 \quad \text{for} \quad T_j < \tau \qquad (2.43)$$

It is preferable to use a non-zero value of λ, probably selected so that the g_j are of the same order of magnitude. If λ is set to zero, this may cause difficulties in evaluating some of the above expressions.

Step 2

For forecasting it is more appropriate to consider separately the processes that constitute $n(\tau)$.

By (2.3)

$$n(\tau) = Rr(\tau) [1 - l(\tau)] \qquad (2.3)$$

and by (2.5)

$$[1 - l(\tau)] = \int_{t=0}^{\tau} L(t, \tau) \, dt \qquad (2.5)$$

The recruitment process $Rr(\tau)$ and the loss process $L(t, \tau)$ are distinct and deserve to be considered separately.

2.9.1. Recruitment Process.

The simplest case is

$$Rr(\tau) = R_0 \qquad (2.55)$$

and

$$[1 - l(\tau)] = e^{-\lambda \tau} \qquad (2.56)$$

giving

$$N_i = R_0 \left[G(\lambda, A, T) \right]_{A=A_i}^{A_{i-1}} \qquad (2.57)$$

142

This is an inevitable starting point. There will be a constant basic rate of recruitment R_0, and other effects, such as may be due to business cycles, changes in pay and conditions of service, and planned changes in the level of recruitment, can be considered as disturbances added to R_0.

2.9.2. Loss Rates

Losses are usually expressed as a proportion of the population.

If $N(t)$ is the population of a certain class of officers then $\frac{d}{dt} N(t)$ is the loss per unit time and if $p(t)$ is the relative loss rate

$$\frac{dN(t)}{dt} = - p(t)N(t) \tag{2.58}$$

$$\frac{d}{dt} \, ln(N(t)) = - p(t)$$

then
$$N(t) = k \exp(- \int_{t_0}^{t} p(x)\,dx) \tag{2.59}$$

and, for most typical functions $p(t)$, this will result in

$$N(t) = kq(t)e^{-\lambda t}. \tag{2.60}$$

Such an exponential decay factor, $e^{-\lambda \tau}$, will usually be present. Loss rates of the order of 2% to 6% per year are common.

The loss rate is likely to be larger for small values of τ. A large proportion of recruits to an organization are likely to leave as soon as they find that the organization does not appeal to them. In the armed forces, recruits are usually obliged to serve for a period of several years before they may leave. It is not unusual for 50% to leave at this opportunity. In this case, $[1 - \lambda(\tau)]$ will have a point of discontinuity.

Having decided on the representations of $Rr(\tau)$ and $[1 - l(\tau)]$ to be used for forecasting it will be usual to validate them by using them to "predict" the present state of the organization. It will probably be necessary to recalculate the A_i, and the other parameters of the model to get a good fit.

2.10. The "Best unbiased estimates" of model parameters

The "best unbiased estimates" of the A_i and other model parameters, are difficult to define and to calculate. If the organization has 8 ranks, then there are 36 statistics available:

> 8 values of N_i
> 8 values of $\overline{\tau}_i$
> 7 values of $\overline{s}_i$ (since $\overline{s}_8 \equiv \overline{\tau}_8$)
> 7 estimates of var(τ_i), if $N_1 = 1$
> 6 estimates of var(s_i) (since $s_8 = \tau_8$).

And these 36 statistics are to be used to estimate 10 or 11 model parameters:
9 values of A_i, A_8 to A_0, except that A_8 may be taken to be $A_8 = -\infty$ or $A_8 = 0$ and the scale factor is arbitrary, and 2 to 4 other parameters of the model, depending upon its complexity.

To employ 36 statistics to estimate 11 parameters is a problem in non-linear regression theory, with 25 degrees of freedom. Some of the difficulties are:

(i) the sample variances var(τ_i) and var(s_i) will have excessive variances for $i = 2, 3$, where N_2 and N_3 are small. (If $N_1 = 1$, Var(τ_1) and Var(s_1) cannot even be estimated).

(ii) The sample means, $\bar{\tau}_i$ and $\bar{s}_i$ have excessive variances for $i = 1, 2, 3$.

(iii) In some organizations, such as the Royal Canadian Navy, promotion from rank 8 to rank 7 seems to be almost automatic after a certain length of service in rank 8. Where this is the case, and where all other promotion seems to follow a model of promotion by ability, then ranks 7 and 8 should be combined.

(iv) The calculated values of var(τ_i) and var(s_i) are given as inequalities, for example

$$\mathrm{Var}(\tau_i) \geqslant - \bar{\tau}_i{}^2 + \frac{1}{N_i} \int_{\tau=0}^{T} \tau^2 n(\tau) \int_{z=A_i}^{A_{i-1}} f(z, \tau)\, dz\, d\tau . \qquad (2.13)$$

If the A_i were fixed numbers, and if $n(\tau)$ were a determined function, then (2.13) would be an equation. If $n(\tau)$ is to be considered to be the expected value of a stochastic variate, then $n(\tau)$ must have an associated variance. If also the A_i must be calculated from (2.9)

$$N_i = \int_{\tau=0}^{T} n(\tau) \int_{z=A_i}^{A_{i-1}} f(z, \tau)\, dz\, d\tau \qquad (2.9)$$

then the A_i will also have variances, $\mathrm{Var}(A_i)$. If the N_i are considered to be statistics, rather than fixed numbers, they will have variances, $\mathrm{Var}(N_i)$. In this general case the $\mathrm{Var}(\tau_i)$ are difficult to calculate, but they are greater than the values given by (2.13).

If $\mathrm{Var}(\tau_i)$ and $\mathrm{Var}(s_i)$ cannot be calculated with sufficient accuracy, then it may not be possible to use the sample variances to fit the mathematical model.

The problem of adjusting the model to get a " best fit " is not further discussed in this paper.

It is assumed that a good fit may be obtained without the use of refined calculations, and that this will be good enough for approximate forecasts.

In any case there is no certainty that such a mathematical model, however well fitted, can provide accurate forecasts.

2.11. General Model

Define $N(\tau)$: the number of officers in the organization whose total length of service does not exceed τ.

Then
$$n(\tau) = \frac{d}{d\tau} N(\tau), \quad \text{if it exists.} \qquad (2.61)$$

But $N(\tau)$ can only be a discrete variable, and so $n(\tau)$ can only be zero or infinite. The use of $n(\tau)$ in the above equations is only justifiable if $n(\tau)$ is treated as an expected (or average value)

$$E \left\{ \underset{\Delta\tau \to 0}{\mathrm{Limit}} \ \frac{\Delta N(\tau)}{\Delta\tau} \right\}$$

$$n(\tau) = \frac{d}{d\tau} E[N(\tau)] \qquad (2.62)$$

and then $n(\tau)$ must have an associated variance

$$\mathrm{Var}(n(\tau)) = E \left\{ \underset{\Delta\tau \to 0}{\mathrm{limit}} \ (\frac{\Delta N(\tau)}{\Delta\tau} - n(\tau))^2 \right\} \qquad (2.63)$$

This difficulty is avoided by using Stieltjes integrals throughout, so that for (2.2)

$$N = N(T) = \int_{\tau=0}^{T} dN(\tau) \qquad (2.64)$$

for (2.10)

$$N_i = \left[\int_{\tau=0}^{T} F(A, \tau) \, dN(\tau) \right]_{A=A_i}^{A_{i-1}} \qquad (2.65)$$

for (2.12)

$$\bar{\tau}_i = \frac{1}{N_i} \left[\int_{\tau=0}^{T} F(A, \tau) \tau dN(\tau) \right]_{A=A_i}^{A_{i-1}} \qquad (2.66)$$

for (2.13)

$$\mathrm{Var}(\tau_i) \geqslant -\bar{\tau}_i^2 + \frac{1}{N_i} \left[\int_{\tau=0}^{T} F(A, \tau) \tau^2 dN(\tau) \right]_{A=A_i}^{A_{i-1}} \qquad (2.67)$$

for (2.17)

$$m(A_i) = \int_{\tau=0}^{T} f(A_i, \tau) dN(\tau) \qquad (2.68)$$

for (2.33)

$$\bar{s}_i \cdot \underline{\Delta} \bar{\tau}_i - \frac{1}{m(A_i)} \int_{\tau=0}^{T} f(A_i, \tau) \tau dN(\tau) \qquad (2.69)$$

for (2.39)

$$\mathrm{Var}^*(s_i) \underline{\Delta} \mathrm{Var}(\tau_i) + (\bar{\tau}_i - \bar{s}_i^*)^2 - \frac{1}{m(A_i)} \int_{\tau=0}^{T} f(A_i, \tau) \tau^2 dN(\tau). \qquad (2.70)$$

Similarly define $R(\tau)$: the total number of recruits from $\tau = 0$ to τ.
Then (2.3) would become

$$N(\tau) = \int_{t=0}^{\tau} [1 - l(t)] dR(t) \qquad (2.71)$$

except that if $N(\tau)$ and $R(\tau)$ are both required to be discrete variables, then (2.71) must be replaced by a stochastic process. But then $N(\tau)$ would become a stochastic variable, and it would be permissible to consider its expected value $E(N(\tau))$ as being a continuous variable so that

$$n(\tau) = \frac{d}{d\tau} E(N(\tau)).$$

For an accurate model $R(\tau)$ and $N(\tau)$ should be treated as discrete variables, with $N(\tau)$ being derived from $R(\tau)$ by a stochastic process of attrition, but then the results obtained by this refined method are unlikely to be very different from the results obtained by using $n(\tau)$ and $Rr(\tau)$ as if they were bounded variables.

2.12. Rank-dependent Loss Rates

In practice, it seems that the loss rate $L(\tau)$ is dependent upon the present rank of the officer.

$$L = L(\tau, \ i) \qquad (2.72)$$

Then

$$l(\tau, \ i) = \int_{t=0}^{\tau} L(t, \ i)\,dt \qquad (2.73)$$

$$N_i = R \int_{t=0}^{\tau} r(\tau)(1 - l(\tau, \ i)) \int_{z=A_i}^{A_{i-1}} (z, \ \tau)\,dz\,d\tau . \qquad (2.74)$$

This is an awkward equation to solve, and is not considered in this paper.

3. PARTICULAR MODELS FOR PERSONNEL INVENTORY PREDICTION

Editorial Note — The paper as submitted contains an extensive discussion of particular examples. For reasons of space these have had to be omitted. Their titles are listed below; and further details could be sought direct from the author.

3.1. Model of Promotion by Seniority.

3.2. Simple Normal Model of Consistent Promotion.

3.3. Binomial Model of Haphazard Promotion.

3.4. Poisson Model of Haphazard Promotion.

3.5. Poisson Model of Consistent Promotion.

3.6. Normal Stochastic Model of Haphazard Promotion.

3.7. Normal Stochastic Model of Consistent Promotion.

(Special cases — consistent recruitment and loss rates — are considered for 3.3, 3.4, 3.5, 3.6 and 3.7 above)

Not all of the models are complete.

4. CONCLUSION

A general model for personnel inventory prediction has been presented, and the results have been outlined for some of the simpler special cases.

This paper is an account of work in progress, which is incomplete. The following tasks remain:

(a) The work on the models listed in section 3 needs to be completed, with the integrals and series expressed in terms of standard functions, where these exist.

(b) A wider range of special cases needs to be considered.

(c) The level of achievement for each rank needs to be expressed as an explicit function of the number in each rank, as an integral, a series, and, if possible, in terms of standard functions.

(d) For each model, the results need to be expressed in a form suitable for evaluation by a digital computer.

(e) For each model, a set of numerical results is required for a wide range of values of the parameters. From these results it may be possible to derive empirical rules that will guide the application of this type of model.

(f) These models need to be applied to the study of an existing organization.

(g) A detailed search of the literature is required to ascertain whether this approach has been adopted previously, or whether it corresponds to some other problem which has been studied.

(h) Further and deeper study will be given to the general model.

(i) Further study will be given to the recruitment process, defined by $n(\tau)$, $r(\tau)$ and $L(t, \tau)$.

(j) The problems of randomized and extended models will be studied.

(k) The statistical problems involved in the estimation of parameters will be studied.

If several organizations can be characterized by similar models of consistent promotion, then it will be possible to compare the criteria for promotion for each organization. First of all the levels of achievement must be standardized in some manner. For example one might change the scale factors so that the average rate of achievement is the same for each organization. Then, when each officer is promoted, his level of achievement can be deduced, and, divided by his total length of service gives his average rate of achievement. The average rates of achievement for a large group of officers can be correlated with their personal characteristics; such as their I.Q. scores. It may then be possible to assert that officers with high I.Q. scores are promoted at a faster rate in one organization than in another. If enough personal data are available, it may be possible to evaluate the qualities necessary for promotion in each organization. If means can be found to compare the effectiveness of several organizations, it may be possible to find some relation between effectiveness and method of promotion. It would be a very satisfactory result if it could be shown that the more effective organization was that which gave more promotion to its more intelligent officers.

5. BIBLIOGRAPHY

1. Feller, W., *An Introduction to Probability Theory and its Applications*. 2 Volumes. Wiley 1957 and 1966.
2. Parzen, E., *Stochastic Processes*. Holden-Day Inc. 1962.
3. Abramowitz, M. and Stegun, I.A., *Handbook of Mathematical Functions*. National Bureau of Standards, 1964 and Dover Publications, 1965.
4. Erdelyi, A., Magnus, W., Oberhettinger, F., and Tricomi, F.G. *Tables of Integral Transforms, Volume I* McGraw-Hill, 1954.
5. Fraser, D.A.S., *Statistics, An Introduction*. Wiley, 1958.
6. Cramer, H., *Mathematical Methods of Statistics*. Princeton University Press, 1946.
7. Cramer, H., *Random Variables and Probability Distributions*. Cambridge Tracts in Mathematics No.36, Cambridge, 1937.
8. Cox, D.R. and Miller, H.D., *The Theory of Stochastic Processes*. Methuen, 1965.
9. Dill, W.R., Gaver, D.P., and Weber, W.L., Models and Modelling for Manpower Planning. *Management Science* Vol.13, No.4, December 1966.
10. Merck, J.W., A Mathematical Model of the Personnel Structure of Large Scale Organizations Based on Markov Chains. Unpublished Ph.D. Dissertation, Duke University, 1961.

A Possible Application of Dynamic Programming to the Scheduling of Personnel Training

E.L. LEESE
DEFENCE OPERATIONAL RESEARCH ESTABLISHMENT,
OTTAWA

I. INTRODUCTION

In recent years there have been many studies of the management of inventory. Some of these seek to determine rules for ordering stock which are " optimum " in some sense. The studies normally assume that demands for stock items occur in a random fashion, and that new stock items cannot be obtained as soon as they are ordered. One seeks to determine an " ordering policy " which will minimize the expected total cost of the operation over some prescribed period of time. Costs normally include the cost of holding stock in inventory, and the cost of ordering new items. In addition, a " penalty cost " is sometimes assessed in cases in which demands cannot be immediately satisfied from the stock in hand or on order.

There is an analogy between this problem and the problem of training personnel to fit them for new duties. Indeed, if the meanings of the various " inventory " quantities are suitably changed, it appears possible to translate the inventory problem directly into a personnel training problem. This paper investigates the possibility of doing this, and of applying a mathematical model, recently developed by Prof. P.R. Beesack (Reference (1)) for the inventory problem, to a problem of personnel training.

The mathematical details of the method will not be given in full. They are available in Reference (1). This paper merely describes the model, lists the assumptions used, and gives numerical results for a specimen case.

2. DESCRIPTION OF PERSONNEL PROBLEM

We study the problem of training groups of men so that they can take on jobs of a certain type. We start with a (small) pool of trained men, and a (large) pool of untrained men. As time goes on, there are demands for the services of trained men. These demands arise randomly, but the statistical distribution of the demands is assumed to be known. If trained men are available to satisfy a demand, they are supplied at once.

At each of a number of (equal-spaced) times, a review is made of the number of men currently in the " trained " pool, and of the number of demands (if any) which have not currently been met. On the basis of the review, a decision may be made to start training a certain number of people. However, there is naturally a time lag between the decision to train a new group of men, and the completion of the training of this group.

Time is divided into a number of (equal) periods, the start of each period corresponding to the time at which the above periodic review is made. The whole system is to be studied for some finite number of such time periods.

One can set up rules, of various kinds, which will determine the training action required at each of the review periods. If we specify a set of rules (or " training policy "), we can work out, for each time period, the proportion of demands for trained men which can be immediately satisfied from the pool of trained men. The expected overall proportion of such demands which are immediately satisfied is a reasonable measure of the " service level " provided by the system.

If we change the rules (" training policy ") we change the service level. We can increase the service level by adopting a " generous " training policy which ensures an ample supply of ready-trained men in the pool. But this may be wasteful, since the pool of trained men are not necessarily fulfilling a useful function while they wait for suitable employment.

The problem is to design a set of rules which provides at least a certain specified service level, but which minimizes the overall cost of the system. This cost includes a " holding cost " associated with, and proportional to, the size of the pool of trained men who are waiting for suitable work. In addition, each time training action is initiated the system incurs a " training cost ". This training cost includes two components,

(i) a " set-up " cost, associated with the setting up of the training procedure. This is independent of the number of men to be trained.

(ii) a " variable " training cost which is proportional to the number of men to be trained.

3. MATHEMATICAL SPECIFICATION OF PROBLEM

We must now translate the above problem into mathematical terms. We assume that we are concerned with the study of the process over $(\lambda + N)$ time periods, the start of each period corresponding to the time at which a periodic review is made. The lag between making a decision to train a group of men, and the completion of their training, is assumed constant and equal to λ time periods.

In each of the $(\lambda + N)$ time periods there may be demands for trained men. The statistical distribution of the size of the demand, d_i, in period i, is assumed known for each period. In other words we know the distribution functions,

$$\phi_i(k) = \text{Prob.} \ (d_i = k) \tag{1}$$

for $k = 0, 1, 2 \ldots$ for all periods $i = 1, 2 \ldots (\lambda + N)$.

It is assumed that these distribution functions are independent from period to period.

At the start of each period the situation is reviewed. At the start of period i we know:

u_i = the number of trained men in the pool, now available for duty,
v_i = the number of men who are now being trained, but whose training is not yet complete,
w_i = the total number of trained men who have been demanded, but not supplied, in past periods.

If, instantaneously, the training of the v_i men were completed, and the unsatisfied demands for the w_i men were met, the net number of trained men available would be

$$x_i = u_i + v_i - w_i \tag{2}$$

Note that in some situations x_i could be negative.

On the basis of the observed values of u_i, v_i, w_i for period i (and of the history observed for all previous periods), we make a decision to initiate the training of a group of z_i men. (z_i can be zero). After this decision is made, a group of $z_{i-\lambda}$ men, who began their training λ periods ago, complete their training and join the pool of trained men. For the remainder of period i, all that may occur is a fresh demand for d_i additional trained men.

In each period we can specify rules which enable us to choose z_i from a knowledge of the values of (u_i, v_i, w_i) in the current period and in past periods. This amounts to specifying z_i as a function of these variables. In other words a " training policy ", or choice of rules for deciding on training action, amounts to the specification of a set of functional relationships between $z_1, z_2, z_3 \ldots$ and the appropriate u, v, w variables.

We must now specify the costs of operating the system. In costing the system we introduce a discount factor $\alpha = 100/(100 + r)$ where r is the interest rate (%) per time period. In estimating the training cost corresponding to a decision, made in period i, to train z_i men, we assume that the " set-up " cost K is incurred at the time we decide to train the men, but that the " variable " training cost Cz_i is paid only at the time the training is completed (at period $(\lambda + i)$). Hence the total training cost for period i is

$$c(z_i) = K\,\alpha^{-\lambda} + cz_c \ (\text{if } z_c > 0); \ = 0 \ (\text{if } z_c = 0) \tag{3}$$

To this we must add the " holding cost " for period i, which is a constant (Ic) times the maximum number of men in the " trained " pool in period i.

If we have specified a training policy, we can readily derive an expression for the expected total cost of the operation, in terms of the variables mentioned above.

In addition we can derive an expression for the " service level ", which is taken as the ratio of the expected total number of demands which are satisfied immediately, to the expected total number of demands.

Our problem now is to choose a training policy which minimizes the expected total cost of the operation, while providing a service level which equals or exceeds some specified amount.

4. SOLUTION OF THE PROBLEM

The mathematical details of the solution will not be given here. They are available in Reference (1). However, we note that we are trying to minimize a quantity (expected total cost) which is the sum of a number of quantities each relating to one particular period, by suitable choice of a number of functions z_i each dependent on the situation in the current and in all previous periods. The technique which naturally suggests itself for this problem is dynamic programming. However, we have to maximize the expected cost subject to a side constraint. Hence we expect to have to use the Lagrangian Multiplier technique.

It turns out (as is fully explained in Reference (1)) that our problem can indeed be solved by these techniques. Moreover the optimum solution is of a fairly simple form. The optimal set of functions z_i can be specified simply in terms of the variables x_i defined in equation (2). In fact, for any period i which is one of the first N periods we have

$$\left. \begin{aligned} z_i &= S_i - x_i \quad \text{if} \quad x_i < s_i \\ &= 0 \qquad\quad \text{if} \quad x_i \geqslant s_i \end{aligned} \right\} \tag{4}$$

In other words, for period i, if the value of x_i is less than a certain critical value s_i, we make a decision to train an additional $(S_i - x_i)$ men. If however the value of x_i is greater than or equal to s_i, we do not start any new training in period i.

This type of policy is usually known as an (S, s) policy in inventory management theory. The method of obtaining the values of S_i and s_i for the various periods is explained in detail in Reference (1). As is obvious from commonsense, there is never any point in starting any training in any period $i > N$ since the training would not be complete by the end of the whole operation.

5. A NUMERICAL EXAMPLE

To see how the above method works, we give the results of a (hypothetical) numerical example. In this example the assumptions are as follows:-

$\lambda = 2$ (time lag, in periods, between initiation and completion of training)
$N = 10$

$\lambda + N = 12$ (total number of periods over which the operation of the system extends)

$x_1 = 10$ (initial number of men in " trained" pool)

$\phi_i(k) = {}^{10}C_k(\frac{1}{2})^{10}$ (statistical distribution of demand for trained men is binomial, with maximum demand 10 and mean demand 5 for each period)

$\alpha = 0 \cdot 945$ (cost discount factor, corresponds to 6% interest rate per period)

$K = 20$ (" fixed" component of training cost)

$c = 50$ (cost per man for " variable" component of training cost)

$Ic = 7 \cdot 5$ (cost per man associated with " holding" cost for a given period)

Required service level, at least 90%.

The solution developed by Prof. Beesack was translated by Mr. D. W. Dewar into a (FORTRAN IV) computer program, and a number of numerical cases (including the one just detailed) were run on the IBM 360 Model 65 in Ottawa. The solution for the above case is given below: -

TABLE I

Optimum Training Policy

Period (i)	1	2	3	4	5	6	7	8	9	10
Value of S_i	17	17	18	18	18	18	18	18	18	13
Value of s_i	15	15	15	15	16	16	16	16	16	11

With this training policy the expected total cost is 2353.83, while the service level provided is 90.737%. (Since the values of the S_i and s_i must be integers, it is of course not possible to achieve a service level of exactly 90%.)

6. CONCLUSION

This paper does not present any new results. Its only object is to draw the attention of personnel managers to the possibility of using techniques already developed for inventory management, in solving analogous problems of personnel management. Discussions will now be held with Canadian Forces service officers to discover whether the above model needs modifying to make it appropriate for practical personnel management situations. It is hoped that the model, when suitably modified, will eventually be useful to the staff officers of Canadian Forces in the efficient management of training resources.

REFERENCES

1. Beesack, P. R. A finite horizon dynamic inventory model with a stockout constraint. *Management Science*. Vol. 13, No. 9, May 1967, pages 618-630.

Application of Actuarial Techniques to Officer Career Planning

E. JONES

MINISTRY OF DEFENCE (U.K.)

1. INTRODUCTION

This talk is concerned with career planning in the usual case of a graded staff in which numbers at each level are fixed by the needs of the work and promotions occur only when there are vacancies in the grade above. Points will be illustrated by reference to the Executive Class of the Civil Service and to a hypothetical Royal Navy officer branch. The methods described have been used for RN officer planning for 20 years or so, and on a less regular basis for civilian staff planning in the Navy Dept. also.

2. ULTIMATE AND SHORT TERM POSITIONS

In the long run the complement structure (i.e. the proportions of posts in each grade) is the predominant factor determining career prospects but in the short term the position will depend very much on the characteristics of the age distribution of present staff and on whether there is, or has recently been, any expansion or contraction. Changes in entry and retirement ages and in wastage rates also react on career prospects.

In assessing future prospects two different approaches are therefore made. Firstly, a model is constructed to show the theoretical steady state position assuming ultimate stability in size and age distribution of the staff. The validity of such theoretical models in dealing with current practical problems will be discussed later. Secondly, the existing staff is projected by age and grade up to about 10 years ahead in order to forecast retirement and wastage losses, and hence promotions and recruiting needs – taking into account any foreseen changes in the size of the staff.

Planning decisions are based on study of both the steady state model and the projections of existing staff. This helps to minimise the risks of solving short-term problems by measures which may create difficulties years later.

3. THE SERVICE TABLE

Application of these methods depends on soundly based prediction techniques for staff subject to probabilities of wastage which vary with age, length of service and, possibly, grade. The basic mathematical problems are of the same type as those underlying the operations of life assurance companies and pension funds, and the forecasting of national populations – and so similar actuarial life table techniques are used. It is of interest that these have also been found applicable in quite different spheres e.g. in assessing replacement policies for aircraft and vehicles. When applied to a staff the life table is more appropriately termed the " service table ".

The service table of a male staff recruited at age 18 and serving until 60 is shown, in graphical form, in Figure 1. This is based on annual wastage of 5% of mean strength for the first 5 years after entry and 2% thereafter. The bottom line represents an arbitrary 100 entries at age 18 and the sloping line shows how this number diminishes as the years go by. (Table 1, on page 154, deals with the same example).

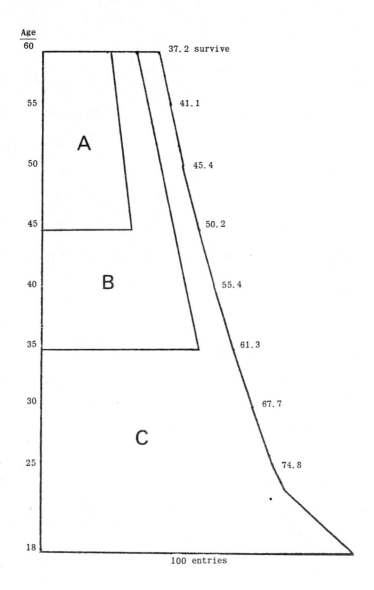

Fig. 1: MALE CIVILIANS ENTERING AT AGE 18
AND SERVING UNTIL 60

TABLE 1

Career prospects – examples

Grades A, B, C = 15%, 25% and 60% respectively of total strength

Average promotion age	Career factor to B	Yearly number of promotions	Average promotion age	Career factor of *all* staff to A	Yearly number of promotions
38½	100%	57	51	100%	45
37	91%	54	50	90%	41
35	82%	50	45	57%	29
30	65%	44	40	41%	23

The service table illustrates the career factors underlined above viz:-

82% of the 61 survivors at age 35 promoted to B

57% " " 50 " " " 45 of *all* staff promoted to A

i.e. 70% of survivors *in B* at age 45 promoted to A

The table assumes annual wastage of 5% of mean strength each year up to age 23 exact and 2% thereafter. The base line of the service table is arbitrary and the diagram can be scaled up or down as required. The 100 entries a year on these wastage assumptions would give a steady state strength of 2,479.

In general, if $l_x dx$ denotes total staff in all grades at exact age x, then

$$l_{x+t} = l_x \exp \left\{ - \int_0^t \mu_{x+r} \, dr \right\} \text{ where } \mu_x = \frac{-1}{l_x} \frac{dl_x}{dx}$$

and total strength between ages x and y exact is $\int_0^{y-x} l_{x+t} dt$.

In practice, a convenient method of estimating μ_x is to analyze withdrawals and strengths by year of birth: e.g. wastage in 1966 of staff born 1940 related to the mean strength of such staff over the year 1966 gives an estimate of μ_{26}. The probability of surviving in service for one year from age 25½ exact is not $(1 - \mu_{26})$ but $\exp(-\mu_{26})$, approximately.

154

Looked at vertically, the diagram shows the age, composition and size of the staff which would result eventually if 100 recruits joined each year and wastage remained as assumed i.e. it shows the steady state position. The sub-division into grades A, B and C will be discussed presently.

The assumption of such a simple wastage pattern in Figure 1 is solely for convenience in simplifying the calculation of career prospects for illustrative purposes. The service table method is, of course, equally applicable if wastage varies from age to age, or if staff enter at different ages and wastage is a function of both age and length of service. Brief reference to the general mathematical relationships between strengths and wastage rates is given in Table 1.

4. WASTAGE INVESTIGATIONS

An investigation of past wastage is an essential preliminary to constructing a service table. The observed wastage rates would be smoothed to remove random fluctuations and, as they are to be used for forecasting, may be adjusted to allow for trends if analyses by cause of loss shows this to be desirable. The depth to which the wastage investigations are taken would depend on how much data are available. It may sometimes be necessary to adopt fairly arbitrary rates based on a comparable staff.

The basic process of relating actual losses at each age to the appropriate strengths at risk in order to produce rates itself involves technicalities. For example losses may be related either to strength at the beginning of the year (with adjustments for entries) or to mean strength over the year. These give different measures and affect the construction of the service table. There is a considerable body of actuarial doctrine in these matters – but undue refinements are inappropriate in the manpower planning context.

5. A SIMPLE CAREER STRUCTURE MODEL

Turning again to Figure 1, it is assumed that the numbers in the grades A, B and C represent 15%, 25% and 60% respectively of total strength. The diagram shows all promotions to B and to A to occur at ages 35 and 45 respectively. These are averages and promotions would be spread each side. The ratio of the total number of promotions into a particular grade to the number of survivors at the average promotion age is usually a good approximation to what we term the " career factor " to that grade – viz the probability, excluding wastage risks, that a recruit will ever be promoted to that level. Table 1 gives a few of the possible combinations of career factor and age on the stated assumptions – and Figure 1 shows one of these solutions.

Average promotion age and career factor are the opposite sides of the same coin and it is meaningless to quote one without the other. If operating, say, a low age/low career factor policy it would not be possible to switch rapidly to a high age/high career factor basis without a change in strengths in view of the larger number of promotions entailed. If strengths are to remain constant it would be necessary to continue for a time with the existing number of promotions but to make them at higher ages – so that numbers of retirements and hence promotions would eventually rise to the new level required.

It will be apparent that it is the ratios between A, B and C (see Figure 1 and Table 1), and not the actual numbers which determine ultimate career prospects. These ratios between numbers in the different grades often remain relatively stable when total staff numbers are changing. Steady state career factors on one target strength may not therefore be much different when recalculated on a new strength. This is the main reason why the steady state model, although a theoretical concept, has practical value. But even though the *ultimate* prospects may be much the same on the new as on the old strength the actual process of moving from one to the other would, of course, have repercussions on promotions. A steady state model is particularly useful in assessing

155

a change in conditions the effects of which would not become felt for many years
(e.g. a higher retiring age for future new entrants).

6. CIVIL SERVICE EXECUTIVE STAFF MODEL

A more complex model is needed for Executive Class staff in the Civil Service. Direct
entrants leave school at around age 18 with G.C.E. Advanced level passes and join over
a span of ages. There is also a very substantial flow of promotions from the clerical
grade from under age 30 to over age 50. Both men and women are employed; women having
higher wastage rates. Further, there are more than three grades but this does not
introduce any new principles.

The model must allow for the fact that in view of their better educational qualifications and earlier start as Executives, the direct entrants will on average have better
career prospects than the promotees from the clerical staff. Further, the prospects of
the promotees will diminish as their age at entry into the Executive Class increases –
on grounds of quality and because of the shorter period of future service left.

A planning scheme is drawn up along the lines of Table 2 in which the numbers are
hypothetical. The distribution of the intake by type and age in column (3) would be
based on past experience and on policy regarding future ratios of men to women and of
direct entrants to promotees. Determination of the assumptions in columns (4) and (6)
regarding the way in which the career factor will vary between different groups is
likely to present more difficulties. An approximation to career factors actually
attained in the past can be obtained from the distribution by grade of the survivors of
each cohort just after the final promotion has been made – the career factor to grade B
being the ratio of those in A and B to the total still serving at that age. The
observed career factors would however reflect past conditions when the proportions of
higher posts may have been different or there may have been other disturbing influences.

Evaluation of the scheme in Table 2 using appropriate service tables gives g and h
and hence the whole ultimate promotion pattern. One object of the investigations might
be to assess the career implications of changing the proportions of women or of
promotees. A general point can be made. As women have higher wastage rates than men,
proportionately fewer will reach the higher ranks even if career factors are the same.
Women therefore in a sense " subsidize " the careers of men and, by definition,
promotees from the clerical class " subsidize " the direct entrants.

7. RN OFFICERS

7.1. Structure and Planning Principles

Turning to Royal Navy officers, Figure 2 illustrates the steady state position in a
hypothetical branch in which entry, promotion and retirement ages are similar to those
of Seaman officers. But the planned strengths and career factors are hypothetical.

There are three distinct entry streams with different conditions and prospects.
Figure 2a relates to Supplementary list officers who enter on 10 year commissions with
the option of leaving after 5 years. There are prospects of moving sideways into the
General List or of being offered pensionable service to age 50.

Figure 2b represents the General List – the main body of permanent career officers
consisting largely of Dartmouth cadets but including graduate entrants and exceptional
young naval ratings selected for Dartmouth training at about age 18.

Figure 2c refers to Special Duties list officers – these are promoted from naval
ratings at an average age of about 31 for more limited duties than those of General List
officers.

The General List entry is fixed to give a specific career factor to Commander – this
being a planning target and not a guarantee. Figure 2 takes this to be 60% at the
average promotion age of 38. The General List entry is therefore based on the estimated

TABLE 2

Hypothetical career planning scheme – Executive staff (Civil Service)

Type of intake (1)	Average age of entry groups (2)	Percentage Distribution of total intake (3)	Career factor to grade B (4)	At average age (5)	Career factor from grade B to A (6)	At average age (7)
Males						
Direct entry	20	30%	g	35	h	45
Promotees	30	20%	$(.8)g$	45	$(.6)h$	55
=	40	15%	$(.4)g$	55	–	–
=	50	10%	–	–	–	–
Females						
Direct entry	20	10%				
Promotees	30	7%	as above		as above	
=	40	5%				
=	50	3%				
		100%				

" Promotees " = intake into the Executive Class by promotion from the Clerical grade.
In practice a larger number of age groups might have to be considered.

Fig. 2a: SUPPLEMENTARY LIST (S.L.)

(10 YEAR COMMISSION WITH
BREAK POINT AT 5 YEARS)

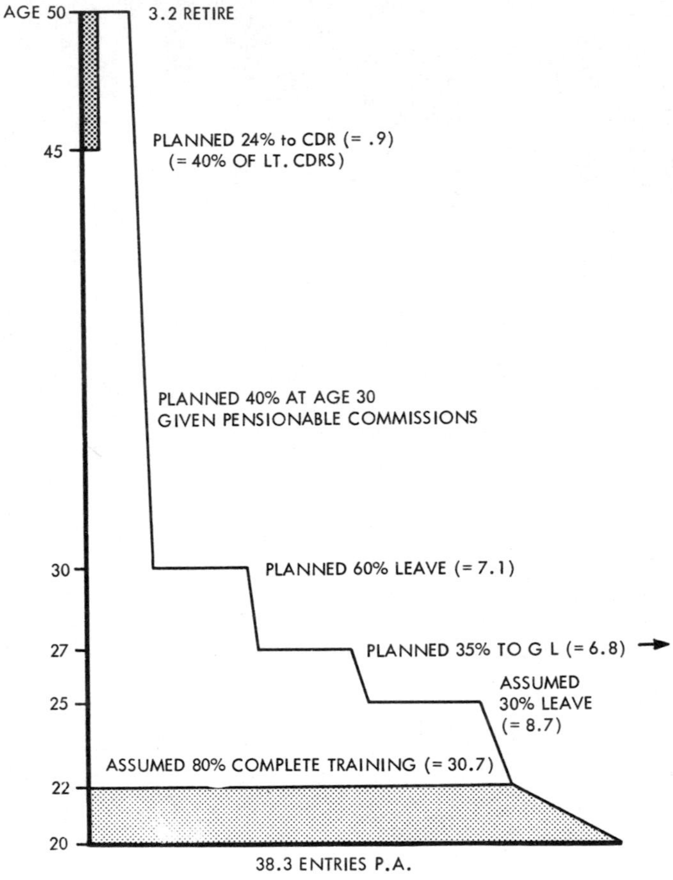
AGE 50
45
30
27
25
22
20
3.2 RETIRE
PLANNED 24% to CDR (= .9)
(= 40% OF LT. CDRS)
PLANNED 40% AT AGE 30
GIVEN PENSIONABLE COMMISSIONS
PLANNED 60% LEAVE (= 7.1)
PLANNED 35% TO G L (= 6.8) →
ASSUMED
30% LEAVE
(= 8.7)
ASSUMED 80% COMPLETE TRAINING (= 30.7)
38.3 ENTRIES P.A.

Notes

The planned strengths and planned promotion prospects are hypothetical.

Promotion and other percentages quoted relate to numbers still in service at that point.

In practice entries and promotions occur over a range of ages - not at single points as shown above for simplification

G.L. Lt. Commanders can retire between 40 & 50 - an arbitrary three-point scheme is used above.

G.L. Captains retire at 55 or after 9 years as Captain if earlier - giving an average age of just under 55.

Fig. 2: HYPOTHETICAL

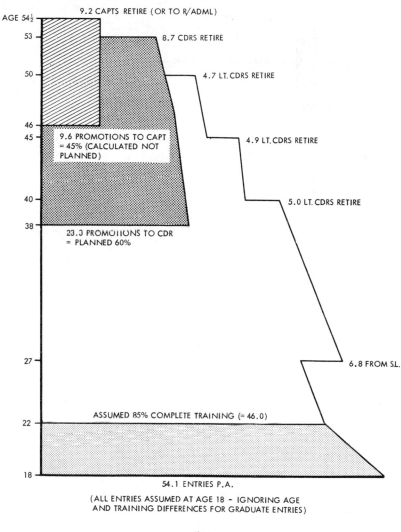

9.2 CAPTS RETIRE (OR TO R/ADML)

AGE 54½

8.7 CDRS RETIRE

4.7 LT. CDRS RETIRE

9.6 PROMOTIONS TO CAPT = 45% (CALCULATED NOT PLANNED)

4.9 LT. CDRS RETIRE

5.0 LT. CDRS RETIRE

23.3 PROMOTIONS TO CDR = PLANNED 60%

6.8 FROM S.L.

ASSUMED 85% COMPLETE TRAINING (= 46.0)

54.1 ENTRIES P.A.

(ALL ENTRIES ASSUMED AT AGE 18 - IGNORING AGE AND TRAINING DIFFERENCES FOR GRADUATE ENTRIES)

Key

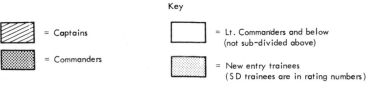

= Captains

= Commanders

= Lt. Commanders and below (not sub-divided above)

= New entry trainees (S D trainees are in rating numbers)

CAREER STRUCTURE

(continued on p. 160)

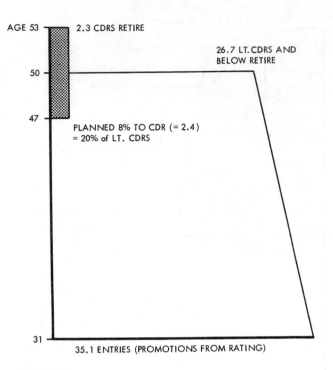

TABLE 3: SUMMARY OF STRENGTHS

	G.L. ex Age 18 entry	G.L. ex S.L.	S.L.	S.D.	Total
Flag Officers (not shown)	9	1	–	–	10 *
Captains	69	11	–	–	80 *
Commanders	217	35	4	14	270 *
Trained Lt.Cdrs & below	718	82	240	600 *	1640 *
	1013	129	244	614	2000 *
New entry Trainees	200	–	69	–	269
Overall total	1213	129	313	614	2269

* these are the target strengths specified – all other figures obtained by calculation

numbers of Commanders and above needed about 20 years later. The shape and size of the
Navy so far ahead is speculative but the best assessment is made on a conservative
basis. An unforeseen reduction of say 10% in the size of the Navy would itself mean that
the actual career factor might turn out to be about 55% instead of the planned 60%,
which would not be a serious divergence. A really substantial reduction in the Navy
would be likely to entail a formal redundancy scheme, in which event the aim would be to
spread the reductions over all categories and ages in such a way as to maintain as far
as possible the career prospects originally planned.

The fact that the General List entry is determined solely by career prospects means
that it is fixed quite independently of the number of junior officers required and
cannot be varied to meet short term fluctuations in strengths or requirements. This
gives maximum stability in General List career prospects but means greater dependence on
the other two officer streams to cope with fluctuations. This approach also requires
maximum stability in numbers of promotions to Commander from year to year, subject to the
need to produce the correct strengths. Minor fluctuations are therefore smoothed out by
fixing promotion rates which it is hoped can be used for 2-3 years ahead. They are
reviewed regularly and altered when necessary.

In producing Figure 2 the first step is to deal with SD officers – the numbers being
fixed by the number of suitable posts and by the promotion potential amongst naval
ratings. The other two streams are closely interlocked because of the planned transfer
of 35% of SL survivors to the General List at age 27, where they enjoy the full GL
career prospects. The set of entry rates shown represents the unique solution to the set
of assumptions regarding strengths and retirement ages, etc., specified in Figure 2 and
Table 3. A fuller account is given in an article on officer career planning published in
the Operational Research Society Journal.

If the plan in Figure 2 were accepted the General List entry would become 54 at
once because it is based on long term considerations and not the present position. The
SD intake would not necessarily become 35 immediately – the balance between supply and
demand for officers over the next few years would be taken into account. The SL intake
would depend even more on short term forecasts and might be quite different from 38 for
some time.

7.2. Career Implications of Different Entry Streams

Just as women entries and promotees from the clerical grade enhance the career
prospects of male direct entry executives so do SL and SD officers enhance the prospects
of the General List which would otherwise only be 35% to Commander instead of 60%. But
whereas such enhancement is something of a by-product in the case of civilian staff, it
is specifically planned for in the case of RN officers by employing the three distinct
streams. This career aspect is not however the sole reason for having the Supplementary
and Special Duties Lists. They are in any case needed to give greater flexibility in
strengths, to meet certain manning needs (e.g. aircrew) and to give an outlet to naval
ratings.

It is clearly desirable that employees in all walks of life should have full
opportunities to rise as high as their potentialities will take them. It is an interesting reflection that this socially desirable policy improves prospects of both naval
ratings and career officers, and so makes it possible to offer better terms to attract
the more highly qualified entrant.

8. PROJECTION OF RN OFFICER STRENGTHS

Turning to the question of projections of existing strengths, projections up to
10 years ahead are produced every six months or so for each Royal Navy officer branch,
rank and entry stream. These forecasts are compared with estimates of requirements over
the next 10 years in order to review current promotion rates and SL and SD entry
targets. These comparisons in conjunction with the steady state calculations also

provide the basis for many policy decisions dependent on the numerical position.

Progression of RN officers up the career scale is based on seniority; only retirements being governed by age. All promotions within each cohort take place over a fairly narrow and specific seniority zone – thus all promotions to Captain might occur between 7 and 9 years seniority as a Commander.

Projections start with a complete age and seniority distribution of current strengths in each rank. The number at seniority x is diminished by the appropriate probability of wastage to give the survivors at seniority $(x + 1)$ a year later, due allowance being made for the spread of the planned annual promotion rates over the promotion zone. At the end of the zone, those remaining unpromoted then have to be projected by age to allow for retirements. This switch from a seniority to an age projection basis introduces some complications. In view of the precisely defined promotion zones, short term trends in career-factors can be derived readily from the forecasts.

9. CIVILIAN STAFF PROJECTIONS

In the case of civilian Executive staffs existing strengths are first projected by age for one year only. This gives forecast numbers of promotion vacancies in grades A and B and entries into grade C. Age specific probabilities of promotion from B to A based on the accumulated experience of recent years are then applied to the current staff in B and the resulting promotions at individual ages scaled up or down to accord with the total number of promotion vacancies already forecast – similarly with promotions from C to B. The procedure is then repeated for each subsequent year of the forecast period. It is necessary to divide the staff into groups of entry ages and deal with each group separately in order to allow broadly for seniority and also for the fact that promotion prospects vary with entry age as indicated in Table 2. All this involves a substantial volume of computations – which however lend themselves to computer processing.

The use of age-specific promotion rates based on the past is, of course, simply a device for arriving at a sensible age-distribution of promotions in view of the wide spread of promotion ages and the fact that, unlike the case of RN officers, there are no specific promotion zones. The total numbers of promotions allowed for each year are based solely on the forecasts.

Whether forecasting RN officers or civilians it may occasionally be necessary to use wastage rates which vary in time as well as with age – e.g. if an important change in medical standards for invaliding were contemplated.

10. SUMMARY

To sum up briefly: steady state models are a valuable planning aid in indicating long term career prospects and in providing a ready means of assessing the career implications of alternative schemes. They play a special part in RN officer planning in that the current recruiting rate for GL officers is actually the steady state figure. Projections of existing strengths are also of fundamental importance but mainly for comparing supply and demand, for fixing entry targets (other than GL officers) and estimating numbers of promotions in the short term. Owing to the time scale and possible existence of temporary factors affecting promotion these projections give only a limited view of future trends in career factors. But such planning methods are designed to provide practical answers to practical problems and have been used for a good many years.

A Model of Defence Manpower Availability

W.V. WEBB

MINISTRY OF DEFENCE (U.K.)

INTRODUCTION

The number of men that a country requires in its armed forces is determined by military commitments for its own defence and for the fulfilment of treaty arrangements with other countries. The recruiting targets necessary to achieve and maintain this strength, including men under training, can then be set.

These targets may be met by voluntary recruitment supplemented by conscription or selective conscription, and many countries use this dual method. In Great Britain conscription was discontinued in 1961. Sufficient time has now elapsed for most of the effects of conscription to have worn off, and the British Armed Forces may be regarded as an example of forces maintained entirely by voluntary recruitment. Under such a system it is prudent to compare target requirements with forecasts of the probable future achievements regarding recruitment and strength so that problems may be foreseen in time for remedial action to be taken.

This paper considers in general terms some of the factors affecting such forecasts, and then examines numerically the effect of changes in two of the factors by means of a hypothetical model. The two factors considered are the total number of births and the average age of recruitment.

NATIONAL MANPOWER

Recruits for the armed forces can come only from the pool of national manpower over the minimum school leaving age — at present 15. The total number of men available are the survivors of those born in past years, adjusted for net migration, for those who are continuing in full-time education, and for those few who, because of permanent incapacity, are neither in education nor employment.

Many of the recruits to the armed forces come straight from full-time education, and the primary numbers available for recruitment may be taken as the outflow from the educational system. Apprentices and other civilian trainees also customarily enter their training on leaving full-time education. This training often lasts four or five years and those who enter upon it are unlikely to provide many recruits to the armed forces.

Of those available for the armed forces, however, not all are suitable. Certain minimum standards regarding education, ability, physique and character have to be met. In addition the need to maintain physical fitness means that those in the armed forces cannot serve to as high an age as they could in civil employment. This imposes a limitation on the ages of recruitment and most recruits are obtained at ages 15 to 19. Although men do join the forces at ages up to 33, the numbers diminish rapidly as the age increases.

Suppose then that a certain proportion of those born in a particular year are known to have joined the forces voluntarily, can it be assumed that in future a similar proportion of each birth cohort will join the armed forces? And can we also assume that the age-spread will be the same as before? There are a number of changing influences which come immediately to mind.

The resources which other employers are prepared to devote to recruiting may have a noticeable effect on the armed forces and this may be linked to the economic circumstances of the country as a whole.

Another factor is the tendency of children to stay on longer in full-time education. It would be unrealistic to assume, without supporting evidence, that those who in future leave full-time education at 18, will be as likely to join the armed forces as those, who, in the past left at say 17. For instance they may have obtained higher qualifications in full-time education than those leaving at the younger age and hence would be eligible for a wider range of occupations.

A different complication is that migration since the war has brought about a change in the ethnic composition of the population. Births among immigrants and their descendants will constitute an increasing proportion of future births. Both the rate of application to join the armed forces and the ability to pass the various acceptance tests, may be different for the children of these immigrants from the corresponding factors for the indigenous population.

Some other factors may also be important: the increasing use of automation may diminish competition; the influence of the industrial training boards established by recent legislation may diminish the advantages of technical training in the forces; the general climate of opinion towards the armed forces can react on recruitment; the shrinking opportunities for service overseas may reduce the attractiveness of a service career.

If a decline in recruitment occurred, the forces might be able to mitigate its effect on strengths if they could encourage men to remain longer in service. Effective service might also be increased if higher ages at recruitment, carrying with them higher educational qualifications, and new training methods permitted shorter duration of training. The problems are numerous and complex and a great deal of research and study goes on all the time towards solving them, but they are outside the scope of this paper.

THE HYPOTHETICAL MODEL

The numbers available for recruitment depend in the first instance on the outflow from full-time education. The outflow is determined by the number of births that have occurred in past years, adjusted for deaths and net migration, and the ages at which boys leave full-time education. The observed tendency to stay on longer at school is likely to continue and to be accentuated by the planned increase from age 15 to 16 in the minimum school leaving age. This tendency is expected to cause an increase in the average age at recruitment to the armed forces. Changes in the number of births and in the average age at recruitment are features we have to accept and adjust to, and these are the only factors which are varied in the model.

Other factors are assumed to remain constant throughout the period investigated, although as already indicated, many of them could be influenced by appropriate changes in the conditions governing entry, training and service. Thus in the model constant length of service, wastage and re-engagement rates have been assumed irrespective of age at entry, and the strength at the start of the period has been run-down in conformity with these assumptions so as to avoid any distortion of the results. To simplify the arithmetic, recruitment has been assumed to occur only at the main ages of entry.

If the total number ultimately recruited from each birth cohort does not change there will nevertheless be a drop in annual recruitment so long as the average age of recruitment of boys born in successive years continues to increase. The effect on the strength of the armed forces lasts for a considerably longer time than the effect on annual recruitment, and does not completely wear off until a period of years equal to the sum of the period of shortage in recruitment and the maximum length of service of these recruits has elapsed.

Similar results are obtained if there are changes in the numbers recruited from each birth cohort.

164

The model deals only with the total numbers and does not attempt an analysis by quality. When considering the results obtained from the model it is important to bear in mind that variations in the numbers with special qualifications or skills may be quite different from those in the overall total.

PREDICTIONS FROM THE MODEL

The diagram shows four graphs all with the same time scale for ease of comparison, which should be considered in two pairs. The graphs showing level of recruitment (marked A) display changes in recruitment which lead to the changes in strength indicated by the graphs of relative strength (marked B). The implications of these predictions will be discussed in detail.

The changes in recruitment shown by graph A1 are the result of assuming that there will be an increase in the average age at recruitment throughout the period and that the total number of recruits obtained from each birth cohort will be a uniform proportion of the actual numbers of male births in the United Kingdom. The increase in the average age at recruitment is greatest among those recruited from the birth cohort first affected by the expected change in the school leaving age, and shows up as a discontinuity on the graph. The recovery in strength (see B1) occurs a few years after the recovery in recruitment.

Reasons have already been given why it may be unrealistic to assume that voluntary recruitment will bring in the same proportion of each birth cohort. In conditions of full employment competition from other employers may be enough to reduce the proportion of each birth cohort who enter the armed forces, and an alternative basis for forecasting must be sought which would make allowance either directly or indirectly for this.

The limited information so far available suggests that, in a period not subject to major changes in conditions affecting recruitment, the number recruited at a given age may bear a nearly constant relationship to the number available for recruitment. At the youngest age, this number is the outflow from full-time education. At other ages the number available may be taken as the number leaving full-time education plus those of the same age who left full-time education earlier, and who are not yet committed to a chosen career. Thus those who have already entered upon a course of professional training or apprenticeship which extends beyond the main ages of entry to the forces would be excluded. Those who have entered the forces at a younger age, or who have applied and been rejected for the forces would also be excluded. The relationship would have to be tested over a period of years to confirm its validity, but until this can be done it seems reasonable to use it as an experimental basis for forecasts.

Factors of this kind were worked out on a basis consistent with other elements in the model and assumed to remain constant from 1967 onwards. The resulting variations in the level of recruitment and the corresponding changes in strengths are illustrated in graphs A2 and B2. The level of recruitment is lower than that based on a uniform proportion of each birth cohort, particularly after 1971, and the corresponding strength of the forces also falls increasingly below the earlier estimate with passage of time.

The marked divergence after 1971 of the estimates on the two bases is caused by the severity of the assumption made on the second basis that the numbers recruited after 1971 can be assessed by applying the same factor to age 16, for example, after that date as before, in spite of the assumed disappearance of 15 year old recruits as a result of the increase in minimum school leaving age. This is tantamount to saying that the attitude of those who would otherwise have joined the forces at age 15 will change to that of those who now join the forces at age 16. In the event, it may well be found that the rate of joining will increase at age 16, and recruitment will be at a level between that indicated by the two graphs. A closer estimate might be obtained nearer the time with the·aid of an attitude survey among those who are going to be affected by the change in school leaving age. At the present time it can be said, however, that variations in the number of births, and in the age of recruitment are likely, other

CHANGES IN LEVEL OF RECRUITMENT AND RELATIVE STRENGTH OF THE ARMED FORCES
DERIVED FROM THE HYPOTHETICAL MODEL

(1) recruitment from each birth cohort proportional to the number of births
(2) recruitment of a constant proportion of the numbers available at each age

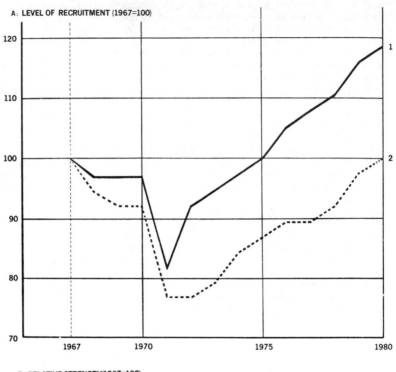

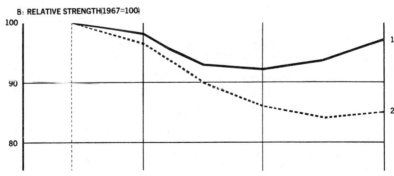

CALENDAR YEAR

factors remaining constant, to cause a fall in recruitment during a period of about ten years, and to cause a decline in strength to about 90 per cent of the present strength by the late 1970's.

FURTHER RESEARCH

Steps are being taken to extend the range of statistics available. This may take a long time to complete and some of the information may be obtainable only at a national census. The intention is to construct more sophisticated models which would cater for variations in as many factors as possible which can be isolated and expressed in mathematical form. Various levels of qualification and technical skill would be incorporated, and forecasts by quality and geographical region attempted.

Part II THE WORKING OF MILITARY SYSTEMS

Research from the Point of View of Decision Makers and Senior Administrators

L.J. DUNNETT

PERMANENT UNDER-SECRETARY OF STATE
MINISTRY OF DEFENCE (U.K.)

My task today is to talk to you about research from the point of view of decision makers and senior administrators, with particular reference, of course, to manpower research in the defence context. This happens to be a subject in which I am particularly interested, since I was Permanent Secretary for four years in the Ministry of Labour before I came to the Ministry of Defence a year ago.

First may I say a word about research and senior administrators? Clearly good administration should be lively administration and forward looking. If one were to make a criticism of public administration as it operates in the United Kingdom it would be that too many administrators regard it as their prime duty to keep the " in " tray clear. But if administration is to be forward looking and lively, clearly it must be served by, and make full use of, forward looking research. Society is changing so fast and technology advancing so quickly that any forward planning that is not so supported is not going to be very successful.

When I refer to research, I mean research in all those areas and in all those disciplines that may have a contribution to make to the kind of forward planning to which I have referred. Manpower research involves, of course, economists and statisticians, but there are important contributions to be made also by the sociologists, the psychologists, and the social anthropologists.

I. THE RECENT GROWTH OF INTEREST IN MANPOWER PLANNING

In a paper prepared for me recently, the statement was made that the need for manpower planning and manpower research has become widely apparent in the United Kingdom only in the last five years and that it was worth considering why wide interest in manpower was so recent. (If I were to be immodest, I might observe that it was exactly five years ago that I became Permanent Secretary of the Ministry of Labour, but as you all know post hoc does not necessarily mean propter hoc.)

What then has created this wide interest in manpower? One view is that the first condition necessary before an extensive interest can develop is that there should be a general awareness of the risk of shortage and that a shortage may hamper the fulfilment of the plans of Government Departments, of industry and of managements generally. When managements become aware that manpower is a scarce resource and that the unaided market mechanism cannot provide the requisite skills at the right time and place, then managements begin to pay as much attention to manpower as they do to other factors. They begin to realize that people are their most valuable asset.

Now, of course, there is a good deal of truth in that view, but it is, I think, deficient in certain respects. I think it fair to point out that the growing interest in the United Kingdom in manpower planning stemmed from, or at any rate was actively fostered by, the interest in national planning and from a dissatisfaction with the stop-go working of the economy. Perhaps I could say a brief word on these related topics.

As soon as people began making a national plan, i.e. asking themselves what would be involved in promoting and sustaining a faster rate of economic growth, say 3% or 4% per annum, the importance of manpower, particularly skilled manpower, stood out like a sore thumb. What was also immediately apparent was that the working population in the United Kingdom is likely, over the next 10 to 15 years, to grow very little indeed, which meant that if anything like a 4% rate of growth was to be achieved, much better utilization of labour and greater productivity were essential. All experience since the war has shown that when the economy is in a boom condition shortages of labour develop in most areas of the country. In such a situation wage rates get out of control, balance of payments crises ensue, and it then becomes necessary to apply the brakes.

It was, I think, out of this kind of thinking that the current interest in manpower planning and manpower research developed. It was essentially, however, an activity that started in the Government Departments concerned, particularly the DEA and the Ministry of Labour, and even now I doubt whether the majority of managements in industry give the subject all the attention it deserves.

I have mentioned the importance, if sustained growth is to be achieved, of obtaining higher productivity. Perhaps I could say a few words on this subject now.

2. MEANS OF ACHIEVING HIGHER PRODUCTIVITY

2.1. Technological Change

Improved technological efficiency and technical innovation are probably the least painful sources of increased productivity. But technological change may create an accelerating need for redeployment of manpower between skills, between occupations, between employers, between industries and between localities.

If the benefits of technological change are not to be dissipated in the future as they have so often been in the past, in the form of under-utilized resources (and particularly in the forms of over-manning, localized unemployment and scarcity of essential skills) then the future deployment of manpower must become a major preoccupation of Government and managements. At both the national and the employer levels we must make a better co-ordinated attempt to foresee change and provide for it.

2.2. Improved Management

Improved management is another and obvious way in which improved productivity can be achieved. Better manpower planning is one aspect of improved management. Another is the use of the various management services and management sciences which aim at better utilization of current as well as future resources. In step with the growth in awareness of the importance of manpower resources in the United Kingdom there has been a remarkable upsurge of interest in the management sciences. The creation of new University Business Schools and University Departments of Management and of Operational Research, most of which have a declared interest in manpower planning and research, is one result of this new interest. Job analysis, training research, advanced computer schemes and management information systems are some of the aids for management which are now accepted as essential.

2.3. The Importance of Sociological Research

There has also recently been a growing awareness of the value of sociological research as a source of improved management. Fact-finding and attitude or opinion surveys are an obvious branch of sociological work which can help to improve the knowledge of management. Then again there is the growing range of studies of group-conflict, organizational change and resistance to change. Resistance to change (whether it be given the label " restrictive practices " or " adherence to tradition ") can cause inefficient use of manpower resources in any organization. Industrial managers, civil servants, scientists, trades unionists and members of the Armed Forces are all capable of resisting change. One of the potentially most valuable contributions which the sociologist can make is to produce in us an awareness of our own tendency to resist change because it is change. Conflict between the established orders on the one hand, and the need for new specialisms and new forms of organization on the other can distort assessments of future manpower needs, and hence diminish the chance that these needs will be met.

3. MANPOWER RESEARCH AND THE ADMINISTRATOR

Against this background, what are the factors arising from manpower research and planning which concern the administrator? First, of course, there is the accuracy of the forecasts of manpower supply and demand. Everyone concerned with manpower planning and research understands the great difficulty of producing realistic forecasts, for even a few years ahead, of the demand and supply of different types of skill. The challenge presented by this forecasting, with its delicate balance of practical and theoretical issues, is one of the most difficult with which the statistician has to deal. But when the forecasts have been made, and the limits of their reliability established, it falls to the administrator to decide on the action that must be taken on both the demand and supply sides of the equation.

For example; it may be necessary to take action to increase the supply of certain types of manpower, so demanding investment in education and training and in employment advisory services. Again, especially in the light of the rapid change which is a feature of the modern economy, schemes of re-training will often be required. Another problem may be the promotion of mobility between occupations and between geographical regions. This may require changes in wage structures, pension arrangements, measures of compensation and the provision of housing. All this must be done in this country against the background of a prices and incomes policy which, while providing for wage increases where they are essential for the re-distribution of labour, places severe limits on the wholesale use of monetary incentives to secure change.

These are just some of the administrative problems that arise from manpower research and planning and they are problems which occur both on the national scale and within the individual organization, be it firm or Government Department. Finally, of course, one of the problems to be considered is the level of resources to be invested in manpower planning and its ancillary services, such as re-training schemes, employment exchanges and the like. In theory, one might continue to invest in these services so long as the benefits they produced outweighed costs; but such a calculation is by no means easy to make. For example, how should one estimate the benefits arising from such services? Are they adequately measured by the increase in money incomes enjoyed by those who receive the benefit of the services? Or should we look for a measure in terms of savings, e.g. in the cost of looking for jobs, in the time spent between jobs, in lower recruitment costs, in lower employment benefits and so forth? These are clearly not exclusive approaches to this problem. But I mention them as illustrations of the need to produce some kind of estimate of the benefits arising from manpower planning and its associated services in order to make some reasoned judgment of how far one should go with the expansion of manpower research and associated policies.

4. MANPOWER RESEARCH IN THE DEFENCE CONTEXT

I have been talking so far about manpower research in the general national economic context. I would like to turn now to the problems of manpower research in relation to defence.

The first point I want to make is that, of course, in any democracy the broad allocation of resources as between various competing needs lies at the heart of politics. As Aneurin Bevan once said, politics is about priorities. I think we would be deluding ourselves if we thought that at the present time the voting populace as a whole gave defence a very high priority. Conflict between defence expenditure and social expenditure has, of course, a long past history behind it; it is still one of the primary problems of our time. The result is that pressure on the Services to obtain the maximum effectiveness from the resources available to them is as great as it has ever been. The need to improve efficiency in the business sense is paramount.

Then again, changing social attitudes require us to give deep thought to the methods of manning the forces. In the United Kingdom we no longer use conscription; we rely on voluntary recruitment. All the signs are that people are becoming increasingly reluctant to accept long engagements and are inclined to view them as undesirable restrictions on the freedom of individuals to change their jobs. This situation creates a need for careful research to establish what are the optimum forms of engagement structure, having regard particularly to current social attitudes and our ability to obtain enough recruits. In other words, we will have to give a lot of new thought to the problems of the size of the manpower force which Society is prepared to see allocated to defence and the price which Society is prepared to pay to recruit and retain such a force.

There are three other matters to which I should like briefly to refer. The rate of technical change, the specialized nature of the work and the comparatively short effective service life of armed forces manpower, makes the proportion of the Armed Forces devoted to training very high in comparison with industry. For that reason alone research into new methods of training and improved assessment of personnel aptitudes and potential are particularly important.

Secondly, we have to keep a careful eye on what is happening in the country's educational system. An increasing proportion of boys are staying longer at school and obtaining improved qualifications of one sort or another, and an increasing proportion are being retained in full-time education in the Universities and equivalent Institutions. Forecasts show a diminishing number of boys leaving school at the ages and with the qualifications from which most of our recruits have traditionally been drawn. This supply outlook, coupled with our increasing demand for advanced skills may well require us to adopt a radically new approach to the concept of rank and line/staff relationships in the Forces.

Industry is finding itself faced with similar problems and it was for reasons of this kind that over the last few years the Ministry of Labour has been instrumental in creating by Statute new Industrial Training Boards, of which, in due course, there will be close on 40. This by itself is an indication of the importance which is now attached in this country to industrial training and manpower planning as a whole.

Thirdly, I often feel that the Services get less than their due credit for the value to the country of the substantial output from the Forces each year of valuable skilled manpower. In considering the value the country obtains from its investment in defence, this is a factor which is too often ignored.

5. DEFENCE MANPOWER MANAGEMENT

I said in the introduction to this paper that the need for manpower planning and manpower research has become widely apparent in the United Kingdom only in the last five years. This is not to say that manpower planning and manpower research did not exist before then. In fact, the Armed Forces in the United Kingdom have been engaged in these activities for many years and they can fairly claim to have pioneered manpower planning and several branches of research. What we now need to do is to build on the foundations already laid the best possible organization for planning and research we can afford with a view to achieving more effective management and better-informed decisions. And, indeed, this is just what we are doing.

In the higher reaches of our manpower management structure we now have a member of the Government – the Minister of Defence (Administration) – who has as one of his primary responsibilities the oversight of manpower management throughout the Defence Forces; and we have a serving officer of four-star rank – the Chief Adviser (Personnel and Logistics) – with an overall responsibility for all Armed Forces personnel.

We have also recently created a Defence Manpower Studies Unit under the direction of a Chief Statistician which will be responsible for accelerating and co-ordinating work in the planning and research field. It will be responsible, for example, for the co-ordination of the manpower " management information " systems of the three Services, involving systematic examination of data sources and flows, management requirements and computer facilities. It will be developing, by further improvement of single-Service methods, a range of advanced forecasting techniques. It will aim at increased precision and continued refinement of information, bearing in mind the need to minimize the very real risk that management may be misled by vague terminology, and by too hazy a notion of the meaning of words which are used as expressions of quantity and of quality or qualification.

Much of the work of the DMSU will involve team-work by statisticians, economists, behavioural scientists and others and much of it could be classified as operational research. We believe that the Unit will provide valuable and interesting experience of the use of the multi-disciplinary attack on manpower problems by a small team located within management. The staff of the unit will work closely not only with the management and policy departments of the three Services and the Central Defence Staffs, but also with the Staffs of several other Government Departments which are involved in manpower and economic policy. They intend also to work closely with a number of University departments and other research organizations who have interests in these fields, and we are most encouraged by the interest which several of these are taking in our affairs. We are pleased, too, with the interest taken by a number of industrial concerns, and by our friends overseas. We have gained, and hope to continue to gain, a great deal from the exchange of ideas and experiences with them.

No hard and fast rules about the staffing and future of the Unit are being made. The Unit will have to justify itself by its results. The work done will need to be of first-class quality from the professional and academic point of view, but will also have to be done with speed and efficiency. Policy decisions must often be taken at short notice, and cannot await the setting-up and carrying through of lengthy research programmes. The new Unit, therefore, will need to serve the needs of management, not only by making sure that the best available management-information is supplied as required, but also by trying to anticipate future needs when it is setting up data banks, computer-based models and research programmes. It will need to keep itself very well informed of developments and likely developments throughout the manpower field, and it is for that reason that we have located the Unit at the heart of the management structure.

6. CONCLUSION

To sum up, I have tried to indicate the importance which is now attached in the United Kingdom to manpower research in the national context and the increasing import-ance which we attach to it in the defence context. I am quite sure that as society changes, we may also have to change our views pretty radically about the type of men and women who are prepared to join the Services, the training they expect to get in the Services, and the periods for which they are prepared to serve. It is because of the vital importance of all these problems that I so welcome the holding of this conference in London and how much we look forward to seeing the results of your deliberations.

The Role of Research in Military Manpower Management

EUGENE T. FERRARO
DEPUTY UNDER SECRETARY (MANPOWER)
DEPARTMENT OF THE AIR FORCE (U.S.A.)

I. INTRODUCTION

Just fifty years ago this month, a long and fruitful partnership was initiated between the behavioural scientists and the United States Armed Services. On August 17, 1917, a Division of Psychology was established in the Medical Department of the War Department. Its staff, consisting of a handful of bright young psychologists, had as its assignment the application of the emerging techniques of psychological testing to some of the unprecedented manpower and personnel problems generated by the World War I mobilization. Among the contributions of this and associated groups were the Army Alpha and Beta tests, as well as other major innovations in personnel selection and classification.

These innovations, I might add, were not accepted without some trepidation on the part of those accustomed to more traditional techniques of handling military personnel matters. Three official investigations were conducted into the operations of this brash young group of scientists – the " whiz kids " of their day; but, military psychology survived these initial trials quite well. And, over the years, the contributions of the behavioural scientists to military manpower management have been progressively broadened to such additional functions as performance evaluation, training methodology, job analysis, human engineering, retention and morale studies, personnel systems analysis and demographic research – among others.

It would be tempting to dwell on the past and present accomplishments of research in these diverse areas. Many of you here are, however, far more familiar with these than I am. One tangible indication of the importance of this research in our defense effort, however, is the level of funds currently allocated for these activities within the Department of Defense. During the past fiscal year, a total of over $20 million was budgeted for manpower and personnel research studies in the Department of Defense; and even this sum, in the light of what confronts us, is now recognized as far less than adequate.

About half of the research supporting our personnel and training functions is performed by six research laboratories – two each in the Army, Navy and Air Force. Their staffs include about 350 professional personnel at the present time, mainly drawn from the behavioural sciences. More than a dozen other research centres or activities with primary missions in such related fields as medical research, human engineering or weapon systems analysis also perform certain research projects related to manpower and personnel management problems.

The efforts in all of these centres have resulted in such innovations as the Air Force Qualitative and Quantitative Personnel Requirements Information, i.e., the QQPRI system which enables us to predict manpower and training needs which will be generated by weapon systems under development. In addition, our research funds support a number of projects performed by universities and other nongovernmental research organizations.

Almost immediately after joining the Department of the Air Force in June 1966, I made a point of visiting the principal Air Force activities engaged in personnel research: the Personnel Research Laboratory in Texas and the Behavioural Sciences Laboratory in Ohio. I also visited the various activities of the Air Training Command, the Air University, and the Air Force Academy to see how the education and training function was being performed and to determine the actual and possible impact of research on their performance.

I also consulted intensively with Mr. Thomas Morris, the Assistant Secretary of Defense (Manpower), and with my counter-parts in the other Service Departments to get a broader appreciation for the total personnel research effort.

Several facts soon became evident:

(i) The key professional staffs in all our personnel research activities are highly qualified; and they have accumulated some valuable data, and achieved some notable results.

(ii) There is present a challenge to both top manpower and personnel management officials and those directing and performing research to attain superior two-way communications between these major factors of an effective personnel system. Those of us in the management sector can insure that the researchers have available to them an appropriate perspective to identify the problem areas in which we will most need personnel research contributions in the coming years. We can also improve the utilization of the data and results attained in our research effort by making it more widely available to all segments of the personnel system. This better communication and perspective, I believe, will help to direct our research effort toward improvement of the personnel system as a whole, rather than toward specific functional areas as has sometimes been true in the past.

2. THE PATTERN OF PERSONNEL RESEARCH TODAY

A broad functional classification of research projects funded in the past fiscal year shows that the largest single area of research support was for training methodology, which alone accounted for a total of nearly $15 million, or 65%, of the total Department of Defense manpower and personnel research effort. Three other areas — namely, general psychological research, operational performance evaluation and job analysis-type studies — accounted for most of the balance. All other categories of manpower and personnel research, including selection methods, supply and requirements, planning systems, studies of retention and morale, and of the personnel distribution and assignment systems, among others, accounted for less than $3 million, or about 12.5% of the total.

Within the last mentioned manpower and personnel area, the bulk of the research effort may — I believe — be described as follows:

First, it consists of applied or developmental research geared to the production of a specific management tool or method, such as a revised training curriculum, a more effective measure of operational performance, a better selection test, or an assessment of task requirements for particular functions or occupations.

Second, in developing these new personnel and training tools, the approach has generally been one of " sub-optimization ". A personnel selection or aptitude test is validated, for example, in terms of its ability to predict success or failure in particular training courses. A training curriculum or methodology is geared to assure more efficient training in a specific course or group of courses, and so forth.

Finally, because of the nature of the projects the research has been very largely conducted by one scientific discipline, namely psychology, in association with methodologists, such as operations researchers and statisticians.

In this context, it may be helpful to cite some of the findings of a critical self-analysis conducted by one of the major training research activities of the Defense Department. This analysis focused first on those factors which contributed to the successful implementation of its research products and, conversely, on those conditions which hindered their acceptance.

Among those factors which contributed to successful implementation were listed –

(i) Timeliness – " The product filled a recognized instructional gap ... ".

(ii) Command Interest – " There was a strong operational command interest to include that of a subordinate command ".

(iii) Product Engineering – " The end product was a plug-in item specifically engineered for a given situation ... ".

(iv) Concreteness – " A material item, such as a complete lesson plan or a training device with user handbook, was provided".

(v) Personal Interest – " An individual officer or officers became convinced of the worth of the product, and were willing to serve as forceful and determined proponents".

(vi) Zeitgeist – i.e., " some other Service, foreign army, or civilian institution had accepted the product or a similar one. In other words, the product was not excessively novel".

The unused research products, in turn, generally lacked these characteristics. They suffered from handicaps of poor communication, lack of timeliness or strong command interest, or they may have been too costly. In particular, they were less likely to be adopted if they were more far-reaching in their impact upon the system, if they required many related changes in procedures, and – as the writer expressed it – " if the product appeared to question a 'sacred cow', that is, attack current practices, individual competence, tradition, or long-accepted doctrine".

This self-appraisal suggested that the researcher, at least in this organization, has been discouraged from initiating recommendations of large scope, with potentially major impacts upon the personnel system, for the very reason that they might entail a whole cycle of related changes in the system.

Yet, these recommendations of great scope are precisely the issues which top management must face up to, and make decisions about in its daily activities. These decisions may involve a change in manpower procurement strategy, a revision in selection standards, a revised system of compensation, or perhaps a revised policy for officer-career management. All of these decisions have several things in common. They require a clear appreciation of the wide ranging impacts of possible changes upon the personnel system as a whole. Such decisions require a capability to evaluate alternatives in terms of their costs and of their impacts upon force effectiveness. Finally, they may involve judgments of other relevant parameters, including possible implications for national manpower policy beyond the military establishment itself.

3. RESULTS OF PERSONNEL RESEARCH

3.I. Development of Mental Test Standards

One important military personnel policy which has received a great deal of attention in the Department of Defense in the past two years has been the establishment of appropriate mental test standards for qualification for service by our enlistees and inductees. Our Military Services, as you know, have employed for many years a standard psychological screening test, the Armed Forces Qualification Test (AFQT), as the primary measure of mental fitness for service. Those individuals receiving a percentile score of less than 10 have been disqualified by law; those in a marginal passing range with scores from 10-30, inclusive, have been subjected in recent years to a supplementary screening aptitude test battery. The passing requirements under this aptitude test battery have varied, and had become rather severely high in the years immediately preceding our military buildup for Vietnam.

Our mental fitness standards had gradually been raised and, in turn, contributed to a steady increase in rejection rates among candidates for military service from about 24% in the early 1950's to an estimated rate of 35% by 1965. These rates, I might add, include rejections for both medical and moral reasons as well as for failure on the mental tests. Mental test deficiencies account for about one-half of the total rejected.

These high rejection rates became a source of concern at policy levels well before the beginning of our Southeast Asia buildup. These standards had deprived many young men with limited education, but who were potentially capable of serving, of an equal opportunity to enter military service. This included many young men who had come to our recruiting offices and were eager to serve. At the same time, the burden of the military service obligation, through the draft, was being disproportionately borne by other groups in our population. Moreover, these " rejected " men who fell in this marginal group would have been legally qualified for service in the event of a declared national emergency. Farsighted military manpower planning appeared to call for perfecting a capability to effectively train and utilize this so-called " marginal " manpower resource in advance of any such contingency.

In this assessment, we turned our attention first to the mental tests themselves. What were they designed to measure? How reliable were they? It was clear that the aptitude tests were designed for a very specific purpose; that is, to predict success or failure in formal training courses for the higher qualifying mental categories. They were validated against this criterion and appeared to perform this function well; that is, those with high scores on the aptitude tests had a greater chance of successfully completing the course; those with poorer scores, a lesser chance.

This was in essence all that the psychologists, who had developed the tests, could tell us, and perhaps all we could expect from them. Yet, what we needed to know to make an intelligent management decision was much more. First, we required information on the total manpower supply which might be available for service through enlistment or induction under possible alternative lower standards under study. Secondly, we needed estimates, or judgments, on the possible consequences of any modification in the existing standards for our training system as a whole — including basic training, formal specialist training, and on-the-job training. What would be the possible effects upon costs, and upon the ability of the training establishment to produce the required number of fully qualified specialists in a wide range of skills?

Looking beyond the training phase, it seemed even more important to assess the impact of changes in test standards upon military performance — the capability of our commanders in the field to perform their assigned missions. We were particularly concerned about the apparent relationship between low mental test scores and the probable higher incidence of disciplinary problems suggested by earlier experience.

Much of the information which might have been desirable to arrive at judgments of this type was not readily at hand. It was accumulated and developed to the extent possible by the Office of the Secretary of Defence and the Military Departments, from a wide range of sources. It was supplemented by first-hand visits and discussions with those responsible for selection and training of our personnel. From this assessment there did emerge a judgment that a progressive, carefully phased reduction in our aptitude standards was both feasible and desirable.

3.2. Project 100,000

This program, which has just been described and which was announced by Secretary McNamara in 1966, is referred to by us as Project 100,000 since the Secretary stated this as a goal for the number of additional men, not previously qualified, who would be accepted in this coming year under our revised standards. This program, I should emphasize, is not merely a reduction in standards. What makes the current effort unique is the conscious effort of management to accomplish this broadening of our manpower procurement base while maintaining the necessary quality and effectiveness of our operating forces.

From our studies to date, we are convinced that this is a completely realistic objective. To accomplish this objective, we have set ourselves a series of closely integrated tasks to be performed on a phased basis, ranging from improvements in our initial selection procedures to necessary modifications in processing, in training methods and curricula, and to job re-engineering, where feasible.

Against this background, it is relevant to ask, " What role did research play in the decision making process, and what role can research play in support of the implementation of this program? "

In the early phases of our policy review on this project we, of course, had examined a wide range of past personnel research studies. A review of these studies supported our conclusion that the present aptitude test screening procedures were much more relevant to success in academically oriented training courses than they were to actual military performance; at least in those military duties not requiring any great degree of technical skill. They also revealed that the widespread impression among many of our commanders that low mental category individuals necessarily accounted for disciplinary problems was a serious over-simplification of the actual facts. We found, for example, that the fact of high school graduation, irrespective of academic achievement or mental test score, was a much more significant predictor of ability to adjust well in military service than the score on the psychological test, per se. One Air Force study showed, for example, that high school dropouts scoring in Mental Group I, our highest mental category, had twice the frequency of behavioural problems than did high school graduates who received the lowest passing scores, i.e., Group IV' s.

In many other respects, however, the scope of available research to guide policy development in this area was found to be seriously deficient. We did not, for example, have available accurate estimates of the potential manpower supply which would be made available under various possible changes in our test scores or other screening criteria. These estimates were necessarily improvised, and in fact, turned out to be quite realistic; but, I am assured by those responsible for them that this was, at least in part, pure good fortune. Similarly, we lacked a sound factual basis for estimating the capability of each Military Service to utilize individuals from this marginal group in their various jobs. Some research had been initiated in this area but we lacked both a sound methodology and the necessary data in the time frame available. Above all, our review of the available research indicated a fragmentation of effort in which no integrated analysis had been attempted in any Service, of the implications of a reduction in these standards for their personnel system, as a whole. In these areas, we improvised as best we could.

4. THE ROLE OF PERSONNEL RESEARCH IN THE FUTURE

Looking ahead, personnel research can and will however play a very vital role in the re-engineering of our personnel system as initiated by Project 100,000. A series of specific tasks related to our overall program objectives has been developed in close consultation with top manpower officials of the Military Departments and with their research experts.

To begin with, Secretary McNamara directed that we maintain a complete data bank for each individual accepted under this program which will follow him through his entire service career and will continue on beyond that to measure his post-service adjustments and working experiences in civilian life – the latter necessarily on a sample basis. This data bank has already been structured, including provisions for appropriate control groups; and we are already making plans for designing the post-service follow-up of those who will be leaving the service in the next year or two. It will include a comprehensive series of measures of the characteristics and aptitudes, training assignments and performance records of these individuals.

Secondly, we have initiated a number of short range research tasks designed for early implementation under this program. In the area of selection, for example, we are developing supplementary tests to measure the vocational maturity and self-confidence of those newly qualified, at various stages of their service careers. In addition, we are conducting special tests of reading ability to identify those individuals who may need special educational assistance in this vital skill early in their service career. In the area of training, a total of 37 specialist occupation courses have been selected for intensive review and modification in order to facilitate the successful completion of these courses by these men of limited educational achievement. We are exploring the feasibility of job restructuring as a means of increasing the utilization of these men in a broader range of skills. One pilot study, pertaining to the Navy Hospital Corpsman specialty has already been initiated for this purpose.

In the Air Force, we have developed a data base including biographical inventory data and follow-up information on personnel in the Project 100,000 program which will be used to determine correlations between environmental factors and performance. The results of this research project will be used to enhance the effectiveness of our selection process and to isolate societal or locality factors which can be improved by specific training applications. Finally, we are now making plans for a longer-range research and development effort which will include a search for still better and fittingly applicable techniques of selection, training, and job organization.

In this paper, we have selected but one program, Project 100,000, as an illustration of the exciting possibilities for concerted team work between management and the research scientist in the years ahead. There are equally challenging possibilities in many related aspects of military manpower management, in our military recruitment programs, in our efforts to improve retention of personnel, and in the complex area of military compensation and benefits, to name just a few. To realize these potentials will require a more effective relationship between management and the research community.

In order to identify the approach which would offer the greatest opportunity for improving our Air Force manpower and personnel research effort, the Air Force Scientific Advisory Board was requested to have its Ad Hoc Psychology and Social Sciences Panel make a detailed review of the research and analysis efforts within the Air Force.

We are hopeful that the consensus of these observations will provide an improved perspective for making our personnel research effort a more effective management tool. We are making progress toward this goal, and I want to emphasize several areas of particular significance:

(i) Management is taking a greater interest in research

Management has the responsibility for defining clearly the policy issues and problem areas in which research support is most needed. Since research, to be accomplished effectively, requires lead time, management is attempting to anticipate these problems and issues well in advance of the time frame in which the decisions must be made. This is not always possible in our highly dynamic environment; yet, I am convinced we will do a better job than we have in the past.

Management has an equal responsibility for careful and open-minded review of research findings and recommendations. Both the researcher and the manager are in a sense agents of innovation, and innovation means taking risks on new ways of doing things and some challenging of our " sacred cows ".

We have recognized the requirement for management to have the capability within its own immediate staff of communicating effectively to the researcher, defining research goals and tasks in a meaningful language, and – in turn – being capable of reviewing and interpreting technical research findings.

(ii) The personnel research effort is being structured and attuned to meet and anticipate the requirements of personnel management

To make intelligent judgments concerning implementation of research findings, as I have noted above, management must consider the full consequences of any course of action upon the personnel system as a whole – the costs entailed and the impacts upon our overall effectiveness. Management also properly wishes to assess the merits of alternative courses of action and to weigh them on the same scale. To be able to make a maximum contribution to the process of decision making, the research community, I believe, should broaden its own criteria and points of reference. Although specific research studies of the types now generally undertaken will continue to be necessary, we shall attempt in the future to use them as inputs into much more complex models of the personnel system as a whole. These models will be designed to incorporate the increasingly pertinent and accurate inputs we can devise. We shall also assure that they are susceptible to continuing modification as our policy parameters and our technology are changed.

Another adjustment which we are making in our research effort is a more clear delineation of responsibilities for conducting research and for its implementation. If management staffs include professional advisors to furnish " best judgment " advice regularly and frequently, the demands on the researchers' time for such advice will be reduced, and there will be less encroachment on the research effort to accomplish a management function. Of course, the researchers will continue to assist the professional experts in the solution of urgent problems.

(iii) Finally, it is clear that the information and assistance which we need in the area of military manpower management cannot be supplied by any single discipline.

The problems of human behaviour in a complex organization demand for their solution the concerted and integrated efforts of many related disciplines – the psychologist, the sociologist, the economist, and the operations analyst – to name just a few.

I do not believe, moreover, that simple propinquity of scientists from these separate disciplines is the ultimate answer. We intend to get the psychologist to think like an economist, and get the economist in turn to think like a psychologist at least in some measure. In the long run, the answer may well lie in the establishment of a new discipline of manpower science which will blend in one profession the necessary elements of all these separate fields of learning on a truly integrated fashion.

Meanwhile, and until that optimum is attained, I believe that the key to the greatest improvement in effective use of personnel research is to be found in communications. Management will provide the impetus and the guidance. Research will provide a structure and capability which are responsive to the needs of our society and of management. And both will keep the flow of information timely and understandable.

5. CONCLUSION

We are in the process of restructuring the manpower and personnel activities of our Military Departments to bring to them the management skills and techniques which have proven so effective in other areas of defense management, and in research and development generally. This approach to the human resources area can undoubtedly enable us to make still greater gains, but it will require very substantial research to give us knowledge comparable to that we have acquired in the physical sciences.

To perfect the manpower management will require organization strengthening which we have already initiated. Each Military Department has a Deputy Under Secretary for Manpower, and the necessary staff and working relationships with the military staffs are evolving.

We shall follow this initial restructuring with a continuing effort to exercise the organization so that it compiles the data; acquires the experience and expertise to measure and predict the results of new and changing personnel policies, and of new manpower development and utilization programs. We confidently expect a new order of improvement in the management of military personnel resources.

Of even more social significance, however, is the likelihood of greater appreciation of the benefits to be derived from fuller development and satisfaction of the individual in all walks of life, particularly among the disadvantaged or under-utilized. The Military Services have in the past served as leaders in many fields that have had a civil " fall out ". Good examples are the electronics industry and aviation as a whole. The human resources area seems ideally appropriate for similar and extensive gains.

The improvement in management organization, techniques and philosophy for which we are striving will rely heavily on personnel and manpower research and development. Not only will the present levels of research be raised to support necessary programs, but also the position of the research activities and their relationship to the general policy-forming and management officials will be carefully considered and enhanced.

We are conscious of our opportunity to make a major contribution to society through organization and research in a relatively new field – manpower. We anticipate significant gains from our efforts.

Manpower Studies at the Center for Naval Analyses

MARTIN A. TOLCOTT

LT. CDR. J.H. ARMITAGE

CENTER FOR NAVAL ANALYSIS, ARLINGTON, VA.

I. INTRODUCTION

In our society, manpower is a valuable resource. The value of our military manpower goes beyond the simple sum of their pay, allowances, and other forms of pecuniary and non-pecuniary benefits. At a minimum, it includes in addition the estimated value of their future contribution to society. Furthermore, under our form of government there are often political costs involved in decisions to increase our military manpower strength.

The impetus for our work stems from the continual obligation of the Navy, as well as the other services, to ensure that the manpower furnished to them is used as effectively as possible in order to minimize long-term manpower needs, and to provide a rational basis for the assessment of manpower options. Against this background we at the Center for Naval Analyses have directed our efforts toward identifying areas of study which appear most promising to improve the Navy's ability to control and efficiently utilize its manpower.

In this context, we are also attempting to evaluate indicators of manpower strength requirements used by other organizations with the objective of developing a means by which the Navy can more meaningfully express and communicate its manning requirements. On a broader level, we are hopefully building at the Center for Naval Analyses, a capability to identify and address problems of long-range significance to the Navy's Manpower Management sector.

This paper will describe, first, some of our work in making a survey of manpower utilization studies, as evaluated against a concept of how such studies should be contributing to the manpower planning process; second, some of the concepts of manpower planning in industry and other government agencies, including the other services and how they are applicable to Navy manpower planning problems; and third, a description of a way of ordering information by means of which the Navy's manpower planning process might be improved.

2. MANPOWER UTILIZATION STUDIES

2.I. Conceptual Framework

, Decisions as to how best to allocate funds available for studies have always been based more on implicit judgments of priority than on explicit criteria. In our survey of present manpower studies we tried to judge the relative contribution of various types of effort to questions of manpower planning. We did not judge their contribution to other problems. Nor did we compare the relative priority of " manpower planning ", with that of other problem areas. But the urgent need for rational cost-effectiveness criteria reinforces a high priority for studies contributing to the Navy's ability to apply these criteria to manpower, just as it does to hardware systems.

One of the early conclusions reached by our study group was that the term "manpower requirements" really refers to manpower "goals" or "objectives", and that these must be explicitly related to output goals in order to be convincingly expressed and communicated. Further, any specified output goal implies a flow of services which might be produced by alternative levels and "mixes" of manpower (and indeed by alternative mixes of men and machines). Finally, the effectiveness with which resources are used and goals or objectives defined, depends upon explicit knowledge by manpower managers of the costs of the many different mixes of manpower and machines that will produce a desired output.

Figure 1 shows how the cost-effectiveness view of manpower requirements plays a central role in understanding the relationships among various categories of study. The focal point of these relationships is the interaction of *manpower* planning factors with factors of primary concern for *personnel* administration and research.

Studies of the Manpower Planning process are concerned with understanding the available demand and supply options and exercising selected ones through policy decisions. Specifically, the planning level is concerned with the relationships between levels and mixes of manpower and degrees of Naval effectiveness or readiness. Also, since policy decisions must be based on cost comparisons, the cost implications of various manpower options must be known, and development of costing techniques should support the planning effort.

Planning can be aided by management information systems which help planners weigh options against desired accomplishments, predict subsidiary resource needs, and control the utilization of resources. Supporting research on management theory would be expected, leading to improved methods of management decision making and to more promising forms of management organization.

Data for manpower planning should be produced by supporting studies and research in three other broad areas of study: Military Jobs, Training Pipeline and Distribution, and Needs and Attitudes Affecting Retention and Well-Being.

Studies of military jobs involve the structuring of the jobs to be performed, based on work requirements and appropriate organization of functions and tasks to match the abilities of available personnel. They are also concerned with identifying human skills, experience and other characteristics consistent with the accomplishment of jobs at defined levels (or standards) of performance. These studies would include the relative effectiveness and costs of various man-machine alternatives for performing specified functions, and the application of human engineering principles to the design of systems to minimize manning and training requirements. Data from these studies should be used as a basis for estimating the appropriate manning for specific Naval activities, and data from validation studies should be available in manpower management information and control systems, and summarized into more general form to help managers examine and select from available options in planning future systems. In addition, such studies should produce data upon which training programs can be based.

Studies of Training Pipeline and Distribution are concerned with the development and supply of appropriately skilled personnel to fulfill manpower demands. They furnish the methods and criteria for recruitment, selection and classification, training, assignment, and performance evaluation.

Manpower goals established by planners depend on personnel availability and training requirements, since these factors affect manpower costs. Projected information about personnel distribution defines the feasibility of meeting various manpower demand alternatives. Difficult demands may be met by redistribution of skilled personnel, by provision of fewer skilled personnel, or by supplying personnel of lower or different skills. But rationality demands that the effects of these shifts be known in advance.

Thus, manpower planners should be able to look to studies we have categorized as Training Pipeline and Distribution, for concrete information about personnel development and supply: current and projected numbers, capabilities, and developmental costs under varying conditions of demand. Supporting studies in this area should also aim at improving the training and distribution processes.

Studies of Needs and Attitudes Affecting Retention and Well-Being are concerned with

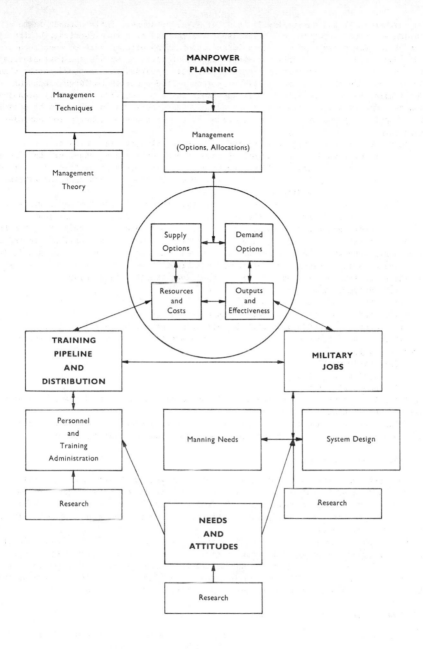

Fig. 1 SCHEMATIC MODEL OF RELATIONSHIPS
AMONG MANPOWER STUDY AREAS

the psychological and physical well-being of Naval personnel. Their purpose is to enhance motivation, morale, and selective retention and to ensure survival, health, and comfort insofar as is possible. To a large extent these efforts must be concerned with individual needs, particularly when they address problems of morale and psychological factors, and to that extent they are more correctly regarded as *personnel* rather than *manpower* considerations. However, if needs and attitudes common to large groups of individuals are found to affect their behaviour in ways significant for Navy planning, then the control and utilization of these people as groups, the development of policies with respect to them, and the costs involved, become matters of concern for manpower planners.

These studies are indirectly related to manpower planning in two ways:-
> (i) Insofar as attitudes affect enlistment and continuance behaviour, and there-fore costs, they should be measured to permit better prediction of future man-power supply, and to allow evaluation of the benefits and costs of alternative policies for modifying the behaviour;
> (ii) Insofar as incentives and environmental protection affect human performance on the job, their effects should be understood to permit better estimates of levels and types of manning needed to achieve specified levels of work output.

As the first step in our approach, a classification scheme was developed in the form of a matrix into which the studies being surveyed could be categorized. The matrix is built around several dimensions, as shown in table 1.

There are four major areas of study, shown down the left-hand column:
  (i) (Primary) Manpower Planning studies
  (ii) Studies of Military Jobs
  (iii) Studies of Training Pipeline and Distribution
  (iv) Studies of Needs and Attitudes Affecting Retention and Well-Being.

Within each of the above focal areas, there are three levels of effort, shown across the top:
  (i) Development
  (ii) Applied Research
  (iii) Basic Research.
Classification of studies into these levels was based on judgment of the nature of the work, rather than on the source of funds.

Within each area and level, there are 21 categories shown in the table, and over 100 subcategories as needed to comprehensively describe the subject matter.

2.2. Data Sources and Methods

The most important source of data for our study was the Research and Technology Résumés maintained by the Defense Documentation Centre for selected groups in the Behavioural and Social Sciences and Biological and Medical Sciences fields. These provide one- or two-page descriptions of research and exploratory development efforts at the work-unit level.

Of a total of about 2000 project descriptions and titles available, about 500 of the most relevant, representing a substantial portion of research and study efforts, were sorted into our classification scheme and summarized to describe their content, funding, and man years of effort. These summaries served as the basis for evaluating the *relevance* and *usefulness* of the efforts to the manpower planning process.

2.3. Evaluation Criteria and Illustrative Findings

To evaluate our material gathered through this survey, we asked ourselves a series of questions.

First: *Do Navy output goals, as now expressed, permit manpower planners to relate them to manpower goals? And can manpower levels falling short of currently stated man-power goals be translated into reduced levels of useful output?*

Most Navy fleet units — especially surface units — are designed to have a multi-purpose capability, although the probability of any of their designed missions actually

TABLE 1

STUDIES CLASSIFICATION SCHEME

Focus	Development	Applied Research	Basic Research
Manpower Planning (Command)	Manpower management	Manpower management techniques	Manpower management theory
Military Jobs	Determination and validation of manning needs Human engineering in specific system design	Job/occupational analysis Man-machine interfaces Group effectiveness	Performance processes
Training Pipeline and Distribution	Personnel and training administration	Selection and assignment Training	Aptitudes, abilities and individual differences Learning and forgetting
Needs and Attitudes Affecting Retention and Well-Being	Incentive development Design for human support and maintenance	Motivation and adjustment Psychological operations Protective health and sustenance materials and procedures	Processes in attitude change Psychophysiology

being called into play varies considerably with their location and the nature of the existing threat. The Navy's work output goals are defined mainly by the number and types of units being planned, and the relationship between manpower goals and work output goals should be explicitly exposed. These relationships are not easy to identify, but the techniques for doing so exist, and some data are becoming available.

One effort that appears promising for relating manpower goals to work output is the United States Navy's readiness analysis program. Unit and fleet commanders have been requested to identify functions which their units must perform under each of three operational alert conditions in three types of threat environment, and to determine the manning necessary to accomplish each function. The manning data will be gathered by the Navy's Manpower Validation Teams. The data which are being submitted are aggregated by ship type and related to the readiness levels specified by the Joint Chiefs of Staff. The importance of this effort lies in its attempt to identify explicit output options in terms of functions which can be performed simultaneously, and to define the conditions under which different readiness levels might be acceptable. The manning data for each function are needed before the effort can fulfill its promise for manpower planning. But when the work is completed, it should be possible for the Navy to better understand, and make more explicit, the specific implications of any reduction in manpower authorizations, at least in terms of functions which can or cannot be carried out simultaneously.

Several other efforts, in our category of military jobs, support this approach. One is a battle manning study designed to determine manpower requirements for specific classes of ships under circumstances placing maximum demand on manpower resources (continuous Condition III). Another is the work previously done on staffing criteria for ship and shore activities, in which workload indicators are identified for each type of function (such as number of messages processed by the communications department), and staffing standards are presented as variables related to the number of work units. This method of deriving and presenting manning needs lends itself to the better understanding of trade-offs between manpower and work outputs.

Predictions are also made of manning and training required in new development systems, before designs are firmed up. Historically these techniques have been applied more to systems and sub-systems than to complete ships. But there appears to be a welcome (although gradual) trend to examine the ship as a whole, and to make explicit the manning and cost implications of alternative ship designs.

A second fundamental question in manpower planning is: *what do we know about the effectiveness of various manpower mixes to accomplish group or team tasks? And have Naval tasks and jobs been organized to use the most economical mixes of manpower?*

The answer is: we know less than we should. Group effectiveness is not easy to measure, and much of the research in group performance is more concerned with inter-actions among people than with performance on realistic Navy tasks.

One significant program of studies is that concerned with ASW crew performance, initiated by the Scientific Advisory Team, ASW Forces Atlantic, and now being extended.

A related effort being sponsored by the Navy Department is an attempt to determine the extent to which existing reporting and information systems can provide data on the operational effectiveness of a unit as a function of the manning levels and mixes aboard. The results should lead to improvements in the management tools available for manpower planning.

The CNA-INS Manning II study was partially concerned with possibilities of varying manning mixes to achieve equally effective outputs at minimal cost. Degree of substitutability among different levels of personnel was determined through interviews with supervisors, and a Cobb-Douglas production function was applied to the data to determine the outputs.

Substitution of manpower, as a resource allocation problem, is a fundamental concern of manpower management. One type of substitution involves interchangeability between Navy and civilian personnel on those jobs which can be performed equally well by either. U.S. military services are under pressure to reduce their use of military manpower even though such reduction, if appropriate analytic tools were available, might be shown to increase costs to the services.

This raises another fundamental question: *what are the cost factors important to the decision makers in the Office of the Secretary of Defense (OSD)?* Cost studies are now exposing many Navy cost factors in some detail. But there are significant manpower cost implications at levels higher than the individual service. OSD is concerned, at the very least, with cost comparisons across services for performance of equivalent military missions. Further, economic studies are making OSD aware of the importance of considering the costs and benefits of alternative policies to society as a whole, and of including among the costs some which are not routinely levied against the service itself. From this point of view the true cost of military manpower is not just the budgetary cost of recruitment, training, compensation, housing, etc. It includes external costs perceived by decision makers but unfortunately not always made explicit by them, such as veterans' benefits and foregone private production, and reduced by the value of social benefits such as lower unemployment. Increasing awareness of this viewpoint may underlie the current emphasis on manpower reduction as well as toward the acceptance of more personnel in the low mental level categories by the Armed Forces.

The question of manpower mixes raises an even more fundamental question: *are the Navy's current manpower labels (rates, ratings, Enlisted Classification Codes, etc.,) easily related to effectiveness of performance in various types of task?* It appears that ratings and pay grades as descriptors of performance capability and of costs can be improved. A Chief Petty Officer in a soft rating, like commissaryman, usually has much more longevity than one in a hard rating like electronics technician. His longevity is costly and it is doubtful if this extra experience is needed in his occupation. On the other hand it may be important when he supervises a work gang. But our ability to describe and measure task performance on the job is so limited that it is difficult to determine what characteristics are most important.

Studies in task dimensions and job structuring are about equally divided between attempts to improve or refine the current Navy rating structure, and more fundamental studies of the dimensions underlying jobs and job structures. These latter studies are attempting to understand and describe tasks independently of the specific equipment used by the worker. They could lead to significant changes in the Navy's manpower planning ability.

Given the manpower categories now in use, can supply needs and distribution options be predicted for any specified demand?

Here there are some sophisticated tools available. The Bureau of Naval Personnel has developed several information systems and simulation models useful in predicting the necessary buildups and lead times for supplying personnel and personnel-related resources.

Other information systems and a proposed operational Data System are designed to provide stores of manpower-related information. At present, they are incomplete, uncoordinated, and data retrieval is difficult, but they will become more useful for analytical and planning purposes when more complete data on personnel characteristics and related operational performance are included.

Another fundamental question is: *what factors cause certain categories of manpower to be in short supply, or to cost more than other categories? And what would be the costs of policy changes aimed at either:*

(i) *increasing the supply of these categories, or*

(ii) *reducing the need for them?*

Among the studies of needs and attitudes, questionnaire surveys have identified expressed attitudes on a wide variety of conditions of Navy life. Pay and time away from home are high on the dissatisfaction list and are presumed to affect retention. More definitive studies relating people's actual experience with their continuance behaviour are in process.

Motivation and stress have been studied extensively among sub-mariners and aviators. Personality and emotional factors in recruits have been identified which predict their later adjustment, although the predictive value is low. Psychological tests have not been broadly evaluated for their usefulness in identifying personnel who might most easily be persuaded — through appropriate treatment — to remain in the service.

2.4. Summary

We have been reviewing studies in the field of manpower control and utilization to determine their relevance and usefulness to the manpower planning process. Manpower planning is taken to be concerned with long-range implications of different levels and mixes of manpower as they relate to levels of Naval effectiveness or readiness and to costs. Manpower requirements can be determined and justified only when these relationships are understood and exposed.

Our review has identified several efforts which are producing data of the type needed for planning. Our first conclusion is that these data must be brought together in a way which permits their interaction to be better understood.

It also appears that other areas of study should be initiated or expanded to contribute to this overall effort:

(i) Data from hundreds of ad hoc studies of specific systems and Naval activities need to be consolidated and codified into a form which shows the trade-offs between design, manning and output.

(ii) Provision needs to be made to incorporate such data into management information systems, to improve tools for planning.

(iii) Current study efforts in work dimensions and job structuring need to be expanded to achieve fundamental improvements in the categories used to express manpower goals.

(iv) New techniques are needed to improve selection, training and performance evaluation of leaders and supervisors.

(v) Study of attitudinal and psychological factors in performance and retention need to be expanded and broadened.

(vi) Studies of group and organizational effectiveness need to be expanded to provide data on realistic operational tasks.

3. MANPOWER PRACTICES IN INDUSTRY AND THE OTHER SERVICES

3.1. Scope

To summarize briefly our work in this area, not surprisingly we found no industrial manpower planning system ready to be adopted for use by the Navy. What we do find is a trend toward so-called systems management which is far from perfectly understood by anybody — including its proponents — and only incompletely and inconsistently applied. We also find some interesting policies and practices which might be considered for adoption by the Navy, once their implications are understood.

Table 2 shows the organizations from which we have gathered data. As you can see, this was essentially a small-sample survey. However, in addition to direct contacts with these primary sources, we have been reviewing results of surveys by the American Management Association and other secondary sources.

The type of data collected includes information on the structure and functions of manpower management organization; general personnel policies and practices; particular policies with respect to jobs on ships, overseas, and in remote locations; and planning factors, standards and documentation where appropriate. Our information is not comprehensive. However, we consider it sufficient to assure us that there is no single, easy answer to Navy manpower planning problems and that the approach we are developing — combined with the other tools already existing or in development — can produce benefits in the long run.

3.2. Conclusions

Perhaps the most important of our conclusions is that in industry, planning consists primarily of establishment of goals, measurement of achievement, examination of options

TABLE 2

ORGANIZATIONS SURVEYED

Industries	Government Maritime
Celanese Corporation	Civilian Manpower Management Office (of the Navy Department)
Federal Electric Corporation (Division of ITT)	
	Environmental Science Services Administration (of the Department of Commerce)
International Basic Economy Corporation (IBEC)	
International Telephone and Telegraph Corporation (ITT)	Military Sea Transportation Service (of the Navy Department)
Sandia Corporation	

Other Military	Secondary Data Sources
Air Force: DCS, Program and Resources – Office of Manpower and Organization; DCS, Personnel	American Management Association Reports
	State Department Data
Army: ACS, Force Development; DCS, Personnel	Private Industrial Surveys
Marine Corps: ACS, G1	

in the use of resources, and exercise of options in reallocating resources (including manpower) to arrive closer to the goals.

Figure 2 shows how these actions are reflected in specific functions performed at the Corporate level – analogous to our planning level and at Division level – more or less analogous to our Type and Unit Commanders. Not all companies accomplish all these functions systematically, but their importance is generally recognized. The salient points are:-

First, goals are established in terms other than manpower: manpower is regarded as one of several types of resource which contributes to the achievement of goals, but at a measurable cost. In this regard, manpower planning takes place within the context of total resource planning, rather than as a separate functional element.

Second, although Divisions may have substantial control over specific policies, such as hiring, firing, advancement, and utilization, they are held accountable for their operational performance, again in terms other than manpower, and may be directed to reduce manpower in certain categories (usually overhead employees) when Corporate Headquarters deems necessary. Future projections and measures of past performance are required reporting tools. Measures such as profits, volume, sales per employee, and total compensation as a per cent of sales, provide industry with useful measures combining cost and effectiveness.

Third, this measurement and control system, combined with the fact that employees can be hired at reasonably short notice from the outside at any level of training and fired with reasonable notice, relieves industry of the necessity to make precise predictions of manpower needs beyond one year into the future. The self-adjusting system can be activated quickly – the aerospace industry has provided several instances of mass layoffs overnight. Mass recruitment takes longer, but compensation policies can be adjusted to the needs if necessary. The relative ease with which personnel are able to shift from one company to another is due to the high degree of transferability of the skills and experience they have acquired. In general however military training is much less transferable to other than military jobs.

Other industrial practices are as follows:

    (i) Many personnel decisions can be made on the basis of an individual's capabilities, potential, and desires, rather than in terms of large groups or categories.

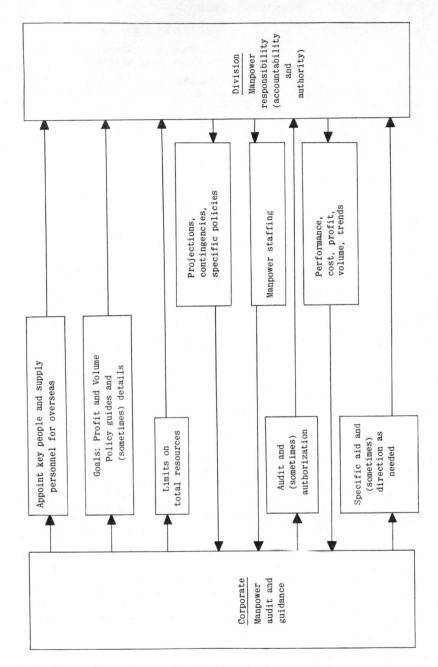

FIG. 2: INDUSTRIAL MANPOWER PLANNING FUNCTIONS –
CORPORATE AND DIVISION LEVELS

192

(ii) Industry makes wide use of professional personnel specialists as well as business management specialists at the planning level.

(iii) Industry operates in a more or less free market, with no long-term obligatory service (except in a few special cases).

(iv) Industry can hire people from the market place at any level, including executives.

(v) There are a variety of fringe benefits which are familiar to all of you.

As part of our survey we obtained data on policies and practices being applied to personnel in jobs with similar characteristics to those found in the Navy – specifically, MSTS (Military Sea Transport Service) crews, contractor technicians on range ships, and contractor personnel in remote and isolated stations. Table 3 shows some of the data. The wage rates shown are those for employees comparable in level and training to an Electronics Technician, Chief Petty Officer. The work hours are those used as a basis for computing basic weekly pay.

The opportunity to earn overtime pay is a strong incentive for MSTS crews and range ship technicians to work longer hours than standard. At remote stations, where overtime pay is not normal, both the hourly rates and the standard work week for computation of weekly rates are higher. Contractor personnel on ships and at remote stations tend to sign up with a specific financial goal in mind, and when they have achieved it, they seek other types of jobs. Reenlistment bonuses are available in some cases, just as in the Navy. MSTS crews are more likely to continue in service, but take advantage of annual leave and a substantial amount of unpaid leave on shore, whenever their financial position permits – thereby diluting their earnings to some extent.

TABLE 3

POLICIES AND PRACTICES FOR JOBS SIMILAR TO NAVY

	MSTS Crew	Range Ship Technicians	Remote Stations
1. Basic Weekly Pay: ETC Equivalent	$170-200	Approximately $150 +	$268-310
2. *Standard* Work Week (Hours)	40	40	54
3. Hardship Pay	Base pay varies with location & ship type.	25% bonus for sea duty	Up to 5% depends on sites.
4. Reenlistment Bonus	----------	-------------	Up to $1200 a year.

Data were also obtained on compensation policies for overseas executives and administrators comparable to officer levels. Many companies use our State Department ratings of overseas locations as a basis for establishing overseas bonuses and hardship differentials, which may range from 10 to 25 per cent of salary.

As we examine the manpower planning process of the military services, several features, shared by all, distinguish them from industry, as shown in Figure 3.

Most important, of course, is the fact that the planning levels within each service are in effect caught between the demands of their user divisions and the constraints imposed by the legislative and executive branches with respect to compensation and related policies, manpower end-strength limits, and budgetary limits. In turn, legislative action produces a manpower supply at low prices, through the draft, but the true costs of manpower supplied through such a pricing system are just beginning to be appreciated.

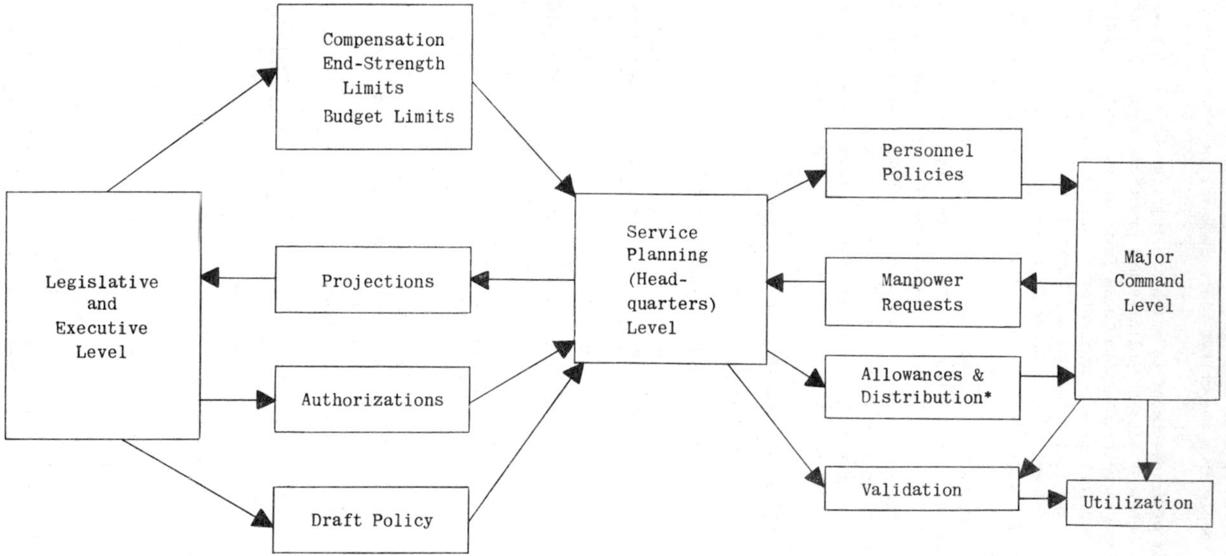

FIG. 3: MANPOWER PLANNING FUNCTIONS FOR ALL SERVICES

* Total manpower is allocated for all services at headquarters level, but services have varying degrees of freedom at major command levels for allocating manpower resources to units.

194

Within the services, the main differences from the industrial planning process are that the manpower user cannot set policy and cannot determine the individuals who will be assigned to him (with very few exceptions). Once assignments have been made, however, the user has almost complete freedom in how he utilizes his personnel, with little explicit responsibility to account for costs or effectiveness. The manpower validation function, exercised by both planners and users, is an attempt to impose a degree of accountability, but validation criteria are not standardized, they do not measure performance effectiveness of the activity as a whole, and they do not include cost measures. In effect, there is little incentive and almost no guidelines for using resources efficiently.

There are a few points of difference between the Navy and the other services which should be noted although these are primarily differences in degree. In the Air Force organization, for example, the manpower planning office is under Programs and Resources, in the Army, under Force Development, while in the Navy it appears more isolated from the other resource planning functions, at least in terms of the organizational structure. All services have on-going manpower validation efforts. The Air Force effort is most extensive (2200 people as compared with the Navy's approximately 400); it is also the most highly coordinated, and most completely documented in a way which permits the data to be extrapolated for planning of new systems or activities. The Air Force's highly centralized system management procedure ensures early and comprehensive planning of manpower requirements for new systems. Finally the Air Force has delegated to its major commands the authority to develop manning tables for their own units, within an overall allocation, and to change these tables within limits without any central action. The Navy and Army allocate and approve changes for all billets centrally. We understand the Army, after finding a centralized system unsatisfactory, is now moving toward a decentralized system. Because of the contrast among our own services, there appears to be justification for further examination of centralization versus decentralization in the manpower requirements determination and management functions.

As we examined the other military services in greater detail, another important distinction emerged. It has often been stated that the Navy is unique because it consists largely of ships, which are multi-mission in character. This characteristic has an important implication for manning standards and criteria.

The Navy relies on staffing criteria and work standards to determine ship manning, as the other services do in determining manning for support functions. The work study techniques by which tasks are analyzed and personnel needs determined and validated, are essentially the same as those used by the other services. They include a substantial amount of judgment along with work measurement, but they reflect the methodological limits of the state of the art. As a basis for the establishment of manpower goals, they are usually not seriously questioned. What may cause concern however, is the degree to which functions which must be performed by each type of activity are established beyond question; this is most critical, and most difficult for the multi-mission Navy ships.

One further comparison among the services is relevant to the problem of manpower planning, namely, their policies with respect to personnel rotation and the implications for manpower requirements.

Table 4 shows the present rotation rate goals expressed by the various services — they are usually stated as goals rather than official policy.

Notice that the Navy appears conservative when compared superficially with the other services; its numerical ratio is two bad to one good, as compared with one bad to two good in most other cases. However, the Navy's goal is specified in terms of billets, while the others are in months. A Navy sea billet includes time in port, although not necessarily home port, and the proportion of time spent at sea varies with the type of ship. For this reason, certain occupational types in the Navy are experiencing significantly different proportions of time at sea than other types. In addition, many shore billets — particularly in certain ratings — are left vacant while sea billets are filled to the extent possible. As a result of these factors, the existence of a 4 : 2 billet ratio does not guarantee a 4 : 2 ratio in actual experience, and Navy personnel are faced with relatively more uncertainty in their planning. Of course, perceptions of "good" and "bad" duty will vary among individuals; however, in some cases they may

TABLE 4

ROTATION RATE GOALS OF U.S. MILITARY SERVICES

	" Bad " Duty	" Good " Duty	Rotation Goals
USAF	Southeast Asia	Non-Southeast Asia	12 bad to 48 good months (in CONUS)
Army	Short tour (RVN, Korea)	Any accompanied	12 bad to 25 good months
USMC	WestPac tour (portal-to-portal)	Non-WestPac	13 bad to 25 good months
Navy	Arduous sea Overseas shore Toured	CONUS shore Preferred overseas shore	4 bad to 2 good billets

differ substantially from official views. The need for rotation billets has been recognized; the Navy's unique characteristic is that its bad billets are not continuously bad. We are examining Navy data on actual rotation experience, by rating, to better understand its relationship to continuance behaviour.

The data gathered from this survey, combined with knowledge based on a short look ahead, leads to some interesting suggestions.

The Defense Department's Resource Management Program, as promulgated by the Secretary of the Navy, places a responsibility on the ship Type Commander to account for the costs of the resources he uses – including manpower. Recalling the findings of our industrial survey, this program is consistent with two industry practices: it considers manpower one of many resources used in the production of an output and it puts accountability at a level analogous to a corporate Division.

However, two processes are presently omitted which should be included:-

One hazard in this program is the possibility that when cost information is reported up the line, decisions may be taken on the basis of this information alone. If two destroyers are found to differ significantly in operating costs, the conclusion may be drawn that one is more efficient. This conclusion would be based on an assumption that they are accomplishing – or are capable of accomplishing – equal functions or outputs, which may not be the case. In industry, costs are evaluated in combination with effectiveness, through measures such as profits and volume. We made the point earlier that one promising measure of effectiveness for Navy manpower appeared to be the one used in the Navy's readiness analysis program – number and type of functions which a ship can perform simultaneously. If manpower costs are going to be accounted for at the ship level, it becomes doubly important to be able to relate these costs to some independent measure of effectiveness, otherwise it will become even more difficult to make manning goals credible. The establishment of effectiveness measures are therefore necessary to avoid a potentially serious problem.

The second omitted process is one which also reflects good industrial management practice. In industry, it is normal to associate accountability with responsibility. Our survey showed a high degree of decentralized authority for policy-making, and in the manpower area, Divisions can usually increase or decrease their staffs within broad limits, as long as their performance is satisfactory. We mentioned previously the Air Force policy which (within limits) decentralizes authority for establishing billets. In the Navy, this would mean extending such authority to the Type Commanders when they are asked to become more accountable, provided they are able to specify their outputs in acceptable units.

3.3. Summary

In summary, our survey of industry and other services has identified several interesting features with potential Navy application. The major ones are as follows:
  (i) Close coordination of manpower planning with total resource planning.
 (ii) Accountability for manpower cost and effectiveness at operating levels – in terms other than manpower.
(iii) Decentralized control of manpower strength – within limits.
 (iv) Wide use of career specialists.
  (v) Documentation of relationships between manpower levels and other indicators of effectiveness at a general level for planning purposes.

4. THE MANPOWER SYSTEM MODEL

4.1. Overall Approach

Recently, with the introduction of " third generation " computers a relatively new management methodology has become practical. This methodology may be described as " systems management ". Underlying the use of the method is the conviction that all the parts of a system are interdependent, and that system efficiency is more a function of the control exercised over the interaction of the system variables than the efficiency of one system element. To illustrate this, the efficiency of an ASW system depends on the interaction between command, communications, weapons and sensors. The control over the interaction between these functions may have far more effect on system effectiveness than the simple efficiency of, say, the sonar.

Accepting this proposition, one can view Navy manpower as a system, and seek to so describe it as to expose not only its constituent parts, but also the interaction of system variables so that control over this interaction can be exercised and the efficiency of the system improved.

The Manpower System is very complex. But the principles underlying the systems approach to manpower planning are relatively straightforward. Thus, while we will be describing a computer model for the evaluation of the manpower system, the only purpose of the computer is to handle the great numbers of data elements and calculations involved. It is therefore an analysis and planning tool and not a computer control system.

In its simplest terms, the approach consists of viewing manpower as a system through which aggregates of people in various categories flow at various rates, producing output services at various costs. The assumption is that the manpower planner wishes to select policy options which will enable specified output goals to be provided on a sustained basis at minimum cost.

The problem is complicated by the following factors:
  (i) Different categories of people produce different outputs, and the degree of substitutability among them must be determined or estimated.
 (ii) Output measures applicable to a total manpower structure have not been devised.
(iii) Different categories of people show differential costs not only as a direct result of compensation policies, type and length of training, etc., but indirectly, through differential attrition, because they may respond in different ways to those policies.

Since manpower in different categories may behave differentially with respect to enlistment, continuance, and performance, we considered it desirable to disaggregate total manpower into many different categories in order to reveal significant relationships. We have not nearly exhausted the possibilities inherent in available data, but have selected a few categories for illustrative study. Our underlying purpose has been to provide manpower planners with an analytical tool by which they can better understand the implications of policy options, and into which new or refined data, or different policy alternatives, may be incorporated from time to time as they become available.

The Manpower System Model is what is known as an heuristic model. This simply means that it is designed to develop a plan which is an improvement over current procedure,

197

and satisfactory in relation to constraints on cost, manpower, and man outputs. It is open-ended, permitting further extension and experimentation on the bases of model results and additional data and parameters. One would like to define an algorithm for the optimization of manpower that could be solved directly; we may eventually be able to do this. Now, however, the variable interactions in the manpower system are far too complex for an integrated single set of equations.

4.2. Assumptions

Before going further, some of the underlying assumptions about the properties of a manpower system need to be described. The basic elements are men, interacting individually and in groups, both within the system and on the system. Unlike machines, the constituents of a manpower system can change the very character of the system itself. The underlying reason is that actions on the system by managers are subject to interpretation by men according to their individual value structures. Unlike a mechanical system, men can elect to leave the system. They do so on the basis of their perceptions of the degree to which the system responds to their needs as they see them.

The Manpower System Model as it has been developed has five implicit elementary assumptions:

First, men's behaviour is *directly* responsive to manpower policies, and *indirectly* and *differentially* responsive based on their perceptions of their environment and their perceived benefits from the policies applicable to them. A pay policy may be perceived not only in terms of purchasing power, but also in comparison with private pay policies, and as a symbol of recognition. Similarly, work hours, training and rotation policies are viewed in several relational contexts and in relation to pay policies. Thus the attrition behaviour of Navy men is not only a response to policies, but also to their perceived relationship to the civilian environment. Many key policies of the Navy mask relationships to men's responsive behaviour and do not facilitate their comparison with the external environment by planners interested in predicting behaviour.

A second assumption is that there are many different mixes and numbers of men which can be combined to produce the same quantity and quality of output services. This means that at the margin, some men in one class are substitutable for men in another. Thus, within limits, we can substitute a larger number of second class petty officers for a given number of first class petty officers or for that matter some number of electronic technicians for fire control technicians.

A third assumption revolves around the classes into which men are divided. Classification is to some extent arbitrary, but its purpose is to aid understanding. We have therefore assumed two dominant manpower categories, rating and longevity. The reasons for this are that most of the direct costs of men are homogeneous with respect to these two classes, and their training, basic education, intelligence, proficiency, and the value of their skills are probably relatively homogeneous.

The fourth assumption revolves around the classes into which man-services are divided. In analyzing work output, we have divided man-services into essentially two groups of classes. The first is place-oriented, like *away from home, at home, TP&P* (transients, prisoners and patients), and *in formal schools*. The second group is skill level, as measured in longevity. Each of these classes has a unique place in the Manpower Systems Model.

Implicit in the class assumptions for men and man-services is a special distinction. Costs are directly attributable to men, but it is the flow of services that men provide which determines the ultimate Navy product, or " Readiness ". Because of this special distinction, classes of men and man-services have been created – to permit the translation of costs of men into costs of product, and numbers and qualities of men into units of output.

The fifth class of assumptions concerns the character of costs in planning and decision-making for future manpower goals, as distinct from Programs, Plans and Budget process costs. The distinction is that the former are equilibrium costs associated with future goals, while the latter are the intermediate dollar expenditure rates along the way. Thus it is meaningful in establishing goals to think of " opportunity costs " – the value of the benefits foregone by using a resource for one purpose as distinct from the best of all possible other purposes.

Costs must also be separated from value, for they may be quite different. We have assumed that Navy men behave as economic entities to the same extent that all men do. Thus the Navy man contracts his services to the Navy in return for benefits of some value. Value is not altered by the price the Navy pays to provide a given benefit but only by a change in the value structure of the individual. Thus the value of a commissary or medical or retirement benefit to a man is conditioned by the extent to which he anticipates he will use, need or receive that benefit.

4.3. Organizational Objectives

The Navy has many techniques for establishing unit manning needs. These include design work study, fleet work study, validation and audit programs, shipboard tests, battle manning analyses, Readiness level manning study, fleet and type commander recommendations and others. We have described some of the ways these efforts will facilitate the better expression of " requirements " at the manning level. These procedures, nevertheless, are only a part of the manpower " Requirements " problem. The questions of the proper mix between military and civilian personnel and the effect of contemplated changes in unit manning on attrition, rotation experience, training, and ultimately total manpower and the costs and output of this total system remain unanswered. Though Navy Program Planning Factors exist for each of these items independently, their interaction in the total system should be more accurately known.

We are faced at the outset with defining working objectives for a manpower system model. We have therefore assumed that Navy manpower objectives are:

" to provide the necessary man-services to operate specified Navy weapons and systems in the operating environment ".

To quantify and operate on such an objective, definitions for these services had to be devised. Thus, we assumed that all out-of-home-port activity of ships and aircraft units, and activities in remote locations, constitute the desired operating environment objectives of the Navy and therefore determine the desired flows of man-services in the operating environment. This is not wholly correct; for example, the ship being over-hauled away from home port is not in the operating environment, but the definition is satisfactory for our purposes.

The Navy is very large and has continuously changing operating environment needs. However, because of limited hardware endurance and logistics, the number of men and units in the operating environment varies little when viewed from the perspective of the total Navy over reasonable periods. It therefore appears that there is a basis for the definition of Navy objectives in terms of flows of man services which can be defined both quantitatively and qualitatively. Given the fractions of each year that all Navy units expect to spend in the operating environment, and the quantitative and qualitative numbers of men on those units, the number of man-years of service from each Navy rating required to meet our operating environment objectives can be computed. Thus, using conventional unit manning tools, with the addition of expected or desired unit movement data, the basic building block of a manpower systems model can be constructed. We have chosen to call this building block " on-the-line " manpower for want of a better term. It is important to remember only that it is man hours of service per year that we are describing by this definition and *not* men. If we can define our " on-the-line " man outputs with reasonable validity (and much work is being done to give added credibility to these values) we can ask a rather basic question. What combination of policies is likely to produce the men necessary to provide these man services in the most efficient manner? To answer this question we must understand costs, we must understand something of the characteristics of men that are considered desirable from management's view, we must understand how men will respond to conditions of their employment and we must understand the options available.

The structure of the Manpower System model presumes that in some ordered way (given any explicit set of all the policies that bear on attrition behaviour), one can predict the attrition rate that would likely result for a given rating and longevity year. The dominant policies in this set would consist of individual pay and benefits, selectivity rate, amount, frequency and timing of formal training, family separation, standards of expected work hours, minimum service to be eligible for advancement in rate and maximum service allowable in a particular grade. Given these policies, an attrition rate predicted therefrom, and empirical data on the cost of training and TP&P per man year, the basic tools to examine the cost and output ramifications of these policies on a given set of " requirements " are at hand.

4.4. Policies

4.4.1. Man Maintenance Cost Policy

We have created a cost model, though it is not complete, designed to produce four different kinds of information:

    (i) the dollar value of annual pay and benefits as they are perceived by individual classes of men;

    (ii) the dollar costs of men as individuals, not necessarily perceived as having value by them;

    (iii) the difference between the prices paid by the Navy for benefits and the value ascribed to them by individuals; and

    (iv) the present values of future benefits both in terms of their prices to the Navy and their present value as perceived by individuals.

These four information categories will be useful in describing the Manpower System in terms of its cost and effectiveness, and they can serve as the foundation for the development of predictors of behaviour.

Navy attrition as a function of longevity for Fiscal Years 1963-1965, derived from data in the Secretary of the Navy's Retention Task Force Report, is presented in figure 4. While we know that attrition rates vary from year to year and by occupation and by pay grade as well, it is the general properties of this curve which are significant. It is quite obvious that the draft plays a large part in influencing attrition at about the four-year point, since this is the first opportunity for men who entered the Navy as a result of draft pressures to leave. But thereafter attrition rates gradually decline to the twenty-year point, when retirement benefits take effect, and then rise sharply.

The shape of this entire curve is certainly conditioned by the value of benefits men perceive at various points in their service careers in relation to private benefits. Thus, the attrition rate is a result of the aggregate policies that serve to define the perceived value of benefits. Benefits provided are direct costs to the Navy, and through changes in the rate at which men flow through the system and the mix of experience that results, many indirect man-costs are incurred. In addition, the output of the force is a direct function of the attrition rate. Is the attrition rate profile on this chart consistent with the most efficient, or cost-effective, manpower system? There are probably many other profiles that are completely feasible with some policy modification. One of the basic problems we are addressing is that of finding those policy sets that will produce changes in the attrition rate, and means of predicting the magnitude of the changes, such that alternate configurations of the manpower system can be identified which have the potential to decrease the cost per unit of output of the Navy.

4.4.2. Selectivity Policy

The Navy Manpower System as we know it is characterized by the introduction of a relatively heterogeneous class of men who are divided after induction based on their education and test scores, into slightly more homogeneous groups. We apply varying amounts of training to these groups and further divide them into homogeneous occupational groups. We then qualitatively differentiate men within groups into skill classes that we call " rate ". All of these processes are accomplished within a time continuum during which each process is repeated as men flow out of the system through voluntary attrition, death, disability, unsuitability, and lastly, by selectivity. The process, then, is one

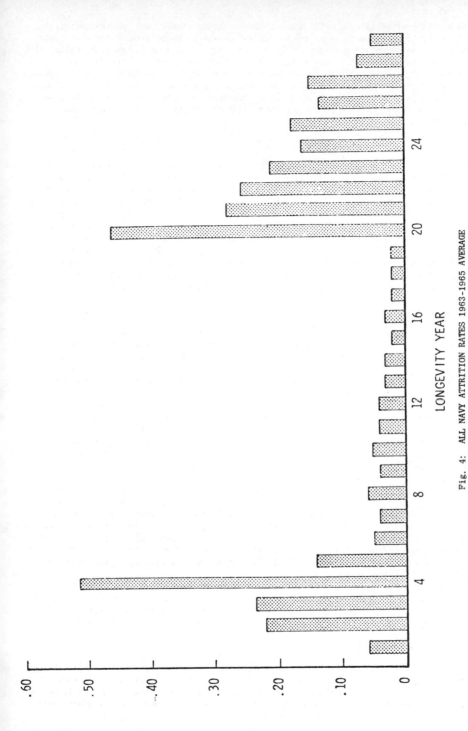

Fig. 4: ALL NAVY ATTRITION RATES 1963-1965 AVERAGE

of continuously differentiating a heterogeneous group of men into successively finer and finer homogeneous classes. The assignment of men to these classes can only occur with time as we gather performance, skill and training data on men as individuals. With the progress of time, however, we continuously identify men who do not fall within any of the usefulness classes for which the Navy has an identifiable need either because their cost exceeds some acceptable class norm or because their output is not equivalent to class standards or both. Thus an explicit management policy, which we have chosen to call selectivity, must be defined to both recognize and provide for this winnowing process.

4.4.3. Training Policy

Another policy, or plan if you prefer, over which the Navy has considerable control is the training profile for men within any given class. Training may be viewed as an investment in " knowledge capital ". This capital resource is subject to both amortization and obsolescence. As a result, it must be provided initially and then continuously expanded and updated with time. Both the timing and amount of training to be applied to any class of men are functions of technology and the stocks of knowledge and skills accumulated in the man inventory of that class. Knowledge, when viewed as a capital resource created by investment in training, inheres in men. Thus when men leave the Navy, they take a valuable capital resource with them. Training profiles are therefore explicit policies that we wish to examine because of their interdependence with the specific configuration of men likely to result from a predicted attrition rate.

4.4.4. Rotation Policy

An important policy variable that appears to interact in a complex way with all other policy variables is the fraction of their careers men may expect to spend in the operating environment, or in what we have chosen to call " on-the-line ". We have previously pointed out the differences between Army, Air Force, Marine Corps and Navy rotation ratio goals. The single most significant difference between the Navy and the other services in the expression of these goals is that the Navy's are in terms of billets while the latter are in terms of man assignments. We have examined man experience in relation to a new set of human experience-based definitions. The data are still being analyzed, but we would like to point out some results obtained so far.

We have calculated the approximate percentage of time spent on-the-line and in the rotation base, rating by rating, by obtaining data on time away from home port or home base by ship type and aircraft squadron, and determining the distribution of the various ratings among ship types, aircraft squadrons and other activities.

We found time actually spent at home port, home base or rotation base activities averages 70 per cent of the time, which approximates the expressed rotation goals of the other armed services. However, we found wide variations among ratings, ranging from 54 per cent of time at home in one rating to 99 per cent in another. It is also interesting to note that if there were no discrepancy between billets and men in the Navy and if the Navy were to meet its desired rotation goal of 4 sea billets to 2 shore billets, nevertheless, there would still be wide discrepancy across ratings in the amount of time men can expect to be at home.

Though there is a high correlation (.86) between per cent of time in shore code billets which are now used as a basis for defining rotation goals and per cent of time in the rotation base as we have defined it; these two indicators give quite different measures of good and bad time, and both show wide differences among ratings.

4.4.5. Work Hour Policy

Hours of work planned for a given class of men is another policy variable that can impact significantly on system costs and effectiveness. Obviously, the output of man services will vary as a function of work hours, but so may we expect the attrition rate to vary. Thus the attrition behaviour of men in response to work hour standards will affect both the number, type and cost of the productive hours of services produced. If we were to assume that men worked 70 hours per week on-the-line (10 hours per day, 7 days per week), 47 hours per week in port (one 4-hour watch every four days) and 44 hours per week in the shore establishment (one 4-hour watch per week), then the average annual work hours would range from a high of 3156 hours in one rating to a low of 2080 for another. Since national average work hours approximate 1860 hours per year, we would expect that attrition behaviour would be significantly influenced by the relative differences that exist. Thus work hours also constitute a policy requiring examination in the context of our Manpower System Model.

4.4.6. Promotion Policy

Much has been said about advancement and promotion policy and the response of men to such policy; however, these policies may be viewed a bit differently in the context of our model. First, as we have said previously, rate is one of the devices we use to separate broad classes of men into more homogeneous usefulness classes. Thus, it defines skill level, hierarchical position, and dominant type of activity. In this sense, rate is an organization hierarchy class of men. Rate is also a man-perceived form of recognition and status and thus attrition behaviour can be expected to vary according to the value men place on these perceptions. Third, the Navy pays different prices for services in different rates, which serve to enhance the recognition accorded higher rate, and to permit the Navy to bid in the market place for more valuable people. Therefore the number of different rates that are useful is conditioned by our need to define separate skill levels so that men may perceive esteem-producing distinctions between themselves and other classes of men, so that we can relate classes of men to jobs to be done, and so that we can measure the competitive prices to be bid for their services in the market place. We now have nine enlisted rates and they are probably sufficient; however, it is useful to constrain service in rate by explicit policy within reasonable limits in order to preserve the qualitative, skill, status, and cost homogeneity functions to be served by the class of men defined by " rate ".

4.4.7. Other Policies

The last set of significant policy variables are those that produce costs but that appear to us to have minimal impact on the attrition behaviour of men. These might be best regarded as qualitative standards for man-related activities and facilities. A second group of these type policies are those that revolve around reimbursement practices for personal costs incurred under special conditions of service and travel. These cost producing practices may be expected to have little impact on attrition behaviour except in their absence; nevertheless, they are significant, and therefore must be accommodated within the Manpower System Model construct.

4.5. Policy Functions

Manpower policies may then be viewed as performing three functions. They set standards for output services and for the production and maintenance of human capital; they fix the costs of men, and they provide a perceptual reference for men to compare their Navy conditions of work and benefits with the external environment. There is not a unique correspondence between a given policy and a given function however, since the same policy may serve all three functions. Thus values must be assigned to each policy in relation to each function it fulfills. Figure 5 illustrates the accumulation of policy defined costs into an aggregate investment in human capital. Only a part of this human capital resource is used in the production of useful outputs and the remainder is lost to the Navy through attrition.

Figure 6 reflects the relationships between man, his external environment, and his behaviour in response to his perceived benefits and the flows of services expected from him. In those cases where the relationships are compatible, he continues to produce real outputs; in those where there are significant inconsistencies, he responds by attriting.

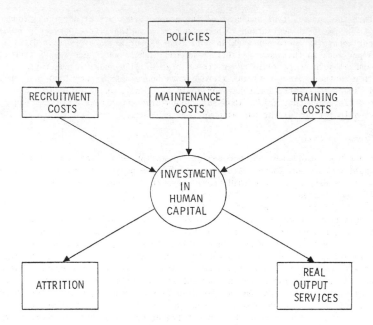

FIG. 5:   COST PRODUCING POLICIES

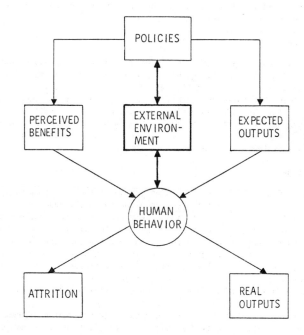

FIG. 6:   BEHAVIOUR PRODUCING POLICIES

4.6. Summary

The organization of the Manpower System Model may now be briefly summarized by figure 7.

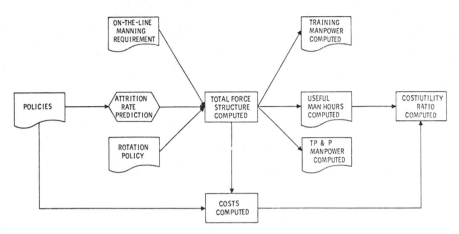

Fig. 7:   THE MANPOWER SYSTEMS MODEL

(i) Given a set of policies examined in relation to men's behavioural response, a prediction can be made of the likely attrition rate that will result. Much work remains to be done to quantify a set of predictors, but we believe a set sufficiently reliable for manpower planning purposes is a realistic possibility within the present state of the art in the behavioural sciences.

(ii) On the basis of a defined on-the-line man services requirement, a predicted attrition rate, and a rotation policy, the number of men by longevity year necessary to produce the desired on-the-line manpower can be computed.

(iii) With a particular training profile and TP&P allowance, the numbers of man years of useful services the force can produce can be defined.

(iv) Given the promotion policy which establishes the grade structure of men by longevity, and compensation and man maintenance policies, the total costs of men can be computed.

(v) By applying a work hours policy to the useful man years of service produced by the force, the costs per useful man hour can also be derived.

The simple efficiency of the force derived from a given policy set might then be measured as the average cost per hour of useful services. We know, however, that hours of service provided by different skill levels within a class of men have correspondingly different values and further that their value is also a function of the relative mix of the different skills available. In order to account for this skill and mix difference, we have developed what appears to us to be a reasonable utility function to quantify an index of utility. This function gives higher value to services provided by men in each succeeding higher longevity year. The relative value of men in one longevity year changes as the number of men in adjacent longevity year classes change. This utility function is similar to, though not quite the same as, the well-known economic production function developed by Cobb and Douglas.

The Manpower System Model computes a measure of the total utility of the force derived from the man hours of useful service the force structure can produce and weighted by the relative values of the different longevity classes of man hours. The division of the total cost of the force by the units of utility it can produce is what we believe is a practical measure for assessing the efficiency of a force produced by a given policy set. In these terms it is then possible to test all other feasible policy sets and variations in operating environment manning to assess their impacts on required total numbers of men, costs, and finally, cost-utility, or cost effectiveness.

We believe that a Systems Model which will demonstrate the costs and changes in output, or cost-effectiveness, that can be reasonably predicted from changes in the numbers and quality of men in the Navy is the most straight-forward way of communicating manpower needs effectively. The implication of such a method of dialogue is an increase in the joint responsibility for manpower planning between the Navy and higher authority, because requirements, or goals as we would prefer to call them, would be directly tied to the policy changes and resources necessary to make them achievable.

The model described is operating with empirical data where it could be obtained within the limits of resources and time. Missing data elements have to this point been simply given assumed arbitrary values as close to reality as we could guess them to test the methodology. These tests suggest to us that an integrated Manpower System Model can indeed by constructed and it can be a powerful aid in the quantification and assessment of manpower planning options.

REFERENCES

References have been deliberately omitted because most relevant material has been obtained from U.S. Department of Defense Research and Technology résumés, Department of the Navy memoranda, and interview data. Sources will be furnished to interested parties upon request if the specific information concerned is not appropriately restricted in its disclosure.

Manpower Studies at the Institute of Naval Studies 1963-1966

ANTON S. MORTON

ARTHUR D. LITTLE INC.

I. INTRODUCTION

I am reporting about studies carried out in the first three years of the Manning Study of the Institute of Naval Studies, the long-range study portion of the Centre for Naval Analyses. The multidisciplinary group who carried out these studies consisted of a biologist (who functioned as project director for the first two years of the project), Naval officers who supplied a link to the Navy and detailed operational knowledge of Navy procedures, a social psychologist with a sound human factors background, a mathematical statistician, a bio-statistician, an operations researcher, an economist, a programmer, and myself, a social psychologist who acted as project director in the third year of the study. In addition, we were fortunate to have the consultant services of Professor Franklin Fisher, of the Department of Economics of the Massachusetts Institute of Technology for the cost/effectiveness study.

2. MANPOWER I

We first carried out a series of three studies. The Multivariate Study of Enlisted Retention (MUSTER) investigated the characteristics of those who re-enlist compared to those who did not re-enlist. I shall discuss this study and its continuation in more detail later. A second study, the Incentive Survey (INSUR) was an initial exploration of additional incentives which might raise the re-enlistment rate and whether it was worthwhile to do so. The third study compared the number on board, compared to the number required, at various kinds of Navy activities, and for Navy Rating Groups.

3. MANPOWER II

Manpower II, Navy Manpower Considerations 1970–1980, consisted of about ten tasks. As part of planning, we carried out an analysis of the operations of the office of the Deputy Chief of Naval Operations for Manpower and Reserves, with a view toward recommending information and analyses to enhance this program. At the request of the Secretary of the Navy, we carried out a study of options open to the Navy with respect to retirement policies, and how a study evaluating the options might be carried out.

The Multivariate Study of Enlisted Retention, (MUSTER) II, on which I shall report in detail, contributed considerable information about the effects of alternate recruiting and selection practices, and about retention. Critical Rating Classification for Retention studied the effects of possible new practices in assigning certain kinds of men with high re-enlistment probabilities to the critical ratings, those which the Navy feels should have the highest re-enlistment rates.

Our studies concentrated in the retention area. The Officer Survey, examined the officer retention situation, characteristics of officers related to high retention probabilities, and incentives and experiences which contributed toward high officer retention. A study

of the Navy from the enlisted man's point of view analyzed answers to open ended
questions which asked men to state in their own terms the advantages and disadvantages
of a Navy career.

A Special Program Evaluation examined the incentive characteristics of special
programs the Navy has instituted to raise the re-enlistment rate, and made suggestions
for other such programs. The Cost Effectiveness Study, which will be reported in more
detail below, examined the costs and benefits of various ways of raising the Navy
enlisted re-enlistment rate.

4. THE COST EFFECTIVENESS STUDY[1]

4.1. Purpose

In the words of the directive, this study concerned "the cost/effectiveness of
retention incentives". In it, we were to "review factors contributing to cost/
effectiveness". For reasons discussed in detail above by Fisher, we took as the Navy's
goal in this study the achievement of given effectiveness levels at least cost. The
method used was that of nonlinear dynamic programming. I shall discuss below in what
ways the model was nonlinear and dynamic. The study simulated what might happen to the
costs and effectiveness of the Navy if any of twenty-three incentive situations,
including the present incentive situation, were to be instituted. The additional
incentives we tested were of five types:

   (i) Educational, such as two years at a junior college for each four years of
      service after the first four.

  (ii) Policy changes, such as increasing markedly the extent of time spent with
      family.

 (iii) Pay, such as a 20% pay raise.

  (iv) Changed fringe benefits, such as a scholarship for dependent children.

   (v) Promotion opportunities, such as promotion to Warrant Officer at the end of
      ten years of enlisted service.

We wished to estimate how the institution of these incentives would affect the Navy's
re-enlistment rate, and thus its effectiveness, and its costs.

4.2. Estimating Re-enlistment Rates for Incentives

We used survey methods to estimate the first-term re-enlistment rate resulting, if
given incentives were instituted. I shall not go into detail on the methods used to
estimate *actual* proportions of men who would re-enlist for a given incentive from
statements of *intention*. I shall simply say that there is a close and consistent
relationship between the actual re-enlistment rate of men of various age groups (derived
from MUSTER) and the percentage of men in each age group who *said* that they intended to
re-enlist, although fewer men at each age group *say* they will re-enlist than actually
do. Relationships like these were used to calibrate the responses of the survey sample
to the new incentives.

---

[1]   Professor Franklin Fisher of the Massachusetts Institute of Technology, Dr. David M. Mityberg,
    Mr. Charles Berndtson, and Mr. Frank Cole all made significant contributions to this study.

4.3. Estimating Costs

It was critical to relate personnel costs per man to longevity year, since costs do vary markedly on this dimension, and since changes in the first-term re-enlistment rate would change the longevity distribution of the Navy. Data were obtained for the following cost categories:

- Basic pay
- Quarters allowance
- Subsistence allowance
- Social security
- Clothing maintenance allowance
- Sea/Foreign duty allowance
- Family separation allowance
- Training
- Clothing allowance
- Procurement
- Transportation
- Medical
- Re-enlistment bonus
- Proficiency pay
- Commissary
- Dependants and Indemnity compensation
- Hazardous duty pay
- Separatee's travel to home of record
- Separatee's unused leave lump sum payment
- Retirement costs

4.4. Estimating Operational Effectiveness

Prof. Fisher discussed earlier some considerations as to the choice of Navy operational effectiveness measures. In our case, what was required was the ability to specify *what combinations* of trained and relatively untrained men *are equivalent in operational effectiveness*. That is, we needed to know only the trade-off among men of different amounts of experience — the number of untrained men worth one partially trained man, for example — in order to specify what is meant by a given level of Navy operational effectiveness.

The simplest example of trade-off factors is the case in which it is believed that the trade-off between men of different experience is a constant, in which, for example, one Chief Petty Officer is worth six undesignated unrated men. In such a case, we need only convert the measurement of the number of men in the Navy by measuring them in efficiency units. Thus, in the example just given, we count every undesignated striker as worth one efficiency unit and every Chief as worth six. Two Navies are then considered to perform the same job if they each have the same number of efficiency units. We may thus compare incentives by fixing a target number of efficiency units (at, for example, the number of efficiency units in the present Navy) and seeking the incentive which achieves that number of efficiency units at lowest cost.

Unfortunately, the real situation is not quite so simple as this. Statements such as "one Chief is worth six undesignated men" are *unlikely* to be truly *independent of the number of Chiefs* and undesignated men. That is, an extra Chief is likely to be worth a great many more undesignated men when Chiefs are in short supply than when there are a great many Chiefs available.

Consider, for example, an extreme hypothetical situation where the Navy had lost all its Chiefs. Replacing each lost Chief by six additional unrated men would certainly not replace the supervisory functions which Chiefs now contribute to Navy operational effectiveness. Alternatively, if the Navy had too many Chiefs, the worth of an extra Chief would be rather less than it is now. If the Navy had too many Chiefs and not enough unrated men, an additional unrated man would clearly be more valuable than an

additional Chief. (We are making the not unreasonable assumption that the Navy would
not wish to compel Chiefs to do the work of Seamen.) In this situation, the conversion
factors which measure men of different experience in a common efficiency unit are *not
independent* of the number of men of each experience class. This situation is depicted
in Figure 2 showing different hypothetical combinations of Chiefs and undesignated
strikers required for a given level of operational effectiveness. If one Chief were
always worth a given number of strikers, the graph would be a negatively sloping
straight line. As it is, on the assumption that one additional Chief is worth less, the
greater the proportion of Chiefs to undesignated strikers, the equal-effectiveness
curve is convex to the origin.

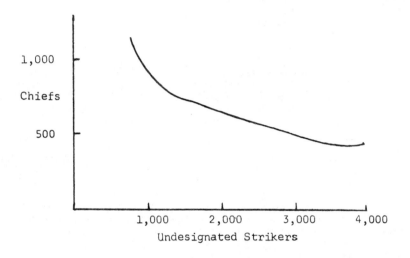

Fig. 1 HYPOTHETICAL EXAMPLE OF EQUAL-EFFECTIVENESS CURVE
FOR CHIEFS AND UNDESIGNATED STRIKERS

Discussion with Naval officers indicated that enlisted men could be grouped into
four experience classes, with substitution within a class assumed on a man-for-man basis.
The least experience class (the first) consisted of all first-year men. Men after their
first year were distributed among the remaining three classes in accordance with the
actual distribution of men in each year-of-service in 1964 by groups of pay-grades. We
assumed that a typical group of inductees would advance in training to match the cross-
section data for the base year.

The Navy's utility function was then defined with the sizes of the four classes as
arguments. The discussions above suggested diminishing marginal rates of substitution
(e.g., rearrangement of personnel just compensating for the loss of an experienced
supervisor becomes more difficult if such men are relatively scarce), and a four-factor
Cobb-Douglas function (used ordinally only) was chosen for analytic convenience.[1] Thus,
denoting the number of men in the ith experience class in calendar year t by Y_{it}, the

---

[1] Our dynamic programming problem made such reasons a bit more compelling than usual. While only
a Cobb-Douglas was used, for this reason, its parameters were varied considerably.

Navy's utility function in year t was taken to be:

$$U_t = Y_{1t}^{\beta_1} Y_{2t}^{\beta_2} Y_{3t}^{\beta_3} Y_{4t}^{\beta_4} \quad ; \quad \sum_{i=1}^{4} \beta_i = 1. \tag{1}$$

4.5. Gathering Data to Estimate Exponents in the Effectiveness Function

To estimate the β_i, over 100 interviews were conducted with experienced supervisors scattered over nine ship types and six occupational groups, asking how many men of a given experience class would just compensate for the loss (or gain) of one man in another class. Given the men on-board, the implied β_i could then be determined for each interviewee from the marginal rates of substitution so described, assuming his utility function to be of the form (1).

	UNIT TYPE ————		RATING————	
PAY GRADE	E-2, E-3	PO 3 DES STR	PO2, POI	CPO, CPOS, CPOM
USEFULNESS CLASS	BASIC (1)	APPREN. (2)	JOURNEY- MAN (3)	CHIEF (4)
ON BOARD	15	7	4	1
	SAME	+2	-1	SAME
	-3	+1	SAME	SAME

Fig. 2   PAY GRADE SUBSTITUTABILITY INTERVIEW FORM

Figure 2 shows a sample of the forms used. In each interview, we ascertained the kind of unit and the rating, (occupational group), which the interviewee supervised. We defined the four experience classes for him and ascertained how many men in each class he had on board. We told him that we were interested in the level of effectiveness attained with different combinations of numbers of men in each experience class. He knew his level of effectiveness with his given mix of men. We then asked him, for example, how many men in the second usefulness class he would need to replace the loss of one man in the third usefulness class. In the example shown, the interviewee indicated two. We encouraged him to think about how he would redivide responsibilities among his division or department in the event of the indicated addition or subtraction of men.

These interviews indicated marginal rates of substitution among men of different experience classes for given ship types and rating groups. These were weighted in accordance with the composition of the Navy by ship type and rating group, and summary rates of substitution derived. We derived one set for the Navy as a whole and another for Electronics Maintenance Personnel. The latter were treated as a separate group because the Navy felt that it had particular interests in raising their re-enlistment, and also because we had hypothesized and found that marginal rates of substitution among experience classes in the Electronics Maintenance group are noticeably different from those in the Navy as a whole. From the paygrade substitutability interviews we derived the Betas for the nonlinear effectiveness formulas.

4.6. Two Effectiveness Functions

Figure 3 shows Betas computed for All Navy and Electronics groups respectively. We can conceptualize the ratios of a pair of Betas as indicating the relative impact upon effectiveness of a 1% change of the number of men in their respective experience classes. For example, in the All Navy formula, a one *per cent* change in the number of men in the second usefulness class will have five times the impact on effectiveness as a 1% change in the number of men in the fourth experience class. Note that if the number of men in any experience class drops to zero in this nonlinear model, total effectiveness drops to zero. It is instructive to compare the Betas. We see that for the All Navy formula, β_1 is almost as large as β_2. However, in the electronics formula, β_2 is more than six times as large as β_1. This indicates that in electronics, a given percentage change in the number of men in the second experience class (PO3's and designated strikers) has six times as much impact on effectiveness as the same percentage change in the number of men in the first experience class (untrained men in electronics). Thus, untrained men in electronics are not worth very much compared to barely trained men; very great increases in their numbers will have relatively little effect on effectiveness of the electronics maintenance part of the Navy.

4.7. How the Model Functions

Now let us see how the model ties together these various concepts discussed above. The model operates alternately with planning and action cycles. In the planning cycle, the model begins with a requirement for the number of men in each experience class needed in each year of the 30-year time frame. It converts these requirements into effectiveness targets by means of raising each Y_i, that is the number of men in each usefulness class stated in official Navy personnel requirements, to the exponent of its β_i, relative impact factor, and multiplying out, as in formula (1). The model begins with the strength of the Navy at the beginning of each year. It then uses survival rates for each longevity year, mapped onto the experience classes, derived from the surveys as indicated above, and from historical data, to attrite men from each longevity year group, and thus derives the number on board at the end of the year in each experience class. (Naturally, the largest attritions take place in the fourth and twentieth longevity years.) Note that we are still in the planning cycle.

Using the relative impact factors, it computes the estimated effectiveness of those expected to remain on board at the end of the year. It then compares this with the effectiveness target for the year and computes a first trial guess at how many men need to be inducted as recruits during the year so that effectiveness on board will equal or exceed effectiveness targets. The model repeats planning for each calendar year, projecting ahead the actual on-board effectiveness for the end of the year, comparing this to the requirements, and planning to induct men as necessary to equal or exceed the requirements (see Figure 4).

It is of considerable interest that the model will equal or *exceed* requirements for any given year. This is because the inputs in a given year will affect not only the total operational effectiveness for that year, but those for succeeding years. In other words, men in usefulness class 1 in year t will be in usefulness class 2 in year $t + 1$ and in usefulness classes 3 and 4 in succeeding years, if they stay in the Navy that long.

The model plans ahead. It inducts men in year t not only to satisfy year t's requirements but so that requirements will be met in future years $t + x$. Thus it is not only possible but in some cases desirable that the model induct a sufficient number of men in any given year, to *overfulfill* that year's requirements, holding these men in the Navy, developing their training and experience, so that when increased needs are to be met in future years, there will be trained and experienced men available to meet them.

The model does this planning ahead in an iterative manner. That is, it starts out with a first guess at the numbers of men that should be inducted for each of the next thirty years and concomitant cost expenditures. It then looks to see if costs can be

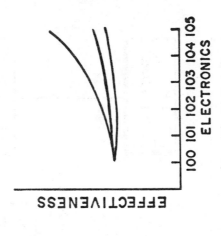

$$\text{EFFECTIVENESS} = Y_1^{.07} \ Y_2^{.45} \ Y_3^{.35} \ Y_4^{.13}$$

ELECTRONICS

100 101 102 103 104 105

EFFECTIVENESS

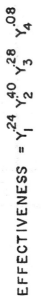

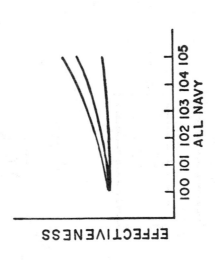

$$\text{EFFECTIVENESS} = Y_1^{.24} \ Y_2^{.40} \ Y_3^{.28} \ Y_4^{.08}$$

ALL NAVY

100 101 102 103 104 105

EFFECTIVENESS

Fig. 3   EFFECTIVENESS VS. INCREASE IN   (1) BASIC   (2) APPRENTICES   (3) JOURNEYMEN (NOT SHOWN)   (4) CHIEFS

213

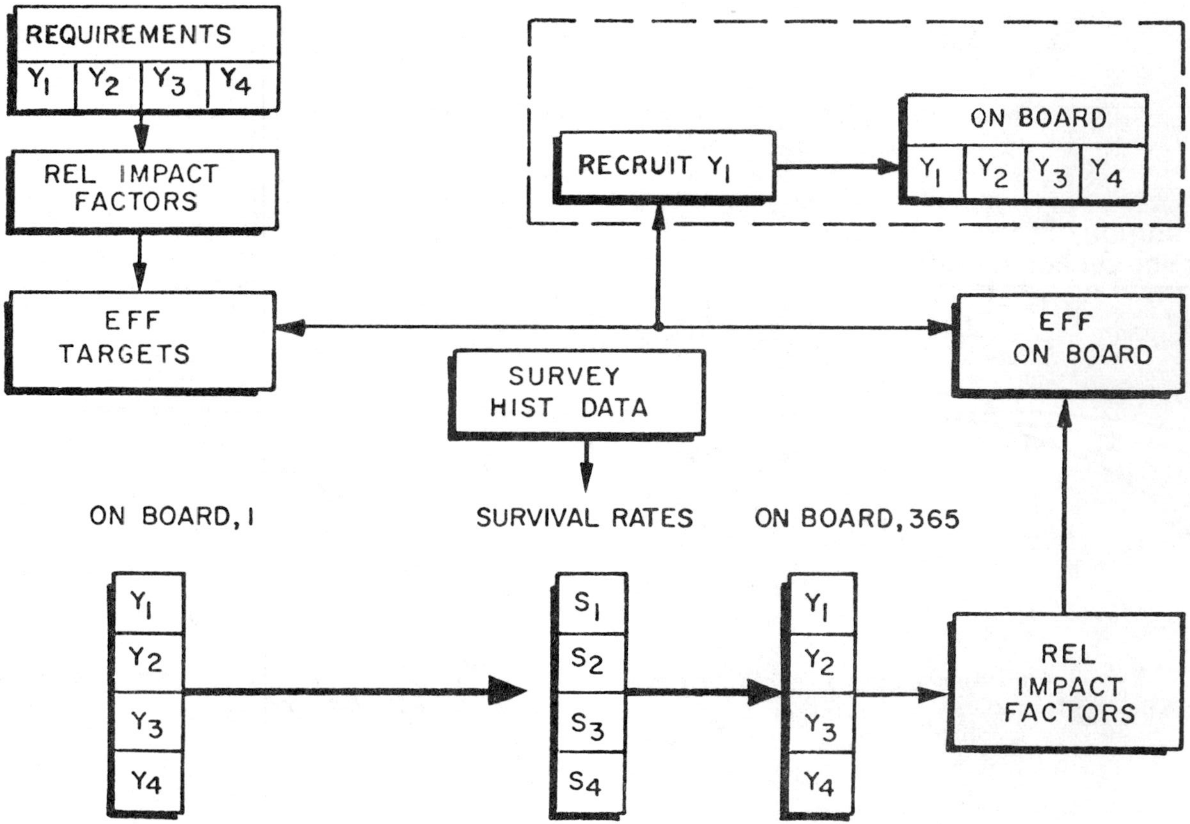

Fig. 4 C/E MODEL, PLANNING AND ACTION

reduced by a slightly different induction pattern. This slightly different pattern then becomes its second guess. Further guesses are assayed, in succession, until the model finds that further manipulations of the annual inputs would result in only insignificant reduction in costs.

At this point, the model decides for a given incentive that it has come to a reasonably optimum solution, to minimize costs over the next thirty years, for a given set of costs per man per longevity year and re-enlistment rates. This is the action phase of the cycle. The model then compares incentives, seeking that incentive which produces or exceeds the required level of operational effectiveness in each of 30 years at lowest cost. When found, that incentive is meaningfully the most efficient one. It produces a Navy which does a *given job* at the *mimimum cost*.

4.8. Discounting

Now, our discussion has so far proceeded as if the introduction of an incentive resulted in a given hypothetical Navy and given costs at one particular future time. This is not the case. Such an introduction has effects on Navy size, experience composition, and costs which last far into the future and which will generally vary in different future years. We must take account of this in our analysis.

In treating this problem, we treated costs and operational effectiveness somewhat differently. Costs are in dollar terms and it is clear in principle how costs in one year should be compared with costs in another and how a whole stream of future costs should be assigned a single value. This is accomplished by computing the *present discounted value* of the cost stream, using a discount rate, 5%, which reflects the trade-off between present and future costs. Operational effectiveness is not discounted, since there is no reasonable way to talk of trade-offs among effectiveness levels in different years.

4.9. Requirements Tracks

We avoided comparison of successive years' operational effectiveness by setting up as targets, and then attaining or exceeding, minimum levels of operational effectiveness which would be achieved by hypothetical Navies. We posited four sets of requirements, two electronics, and two All-Navy, each stretching through the 30-year time frame. The first two sets of OE requirements (one for electronics, the other for the entire Navy) were derived from Navy projected requirements from 1965 to 1980, extrapolated to 1994, assuming no change after 1980. The second two sets of OE requirements derived from our own estimates of strategic considerations for the future Navy.

4.10. Choice of Time Frame

A time frame of 30 years was chosen as a compromise solution in response to the following considerations. First, the typical length of active duty for career men is 20 years, setting a lower bound for the length of the time frame. Second, an increment of some years above this lower bound gave us a reasonable expectation that toward the end of the time frame a steady state would have been reached. Reaching a steady state means that the annual recruit input rates would be relatively constant from year to year, assuming that total requirements do not increase during the last years of the time frame.[1] Third, forecasts of requirements are limited to the next 15 years, so that requirements set up for times after that are open to doubt, the more so, the longer the estimated requirements extend beyond the 15 year time frame. Finally, the discounted costs incurred in years *far* in the future do not exert a strong effect on the total costs integrated over 30 years. For example, with our discount rate of 5%, only $0.23

---

[1] Our costs included *all* the costs incurred during their Navy careers by men inducted in the model, even those inducted toward the end of the time frame. This avoided undesirable end effects.

is added to the summary costs for each dollar spent in the thirtieth calendar year of the time frame. Considering the minimal effect of the costs in year 30 on total costs, it is not worthwhile to extend the time frame beyond 30 years.

4.11. Summary of Model Functioning

We sought those incentives which would achieve in every year in the time frame at least the same operational effectiveness as a specified Navy, at lowest present value of cost. Since, even though we cannot measure operational effectiveness, we can tell in principle when one Navy is more effective than another (by asking which combination of experience and size is preferred), this is a meaningful procedure. It has the advantage of not attempting the comparison of operational effectiveness in different years and the associated possible disadvantage of assuming that no cost saving of any size will compensate for any shortage in operational effectiveness below the minimum specified for a particular year. That disadvantage is largely alleviated, however, by the fact that we tested the sensitivity of the results to two sets of minimum operational effectiveness requirements.

4.12. Sensitivity Testing Results

Since the model involved a number of assumptions, we felt it wise to do some sensitivity testing. First, we found that the results, (ordinally stated) were insensitive to the two kinds of *requirements* assumed. Second, they were insensitive to four kinds of *credibility calibrations*, all variants of the way in which we estimated the proportions of men who *would* re-enlist from those who *said* they would re-enlist for given incentives. Third, in this study, we used a *5% discount rate*. In the previous incentive survey study, we had found that results were insensitive to the differences between 3%, 5% and 7% discount rates. Finally, in this study we found results insensitive to *variations in the Beta weights* in the nonlinear effectiveness functions.

The ordinal insensitivity of results is based on an analysis which showed the ranked cost of the twenty-three incentives, with variations, so that 41 cases were run for each assumption set. Coefficients of concordance among the rankings of costs for all assumption sets were of the order of .99.

4.13. Results - All Navy

Now let us talk about substantive results for the entire Navy. Some of these are shown in Figure 5.

Possibly our most important result, as shown in Figure 5, is that, *to achieve given effectiveness levels*, the manpower-related cost of running The Navy as a whole *increases* as the re-enlistment rate increases within a given range about its present value. I wish to emphasize that the $55-1/2 billion cost Navy attained by a re-enlistment rate of 18% produces the *same* operational effectiveness in each of 30 calendar years as does the 64-1/2 billion dollar cost Navy attained by a re-enlistment rate of 40%. Only the costs differ, because of different re-enlistment rates and the resultant different mixes of experienced and inexperienced men.

This result should not be taken to imply that the Navy should attempt to lower its re-enlistment rate. The price of a very low re-enlistment rate and the relatively low final cost which goes with it is the necessity of inducting very many men in each year of the time frame. Currently the Navy recruits about 100,000 men a year. Depending upon the assumptions made about the relative impact factors of untrained men, the model indicates that a re-enlistment rate of 18% forces inductions of between 117,000 and 121,000 men in the first year of the time frame and 146,000 to 148,000 men in the last year. Even though the low re-enlistment rate seems to lower total costs, it is highly unlikely that the Navy could recruit the number of men required with such a low first term re-enlistment rate, even with the draft.

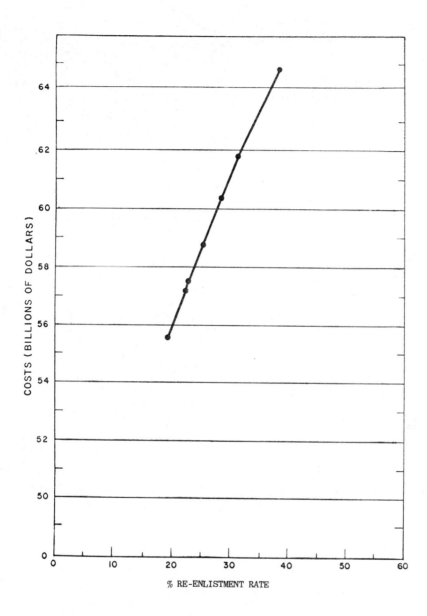

Fig. 5 RE-ENLISTMENT RATE VS. COSTS: ALL-NAVY RESULTS $\beta = 1$

217

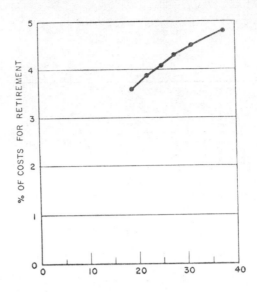

Fig. 6 RE-ENLISTMENT RATE VS. % COSTS OF RETIREMENT: ALL-NAVY RESULTS $\beta = 1$

One reason for what we saw in Figure 5 is shown in Figure 6. As the re-enlistment rate goes up, so does the proportion of men who stay until retirement. As is well known, a man who re-enlists after his first term (4th year) has a very high probability of staying 20 years, until retirement. A re-enlistment rate of about 18% means 3½% of manpower costs go for retirement pay; a re-enlistment rate of 38% means that almost 5% of total manpower costs go for retirement pay. Retirement pay is only part of the story, however. Various active duty costs, such as pay and allowances and training costs, also contribute to the extremely high cost of maintaining a very high re-enlistment rate.

This result seems to contradict frequently held notions which emphasize heavy training costs for first termers and conclude that re-enlisting them will save the costs of training their replacements. First term training costs are indeed sizable; about $4,000 and $2,000 per man in electronics and All Navy, respectively. In addition, however, post first term training costs are even larger for the electronics group (about $4,500 and $5,600 per second- and third-termer respectively) and the same order of magnitude as those for first termers for the All Navy group (about $1,800 and $1,200 for the second- and third-termer respectively). More important, these sizable training costs for experienced men are *not accompanied by commensurate increases in effectiveness* (as measured by the relative impact factors).

4.14. Results - Electronics Maintenance and Repair Group

Table 1 shows costs in billions of dollars for achieving or exceeding the electronics effectiveness goals for a 30-year period, and in terms of cost proportional to those for incentive 000, the Navy as is, with the then-current first term re-enlistment rate of 24.9%. Incentive 103, with lowest costs, enables men to leave the Navy after 10 years of service, with vested rights to retirement pay beginning at age 40. Since we did not know what proportion would avail themselves of this incentive at their tenth year of service, the analysis assumed that a very large proportion would do so. We assumed that all the re-enlistment *increment*, that is the difference between 27.8% and 24.9%, would leave at the end of the year of service nine; in addition we assumed that 10% of those 24.9% who would have re-enlisted for the present Navy incentive package would leave at the end of that year of service.

TABLE 1

ELECTRONICS RESULTS ($\beta = 1$)

INCENTIVE		COST ($ BILLIONS)	PROPORTIONAL COST	RE-ENLISTMENT RATE
103.	VERY MANY RETIRE AT 10 YEARS	7.445	98.9	27.8%
200.	MENTAL LEVEL I, WARRANT OFFICER AT 10 YEARS	7.480	99.3	29.9%
000.	NAVY-AS-IS	7.529	100.0	24.9%
101.	MANY RETIRE AT 10 YEARS	7.539	100.1	27.8%

Incentive 200, the second least costly, involved giving all enlisted men in Mental Group I the opportunity to become Warrant Officers after ten years of enlisted service. We assumed that 75% of the men eligible would avail themselves of the opportunity. Since Mental Group I is the very top few per cent of even electronics men, a highly selected group in themselves, the program would produce about 700 Warrant Officers per year. Part of the reason for the favourable cost picture is that Incentive 200, like Incentive 103, encourages men to leave the enlisted ranks in mid-career. However, because its costs are so close to those for the Navy as is, and within the 1% margin of error involved in the iterations which gave the minimum discounted costs for each program, we did not conclude that Incentive 200 would result in significant cost savings.

By contrast with Incentive 103, Incentive 101 resulted in costs slightly higher than those for the Navy as is. In this, we assumed that only the re-enlistment increment would leave at year 10.

In conclusion, I shall quote from the last few paragraphs of the summary report of this study:

By far the largest difference in relative impact factors between adjacent experience classes exists between classes 1 and 2. This difference exemplifies the real-world difference between untrained and just-trained men. Since this transition is achieved, by and large, within the first term, early retirement at ten years does not make it particularly difficult to meet requirements since it does not affect directly the proportion of men in usefulness class 2. Retirement at ten years does indeed affect (it increases), the proportion of men in experience class 3, while reducing the proportion of men in experience class 4. Since the direct costs of keeping a man in service rise with the length of that service (because pay rises with seniority and retirement benefits accumulate), the early retirement incentives reduce the direct costs associated with having a given time profile of experienced men in the Navy by reducing the average length of service of such men.[1] It is both reasonable and consistent with our results as to the worth of increasing the first term re-enlistment rate, if other things remain equal, to find that the early retirement incentives cost out as more efficient than the present incentive program.

---

[1] This would not be true if the survival rates of men beyond the first term were not already high, since allowing early retirement would be expensive if a substantial number of experienced men left the Navy after ten years with the current incentive program, thus forfeiting retirement rights. In such a case, the early retirement option might not reduce the average length of service of experienced men but would add an additional cost.

We found that as the re-enlistment rate goes up in small amounts, costs go up. Conversely, as the re-enlistment rate goes down in small amounts, costs go down.[1] We also found that the only incentive tested for the electronics cases, which resulted in noticeably lower costs, was one which assumed that many people would leave at year of service 10.

It would seem that additional studies on the effects of lowering survival rates and/ or changing cost structure in mid-career would be in order. The results obtained are clearly a result of fact that, once men have made the transition into year of service 5, they tend to remain in the Navy until retirement.

5. MULTIVARIATE STUDY OF ENLISTED RETENTION (MUSTER)[2]

5.1. Study Population

MUSTER, the Multivariate Study of Enlisted Retention, was based on the complete Enlisted Master Tape of the Navy of approximately 585,000 people. We eliminated about 473,000 because they did not come up for re-enlistment during the time frame of the study, approximately fiscal 1963. About 3,000 men re-enlisted in October 1963. The computer tapes for those who chose not to re-enlist during October were not available, so that we could not compare the re-enlistees with them; these records were not analyzed. About 26,000 men were not eligible or recommended for re-enlistment. These were not included in the study, nor were approximately 1,600 Navy women. About 97,000 men and women were not included in the study because they were Naval reservists, deserter enlistments, men with more than 21 years of service, or women not re-enlisting in our time frame. This left us with about 39,000 men who re-enlisted and 44,000 men who had the opportunity to re-enlist but did not do so in this time frame.

5.2. MUSTER I Analysis

In MUSTER I, we examined some of the relationships between given variables and the other variables considered in the analysis. First, we looked for artifacts, cases where the seeming relationship between variables X and Y was in fact the result of a true relationship between variables X' and Y. In these cases, if we held X' constant, the apparent relationship between X and Y (re-enlistment rate) would disappear.

Second, we looked for interactions: we examined the relationship between two independent variables, X and X', and the re-enlistment rate Y. In some cases, the catalytic interaction between X and X' might make the re-enlistment rate for a bivariately defined subgroup *lower* and in others, *higher*, than one would have predicted from a linear model of X or X' alone.

Finally, we looked for moderator effects. Here, a variable, X' acts as a *moderator* upon the directionality of the relationship between variables X and the re-enlistment rate, Y. As X' varies, the relationship between X and Y varies.

In MUSTER I, we analyzed the relationship between various variables and the re-enlistment rate, for four groups, first termers in electronics, first termers in other ratings than in electronics, career men in electronics, and non-electronics career men.

Figure 7 shows the relationship between mental level and re-enlistment rate. For first termers, both electronics and non-electronics, it is essentially curvilinear. Even disregarding the "no data available" group to the right, we see that those on the extreme ends of the distribution tend to have a higher re-enlistment rate than those in the middle. The first three first term electronics points to the left may be disregarded, since they contain among them fewer than 1% of the population.

---

[1] This result is, of course, contingent upon present US military costs per longevity year.
[2] Dr. Arnold Singer acted as task leader for this study. Significant contributions were made by Dr. Joseph Bryan of the Travellers Research Centre, and Mr. Charles Berndtson.

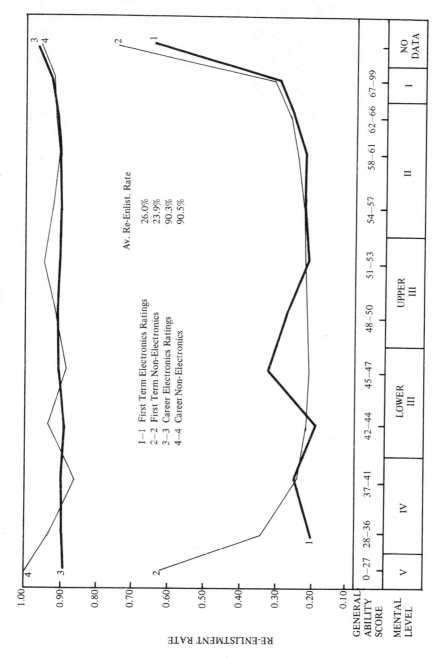

Fig. 7 RE-ENLISTMENT RATE VS. GENERAL ABILITY SCORE AND MENTAL LEVEL

Av. Re-Enlist. Rate

1–1 First Term Electronics Ratings	26.0%
2–2 First Term Non-Electronics	23.9%
3–3 Career Electronics Ratings	90.3%
4–4 Career Non-Electronics	90.5%

These plots are historically significant, in that previous studies had shown that the re-enlistment rate was negatively correlated with mental group. We see here that the Navy is *no* more likely to lose its more intelligent men that it is to lose those in the medium intelligence range. We also see that there is essentially no relationship between the mental group level of career men and their re-enlistment rate.

Figure 8 shows some moderator effects, i.e., the different relationships between years of education, on the one hand, and re-enlistment rate, on the other, for men in different occupational groups. For medical and dental occupational group members, the re-enlistment rate is negatively correlated with years of education. For all non-electronics men, it is, by and large, positively related. The negative relationship also exists for craftsmen and for gun crews. With this kind of data as background, we go on to MUSTER II, the study in which we sought to bring together into a fabric usable by the Navy, relationships like those shown here.

5.3. MUSTER II Purpose

The purpose of this study was, to quote the directive, an analysis of "the independent variables underlying re-enlistment ... so that we could recommend personnel practices to raise the re-enlistment rate".

The purpose of our analysis was to find a set of characteristics known at the end of three days naval service typical of the man who can be expected to re-enlist. Identified by these characteristics, men unusually likely to re-enlist can be classified into various occupations, such as electronic maintenance and repair, where it is relatively more profitable to the Navy to keep a high experience mix of men. Both single characteristics, such as general classification test scores, and joint characteristics, such as combinations of given general classification test scores and age, were used in this analysis.

The method was primarily the Regression Estimation of Event Probabilities (REEP)[1], a nonlinear regression method developed at the Travellers Research Centre, Inc., in Hartford, Connecticut, U.S.A. The method is unusual in that it uses nonlinear combinations of dummy variables, i.e., assigning scores on the basis of presence or absence of given characteristics, rather than the usual continuous scores used in regression work. In addition, we carried out multivariate analyses of re-enlistment rates similar to those used in MUSTER I.

5.4. MUSTER II Results

TABLE 2

FIRST TERM RE-ENLISTMENT RATES

	BIRTHPLACE/RESIDENCE		
	SAME	DIFFERENT	TOTAL
ELECTRONICS	$\frac{1226}{5002} = 24.5\%$	$\frac{546}{1818} = 30.0\%$	$\frac{1772}{6820} = 26.0\%$
NON-ELECTRONICS	$\frac{7214}{33998} = 21.2\%$	$\frac{2974}{10777} = 27.6\%$	$\frac{10188}{44775} = 22.8\%$
TOTAL	$\frac{8440}{39000} = 21.6\%$	$\frac{3520}{12595} = 27.9\%$	$\frac{11960}{51595} = 23.2\%$

---

[1] The purpose of REEP is similar to that of the multiple discriminant function.

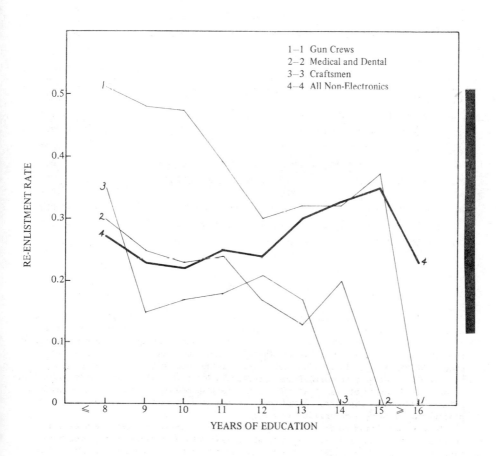

Fig. 8 FIRST TERM RE-ENLISTMENT VS. EDUCATION

Table 2 shows particularly striking results. For first termers we determined
whether their state of birth was the same as their state of residence at the time they
enlisted. Table 2 shows markedly different re-enlistment rates, for both electronics and
non-electronics men, for groups for whom these two states were the same or different.
Relationships like these were used in the regression.

Analyses were done for various groups. I shall show one for first term trainables,
i.e., men in mental level upper III or above. The group was chosen so that results from
it could be applied to the procedure for choosing men in the electronics maintenance
occupation and other "hard skill" occupations.

TABLE 3

SIGNIFICANT PREDICTORS AND REGRESSION WEIGHTS: FIRST TERM TRAINABLES

	CHARACTERISTIC	WEIGHT
0.	ADDITIVE CONSTANT	.579
1.	AT ENLISTMENT, NO PREVIOUS SERVICE AND AGE < 23	− .136
2.	BIRTHPLACE SAME AS RESIDENCE	− .075
3.	MEDIAN STATE INCOME (WHITES) ⩾ $3800	− .077
4.	WHITE AND GENERAL CLASSIFICATION + ARITHMETIC SCORES ⩾ 125	.008
5.	AT ENLISTMENT, AGE ⩾ 23 AND PREVIOUS SERVICE ⩾ 2 YRS., *OR* AGE = 21, 22 AND SERVICE ⩾ 5 YRS.	.354
6.	"EDUCATION DIFFERENCE" 1.00 TO 1.99 *AND* EDUCATION = 12 YEARS	− .052
7.	WHITE *AND* GENERAL CLASSIFICATION + ARITHMETIC SCORES < 110	− .118
8.	ELECTRONICS TECHNICIAN SELECTION TEST < 67 *AND* GENERAL CLASSIFICATION + ARITHMETIC SCORES 110–124.	− .082

DEVELOPMENTAL SAMPLE = 8136

Table 3 shows the significant predictors and their regression weights found in the
analysis. Since REEP variables are all-or-none, scores on each variable are either 1 or
0. Therefore, in order to compute a man's re-enlistment probability, a regression weight
is simply added to the sum, if he has the given characteristic, and not added to the
sum, if he has not. It is thus a simple clerical job to compute regression scores.

Now let us examine the significant predictors for this analysis which was based on a
developmental sample of more than 8,000 men. The absolute magnitudes of the regression
weights reflect the magnitude of the contribution of each variable toward significant
discrimination between re-enlisting or not.

We see that having no previous service and being younger than 23 is a negative
indicator; having enlisted in the state which was one's birthplace another negative
indicator; coming from a state where the income for whites is equal to or greater than
$3800 also negative, etc. Variable 5 is an example of the positive indicators. If either
of the following is true, for a man, .354 is added to his regression score:

(a) At enlistment he was at least 23 years of age and had at least two years of
service.

(b) At enlistment he was 21 or 22 years of age and had at least five years of
service.

Note that the preponderance of negative weights balances out the large and positive
additive constant.

224

Of course, in regression, with enough variables one can fit a curve to an elephant. It is of considerable importance to examine the results when the regression equation shown here was applied to an entirely *independent verification sample* of almost 3,900 men.

TABLE 4

PREDICTED AND ACTUAL RE-ENLISTMENT

	FIRST TERM TRAINABLES	
EXPECTED REENL. RATE	ACTUAL REENL. RATE	PERCENT OF TOTAL
LOW (.158)	.176	36.0
AVG. (.251)	.257	43.5
HIGH (.389)	.340	20.5
TOTAL (.245)	.245	100.0

N = 3869

Based upon their expected re-enlistment scores, the men in the verification sample were grouped into subgroups with low (average .158), average (average .251) and high (average .389) *expected* re-enlistment probabilities. This grouping was done entirely on the basis of the significant regression variables and scores derived therefrom.

The *actual* re-enlistment rates (behaviour three to four years after the predictor variables were entered on each record) were .176 for the low, .257 for the average, and .340 for the high group. Thus, on the basis of information available within three days of induction into the Navy, we had been able to differentiate three groups of men with significantly dissimilar re-enlistment rates. This is useful in helping the Navy to fill about 10% to 15% of its billets because slightly more than 20% of our sample was identified in the high group, 36% in the low group. Thus, for a majority of the sample, we were able to make quite successful predictions about their having, as groups, unusually low or high re-enlistment propensity, respectively. We recommended that the Navy make use of these tools, so that with no major costs, it could channel a large group of unusually re-enlistment-prone men to those occupations where it had the greatest need for a high re-enlistment rate.

New Approaches to the Determination of Shipboard Manning Requirements

CAPTAIN ROBERT G. BLACK U.S.N.

BUREAU OF NAVAL PERSONNEL, WASHINGTON

I. INTRODUCTION

For quite some time we have recognized the need for accurate measures of manpower requirements for work performance both ashore and afloat. Additionally, we need reasonably precise predictions of numbers and kinds of people required in the United States Navy over the next five years.

There are many factors complicating the task of determining current requirements. These factors increase in complexity when trying to predict true manpower requirements five years from now.

For many years we have issued a series of manpower authorization documents for ships and shore activities which set forth an "ALLOWANCE" and a "COMPLEMENT".

The term ALLOWANCE represents our best judgement as to the minimum number and spread of personnel required to carry out all normal operations and training in peacetime, plus a limited capability to "fight the ship'" for relatively short periods of time. The shore activities allowance sets forth the qualitative and quantitative naval personnel required to effectively perform all peacetime tasks.

The COMPLEMENT figure sets forth the rates and ratings required to carry out all missions and tasks in wartime.

The majority of our ships are actually manned at a figure somewhat lower than the peacetime Allowance. Number and spread of personnel on board any ship at any particular time is dependent upon budgetary considerations, re-enlistment rates, critical shortages in certain scarce skills, and many other factors.

When asked to justify our fleet manpower requirements at various review levels within the Navy and the Department of Defense, and to the Bureau of the Budget and the Congress, we were hard pressed to explain and document manpower requirements. All too often it seemed that the best answer we could give was that "experience or judgement indicates that this is the number required". For a new construction ship, our predictive capability was limited. We found ourselves saying that a ship would require "about such and such a number of officers and men" because a similar existing ship had an allowance that called for these numbers. Obviously, there was a need for a more precise system to determine manpower requirements.

2. BACKGROUND

Consequently, more than five years ago we initiated a program to improve our capability to determine the numbers and skill levels of personnel needed to accomplish required wartime and peacetime tasks. Under General Operational Requirement Number 43, the Chief of Naval Operations established the specific goal of improving our measurement and predictive capabilities to the point where we could determine the Navy's manpower requirements with an error of less than 5%.

In 1962 a Staffing Criteria Research Project was established, funded at approximately $250,000 per year, to determine the most economical and accurate methods for determining Navy manpower requirements.

This research project was assigned to the Personnel Research Laboratory, Washington, a field activity of the Bureau of Naval Personnel. For the next year and a half, a group of 16 Industrial Engineers and Management Analysts were recruited to undertake the development of a comprehensive Navy Staffing Criteria System.

The first class of ships studied in depth in this program was the CVS-10 Class, Anti-Submarine Warfare Support Aircraft Carriers. Teams from the Laboratory conducted on-site studies on four ships, and determined that the work performed on board a CVS could be logically divided into 22 functions and 85 subfunctions. A function is an area of work which is distinguished by the requirement for specialized skill or knowledge and is usually performed by a major organizational element or unit. Subfunctions are groups of related tasks or duties performed within the function. At the subfunction level a *workload indicator* or a unit of work is selected as a measure to represent aggregate of related work performed. This led to the development of staffing criteria which are essentially management standards defining relationships of manpower requirements with work to be performed. Table 1 illustrates a typical Staffing Table.

This table sets forth the manpower required in the Inside Electrical Repair shop of a Repair Ship. You see from the Brief "Work Performed Statement", that personnel employed in the shop rewind generators, motors, stators, and armatures; they wind coils and resurface commutators and slip rings. The most appropriate measure of the volume of work performed is the number of work orders processed per month, which has been selected as the workload indicator. The billets required to accomplish varying amounts of work are shown in columns (9) through (17).

Hundreds of tables similar to this one have been developed and promulgated in the U.S. NAVY STAFFING CRITERIA MANUAL FOR ACTIVITIES AFLOAT and the companion volumes for ACTIVITIES ASHORE. By mid 1966, the Afloat Manual contained staffing tables covering all work functions and subfunctions performed on a total of 168 ships. The Ashore Manual contained Staffing Tables covering 35 functions and 240 subfunctions.

3. APPLICATION OF STAFFING CRITERIA

To facilitate use of the Staffing Criteria Tables by planners and allowance writers the Afloat Manual was organized into chapters covering individual classes of ships. Here, for the first time, we felt that we had a documented statement of the peacetime manpower required for each of the ship classes that had been studied. In addition to Staffing Tables in the Manual, individual research reports were published covering the studies on each of the classes of ships. These reports compared the allowances resulting from the rigorous application of staffing criteria with those presently allowed on the Manpower Authorization Documents. In accordance with guidance issued by the Chief of Naval Operations, staffing criteria tables for functions performed ashore were based on a 40 hour workweek, while tables for activities performed aboard combat ships were based on a minimum of 56 hours of work per week while at sea. Where necessary the at sea workweek could be expanded to 70 hours per man.

Using this rationale, application of the criteria to work being performed on ships called for increases more frequently than it called for decreases. There were, however, instances where application of the criteria indicated that a ship's allowance could be substantially reduced.

For example, Table 2 shows how the application of staffing criteria for Repair Ships would effect the allowance of a particular ship. Applying the criteria against the work actually performed for the previous twelve months, it is indicated that the ship's allowance called for 128 more billets than were actually required. From a manpower utilization standpoint the corrective action could be either the assignment of more work orders to the ship or a reduction in the allowance – or some of each.

TABLE 1 STAFFING TABLE

Code No.: 80 30 1.1
Function: REPAIR
Subfunction: Electrical Repair
Subfunction Subdivision: Inside Electrical Repair

Staffing is applicable to Allowance Planning.
Degrees of Readiness Considered: All
Workload Indicator: No. of Work Orders Processed Per Month

	QUALITATIVE REQUIREMENTS							QUANTITATIVE PERSONNEL REQUIREMENTS								
	OFFICER			ENLISTED		CIVIL SERVICE CODE		Increments of Workload Indicator								
BILLET TITLE	Desig	Gr	NOBC	Rate	NEC			31-40	41-50	51-60	61-70	71-80	81-90	91-100	101-110	111-120
(1)	(2)	(3)	(4)	(5)	(6)	(7)	(8)	(9)	(10)	(11)	(12)	(13)	(14)	(15)	(16)	(17)
Shop Supervisor				EMCS									1	1	1	1
Inside Repair Supervisor .				EMC				1	1	1	1	1	1	1	1	1
Assistant Supervisor . . .				EM1						1	2	2	2	2	4	4
Electrician Repairman . .				EM2				3	3	3	4	5	7	8	11	12
Electrician Repairman . .				EM3				3	4	5	5	5	6	7	5	6
Electrician Repairman . .				EMFN				2	3	3	3	4	4	4	3	3
Electrician Helpers . . .				FA				2	2	2	2	3	3	3	3	3
Lathe Operator				MR3							1	1	1	1	1	1
Total Staffing (Enlisted) . . .								11	13	15	18	21	25	27	29	31

Work Performed: Rewinds and repairs generators, motors, stators and armatures. Winds coils, and resurfaces commutators and slip rings.

228

TABLE 2

AR-13 ENLISTED PAY GRADE COMPARISONS

PAY GRADE	OPNAV 1000/2	STAFFING CRITERIA
E-9	6	3
E-8	8	4
E-7	27	35
E-6	91	65
E-5	125	87
E-4	168	130
E-3*	25	81
E-3	164	115
E-2	91	57
TOTALS	705	577

*Designated Striker

Applying the criteria to the work being performed indicates a need for

(1) More Work Orders

or

(2) 128 Fewer Billets

TABLE 3

APPLYING THE SAME CRITERIA TO OTHER AR SHIPS

	OPNAV 1000/2	STAFFING CRITERIA	
AR-8	624	662	+38
AR-23	556	568	+12

Table 3 shows that the application of the same criteria to two other Repair Ships gives different results. The workload of each of these ships was sufficient to justify slight increases in their current manpower authorizations.

4. THE PILOT STUDY

4.1. Planning of Objectives

In the summer of 1966, we had reason to feel that the Staffing Criteria Program was possibly ready to move from the Exploratory Development stage to a full scale operation that would be used in the periodic adjustment of allowances for ships and shore stations.

Before continuing in the development of the staffing criteria research program, a full scale review was undertaken of the entire program. The results of the exploratory stage were evaluated to see if we had accomplished our original mission. Could the allowance writers use the staffing tables as satisfactory documentation to the Department of Defense and to the Bureau of the Budget? Were the staffing tables easily understood? Was there adequate information in the tables to permit users to justify an increase or a decrease in allowance? In other words, were the staffing tables fully documented, and was the format adequate, to assure complete understanding by any user?

Some problem areas were discovered. What was clear to staffing criteria developers caused some difficulty to the users because detailed documentation for allowance changes could not, due to space limitations, be included in the tables.

A pilot study was established, therefore, as a joint effort of researchers from the laboratory and the allowance writers. The study had two major objectives:

> (i) Determine with the greatest possible accuracy the manpower required for a given class of ships.   and
>
> (ii) Present this information in a format acceptable to higher authorities in the chain of command.

A decision was made to use the DD-710 Class of Destroyers for the pilot study, because the U.S. Navy operates 77 destroyers in this class; staffing criteria had been previously developed and published for ships of this class; and this class of ships was one of the first in which our relatively new 3M System had been installed (Maintenance Material Management).

I re-emphasize that the pilot study was truly a joint effort on the part of research personnel and allowance writers. Civilian Industrial Engineers and Management Analysts from the Personnel Research Laboratory worked with the Active duty naval officers charged with the task of writing ship's allowances. Weekly meetings were set up to discuss the progress of the study with high level officers on the staff of the Chief of Naval Operations.

A target date of 30 December 1966 was established for completion of the Study and Documentation of the Manpower Requirements for the DD-710 Class. This date was met. In January 1966, meetings were held with Fleet and Type Commanders to obtain their views on the new method of documenting requirements. Their response was highly enthusiastic and the changes recommended in these meetings were of a minor nature.

4.2. Derivation of Manning Requirements

Let us take a closer look at the manning concepts embodied in the DD-710 Pilot Study. Figure 1 illustrates the factors that determine manpower requirements on a Navy ship.

First, we know that the ship was built for a particular purpose or *mission*. In carrying out this mission a number of *tasks* must be accomplished. For a ship already constructed and in operation, the *size* and *configuration* of the ship are known factors.

The bulk of the manning requirements stem from the necessity to *operate* and *maintain* the equipment required to accomplish necessary tasks.

On the operational side, information is required as to the exact capabilities desired. We need decisions as to which functions must be performed simultaneously. We need decisions as to the length of time a function must be performed. For example, in the Combat Information Centre, do we expect to maintain around the clock air and surface surveillance? If so, do we also expect to maintain continuous ASW surveillance? Which of our weapons are manned in Readiness Condition III for periods of indefinite duration?

For maintenance, we require the best possible information as to the daily, weekly, monthly, and quarterly maintenance requirements established to prevent breakdowns. We need valid estimates of the number of hours that will be required for corrective maintenance. We need to determine from records or work sampling, or other means, the hours required for facility maintenance (painting, chipping, cleaning of compartments and passage ways.)

After we have determined the manpower required for *Operational Manning* and for *Maintenance Manning*, we begin to have a picture of what population we will be dealing with. We can start to compute support requirements. Every additional person on the ship adds to the support requirements. That man must be fed, his clothes must be washed, his hair cut. On larger ships we do his dry cleaning and maintain a cobbler shop. Someone must receive and distribute his mail, and someone else will maintain his pay records.

In the supply department, considered a part of our support manning, *usage* factors will influence the number of line items which must be stocked.

Finally there is one more requirement, and we label that *Administrative Manning*. A ship is no sooner commissioned than it acquires a tremendous volume of directives. As it acquires a population, requirements are established to maintain personnel records on an

Fig. 1   DERIVATION OF ENLISTED MANNING SYSTEM REQUIREMENTS FOR U.S. NAVY SHIPS

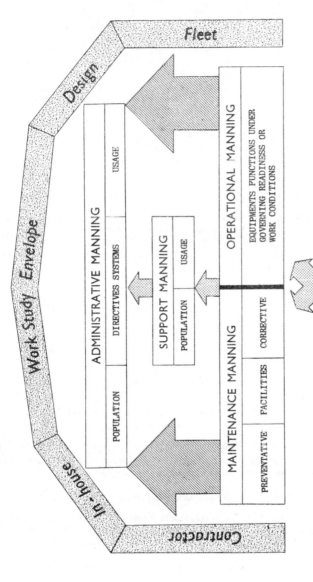

individual and collective basis. Training programs must be provided, examinations administered, disciplinary cases must be processed.

With information developed and recorded concerning *operational* manning, *maintenance* manning, *support* manning, and *administrative* manning, we have a further requirement which we have labelled the "WORK-STUDY ENVELOPE". This work study may be done by contractors, or by "in-house" personnel. It may be a full scale Design Work Study, as in the case of a new ship being built in today's environment, or a study conducted by one of our Fleet Work Study Teams on a ship constructed 20 years ago.

In this final phase all the bits and pieces of information are put together. Here we are finally able to record what each man does in each condition of readiness, what watches he stands, what equipment he maintains, how much time must be allowed for service diversions, delays, leave, TAD, time spent in Sick Bay, etc. We are also looking at requirements other than battle: What special situations or evolutions may prove to be governing? In the case of an oiler, for example, the maximum number of people required is not in a combat situation, but in the replenishment evolution.

We may discover during the work study phase on some ships that the factor which determines the minimum acceptable number of men in the Engineering Function is the number required to get the ship underway in an emergency when three of the four duty sections are on liberty.

4.3. Documentation of Ship Manning

The DD-710 Ship Manning Document seems to represent the best format which has been developed to date for use in the justification of manpower requirements to higher authority. In one sense it is a Table of Organization and Equipment. In fact, consideration was given to the use of this as a title for the documentation. Essential elements listed are:

4.3.1. *Mission and Tasks*

4.3.2. *Doctrinal Constraints*

4.3.3. *Scenario*

For example, the DD-710 manning requirements were stated for the following conditions:
  (i) At sea in wartime or contingency environment.
  (ii) All offensive and defensive functions capable of being performed simultaneously.
  (iii) Other functions not required to be performed simultaneously.
  (iv) Continuous Readiness Condition III – Three Section Watch Basis.
  (v) All maintenance assigned to ship responsibility capable of being accomplished.
  (vi) During inport periods, all requirements are satisfied with four section watch including maintenance, leave, TAD, training, etc.

4.3.4. *Functions as Related to Installed Systems/Equipments*

This portion of the documentation is particularly important since it provides the basis for trade-off decisions. Here we can answer such questions as, "What manpower do we save if we remove a particular piece of equipment and the related function?"

4.3.5. *Basic Manning Criteria (Maintenance, Operational, Support, and Admin)*

You have seen how these building blocks become a part of the whole manpower requirement.

4.3.6. Applied Work Study

Productivity (What level can we expect?)
Service Diversions (How much time must be allowed for these?)
Utility Tasks (What are the hours required? – determine through Work Sampling Techniques.)
Improvements through Method Study.

4.3.7. Manning Requirements Other Than Battle

Here we have a listing of the various evolutions and the manpower required for each.

5. THE CONCEPT OF CONDITIONAL MANNING

It is, of course, quite possible that we will not be able to afford "battle manning" for all of our ships — all of the time. In this event we can employ what I term *"Conditional Manning"*.

(i) If battle manning represents the minimum manpower for wartime operations, any reduction in manning shall be accompanied by a reduction in responsibility to perform associated functions.

(ii) It appears feasible to draft manpower authorization documents using the battle manning as the basic measure of requirements. Billets which will not be filled under "Conditional Manning" would be coded in the manpower authorization document. Functions not capable of being performed under conditional manning would be stated in the manpower authorization.

(iii) The coded billets would serve as a base for mobilization plans.

6. CONCLUSION

Reaction to our new methods of documenting ship manning requirements has been generally favourable. I think it is important to note that the techniques and procedures now used to determine manpower requirements do not vary greatly from those employed in the earlier phases of the staffing criteria program. However, the resulting information is packaged in a format which seems to meet the needs of potential users (allowance writers) and the various reviewing authorities (DOD Systems Analysis, Bureau of the Budget, etc.).

Our research schedule calls for the development of complete ship manning documents for 32 different classes of ships by 1970. At the present time we are conducting studies aboard Guided Missile Destroyers, Nuclear Powered Submarines, and Repair Ships. Over the next two years, through the continued joint efforts of our researchers and line officers, we expect to further refine our work measurement techniques and to improve the documentation format.

The Social Survey in Manpower Research

D.M. MONK

RESEARCH SERVICES LTD., LONDON

I. INTRODUCTION

My justification for addressing this conference is my employment with a survey
research company that has, on occasion, conducted studies into the recruitment and
retention of manpower. Such studies are not commissioned very frequently and what
experience or expertise I have is in the general application of the survey method; not
in a detailed knowledge of manpower research. My intention, therefore, is to indicate
the importance and relevance of the social survey to manpower research and planning, and
to illustrate some of the points with examples from completed studies. However, as part
of my thesis is that the techniques that have been developed for social surveys have
been under-utilized in manpower planning, there will be a bias towards potential rather
than actual use.

2. THE NATURE OF THE SOCIAL SURVEY

The social survey is widely used by commerce, central and local government, political
parties and academic social scientists — yet it is difficult to arrive at a precise
definition. The term has been used to cover sample surveys of well defined populations,
censi of special populations, studies using observational methods only, and studies that
would be regarded by many as experiments rather than surveys. It is, in fact, a collective noun for a number of methods of collecting information about populations on a
systematic basis. Sampling is normally, but not necessarily, employed and many types of
data collection methods may be used.

Under this broad definition the survey method has been used in manpower research for
many years. Thus, to bring the topic to manageable proportions I wish to restrict my
comments to surveys where people are the universe studied, and the objectives of the
studies have included job motivation and attitudes to the work situation in addition to
simple behavioural measures. This excludes a large number of uses of the survey method —
studies of training methods in particular industries, studies of the use made of particular recruitment channels by employers, or studies of salary levels in particular
companies. Such studies present very little difficulty — either conceptually or
administratively — and there are few problems in the interpretation of the data or
definitions to be employed.

2.1. The Advantages of the Social Survey

One of the distinctive features of the social survey is that information is
collected and stored so that the inter-relationships between the various items of
information may be studied. The range of information that may be collected is extensive
and whether it is collected all from the informant, or partly from the informant and
partly from work records, production output or the school examination records, is not
important.

Very powerful analysis techniques have been devised or adapted to deal with the wide range of information, and there is now a greater appreciation of how to cope with information of different types or status. We are now well beyond the point where people commissioning research divided information obtained in surveys into facts and opinions – the former being useful and the latter interesting. The importance of accepting peoples' attitudes, motivations or opinions as relevant facts about the work situation has become fully accepted over the past decade and considerable progress has been made in developing methods of measuring them.

2.2. The Difficulties of the Social Survey

Although there is great potential for the use of the survey method in manpower research, any reading of the literature on studies that have been reported shows that many problems exist. For example, many of the criterion variables researchers would like to use, such as job satisfaction, are very difficult to define in a way that allows similar measures to be applied to different occupations. The range of techniques available for sampling, data collection and analysis means that the social survey is very flexible. However, although this flexibility allows a wide range of options when designing a study so that the particular problem to hand is answered most efficiently, this flexibility has a limiting effect at the analysis stages. Many of the difficulties that have arisen from social surveys stem from requiring answers to problems that were not included in the original specification. This, of course, is true of many scientific studies, but with social surveys there is a tendency to think that because the relevant data has been collected it can be used for any problem where such data are relevant. This is not the case, and sample design, data collection and proposed analysis must all be planned at the initial design stage.

A further difficulty with social surveys in the manpower area is that very few studies have been carried out on representative samples of the work population in general or particular occupations. This leads to the absence of population or industry norms and difficulties in interpreting data. Often this results in people assuming that survey data have a face validity which is unwarranted. Too often data showing, for example, that x per cent of members of a profession would like their son to join the profession have been interpreted on face value without knowing whether the population norm would vary from x per cent, or whether such a question effectively discriminates between types of occupation.

3. CURRENT USES OF THE SOCIAL SURVEY IN MANPOWER RESEARCH

Apart from studies conducted by academic researchers, the use of the social survey in manpower research has been concentrated into two areas: the recruitment of executives or highly qualified technical personnel, and the retention of operatives or clerical grades. This bias is understandable and is probably the same in military thinking on manpower research.

With retention studies the sampling problems are normally simple. The population to be studied is easily defined; normally it is the present employees in a department or company. Occasionally the sample is extended to include employees who have left in a specified time period. Recruitment studies have more complex sampling problems because the definition of the population from which recruits are required is more difficult, and even when a close definition is agreed easily attainable sampling frames are not always available.

A further problem in recruitment studies is the stage at which career choice should be studied. Is it more beneficial to sample graduate engineers with experience in the industry, graduate engineers below a certain age, undergraduates who are studying engineering, people in the science sixth form, or boys about to choose their sixth form course? Understandably the large commercial companies have tended to concentrate on the nearest point to a person becoming an employee – graduates or undergraduates. However, the military recruits its executives at all the levels mentioned and should be concerned with the career choice at each stage.

I will illustrate some of the work that has been carried out by selecting one study from each of the development levels — school, university and post-graduate.

3.1. Career Choice at Pre-University Level

Considerable attention has been paid to the career choice of school children, particularly with regard to the choosing of courses of study. In an economy that is making ever increasing demands for technologists the reasons for this interest are plain. In 1961 it was shown (1) that for every really bright student who chooses an engineering course there are four who choose a science course. Since the ratio of students admitted to universities was less than 1.2, it was clear that engineering departments were not obtaining their share of bright students. The Robbins Report (2) found a similar situation in 1962.

" Technology and the Sixth Form Boy ", the 1961 report referred to above, attempted to examine the extent to which attitudes to science and technology help to explain the choices of study. Very simple questioning methods were used but a relatively clear answer emerged. To quote from the report:-

" The general picture presented in this country then is of science sixth formers who divide the world only rather hazily into 'scientists' and 'technologists' .....
Scientists, they believe, are educated at universities and go on, if they are lucky, to 'do research': research is glamorous, 'interesting', leading always to exciting new discoveries, is not really 'work', and may well make you famous. Technologists, on the other hand, are educated at technical colleges, have low social prestige, are less intelligent and less well paid than scientists, and their work is often 'boring'".

Other studies such as that of School Leavers by Veness (3) and of undergraduates by the Institution of Chemical Engineers (4) have tended to show that choice of career by people leaving school is firstly based on an over-realistic assessment of personal and social limitations, and secondly is made in a state of ignorance of possible careers and advantages of particular careers.

The Robbins Report estimated that about 40 per cent of students received some advice at school about the range of courses open to them at university. One might assume that advice on careers was at a lower level. As chemical engineering is not a subject taught in the sixth form of schools, and few school science masters have been trained as chemical engineers, the Institution of Chemical Engineers carries out an educational program including literature and lectures. To help in this a study was carried out among newly arrived undergraduates in Chemistry, Chemical Engineering and Mechanical Engineering. For convenience the questionnaires were administered in the first week of the first year of their course at university or technical college, but the study may be regarded as a school leaving rather than undergraduate study.

The main conclusions of the project were:-

(i) Chemical engineers at grammar or public schools decide on their course at a considerably later stage than other students.

(ii) Chemical engineers are better informed about the type of work they will be doing after leaving college and the salary levels to be expected. However, the type of work they would like to do is in marked contrast to the distribution of employment by members of the Institution of Chemical Engineers.

(iii) The Institution's literature and activity had had a marked contribution to career choice and knowledge of chosen career.

Additional information was also obtained that enabled the career choice to be related to types of school, subject taught by headmaster and careers master, social background and other topics.

Many studies of this type have been restricted to small subsections of the population and have been designed from a particular standpoint associated with the

236

sponsor. For this reason it is encouraging that Political and Economic Planning are at present carrying out a more broadly based study of the factors influencing career choice and work aspirations. The study will cover both men and women, will be carried out among school leavers, final year students and people in an older age cohort, and will be capable of comparison with similar work being conducted in the U.S.A.

3.2. Career Choice at the University Level

More studies have been carried out at the undergraduate level than with any other section of employees or potential employees. One reason is the obvious desire of large companies to recruit efficiently from among the best graduates. The other is that the undergraduates frequently organize the studies themselves. Job aspiration and likely career choice are normally among the topics included.

Many of the studies that have been carried out on such populations have followed a standard pattern.

(i) Various careers – civil service, teaching, industry, etc. – have been rated on a number of evaluative criteria.

(ii) Within industry particular companies have been evaluated using similar criteria.

(iii) Career choice and commitment is established.

(iv) Background variables such as education, courses studied and home circumstance are recorded.

Such studies have had two main limitations: firstly, the choice of evaluative criteria is often a matter of selecting those that appear relevant, without special work being carried out; and secondly, the results have been evaluated as a simple comparative study between particular careers and companies. Little attempt has been made to determine how the undergraduate perceives his approaching employment and what are the underlying needs that he or she has. What the results do show is that such people have very strong images of particular types of employment and differentiate strongly between careers and between companies within careers.

The only study of which I am aware that includes the military as a career is that carried out by Cambridge undergraduates in 1962, (5). People were asked whether any of a number of possible reasons for rejection applied to a list of possible careers. Removing those people who said they had " no interest ", the results for five selected careers were: -

Reasons for rejecting career

	Armed Forces	Teach-ing	Civil Service	Journ-alism	Large Business Company
	%	%	%	%	%
Low social prestige	12	9	7	16	5
Insecure future	33	1	3	57	11
Work too dull	28	22	56	6	58
Pay too low	13	43	16	7	2
Limited advancement	13	24	19	14	25

Although I would not necessarily recommend the questioning techniques used I think the results are interesting. Similar profiles are obtained for the Civil Service and Large Business Companies. Also reasonably similar are the profiles for the Armed Forces and for Journalism: both score very highly on having an insecure future, but whereas the work of the Journalist is not seen as dull, a considerable number of undergraduates thought of the military life as dull.

3.3. Studies of Particular Occupations

Studies of particular occupations have been restricted to the professions or groups such as " scientists " and " technical staff ". Mostly they have been limited in scope, being carried out by means of postal questionnaires among membership of the various institutes. The exceptions to this are the study of Mechanical Engineers (6) and studies carried out in 1962 and 1967 by a commercial research company.

Perhaps because of the types of population studied the results tend to show a very similar trend in terms of career satisfaction, desire to change employment and future ambitions within their career. This could be due to the results reflecting the actual situation, or due to too little attention being paid to the meaning of satisfaction in different work contexts. There has been a tendency to use the surveys in a descriptive way only, and few attempts have been made to examine the underlying pattern of needs that cause choice of job and satisfaction in a job.

My colleague, Dr.J. Field, has recently carried out a small study into the images held of employment in the building industry, using more sophisticated principal component analysis techniques. He asked school leavers to " give a score out of ten " to a number of job attractions, for example:-

work under supervision,
left to find things out yourself,
high starting wages,
opportunities for promotion,
working with people of same age;

and to the desirability of a number of building industry jobs, for example:-

architects,
labourers,
plumbers.

A principal component analysis of the data shows the following main features:

(i) The first component contrasts labouring with opportunities for promotion – bricklaying, plumbing and plastering are associated with labouring. Working with people of own age and under supervision, given opportunities for promotion – architects and surveyors are the jobs associated with these desired conditions.

(ii) Second components are thought primarily to be associated with figures and charts. Those attracted to such work associate with architects or surveyors in contrast to bricklaying, plumbing and outdoor work generally but are inclined to consider it backroom work likely to involve fewer opportunities for promotion or work with people of the same age.

(iii) A third component contrasts having a high starting wage and being left to oneself. Working indoors and with older people are associated with higher starting wages.

Analysis of the variation per item shows, for example, that 80% of the variation in attitudes to labouring and 77% of the variation in attitudes towards opportunity for promotion are accounted for by the first component and relatively small proportions by the others. On the other hand, attitudes to early responsibility are not accounted for in any of the first five components and the variation remains largely unexplained. If the first three components, those accounting for most variation, are considered it is possible to plot on a globe points referring to occupations located in space which refers to informants, points referring to informants located in space which refers to the occupations and thirdly points referring to job qualities located in space which refers to informants. This provides the map of the underlying structure of the way that school leavers perceive the employment situation in the industry. What normally happens in this case is that the results are plotted on a plastic spherical globe, which enables one to study the dimensions and the clustering of the qualities and the jobs very much

more easily. Using such a map shows that school leavers are not so interested in
particular jobs, they are interested instead in job qualities. These job qualities —
though there must be a certain amount of value judgment in naming them — emerge as

(i) Competitive Achievement:-

Most boys want to be seen to get on. Not only must there be opportunities for
promotion, but they want both to be supervised and be with their own age group.

(ii) Job Content:-

Some boys however are more influenced by the actual nature of the jobs: working with
machinery, working out-of-doors.

(iii) Job Image:-

The significance of individual jobs was of interest. Finding things out and working
with older people were associated with being an architect or surveyor. The individual
trades — plumber, bricklayer — did rather worse. The significance these had were the
absence of the desired qualities of Achievement.

My view is that social surveys will not make any real contribution to the actions
of policy makers until the surveys conducted shift from the mainly descriptive recording
of stated degrees of satisfaction, etc., and simple analyses of such criteria with
demographic and situational variables, to a more analytic approach. Studies of the type
carried out by Field may be applied to any industry and any population. They provide
a map of the manner in which careers are perceived by possible employees and an
explanation of the dimensions that are important in such perceptions. Also, although
they have not been used for that purpose, there is no reason why they should not be
applied to employees in studies of retention of workers.

4. THE POTENTIAL FOR THE SOCIAL SURVEY IN MANPOWER RESEARCH

I said earlier that the social survey has been under-utilized in manpower research,
and I have implied in my comments on current work that where surveys are employed they
have not been used to their full potential. Too many of the studies have been designed
to answer very limited ad hoc problems on specialized samples and too few have attempted
to examine important and fundamental aspects of employment on the general population.

It is possible by comparing census material to estimate the net changes of employment in particular occupations, but only in a sample survey is it possible to examine
total or gross mobility and analyze the factors that are associated with different
levels of mobility. Such large scale surveys might also produce information relevant to
such problems as the economic benefit of different types of education, such as University
or Technical College; or the likely effects of taxation or other government action on
work mobility or entering the work force at all.

There is another major benefit that would stem from the use of social surveys in
this way. I am conscious that this conference program is broadly divided into two
sections. The first has a bias towards econometric, model-building and operations
research aspects of manpower planning, while the second has an emphasis on the work
situation and an occupational psychology approach. My impression as an outsider is that
the two activities are very separate and that survey information on the general work
population would help bring the two approaches together.

Large scale surveys would supply some of the necessary input data for models used
in manpower planning. They would also be able to test on the general working population
some of the hypotheses developed in small scale studies by occupational psychologists,
involving variables such as attitude to work, ambitiousness, work behaviour and education
level. In addition, they would provide population values against which the smaller
factory or industry located studies could be compared.

In the final analysis, however, the social survey is a technique that has value only when policy makers perceive a need for information that will guide their decisions. Thus, I will end by posing some questions:-

(i) How has the relative attractiveness of a career in the armed forces changed in the eyes of young people during the past five years?

(ii) What sources of advice or approval does a young man turn to when considering a career in the armed forces, and which reinforce or negate his joining?

(iii) After segmenting the younger population into different levels of technical training or technical aptitude, how well is the military maintaining its share of better qualified people?

(iv) For promotional purposes, what are the positive features that attract young people and what are the negative features that deter them?

(v) What terms of service in the military have greatest appeal to various groups of the population?

Only if there is a real need for such information will the social survey make a significant contribution to manpower research in the defence context.

REFERENCES

1. *Technology and the Sixth Form Boy*, 1963, (Oxford: Department of Education).
2. *Report of the Committee on Higher Education (Robbins Report)*. Command 2154, 1963. (London HMSO)
3. Veness, T. *School Leavers: Their Aspirations and Expectations*. London, Methuen 1962.
4. The Choice of Chemical Engineers at University or Technical College, *The Institution of Chemical Engineers*, 1964.
5. Cambridge Opinion — unpublished survey, 1962.
6. Gerstle and Hutton, *Engineers: The Anatomy of a Profession*, Tavistock Press, 1966.

Comment

LT. CDR. PAUL D. NELSON, U.S.N.

Mr. Monk's presentation quite clearly demonstrates the necessity for integrating, not only methods and problem areas of study, but also levels of society to be studied with regard to the military. The armed forces personnel come from the civilian society at large and then return to that civilian society. There are at all times reference points in the civilian society and I think that unless we have a firm feeling for that which Dr. Wilkins described as national character and also that which Mr. Monk has described in his various normative studies then we will never be completely in touch with some of the bases for decisions made by military men, e.g. the alternatives which exist when it is time to make a decision as to whether to remain in the Service or not. The fact that young men have a particular view of the military prior to coming into the Service may be somewhat academic by virtue of the fact that they are in some ways compelled to serve in the military. However, the pre-service image has certainly served as a significant base line attitudinally from which military experience allows the man to change or modify his value system as specific attitudes.

In summary I would like to suggest that regardless of what area of work we are engaged in in life the first approach in attempting to define the reward system for work is to look on the surface of the matter. We have been through the satisfaction indices, these are what I might refer to as public indices of reward, but I think in the final analysis the most significant rewards are relatively private, that is, they are contained in such conceptualizations as the individual's system of aspirations and personally perceived achievements and his rewarding experiences as a member of a close cohesive unit – the merit of which has been discussed very well by Dr. Little in some of his writings. Interestingly enough, in almost none of the military research that I have known of have we had much attention paid to the concept of personal influence which has almost taken over social psychology, the person-to-person influence which must exist to some extent in determining various roads that young men take. This is not an easy matter to study and I do not believe that we should study this at the expense of the other types of information, but I suggest, as a concluding remark, that some of our future work might be along – as Mr. Monk has described – more dynamic rather than static concepts.

Selected Tables from Surveys of the United States Military Age Population, Oct-Dec. 1964

HAROLD WOOL

DIRECTOR OF PROCUREMENT POLICY,

U.S. DEPARTMENT OF DEFENSE

In April 1964, a comprehensive study of the draft system was undertaken by the Department of Defense at the direction of the President. A major objective of the study was to assess the possibility of meeting military manpower requirements on a completely voluntary basis in the coming decade. In addition, data were collected to aid in an evaluation of the operation of the existing Selective Service System and of possible alternatives to existing draft selection policies.

In support of this study, a number of statistical surveys were initiated by the Department of Defense. These were designed, generally, to obtain information on the current military service status of men of military service age, to determine key factors influencing decisions of young men concerning volunteering for military service and to help in assessing the effects of draft liability upon their employment and personal plans. The surveys were conducted by the Bureau of the Census for civilians, and the Department of Defense for military personnel. (Other special studies were conducted by the Selective Service System, the Department of Labor, the Department of Health, Education and Welfare, and other Federal agencies.)

Selected tables developed from these surveys are presented in the next few pages. They are followed by a brief technical note on each of the three surveys.

TABLE 1

Estimated Percentages of First-Term Enlisted Personnel
Who Enlisted Primarily Because of the Draft by Service
(Based on Responses to Alternative Survey Questions, October 1964)

	Per Cent Draft-Motivated	
	Would not have enlisted if no draft[1]	Draft or military obligation primary reason for enlisting[2]
All Services	38.0	37.1
Army	43.2	38.6
Navy	32.6	31.5
Marine Corps	42.9	43.1
Air Force	30.4	38.6

[1] Based on responses to question: " If there had been no draft and you had not had any military obligation at the time you first entered on active military service, do you think you would have entered the service? "

[2] Based on responses to question: " What was the single most important reason for your original entry in active military service? "

TABLE 2

RESPONSES OF REGULAR ENLISTED PERSONNEL ON THEIR FIRST TOUR OF ACTIVE DUTY TO:

"WOULD YOU HAVE ENLISTED IF THERE HAD BEEN NO DRAFT?"a

By Selected Characteristics

(Per Cent Distribution)

Selected characteristics	Total	Yes definitely	Yes probably	No probably	No definitely	No idea	Draft* Motivated
(1)	(2)	(3)	(4)	(5)	(6)	(7)	(8)
TOTAL	100.0%	30.1	27.6	20.1	15.2	7.0	38.0
SERVICE							
Army	100.0%	27.1	25.6	20.7	19.4	7.2	43.2
Navy	100.0%	32.3	30.2	17.9	12.3	7.3	32.6
Air Force	100.0%	26.6	26.4	23.8	16.0	7.2	42.9
Marine Corps	100.0%	37.0	28.7	17.4	11.3	5.6	30.4
AGE AT ENLISTMENT							
17 to 19 years	100.0%	34.2	29.5	17.2	12.0	7.1	31.4
20 to 25 years	100.0%	17.6	21.6	29.1	24.9	6.8	57.9
EDUCATIONb							
Less than high school graduate	100.0%	42.9	28.8	11.7	9.7	6.9	23.0
High school graduate	100.0%	27.2	28.2	22.4	14.9	7.3	40.2
Some college or more	100.0%	16.3	23.1	28.3	26.0	6.3	58.0
MENTAL GROUP							
Group I and II	100.0%	25.1	27.4	22.8	18.5	6.1	44.0
Group III	100.0%	33.9	28.0	18.1	12.6	7.5	33.2
Group IV	100.0%	36.6	27.9	14.8	11.8	8.9	29.2

Source: Department of Defense Survey of Active Duty Military Personnel, as of October 1964

a The question asked, "If there had been no draft and you had not had any military obligation at the time you first entered Active Military Service do you think you would have entered the service?"
b At time of entry on active military service.

* NUMBER ANSWERING "NO PROBABLY" OR "NO DEFINITELY" AS A PER CENT OF THE TOTAL, EXCLUDING "NO IDEA".

243

TABLE 3

RESPONSES OF 16 TO 19 YEAR OLD CIVILIAN YOUTH TO:
" WHAT IS THE MOST IMPORTANT FACTOR IN CHOOSING A JOB OR CAREER? "
BY EDUCATIONAL ATTAINMENT

Job Characteristics	Total	Non-High School Graduate	High School Graduate	Some College or More
Chances for further training and learning job skills	24.0%	26.8%	25.1%	7.8%
Steady, secure work	22.9	24.5	22.1	15.3
Interesting work	21.9	18.5	21.8	40.3
Chances for advancement	8.9	7.9	11.4	10.9
Pay	8.6	8.3	9.8	9.1
Freedom to do the job the way I think best	5.8	5.8	4.9	7.4
Highly respected job	2.8	2.7	1.6	4.5
Retirement plans, medical plans, fringe benefits	2.7	3.2	2.2	1.2
Chance to be a leader	2.3	2.4	1.0	3.5

Source: Based on Census Bureau sample survey of civilian men, aged 16-34 years, October 1964.

TABLE 4

COMPARISONS OF MILITARY SERVICE AND CIVILIAN JOBS
IN TERMS OF SELECTED JOB CHARACTERISTICS:
UNITED STATES AND CANADIAN VETERANS

Job Characteristics	United States Veterans[1]			Canadian Veterans[2]		
	Military Better	No Diff.	Civilian Better	Military Better	No Diff.	Civilian Better
Chances for further training and learning job skills	36%	22%	42%	44%	15%	41%
Steady, secure work	47	30	23	44	43	13
Interesting work	20	23	57	24	27	49
Chances for advancement	24	20	56	26	29	45
Pay	2	5	93	13	17	70
Freedom to do the job the way I think best	5	17	78	4	17	78
Highly respected job	14	29	57	26	35	39
Retirement plans, medical plans, fringe benefits	59	16	25	57	33	11
Chance to be a leader	37	33	30	33	45	22

[1] U.S. Census Bureau survey of civilian men, aged 16-34 years, October 1964. Data shown are for veterans under age 25.

[2] Based on Canadian sample survey of civilian men, aged 16-34 years, August — December 1965. (Capt.W.R. Kelley, *A Study of Attitudes Toward Military Service*, Canadian Forces Applied Research Unit, Technical Note 66-7, October 1966, p.8.)

TABLE 5

DIFFICULTIES IN EMPLOYMENT AND FROM " DRAFT UNCERTAINTY "
EXPERIENCED BY ENLISTED PERSONNEL PRIOR TO ENTERING
MILITARY SERVICE, BY AGE OF ENTRY AND EDUCATIONAL LEVEL

Age of Entry	Educational Level			
	All Educational Levels Combined	High School Graduate or Less	Some College No Degree	College Graduate
	Per cent who were told they could not be hired because they might be drafted			
Difficulty in employment				
All ages[a]	20%	17%	35%	40%
17-18 years	11	11	18	—
19-21 years	27	25	34	b
22-25 years	39	34	47	45
	Per cent of men who had difficulties because they were uncertain as to whether they would be drafted			
Difficulty from draft uncertainty				
All ages[a]	21%	16%	43%	51%
17-18 years	8	8	15	—
19-21 years	28	24	40	b
22-25 years	54	49	66	69

[a] Includes small numbers of men who entered service over age 25.
[b] Insufficient data to warrant separate presentation.

Source: Based on Census Bureau sample survey of civilian men, aged 16-34 years,
October 1964.

TABLE 6

PERCENTAGE OF MEN IN SELECTED AGES WITH MILITARY
SERVICE EXPERIENCE, BY EDUCATIONAL LEVEL, 1964

Educational Level	Age Group	
	26 Years[1]	27 - 34 Years[2]
TOTAL	52%	64%
Less than H.S. Graduate	50	58
Less than 8 years	—	30
8 years	—	51
9-11 years	—	70
H.S. Graduate, No College	57	74
Some College, Non-Graduate	60	68
Under 2 years college	—	70
2 years or more	—	66
College Graduate	40	53
Bachelor's degree only	—	71
Graduate study	—	27

[1] Adapted from Selective Service Sample Inventory as of July 1964. Refers to men aged 25-1/2
to 26-1/2 years.
[2] Based on sample surveys of civilian men and active duty military personnel as of October 1964.

245

A. Survey of Civilian Men, Aged 16-34 Years

A survey of a representative nationwide sample of civilian men, aged 16-34 years, was conducted by the Bureau of the Census in October-November 1964 at the request of the Department of Defense. The age range 16-34 years was selected because it included all men in the ages of draft liability as well as youths aged 16 to 18-1/2 years who would be entering the draft-liable age group in the next two years.

The sample selected for this survey included all men in these ages who had been included in the Census Bureau's Current Population Survey (CPS) in May 1964. The CPS is a regular monthly sample survey of the population conducted by the Bureau of the Census, which serves as the basis of national statistics on labor force, employment and unemployment, and of statistics on other population characteristics. The information is obtained from a scientifically selected sample of about 35,000 households in 357 areas throughout the country. Roughly one in every 1,660 persons in the civilian noninstitutional population is included in the survey.

Separate questionnaires were addressed to veterans and to nonveterans, as identified by earlier responses to Census survey questionnaires. The questionnaires, which were of the self-administered type, included items on military service experience, plans and attitudes on the effects of the draft upon both military service plans and civilian employment, and on various social and economic characteristics.

The numbers shown in the tables represent the estimated total noninstitutional civilian male population in the specified age groups with the indicated characteristics. These population estimates were derived by the Bureau of the Census on the basis of a detailed weighting procedure described in a Census Bureau publication, " Concepts and Methods Used in Household Statistics on Employment and Unemployment from the Current Population Survey, " Series P-23, No.13, pp.9-10.

As in all surveys of this type, not all persons responded to all questions. For this reason, the totals in any one table may differ from totals for comparable groups in other tables.

B. Survey of Active Duty Military Personnel

Concurrently with the survey of the civilian male population, a survey was conducted of officer and enlisted personnel on active duty in the four Armed Services of the Department of Defense. A random sample of active duty personnel was surveyed in October and November 1964, including 5% of male enlisted personnel and 10% of male officer personnel, exclusive of personnel temporarily absent from duty, on training maneuvres or otherwise not available for survey. Responses were received from a total of about 80,000 enlisted personnel and 22,000 officers, corresponding approximately to one in thirty enlisted men and one in fifteen officers on active duty.

Separate questionnaires of a self-administered type were addressed to enlisted and officer personnel. The questionnaires generally paralleled in scope those addressed to civilian males with appropriate modifications designed to obtain information on such subjects as military service experience, reason for entry into service, and military career plans.

Separate percentage distributions by Service in tables from this survey are based upon unweighted sample distributions. The percentage distributions for Department of Defence totals have, however, been weighted on the basis of total service strengths, by pay grade, as of October 31, 1964.

C. Survey of Ready Reserve Personnel

A sample survey of members of the Ready Reserve components, including the Army and Air National Guard, was conducted in December 1964 to February 1965, designed primarily to identify factors influencing entry and retention of personnel in the Ready Reserves and the influence of the draft in relation to various relevant characteristics such as age, educational level and employment status. The sample was selected on a random basis, based upon specific terminal digits of reservists' serial numbers. Sampling ratios were established separately for officer and enlisted personnel in each reserve component. Preliminary tabulations, shown here, are based upon responses from 18,482 officers and 27,729 enlisted personnel. These represent 7.1 per cent of all Ready Reserve officer strengths and 1.8 per cent of all Ready Reserve enlisted strengths, respectively, as of 30 November 1964.

Tabulations from this survey are based upon unweighted distributions.

Attitudes: Procurement, Performance and Retention

LT. CDR. PAUL D. NELSON, U.S.N.
NAVY MEDICAL RESEARCH INSTITUTE
BETHESDA, MARYLAND (USA)

When first invited to chair a panel at the present symposium, I had understood the topic of our focused attention to be that of retention in the armed forces. In our vernacular retention connotes that behavioural event in which, by agreement of military management, the individual service member voluntarily remains in the military organization beyond his initially obligated tour of duty, perhaps for a career. To function effectively, it is doubtful that any military organization in the free world can afford 100% retention except perhaps under the most unusual of circumstances for relatively short periods of time. But in order to provide continuity through experience and effective leadership there must be some optimal level of retention, determined at least in part by the following conditions:

(i) size and rank structure of the military as determined by defense commitments and political-legal restrictions;

(ii) civilian manpower resources and the functions to be fulfilled within the military organization; and

(iii) the economics and technological state-of-the-art of training systems within the military establishment.

Those and other considerations are in fact being addressed by other delegates to this manpower symposium. As a social psychologist I am also interested in those aspects of the retention problem which have to do with the individual's decision to remain in the military, a problem of personal motivation based upon interests, attitudes, and basic value systems. What is it, in other words, that leads some individuals to a decision to remain in the military while others leave? Hopefully, but not always realistically, those individuals whom management is most interested in retaining would similarly be most highly motivated to remain in the military.

Having invited the participants of this panel to share their research which bears on the content of such motivation, I would like to focus slightly more upon the strategy and methodology of retention motivation studies. The first step in this direction was to modify the title of our panel's topic to read " attitudes and values: their relevance to procurement, performance and retention ", denoting that study of attitudes as they pertain to retention must be dynamic and longitudinal in scope. If we were to apply a prediction model to retention, it would be most efficient for us to be able to identify as early as possible those individuals most likely to choose to remain in the service. Not that such individuals would be the only ones initially inducted, since we would not be striving for 100% retention. But expensive training assignments and career planning might be made more efficient by such early information.

There is little conclusive evidence that pre-service characteristics and attitudes at the time of procurement are powerful predictors of decisions to remain in the service, when the latter are made from two to four years after entry into the military service. This is not to say that such early information is of no value. We know, for example, that pre-service characteristics are related significantly to adjustment in military service, particularly among enlisted personnel in our armed forces. The fact that completion of twelve years of formal schooling is one of the best early indicators of adjustment may be attributable at least as much to the motivational aspects of continuing and completing a schooling program as to what is learned in the formal curricula. Then too I am reminded of some data we collected in studies of voluntary attrition among officer-candidate naval aviator trainees in which it was noted that a history of " failure to complete ", even among their parents, was significantly related to trainees voluntarily dropping out of pilot training.

For the most part, though, our ability to predict events two to four years in the future, whether it be performance or motivation, is so modest that we must look further to the intervening events. That is, we must update our knowledge about individuals as they proceed through military life experiences. Hopefully, we could develop a contingency model of prediction, starting with a matrix of information about the individual when he enters the military service and modified by the inputs derived from his military experiences, his performance and his attitudes.

Simply assessing the state of attitudes at a point in time does not allow full understanding of the meaning of those attitudes. Bem, a psychologist at Carnegie Institute of Technology, recently postulated, with supporting experimental data, that attitudes are to a great extent a function of the enacted behaviours which precede them.[1] Certainly this makes sense to the attitude theorist whose notions are predicated upon the significance of past experiences. But it serves to alert those whose approach begins with the attitude as an entity in itself to be judged in utility only as a predictor of some subsequently, and hopefully, dependent behavioural event. This is not in contradiction to such results as those of Stouffer's classical study of attitudes as predictors of combat effectiveness among American soldiers in World War II.[2] Even there, the basis for overtly similar attitudes differed as a function of the past experience of the troops studied. But it does serve to emphasize the interdependency between attitudes and non-verbal behaviours over time. A contingency model would allow attitudes revealed at point in time " x" to be evaluated in terms of behaviour both prior and subsequent to that point in time. Thus, we need to look at the individual from procurement through performance in the military to gain best understanding of his attitudes concerning retention.

Perhaps most important for us to pursue, more than we have, at the time of procurement and thereafter, are the individual's values and goals, short term and long term, abstract and concrete. The individual's aspirations and his perception of likelihood achieving the same should be given more attention. In retrospect the individual's sense of the past, of the present and what in life he wants and expects in the future should be ascertained.

Strong, in a lecture on satisfactions and interests published nearly ten years ago in *The American Psychologist*, emphasized the utility of a dynamic concept such as motivation, in contrast to often relatively static concepts of job satisfaction, in predicting future behaviour.[3] Vroom, in his now classic writing on work motivation, postulates the interaction of a value orientation (i.e. a goal) with perceived probability of achievement of such a goal as resulting in action, with the individual's perception of action outcome providing feedback for the modification of the two antecedent properties.[4] Despite such formulations we still find attempts being made to assess attitude states solely in rather static terms of job satisfactions (including the " chow ") in hopes that such will relate to such future behaviours as performance on the job and decisions to remain in the military.

Again, this is not to say that job satisfactions are unimportant in shaping the course of future behaviours, but merely that they are insufficient bits of information in and of themselves, particularly when assessed at isolated points in time with relatively little focus upon the experiences and attitudes which preceded them. Salaries of military personnel are probably discussed as much as any job factor in regard to retention. There are few, if any, persons I am sure who would not appreciate higher wages in our societies, especially in partial reward for those inconveniences unique to military life, ranging from long separations from family to the risking of one's life. But salary, in and of itself, I propose, is not the answer to more effective retention.

In a very basic sense, it is probably the individual's striving to achieve personal meaning in life, to be challenged, and to feel recognized, if only indirectly, which serves to motivate men. Dunnette, in reviewing a series of studies directed at testing Herzberg's theory of job satisfactions, cites the three factors of perceived achievement, recognition and responsibility as consistently salient in attitudes towards one's job. [5, 6]

The interpretation of expressed attitudes, goals, values, and even satisfactions must be made in terms of the status in life from which the individual has entered the military service and the alternative opportunities he perceives to lie in the future. Relevant to this notion are two concepts generated by Stouffer, namely " relative deprivation" and " intervening opportunities", seemingly simple in nature, but patently valid and far too often neglected by students of attitudes. [7] The former concept suggests that individual differences in present attitudes must to some extent be weighed in terms of individual differences in past and current life circumstances and also concomitant differences in perceived status relative to peers, now often referred to as social comparison. The concept of " intervening opportunities", while generated to explain migration patterns in population shifts, could be equally useful in evaluating decisions made by military personnel about relative assignments and career options.

I am reminded of two separate findings in studies of naval aviator trainees, again, which possibly reflect Stouffer's two concepts. They at least emphasize the relativity of value systems among military personnel, even among those who in this instance are frequently pooled into a single and seemingly homogeneous category of personnel – namely aviators.

The first illustrates something of a career-type decision. About ten years ago a change was implemented in the contract status of aviator trainees to lengthen the tour of duty after pilot training. Since the men were all volunteers on a specific contract, those already in training were provided a time period during which they could decide to accept the new contract or reject it and be released from active duty with no ill effect. Having much background data on these young men, several of us were able to intensively study the decisions made. Of all the data available, those which were interpreted by us as reflecting generational occupational mobility appeared highly related to the decisions made. The young men whose fathers' *and* paternal grandfathers' occupations were both in what we call professional categories (i.e., law, medicine, and business management) decided in disproportionate numbers to leave the service. The others, particularly those whose paternal grandfathers had been unskilled and whose fathers had moved up the occupational prestige ladder to skilled or white collar jobs, decided in disproportionate numbers to remain in the service for the longer tour of duty. It is as though for the first group military service in officer status is an assumed part of a young man's experience before continuing the family tradition of professional pursuits and that simply having volunteered and been accepted for such experience was sufficient qualification. For the other group, being a military officer, and aviator in particular, possibly represented a major upward shift in occupational mobility within the family tradition. Thus, goals, opportunities and perceived status in retrospect and prospect were conceivably all at issue.

The second illustration was derived from a recent report by Berkshire. [8] Some time ago several of us had worked on the problem of recruiting appeals for naval aviators. Among other things we attempted to assess the extent to which young men attribute such factors as prestige and job security to naval aviation. The individual was required to rank naval aviation on those factors relative to a set of approximately twenty alternative occupations (including the Air Force!). Berkshire recently utilized that scheme to develop measures of motivation possibly related to voluntary attrition, or lack of same, from flight training. The data were developed on two groups of trainees, one of which were college graduates commissioned as officers before flight training. The other group were not college graduates and would not be commissioned until the end of flight training, attrition from which would revert a man to enlisted status.

Over and above the Mechanical Comprehension Test, which is one of the better general predictors of flight training success, both the prestige and security measures contributed significantly in multiple regression against the success-attrition criterion, but differently for the two groups of trainees. For the officer college graduate group, the prestige measure was related to completion of training. At that, it was the prestige of being an aviator relative to non-aviator flight officer which was important. For the non-commissioned trainees who did not have a college degree security rather than prestige was the important variable. For the college graduate group the availability of an abundance of attractive occupational pursuits possibly reduced the value at their age of job security. Furthermore they were already officers but were most intent on being aviators. Nothing short of being an aviator would do within their personal scales of aspiration. For the other group with neither college degree nor military commission, the opportunity to realize a secure professional job, granted its prestige, was perhaps a more realistic striving. This was an opportunity for them to achieve a position which could compensate for some lack of civilian schooling and if they did well, to continue in that career field if they so wished.

Our data in the Navy is not exclusive to the aviator groups. Gunderson has found that enlisted naval personnel tend to choose (or perhaps are chosen for) occupations within the service which are similar in socio-economic characteristics to general indices of their parents' socio-economic status as judged by parental education and father's occupation.[9] Thus, the extent to which values and attitudes about work in the military are a function of background, continuously subject to modification by actual experience in the military, would be worth more intensive study.

Among enlisted personnel the concepts of opportunity and achievement are worth exploring, for example, in regard to advancement in rank. Conceivably a bright, motivated, effective young enlistee can achieve half the rank levels available to an enlisted man during his first four years of enlistment. If he were to stay in the service for a minimum career of twenty years this means that he has accomplished half his level of aspiration in only one fifth of his career time. What effect does this have upon a young man's motivation? Does such promotion relative to rank structure opportunity possibly deter from the challenge even though it is probably intended to reward and attract him? One might suggest that such enlistees can always aspire to commissioned officer status. Many do so aspire, make it, and do a fine job. But since we are discussing value systems, what of the military culture with its officer-noncom distinctions and how do those affect the attitudes of men who shift from one category to the other? Anecdotally, one often hears of the " no man's land " between enlisted and officer status. Then too, different branches of the military organization may have different norms or prevailing attitudes concerning such status shifts. I suspect that in some branches of our armed forces, having previously served well as an enlisted man is prestigious to an officer for " he then knows " the problems of his men and has come up the hard well-fought way. Once more, however, we have more speculation than data – data which might very well be relevant to the problem of retention.

Differences in attitudes, taken in the sense of motivations, among various components of the military service deserves much further attention. I do not at all consider it unprofessional for us to try, as modestly as we are able, to better understand such concepts as loyalty, pride and the value of " serving ". I refer here not only to national loyalty or to loyalty to the Navy or the Army but loyalty within those larger social systems. I have often informally referred to our Navy, and it probably holds true for other armed services, as a system of special forces, each with something of its own traditions and esprit de corps. The Marines, the Seabees, the aviators, the " tin-can sailors " and the submariners are well known examples. Yes, I think that Janowitz's comments on the new military are probably valid, that the old culturally homogeneous and family-heritage-oriented system of the military has changed into a complex technologically-oriented and culturally heterogeneous social system.[10] But even within this new organizational form I consider the challenge to be great for the social scientist to depict new strains of heritage. The effect on attitudes and behaviour of belonging and perceiving a personal contribution to the effectiveness of a " special " unit is probably great. I have in mind more than simply the abstraction of loyalty to one's unit or type of " special " force; here I refer to the concreteness of interpersonal loyalty, the importance, if you wish of the " buddy " concept described so well by Stouffer in the already cited World War II studies and by Little in his studies of the Korean conflict.[11] To what extent are personal influences among men who have served so closely together in face of adversity related to attitudes and such specific behaviours as remaining in the military?

Perhaps somewhat obtusely, I have tried to touch upon what I consider challenging considerations for those of us concerned with attitudes, particularly as they ultimately relate to retention in the military. We may not be able to develop information which can be practically implemented in such a way as to improve the retention of men we most want on a career basis. But it is important nevertheless for us to understand the attitudes and values which develop in young men during military service for their effect may be just as great in the context of civilian society to which most of the men return after obligated service. Even among those who remain in the service we must consider the implications of attitudes for further effective service and such pragmatic matters as assignments and career patterns. We could do nothing worse perhaps than to retain potentially effective leaders, commissioned or non-commissioned, technical specialists or generalists, and fail to realize that potential through mismanagement of their roles within the military.

That monument of attitude research within the American military system, referenced several times in this discussion, organized by the late Samuel Stouffer and his colleagues, namely *The American Soldier*, was based upon some 300 surveys of more than half a million men. It was referred to by the *American Sociological Review*, in 1949, as " one of the most significant contributions to the social sciences during the last twenty years ". Now, nearly twenty years later, one would not be too far wrong in making the same statement. Of greatest significance in those works were the insights Stouffer had about the meaning of the vast amount of data accumulated, the psychological concepts generated.

This is not to discredit those who have in many ways advanced the state of the art in attitude research since 1949. But it is my general impression that we have not pursued to the best of our ability many of the concepts generated twenty years ago. We will always have a need in the military, as in industrial organizations, to assess current satisfactions, dissatisfactions, and interests regarding the day-to-day life circumstances of one's job (i.e. the food, recreation, work schedules, etc.). But we will not enhance our understanding of man's behaviour by clinging only to those types of surveys.

The military setting affords a most unique opportunity to do what so many behavioural scientists feel is necessary but which so few foresee the time or patience to carry out, namely to conduct systematic longitudinal studies by cohorts. This seems a most sensible way in which to gain better understanding of the attitudes of men in the military.

Interestingly enough, among all the surveys listed in the volumes of *The American Soldier* not one had to do specifically with retention or career choice. That was an epoch in which national emergency necessitated the induction of masses of men to end the war. The concern of the times toward the end of World War II, as evidenced in the writings of Stouffer, was " return to civilian life ". Yet many men remained in the service following the war. Many had voluntarily entered the service, of course, during the 1930's in time of economic depression. But it is to no small extent a consequence of those who entered during the war and remained in the service that our armed forces have in recent years been critically concerned with the problem of retention, since the 20-30 year military career of those earlier entrants is drawing to a close.

We have perhaps overlooked the opportunity during these past twenty years to systematically evaluate the attitudes of even younger generations who have served in the armed forces. Our research in the military has, during the past twenty years, been heavily committed, as well it should, to the matter of rendering man effective in a rapidly growing system of technology, the concept of man-machine integration. Had we placed a continued and proportionate emphasis upon the human qualities of man's experience in the military we might be in better standing at this hour as regards such matters as retention.

But let us move on, in the spirit of those whose good work has been presented here and of others who have contributed in recent years, heeding as we go the final words of a Stouffer lecture at Harvard: " As further research in social psychology in the Armed Forces goes forward we may expect increasing advances in our knowledge of the theory of social attitudes and of techniques – for testing applications of the theory. These tools are in their infancy. There is a challenge to imaginative and resourceful officers of the Army, Navy, and Air Force to lead in developing them to still greater effectiveness ".

REFERENCES

1. Bem, D.J. " Self-Perception: The Dependent Variable of Human Performance ". *J of Organizational Behaviour and Human Performance*, Vol.2, No.2, May 1967, pp 105-121.
2. Stouffer, S.A. et al. *The American Soldier: Combat and Its Aftermath*. Princeton, N.J.: Princeton University Press, 1949, pp 3-58.
3. Strong, E.K. Jr., " Satisfactions and Interests ". *The American Psychologist*, Vol.13, No.8, Aug 1958, pp 449-456.
4. Vroom, V.H. *Work and Motivation*. New York: John Wiley & Sons, 1964.
5. Dunnette, M.D. et al. " Factors Contributing to Job Satisfaction and Job Dissatisfaction in Six Occupational Groups ". *J of Organizational Behaviour and Human Performance*, Vol.2, No.2, May 1967, pp 143-174.
6. Herzberg, F. et al. *The Motivation to Work* (2nd ed). New York: John Wiley & Sons, 1959.
7. Stouffer, S.A. *Social Research to Test Ideas*, New York, The Free Press of Glenco. 1962 pp 13-38, 68-112.
8. Berkshire, J.R. " Evaluation of Several Experimental Aviator Selection Tests ". Pensacola, Fla: *NAMI-NAMC Report 1003*, March 1967.
9. Gunderson, E.K.E. " Socioeconomic Status and Navy Occupations ". *Personnel and Guidance Journal*, Vol.44, 1965, pp 263-266.
10. Janowitz, Morris (ed). *The New Military*. New York: Russell Sage Foundation, 1964.
11. Little, R.W. " Buddy Relations and Combat Performance ". In Janowitz (ed), *op cit.* pp 195-224.

Comparaison de Techniques D'Enquête

U.J. BOUVIER

CENTRE D'ETUDES SOCIALES
DES FORCES ARMEES BELGES

I. RECHERCHE A LA FORCE AERIENNE

Une recherche à la Force Aérienne Belge a utilisé concurremment trois techniques dont un questionnaire à réponses libres et un questionnaire avec réponses à choix forcé. Les réponses libres ont pu être groupées assez valablement sous les mêmes rubriques que celles du questionnaire à choix forcé. Je voudrais comparer les résultats des deux questionnaires.

On a d'abord demandé aux sujets : "Quels sont les motifs de satisfaction que vous trouvez dans votre vie à la Force Aérienne?"

La deuxième question était : "Rencontrez-vous ou avez-vous rencontré des difficultés en ce qui concerne votre vie à la Force Aérienne? Si oui, quelles sont ces difficultés?"

Quand ils avaient répondu à ces deux questions, on leur présentait successivement un questionnaire à choix multiple où figuraient une quinzaine de motifs de satisfaction parmi lesquels ils devaient choisir et marquer leurs choix par des croix. Sur un second questionnaire figuraient une vingtaine de difficultés; des croix devaient aussi marquer les choix.

Pour comparer les résultats, un premier problème se posait. Fallait-il comparer des pourcentages de sujets par motif ou des fréquences de choix? Il se fait que le nombre de motifs exprimés par chacun influe assez fortement sur les pourcentages de sujets qui choisissent certains motifs. Si chaque sujet cite plusieurs motifs, le nombre de fois qu'un motif sera choisi sera généralement plus grand que si chaque sujet n'exprime qu'un choix. Or il se trouve que le nombre moyen de choix exprimés est très différent d'une technique à l'autre. Aussi, plutôt que de calculer les pourcentages de sujets qui choisissent chaque motif, avons-nous préféré calculer les fréquences relatives d'apparition des motifs. Pour chacune des techniques, la somme des fréquences est égale à cent.

I.I. Motifs de satisfaction

Nous avons dressé un tableau, donnant par rapport au nombre de réponses, la fréquence relative de chaque motif de satisfaction (tableau 1). Ce tableau pour les motifs de satisfaction distingue les sujets d'expression française 2.065 sujets, de ceux d'expression néerlandaise 2.944 sujets. Dans chaque régime linguistique on trouve les fréquences calculées pour le questionnaire à choix multiple et celles pour les questions ouvertes.

(i) On est d'abord frappé par le parallélisme entre les 2 régimes linguistiques. L'analogie est assez grande pour les réponses à choix multiple; elle est moins grande pour les questions ouvertes pour lesquelles quelques écarts sont assez importants:

	Fr	Ne
esprit de camaraderie	12,3	5,9
fonction remplie à l'armée	14,8	10,1

(ii) On est surtout frappé par quelques écarts sérieux entre les deux techniques

	Fr		Ne	
	Ch. Mul.	Ouv.	Ch. Mul.	Ouv.
équipement gratuit	9, 5	2, 3	10, 5	2, 9
soins médicaux	8, 7	2, 1	8, 8	1, 5
influence morale de l'armée	6, 6	1, 1	6, -	0, 3
fonction remplie à l'armée	6, 3	14, 8	6, 5	10, 1
possibilité d'avenir	4, 4	8, 1	4, 1	7, 5
attitude des supérieurs	2, 2	9, 8	3, 9	11, 2
discipline	1, 8	5, 5	1, 4	6, 4

TABLEAU 1

FREQUENCE DES MOTIFS DE SATISFACTION

MOTIFS DE SATISFACTION	FRANCAIS		NEERLANDAIS	
	Choix multiple	Questions ouvertes	Choix multiple	Questions ouvertes
Avantages financiers	15, 1	12, 4	14, 2	10, 6
Congés et permissions	11, 5	7, 2	12, 6	10, 4
Esprit de camaraderie	10, 4	12, 3	9, 6	5, 9
Equipement gratuit	9, 5	2, 3	10, 5	2, 9
Soins médicaux	8, 7	2, 1	8, 8	1, 5
Difficultés moindres que dans la vie civile	7, 5	5, -	5, 2	7, 6
Influence morale de l'armée	6, 6	1, 1	6, -	0, 3
Fonction remplie à l'armée	6, 3	14, 8	6, 5	10, 1
Possibilités d'avenir	4, 4	8, 1	4, 1	7, 5
Logement, chauffage, éclairage à bon marché	4, -	3, -	2, 7	2, 4
Activités typiquement militaires	3, 2	3, 2	2, 7	1, -
Prestige de l'armée et de l'uniforme	2, 5	3, 1	2, 4	0, 7
Nourriture	2, 3	2, 9	4, 3	4, 7
Attitude des supérieurs	2, 2	9, 8	3, 9	11, 2
Loisirs nombreux	1, 9	2, 4	3, 1	2, 5
Discipline	1, 8	5, 5	1, 4	6, 4
Autres motifs (divers)	2, 1	4, 8	1, 9	14, 3
Nombre moyen d'avis	3, 8	1, 3	4, 1	1, 4

I.2. Difficultés rencontrées

Le tableau 2, pour les difficultés, est le correspondant du précédent.

(i) Pour celui-ci aussi, il y a une assez grande analogie entre les 2 régimes linguistiques, cependant moins bonne pour les questions ouvertes, où l'on trouve

	Fr	Ne
répartition du travail	11, 5	5, 7

(ii) Ici encore on est frappé par quelques grands écarts

	Fr		Ne	
	Ch. Mul.	Ouv.	Ch. Mul.	Ouv.
problèmes d'ordre financier	13, 9	22, 7	12, 2	25, 4
promesses non tenues	9, 2	3, 4	7, 1	2, 2
organisation du travail	7, 7	2, 5	8, -	1, 7
instabilité (garnison ou fonction)	4, 9	-	5, 9	-
répartition du travail	2, -	11, 5	2, 3	5, 7

I.3. Considérations

(i) Le parallélisme satisfaisant entre les deux régimes linguistiques, pour chacune des techniques prises séparément, est un élément encourageant. Puisqu'il s'agit de deux cultures présentant quand même quelques différences on n'aurait pas été surpris que les réactions soient, elles aussi, différentes. S'il y a une assez grande analogie entre les réponses, on peut penser que c'est parce que les techniques atteignent "quelque chose d'assez stable", même si ce "quelque chose" diffère d'une technique à l'autre.

Par exemple "quelque chose d'assez stable" qui se retrouve par les deux techniques, ce sont les éléments d'ordre financier qui apparaissent en tête par les deux techniques, dans les deux régimes, tant comme motif de satisfaction que comme difficulté. Il est difficile de ne pas croire qu'il s'agit d'un élément important.

Il en est d'autres qui apparaissent avec des fréquences importantes pour chacune des techniques. Quelques-uns des motifs classés en tête des tableaux sont dans ce cas.

Par contre on sera amené assez naturellement à considérer que les motifs dont les fréquences sont faibles pour les deux techniques ne présentent guère d'importance pour l'ensemble des sujets interrogés.

(ii) Pour ce qui ne se retrouve pas de la même façon par les deux techniques, on doit choisir une stratégie d'interprétation : ou bien accepter tout ce qui apparaît soit par l'une soit par l'autre technique, ou bien se donner un critère de choix. Tout accepter nous met en présence de contradictions assez désagréables et il semble qu'il vaut mieux chercher un critère de choix.

Il est remarquable que lorsque les écarts sont très importants, ils sont dans le même sens pour les 2 régimes linguistiques. Nous devons cependant signaler trois exceptions, quoique les écarts ne soient heureusement pas très grands :

	Fr		Ne	
	Ch. Mul.	Ouv.	Ch. Mul.	Ouv.
difficultés amenées dans la vie familiale	8,5	5,8	5,5	7,5
esprit de camaraderie	10,4	12,3	9,6	5,9
difficultés moindres que dans la vie civile	7,5	5,-	5,2	7,6

Si, pour faciliter la recherche d'une hypothèse d'interprétation, nous faisons abstraction des exceptions, qui ne sont d'ailleurs pas trop criantes, nous pouvons nous baser sur le fait que les écarts sont dans le même sens dans les deux régimes linguistiques pour prendre confiance dans leur permanence et les interpréter sans trop de crainte.

Une constatation pourrait, semble-t-il, nous servir de point de départ. Le nombre moyen d'avis exprimés est bien plus grand pour la technique à choix multiple que pour les questions ouvertes. Il est deux fois plus grand au tableau des difficultés et trois fois plus grand au tableau des motifs de satisfaction.

Peut-on attacher un sens à cette observation? En réponse à une question générale, tant pour les éléments satisfaisants que pour les autres, il y a des chances que les dernières frustrations subies et les satisfactions ressenties récemment, seront les premières auxquelles chacun songera. Il s'agit de réponses "de premier jet" en quelque sorte, surtout influencées par le présent, par l'actuel.

A en juger par le nombre moyen d'avis exprimes aux questions ouvertes, les sujets ne font pas d'efforts pour trouver plusieurs motifs : les moyennes sont 1, 3 et 1, 4 pour les motifs de satisfaction et 2, 1 pour les difficultés.

Par contre, si l'on propose de choisir dans une liste nombreuse, peut-être surtout si l'on doit ranger, on est presque nécessairement amené à réfléchir, à peser, à comparer. La réponse sera plus élaborée et aura des chances de contenir des éléments situés à d'autres niveaux.

En outre, s'il y a réflexion, retour sur soi, comparaison, on peut s'attendre à ce que le nombre de motifs exprimés soit assez grand.

On ne devrait pas être surpris d'ailleurs que les éléments cités, s'ils sont réfléchis, soient aussi nombreux pour les motifs de satisfaction que pour les difficultés, tandis que s'il s'agit d'éléments du vécu, qui soient encore actuellement ressentis, il y ait plus de frustrations dont l'action persiste, que de satisfactions. C'est ce qui apparaît, le rapport étant, aux questions ouvertes, de trois difficultés citées pour deux motifs de satisfaction.

I.4. Interprétation

Quelle pourrait être l'interprétation des résultats dans cettte optique?

(i) Aux motifs de satisfaction, nous dirions que les problèmes
de l'équipement gratuit
des soins médicaux
de l'influence morale de l'armée
ne sont guère ressentis de façon immédiate, mais que, à la réflexion, un assez grand nombre de sujets leur reconnaissent une importance assez grande.

Il semble naturel que ces trois motifs ne soient pas vécus intensément, mais qu'ils soient mieux appréciés sur un plan plus rationnel.

TABLEAU 2

FREQUENCE DES DIFFICULTES

DIFFICULTES	FRANCAIS		NEERLANDAIS	
	Choix multiple	Questions ouvertes	Choix multiple	Questions ouvertes
Problèmes d'ordre financier	13,9	22,7	12,2	25,4
Promesses non tenues	9,2	3,4	7,1	2,2
Difficultés amenées pour la vie familiale	8,5	5,8	5,5	7,5
Organisation du travail	7,7	2,5	8,-	1,7
Attitudes des supérieurs	6,9	10,8	5,9	7,8
Peu de perspectives	6,9	14,1	8,1	11,6
Congés et permissions	5,3	2,9	4,7	4,3
Injustices	5,-	1,7	5,4	3,3
Instabilité (garnison ou fonction)	4,9	-	5,9	-
Nourriture	3,8	2,-	2,4	1,7
Discipline et punitions	3,6	3,4	4,6	3,9
Matériel ou équipement insuffisant	3,6	2,5	2,5	1,3
Manque de liberté	3,5	0,5	3,3	1,4
Information sur le service	3,1	0,8	5,7	0,5
Nature des prestations	3,1	5,-	2,3	6,2
Possibilités de délassement	2,4	1,1	4,1	1,6
Répartition du travail	2,-	11,5	2,3	5,7
Hygiène et soins de santé	2,-	2,3	3,3	4,8
Conditions de logement	1,2	1,5	2,6	1,9
Attitudes et comportement des camarades	0,7	0,7	1,1	0,4
Mauvaises influences de l'armée	0,7	-	0,8	-
Autres difficultés diverses	1,9	4,7	2,4	6,8
Nombre moyen d'avis	4,3	2,1	4,5	2,1

Par contre, nous dirions que
 la fonction remplie à l'armée
 les possibilités d'avenir
 l'attitude des supérieurs
 la discipline
sont de nature à provoquer des satisfactions assez vives dans l'immédiat, mais
que la plupart des sujets sont capables de "faire la part des choses" pour,
à la réflexion, faire une classification assez sereine qui diminue l'importance
relative de ces éléments.
Il faut remarquer que pour
 la fonction remplie à l'armée
 et les possibilités d'avenir
les résultats des 2 techniques ne sont quand même pas trop différents. Tout en
gardant une certaine importance à la réflexion, ce serait surtout par
impression immédiate que ces éléments paraîtraient satisfaisants.

 Dans la perspective que nous avons adoptée, on pourrait penser que le côté
valorisant, flattant l'amour-propre, serait en cause, plutôt que l'aspect
sécurité d'emploi.

 L'attitude des supérieurs serait ressentie de façon très vive dans l'immédiat, mais ne garderait qu'une importance assez faible comparée aux
autres éléments. Il en serait de même pour la discipline, à un degré moindre.
Je signale que cet échantillon est formé pour la plus grande part de sous-
officiers.

 Toujours dans notre perspective d'interprétation, on pourrait penser que
lorsque ces motifs sont cités en réponse aux questions ouvertes, c'est leur
côté flatteur, leur aspect valorisant qui seraient en cause. Tandis qu'au
questionnaire à choix multiple, ce serait plutôt l'aspect sécurisant de ces
éléments.

(ii) Pour les difficultés rencontrées, nous dirions que
 les promesses non tenues
 l'organisation du travail
 l'instabilité
ne sont guère vécues dans le présent, mais que, à la réflexion, comparativement
aux autres éléments, ils acquièrent de l'importance.

 A l'opposé, les problèmes d'ordre financier seraient ressentis beaucoup
plus vivement dans l'immédiat, quoique considérés encore comme très importants
à la réflexion et comparativement aux autres. Il semblerait que des problèmes
de
 répartition du travail
se soient posés au moment de l'enquête ou peu de temps avant, surtout dans des
unités d'expression française, mais qu'ils auraient été ramenés à des
proportions plus modestes à la réflexion.

 Peut-on dire que notre hypothèse interprétative soit, a posteriori, en
accord avec le bon sens? Nous pensons que, si les échantillons avaient été
plus homogènes, les motifs auraient pu se partager plus nettement en une partie sentie ou vécue et une autre partie plus raisonnée. L'hétérogénéité des
échantillons est peut-être telle que les mêmes motifs ne sont pas sentis de la
même façon par chaque catégorie, et qu'ils n'ont pas non plus la même
importance sur le plan rationnel. Aussi voudrais-je consacrer quelques minutes
à une autre étude comparative avec des échantillons homogènes.

2. RECHERCHE A LA FORCE TERRESTRE

2.1. Motifs de s'engager ou de ne pas s'engager

Une recherche, sur environ 2.500 miliciens de la Force Terrestre, a porté sur les motifs de s'engager ou de ne pas s'engager à l'armée. Pour une partie d'entre eux, on a utilisé un questionnaire à réponses préparées, parmi lesquelles on leur demandait de choisir en rangeant leurs choix. Nous avons utilisé les résultats, d'une part en pondérant les choix, d'autre part sans les pondérer. A l'autre partie des sujets, choisis au hasard, on a demandé de faire une rédaction "pourquoi je m'engage" ou "pourquoi je ne m'engage pas" en mentionnant les avantages, les désavantages et éventuellement d'autres considérations. Les éléments relevés dans ces rédactions libres ont pu être groupés sans trop de difficultés sous les mêmes rubriques que celles du questionnaire. Je n'ai retenu, pour cet exposé, que les échantillons des non désireux de s'engager; les autres échantillons sont beaucoup plus petits (28 Ne et 31 Fr).

Pour chacune des techniques on a calculé la fréquence d'apparition de chaque motif par rapport à l'ensemble des choix exprimés. J'appelle également "fréquences" les calculs faits en tenant compte des pondérations.

J'ai choisi parmi la cinquantaine de rubriques qu'on a relevées, celles pour lesquelles les différences de fréquences sont assez grandes. Ces rubriques couvrent d'ailleurs plus de 60% des fréquences. Vous les voyez au tableau 3. 920 sujets d'expression néerlandaise ont répondu au questionnaire en ordonnant leurs choix; 60 n'ont mis que des croix. Les chiffres sont respectivement 489 et 203 pour ceux d'expression française. Par ailleurs, deux autres échantillons de 375 néerlandais et 385 français ont rédigé librement.

On voit qu'il y a une assez grande analogie entre les deux régimes linguistiques. D'autre part, les "fréquences" ne sont guère différentes pour le questionnaire quand les choix sont pondérés et quand ils ne le sont pas.

Si l'on compare questionnaire et rédaction libre qui, je le rappelle, concernent des échantillons différents, on voit que, pour les rubriques que nous avons retenues, il y a des différences considérables, *toujours dans le même sens dans les deux régimes linguistiques.*

Ce qui indique qu'il est peu probable que ces différences soient dues aux échantillons, choisis au hasard, mais qu'il faut les rapporter plutôt aux techniques utilisées.

Il vaut la peine de souligner que c'est pour plus de 60% des fréquences totales qu'il y a des différences assez grandes entre les résultats des techniques. Il faut admettre que les questionnaires et la rédaction libre ne permettent pas de constater la même chose. Pour les rubriques reprises au tableau 3, ce qui paraît important si l'on s'en rapporte aux questionnaires, semble l'être beaucoup moins par la rédaction libre, et vice-versa.

2.2. Interprétation

Pouvons-nous tenter la même interprétation qui nous a servi pour la recherche précédente?

Il y a une différence quant aux nombres moyens d'avis exprimés. Ces nombres sont le plus élevés pour la rédaction libre. Ceci est en opposition avec ce que nous avons constaté a la Force Aérienne. Mais aussi, ce n'est pas la même chose de répondre à des questions ouvertes ou bien de rédiger un texte. Quelqu'un qui est sollicité de "faire une rédaction" se croit généralement obligé d'écrire assez longuement. En fait, la plupart des rédactions avaient au moins une page. Pour remplir une page ou deux, il faut trouver des choses à dire...! Cette sollicitation ne suffit-elle pas à expliquer le grand nombre d'avis émis par cette technique?

A la différence près du nombre des motifs, il nous semble que les conditions d'expression sont à peu près les mêmes que pour les questions ouvertes. A l'occasion d'une rédaction libre, les avis sont émis sans une revue préalable de tous les éléments du problème. Ce qui a le plus de chances de se manifester, c'est le ressenti actuel, le

TABLEAU 3

FREQUENCE DES RAISONS

DE NE PAS S'ENGAGER A L'ARMEE

	Ne			Fr		
	N = 920		N = 375	N = 489		N = 385
	Questionnaire non pondéré	Questionnaire pondéré	Rédaction libre	Questionnaire non pondéré	Questionnaire pondéré	Rédaction libre
1 Peu de possibilité d'avenir	4,9	5,8	2,2	5,3	5,9	0,9
2 Congés et permissions	8,4	8,8	3,0	8,1	8,5	3,2
3 Loisirs	3,5	3,0	1,8	4,1	4,2	1,0
4 Discipline et punitions	5,4	5,6	10,2	5,2	4,5	6,1
5 Eloignement de la famille	6,3	6,8	5,2	7,9	8,0	3,8
6 Trop peu de liberté	5,0	4,8	10,0	4,9	4,9	8,9
7 Trop peu de liberté d'opinion	6,1	6,3	2,2	6,3	6,3	2,0
8 Manque de respect de l'homme	8,6	9,2	4,7	7,9	9,1	4,4
9 Plus de possibilités dans la vie civile	8,6	10,0	5,8	5,8	5,9	4,5
10 Activités typiquement militaires	2,1	1,5	3,6	1,2	0,7	4,9
11 L'armée est une perte de temps	0,3	0,3	7,6	0,2	0,2	8,1
12 Déjà une profession dans le civil	0,1	–	0,1	0,1	0,01	4,4
13 Corvées	–	–	1,5	–	–	4,6
Nombre moyen d'avis	4,5	4,7	6,-	3,7	4,8	5,2

vécu présent. Ce sont les frustrations récentes, les ressentiments de surface aussi.
Tandis que si une liste de motifs est présentée, les sujets sont amenés à comparer ces
motifs, à les peser, à réfléchir. D'autres niveaux de la personnalité sont impliqués.

Ayant considéré les différences et les ressemblances, il nous a semblé pouvoir encore
tenter la même interprétation qu'à la recherche précédente. Si nous le faisons nous trou-
vons que

> la discipline et les punitions
> le manque de liberté
> la perte de temps à l'armée
> les activités typiquement militaires

sont probablement la source de frustrations, qui sont resenties vivement dans l'actuel,
mais qui sont de surface et qui perdent beaucoup d'importance pour les sujets si ceux-ci
réfléchissent, s'ils comparent, c.à.d. s'ils accèdent à un autre niveau d'appréciation.
Le grief "perte de temps à l'armée" ressenti si fort semble-t-il, probablement à
"fleur de peau", disparaît à peu près complètement au moment des comparaisons.
A l'opposé, nous voyons que

> le peu de possibilités d'avenir
> les congés et permissions
> le trop peu de liberté d'opinion
> le manque de respect de l'homme

qui paraissent très peu ou peu ressentis de prime abord, acquièrent plus d'importance si
le jugement se réfère à de nombreux éléments d'appréciation.

Il est remarquable que les motifs qui prévalent au questionnaire se rapportent à de
hautes valeurs humaines (liberté d'opinion, respect de l'homme) ou en tout cas à des
perspectives d'avenir. Par contre, les motifs qui prévalent dans les rédactions libres
concernent les contraintes de la vie quotidienne, les activités gênantes ou dont
l'utilité n'est pas très sensible. Dans cette perspective, c'est dans un sens restreint
qu'il faudrait entendre le "manque de liberté" que nous avons cité tout à l'heure.

Dans l'ensemble, pour ces échantillons homogènes, il nous paraît que notre interprétation ne heurte pas le bon sens.

3. CONCLUSION

Si l'on considère le questionnaire à choix multiple d'une part et les questions
ouvertes ou la rédaction libre d'autre part, et si l'on admet la façon dont nous avons
interprété les résultats des deux études rapportées, il faut admettre aussi que chacune
des techniques peut apporter des renseignements d'un certain niveau. Le choix de la
technique dépendra du niveau auquel on s'intéresse.

Par exemple, si l'on veut connaître les "points chauds" d'un climat, les zones
sensibles du moment, des techniques d'expression libre sembleraient indiquées. Par contre,
il vaudrait mieux préparer des listes d'éléments à choisir si on désire explorer des
couches plus stables et peut-être plus profondes.

Attitude Research in the United States Air Force[1]

ERNEST C. TUPES

PERSONNEL RESEARCH LABORATORY

LACKLAND AFB, TEXAS

I. INTRODUCTION

Studies of attitudes have been a part of the research program of the Air Force Personnel Research Laboratory since the late 1940's, although the emphasis and priority given this type of research has varied markedly from year to year. In the early period, the interest was mainly in the areas of re-enlistment attitudes of airmen and of attitudes toward flying of pilot and navigator trainees. Then for a few years our studies were primarily concerned with the Air Force Reserve Officer Training Corps cadet and his attitudes toward his AFROTC training; his later pilot and navigator training; and an Air Force career. Reports of these studies are listed in the reference section of this paper which contains all attitudinal studies carried out by Personnel Research Laboratory.

In general they lead to the following conclusions: Attitudes seem to play an important role in determining whether an individual will complete a training program but not how well he will perform in that program. Re-enlistment and career attitudes are quite complex and unless measurement of these attitudes is carried out within carefully defined subgroups many valid relationships will be hidden. Finally, with respect to prediction of re-enlistment behaviour the low end of the attitude scale may be quite predictive but the high end is frequently of zero validity. That is, in the operational setting, if an individual admits he is negatively inclined toward some aspect of military life you can believe him, but statements of positive attitudes are not necessarily dependable.

Around 1960 it became Air Force policy that no person could become a commissioned officer without at least a bachelor's degree. Since the percentage of college graduate officers who made a career of the Air Force had always been quite low, it seemed apparent to task scientists at Personnel Research Laboratory that the problem of officer retention would soon become acute. Consequently a series of studies of career attitudes of Air Force officers was started and research in this area is still receiving considerable emphasis. I will review briefly two of these studies and then spend the remainder of my time in describing an on-going long range follow-up study of attitudes and attitude changes in a group of officers commissioned in late 1963 and early 1964.

2. OTS ATTITUDE STUDIES

With the initiation of the Officer Training School (OTS) program in 1960 (this is a twelve week course for college graduates leading to a commission as second lieutenant), Harding and others developed an attitude questionnaire which was administered to a number of OTS classes a week or two before graduation. This questionnaire had several purposes. First, it was desired to obtain an indication of OTS students' attitudes, motivations,

---

[1]   This paper was presented in conference by Col. James H. Ritter, U.S.A.F.

and reactions to OTS and to the Air Force. Second, the data would be used in the development of a retention scale. Third, a fairly new technique in attitude measurement called the Importance-Possibility Scale would be tried out. In this scale the respondent is given a list of 22 job characteristics or rewards such as "have competent supervisors", "do a great deal of travelling", and "obtain a good salary". He is asked to rate each characteristic on a five point scale with respect to its importance to himself and then to rate each characteristic again, this time with respect to the possibility of his obtaining each characteristic in the Air Force. This technique is based on the assumption that easy attainment of a reward is not enough but that the reward in addition to being attainable must also be of importance to the individual. Presumably if an officer saw little chance of obtaining in the Air Force those characteristics which were important to him he would not be inclined to make a career of the service. The questionnaire was administered anonymously to 588 male OTS students and with name identification to 276 male OTS students. This latter group was followed up with a similar questionnaire after 18 months on the job.

Certain results of the analyses are quite interesting. The first is concerned with shifts in expressed career intent over the 18 months after OTS graduation. As indicated

TABLE 1

OTS Responses to Career Intent Statement

| | AT GRADUATION | | AFTER 18 |
	Anon.	Signed	MONTHS
YES	35%	34%	43%
MAYBE	59%	63%	40%
NO	06%	03%	17%
N	588	211	211

Product-Moment Correlation
Between Career Intent at
Graduation & 18 Mos = .37

in Table 1, the percentage stating they planned an Air Force career rose from 34% to 43%, and the percentage stating they definitely did not plan an Air Force career rose from 3% to 17%. Whether these increases, which are offset by a decrease from the undecided group from 63% to 40%, represent actual attitude changes, or simply increased willingness to commit themselves cannot of course be determined from the data. In Table 2 are shown the same data when the sample is subdivided on the basis of the career field of assignment. It can be seen that the career groups differ markedly, with the Science and Engineering group showing a small decrease in the Yes response and a large increase in the No response.

Table 3 illustrates the validity of two scales developed to predict career intent. The Retainability scale is based upon 14 selected questionnaire items answerable at the time of application for OTS. The Importance-Possibility scale score is based on response differences found in another follow-up study of a large sample of officers some of whom were still on active duty after serving their obligated tours and some of whom were inactive. Both of these scales have quite respectable validity and it appears that either would be quite effective screening devices for reducing the percentages of individuals with low career intent among the applicants selected for training.

TABLE 2

OTS RESPONSES TO CAREER INTENT STATEMENT BY CAREER FIELD

CAREER FIELD		AT GRADUATION	AFTER 18 MONTHS
RATED	Yes	43%	53%
	Maybe	55%	42%
	No	02%	05%
	N	124	124
SCIENCE & ENGINEERING	Yes	18%	13%
	Maybe	74%	35%
	No	08%	52%
	N	23	23
OTHER	Yes	25%	34%
	Maybe	72%	38%
	No	03%	28%
	N	64	64

Correlations:
Rated   .34
S & E   .34
Other   .29

TABLE 3

PREDICTION OF CAREER INTENT

PER CENTS FAVOURABLE IN CAREER INTENT

	AT GRADUATION		AFTER 18 MONTHS
	ANONYMOUS	SIGNED	
RETAINABILITY SCORE:			
Above 2.3	59%	57%	62%
Below 2.3	12%	12%	25%
IMPORTANCE-POSSIBILITY SCALE SCORE:			
Above 18.25			70%
Below 18.25			16%
TOTAL GROUP:	35%	34%	43%

Correlations:
 Retainability Score
  Anon.   .58
  Signed   .60
  18 Mos   .53
 Import-Poss Score
  18 Mos   .51

3. ATC ADVISORY BOARD SURVEY

In 1964 at the request of the Air Training Command Advisory Board, Personnel Research Laboratory designed and administered a survey of career attitude to an approximately 20% sample of all active duty Air Force officers with six years or less of service. Included were questions of a demographical nature (age, grade, etc.,); sociological (parents' income and respondents' financial condition); judgemental concerning military training; and attitudinal toward various aspects of military service of the respondent, his family and his parents. Also included was the Importance-Possibility Scale. Of the total of 7800 surveys mailed out, each addressed to a particular individual, 5800 were returned of which 5000 were usable. Because of the number of variables involved and our previous findings of the inter-dependence of career attitudes and these variables, the analyses were quite complex and in fact will not be complete until a behavioural criterion (whether or not in an active duty status after completion of the obligated tour) is available. Thus only a summary of the more important and interesting correlates of career intent will be presented here. Because of the heterogeneity of the sample with respect to certain variables (regular/reserve status, length of service, and source of commission) known to be related to career intent, the effects of these variables were held constant in analyses of the relationships between all other variables and the statement of career intent.

TABLE 4

MULTIPLE CORRELATIONS OF BASE-LINE VARIABLES WITH CAREER INTENT

	Multiple Correlation
Regular/Reserve Status	.26
Length of Service	.35
Source of Commission	.40
All Three Combined	.47

Table 4 shows correlations between the three "base-line" variables and the career intent criterion. Table 5 presents the relationships between demographic variables and

TABLE 5

MULTIPLE CORRELATIONS OF DEMOGRAPHIC VARIABLES WITH CAREER INTENT

	R	Net R[a]
Career Field	.32	.14
Grade	.26	.10
Type Training Received	.41	.20
Major Air Command	.17	.17
Aeronautical Rating	.28	.10
College Major Subject	.32	.10

[a] Length of Service, Regular/Reserve
Status and Source of Commission
held constant

career intent both without and with the three "base-line" variables partialed out. All the correlations are statistically significant but are numerically quite small. The stronger relationships found between attitudes and career intent are shown in Table 6.

TABLE 6

MULTIPLE CORRELATIONS OF SELECTED ATTITUDINAL VARIABLES WITH CAREER INTENT

	R	Net R^a
Wife and Parents' Attitudes Toward Air Force Career	.55	.49
Challenge of AF Job vs Civilian Job	.51	.42
Frequent Residence Changes	.40	.35
Job in Area of College Major	.36	.17
Importance vs Possibility of:		
Feeling of Accomplishment	.47	.44
Competent Supervision	.35	.33
Have Say in Future	.36	.32
Intelligent Personnel Policies	.30	.32
Promotion on Ability	.30	.30
Competition with Fellow Officers	.33	.28

^{a}Length of Service, Regular/Reserve
Status and Source of Commission
held constant

After the actual in/out criterion matures on this sample additional analyses will be carried out aimed at determining the overall level of prediction which may be obtained from the survey items taken all together and grouped in several ways.

4. OFFICER FOLLOW-UP SURVEY

The final study to be discussed is a year by year follow-up over a five year period of 5600 officers receiving their commissions between mid 1963 and early 1964. The purpose of this study is to attempt to determine critical points in the early service of officers when career attitudes and/or related attitudes change, and to continue the earlier work on the development of retainability scales which might be used in the screening of applicants for the various commissioning programs. A survey, similar to the others described above except that the biographical section was greatly expanded, was administered to the sample either just prior to or immediately after commissioning. Each year the entire sample is resurveyed with essentially the same attitudinal items so that changes may be determined. It will of course be several years before the data are complete but in the meantime several preliminary analyses have been carried out. This sample, it may be noted, is homogeneous with respect to length of service and grade so that only source of commission need be taken into account (regular/reserve differences except those as a function of commission source will not be a factor for another year or two).

The group has now been surveyed three times: prior to commissioning; after one year of active duty; and after two years of active duty. Figure 1 shows per cents planning an Air Force career by year of survey for six source of commission groups: Air Force Academy (AFA); the Military and Naval Academies (USMA-NA); Air Force Reserve Officer

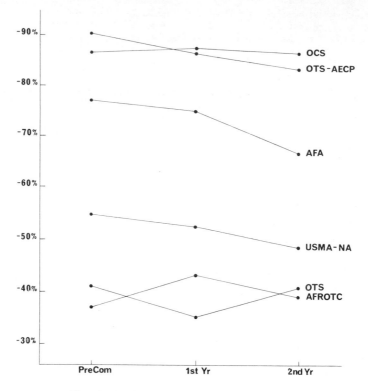

Fig. 1 PER CENTS PLANNING AIR FORCE CAREER

Training Corps (AFROTC); Officer Candidate School (OCS); Officer Training School (OTS); and officers commissioned through OTS by way of the Airman Education and Commissioning Program (OTS - AECP) – this latter is a means by which bright enlisted men with two years of college earn their Bachelor's degrees at Air Force expense and then go through OTS. Of interest is the fact that the two groups most favourable toward an Air Force career are OCS and OTS-AECP. Both of these groups consist of former enlisted men with previous military service. Also of interest is the fact that Air Force Academy graduates are appreciably more favourable toward Air Force careers than are graduates of the Military and Naval academies who transferred to the Air Force. In Figure 2 are shown the per cents of each commissioning source who state they do not intend to make the Air Force their career. It might be pointed out that even among the groups least unfavourable there is a steady year-by-year increase in the per cents not planning a career.

Correlations were computed between the career intent statements in the three yearly surveys and these are shown in Table 7. The correlations are moderately high but low enough to indicate that from 50% to 80% of the various samples responded differently to the 1st year survey and 60% to 85% to the 2nd year survey than they did to the pre-commissioning survey.

Item analyses of the precommissioning survey were carried out against the career intent statement for half of each source of commission group. In general a fairly clear-cut pattern emerged. The officers favourable toward a career are more likely to be married; to have a somewhat lower economic background; and to have had a more transient

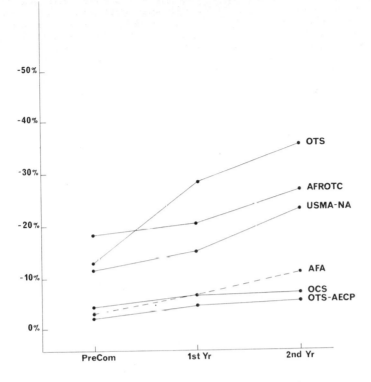

Fig. 2   PER CENTS NOT PLANNING AIR FORCE CAREER

TABLE 7

CORRELATIONS BETWEEN CAREER INTENT STATEMENTS AT VARIOUS TIMES

Product Moment Correlations

	PreCom-1st Yr	PreCom-2nd Yr	1st-2nd Yr
Officer Candidate School	.69	.56	.87
Air Force Academy	.46	.41	.66
Military & Naval Academies	.55	.39	.74
AFROTC	.55	.47	.68
OTS	.60	.46	.68
OTS-AECP	.55	.57	.80
All Sources Combined	.60	.51	.71

unsettled home life. More of this group began working early; attended a state university where they were in the middle third of their class, obtaining their degrees in areas other than science or engineering. Their parents and wives generally have a positive attitude toward an Air Force career. On the other hand, the noncareer officers had a more stable home life; are single; desire to settle down in a particular area; went to a private college where they joined a fraternity; specialized in science or engineering and were in the upper third of their class. Based on these item analyses a Retainability Scale was developed and validated as shown in Table 8. As can be seen the validities of the scale differ little from group to group, and even against the 2nd Yr criterion the validities are significant.

TABLE 8

VALIDITIES OF PRECOMMISSIONING RETAINABILITY SCORE FOR PREDICTION OF CAREER INTENT

	Correlations Between Retainability Score and Career Intent Statement		
	PreCom	1st Yr	2nd Yr
Officer Candidate School	.48	.36	.13
Air Force Academy	.57	.45	.38
Military & Naval Academies	.56	.44	.28
AFROTC	.63	.44	.40
OTS	.62	.47	.38
OTS-AECP	.47	.44	.42
All Sources Combined	.61	.46	.40

TABLE 9

VALIDITIES OF IMPORTANCE-POSSIBILITY SCALE SCORES FOR PREDICTION OF CAREER INTENT

	Correlations With Career Intent Statement of Pre-Commissioning Imp-Poss Scale Scores		
	PreCom	1st Yr	2nd Yr
Harding Key	.21	.13	.12
Total Possibility	.35	.26	.23
Total Importance	.01	.01	.01
Total Imp and Poss	.19	.12	.11
Sum of Items on Which 1 − P > Zero	-.38	-.27	-.24
Sum of Items on Which 1 − P < Zero	.06	.05	.05

Several different types of scores have been developed from the Importance-Possibility scale and the validities of some of these scores for all sources of commission combined are shown in Table 9. The first gives the validities of the original Harding key — based

upon empirical comparison of active and inactive officers. The validity of this key in
the present study is much lower than that found by Harding. The other scores have
validities based upon *a priori* rather than empirical considerations. To obtain these
scores each job characteristic alternative was assigned a weight ranging from *1* for a
response of No Importance or No Possibility to *5* for a response of Extremely Important or
Very Good Possibility. Various combinations of these weighted item responses were then
obtained. Briefly it appears that the more characteristics an officer sees as possible
in the Air Force the more likely he is to be career minded. It also appears that the
importance he attaches to these characteristics *per se* is of little moment as long as he
thinks there is a good possibility of obtaining each characteristic he considers
important. In fact the greater the discrepancy between Importance and Possibility the
greater the chances that an officer will not plan to make a career of the Air Force.

REFERENCES

This list contains all relevant Air Force Personnel Research Laboratory reports in the
area of attitude study and measurement. Copies of any of these reports may be obtained
by a request, through official channels, to:

Personnel Research Laboratory

Lackland Air Force Base

San Antonio, Texas

Berkeley, M.H., & Brokaw, L.D. *Stability of WAF attitudes as measured by WAF attitude survey
BE-CE501GX.* AFPTRC-TN-56-72. Lackland AFB, Tex.: Personnel Research Laboratory, Air Force
Personnel and Training Research Centre, June 1956.

Bowles, J.W., & Torr, D.V. *An attitude survey of AFROTC cadets.* AFPTRC-TN-55-40. Lackland AFB,
Tex.: Personnel Research Laboratory, Air Force Personnel and Training Research Centre,
November 1955.

Cureton, E.E. *Dimensions of airman morale.* WADD-TN-60-137, AD-245 845. Lackland AFB, Tex.:
Personnel Laboratory, Wright Air Development Division, June 1960.

Cureton, E.E. & Sargent, B.B. *Factor-analytic reanalysis of studies of job satisfaction and morale.*
WADD-TN-60-138, AD-248 076. Lackland AFB, Tex.: Personnel Laboratory, Wright Air Development
Division, July 1960.

Downey, R.L., Jr., Harding, F.D., & Bottenberg, R.A. *Ratings by officer groups of importance and
obtainability of selected job characteristics.* PRL-TDR-64-4, AD-437 954. Lackland AFB, Tex.:
Personnel Research Laboratory, Aerospace Medical Division, February 1964.

Ewing, Faye & Alvord, R.W. *USAF officer career decisions: Predictability of initial career intent.*
PRL-TR-65-2, AD-613 333. Lackland AFB, Tex.: Personnel Research Laboratory, Aerospace Medical
Division, February 1965.

Fitzpatrick, R., & Cullen, J.W. *Prediction of airman re-enlistment.* AFPTRC-TR-57-12, AD-146 416.
Lackland AFB; Tex.: Personnel Laboratory, Air Force Personnel and Training Research Centre,
December 1957.

Flyer, E.S., & Carp, A. *Retention of rated AFROTC officers.* AFPTRC-TN-57-126, AD-134 258. Lackland AFB, Tex.: Personnel Laboratory, Air Force Personnel and Training Research Centre,
October 1957.

Flyer, E.S., & Potter, N.R. *Characteristics of basic airmen willing to volunteer for a six-year
tour in missile squadrons.* WADC-TN-59-35, AD-210 476. Lackland AFB, Tex.: Personnel
Laboratory, Wright Air Development Centre, February 1959.

French, Elizabeth G. *Relation of an indirect measure of attitude to expressed military attitude.*
AFPTRC-TN-55-72. Lackland AFB, Tex.: Personnel Research Laboratory, Air Force Personnel and
Training Research Centre, December 1955.

French, Elizabeth G., & Ernest, R.R. *The relation between authoritarianism and acceptance of
military ideology.* AFPTRC-TN-56-34. Lackland AFB, Tex.: Personnel Research Laboratory, Air
Force Personnel and Training Research Centre, February 1956.

Harding, F.D., & Bottenberg, R.A. *Contribution of status factors to relationships between airmen's
attitudes and job performance.* ASD-TN-61-147, AD-272 050. Lackland AFB, Tex.: Personnel
Laboratory, Aeronautical Systems Division, November 1961.

Harding, F.D., & Bottenberg, R.A. *Attitudes and career intentions of Officer Training School
students.* PRL-TDR-62-8, AD-289 872. Lackland AFB, Tex.: Personnel Research Laboratory, Aerospace Medical Division, May 1962.

Harding, F.D. & Downey, R.L. Jr., & Bottenberg, R.A. *Career experiences of AFIT classes of 1955
and 1956.* PRL-TDR-63-9, AD-403 830. Lackland AFB, Tex.: Personnel Research Laboratory, Aerospace Medical Division, April 1963.

Harding, F.D., & Wong, K.K.L. *Attitudes and career intentions of Officer Training School graduates*. PRL-TR-64-26, AD-610 056. Lackland AFB, Tex.: Personnel Research Laboratory, Aerospace Medical Division, October 1964.

Kaapke, L.D., Tupes, E.C., & Alvord, R.W. *A multiple linear regression analysis of officer career attitudes*. PRL-TR-65-16, AD-627 651. Lackland AFB, Tex.: Personnel Research Laboratory, Aerospace Medical Division, October 1965.

Kamenetzky, J., & Schmidt, H. *Effects of personal and impersonal refutation of audience counter-arguments on attitude change*. AFPTRC-TN-57-102, AD-134 223. Lackland AFB, Tex.: Personnel Research Laboratory, Air Force Personnel and Training Research Centre, July 1957.

Kaplan, Margorie N., & Alvord, R.W. *USAF officer evaluation system survey: attitudes and experience*. PRL-TR-65-17, AD-628 551. Lackland AFB, Tex.: Personnel Research Laboratory, Aerospace Medical Division, November 1965.

Moltz, H., & Thistlethwaite, D.L. *Attitude modification and anxiety reduction*. AFPTRC-TN-55-37. Lackland AFB, Tex.: Personnel Research Laboratory, Wright Air Development Division, November 1955.

Nolan, C.Y. *Attitude differences among disparate Air Force specialties*. AFPTRC-TN-56-88. Lackland AFB, Tex.: Personnel Research Laboratory, Air Force Personnel and Training Research Centre, June 1956.

Thistlethwaite, D.L., Moltz, H., Kamenetzky, J., et al. *Effects of basic training on the attitudes of airmen*. AFPTRC-TN-55-3. Lackland AFB, Tex.: Personnel Laboratory, Wright Air Development Division, June 1955.

Thistlethwaite, D.L., de Haan, H., & Kamenetzky, J. *The effects of "directive" and "non-directive" communication procedures on attitudes*. AFPTRC-TN-55-39. Lackland AFB, Tex.: Personnel Laboratory, Wright Air Development Division, November 1955.

Thistlewaite, D.L., & Kamenetzky, J. *Attitude change through refutation and elaboration of audience counterarguments*. AFPTRC-TN-55-49. Lackland AFB, Tex.: Personnel Laboratory, Wright Air Development Division, November 1955.

Thistlethwaite, D.L., Kamenetzky, J., & Schmidt, H. *Factors influencing attitude change through refutative communications*. AFPTRC-TN-56-64. Lackland AFB, Tex.: Personnel Laboratory, Wright Air Development Division, June 1956.

Thorndike, R.L., & Hagen, Elizabeth P. *Attitudes, educational programs and job experiences of airmen who did not re-enlist*. AFPTRC-TR-57-2, AD-134 209. Lackland AFB, Tex.: Personnel Laboratory, Wright Air Development Centre, June 1957.

Tupes, E.C., & Cox, J.A. *Prediction of elimination from basic pilot training for reasons other than flying deficiency*. Research Bulletin 51-1. Lackland AFB, Tex.: Human Resources Research Centre, Air Training Command, February 1951.

Tupes, E.C., & Yarnold, J.K. *Military attitude as a predictor of Air Force success; preliminary studies of the attitude survey*. Research Bulletin 52-23. Lackland AFB, Tex.: Human Resources Research Centre, Air Training Command, July 1952.

Tupes, E.C., Bowles, J.W., & Toor, D.V. *Predicting motivation for flying training among senior AFROTC cadets*. AFPTRC-TN-55-18. Lackland AFB, Tex.: Personnel Research Laboratory, Air Force Personnel and Training Research Centre, July 1955.

Whitlock, G.H., & Cureton, E.C. *Validation of morale and attitude scales*. WADD-TR-60-76, AD-242 359. Lackland AFB, Tex.: Personnel Laboratory, Wright Air Development Division, June 1960.

Whitlock, G.H. *The status of morale measurement, 1959*. WADD-TN-60-136, AD-243 825. Lackland AFB, Tex.: Personnel Laboratory, Wright Air Development Division, May 1960.

Job Satisfaction in the Royal Air Force

GILBERT JESSUP

MINISTRY OF DEFENCE

Social research began in the Royal Air Force in 1954 with an experiment at one operational unit, RAF Benson (1). Conditions of the unit were systematically changed in the three phases of the experiment. First a number of the petty restrictions normally imposed on airmen were removed. Second, improvements were made in the personal and domestic facilities provided for airmen. Third, certain organizational changes were implemented with the aim of producing greater cohesion among the sub-groups on the unit. Morale on the unit was assessed prior to the experiment and after each of the three phases by means of questionnaire scales. The level of morale was also assessed at four control stations in the same command as Benson on each of the four occasions. The results of the experiment were contaminated by a number of extraneous factors, particularly the "Hawthorne" effect in that the personnel at Benson recognized that they were taking part in an experiment. In fact the situation was further complicated because the airmen heard that improvements were to take place before the experiment began, which gave a boost to the initial measure of morale, and the actual changes did not altogether live up to expectation. No gain, and in fact a slight drop in morale followed phases one and two of the experiment, but a significant gain occurred after phase three – the organizational changes. The level of morale at the control stations did not vary significantly over the period of the experiment.

The experiment at Benson was stimulated by considerations of the retention of personnel or internal recruiting. It was felt that improvements in service conditions would result in a higher rate retention of personnel on the unit (as measured by the numbers re-engaging for a further period of Service) but no such increase resulted. This may have been due to the fact that the airmen recognized that the changes were not general throughout the RAF and that they would sooner or later be posted from Benson or it may be that the changes were not sufficient to change basic attitudes to the service.

The Benson experiment illustrates some of the difficulties in experimentally manipulating the service environment, and assessing the effect on the attitudes of personnel, even when the opportunity exists. For this reason we have relied primarily on survey techniques in our social research.

We have performed a number of surveys to find what factors are related to the decision to re-engage or leave the service at the end of an airman's initial engagement. One study on internal recruiting by P.J. Sadler in 1957 (2) was based on the questionnaire responses of a sample of 2,417 airmen at seventeen RAF units. The questionnaire used in this, as in most RAF studies, consisted primarily of multiple-choice items plus a few open-ended questions. The attitudes of those intending to leave the service were compared with those intending to re-engage for a further period. It is difficult to generalize about the results of such a survey. Although the major reasons for leaving given by the total sample of those leaving were (a) insufficient pay, (b) service restrictions and, (c) poor accommodation, further analysis shows that it is primarily the younger airmen who suffer in these respects and that for the more mature, married airmen, generally living with his wife and children off the unit, a different pattern emerges. Their major problems were (a) family separation or the possibility of same, (b) their children's education, because of frequent moves, and (c) poor promotion prospects in some instances. Apart from age and marital status, further analysis by trade, rank, and so on is required to get a meaningful picture of the motives involved in the decision to stay or leave. The isolation of causes is complicated by the fact that these dimensions interact with each other.

Our social research programme in recent years has concentrated on the measurement of job satisfaction and the factors to which it is related. It is recognized that the basis of healthy recruiting, of the retention of personnel, and it is hoped of their performance, is providing airmen with a satisfying working and living environment. This of course depends very much on the social and psychological climate as well as on physical and material conditions.

Over a period of three years, from 1962-1965, we were called in to survey 16 units in six home and one overseas command. Our primary concern in these surveys was to ascertain the level of morale or job satisfaction and the associated factors in the particular units. But as a basically standard procedure was applied at each of the 16 units some useful generalizations about the RAF can be obtained by an analysis of the accumulated data. In all we have completed questionnaires from 4,820 airmen.

Job satisfaction varies appreciably according to the trade group in which an airman works. On one measure, for example, the trades ranged from Air Defence Operator, in which only 30 per cent express high job satisfaction to Air Traffic Controller in which 70 per cent express high job satisfaction. This compares with the average of 46 per cent for the total sample. The differences between these two trades mentioned can easily be understood in terms of the nature of the jobs performed. Although the two jobs have some similarities the Air Traffic Controller is doing a job which is obviously important, he is in the centre of things and knows what is going on, he has rapid feedback of results of his work. The Air Defence Operator, on the other hand, is rather remote from the unit, does not so easily recognize the importance of his task and has practically no knowledge of the results of his work. Added to this the dissatisfied Air Defence Operator does not have a skill which he can transfer to civilian life whereas the Air Traffic Controller does.

Job satisfaction also increases steadily with rank as airmen move up the hierarchy after a slight drop during the first few years of an airman's career. 39 per cent of air craftmen express high job satisfaction compared with 75 per cent at Flight Sergeant level with the intermediate ranks falling in between. Job satisfaction among airmen is significantly related to:

   (i) interest expressed in work

  (ii) knowledge of purpose of tasks performed

 (iii) knowledge of results

  (iv) doing a job which requires the use of the skills for which the airman has been trained

   (v) use of abilities and intelligence

  (vi) pace of work (even rather than fluctuating)

 (vii) number of hours spent actually working as opposed to being present at work (the optimum being 6–8 hours per day)

(viii) working normal hours (as opposed to shifts)

  (ix) pride in section

   (x) estimated efficiency of section

  (xi) encouragement to offer suggestions

 (xii) confidence in use of suggestions offered (i.e. feeling of participation)

(xiii) number of superiors issuing orders

 (xiv) freedom from domestic problems

  (xv) physical working conditions (temperature, lighting, ventilation).

The majority of these factors have, of course, been found important in industrial studies. Our analysis has in general confirmed that they also apply in a military setting.

A large proportion of the variance in job satisfaction among airmen can be attributed to factors within the control of first line supervisors. This was also the conclusion of a job satisfaction survey carried out recently in the United States Air Force by Cantrell, Hartman and Sims, 1967, (3). It might be added in this context that the results of our research in this area are widely used in RAF management training programs.

The relationship between job satisfaction and performance is not clearly established. However, there is evidence that job satisfaction is positively related to satisfactoriness as assessed by the airmen's section commander. It is difficult to obtain objective performance criteria on individuals.

More recently we have been engaged on a research program to discover how the organization of an operational unit affects the attitudes of the personnel on the unit. We are interested in how the attitudes at different levels in the organization are related; for example, the extent to which the attitudes of a section commander can affect the attitudes of the men he commands. We are concerned with group cohesion and its relationship to job satisfaction and such questions as the variance in job satisfaction within working groups and between working groups and thus the degree to which job satisfaction can be accounted for by group factors. We are further interested in the proportion of variance in job satisfaction that can be accounted for by service conditions as opposed to the variance due to the differences in personality of the individual airmen.

At present we are performing a comparative study of three selected units. We are interviewing all the officers and administering questionnaires to all the airmen on each unit. We have so far only performed a preliminary analysis on some of the data. The correlation between job satisfaction and group cohesion ($r_t = 0.19$) although quite small is statistically significant.

The relationship between size of working group and job satisfaction does not appear to be important in a service setting although there are indications that men in groups of 6–11 are slightly more satisfied than smaller or larger groups. Groups of this size also appear more cohesive. This factor has not been fully analyzed and it may be an artifact of the type of work performed by groups of this size.

REFERENCES

1. Sadler, P.J., (1955) Benson Experiment, *Air Ministry, Science 4 Memo No 50.*
2. Sadler, P.J., (1958) Internal Recruiting Survey (RAF), *Air Ministry, Science 4 Memo No 69.*
3. Cantrell, G.K., Hartman, B.O. & Sims, L.S., (1967) Factors in Job-Satisfaction: A Followup, *USAF School of Aerospace Medicine, SAM-TR-67-21.*

Attitudes and Values as Predictors of Military Performance

WALTER L. WILKINS

U.S. NAVY MEDICAL NEUROPSYCHITRIC
RESEARCH UNIT, SAN DIEGO.

I. INTRODUCTION

Research upon aptitudes, so presciently summarized by Clark Hull in 1928, has reached, in military and industrial psychology, an enviable position of acceptance, of solid results – indeed, of indispensability. Yet the proportion of the variance the selection experts account for through their reliable tests is far from satisfying. When long-term adjustment is assessed, when military competence, is measured, the predictive validity of the tests of aptitude and of the bare demographic factors, like age or educational level attained, while statistically gratifying, is practically disappointing There is plenty of room left for possible predictions based on motivation, or values held, or non-cognitive factors generally considered. Yet the measures of these things are technically and theoretically (substantively) far from adequate.

I am reminded of a comparison made in another context fifteen years ago by Lee Cronbach. He asked, in considering the assessment of school children's adjustment, whether a classroom teacher was helped more by the results of a Stanford-Binet or the results of a Rorschach. The Stanford-Binet, administered by an experienced psychologist, gave a remarkably reliable measure of the aspects of the child's intelligence that were related to success in the common branches of the elementary school. Yet this very exact measure tapped something which an experienced teacher was presumably tapping daily by the routine learning exercises, and the test often added very little to the teacher's knowledge of the child. The Rorschach, on the other hand, again administered by an experienced child psychologist, added a great deal to the teacher's knowledge of the child, and in areas of development – emotional, dynamic, motivational – which the teacher's daily set tasks did not assess. Unfortunately, the proportion of good and of poor information – of wheat and of chaff – in this new information could not be determined. So, as Cronbach posed the question, does one wish in a particular instance to have a very small amount of new information about a child, but to have this information very reliable indeed? Or does one want a great deal of information about a child of which fifty per cent, say, might be new and significant information and fifty per cent new and significant misinformation?

Well, we hold no brief for the Rorschach in our laboratory – we think it may well be useful in clinical situations although of very limited use in most assessment situations – but we *do* feel that much more time and effort put in to tests, unless a new breakthrough of a Binet is forthcoming, will bring about modest results. And we hope that a mounting of research effort in the motivational aspects of military adjustment will have handsome results.

2. ATTITUDES

We must admit, at the outset, that our efforts to "get a handle" on attitudes and values and motivations are as unsuccessful as anyone else's. Further, we must admit that our efforts in measuring relevant attitudes give predictive validities well below those we find for the standard predictors – level of schooling, age, and intelligence test results – when one predicts performance. We have some modest successes – notably, I think, in the prediction of adjustment of wintering-over parties in the Antarctic continent, and in prediction of short-term adjustment of men exposed to physical trials of a severe sort – such as the training of underwater swimmers. But in general our applications of attitudinal test results have resulted in very modest predictions indeed.

I wish to report on some results of an application of a revision of Richard Snyder's test items, developed on Army recruits when he was a scientist at Human Resources Research Office, to Marine Corps personnel on whom we have good criterion information, and then to express a hope as to what the next steps might be.

It may be recalled that Snyder's laboratory is primarily a *training* laboratory and that he was interested in the relation of attitudes which might be tapped on a Likert-type set of items to variables in the recruit training situation. He found that the composition of the basic training platoon had a great deal to do with attitudes favourable or unfavourable to military service. Since men with the most favourable attitudes toward the Army tend strongly to be volunteers, he advised having a sufficient number of volunteers in all training platoons to assure a mean favourable attitude throughout. He also found, by the way, that volunteers tend to be somewhat younger and to have somewhat less schooling than nonvolunteers. More than this though, is the fact that volunteers bring enthusiasm which draftees lack at least initially. He went on to say about volunteers, "Doubtless they include a considerable proportion of young men who are not well motivated, who have little self discipline, and who are pretty hard to handle. However, they include a great many men who are bright, ambitious, and well-disciplined; and who enter the service with a very real interest in soldiering. It is the latter group about whom we are most concerned, for if they find the Army a situation in which a high premium is placed on docility, conformity and the ability to stay out of trouble, and if it is further a situation in which there is no significant reward for extra effort to acquire the really most important skills and knowledge of the soldier, then we believe they will truly become disillusioned."

The Marine Corps attitude data we have been analyzing are byproducts of a longitudinal study of military adjustment, having special emphasis on health and illness, especially psychiatric illness, and reports on various segments of the study have been made by Newell Berry, John Plag, and Paul Nelson (1966, 1967). Since, at the time of collection of the initial data on recruits, the Marines were all volunteers, at least in the sense of not being draftees, we are unable to validate directly the Snyder conclusions about volunteers and draftees. But we can certainly say that the Marine data corroborate the Army data.

The principal results of the attitude studies can be quickly summarized. At the outset, many Marines enlist for less than positive reasons. If one added to those who admitted that if there had been no Army draft they would have been unlikely to join, those who admitted that if they had had a satisfying job they would not have joined, one gets a sizeable majority. But they *were* volunteers and it is interesting to note that after training commenced, their opinions of the Marine Corps went up. One of the things which made the Corps more favourably regarded was *discipline*. I presume that nobody really *loves* discipline. The few monks among psychologists, at least as far back as T.V. Moore, have testified that not even monks in the monastery possess a true liking for discipline, accustomed to it as they presumably are. That adolescent males should *like* discipline would be too much to expect, even in less rebellious decades than ours – but it remains that adolescents may, as some clinical psychologists pointed out a decade ago, *need limits*. Perhaps it may be more accurate to say that adolescent males may feel a valid sense of satisfaction at achievement of the group which is facilitated by the limitations on the individuals in the group. Nearly every man who has gone (successfully) through military training has been aware of the sense of accomplishment of the training group he belongs to and the shining faces on graduation day testify to the sense. Marines appreciate the need for discipline – unit discipline and self-discipline, and their attitudes toward discipline are positive.

Yet discipline is not easy to get used to. While it is easier to bear than the young man feared it might be, it is not enjoyable. When a young man lines up with his rankless peers before a formidable-looking sergeant and his mind is filled with the anecdotes his uncle or his father told, he may well wonder about the physical and psychological stamina he may need to get through the next few months and have some doubts as to his possession of such stamina. Yet the great majority do muster the necessary grit and not only survive the physically demanding routines – they build themselves up doing so – and the resulting change in attitude is not only toward the Corps, it is also a building of confidence in one's self as well.

We found for the Marines, as Snyder had found for the Army, that the bulk of recruits thought that the training could have been tougher and they would still have made it. On this point, we are not at all sure that the best judge of the toughness of recruit training should be a newly graduated recruit. The recruit's judgement may be about as valid as the judgement of the new doctor of philosophy about the rigours of the Ph.D. examinations.

So we may summarize the attitudes, in general, as follows: The Marine Corps, in its recruit training, is able to capture the attention of young men. The exercise, the food, the new things to learn, the group spirit combine to create a feeling of accomplishment. The attitude items reveal that the work is hard, challenging, rewarding. Just about every recruit is in better physical shape as a result of training and is more self-confident as a result of this. And while aware of the demanding nature of Marine Corps discipline, the men at the close of recruit training are completely agreed that the discipline is good for them. And there is general agreement on the necessity for the Corps to make the recruits more or less alike – to discourage, at least in basic training, the differences among men.

Getting along in the immediate military organization is definitely related to several sets of attitudes. I mentioned that a recruit's judgement of the Corps goes up during recruit training. Attitude items related to rise in opinion of the Corps are the recruit's estimate that the recruit training instruction is good, that Marine Corps makes a man of one, that discipline is good for a person, that the men are respected by non-commissioned officers, who are well qualified and know how to get the best out of the men.

Attitude items clustering around the estimate of finding Marine Corps life enjoyable include the realization: that the man learned a good deal, that good work was noticed and commended by officers who were understanding, and that the officers and NCO's respected the men.

Other significant clusters of attitude items associated with generally positive motivations included those relating to good instruction by well-qualified and experienced instructors, those relating to mutual respect within the Corps with the individual Marine regarded as an individual, no one jumped on unfairly, and with reasonable explanations for regulations. This mutual respect, if we regard the item inter-correlations correctly, is based on respect for competence as well as for authority, and also by a belief that officers and NCO's are quite willing to take the same risks and lead the same arduous life that their men lead. Still another set of items associated with positive motivation is that related to the possibility that the Corps does a reasonable job of assigning men to slots for which they have some aptitude and interest. Specific items include: officers understand the needs of their men, NCO's understand the needs of the men, there are no favourites in the Corps, the Corps encourages men of ability, the Marines train well; but also – the Marines eat well!

We were also able to run this set of attitudes of recruits against some handy criteria of effectiveness four years later. Over this period of time, the individual attitude items lose their validity, if they possess any, to predict soldierly effectiveness. A simple norm for a reasonably effective Marine, on paper, is ability enough to finish a four-year enlistment (15 to 18% do not), and to be acceptable enough to warrant re-enlistment. Ability to get promoted is patently related to such a criterion (.507). So is keeping out of trouble – what Berry called, "the administrative nuisance". If a young man can avoid being a nuisance to his organization, he generally will wind up effective, (.309), and being raised in pay (.371), and be marked favourably by his officers (.304). But individual attitude items do not correlate with these criteria. The attitudes toward military service, while stable, can be presently measured with little more significance than shown in World War II by Stouffer and his colleagues.

3. VALUES AND MOTIVATION

Another aspect of the problem of motivation for military service is that relating to inefficiency of performance for psychiatric reasons. It is widely accepted that of all soldiers and sailors who leave the service before their obligated periods of service are completed, at least half leave for psychiatric reasons. Assessment of "medical" disability records certainly suggests that at least 50% of such cases are of men whose problems were psychiatric or who couldn't learn the basic materials for psychiatric reasons – if not just too slow to compete with their peers in the service. While much psychiatric disability may be largely the result of self-interest, no reliable estimate is possible of how much.

Men who are drafted into the armed forces, even highly intelligent ones like physicians or psychologists, are in all likelihood not following an occupation which was first in desirability during their academic lives. Many men would like to escape from a life which involves danger, monotony, unsolicitous supervisors, and the lack of affectionate family contacts. Small ills are, unconsciously no doubt, blown up to psychosomatic disorders in severe cases, and into passive aggressive models of poor performance in lesser cases. A man facing the dangers of combat can work up symptoms which, because of their psychotic or neurotic nature, can obtain him an honourable discharge. Poor motivation is thus a recognized source of cost in military services – and this does not even consider the question of secondary gain – from pensions in countries where pensions are a part of the picture. In recent years, of course, the recognition of these considerations has led to a decline in the use of medical diagnoses, with their honourable connotations, to cover poor motivation, and nowadays very few men in uniform are sent back to civil life without a full opportunity to test their competencies at a variety of military tasks. Still, the largest loss of manpower to the services (in peace time) is discharge for psychiatric cause. When there is added to this the discharge from the service of the antisocial acting out of the impulsive and aggressive serviceman, whose problems may well be complicated by a psychiatric condition, the number is impressive and the cost so large as to stagger the economists who tally costs.

But this is not at all to imply that psychiatric illness is a necessary result of poor motivation nor to imply that illness is feigned. A young man who, because of constitutional weaknesses or unfortunate early life circumstances, enters military life with psychological disabilities may well find that the stresses of military life exacerbate his previously annoying symptoms into crippling symptoms. His desperate attempts to keep up with his fellows physically and psychologically may put too much of a strain on his marginal resources and he may break down. Or another man, adapting well enough to the initial recruit training demands, finds the cumulation of boredom alternating with hazard too much to live with and he acts out against the conformity-demanding life. The first of these should not be counted as poor motivation, in all likelihood, although the second probably should be counted.

Among the problems of military selection there is one of particular interest in our laboratory. There is a small but significant proportion of young men entering the service who look very inadequate – indeed, worse than marginal – during the first few days and weeks, so that training officers frequently despair of keeping them. There is another small but again significant number who look acceptable, even fairly good, who do not really have the inner fortitude to do a good job in military life. Mistakes in identifying such cases can be expensive. At the present time, we lack reliable ways of identifying both of these groups.

Values, like attitudes, can be measured in military organizations by psychological instruments which are psychometrically sophisticated, but far from satisfactory. The newest of the widely accepted scales, Leonard Gordon's *Survey of Interpersonal Values*, has been used by him with certain Army samples and by us with Antarctic volunteers (Gunderson and Nelson). In the Antarctic wintering-over parties the SIV was found to be "sensitive to differences in current social status and generally insensitive to differences in familial and cultural background". Low rank in the organization and in-experience were associated with needs for support and encouragement. Religious devotion was associated with benevolent attitudes toward others. Higher educational level was associated with willingness to exercise leadership. While predictions from such scales of values, as from the older Allport-Vernon-Lindzey scale, are somewhat disappointing, they are of considerable value in measuring changes within a population over time. Gunderson, for example, has shown how changes in Gordon's "benevolence" develop over a year on the ice. And the attitude scales administered during recruit training to the Marines were again used after two years, when a battalion returned from service in Okinawa. The suggestion here is that instruments assessing values and attitudes, while adding little to predictive validity for individual servicemen, may be profitably used for assessment of change during service life.

Research is needed on one more aspect of motivation − one which would go beyond aptitudes, interest in military life, motivation for the particular assigned task, compatibility with the group members, attitude toward service − and that is what is sometimes referred to as national character − the common traits of personality and of character which might be said to be typical of the people of a nation. If we had valid measures of such a construct, we might assess the morale of the individual serviceman or of the functioning unit by comparing it with some theoretical national norm. Aside from the factorial work of Raymond Cattell and the work summarized by Duijker and Frijda, very little has been done by psychologists with this concept, which may of course belong to political science or anthropology. Anthropologists like Margaret Mead have noted how a deep, and perhaps largely unverbalized and informal set of sentiments and values may be powerful in motivation − perhaps more powerful than more easily verbalized values. Whether the modal personality described by Inkeles and Levinson, or some other approach to national character, might be used, is uncertain. Duijker and Frijda caution, however, that a good number of nations may have multimodal − or perhaps less fortunately, bimodal national characters, so that accurate assessment seems presently unlikely.

4. CONCLUSION

The reports from our laboratory certainly corroborate the facts, known to all of you − indeed to which many of you have contributed significantly − that the prediction of effective performance in military life, as in so many other occupational areas − is most reliably made when the predictors emphasize significant items from the life history and good measures of aptitudes in the cognitive area. John Plag, of our group, has published data on the usefulness of measures of intelligence, of level of schooling attained, and of life age in the prediction of acceptable service over a four-year period. And Eric Gunderson and Paul Nelson, have done similar studies on the wintering-over scientists and sailors in the Antarctic.

Our predictive validity coefficients are of the magnitude set by Edwin Ghiselli in his recent *Validity of Occupational Aptitude Tests*. Coefficients of these levels, while allowing selection at better than chance levels, and while very useful indeed for large scale selection programs, leave most of the variance unaccounted for. Improvement, then, *should* be possible, but seems unlikely to come from exquisite refinements of present measures of intelligence, or subtler measures of educational attainment. The improve-ment in identification of who *will* be effective, as distinguished from who *can* be effective, must come in the areas of values held, motivations, attitudes. There is certainly a large and impressive literature of battle that tells us that spirit often makes the difference. And off the battlefield, say in sport, we have all seen teams of somewhat lesser strength or skill overcome the greater ones. When we bet on sports events, of course, we place our wager on the best measures of skill and strength and past performances we can find – and so we study the Daily Racing Form or the batting averages. But we would like to do better in predicting human performance than the Daily Racing Form does with horses (which is hardly better than chance and requires careful study). If we wish to learn whether a pole vaulter will, on this particular day, be able to soar seventeen feet over a bar, we surely will be curious about his health and strength – but his *desire* today will be more likely to be of value to us in our estimates of his performance.

Many psychologists feel uncomfortable with concepts of value, of motivation, of attitudes – generally because any scientist is uneasy with concepts not very amenable to exact measurement. At the present state of our knowledge, values are perhaps too ill-defined or too personal or too complex to allow measurement acceptable to the psychometric theorists. There is however, a new surge of interest in measures of these features of human life – not only among the personologists, like Abraham Maslow and Carl Rogers, who have never been distracted from their attention to the central factors of human behaviour, and the clinicians who must concern themselves daily with the motivations of their clients and patients, but also among the developmental psychologists who are again turning attention to the ways in which values develop in adolescents – including the late adolescents who are the typical recruits in our training centres.

Certainly since the time of G. Stanley Hall we have all known that adolescence is a time of critical importance, precisely because the values learned when we were pre-schoolers became, as it were, fixed – or perhaps for some of us, became unfixed. As Erik Erikson, in his *Childhood and Society*, has formulated it, adolescence is a time of the restructuring of a sense of personal identity. The preschooler gives a naive response to the question, "Who are you?" but the adolescent asks himself, "Who am I?" and makes an answer – hopefully self-consistent and integrative, but not always. The institutions of the social order – the family, the church, and the school – help to set guidelines for the answer the adolescent gives to his own question, as well as to the related questions, "What is the purpose of life?" and "What will I make of my life?"

With the increasing rejection of adult values on the part of adolescents, we have learned to look at the peer culture to see how the adolescents' peers help him to formulate his value system. For the minority of youth who enter the armed forces, a surprisingly effective combination of adult (military) and peer norms brings about, for a noticeable majority of trainees, a dramatic, although not necessarily permanent, reformulation of life goals and values.

In a pluralistic society like that of the United States of America there are conflicts about values and these conflicts affect the morale of young people. The most easily cited conflict is that between the natural striving for independence from adult authority so typical of middle and late adolescence and the teenager's need for and dependence on guidelines set by adult society. The authority of the military is likely to be fairly inflexible, at least as compared with paternal or magisterial authority. I'm sure we've all been amused at the plight of the youth who flees the strictness of home or high school and chooses, say, the Marine Corps as an escape from the restrictions he found so confining!

Conflicts in values provoke anxiety, the clinicians tell us. Clinical psychiatrists and psychologists in recruit training facilities spend their time helping young men resolve the anxieties which have arisen during training – conflicts about self and organization, about goals and life patterns and careers. A potent factor in helping these clinicians to help the young men is the very stability of the organization and a powerful aid in resolution of value conflicts. The Navy is an institution of many years existence and an honourable history. So, too, the Army and the Marines. So, when a young man asks himself, "Who am I?" he can give a partial answer in saying, "I'm a Marine!" The military, with its constant emphasis on such things as honour, efficiency, pride of outfit, the sense of sharing with close companions the adventure and the peril of a manly and hazardous life, can help provide a set of personal values for many a young man somewhat perplexed in his adolescent identity crisis – and this personal set of values, if integrated from those he learned at home, at church, and at school, may be realistic and concrete enough so that they can be applied to everyday problems faced not only as a military person but also as an adult responsible citizen (Rooney).

REFERENCES

Duijker, H.C.J., and Frijda, N.H. (1960), *National character and national stereotypes.* Amsterdam: North Holland Publishing Company.

Ghiselli, Edwin E. (1966), *The validity of occupational aptitude tests.* New York: Wiley.

Gordon, Leonard V. (1960), *Manual for survey of interpersonal values.* Chicago: Science Research Associates.

Gunderson, E.K.E., and Nelson, Paul D. (1966), Life status and inter-personal values. *Educational and Psychological Measurement*, 26(1), 121–130.

Inkeles, Alex and Levinson, D.J. (1954), National character: the study of modal personality and sociocultural systems. In G. Lindzey (Ed.), *Handbook of social psychology II.* Cambridge, Massachusetts: Addison-Wesley.

Nelson, Paul D., and Berry, Newell H.. (1966), Attitudes of Marines during first enlistment. *Navy Medical Neuropsychiatric Research Unit Report 66-21.*

Rooney, John J. (1965), Developing values in adolescents. *National Catholic Guidance Conference Journal*, 9(3), 157–164.

Stouffer, S.A., Suchman, E.A., Devinney, L.C., Star, S.A., and Williams, R.M., Jr. (1949), *The American soldier: Adjustment during Army life I.* Princeton: Princeton University Press.

Cultural Training and Assimilation[1]

HARRY C. TRIANDIS

UNIVERSITY OF ILLINOIS, U.S.A.

I. THE PROBLEM

I would like to discuss the problem of how to prepare a person for a foreign assignment. Perhaps I should begin by establishing that there is a problem.

In 1965 I studied a sample of American business men and military officers stationed
in Greece, and their Greek counterparts. I was surprised by the *very* considerable dissatisfaction of these Americans with their assignment. While living in an almost ideal
climate, in a modern city (with a rich cultural heritage) they were unhappy with their
environment (Triandis, 1967a).

What is the source of this dissatisfaction?

We have examined several hypotheses but I only have time to give you our conclusion.
From an American point of view, there are both undesirable and desirable Greek
characteristics. Those Americans who have stayed in Greece long enough to understand the
culture have learned " to live with " the " undesirable " traits and they have also
developed the ability to see a number of " desirable " Greek traits. But the majority
of the short-stay Americans see mostly the undesirable traits; and that explains their
dissatisfaction.

In sum, the undesirable Greek characteristics are perceived by both the old-timers
and the newcomers but the old-timers *understand* these characteristics and are not
puzzled by them. The old-timers also accept these characteristics and are not rejecting
Greeks and Greece because of the presence of these characteristics. Furthermore, some
good characteristics become salient with the length of exposure and they gradually out-
weigh the undesirable characteristics.

We are thus faced with the following problem: How can we prepare an American going
to Greece, by teaching him about certain aspects of Greek culture, so that he will
understand and accept the Greek traits he considers as undesirable and appreciate the
desirable ones.

First, let us examine how Americans and Greeks perceive each other.

2. HOW DO AMERICANS AND GREEKS PERCEIVE EACH OTHER?

My Greek colleague, Vasso Vassiliou, and I [Triandis and Vassiliou (1966)] studied
the stereotypes of Americans and Greeks. We started the investigation with informal
interviews with Americans working in Greece and with Greeks working with Americans. We
asked these people to characterize co-workers of the other culture. By means of this
approach we obtained one hundred characteristics which were frequently mentioned by
these samples. We reduced this list of characteristics to forty that appeared to be

---
[1] This study was supported by the contract to study Communication, Co-operation and Negotiation
in Culturally Heterogeneous Groups between the University of Illinois and the Advanced
Research Projects Agency and the Office of Naval Research (Contract NR 177-472, Nonr 1834(36);
Fred E. Fiedler, Lawrence M. Stolurow and Harry C. Triandis, Principal Investigators.)
Fred E. Fiedler, David Summers and Pola Triandis made valuable comments on an earlier version
of this manuscript.

relatively independent of each other, and less ambiguous than the remaining sixty. We
then employed a structured instrument [with a semantic differential format], such as is
shown in Figure 1. In this way we were able to obtain the stereotypes of Americans
toward Greeks and of the Greeks toward Americans plus the self-perceptions, or auto-
stereotypes, of the two groups.

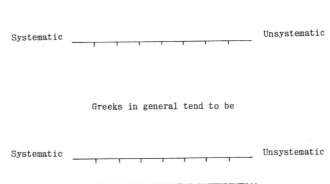

Fig.1 EXAMPLE OF SEMANTIC DIFFERENTIAL
FORMAT USED TO STUDY STEREOTYPES

We (Vassiliou and Triandis, in preparation) examined the responses of eight
hundred Greeks and four hundred Americans. The Greeks were a representative sample of
the population of the two largest cities in that country.

Now that I have outlined our approach, what are some of our specific findings? Using
the instrument of Figure 1 and in very summary form we discovered that Americans saw the
Greeks as *inefficient*, [unsystematic, lazy, inaccurate, uninterested in planning their
work, careless in its execution, oversensitive to criticism], *suspicious*, *emotional*,
[extrapunitive, arrogant] *dogmatic*, [rigid] and *generally difficult to get along with*.
The Greeks saw the Americans as *accurate*, [systematic] and *efficient*, but also *dull*,
naive, *cold* and *arrogant*.

How can we understand these perceptions? In our analysis of subject consistencies in
stereotype responses we have adopted the theoretical views of Don Campbell (1967).
Campbell argues that cultural differences exist and that what is being obtained in
stereotypes are perceived accentuations of the existing differences. In other words,
when Greeks are very high on some characteristic and Americans are very low, the
characteristic will appear in their respective stereotypes. It is the *difference* in the
mean value of a characteristic that determines the probability of its appearance in the
stereotype.

This theoretical view, which is supported by some evidence, suggests that we can
understand Greek national character by using the perceptions of the Americans in Greece
as well as the self-perceptions of the Greeks. We can begin with the stereotypes and
develop hypotheses; then test these hypotheses with other kinds of data.

In other words, let us assume that the stereotypes accurately reflect the mean
differences in the values of the characteristics. Are they consistent with an analysis
of the ecology and history of the two cultural groups? The following analysis will provide an affirmative answer to this question. We will further show that a number of
social psychological analyses of the responses of subjects to various questions are
consistent with our theory of the essential features of Greek national character.

The major thesis of the present paper is that if an American is exposed to such an
analysis of Greek national character, he will be helped in his adjustment to Greece.

This argument, if generalized, would suggest that any culture can be analyzed in the same fashion and the adjustment of any group to any culture can be improved if we follow this approach. Such generalizations require further research. In the present paper we will simply illustrate our approach.

We will begin with an analysis of Greek culture in historical perspective.

3. GREEK CULTURE IN A HISTORICAL PERSPECTIVE

In order to understand a culture one must understand the development of the attitudes, norms, values and behaviour patterns that characterize it. To accomplish this it is useful to examine briefly the geography and history of the particular country.

Attitudes, norms and values develop because they are extremely helpful to individuals, in understanding their world, in defending their self-esteem, and in acting efficiently in the world. Thus, the major determinants of subjective culture may well be found in the ecology and history of a group of people.

Greece is a highly mountainous country, cut up by the sea in ways which create considerable isolation for many segments of its population. As a result, the social environment of the average Greek is limited and he is most powerfully identified with his island, his valley or his small town. Greece is also low on natural resources. The natural infertility of the rocky soil was enhanced by the ancient Greeks who undertook a program of deforestation which has depleted and eroded the surface of a large part of the country. As a matter of fact the ancient Greeks were very proud of their destruction of the forest. Plato boasted that a large area around Athens was " civilized " because it was no longer wooded. As a result, it is hard to raise crops except in two or three fertile plains, such as Thessaly. While the country is scarce in resources it has simultaneously experienced considerable pressures from expanding population. The use of the sea and the emigration of a large number of Greeks, however, has prevented the standard of living from falling.

The major cultural influences of modern Greece have come from Byzantium and the three-hundred-and-fifty-year long Turkish occupation. The Byzantines had several Christian and nationalistic concepts which are still found in modern Greece. At the same time there are unmistakable remnants of Turkish influence in the popular music, the food, and certain social customs of modern Greece. Thus, modern Greece is culturally a part of the Middle East as well as of Europe.

Among the most significant historical events which have probably been influential in moulding the Greek national character we should include the fall of Constantinople in 1453, which placed the Balkans under the domination of the Turkish Empire. The Turks used the intellectual Greeks as their clerks which helped in the preservation of Byzantine values. The resistance against the Turks continued in the mountains. Thus, modern Greek national character was moulded by the ideal of the guerrilla fighter. Another influence came from the fear of abduction of boys by the Turks. This is because the Turks undertook, as early as 1330, a program of recruiting an independent military force by abduction of seven- to eleven-year-old male Christian children and placing them in specially formed schools for soldiers. These were the so-called Janissaries. Between 1330 and 1826, when the Janissaries were disbanded, the threat of Turkish abduction of the male child was real and relevant.[1] This threat probably had a significant impact on Greek child rearing practices, which have in turn determined certain aspects of modern Greek national character.[*] Specifically, it made mothers exceedingly controlling. This control included a good deal of over-protection (Vassiliou, 1967).

---

[1] " Janissaries ", *Encyclopaedia Britannica*, Vol.12, (Chicago, 1957), p.890.

[*] *Editorial Note*: This was sharply questioned by several conferencers but it does not seem appropriate to interrupt Dr. Triandis' whole argument to discuss a single historical or psychological point, particularly in view of the *caveats* he enters at the end of his contribution.

The Greek Revolution began against the Turks in 1821 and lead to a series of wars which continued intermittently for the next one hundred years. During this period the modern Greek state was formed by importing political institutions such as government ministries, parliaments, etc., from Western Europe. Instability in political life has characterized this period. Several revolutions occurred. The Second World War was especially damaging and was followed by several years of conflict with communist supported guerrillas.

From a psychological point of view the significance of these events is that in the last several hundred years the Greeks have had very little control over their personal life. Much of their behaviour has been directed towards meeting crises created by war or revolution. As a result they have developed exceedingly effective procedures for meeting crises, but neglected skills for long term planning. Clearly one cannot plan when one does not know the outcome of next month's events.

This introduction to Greek geography and history will allow us to examine some of the basic features of Greek culture by looking at certain probable determinants of these features. To repeat, we have the characteristics of:

(1) scarce resources and keen competition for them,

(2) the reaction to the domination by an autocratic government, including the manly ideal of a " hero " fighting in the mountains,

(3) fear of loss of boys by abduction with the resultant overprotectiveness of mothers,

(4) the importation of institutions from abroad and

(5) low control over the environment.

4. GREEK NATIONAL CHARACTER

Let us now turn to an examination of some significant features of Greek national character.

4.1. The Ingroup

The factors which were discussed in the previous section have resulted in a definition of the " ingroup " which is somewhat different for Greeks than it is for Western Europeans or Americans. The Greek ingroup may be defined as " my family, relatives, friends and friends of friends ". Within the ingroup the appropriate behaviours are characterized by co-operation, protection, and help. Not only are these associative behaviours appropriate but the concept of the *philotimo*, requires that a person *sacrifice* himself in order to help members of his ingroup. The functional significance of such ties, among members of the ingroup, is clear. It is easier to survive in a highly competitive world as a member of a group of people who co-operate and help each other. In contrast to the ingroup the " outgroup " consists of anyone who is not at least an acquaintance.

Let us consider some examples to clarify the meaning of these distinctions. Americans living in Greece have been frequently surprised by the extreme rudeness of Greeks in public places; for example, in buses. Why would a young man shove a little old lady aside so he can get in first into a bus? It is perhaps that the little old lady belongs to his outgroup and there is no norm that *requires* that he protect, help, or give her his place.

By contrast the principle of the *philotimo* operates within the ingroup. It states that a " good " person must sacrifice himself for the good of the ingroup. This means, for example, that a brother must wait until all his sisters are married and have been given a generous dowry, before he embarks on matrimony. The notion here is that *all* the resources of the family must be applied to the task of providing the dowries, since this is the best way to assure the girls, of the family, of a good life. To take another example, a family may spend its entire month's entertainment budget on one single guest. The explanation here is that the guest becomes a member of the ingroup and members of the ingroup must sacrifice themselves for him. Such behaviour would appear extremely exaggerated in Western Europe and the United States. Why should one do without entertainment money for a whole month just for one guest?

The existence of such clear distinctions between ingroup and outgroup makes Greeks appear extremely suspicious when they first meet a person they do not know. The newcomer has to be classified and until this happens he remains *in limbo*. If he is classified in the outgroup all kinds of competition and unfair play are " par for the course ". If he is classified in the ingroup every kind of help is likely to come his way. For example, when a Greek calls another Greek on the phone the response is likely to be very suspicious and unco-operative, until some kind of a bond is established. The bond may be a mutual friend, or one may mention the same village or island birth place. Once the bond is established it is possible to " do business " but if the bond is not established the relationship remains extremely formal and almost hostile.

Americans also have trouble understanding Greek relationships with authority figures. The reason is that Greeks reject outgroup authority figures. This syndrome is characterized by attempts to undermine authority and consider the self as the only person competent to do an important job.

Greek relationships with authority may be described as follows: the high status Greek is a benevolent dictator in the ingroup and receives submission from his subordinates. [Perhaps as a result of this Greece has an extremely low delinquency rate.] On the other hand in the outgroup the high authority Greek is suspicious, feels that his subordinates are rebellious and acts oppressively towards them. The subordinates on their part avoid him, dislike him, and attempt to undermine him while their behaviour frequently appears subservient. There are exceptions to these points, for example the boss can be seen by his subordinates as a member of their ingroup, if he is unusually warm and helpful. The Greek attitudes towards outgroup authority figures may be understood in the context of our previous discussion about the several hundred years of hostile regimes and the unadapted importation of political institutions from abroad.

5. EMPIRICAL SUPPORT FOR THE ANALYSIS OF GREEK CULTURE

In order to test some of the theoretical notions that have been obtained from our analysis, we have developed a variety of instruments. I will not take the time to describe all of them to you, but I will give you an example of the work we have done with one of our instruments, the role differential, so that you can see how the theoretical analyses which have just been presented can be tested with empirical data (Triandis, Vassiliou and Nassiakou, 1967a).

5.1. Description of the Instruments

Figure 2 presents an example of the behavioural differential. In this example the father is the actor and the son is the person acted upon. The subjects indicate whether it is appropriate in their culture for the father to behave, as indicated under the scale, in relation to his son.[1] We thus obtain judgements of what behaviours are

---

[1] Note that there are three distinct domains that must be sampled in developing this instrument; it is necessary to have (1) a representative sample of the roles employed in a particular culture, (2) a sample of the social behaviours that are likely to occur in that culture and (3) a representative sample of the population of that culture. In our studies with the role differential we have attempted to sample systematically all three of these domains. In order to be able to state that one culture is different from another culture in the way members of these cultures perceive roles it is important to discover culture-common dimensions of role perception for without them it is impossible to compare roles across cultures.

Our strategy has been to elicit behaviours directly, through sentence completion procedures. In each culture a large sample of social behaviours (in one study we had 6,000 in each culture) is subjected to facet analyses, in order to obtain a smaller and maximally heterogeneous sample of behaviours.

Father-Son

Would _____ ı _____ ı _____ ı _____ ı _____ ı _____ Would not

hit

Would not _____ ı _____ ı _____ ı _____ ı _____ ı _____ Would

admire the ideas of

Would _____ ı _____ ı _____ ı _____ ı _____ ı _____ Would not

obey

etc., etc.

Fig. 2   EXAMPLE OF A ROLE DIFFERENTIAL FORMAT

appropriate in each role. The behaviour scales are intercorrelated. The next step is a factor analysis of the scales. By means of this procedure it is possible to obtain factors that are culture-common as well as factors that are culture-specific. The role perceptions of two cultures are then compared only on the culture-common factors. In the particular example of comparisons of Greeks and Americans we discovered four culture-common factors:

(1) *association* (to stand up for, co-operate with, reward) versus *disassociation* (to be enemy of, to grow impatient with, to be indifferent to),

(2) *superordination* (to command, to reprimand, to appoint) versus *subordination* (to ask for advice, to ask for help, to apologize),

(3) *intimacy* (to marry, to kiss, to pet), and

(4) *hostility* (to annoy, to quarrel with, to complain to).

These four factors appear to be the basic culture-common factors of interpersonal relations which describe roles.

Corresponding to this structure of interpersonal relations is the structure of roles. In short, roles:

(1) may be associative or disassociative,

(2) may involve a superordinate person interacting with a subordinate, or a subordinate interacting with a superordinate,

(3) may be intimate or formal, and

(4) may involve conflict and therefore hostility, or no conflict and no hostility.

In this brief presentation I am unable to give you any of the technical details involved in this type of work. However, I wish at this point, to summarize by saying that with the procedures that we have employed so far we have discovered a large number of cultural differences which appear to be interrelated in highly meaningful ways and this allows us to develop some understanding of the way different people in different cultures look at their social environment.

5.2. Summary of Relevant Data

We have tested some of the theoretical notions presented earlier by comparing the responses of Americans and Greeks to our role differentials. If the theoretical notions presented above are valid, then there should be a difference in the way Americans and

Greeks perceive roles in the ingroup and the outgroup (using the Greek definition of an ingroup). Specifically, in roles classified as belonging to the Greek ingroup, i.e., family and friends, there should be more affect and intimacy; in roles classified as belonging to the Greek outgroup there should be less affect and intimacy than in the corresponding American roles.

To test this deduction, we classified roles according to whether they involve a high status person acting toward a low status person or the reverse. In our comparisons of American and Greek role perceptions we discovered an extremely strong pattern which may be summarized as follows: in ingroup roles in which a high status person acts toward a low status person, the Greek roles show higher affect, intimacy, rejection and super-ordination than do the American roles. In other words, the high status ingroup Greek is seen as a benevolent dictator who will reject people who do not follow his instructions and will act with considerable superordination toward his subordinates. In outgroup roles the opposite is true. That is, relative to the American roles of this type the Greek role perceptions show less affect and also less rejection. In other words there is an aloofness in the Greek perception of the high-to-low status roles within the outgroup.

A similar pattern can be seen in the perception of the low-status-to-high-status roles. Such roles within the ingroup are characterized by high affect, intimacy and high subordination. In other words, the low status member willingly and warmly accepts the leadership of the benevolent dictator within the family. But it is quite a different story in the outgroup. There, he shows low affect and general avoidance of the authority figures.

Another way of looking at the ingroup-outgroup relationships is to examine the position of roles in a two-dimensional space defined by the dimensions of *intimacy* and *affect*. You will recall that these were two of the four dimensions that were found to be culture-common in the work that we have completed with role differentials. In Figure 3

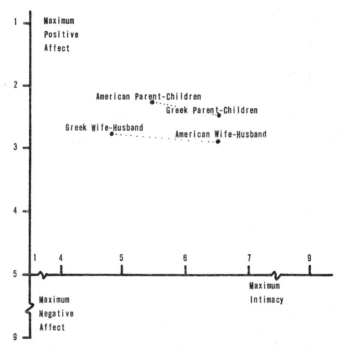

Fig. 3 THE PERCEPTION OF NUCLEAR FAMILY ROLES
BY AMERICANS AND GREEKS

you see the way the nuclear family roles are perceived by Americans and Greeks. You note that Greeks see more intimacy between parents and children than do Americans. On the other hand they see less intimacy between husbands and wives than do Americans. In Figure 4 you see the perceptions of Americans and Greeks, of friends and bosses. Notice here that the Greeks see greater intimacy with friends than do Americans, but less intimacy and some negative affect in the case of bosses.

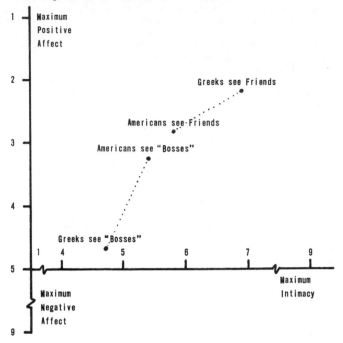

Fig. 4 THE PERCEPTION OF FRIENDS AND " BOSSES "
BY AMERICANS AND GREEKS

The border line of the Greek ingroup, according to our data, is a point between friends and acquaintances on the one hand, and authority figures or competitors on the other. At the same time we note that Americans see less intimacy between themselves and their relatives and friends than do Greeks. Finally, in Figure 5 you can see the position of the role of guest as well as the position of conflict roles on the intimacy and affect dimensions. Note that outgroup roles are seen in Greece as subject to more intimate but also more affectively negative behaviours than is the case for Americans. [1]

I believe that these data regarding role perceptions lend support to the importance of the ingroup-outgroup distinction in Greece.

---

[1] For those who are helped by " translations " of cultural concepts we state that the principle of the *philotimo* plays, in the Greek ingroup, the same role that the principle of *fairness* plays within the Anglo-American ingroup. For example, it is possible to appeal to this principle, when you are talking to a member of your ingroup, and expect " good results ". The principle of the philotimo not only requires fairness, but also sacrifice. Thus, a brother who lost much money can expect a substantial sacrifice from one of his brothers, so that he may be helped from his unfortunate position. Thus, the philotimo implies more than fairness, but it operates within a more limited group.

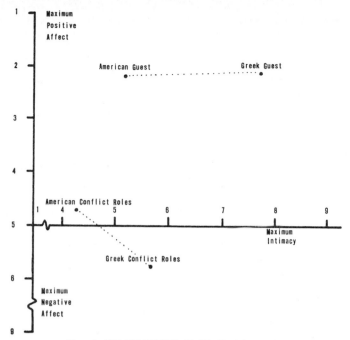

Fig. 5   THE PERCEPTION OF GUESTS AND CONFLICT
ROLES BY AMERICANS AND GREEKS

6. THE EXPLANATION OF OTHER GREEK CHARACTERISTICS

I will now return to the stereotypes of the Americans in Greece. You will recall
that they perceive Greeks as suspicious and difficult to get along with. In view of the
cultural differences in the perception of the ingroup and outgroup roles these judgments
do not appear surprising. Perhaps if an American is trained to understand the Greek
ingroup, the principles of how to become a member of it, and how to employ the Greek
philotimo in order to accomplish his mission in Greece, he will find the Greeks much
easier to get along with.

You will also recall the American characterization of Greeks as oversensitive to
criticism, extrapunitive, arrogant, dogmatic, rigid, and emotionally uncontrolled.

How can we explain such stereotypes? I believe that an analysis of Greek child rearing practices may throw some light. You will recall that I mentioned in my discussion
of Greek history that Greek mothers were found to be exceedingly overprotective. This
point is further documented by Vassiliou (1967). This is particularly true for their
relationships with boys. It is quite likely that the several hundred years of fear of the
abduction of boys, mentioned earlier in this paper, are at the root of this extreme
behaviour. The result of this overprotection is that Greek boys become overdependent on
their mothers.

On the other hand, the social status of Greek mothers is very low, unless their
sons are heroes or overachievers. Thus, they are under pressure to inspire them towards
achievement. As a result while they make their boys overdependent, at the same time they
tell them that they are heroes and that they must excel in a highly competitive world.

This inconsistent pattern of child rearing, which emphasizes overdependence on the
one hand and achievement on the other, leads, I believe, to a low self-esteem with a
facade of high self-esteem (see also, Vassiliou, 1967). Low self-esteem can be seen in
an unusual sensitivity to criticism and in extrapunitiveness. It is very difficult for
most modern Greeks to admit that they are wrong.

The facade of high self-esteem is interpreted by Americans as arrogance, dogmatism and as an attempt to appear omniscient and omnipotent. Americans in Greece have often found their Greek co-workers " exasperating " because of these traits. The conflict between the real self and the facade also leads to emotionalism and an extreme style of expression.

Finally, recall the American stereotypes of inefficiency, inaccuracy, lack of planning, etc. To understand these traits we must remember the low control of the environment which has characterized Greek life during five hundred years. This feature of the environment leads to a syndrome that may be called " poor working habits ". This is characterized by lack of planning, little attention to detail, and careless execution of work. Planning behaviour requires reinforcement. When it is seldom reinforced it does not develop.

It seems understandable that many of these traits are exasperating to an American. He cannot understand why Greeks plan so little, are so unsystematic, so careless in executing their work, so oversensitive to criticism, so extrapunitive, react to authority in such unusual ways, etc. The thesis of the present paper is that if the American sees these traits in their ecological and historical context, he may:

(1) be less disturbed by them and

(2) be more effective in working with Greeks. These last two points are at this stage only hypotheses subject to further research.

To summarize, evidence from both historical analysis and social psychological data converges on an explanation of why Americans feel confused in their relationships with Greeks. It points to a difference in the definition of the ingroup in the two cultures; a difference in the importance of the ingroup; the use of the principle of the *philotimo*, as opposed to the principle of fairness; a different pattern of relationships with authority figures; a peculiar self-esteem having a facade that is very different from its real essence; and a culture which has not been able to practise planning in the way that Western Europe and America have been able to do. The thesis of this paper is that these facts can be taught. An American can learn the concepts and skills to understand Greek culture if he is exposed to the right kind of training.

7. AN APPROACH TO CULTURAL TRAINING

I now wish to turn to a different topic and examine the question of how to train an American to be effective in another culture. The approach that was initiated by our group in Illinois, which includes in addition to Fred E. Fiedler, Larry M. Stolurow and Charles Osgood, was to construct what we call *Culture Assimilators*.

These assimilators consist of a series of episodes in which an American is presented with a problem. The problem may be how to behave correctly or how to interpret the meaning of a particular social behaviour. For example, one might mention what is apt to happen if the American in Greece telephones somebody he does not know. The response is likely to be quite negative and suspicious and to a foreigner even slightly hostile. The American may feel less threatened if he knew that in fact it is the *normal* response that any member of the outgroup will receive and there will be a switch to a completely different response after one becomes a member of the ingroup. This can occur when one has been classified as a guest.

The episode that might be used in a culture assimilator, to illustrate this condition, could simply involve an American telephoning a Greek and receiving a cold response. The trainee is then asked to pick one of several possible interpretations. If he picks the incorrect explanation for the Greek response he is told that he is wrong and is asked to return to the question and pick another interpretation. He continues choosing explanations until he comes across the correct one. He is then praised and given an elaborate explanation of why the interpretation is correct. This is then used as a basis for explaining some of the cultural concepts that we have been discussing such as the notions of the outgroup, the ingroup, Greek suspiciousness until a foreigner is " classified " in the ingroup or outgroup, etc. Our evidence suggests that people who are trained with a culture assimilator become more effective in their inter-personal relations (Chemers, Fiedler, Lekhyananda and Stolurow, 1966).

Nayer, Touzard and Summers (1967) found that culture-assimilation training improves the interpersonal effectiveness of Americans working with Indians, from the point of view of the Indians, but not from the point of view of the Americans. In other words, the Indians saw the culturally trained Americans as more effective than the non-culturally trained; the Americans did not see themselves as more effective when they were trained than when they were not trained.

[There are still a number of questions left, in the development of assimilators. Some of these questions concern the relative emphases that should be given in cultural assimilator training. For example, should one attempt a *general* sensitization to the problem of the appropriate interpersonal behaviours in other cultures or should one be very specific in explaining the particular behaviour patterns that are most effective in different situations? Should one emphasize interpersonal relations and the way members of the other culture behave in different role relationships or should one emphasize the way the members of the other culture " look at the world ", that is their particular way of perceiving the world and their attitudes toward the issues that are going to be central to the negotiations between the visitor and his host? Should we emphasize cultural differences or cultural similarities?]

I would like to complete this presentation by issuing a number of caveats.

(1) I am not claiming that the features of Greek national character which I have described above are unique to Greece. There are obviously such features to be found in other countries of the Middle East or Southern Europe.

(2) The arguments about the way the ecology and history have determined the particular aspects of Greek national character that I have discussed are specu-lative and need a great deal of further research. My defence for using such arguments is, (a) they allow the trainee to make sense out of a rather complex social situation and (b) they are highly plausible in view of what we know about the formation of attitudes.

(3) There is much need for further research in testing the effectiveness of culture assimilation programs.

8. SUMMARY

I believe that what we have accomplished on our current project may be summarized as follows:

(1) We have developed a number of very reliable multi-dimensional and rather subtle procedures for the analysis of the way people in different cultures perceive the world around them. [Triandis (1967b), Triandis, Vassiliou and Nassiakou (1967b), and several reports in preparation.] The present paper presented data from only one of our procedures, the role differential, to illustrate our approach.

(2) Some of these procedures have led to significant theoretical developments (Foa, Triandis and Katz, 1966; Foa and Chemers, 1967; Triandis, Vassiliou and Nassiakou, 1968).

(3) We have also found ways of combining the information into training programs that appear to improve the effectiveness of interpersonal behaviour.

If we proceed with this work there is strong hope that we will be able to both improve our understanding of the determinants of effective interpersonal behaviour and the way to train people to improve their performance in face-to-face relations with members of other cultures.

REFERENCES

Chemers, M.M.; Fiedler, F.E.; Lekhyananda, Duangduen; and Stolurow, L.M., (1966), " Some effects of cultural training on leadership in heterocultural task groups ", *International Journal of Psychology*, 1., pp. 301-314.

Foa, U.G. and Chemers, M.M., (1967), " The significance of role behaviour differentiation for cross-cultural interaction training ", *International Journal of Psychology*, 2., pp. 45-57.

Foa, U.G.; Triandis, H.C. and Katz, Evelyn W., (1966), " Cross-cultural invariance in the differentiation and organization of family roles ", *Journal of Personality and Social Psychology*, 4., pp. 316-327.

Naiar, E.S.K.; Touzard, H. and Summers, D., (1967), " Tasks and mediator orientation in heterocultural negotiation ", Urbana, Illinois: *Group Effectiveness Research Lab, University of Illinois, Technical Report* No.54.

Triandis, H.C., (1967a), " Interpersonal relations in international organizations ", *Organizational Behaviour and Human Performance*, 1., pp. 26-55.

Triandis, H.C., (1967b), " Towards an analysis of the components of interpersonal attitudes ", in Carolyn W. Sherif and Muzafer Sherif (Eds.) *Attitude, Ego-Involvement and Change*, Wiley, New York, pp. 227-270.

Triandis, H.C. and Vassiliou, Vasso, (1966), " Frequency of contact and stereotyping ", Urbana, Illinois: Group Effectiveness Research Lab, University of Illinois, Technical Report No.43. (In print as journal article in the *Journal of Personality and Social Psychology*.)

Triandis, H.C.; Vassiliou, Vasso; and Nassiakou, Maria, (1967a), " Some studies of subjective culture ", Urbana, Illinois: *Group Effectiveness Research Lab, University of Illinois, Technical Report* No.45. (In print in a monograph of the *Journal of Personality and Social Psychology*.)

Triandis, H.C.; Vassiliou, Vasso; and Nassiakou, Maria, (1967b), " Some cultural differences in the perception of social behaviour ", Urbana, Illinois: *Group Effectiveness Research Lab, University of Illinois, Technical Report* No.49. (In print in a monograph of the *Journal of Personality and Social Psychology*.)

Triandis, H.C.; Vassiliou, Vasso; and Nassiakou, Maria, (1968), " Three studies of subjective culture ", *Journal of Personality and Social Psychology* (Monograph) in press.

Vassiliou, Vasso, (April, 1966), " Personal Communication ".

Vassiliou, G., (1967)," Aspects of parent-adolescent transaction in the Greek family ". In G. Kaplan and S. Lebovici (Eds.) *The adolescent in a changing world*. N.Y. Basic Books.

Discussion

U.J. BOUVIER

Les divers essais de collaboration entre peuples de cultures différentes, dont nous avons été témoins ces derniers temps, se sont assez souvent soldés par des échecs. Ceux qui viennent pour aider, le plus souvent tentent de transformer la culture de l'autre: ils arrivent avec une âme de missionnaire et sont animés de prosélytisme. On peut croire que leur comportement est basé sur une adhésion candide à leur propre culture, et une non acceptation de celle de l'autre.

Lorsqu'un effort est fait vers l'autre, il s'agit généralement au premier stade d'un essai de tolérance. Sachant que sa propre culture est la meilleure, sinon la seule bonne, on essaie de tolérer les manifestations de l'autre culture. Par exemple, la bonne façon de manger c'est évidemment de tenir la fourchette dans la main gauche et le couteau dans la main droite. Mais grâce à un sérieux effort, nous parvenons à ne pas montrer dans quelle piètre estime nous tenons ceux qui coupent d'abord leur viande, puis prennent la fourchette dans la main droite et mettent la main gauche sur la cuisse.

Si l'effort est plus grand, on peut aller jusqu'à essayer de comprendre les autres. Peut-être l'assimilateur de culture de l'équipe d'Illinois aurait-il pu, après un entraînement judicieux, éviter quelques erreurs à des gens de bonne volonté, dans des occasions qu'il n'est pas nécessaire que je rappelle.

Peut-être y a-t-il aussi des sujets mieux disposés encore et qui peuvent arriver à un troisième stade, celui d'estimer une autre culture, d'apprécier ce qu'elle recèle de grandeur et de noblesse? Par exemple, peut-on se proposer, après entraînement, d'amener un occidental à estimer une culture orientale ou africaine, en dépit des tabous et du manque d'efficacité? Lorsque TRIANDIS nous définit les concepts de ingroup et de outgroup et qu'il nous en montre les implications, n'est-on pas forcé, non seulement de comprendre les comportements en rapport avec ces concepts, mais encore restera-t-on indifférent à la grandeur, à la noblesse de certaines de ces conduites. Le dévouement, l'esprit de sacrifice qu'implique le " philotimo " ne sont-ils pas de nature à susciter l'admiration, même de ceux que leur culture a accoutumé d'agir avec probité (" fairness ") seulement? Il ne fait pas de doute que la méthode de TRIANDIS peut conduire non seulement à plus de compréhension, mais aussi à de l'estime, sinon à de l'admiration.

Mais je crois savoir que l'équipe d'Illinois n'a pas d'ambition philanthropique et ne se donne pas pour but d'améliorer le niveau moral ni des uns ni des autres. Je pense que leur objectif, moins ambitieux sur le plan de l'éthique, est axé essentiellement sur l'efficacité. Ils s'intéressent au fonctionnement des groupes, mais dans la mesure seulement où le rendement à la tâche peut être amélioré. La préoccupation de FIEDLER n'est pas d'améliorer les relations entre le chef et les membres du groupe, ni d'aider au développement d'attitudes favorables à l'organisation, mais seulement de rendre des organisations plus efficaces, en ce sens que les tâches soient mieux faites ou plus rapidement. De même, je crois que TRIANDIS borne ses ambitions à essayer d'augmenter le rendement de quelqu'un qui doit travailler avec des personnes d'une autre culture que la sienne. Pour cela, il s'agit de détecter les éléments susceptibles de provoquer des heurts ou d'être des freins. Les hypothèses élaborées à la suite de cette recherche peuvent servir à entraîner le personnel. La dernière phase est un test d'efficacité et cela en voyant seulement si l'entraînement a réussi à augmenter le rendement.

Faut-il louer l'équipe d'Illinois d'avoir ainsi défini ses objectifs? D'aucuns regretteront peut-être qu'ils soient trop limités? Par contre, cela présente le très grand avantage de fournir des critères objectifs indiscutables. Telles que les recherches apparaissent en tout cas, leur importance saute aux yeux du point de vue militaire.

Pour ne dire qu'un mot des recherches du professeur FIEDLER,* je désire signaler qu'elles nous ont paru tellement importantes pour les Forces armées que, stimulés par son exemple, nous avons entrepris une expérience sur la formation au commandement de petits groupes et sur le transfert de cette formation. Je signale en passant que, d'après nos expériences, les résultats seraient positifs, tant pour la formation directe que pour le transfert.

Quant aux recherches du professeur TRIANDIS, leur valeur ne peut apparaître mieux qu'au sein de cette assemblée. Je crois que dans l'esprit de ses fondateurs, l'OTAN devait être une organisation de collaboration entre peuples dont les cultures n'étaient pas toutes semblables. Les différences de cultures ne semblent pas être un handicap trop lourd pour ce qui concerne les scientifiques, mais je n'oserais pas affirmer qu'il en fût de même pour tous. En tout cas, le fonctionnement des états-majors interalliés comme la conduite d'unités mixtes, risquent de poser de sérieux problèmes d'affrontement de cultures. On peut s'étonner que l'OTAN n'ait pas favorisé, plus qu'elle ne l'a fait, les recherches sur le plan interculturel. L'OTAN n'est pas une organisation a but philanthropique, mais ne devrait-elle pas être soucieuse du rendement, dans le sens, semble-t-il, où l'entend l'équipe d'Illinois?

Avant d'examiner un autre aspect de ces recherches, je voudrais exprimer un regret. Dans les études de TRIANDIS, la référence est la culture américaine. Comme il serait désirable que des grecs, des hindous, des africains, se fondant sur l'écologie et l'histoire des USA, de l'Europe, de la Belgique par exemple, élaborent et testent des hypothèses sur les cultures américaine, ou belge ... Comme il serait instructif de se voir dans différents miroirs!

Le professeur TRIANDIS n'a malheureusement pas disposé du temps suffisant pour nous exposer complètement les techniques qu'il a utilisées. Il nous a parlé de celle qu'il appelle " sémantique différentielle " qui est une échelle telle que celles élaborées par Osgood ou utilisées par FIEDLER. On aurait aimé avoir quelques précisions sur leur emploi. Il ne paraît pas qu'il s'agisse d'échelles métriques, or il semble qu'on ait calculé des intercorrélations entre échelles. Cela soulève quelques problèmes.

L'autre point que je voulais soulever est un bon exemple de différence de cultures qui amène des incompréhensions. Il y a une culture des adeptes de l'analyse factorielle et une culture des opposants. A notre époque, les adeptes paraissent de loin les plus nombreux et comptent dans leurs rangs des hommes très distingués et très éminents. J'appartiens à la culture des opposants. Ceux qui appartiennent à la culture des adeptes semblent croire, ou presque, qu'une découverte ne peut être faite que grâce à l'analyse factorielle. Je me berce de l'illusion d'avoir démontré que les éléments qu'on pourrait mettre en évidence, par une analyse dans une population, auraient des relations dépendant de la structure de la population, et seraient donc contingents, c'est-à-dire variables d'une population à une autre. Cela me paraît un très lourd handicap mettant en question les résultats de toute analyse. Mais les écrits des tenants d'une culture n'influencent guère ceux de l'autre culture. L'ingroup et l'outgroup sont nettement définis et les cloisons sont étanches. La suspicion à l'égard de ceux de l'outgroup est très grande.

Ce que je voudrais dire, c'est ceci. Le professeur TRIANDIS a découvert que certains types de comportements pouvaient être distingués en groupes parents, caractérisés par: l'association, la subordination, l'intimité, l'hostilité ou leurs pôles opposés, et qui correspondraient à la structure des rôles. Les comportements exemplatifs qu'il donne pour illustrer chacun de ces groupes permettent de voir assez clairement le contenu de chacun d'eux. Ces exemples permettent aussi de voir, comment, par simple examen des diagrammes des réponses, il serait possible de constituer ces groupes.

Autrement dit, les facteurs en question auraient très probablement pu être trouvés tout aussi bien sans analyse factorielle, et cela doit les mettre à l'abri des critiques

---

* See Section VI, Leadership, below. *Ed.*

que l'on pourrait diriger contre celle-ci. Que l'on croie ou que l'on ne croie pas aux méthodes d'analyse factorielle, cela ne peut affecter la valeur des résultats de TRIANDIS, puisque ceux-ci ont pu ou pourraient être trouvés autrement.

Peut-être, jusque maintenant, n'ai-je pas dit très explicitement combien j'apprécie les beaux travaux de l'équipe d'Illinois? Pour finir, permettez-moi d'être votre interprète pour remercier ces chercheurs de leur effort et de leur apport.

Marginal Manpower:
Introductory Remarks

SAMUEL H. KING

Three of my colleagues and I from the United States will present accounts —
admittedly rather sketchy — of efforts of the U.S. military services to understand the
problems associated with the use of men classed as marginal and to find ways in which
these men can be trained and used to advantage in the Armed Forces.

The first paper, which will be broad and thin rather than intensive, will cover
historical aspects of the problem, stopping short of contemporary activities. Commander
Newell Berry, Scientific Liaison Officer in the Office of Naval Research, London, will
then deal with selection as it affects marginal manpower, emphasizing studies that are
ongoing or recently completed. In the third paper, Drs. John Taylor & Wayne Fox of the
Human Resources Research Office of The George Washington University, will compare the
results of training below average people with the results of training men with average
and high aptitude. Our last speaker, Mr. Sidney Friedman, who is in the Office of the
Under Secretary of the Navy, will report on additional efforts to improve and measure
the utilization of marginal manpower.

Research on Marginal Manpower: Historical Perspective

SAMUEL H. KING

EMMA E. BROWN

OFFICE, CHIEF OF RESEARCH AND DEVELOPMENT,
DEPARTMENT OF THE ARMY (U.S.A.)

I. INTRODUCTION

A military commander naturally wants the best help he can get in his organization. By definition, the "best" can perform better than others. They can train and lead others. Their efforts can often compensate for the inadequate performance of the less able. An organization of high caliber personnel can presumably accomplish its mission more successfully. The logical objective of selection under normal conditions, then, is to pick those who can be expected, beyond a reasonable doubt, to perform well.

When an organization is forced to expand rapidly, however, the conditions a commander faces when he doubles or triples his work force are not mere extensions of normal conditions. His organization is completely altered in nature. He must devise – or improvise – a new system of sorting individuals and placing them in different jobs. The jobs themselves may have to be redefined, broken up into smaller segments, perhaps, or the duties made more homogeneous. Training, administration, supervision, discipline must be drastically adjusted. Add to these adjustments the fact that the commander may not know what he can expect of the incoming personnel, and that the organization has had no experience in dealing with personnel of such a wide range of competence.

Among the influx of workers there will be some termed marginal. How much of the difficulties of the expanded organization stem from the rapid buildup and how much from acceptance of the underqualified he does not know and perhaps he cannot establish.

2. MARGINAL MANPOWER IN WORLD WAR I

This is the problem that faced military management at the beginning of World War I and, I must add regretfully, at the beginning of World War II. The following observations are taken from a report on the Personnel System of the United States Army written in 1919. [1]

"The American Army was a small one and accepted only physically fit men who could read and write. When war broke out, the part our country would play before a settlement could be reached was underestimated".

With a seemingly unlimited supply of men eligible for service, manpower planners apparently saw no reason to change the high standards for military service that had been in effect. Soon, however, the selective draft fell short of producing the required numbers. Training and assignment programs had to be shifted continually, even while operations were under way. The most logical way to induct more men was, of course, to reduce the standards for acceptance. This was done. Again I quote: "Through all this, however, was an undercurrent and growing feeling that we were not utilizing manpower to the best advantage, and that sooner or later our seemingly unlimited supply of men would give out and we must begin to adopt the French and English experience of conserving our manpower in every way. Even if our supply had been truly unlimited, growing industrial needs at home, and the extravagant plan of retaining tens of thousands of strapping perfectly fit men in noncombat positions in this country or behind the lines overseas became more and more apparent".

With the first draft call for "limited service" men in June 1918, men deemed unsuitable for immediate military service began to arrive at the training camps. The Army was now getting men it did not know how to use – and in large numbers. To salvage men who were substandard, be it for mental, physical, or moral reasons or for language deficiency, the Army formed Development Battalions. The stated purpose of these battalions was to fit men for general – as opposed to limited – service, thus augmenting the manpower supply. Only those whose defects were judged remediable were assigned to the battalions. In the six months of their operation (from May to November, 1918), some 230,000 men were in the Development Battalions for varying lengths of time. At the end of their stay, about 50 per cent were adjudged able to be of some utility to the Army, either as combat soldiers or in limited service jobs. These men were transferred to operational units. Whether they fulfilled the promise, we have no way of knowing. Evaluation of the remedial programs was not in terms of later performance. Hence, no guidelines resulted from World War I – only an unheeded warning that our nation should be better prepared to use men of all degrees of capability in any future emergency.

3. MOBILIZATION - WORLD WAR II

World War II was a mammoth replay of World War I. Again, the Armed Forces started out by raising the standards. These standards then had to be progressively lowered as demand increased and draft eligibles meeting the standards dwindled in number. Again, problems associated with those men considered marginal were not adequately prepared for. True, we find in documents early recognition that in a period of mobilization the services would have to make use of illiterates, non-English-speaking enlisted men, men with physical limitations, men who would be difficult to train, aliens, conscientious objectors.

At the inception of the draft late in 1940, the literacy qualification was the same as that governing acceptance prior to the emergency – the ability to understand "simple orders in the English language". In May 1941, the requirement was changed to the capacity to read and write the English language at fourth grade level. In August 1942, the standard was lowered to admit men who did not meet the literacy standard provided they had the intelligence to absorb military training rapidly. Standards were changed again and again. Between 1940 and 1945, there were 25 changes in military policy on the induction of men who were in some way marginal.

Under the higher standards, and while the manpower resources of the country were still at high level, many well qualified men – some overqualified – had been placed in technical and administrative units. By the time overseas combat needs became acute in 1943 and 1944, these men had come to represent a decided investment in needed skilled manpower. In the case of the Army, they were the object of a tug-of-war between the technical services who needed their competence, and the Army Field Forces who were unwilling to accept lowered qualifications for their fighting men. The dilemma faced by manpower planners was whether to take the high calibre, well qualified men from technical and administrative jobs for which they had been trained and transfer them to combat jobs, or to put men inducted under lowered standards in combat jobs. The outcome was that large numbers of the highly trained specialists were transferred to the combat arms. In effect, the expensive training they had received was wasted and it was necessary to train an influx of lesser qualified troops to fill their jobs. How competently the jobs were filled we do not know.

Consider the situation not only in terms of cost, but in terms of effect on individuals who saw their skills unused, on units whose pride in their competence deteriorated, on commanders who felt their mission threatened, and lastly on the men of marginal ability whose worth was deprecated by the attitude of commanders and fellow servicemen and who perhaps found themselves unable to do what was expected of them.

4. SPECIAL TRAINING UNITS OF WORLD WAR II

When minimum literacy was abandoned as an induction standard, the Army, as well as the other services, accepted the necessity of providing literacy training to fit the marginal serviceman to take his place in the military environment.

For guidelines to this training, the Army went back to the period between wars. Thousands of young men in the Civilian Conservation Corps had been given Army-like training, administered by the Army, between 1933 and 1943. Objectives were non-military. The aim was to provide employment for young men during the depression, to use their services in conservation programs which might otherwise not have been undertaken, and most important, to equip the trainees to find jobs after they left the camps. In running these camps, the Army had gained experience in training, even rehabilitating, young men who were substandard in one or more respects. Training methods and instructional materials developed in the Civilian Conservation Corps — sometimes, admittedly, through trial and error — became the point of departure for the creation of plans and materials for the Special Training Units established for marginal personnel during World War II.

These Special Training Units were designed to bring the illiterate to fourth-grade level in reading, writing, and arithmetic and to give him training in military practices so that he could take his place acceptably in a regular unit. The intention was that the graduate of these Units arrive as part of the regular replacement flow and not as a marked individual. This consideration was important. As the public school student in a class of slow learners, whether it be designated as ungraded class, fourth track, or by some other euphemism, knows why he is in that class — and knows that others know also — so the marginal serviceman singled out for special attention finds himself handicapped by that very attention. Trainers, cadre, job supervisors may tend to evaluate a man low in performance if they know, and few do not know, that he has been classed as marginal. They are likely, consciously or unconsciously, to look more closely for inept behaviour in a man who bears the label "marginal" than in men not so stigmatized. There may also be a tendency to interpret as inept, behaviour which in a non-marginal would not be so characterized.

One example: During World War II, examinees were grouped in five categories, based on scores on the general mental test given at induction. Field commanders complained that they were getting too many men in the lowest mental category. The Department of the Army then arbitrarily decreed that the top half of the lowest category would henceforth be included in the next higher category. Complaints from commanders practically ceased, although they were getting exactly the same proportion of low quality men as before.

The Special Training Unit program came to an end in 1945. From the standpoint both of the research scientist and of the manpower planner, the most telling shortcoming of the program was failure to follow up a significant number of graduates in their later assignments. There was an elaborate end-of-course achievement testing program, but whether successful completion of the course bore any relation to success as a soldier, again we must confess that we do not know.

5. MARGINAL MANPOWER STUDIES — POST WORLD WAR II

In the reduced military forces following the war, there was no place for any but those fully meeting standards of trainability for entry into service. Indeed, selection and classification devices became more elaborate with the introduction of differential aptitude batteries in all the services. Hostilities in Korea again called attention to the fact that our human resources are not inexhaustible and led to sporadic and for the most part abortive attempts to explore courses of action. During 1950 and 1951, partial mobilization appeared to offer an opportunity to study the effects of retention by the services of men who could not be trained to a minimum level of literacy in a reasonable length of time. Was there room in the services for men who could not read or write but who could acquire certain low level skills? An all-service committee worked out a plan for research, but the research was never undertaken.

During 1953 and 1954, the Army established its own working group to study problems associated with the physical, mental, and moral marginal. The purpose was to develop a plan of action with particular emphasis on mobilization. The members of the group succeeded in indicating voids in knowledge needed for planning and pointed up inadequacies in policy, but developed no plan.

Early in 1953, the then Assistant Secretary of the Army directed that an experimental study be conducted on marginal manpower. This study was to be by far the most comprehensive research effort undertaken in this area. The basic question as stated by the Assistant Secretary was: "Will we or will we not utilize all manpower in the event of a future emergency?" Background research was concentrated and thorough. New approaches were sought which would produce empirical data to help answer the question: What kinds of men, among those classified as marginal, with what kinds of training, can do what in the Army, how well, and at what net gain or loss to the Army? The plans as blocked out into defined areas were designed to avoid the pitfalls of previous research on the utility of the borderline serviceman. I am sorry to report that the program was closed out in January 1957, a few weeks prior to the date set for the planned induction into the Army of 1500 men who were to constitute the experimental marginal group.

In the summer of 1953 also appeared the first volume of a series of four[2] reporting on a comprehensive study of the men we have called marginal and the use of this resource during World War II. The studies were conducted as the Conservation of Human Resources Project established in the Graduate School of Business of Columbia University in 1949. The four volumes delineated the magnitude of the problem faced in World War II: almost two million men examined during the war were found to be illiterate or very slow learners who could barely read or write; an estimated one million men were rejected because they were considered mentally disturbed; almost three-quarters of a million men already in service were discharged for ineptness or personality disorders. In sum, of the more than 18 million men examined for military service during World War II, over five million were rejected by the Armed Services.

The rejection rate was not the only reason given for thorough examination of World War II manpower policies. According to statistics compiled under the project, the policy governing separation from the services in September 1943 resulted in the Army's requiring the induction of 100 men to obtain a net increase of five enlisted men. Men were being accepted who did not meet general duty standards at the same time men were being released for like disabilities. This fact and other analyses led the authors to conclude that ... "the sudden and spectacular changes in the numbers declared to be ineffective could only reflect changes in organizational policy and procedures". Another way of conveying the same concept is to ask: Is being marginal a characteristic of the individual or is it determined by the organization?

The Conservation of Human Resources studies brought into relief the sociological implications of military policy with respect to the marginal population of the nation. The authors reached the following conclusions:

(1) The military services relied too heavily on formal education and mental aptitude test scores as a screen.

(2) Special training and assignment for marginal men had not been thoroughly enough explored.

(3) The personnel and medical systems and policies were not well integrated.

(4) "Live" experimentation should be conducted to evaluate the performance of illiterate or poorly educated men after training.

(5) Manpower planning prior to World War II had not examined the true nature of the nation's human resources or related such findings as were available to projected requirements.

6. STUDIES IN TRAINING THE ILLITERATE OR MENTALLY MARGINAL

Several research projects designed to evaluate the effects of special training on men defined as mentally marginal were conducted during and immediately following the Korean conflict. The most carefully designed and controlled of these were the Fort Leonard Wood project conducted by the Army and "Project 1000" conducted by the Air Force.

The Leonard Wood research was conducted to determine whether special training given to marginal men was effective in increasing their military usefulness. Earlier studies had not fulfilled the purpose, since none had yielded a clear estimate of the effects of special training in terms of an unambiguous comparison between the performance of men who had been given special instruction and similar men who had not. Groups of marginally literate men were given three weeks of either special literacy training (reading, writing, and arithmetic), or special pre-basic military training, or a combination of the two. The groups given the various types of training were then sent through regular basic training. At the end of eight weeks of basic training, no differences of practical significance were found between men who had received special training and those who had not, on either written tests or basic training performance. Nor were any differences found between the groups in measures of attitudes and adjustment to the Army.

Findings of Project 1000 confirmed the findings of the Leonard Wood study. Special training in Project 1000 was of longer duration and the follow-up and assessment of the men was more elaborate and comprehensive. For an experimental group, the Air Force provided six weeks of special training in addition to six weeks of regular basic training. The special training consisted primarily of additional basic training but included 45 hours each of training in language arts and arithmetic. A matched group of airmen was given only the six weeks of regular basic training. When the two groups were compared, the special training was found to have had no effect either at the end of basic training or after eight months of service.

7. CHANGING SELECTION POLICIES

It was also during the 1950's that attention focused on achieving greater flexibility in the utilization of the differential aptitudes represented in the service populations.

When the number of servicemen was being reduced in 1957–58, all Army enlisted men were declared eligible for discharge who were not above a specified level on at least three special aptitudes. From 1958 until late 1965, the Army required that inductees who scored low on a measure of general ability be above a specified level on at least two special aptitudes. Since late 1965, there has been a successive lowering of mental standards for entry.

8. CONCLUSION

The resumé I have given evidences a growing concern about marginally able men and successive, if disparate, efforts to find satisfactory ways of defining their role in the Armed Forces. I wish I could say the efforts had been productive. The reality is that we are even now very little ahead of where we were at the beginning of World War II. We still do not know how useful the man called marginal can be to the services, nor the best way to make use of the contributions of which he is capable. We do not even know whether, or to what extent, a man has to be able to read and write in order to function in some military jobs.

How do we determine whether, or at what point, the absorption of men of low capabilities impairs the effectiveness of the Armed Forces? Mathematical models have been developed to estimate, within narrow limits, the effects of manpower policy changes on the nation's defence establishment, but when we come to the utilization of men who are on the borderline of acceptability, crucial information is lacking. The programs I have touched upon have been piecemeal attempts to obtain partial answers to partial questions. The responsibility has not always been that of the seeker of information. Administrative and cost considerations have loomed large, and there was no hard evidence that the contribution of marginal manpower would justify the added expense.

That the problem has a long history should not cause us to lose sight of its ever-changing nature. Environmental and cultural changes alter the position of the marginal. To what extent is technology reducing or increasing the number of jobs he can learn to perform? To what extent should the problem be viewed in the context of the nation as a whole as opposed to a problem only for the Armed Forces?

A major effort has now been set in motion to improve and to measure the effectiveness of marginal manpower programs in the Armed Forces. This work has strong Department of Defense support. Different aspects of the objectives and plans and activities of this most recent program will be mentioned in following contributions.

REFERENCES

1. Committee on Classification of Personnel in the Army. *The Personnel System of the United States Army: Volume I, History of the Personnel System*. Washington, D.C., 1919.
2. Graduate School of Business of Columbia University, Conservation of Human Resources Project. *Progress Report, Summer 1953*. The four volumes, all published by the Columbia University Press. New York, New York were:
   Ginzberg, Eli, and Douglas W. Bray. *The Uneducated*. 1953.
   Ginzberg, Eli, *Breakdown and Recovery*. 1959.
   Ginzberg, Eli, *Patterns of Performance*. 1959.
   Ginzberg, Eli, *The Lost Divisions*. 1959.

Contemporary Studies in Military Selection

COMMANDER N.H. BERRY, U.S.N.

U.S. OFFICE OF NAVAL RESEARCH,

LONDON.

The aims and problems of contemporary military selection are the same as those faced by Joshua before Jericho: Finding the proper number of men with the appropriate aptitudes, motivation, and training who will do well in battle. In the United States as late as the Spanish-American War it was not uncommon for civilians who wanted to be commanders to raise, equip and train their own forces. When they were satisfied that their men were ready for combat, they were presented to the regular armed forces for use. Since that time, society and the art of war have become so sophisticated that the recruitment and basic training of military personnel has become a staff function which seeks to provide the commander in the field with the calibre of personnel required to carry out assigned missions.

As is typical of staff functions, these have tended to become more and more specialized. So much so, that the term "military selection" connotes a vast array of target populations: Who shall initially enter the armed forces; after they are accepted, who shall be retained; which ones shall be given specialized training for specific jobs in specific weapons systems; who should be promoted; among a pool of volunteers for hazardous duty, which ones shall be accepted; and even a decision to return to duty members from the sick list with certain classes of illness is a selection problem, although one that perhaps too frequently is surrendered solely to medical judgement.

It is of course obvious that personnel selection systems must adjust to changes in the available manpower pool. That adjustment is essentially in the risks the system is prepared to take. In time of general mobilization for a full-scale war, the system can afford high risks on initial output into the armed forces because of the pressure of time and because the economic costs of false acceptance are lost in the gigantic sums involved in total war. During times of economic distress, such as the depression in the 1930's, a selection system can demand a very low risk in initial acceptance simply because there are many, many applicants for each opening in the military. This is fortunate inasmuch as the cost of false acceptance in this context is much more obvious and relatively greater in the military budget than in time of war. Thus, an important requirement in military selection systems should be a constant feedback to it from the consumer (the field commander) as to changing requirements, and a constant monitoring of the characteristics of incoming personnel to detect significant changes which might alter the predictions made by the selection system.

As an example of the latter aspect, it is well known that completion of high school before enlistment or induction is the single most powerful predictor of success in the armed forces of the United States. Naturally, if the percentage of enlistees or inductees completing high school should suddenly rise to 70% or 80% (it usually hovers around 50%), that variable would lose much of its predictive power. If it rose to 100%, my statistician friends tell me that it would drop out of the predictive formula altogether.

A second measure in the evaluation of military selection research is: What is the criterion to which the system is seeking to predict? I mentioned earlier a tendency to compartmentalize selection research into entry problems, classification and training problems, and special duty problems. There seems to be a risk here that the recruiter's success is measured by how many of the applicants he sends to the Armed Forces Examining Stations are enlisted; or, of evaluating those involved in basic training, by how many recruits take part in a graduation review; or, that systems sending certain men to special schools will be judged on how many of them complete the school. I am of course referring to using intermediate criteria only.

While it is true that the first and most important criterion in selection research is survival in a system, sheer avoidance of premature separation is not enough. There are many men who manage to complete their employment contract in the military, but only by the skin of their teeth and the fact that there is no one with which to replace their warm bodies in the table of organization. Research in military selection should then always include a more long-range criterion than sheer survival. This turns out to be much easier to establish for enlisted personnel than for officers. Enlisted members engage for a definite period of service, which they complete or not. If they complete it, did the line recommend them for re-enlistment? There are many other subsidiary criteria with which to distinguish between the "good, better, and best" of the effective enlisted man. This is of course using a "company criterion", that is, the line commanders (management) are the final judges of the quality of the product of the selection system.

To illuminate this point, Dr. John A. Plag of the Navy Medical Neuropsychiatric Research Unit, San Diego, California, followed a cohort of 11,000 sailors for a full enlistment period. Under procedures applying at the time that he collected his sample (1960), of those arriving at a Navy training centre, 8% did not complete recruit training; within two years an additional 8% were prematurely separated; and for the four-year enlistment period, 25% were judged to be overall ineffective (did not complete the enlistment or were not recommended for re-enlistment). Using essentially the same criterion for selection success in the Army and Air Force, the same four-year 75% – 25% rate was found. For the Marine Corps, the success rate is roughly 80% – 20%. Using the same criterion, Plag then determined the success rate of sailors assigned to various Class A schools upon graduation from recruit training. He found those rates ranging from 94% for those entering Electronics school to 80% of those assigned to a hospital corps school. (Approximately 50% of his sample graduating from recruit training were sent to a class A school.) LCDR Nelson and I, in following a cohort of approximately 13,400 Marines for a full enlistment period, found that of those Marines assigned to Infantry or Mechanical MOS Groups, 81% were effective; while of those assigned to Clerical or Electronic-Electrical MOS Groups, 91% were effective.

My point is that if the selection process is evaluated at the recruiting level for the Navy, which of the various criteria should be applied? Graduation from recruit training (92% successful); at the two-year level (84% successful); or, effectiveness for the first enlistment (75% successful); or, is production of effective Electronics technicians or Hospital Corpsmen the important standard (94% and 80% success rates respectively)?

Many of us here will recall Raines Wallace's question regarding the criterion question: Criterion for what? It is entirely possible that too many times selection research in the military is compromised by the pressure of time or demands from higher levels for information as of yesterday. In the tradition of obedience in the military services, perhaps we sacrifice sound sampling procedures, adequate criterion definition, or sloppy measurement of a good criterion to prove how useful we are. It might be better when asked for *immediate* results if we emulated the oracle at Delphi: Sat on our chairs over the smoke of pressure and chewed exotic leaves before giving expedient answers. Granting the assumption I have made that selection research in the military is a staff function, then it would follow that the first responsibility of a staff is to give sound advice. If, in the opinion of the research staff, the terms of the question asked is not researchable, or render it impossible to do a good piece of research to throw light on the problem, then we should say so. Executive levels in the military establishment must be educated to the fact that personnel research takes time (necessary to collect meaningful and relevant criterion data), and that, perforce, its results are always behind the immediate present. A "can do" spirit is laudable, but does it always yield answers which contribute to sound, workable personnel policies?

I should like to advance the proposition that with the present state of the art of personnel selection in the military, everything that can meaningfully be said has been said. Given the criterion splits that seem very stable over the past few years (75% successful and 25% unsuccessful), it is extremely doubtful that someone is going to find another bit of demographic data, or invent another sort of questionnaire, that will significantly improve on selection of men entering the armed forces.

I think it is time that personnel research turned from the pursuit of the Holy Grail of increased multiple R's and turned its attention instead to the environment of the military services to find those aspects which tend to assist in or detract from adjustment. For instance, in the Navy and the Marine Corps recruit training facilities, most of the loss occurs within the first three weeks. Why? Is it the haircut, the sudden imposition of a rigid system of conduct rules, homesickness, lack of privacy, or combinations of those elements? To answer questions like these means utilizing methodologies and the results of social psychology in addition to the classical industrial psychology approaches. I am of the further opinion that research designs in military personnel studies in the future should adopt a longitudinal, epidemiological approach in which a cohort of subjects is followed on a name-by-name basis, and that multiple criteria of success be utilized.

In summary, I take the position that:

(1) Contemporary military selection has become a staff function to the line of the armed forces, who are the customers of any research done in this area;

(2) It is the responsibility of a staff to give the best advice it can to the line. This includes advising the line when it has asked a question which is not researchable, or where the answer is already known from previous studies. The personnel research staff should also be ready to educate its executive that experimental design is best left in the hands of the research expert, rather than merely fill research prescriptions handed down from on high;

(3) Military selection research results have demonstrated that three out of four young men entering the armed forces are able to complete their enlistments and to be recommended for re-enlistment, which argues for a highly successful selection system. However, I doubt that the selection system can be meaningfully improved over that ratio by looking for other demographic information or paper and pencil tests; I therefore recommend that personnel research in the military turn its attention to the environmental factors in the system, with particular reference to basic and specialized training periods, to identify those factors which enhance or detract from a young man's adjustment to the armed forces.

Differential Approaches To Training[1]

JOHN E. TAYLOR

WAYNE L. FOX

HUMAN RESOURCES RESEARCH OFFICE
THE GEORGE WASHINGTON UNIVERSITY

I. INTRODUCTION

The U.S. Army has the requirement to provide training in a wide variety of military jobs to men who are found across the entire spectrum of mental aptitude. There is little information on how, or if, differential training should be conducted for men of differing aptitude levels and little is known particularly about how men of marginal aptitude should be trained.

The ultimate objective of the research being reported here is to develop procedures for achieving effective training at all aptitude levels for men in high-density military jobs. In order to accomplish this, it is necessary to map out the relationship among instructional methods and trainee aptitudes in the acquisition of military skills and knowledge.

The research effort has been divided into three phases. The *first phase* involves the development of a battery of training tasks and the subsequent collection of baseline learning data for trainees of different aptitude levels. The *second phase* involves experimentation with training methods in an attempt to improve performance of the less apt. *Phase three* will be a field validation of those training methods found to be most effective.

TRAINING TASK BATTERY

| | TYPE OF MILITARY JOB | | |
	COMBAT	COMBAT SUPPORT	TECHNICAL
PROBLEM SOLVING	T_{14}	T_{15}	
PRINCIPLES	T_{11}	T_{12} T_{13} →	
CONCEPTS	T_9	T_{10} →	
MULTIPLE DISCRIMINATION	T_7 T_8 →		
VERBAL CHAINING		T_5	T_6
MOTOR CHAINING	T_3 T_4 →		
STIMULUS-RESPONSE	T_1 T_2 →		

(vertical axis label: LEVELS OF COMPLEXITY)

Fig. 1

---

[1] The research reported in this paper was performed by HumRRO Division No. 3 (Recruit Training), Presidio of Monterey, California, under Department of the Army contract with The George Washington University.

308

Figure 1 depicts the strategy used for the development of the training task battery. We based the selection of tasks on two criteria. First, each task must have elements in common with those skills and knowledges required in the majority of high-density military jobs. We have divided the military jobs into three categories: *Combat,* which includes such jobs as infantryman, armor crewman and artilleryman; *Combat Support,* which includes such jobs as cook, supply clerk and vehicle driver: and *Technical,* which includes jobs such as missile-operator, radio repairman and electronic technician.

The work of Robert Gagné (1) provided the basis for the second criterion used in task selection. Gagné defines eight different types of learning which he orders from classical conditioning to problem solving, that is, from simple to complex. The nature of Army jobs precludes exact adherence to Gagné's eight-level hierarchy of learning types, but we have adopted the seven levels shown in Figure 1.

The 15 tasks included in the battery are numbered successively, from simple to complex. The arrows indicate that a particular task has elements in common with more than one of the job categories. We plan to have at least two tasks at each complexity level and, of course, several for each job category. At present, eight of the tasks are fully developed and the other seven are in various stages of development.

Phase I baseline learning data will be presented for high, middle and low aptitude trainees on six tasks and Phase II methods experimentation data will be presented for two of the tasks.

2. METHODS AND RESULTS

2.1. General

The data are based upon the performance of 143 U.S. Army trainees divided into three groups on the basis of their Armed Forces Qualification Test (AFQT) scores.

The high group $(N = 52)$ included trainees with AFQT scores between 90 and 99, the middle group $(N = 30)$ included trainees with scores between 45 and 55, the low group $(N = 61)$ included trainees with scores between 10 and 21.

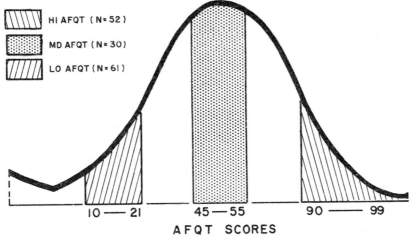

DISTRIBUTION OF AFQT SCORES BASED ON STANDARDIZATION SAMPLE

Fig. 2

Figure 2 indicates how our groups fell in the overall AFQT standardization distribution (2). Trainees were unsystematically selected from the Army reception station at Fort Ord, California. All were newly inducted, had no prior military experience and were awaiting assignment to Basic Combat Training.

For the Phase I baseline data collection, instructional methods designed to optimize training conditions were adopted. Where practical, instruction was automated, using audio-visual presentation. Verbal instructions were given in simple language with ample pictorial examples. All training was conducted individually with a live instructor present to give prompts, answer questions and provide immediate knowledge of results after each response. The material was presented in small segments. Instructions were repeated or reviewed, as appropriate and practice was provided on every trial. In short, training procedures were tailored to give the lower aptitude trainee every advantage.

2.2. Tasks I and 2 - Sequential Monitoring

The first two tasks which I wish to discuss, T_1 and T_2, are sequential monitoring tasks which fall at the simplest level of complexity. In fact, they are so simple that no learning is required for performance. These tasks have elements in common with many military jobs in all three of our categories.

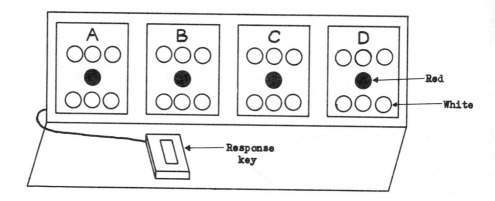

Fig. 3

T_1 is a Simple Sequential Monitoring Task. The trainee was told that this "control" panel (Figure 3) was part of a communications system that became overloaded when a red light came on. His task was simply to "reset" the control panel by pressing the lever when a red light appeared. The control panel apparatus was programmed so that white lights flashed intermittently across the panel accompanied by loud clicking noises. After an interval which varied from 15 to 205 seconds, the white lights went out and one of the four red lights came on. The trainee was required to "reset" the panel a total of 20 times over a 40 minute period. Records were made of response latency, accuracy and the variability of response for each trainee. Data have been collected on 15 high and 17 low aptitude trainees.

T_2 is a Choice Sequential Monitoring Task and uses the same apparatus as the previous task except for additional response levers (Figure 4). The trainee was to respond to one of the four red lights, labelled A, B, C, or D, by pressing the corresponding lever. All procedures and programming were identical for both tasks.

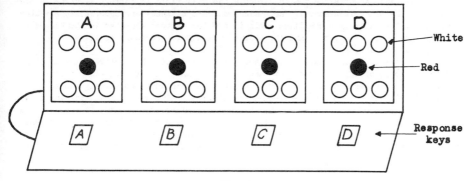

Fig. 4

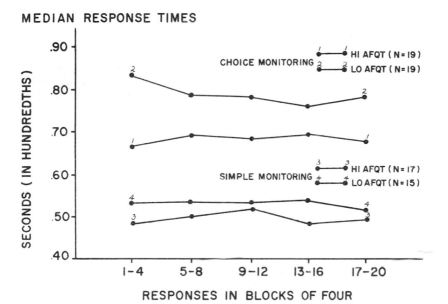

Fig. 5

Figure 5 shows response latencies for both groups on both tasks over the 20 responses, which are grouped into five blocks of four responses each. We had expected to find no difference between high and low aptitude trainees, but as you can see there were consistent and significant differences in response latency. As expected, the task requiring choice yielded longer response times. In addition, the individuals in the low aptitude group exhibited more variability and made a significantly greater number of false or incorrect responses on both tasks.

2.3. Task 3 - Motor Chaining

The next task, T_3, was a rifle assembly task falling at the next higher level of complexity. Rifle assembly is primarily a fixed-procedure motor chaining task and has elements in common with a variety of military jobs.

311

In this task, the trainee was to assemble the M-14 rifle in correct sequence as prescribed in the Army Field Manual. The trainee watched a video-tape showing step-by-step
assembly of the rifle by a qualified rifle instructor. After each step in the assembly
sequence, the tape was stopped and the trainee was allowed to complete the same step on
a rifle provided him.

On each trial, if the trainee could not perform the step, he received prompts from
the instructor, including direct assistance, if necessary. After each video training
trial, the subject was given a test trial where he attempted to completely assemble the
rifle; if he could not, prompts were again available. A minimum of three training trials
was given to each man. When the trainee felt no more video training trials were necessary,
he then received test trials until no further prompts were required and no improvement
in performance occurred across three consecutive trials. A record was made of the time
taken to complete each step in this sequence and the number of prompts required before
the assembly was completed.

Data on the rifle assembly task were collected on 23 high, 30 middle, and 23 low
aptitude trainees. Figure 6 shows time-of-assembly scores for all three groups. Note

MEAN RIFLE ASSEMBLY. TIMES

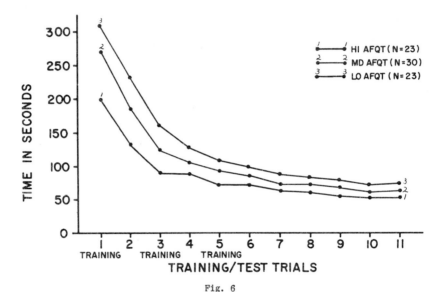

Fig. 6

that the middle group tends to fall midway between the high and low groups. Here, too,
because the task was relatively simple, fixed and motor, we expected no differences
among the groups. The low group, however, took about twice as long to learn as the high
group and, in addition, they required three times as many prompts. Clearly, all of the
trainees could perform the task, but there were differences on the initial ability to
profit from instruction, the amount of help needed and the ultimate level of performance.

2.4. Task 6 - Verbal Chaining

T_6 is a missile preparation task having elements common to several technical jobs.
It is primarily a fixed-procedure *verbal*-chaining task where the trainee is to learn to
perform 34 sequential steps of a procedure for launching a missile.

The subject was trained to perform the 34-step sequence on a specially designed training device which simulated a missile control panel. The proper procedure was demonstrated by an instructor and the trainee was provided a written checklist containing the 34 steps in proper order. The instructor read each step to the trainee and provided prompts, if necessary, in addition to those automatically programmed on the simulator.

The training device automatically recorded errors, total time and the number of prompts required to complete the sequence. Training continued until the trainee could complete the 34-step sequence with fewer than five prompts or until he had received a total of 15 trials. The trainee was given a prompt if he didn't respond within a given time.

Data have been collected on 20 high, 26 middle, and 21 low aptitude trainees. Figure 7 shows the average number of trials required to reach criterion for each of the three

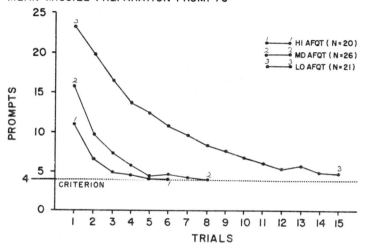

Fig. 7

groups. The term "prompts" on the ordinate indicates the number of times that time ran out before the correct response was given and the man required a prompt. Clearly, the rate of learning was markedly different for the three groups.

Figure 8 shows the proportion of trainees meeting criterion on each trial. Note that at Trial 5, 95% of the high aptitude trainees had reached criterion, while 69% of the middle and only 9% of the low aptitude trainees had attained criterion performance. It can be seen that some of the low group were able to master the task very early while some of them never did. This has relevance when we consider possible differential sorting, training, and classification for the low aptitude personnel. One problem confronting us is to determine how to identify these faster learners who enter Army service labelled as low aptitude trainees.

2.5. Task 7 - Multiple Discriminations

For the last two tasks to be discussed, we have gathered both Phase I baseline data and Phase II methods experimentation data.

PERCENTAGE MEETING MISSILE PREPARATION CRITERION

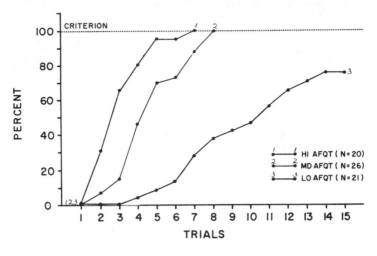

Fig. 8

The first of these two tasks, T_7, involved rote memory and fell at the level of multiple discrimination. This type of rote memory task has elements in common with many military jobs.

In Method A, the trainee was required to learn 26 military symbols taken from Army Field Manuals. Each symbol was placed on a 5″ by 8″ card with an artist's representation of the thing, place, or event symbolized; for example, a convoy. After a pretest, the subjects were shown each card and the instructor read aloud the name of the symbol. The trainee used the cards for a series of study periods. After each study period, the trainee was asked to identify the 26 symbols on a specially prepared answer sheet. He could either write the name of the symbol or say it aloud. A record was kept of the number of symbols correctly identified per trial.

Data were collected on 25 high, 30 middle and 25 low aptitude trainees. Figure 9 shows the average number correct for the three groups on each trial for Method A. Learning rates for the three groups are clearly different with the low aptitude group taking about three times as long to learn as the high aptitude group.

Under Method B, trainees were required to learn 12 of the same military symbols. A traditional paired-associate presentation of the stimulus, or symbol, was followed by a presentation of the stimulus-response pair – in this case the symbol and its appropriate label. As before, trainees could write their response or say it aloud. Trials were repeated until the trainees had learned all 12 symbols.

Data were collected on 14 high and 15 low aptitude trainees (Figure 10). All of the high aptitude trainees met criterion by the fifth trial, while the low aptitude trainees were not at criterion until the 14th trial.

To correct for different list length, Figure 11 presents the findings for both Method A and B in terms of the per cent correct on each trial. We see that the high aptitude trainees were superior to the low under both methods. However, note that even though there were more than twice as many symbols to be learned under Method A, this method resulted in superior performance. Apparently, it made a difference whether this kind of material was presented in mechanical-rote fashion (Method B) or in a fashion that permitted the trainees considerable freedom in organizing the materials themselves (Method A).

314

MEAN MILITARY SYMBOLS CORRECT
METHOD A

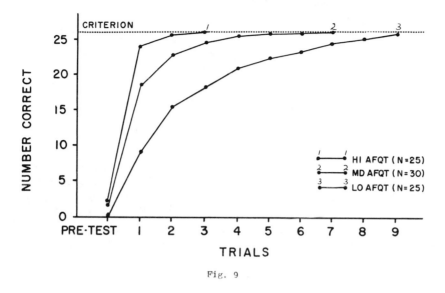

Fig. 9

MEAN MILITARY SYMBOLS CORRECT
METHOD B

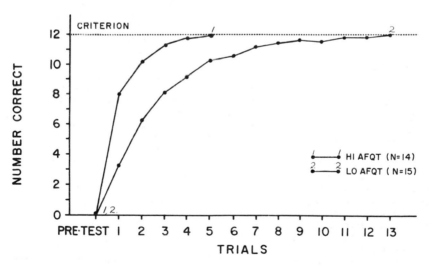

Fig. 10

PERCENT MILITARY SYMBOLS CORRECT
METHOD A VS. METHOD B

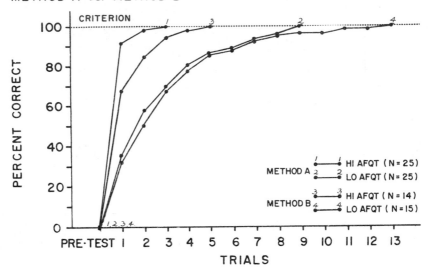

Fig. 11

2.6. Task II - Principles

The last task I will present is T_{11}, a combat plotting task which involved the learning and applying of principles. The trainee had to learn the concepts of range and bearing and apply them in an intersection problem, accurately estimating the position of a target from information describing its range and bearing.

Under Method I the combat plotting training was conducted via T.V., using a co-ordinated tape-slide presentation. The material was presented in small steps, using simple language and pictorial examples, with practice on sample problems.

The trainee was required to make plots on specially prepared plotting paper. Immediate knowledge of results was given to the trainee after each plot and instructions were repeated after each trial of ten plots, if required.

Data were collected on 25 high, 28 middle and 24 low aptitude trainees (Figure 12). These curves are consistent with those previously presented. The high and middle groups quickly mastered the task. They reached criterion in only three or four trials while the lower groups took considerably longer.

Method II consisted exclusively of verbal instruction presented in lecture format, much like the typical classroom lecture. Trainees were also under greater time pressure to make the plots and did not receive immediate knowledge of results after each response.

Data are only available on 10 high and 10 low aptitude trainees (Figure 13). The high aptitude group had little trouble mastering the task, but with the lecture-only method, trainees in the low aptitude group did not master the task and all indications were that they never would.

Figure 14 presents both sets of data. It is obvious that training method becomes critical for the low aptitude trainees.

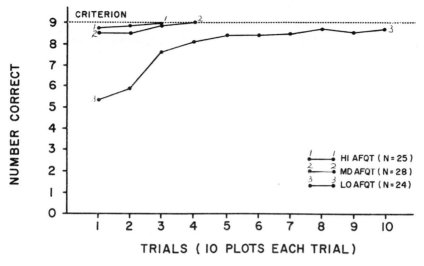

Fig. 12

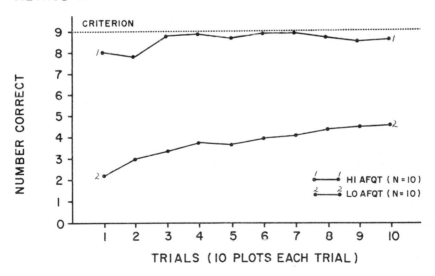

Fig. 13

MEAN COMBAT PLOTS CORRECT
METHOD I VS. METHOD II

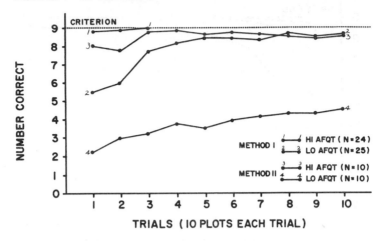

Fig. 14

3. SUMMARY AND CONCLUSIONS

Learning performance was found to be directly and highly related to aptitude level. This relationship held across a variety of tasks and also along a hierarchy of complexity varying from simple stimulus-response, through motor, verbal chaining and multiple discrimination, to principles learning tasks. In some tasks, the differences among the aptitude groups were in rate of learning only; in other tasks, the groups differed both in rate and in final levels of performance.

Performance was found to be related to training method for both high and low aptitude groups. In fact, at the level of principles learning, method of instruction was critical in whether the low aptitude group learned at all.

Further, it was found that the performance of individuals was highly consistent across tasks. Those who did poorly on one task, generally did poorly on all; those who did well on a given task, did well on all. This contradicts the general belief that though a person may be poor at, say, cognitive tasks, he will excel in motor tasks.

The picture we have gained of the low aptitude trainee is that he does poorly on all tasks, taking an average of two to three times as long to learn as the higher aptitude trainee. On some types of tasks he is not capable of reaching the same level of final performance as the higher aptitude trainee. However, he can eventually learn to perform a variety of tasks if the training methods have been carefully selected and organized to insure his assimilation of the instruction.

Most efficient training of men at all levels apparently will depend upon the recognition of individual differences in aptitude which require the design of instructional programs compatible with differences in learning rate and final performance capabilities.

REFERENCES

1. Gagné, Robert M., (1965) *The Conditions of Learning*, Holt, Rinehart & Winston, Inc.
2. Department of the Army, (1965) *Marginal Man and Military Service, A Review*.

Additional Efforts to Improve and Measure the Effectiveness of Marginal Manpower Programs in the Armed Forces of the United States

S. FRIEDMAN

OFFICE OF THE DEPUTY UNDERSECRETARY (MANPOWER)

U.S. NAVY DEPARTMENT

1. INTRODUCTION

As the final contributor on Marginal Manpower, I should like first to refer briefly to some of the remarks made in the previous papers.

Dr. King's historical perspective of research on Marginal Manpower in the U.S. military services concluded with a statement that "a major effort has now been set in motion to improve and measure the effectiveness of marginal manpower programs in the Armed Forces". He added that this effort "has strong Department of Defense support".

Commander Berry directed his remarks to the need for changes in selection systems which must accompany changes in the manpower force as well as the importance of considering longer-range criteria than merely survival in the service. He cited some relatively new and important follow-up studies which have been and are still being carried out by Dr. John Plag at the U.S. Navy Medical Neuropsychiatric Research Unit in San Diego, California.

Dr. Taylor's remarks with reference to the efforts of the Human Resources Research Office in the area of training research were most exciting and, I believe, truly promising.

I should like to point out that the last two papers are but parts of a very extensive and intensive research program which has been given both impetus and support (including financial, I might add) by the Department of Defense. I will attempt in the time allowed me to describe briefly three research projects which are planned by the Navy and to mention in passing some of the Army and Air Force efforts.

2. IMPROVING SELECTION PROCEDURES (USN)

I have chosen the three Navy examples to represent essentially different approaches to the general problem of improving marginal manpower utilization in the Armed Forces. The first is an effort to further improve our selection procedure. This effort has been planned and will be conducted at the U.S. Navy Personnel Research Activity, under Dr. Bernard Rimland and his staff. His approach attempts to consider that the Marginal Manpower category is itself a heterogeneous group, not only because it covers a cognitive range of 20 percentile points on the Armed Forces Qualification Test, but also because of wide variations in the cultural and educational factors believed to affect test performance. Rimland's approach also considers the following:

(i) while our existing test validities are high enough to be decidedly useful, they are still low enough to warrant serious investigation and study for improvement;

(ii) selection testing has been largely oriented toward identifying lower aptitude men so that they might be rejected;

(iii) most selection tests have emphasized intellectual performance required in formal school instruction which ignores the prediction of later on-the-job performance (a weakness also referred to by Commander Berry); and

(iv) available computer technology now provides the wherewithal for detailed analysis heretofore not possible.

Specifically then, with the foregoing considerations in mind, a series of new experimental tests will be administered to a sample of incoming recruits, including both marginal recruits as well as others. The new tests will include, but not be limited to the following:

2.1. The Memory for Numbers Tests

These have been specially adapted for this project from materials devised by A.R. Jensen of the University of California, Berkeley. Professor Jensen's work had discovered digit span to have quite good validities against school criteria, to be relatively uncorrelated with standard intelligence tests, and to show *similar mean scores* for "culturally disadvantaged" as well as middle class children.

2.2. The Hand Skills Test

This test has been shown in a number of Navy studies to measure perseverance and motivation under stress. It requires the subject to make a long series of tally marks in boxes on his answer sheet, under carefully controlled time limits.

2.3. The Manual Speed Test

This is an adaption of the Hand Skills Test intended to provide a machine scorable form, if the H–S Test proves valid.

2.4. Other Tests

Other tests being considered include a group form of the Porteus Maze test, an Oral Directions test, and some appropriate instruments suitable for measuring interest and motivation among marginal personnel.

Attempts will be made to relate test performance to a variety of criteria including such things as early discharge, as well as willingness of commanding officers to recommend individuals for re-enlistment.

I should like to point out that we may not have to wait too long for preliminary results of this research. Some data collection was begun several years ago, and while not all new tests were in this original body of data, sufficient relevant criterion data are now available to permit fairly extensive analyses, and hopefully some significant findings.

3. MAXIMIZING THE PERFORMANCE OF MARGINAL PERSONNEL (USN)

The second Navy effort which I will describe is being planned at the U.S. Navy Personnel Research Activity, under the aegis of Dr. Earl I. Jones, Director of the Navy Training Research Laboratory. The basic aims of this effort will be to enhance and utilize the capabilities of marginal personnel in a manner such that their performance in military jobs will be maximized.

The approach which will be taken to meet these broad aims is divided into four research tasks, as follows:

(i) Identification of Job Elements and Jobs suitable for Marginal Personnel. *Objective*: To identify a representative set of job elements and jobs which marginal personnel can be trained to perform at a completely adequate level.

(ii) Measurement and Training of Basic Skills for Marginal Personnel. *Objective*: Certain fundamental skills, particularly those associated with communication, are basic to learning most jobs or elements of jobs. These skills include oral communication, reading, arithmetic, and ability to use hand tools. The objective of this research will be to develop or select standardized ways of measuring these skills; to establish criteria of the performance levels in these areas that are necessary for entry into training for representative military jobs; and to develop and evaluate methods for training these basic skills.

(iii) Development and Evaluation of Methods for Efficient Training of Marginal Personnel in the Performance of Selected Job Elements. *Objective*: Job elements which marginal personnel can be trained to perform at an acceptable level will have been identified by previous research. The purpose of this research will be to develop and evaluate efficient training methods for those elements.

(iv) Determination of Optimal Sequences for Training in the Elements of Jobs and the Integration of Elements into Complete Jobs for Marginal Personnel. *Objective*: Previous research will have identified job elements for which marginal personnel can be successfully trained, and methods for training in these elements will have been developed and evaluated. The purpose of this research will be to determine optimal sequences for training in the elements of representative jobs and procedures for integrating elements into complete jobs. A primary goal will be to seek principles which may be applied to many jobs.

(v) In addition to these plans in the area of training research, the Navy has endeavoured to modify as necessary three training courses to accommodate small groups of marginal personnel. These include Commissary School training, Equipment Operator training and Aviation Structural Mechanic training. These course modifications are being carried on with small groups of marginal personnel introduced into each of the courses of training. Course evaluations are made on a continuous basis and changes and/or extensions in the courses are made as necessary. Up to the most recent reports no significant problems have been encountered, with the exception that some deficiency with respect to reading ability levels has been observed in the training of marginal personnel in the Aviation Structural Mechanic course.

It is anticipated that there will be a tie-in between the findings from these initial course studies and the planned more fundamental research efforts previously mentioned.

4. JOB RESTRUCTURING (USN)

The third Navy effort which I will mention briefly concerns "job restructuring". This effort will be conducted under the aegis of the Bureau of Medicine and Surgery, with the co-operation and assistance of the Bureau of Naval Personnel. The basic objective of the study is to determine the feasibility of job restructuring within the Hospital Corpsman rating.

Broadly stated, the study will undertake through interview, questionnaire, and direct observation techniques to:

(i) delineate the job functions (requirements or duties expected) of hospital corpsmen and other auxiliary personnel in major Navy medical care facilities;

(ii) define the actual work, and the methods by which it is carried out by hospital corpsmen, of all rates and Navy Enlisted Codes;

    (iii) define qualifications for various types of job functions in terms of experience (including training) and psychological attributes of persons filling such jobs;

    (iv) define the environmental context (to include amount and quality of supervision required and interpersonal coordination) of various jobs;

    (v) determine the extent to which certain elements of various existing jobs could be clustered into new and separate set of job functions; and

    (vi) assess similar job functions and training requirement surveys, for comparison with Navy programs, already conducted in certain civilian medical care facilities by the American Hospital Association and the United States Public Health Service.

This research will be conducted on a contract basis for the Bureau of Medicine and Surgery. It is anticipated to be completed in about a year.

5. OTHER SERVICES

At this point, I should like to cite briefly, some additional examples of efforts being conducted by the Army and Air Force, as well as one, which I think is most important, that was designed by the staff of the Assistant Secretary of Defense (Manpower), with the cooperation and assistance of Army, Navy, Air Force and Marine Corps representatives.

5.1. U.S. Army

Examples of additional Army efforts which are presently underway and which show promise of payoff in the not-too-distant future, involve the development of five special training courses. These courses have been redesigned specifically for the purpose of attempting to train groups of marginal personnel who by previous standards were not considered eligible for entrance into these courses. The courses involve training for the following specific jobs: Supply Clerk, Wheel Vehicle Mechanic, Engineer Equipment Maintenance, Marine Hull Repair, and Telephone Switchboard Operator. While the specific changes in each school or course may differ, it is most interesting to note the following common elements in each effort to redesign of the particular course;

    (i) Course objectives are being carefully reviewed and validated.

    (ii) Course materials are being simplified. Changes being made include modifications to lesson plans, development of new and improved handout materials, and modification of student workbooks.

    (iii) New teaching aids and techniques are being reviewed and introduced into courses as appropriate. These include programmed textbooks, new visual aids, and closed circuit television.

    (iv) Need for integrating literacy and vocational training is considered in each situation. (So far this has not been found necessary.)

    (v) Tests used to evaluate school performance are being reviewed. Generally the aim is to modify existing or develop new performance type tests.

    (vi) For each course a special effort is being devoted to the development of a design and procedure for evaluating the effectiveness of the particular training program.

5.2. U.S.A.F. and the Marine Corps

The Air Force is devoting similar efforts, as is also the Marine Corps, in the general area of redesigning selected training courses, and endeavouring to train some small numbers of marginal personnel in such courses. The Air Force has selected a sizable number of courses for this effort, and include the following kinds of Air Force jobs:

Outside Wire & Antenna Systems Installation and
   Maintenance Specialist
Automotive Repairman
Special Vehicle Repairman
Machinist
Metals Processing Specialist
Pavement Maintenance Specialist
Protective Coating Specialist
Plumbing Specialist
Water & Waste Processing Specialist
Fire Protection Specialist
Air Freight Specialist
Communications Centre Specialist
Administrative Specialist
Photographer
Fuel Specialist (Petroleum)
Material Facilities Specialist
Air Policeman
Telephone Equipment Installer
Electrician
Marine Corps efforts in this area include special courses in Combat Engineers and
Motor Vehicle Operators training.

5.3. Assistant Secretary of Defense (Manpower)

Insofar as the study designed by the ASD (Manpower) staff is concerned, I must again
be most brief, although I do not wish to detract from its importance. A short description
can perhaps best be accomplished by simply paraphrasing its objectives, which are to

   (i) follow-up each individual who entered the service under reduced selection
     standards,

  (ii) document his service experiences including his specific educational attainments,
     and

 (iii) follow-up each individual, as feasible, in his return to civilian life, in an
     effort to assess the direction and extent to which his service experiences
     have enabled him to achieve or attain educational and vocational goals which
     might otherwise not have been available to him. This constitutes a new look at
     ways of assessing national manpower resources and their contributions to the
     national welfare as a whole.

6. CONCLUSION

In conclusion, and in consideration of the entire area of military personnel
research, I should like with your indulgence to refer to a Summary of Proceedings which
I prepared a little over seven years ago at an invitational Tri-Service Conference on
Selection Research (in the Armed Forces of the United States). (1)

In this summary I pointed out "that selection research *per se* was no longer a neat,
well-defined area to which military research psychologists could confine their efforts
profitably". I feel that I could have made the same statement then with respect to
training research and occupational research. I tried to point out then, and feel the
same way now, that selection research (and training research and occupational research)
is inextricably interwoven with research on other personnel operations and procedures
and that much needed improvements in techniques are in various stages of development for
handling the problems as they are beginning to take shape. I said further that "much of
this, of course, has been recognized to some extent in the past. Indeed, no military
research psychologist ever really confined himself to selection research alone; he has

always been concerned with the criterion problem, optimization of assignment procedures and the like".

I believe that what was then new and is now better understood is that the systems approach provides an integrating element to areas of effort which previously may have lacked adequate Gestalt. As I said then, "all of this serves to foreshadow an era in which efforts in the broad area of psychological measurement and prediction, enhanced by broader horizons, will successfully meet greater challenges and yield more productive and more meaningful results for the planning and implementation of military personnel policies and procedures ".

I feel that my observations seven years ago are still pertinent at this time. The need for better integration and coordination of what one may regard as subspecialties in the area of psychological measurement and prediction must be recognized and satisfied. Those who study selection research must consider carefully the training content, methods, and evaluative measures which are employed by educators in the system, as well as the research which may be conducted by other psychologists in their efforts to improve these elements of training. They must also consider the operational assignment procedures, as well as efforts of operations research to improve these procedures. Not to be ignored are considerations relating to the utilization and performance evaluation of personnel originally selected by their techniques.

Similarly, the training researcher must consider the efforts of selection researchers and their techniques to effect improvements, not only in selection but also in assignment and utilization. The same could be said for researchers engaged in any segment of the personnel system. I am glad to detect evidence in the efforts you have heard discussed during this meeting that this type of approach is being considered and utilized.

It is only by these kinds of considerations and careful attention to the interaction effects of the various subsystems that most promising results of such efforts can be achieved. Fortunately, as I have indicated in my reference to Dr. Rimland's planned research, the availability of computers and the sophisticated modelling techniques should enable us to achieve our goal, which is to make the most effective use of manpower in the Armed Forces.

REFERENCE

1. Proceedings, Tri-Service Conference on Selection Research, *ONR Symposium Report ACR-60*, pp. 271–273.

The Measurement of Physical Proficiency: A Problem in Skill Classification

EDWIN A. FLEISHMAN

AMERICAN INSTITUTES FOR RESEARCH

WASHINGTON, D.C.

I. INTRODUCTION

One area of concern, with regard to our manpower resources, is that of physical fitness. I was asked at this conference to describe some recent research on the dimension of physical fitness and their implications for fitness measurement. However, I also want to discuss some more general issues which bear on the larger problem of skill classification.

The subject of physical fitness received increased attention in the United States several years ago. The President had been shown a report which indicated that U.S. youth scored lower than European youth on certain physical fitness tests. He then appointed a Council on Physical Fitness to look into the problem and there was a great deal of activity generated in developing fitness programs. However, interest and activity are not enough. There were many alternatives available and the experts are not all agreed on the proper direction of efforts. There is a need for specific guidance on how to assess physical proficiency, the progress of individuals and the effectiveness of particular programs.

To meet this need a project entitled " The Development of Criteria of Physical Proficiency " was sponsored by the Office of Naval Research. The objectives of this project were:

(a) to identify the components of physical proficiency which need to be assessed, and

(b) to recommend appropriate procedures to measure these components.

The project represented the most concerted effort, thus far, to find out what it is that current fitness tests actually measure, to discover which tests measure the same or different abilities, to classify existing and new tests in terms of abilities measured and to provide indices of how well current tests measure each ability.

The project on physical fitness is part of a large program whose major concern is the development of a taxonomy of human performances, which is useful for classifying and describing human tasks. The absence of generalizable categories of human performance is one of the major " state of the art " problems. Harold Wool has pointed up the problem of transferability of skills that need to be faced. He emphasized transferability from one job to another and from military to civilian jobs. Martin Tolcott referred to the need to identify the dimensions underlying job structure and the need to understand general job dimensions independent of specific jobs. There is a need for useful categories to describe the dimensions of skills. It is within this broader context that I would like to discuss our work.

So, before describing the physical fitness research let me provide some conceptual as well as research background.

2. THE PROBLEM OF TASK TAXONOMY

A fundamental prerequisite to the effective operation of any man-machine system is the acquisition, performance and retention of skilled behaviours. For many years psychologists have studied training and performance, often in applied contexts, under numerous task and environmental conditions and have accumulated vast quantities of data. And yet, as new systems are conceived for the exploration of space, for defense, for command and control, it appears that problems of skill identification, training and performance must be restudied almost from scratch.

Superficially, each new system differs from other systems with respect to application, mission, technology and apparently in its task demands on its human operators. No two task analyses are ever quite the same. No two systems ever have identical job requirements. No training device or simulator ever quite seems to fit the requirement of any system except the one for which it was developed. Is it reasonable to conclude that the tasks of men in systems are so varied that there are no common dimensions with respect to the basic abilities required, the types of training needed for job proficiency, or the degradation of skilled behaviour under given environmental conditions?

The problem is not only one of finding ways to generalize principles from one operational system to another. It also involves the generalization of findings from the laboratory to operational tasks. One reason why much of current research in the experimental laboratory appears so sterile to those who try to apply it to real-life training situations is the lack of concern for the problem of task dimensions. This is often true for laboratory studies of the effects of learning, of environmental factors, the effects of motivational variables, the effects of drugs, etc., on human performance. It is not too long ago when a favourite distinction was between " motor " and " mental " tasks or between " cognitive " and " noncognitive " tasks. Such distinctions are clearly not very helpful in generalizing results to new situations, which involve a complex array of tasks and skills not adequately described by such all-inclusive terms. Tasks selected in laboratory research are not often based on any clear rationale about the class of task or skill represented. Most learning theory is devoid of any concern about task dimensions and it is this deficiency which, many feel, makes it so difficult to apply these theories in the real world of tasks and people. What is needed is a learning and performance theory which ascribes task dimensions a central role.

Categories which conceive of man-task interactions in terms of classes of functions certainly would seem to be steps in the right direction. Categories one sees used include categories like discrimination, identification, sequence learning, problem solving (Gagné, 1964); another system (Miller, 1965) uses interpretation, short-term and long-term memory, decision making; Alluisi (1965) uses categories such as vigilance processes, memory functions, communication functions, intellectual functions, procedural functions, motor skills.

These categories may turn out to be highly useful in both (a) organizing performance data into categories of consistent principles, and (b) allowing more dependable predictions from laboratory to operations and from one operation to another. The demonstration, of course, still needs to be made. One needs to recognize, naturally, that these approaches are initially arm-chair rational descriptive approaches. And there is nothing wrong with this, provided the necessary experimental predictive work is carried out to test the utility of these systems. However, I am sceptical that any small number of categories is going to be sucessful. Everything known about the correlations among human performances indicates a greater degree of specificity than this and considerable diversity of function within these categories. Since there are many types of human functions within each sub-area, one probably cannot generalize too far within each area. It is my feeling that we will just have to admit that human performance is complex and consists of many components. The problem is to simplify the description as far as we can, seeking all the while to find the limits and generality of the categories developed. And the selection of measures, diagnostic and representative of these categories, is an empirical rather than an arm-chair question.

A major point I want to stress is that there are empirical-experimental approaches
to developing task taxonomies and that we already know quite a bit about task dimensions
from experimental-correlational studies already completed and that these allow us to be
much more specific about task dimensions than do the more general categorical terms
previously described. And I believe that combinations of experimental and correlational
methods can develop a taxonomy of human performance which is applicable to a large
variety of tasks and situations.

2.1. Conceptual and Methodological Framework

First I would like to define some concepts which have been developed.
I find it useful to distinguish between the concepts of " ability " and " skill ".
As we use the term, *ability* refers to a more general trait of the individual which has
been inferred from certain response consistencies (e.g., correlations) on certain kinds
of tasks. Some abilities (e.g., colour vision) depend more on genetic than learning
factors, but most abilities depend on both to some degree. In any case, at a given stage
of life, they represent traits or organismic factors which the individual brings with
him when he begins to learn a new task. These abilities are related to performances in
a variety of human tasks. For example, the fact that spatial visualization has been
found related to performance on such diverse tasks as aerial navigation, blueprint
reading and dentistry, makes this ability somewhat more basic.
The term *skill* refers to the level of proficiency on a specific task or limited
group of tasks. As we use the term skill, it is task oriented. When we talk about
proficiency in flying an airplane, in operating a turret lathe, or in playing basketball, we are talking about a specific skill. Thus, when we speak of acquiring the skill
of operating a turret lathe, we mean that this person has acquired the sequence of
responses required by this specific task. The assumption is that the skills involved in
complex activities can be described in terms of the more basic abilities. For example,
the level of performance a man can attain on a turret lathe may depend on his basic
abilities of manual dexterity and motor coordination. However, these same basic abilities
may be important to proficiency in other skills as well. Thus, manual dexterity is
needed in assembling electrical components and motor coordination is needed to fly an
airplane.
Implicit in the previous analysis is the important relation between abilities and
learning. Thus, individuals with high manual dexterity may more readily learn the
specific skill of lathe operation. The mechanism of transfer of training probably
operates here. Some abilities may transfer to the learning of a greater variety of
specific tasks than others. In our culture, *verbal* abilities are more important in a
greater variety of tasks than are some other types of abilities. The individual who has
a great many highly developed basic abilities can become proficient at a great variety
of specific tasks.
Elsewhere (Fleishman, 1964; Gagné & Fleishman, 1959) we have elaborated our analysis
of the development of basic abilities. This included a discussion of their physiological
bases, the role of learning, environmental and cultural factors and evidence on the rate
of ability development during the life span. With this much conceptualization in mind,
we can say that in much of our previous work one objective has been to describe certain
skills in terms of these more general ability requirements.
The original impetus for this program was a very applied problem. While I was with
the Air Force Personnel and Training Research Center, one of our missions was to build
better psychomotor tests for the prediction of pilot success. The wartime Air Force
program had been highly successful in developing such tests. For example, the Complex
Coordination Test had consistent validity for pilots. This seems not surprising, since
the test seemed to be a " job sample " of aspects of the pilot's job. The pilot does
manipulate stick and rudder controls. But there were many tests which had substantial
validity but did not at all " resemble " the pilot's job. Cases in point are the Rotary
Pursuit and Two Hand Coordination Tests. And there were other tests which seemed to
resemble aspects of the pilot's job but had no validity. So it seemed to me that the

first step was to discover the sources of validity in these tests. What ability factors were there in common to a great variety of psychomotor tasks and which of these were common to pilot performance and other Air Force tasks? (See e.g., Fleishman, 1953, 1956; Fleishman & Hempel, 1956.)

Perhaps a not too extreme statement is that most of the categorization of human skills, which is empirically based, comes from correlational and factor-analysis studies. Many of these studies in the literature are ill designed or not designed at all. This does not rule out the fact that properly designed, systematic, programmatic, correlational research can yield highly useful data about general skill dimensions. We can think of such categories as representing empirically derived patterns of *response consistencies* to task requirements varied in systematic ways. In a sense this approach describes tasks in terms of the common abilities required to perform them. As an example, let us take the term "tracking", a frequent behavioural category employed by laboratory and systems psychologists alike. But we can all think of a wide variety of different tasks in which some kinds of tracking are involved. Can we assume that the behavioural category of tracking is useful in helping us generalize results from one such situation to another? Is there a general tracking ability? Are individuals who are good at compensatory tracking also the ones who are good at pursuit tracking? Do people who are good at positional tracking also do well with velocity or acceleration controls? What happens to the correlations between performances as a function of such variations? It is to these kinds of questions that our program was directed.

2.2. Some Previous Research

In subsequent years we have conducted a whole series of interlocking, experimental, factor-analytic studies, attempting to isolate and identify the common variance in a wide range of psychomotor performances. Essentially this is laboratory research in which tasks are specifically designed or selected to test certain hypotheses about the organization of abilities in a certain range of tasks (see, e.g., Fleishman, 1954). Subsequent studies tend to introduce task variations aimed at sharpening or limiting our ability-factor definitions. The purpose is to define the fewest independent ability categories which might be most useful and meaningful in describing performance in the widest variety of tasks.

Our studies generally start with some gross area of human performance. Thus, we have conducted studies of fine manipulative performances (Fleishman & Ellison, 1962; Fleishman & Hempel, 1954a), gross physical proficiency (Fleishman, 1963, 1964; Hempel & Fleishman, 1955) positioning movements and static reactions (Fleishman, 1958a), and movement reactions (Fleishman, 1958b; Fleishman & Hempel, 1956).

Thus far, we have investigated more than 200 different tasks administered to thousands of subjects (*Ss*) in a series of interlocking studies. From the patterns of correlations obtained, we have been able to account for performance on this wide range of tasks in terms of a relatively small number of abilities. In subsequent studies our definitions of these abilities and their distinctions from one another are becoming more clearly delineated. Furthermore, it is now possible to specify the tasks which should provide the best measure of each of the abilities identified.

There are about 11 psychomotor factors and 9 factors in the area of physical proficiency which consistently appear to account for the common variance in such tasks. Before turning to the physical proficiency area let me list some of these psychomotor factors.

(i) Control Precision

This factor is common to tasks which require fine, highly controlled, but not over-controlled, muscular adjustments, primarily where larger muscle groups are involved (Fleishman, 1958b; Fleishman and Hempel, 1956; Parker and Fleishman, 1960). This ability extends to arm-hand as well as to leg movements. It is most critical where such adjustments must be rapid, but precise.

(ii) Multilimb Coordination

This is the ability to coordinate the movements of a number of limbs simultaneously and is best measured by devices involving multiple controls (Fleishman, 1958b; Fleishman and Hempel, 1956; Parker and Fleishman, 1960). The factor has been found general to tasks requiring coordination of the two feet (e.g., the Rudder Control Test), two hands (e.g., the Two Hand Pursuit and Two Hand Coordination Tests) and hands and feet (e.g., the Plane Control and Complex Coordination Tests).

(iii) Response Orientation

This ability factor has been found general to visual discrimination reaction psycho-motor tasks involving rapid directional discrimination and orientation of movement patterns (Fleishman, 1957a, 1957b, 1958b; Fleishman and Hempel, 1956; Parker and Fleishman, 1960). It appears to involve the ability to *select* the correct movement in relation to the correct stimulus, especially under highly speeded conditions.

(iv) Reaction Time

This represents simply the speed with which the individual is able to respond to a stimulus when it appears (Fleishman, 1954, 1958b; Fleishman and Hempel, 1955; Parker and Fleishman, 1960). There are consistent indications that individual differences in this ability are independent of whether the stimulus is auditory or visual and are also independent of the type of response which is required. However, once the stimulus situation or the response situation is complicated by involving alternate choices, reaction time is not the primary factor that is measured.

(v) Speed of Arm Movement

This represents simply the speed with which an individual can make a gross, discrete arm movement where accuracy is not the requirement (Fleishman, 1958b); Fleishman and Hempel, 1954b, 1955; Parker and Fleishman, 1960). There is ample evidence that this factor is independent of the reaction-time factor.

(vi) Rate Control

This ability involves the making of continuous anticipatory motor adjustments relative to changes in speed and direction of a continuously moving target or object (Fleishman, 1958b; Fleishman and Hempel, 1955, 1956). This factor is general to tasks involving compensatory as well as following pursuit and extends to tasks involving responses to changes in rate. Our research has shown that adequate measurement of this ability requires an actual response in relation to the changing direction and speed of the stimulus object and not simply a judgment of the rate of stimulus movement alone.

(vii) Manual Dexterity

This ability involves skilful, well directed arm-hand movements in manipulating fairly large objects under speeded conditions (Fleishman, 1953b, 1954; Fleishman and Hempel, 1954b; Fleishman and Ellison, 1962; Parker and Fleishman, 1960; Hempel and Fleishman, 1955).

(viii) Finger Dexterity

This is the ability to make skill-controlled manipulations of tiny objects involving, primarily, the fingers (Fleishman, 1953b, 1954; Fleishman and Hempel, 1954a; Parker and Fleishman, 1960; Hempel and Fleishman, 1955; Fleishman and Ellison, 1962).

329

(ix) Arm-Hand Steadiness

This is the ability to make precise arm-hand positioning movements where strength and speed are minimized; the critical feature, as the name implies, is the steadiness with which such movements can be made (Fleishman, 1953b, 1954, 1958a, 1958b; Fleishman and Hempel, 1955; Hempel and Fleishman, 1955; Parker and Fleishman, 1960).

Of course, there are detailed descriptions of the operations involved in each category; some of them are more general in scope than others. But it is important to know for example, that it is not useful to talk about strength as a dimension, but that in terms of what tasks the same people can do well, it is more useful to talk in terms of at least four general strength categories which may be differentially involved in a variety of physical tasks.

Perhaps it might be useful to provide some examples of how one examines the generality of an ability category and how one defines its limits. The definition of the Rate Control factor may provide an example. In early studies it was found that this factor was common to compensatory as well as following pursuit tasks. To test its generality, tasks were developed to emphasize rate control, which were not conventional tracking tasks (e.g., controlling a ball rolling through a series of alleyways). The factor was found to extend to such tasks. Later studies attempted to discover whether emphasis on this ability lies in judging the rate of the stimulus as distinguished from ability to respond at the appropriate rate. A task was developed involving only button pressing in response to judgments of moving stimuli. Performance on this task did *not* correlate with other rate control tasks. Finally, several motion picture tasks were adapted in which S was required to extrapolate the course of a plane moving across a screen. The only response required was on an IBM answer sheet. These tasks did not relate to the core of tasks previously found to measure " rate control ". Thus, our definition of this ability was expanded to include measures beyond pursuit tasks, but restricted to tasks requiring the timing of a muscular adjustment to the stimulus change.

A similar history can be sketched for each ability variable identified. Thus, we know that S must have a feedback indicator of how well he is coordinating before the Multilimb Coordination factor is measured; we know that by complicating a simple reaction-time apparatus, by providing additional choice reactions, we measure a separate factor (Response Orientation), but that varying the stimulus modality in a simple reaction-time device does not result in measurement of a separate factor.

Some later studies, using experimental-correlational approaches, provided encouraging results which indicate that it is possible to build up a body of principles through systematic studies of ability-task interaction in the laboratory (e.g. Fleishman, 1956). The approach is to develop tasks which can be varied along specified physical dimensions, to administer these tasks, systematically varied along these dimensions, to groups of *S*s who also receive a series of " reference " tasks, known to sample certain more generalized abilities (e.g., " Spatial Orientation ", " Control Precision ", certain " Cognitive Abilities "). Correlations between these reference tasks and scores on variations of the criterion task specify the ability requirements (and changes in these requirements) as a function of task variations. Thus far we have studied tasks varied along the following dimensions: degree of rotation of display panels relative to response panels; the predictability or non-predictability of target course or response requirements; the extent to which the task allows S to assess the degree of coordination of multiple limb responses; the degree of stimulus-response compatibility in display-control relationships; whether there is a constant " set " or changing " set " from one stimulus presentation to the next; whether or not certain kinds of additional response requirements are imposed in a visual discrimination reaction task; whether or not certain kinds of feedback are provided. Hopefully, once such principles are established, it should be possible to look at new tasks, operational or otherwise and specify the ability requirements.

There is a whole area of work which I cannot describe here today, which relates the taxonomy developed to problems in skill learning and training of more complex tasks (summarized most recently in Fleishman, 1966, 1967). These studies trace the role of the ability components at different stages of proficiency during training (Fleishman and Hempel, 1954, 1955; Fleishman and Fruchter, 1960; Parker and Fleishman, 1960). Instead I want to turn now to the specific studies of identifying the dimensions of physical fitness. These studies generally follow the experimental-correlational pattern and factor analytic approach just described. This involves the development of experimental batteries of tasks hypothesized to measure certain factors; administering the batteries to large samples of subjects, obtaining the intercorrelations among performances and reducing the correlation matrix by factor analysis methods.

3. RESEARCH ON PHYSICAL FITNESS DIMENSIONS AND MEASUREMENT

3.1. Literature Integration

The project had several phases. The first phase consisted of a comprehensive review of the literature on previous and currently used physical fitness tests. The literature in this area is replete with terms like " velocity", " speed", " explosive and static strength", " muscular endurance", " stamina", etc. Are these useful categories? Which categories of performance represent essentially different abilities and tests to measure them. The primary objective of this review was to examine the correlations found among such tests and to describe the factors they are presumed to measure. Special emphasis was placed on reviewing previous factor analysis studies of physical fitness tests in order to compile a comprehensive catalogue of tests according to the factors they seemed to measure (Fleishman, 1964a). It was possible to integrate these factors into a meaningful schema and the main conclusion was that commonly used test batteries do not cover the range of possible fitness factors and many of the tests which are used overlap with one another in the factors measured. Fourteen possible factors were described and questions were raised about other possible factors. The review was probably the most extensive integration ever attempted in this area and served as a basis for our follow-up studies.

3.2. The Experimental Studies

Considerable pre-testing of more than 100 tests was carried out with the objective of providing better measures of the hypothesized factors. The most reliable tests from these pre-tests were included with more familiar tests in two large scale studies with United States Navy recruits. The design of these studies allowed for the confirmation or redefinition of the hypothesized factors as well as for the isolation of new factors. Testing teams, under the supervision of the Yale University project, were established at the Great Lakes Naval Training Center, Illinois and at the San Diego Naval Training Center, California. At Great Lakes, 30 tests designed to measure different factors in the areas of strength and endurance were administered; at San Diego, 30 tests in the areas of flexibility, balance, speed and coordination were administered. At each Center all the tests were administered to more than 200 Navy recruits. Correlations among all these tests and background variables were obtained and subjected to factor analysis studies. Where previous factor analytic studies had focused on relatively small test batteries, here it was possible to combine alternative measures of practically *all* previously identified factors within these two large scale studies. Both of these studies provided better definitions of the factors that need to be assessed for a more comprehensive evaluation of physical proficiency and provided recommendations for tests most diagnostic of these different factors. In all, it was possible to explain the correlations among these 60 different tests in terms of 11 primary factors. A few of these factors were quite specific (e.g., those confined to balancing weights) and were not considered further, but the more general ones were retained for further study.

To illustrate the research strategy let us examine more closely the design of the study to identify ability factors in the area of strength. *Figure 1* lists the experimental and existing tests utilized in the study. Tests were chosen so that some emphasized flexor and others extensor muscles, some emphasized leg and others arm or trunk strength, some emphasized short and long runs. Others emphasized continuous, repeated, or minimal strain, some were timed or untimed. The design made it possible to examine the correlations among tests given to the same subjects to answer questions such as the following: Do we get two factors separating flexor or extensor muscles? Is there a general strength factor common to all these tasks? Does prolonged strain on muscles (pull-ups, push-ups) introduce a new factor (e.g., endurance), compared with tasks using the same muscles in a shorter but speeded period (" Do as many push-ups as possible in 20 seconds ")? Are there factors common to muscle groups (arms vs. legs) as distinguished from factors dependent on the pattern of activity? What is the role of strength in running tasks? *Figure 1* shows the possible factors that could have been obtained when we examined the actual relations among performances.

3.3. Experimentally derived factors and description of tests

A similar design was followed in the areas of speed, flexibility, coordination and balance. The intercorrelations may be seen elsewhere (Fleishman, 1964). For the present we will merely summarize the factors that emerged from these studies and the tests which had the highest factor loading (correlations with that factor). By examining the tests which grouped together on the same factor it was possible to define the factors. The factors identified and the test found to best measure each factor, are as follows:

(i) Extent Flexibility Factor

Ability to flex or stretch the trunk and back muscles *as far as possible* in either a forward, lateral, or backward direction.
Extent Flexibility Test: (Originally called Twist and Touch.) The subject stands, with his left side toward the wall, and arm's length away from the wall. With feet together and in place, he twists back around as far as he can, touching the wall with his right hand at shoulder height.

(ii) Dynamic Flexibility Factor

The ability to make repeated, *rapid*, flexing movements in which the resiliency of the muscles in *recovery* from strain or distortion is critical.
Dynamic Flexibility Test: (Originally called Bend, Twist and Touch.) With his back to the wall and hands together, the subject bends forward, touches an " *X* " between his feet, straightens, twists to the left and touches an " *X* " behind him on the wall. He repeats the cycle, alternately twisting to the right and to the left, doing as many as possible in the time limit.

(iii) Explosive Strength Factor

The ability to expend a maximum of energy in one or a series of explosive acts. This factor is distinguished from other strength factors in requiring mobilization of *energy* for a burst of effort, rather than continuous strain, stress, or repeated exertion of muscles. The two tests chosen to represent this factor emphasize different specific activities.
Shuttle Run Test: Twenty yard distance, covered 5 times for 100 yard total.
Softball Throw Test: The subject throws a 12" softball, as far as possible without moving his feet.

(iv) Static Strength Factor

The maximum *force* which a subject can exert, for a brief period, where the force is exerted continuously up to this maximum. In contrast to other strength factors, this is the force which can be exerted against external objects (e.g., lifting heavy weights, pulling against a dynamometer), rather than in supporting or propelling the body's own weight.

FIGURE 1

POSSIBLE STRENGTH FACTORS HYPOTHESIZED IN THE EXPERIMENTAL TESTS

	Dynamic Strength Arms		Dynamic Strength		Endurance			Explosive Strength		Dynamic Strength	Static Strength	Explosive Strength	Arm Strength	Leg Strength
	Flex.	Ext.	Legs	Trunk	Dynamic	Static	Runs	Arms	Legs					
1. Leg Lifts (in 15 sec.)			X							X				
2. Push-ups (in 15 sec.)		X								X			X	
3. Reverse Sit-ups				X						X				
4. Deep Kneebends			X							X				X
5. Sit-ups				X						X				
6. Squat Thrusts			X							X				X
7. Pull Weights	X										X		X	
8. Hand Grip											X		X	
9. Push Weights – Arms		X									X		X	
10. Arm Pull – Dyna.										X	X		X	
11. Push Weights – Feet			X								X			X
12. Trunk Pull – Dyna.											X			
13. Rope Climb	X									X			X	
14. Dips (in 10 sec.)										X			X	
15. Vertical Jump									X			X		
16. Dips (to limit)		X			X					X			X	
17. Standing Broad Jump									X			X		
18. Leg Raiser				X						X				
19. 10 Yard Dash							X		X			X		
20. Bent Arm Hang	X					X							X	
21. 50 Yard Dash							X		X			X		
22. Chins (to limit)	X				X					X			X	
23. Shuttle Run							X		X					
24. Chins (in 20 sec.)	X									X			X	
25. Medic. Ball Put (stand.)								X				X	X	
26. Hold Half Sit-up				X		X				X				
27. Medic. Ball Put (sit.)								X				X	X	
28. Hold Half Push-up		X				X							X	
29. Softball Throw								X		X		X	X	
30. Push-ups (to limit)		X			X					X			X	

Possible Primary Factors — Possible General Factors

333

Hand Grip Test: The subject squeezes a Narragansett Company grip dynamometer, as hard as possible.

(v) Dynamic Strength Factor

The ability to exert muscular force *repeatedly* or continuously over time. It represents muscular-endurance and emphasizes the resistance of the muscles to fatigue. The common emphasis of tests, measuring this factor is on the *power* of the muscles to propel, support, or move the body repeatedly or to support it for prolonged periods.

Pull-Ups Test: The subject hangs from bar with palm facing his body, and does as many pull-ups as possible.

(vi) Trunk Strength Factor

This is a second, more limited, dynamic strength factor specific to the trunk muscles, particularly the abdominal muscles.

Leg Lifts Test: While flat on his back, the subject raises his legs to a vertical position and lowers them to the floor as many times as possible in the time limit.

(vii) Gross Body Equilibrium Factor

The ability of an individual to maintain his equilibrium, despite forces pulling him off balance, where he has to depend mainly on non-visual (e.g., vestibular and kinesthetic) cues. Although also measured by balance tests where the eyes are kept open, it is best measured by balance tests conducted with the eyes closed.

Balance " A " Test: Using his preferred foot and keeping his hands on his hips, the subject balances for as long as possible on a 3/4 inch wide rail.

(viii) Stamina Factor

The capacity to continue maximum effort, requiring prolonged exertion over time. This factor has the alternate name of " cardio-vascular endurance ".

600 Yard Run-Walk Test: The student attempts to cover a 600 yard distance in as short a time as possible.

3.4. The National Study

The next step in this program was to establish *standards* for evaluating the performance of *individual* boys and girls on the separate tests. Tests found to be most reliable and diagnostic of the different factors were assembled into " batteries " and administered to high school students throughout the country.

In all, 14 tests found to cover 9 basic factors were administered to more than 20,000 boys and girls, between the ages of 12 and 18, in 45 cities throughout the United States. (The list of cities and description of the cross-sections achieved is presented elsewhere) (Fleishman, 1964a). This phase produced the norms (percentile tables) for these tests, as well as developmental curves showing changes with age on the different physical fitness components for the 14 tests. Finally, 10 tests were recommended as the most efficient and reliable for measuring the 9 basic factors. These tests have been called the *Basic Fitness Tests*.

Table 1 presents the reliabilities and factor loadings for the tests in the battery.

Norms and developmental curves for these tests may be found elsewhere (Fleishman 1964a, 1964b). Additionally, a record keeping system, called the Performance Record (Fleishman, 1964c) was developed to provide fitness profiles, conversions of raw scores to percentiles, a " fitness index ", and the plotting of progress as a function of conditioning programs.

TABLE 1

RELIABILITIES AND FACTOR LOADINGS OF THE TESTS

Test	Primary Factor Measured	Relia-bility	Primary Factor Loading	Other Factor Loading
1. Extent Flexibility	Extent Flexibility	.00	.49	—
2. Dynamic Flexibility	Dynamic Flexibility	.92	.50	—
3. Shuttle Run	Explosive Strength	.85	.77	.39 (DS)
4. Softball Throw	Explosive Strength	.93	.66	.32 (SS)
5. Hand Grip	Static Strength	.91	.72	—
6. Pull-Ups	Dynamic Strength	.93	.81	—
7. Leg Lifts	Trunk Strength	.89	.47	.32 (DS)
8. Cable Jump	Gross Body Coordination	.70	.56	—
9. Balance A	Gross Body Equilibrium	.82	.72	—
10. 600 Yd. Run-Walk	Stamina (Cardio-Vascular Endurance)	.80	—	—

3.5. Summary of Findings and Implications

The fruits of this research program are of several sorts. First we have a better understanding of the structure of the physical fitness areas — the dimensions which best describe the variety of performances called for by the plethora of available physical fitness tests. It is seen that a relatively small number of such dimensions (or factors) account for these diverse performances. In this sense the program was scientifically useful in bringing additional order to this field and in simplifying our descriptions of what needs to be measured in this area.

These results confirm that " physical proficiency " is not a single general ability; rather physical proficiency can best be described in terms of a number of broad, relatively independent factors. The same individuals may be high on some factors and low on others. In these terms, the more factors an individual scores high on, the more " physically fit " he can be said to be. The results also allow more precise definition of each fitness factor than was possible before.

A second category of results includes the many specific facts discovered about the nature of physical proficiencies and their interrelationships. For example, we now better understand the role of muscular endurance in strength tests, the relations between capacities of flexor and extensor muscles and the primary abilities that account for running speed. Also confirmed is the distinction between two primary flexibility factors and the generality of static strength across different muscle groups.

The " developmental curves " derived from the research are additional results in this second category. These curves show the rate of " growth " of the different physical proficiencies from age to age (Fleishman, 1964a). It was found that the curves for girls differed in form from those for boys in showing more marked developmental stages. For the boys the shapes of most curves were similar, but there were different critical ages at which the curves levelled out, depending on the factor measured.

Especially illuminating were the detailed analyses of strength tasks. Any characterization of individual strength which ignores one or more of the four strength factors identified is incomplete.

Since several factors were found to extend across different muscle groups (e.g., limbs and trunk), this points up the importance of " central " factors in physical fitness in addition to those reflected in the specific muscle apparatus. Such central factors include central nervous system involvement, responses to kinesthetic feedback mechanisms, heart and circulatory system development, general energy level, etc.

A third category of results of this research relates to specific fitness *measurement principles* discovered. We now know that variations in test procedure produce given variations in the fitness factors measured and in the reliability of the measure. For example,

a) speeded administration (timed) of a Dynamic Strength test reduces its " purity " and brings in a second factor (Explosive Strength);

b) longer Shuttle Run tests are more reliable than shorter ones in use;

c) simple dynamometer tests are preferred (over weight lifting tests) as measures of Static Strength;

d) a Gross Body Equilibrium factor is best measured by one-foot, rail standing tests with the eyes closed;

e) a Leg Lifts test is more valid and reliable than Sit-ups for measuring Trunk Strength.

A fourth major kind of outcome was the specification of the most efficient, practical and reliable tests for measuring each factor and their assembly into a battery of *Basic Fitness Tests*. This battery, which will undoubtedly be further improved by additional research, is based on our present state of research knowledge. A major phase of this work was the development of normative standards for the tests on a much larger national sample than has been possible heretofore. Simplified interpretative tables were provided for ages 12 through 18. Improved methods of evaluating and interpreting individual performances were developed, using modern measurement principles. These included forms for profile analysis, computation of a simplified Fitness Index and evaluation of the rate of progress.

There are, of course, still many unanswered questions. Some of the most intriguing questions concern the nature of " coordination " and " agility " . A concerted effort needs to be made to see if these are usefully considered " separate " abilities or if we can account for such performances in terms of the factors already identified. Additional studies would involve a greater variety of " coordinated " performances than it has been possible to include so far. The use of our battery of factor tests, in the same study with these complex tests, should allow us to specify how much of the variance in such performances we still need to explain. At present, a Multilimb Coordination factor appears distinct from any Gross Body Coordination factor. The former is involved in perceptual-motor tasks involving simultaneous use of multiple controls (feet-hand, two-hand, two-feet), where the subject is typically seated. The latter appears to require movement of the entire body.

There is a need to use these factor tests to predict more complex skilled performances. This would tell us what portion of such performances are specific to the individual skills and how much is relatable to the physical fitness factors identified in our present program. There is also the practical question of how valid our factor tests are in predicting performance in complex jobs involving physical skills.

We also need to know more about the trainability of these component abilities and the degree of transfer of training across tasks representing the same factor. We would expect high transfer between tasks on the same factor and low transfer between factors. A more interesting question is the amount of transfer of training from these skill components to more complex skilled performances.

3.6. Toward a Concept of Fitness

Before closing this section, it may be well to return to an examination of the concept of " physical fitness " . Throughout we have used the term to refer to the functional capacity of individuals to perform certain kinds of tasks requiring muscular activity. This is clearly an operational definition which is useful. Within the scope of this definition our work has specified the dimensions of such performances which need to be measured and has indicated diagnostic tests for this measurement. We re-emphasize this specific definition of physical fitness since the term is often used uncritically, in a broader sense, as equivalent to physical health.

It is obviously incorrect to equate fitness in the " performance " sense with general health. The discovery of the precise relations between organic and functional meaning, should be the objective of concerted research efforts. Such research, should lead to a broader concept of physical fitness, its components, and their relationships.

4. IMPLICATIONS FOR MILITARY CONTEXTS

The factors described provide a way of looking at jobs requiring physical performances in a more analytic way; they provide a way of describing such jobs.

The results suggest possibilities for screening and differential classification. There has been only limited research on this with other physical performance measures. There is need for more validity data.

(i) *Fitness for Combat*. The Army has a Physical Combat Proficiency Test administered annually or semi-annually. These include time to run one mile, crawling time, time to run, jump, change direction and grenade accuracy. This battery has not been validated, but has been correlated with our Basic Fitness Tests. The correlations are all in the expected directions, but the study showed the current Army test to be not as complete as the Basic Fitness Tests in covering the physical proficiency factors.

The Marine Corps has a Physical Readiness Test (Rope Climb, Creeping and Crawling, Fireman's Carry, Step Test, 3 Mile Run and Walk). However, they are changing to a " Physical Fitness Test ", which includes pull-ups, leg raises, squat thrust, 3 mile run and broad jump. No standards have yet been established and it is not clear how these particular tests were chosen.

Before a recruit can leave his Basic Training Centre he must pass the Physical Readiness Test. After Basic Training he is tested four times a year during his career up to age 40. This is entered in his record; if he fails he is to take *remedial* programs. Each Command differs in how this is administered; however, it appears that such tests are not used in assignment.

Some selected schools have other adaptations of these tests; e.g., Airborne Troops have to exceed certain minimums. In general, however, the measures used are not based on research.

(ii) The results of our research suggest *possible applications for marginal people*, where there is interest in who may be assigned to jobs with more physical than mental demands.

Another use is in the evaluation of training programs and conditioning programs, where one needs to identify weaknesses of individuals and of programs.

Still another application is in research on factors affecting human performance. These tests have been used in studies in the laboratory and in the field in evaluating a variety of such effects. For example, *Figure 2* shows one study carried out at the American Institutes for Research on the effects of a given dosage of a drug on human performance (Elkin, Fleishman, *et. al.*, 1965). The Figure compares the gross effects, the time to reach maximum effect and the period required to return to base line levels for several skills. The differential effects on different component abilities, including physical proficiencies, can be seen. Some abilities are more affected than others. A further phase of this work is to include the testing of such effects on complex tests. The question is whether our laboratory results using component ability measures, could have predicted drug effects on the complex tasks.

Measures of these abilities as well as of the other psychomotor abilities described are being used in a variety of studies of the effects of different environment (e.g., high altitude), diets and stressors on performance.

Finally, let me simply re-emphasize (see Fleishman, 1967) that much more work is needed in developing a more analytical framework about human skills which will increase our generalizations about human capabilities and limitations. Such information should also increase the effectiveness with which we utilize our manpower resources.

Fig. 2   COMPARATIVE TIME HISTORIES OF EFFECTS OF A DRUG ON REPRESENTATIVE PERFORMANCE TESTS

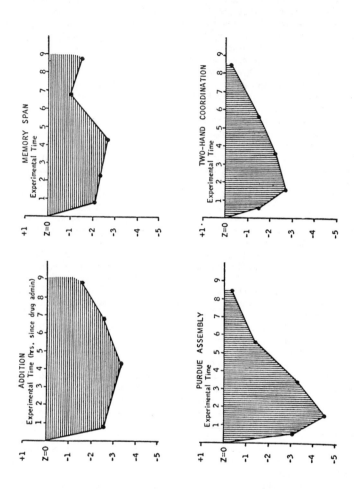

Fig. 2 (Continued)

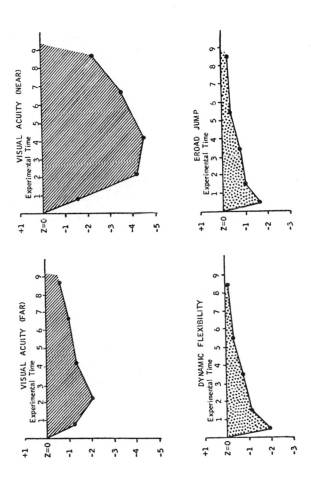

REFERENCES

Alluisi, E.A. and Thurmond, J.B. (1965) Behavioural effects of infectious diseases: Annual Progress Report. University of Louisville, *Perf. Res. Lab. Rep.*, No. PR-65-3.

Elkin, C.H., Fleishman, E.A., *et al* (1965-Oct.) *Effects of Drugs on Human Performance. Research concepts, Task development and Preliminary studies.* A.I.R., Washington Office.

Fleishman, E.A. (1953a) A factor analysis of intra-task performance on two psychomotor tests. *Psychometrika*, 1953, *18*, No. 1.

Fleishman, E.A. (1953b) Testing for psychomotor abilities by means of apparatus tests. *Psychol. Bull.*, 1953, *50*, 241-262.

Fleishman, E.A. (1954) Dimensional analysis of psychomotor abilities. *J. exp. Psychol.*, 1954, *48*, 437-454.

Fleishman, E.A. (1956) Psychomotor selection tests: research and application in the United States Air Force. *Personnel Psychol.*, 1956, *9*, 449-467.

Fleishman, E.A. (1957a) A comparative study of aptitude patterns in unskilled and skilled psychomotor performances. *J. appl. Psychol.*, 1957, *41*, 263-272.

Fleishman, E.A. (1957b) Factor structure in relation to task difficulty in psychomotor performance. *Educ. psychol. Measmt.*, 1957, *17*, 522-532.

Fleishman, E.A. (1958a) An analysis of positioning movements and static reactions. *J. exp. Psychol.*, 1958, *55*, 13-24.

Fleishman, E.A. (1958b) Dimensional analysis of movement reactions. *J. exp. Psychol.*, 1958, *55*, 438-453.

Fleishman, E.A. (1964a) *The Structure and Measurement of Physical Fitness.* Englewood Cliffs, N.J.: Prentice-Hall, 1964.

Fleishman, E.A. (1964b) *Examiner's Manual for the Basic Fitness Tests.* Englewood Cliff, N.J.: Prentice-Hall, 1964.

Fleishman, E.A. (1964c) *Performance Record for the Basic Fitness Tests.* Englewood Cliffs, N.J.: Prentice-Hall, 1964.

Fleishman, E.A. The Basic Fitness Tests. (1966) *Journal of the International University Sports Federation*, F.S.V.V. Bulletin 8E Series, No. 2, July, 1966, pp 125-130.

Fleishman, E.A. (1967) Development of a behaviour taxonomy for describing human tasks: a correlational-experimental approach. *J. appl. Psychol.*, 1967, *51*, 1-10.

Fleishman, E.A. and Ellison, G.D. (1962) A factor analysis of fine manipulative performance. *J. appl. Psychol.*, 1962, *46*, 96-105.

Fleishman, E.A. and Fruchter, B. (1960) Factor structure and predictability of successive stages of learning Morse code. *J. appl. Psychol.*, 1960, *44*, 97-101.

Fleishman, E.A. and Hempel, W.E., Jr. (1954) Changes in factor structure of a complex psychomotor test as a function of practice. *Psychometrika*, 1954, *18*, 239-252.

Fleishman, E.A. and Hempel, W.R., Jr. (1955) The relation between abilities and improvement with practice in a visual discrimination reaction task. *J. exp. Psychol.*, 1955, *49*, 301-312.

Fleishman, E.A. and Hempel, W.E., Jr. (1956) Factorial analysis of complex psychomotor performance and related skills, *J. appl. Psychol.*, 1956, *40*, 96-104.

Gagné, R.M. (1964) *Conditions of Learning.* New York: Holt, Rinehart and Winston, 1964.

Gagné, R.M. and Fleishman, E.A. (1959) *Psychology and Human Performance: An Introduction to Psychology.* New York: Holt, Rinehart and Winston, 1959.

Hempel, W.E., Jr. and Fleishman, E.A. (1955) A factor analysis of physical proficiency and manipulative skill. *J. appl. Psychol.*, 1955, *39*, 12-16.

Miller, R.B. (1965) Task analysis and task taxonomy: inventive approach. Contribution to symposium on " Task Taxonomy and its Implication for Military Requirements ". APA Convention, 1965.

Parker, J.F. and Fleishman, E.A. (1960) Ability factors and component performance measures as predictors of complex tracking behaviour. *Psychol. Monogr.*, 1960, *74*, No. 16 (Whole No. 503).

Task Analysis for Training

J. ANNETT
K.D. DUNCAN
DEPARTMENT OF PSYCHOLOGY
UNIVERSITY OF HULL

I. TASK ORIENTED TRAINING

Recent years have seen an increasing emphasis on the need for statements of instructional objectives derived from job performance and in a sufficiently operational language to generate test situations whereby instruction can be evaluated, (e.g. Wallis 1966). However, it is one thing to advocate training based on task analysis, but quite another to indicate a general method of analyzing tasks for this purpose – as the extent of the literature on task analysis testifies. If there is a weak link in the technology of training it is surely here.

2. HIERARCHICAL DESCRIPTION OF TASKS

A major difficulty, and one of the first to be encountered, is that a complete description of the execution of a task will *include* the information required for training, but will usually include much else as well. What is needed is some explicit rule or guide as to what to record for training purposes and at what level of description to operate. The rule which we would propose is as follows. Begin with the most gross description of performance and ask two questions:

(1) what is the estimated probability, *without* training, of inadequate performance and

(2) what would be the estimated *cost* to the system of inadequate performance? When these two values, or more precisely their product, is unacceptable to the system, then the original statement of performance is re-described in more detail.

Several subordinate "units" of performance may thus be described, and again the decision as to how far to pursue the description to still lower levels of sub units is governed by the foregoing rule. The analysis ceases, either when the values specified in the rule are acceptable to the system, or when training requirements for adequate performance are clear.

Thus, for a given task the analysis may cease at a number of different levels for different sections or sub units of the task and there is complete flexibility with regard to the degree of detail employed. Description, then, is not necessarily at the microscopic level (e.g. sensorimotor process chart) though on occasion it might be when so required by the rule. This approach is not unlike that advocated by Gagné (1962 a), for programming conceptual learning except that (1) it recognizes that *any level of probability* of successful performance may sometimes be acceptable, whereas Gagné's approach would perhaps require near certainty, and (2) it recognizes the cost factor in practical training situations.

A task is thus regarded as a hierarchy of operations and sub-operations. Any operation in the hierarchy will have an identifiable input or cue, an output or response, and possibly response feedback – though whether these are separately described and in

what detail will be determined by application of the same rule, i.e. probability that
without training, cues will be received, responses correctly executed and the cost to
the system if they are not.

The estimation of the two values in the decision rule should obviously be as exact
as possible but the difficulty of estimating them is acknowledged. We have summarized
elsewhere methods and concepts already in the literature which may be utilized for this
purpose (Annett and Duncan, 1967).

3. THE ANALYSIS OF TASKS

3.1. Part-Task Training

Having isolated in appropriate detail, those features or components of the task
which constitute the training problem, we would not, however, have specified a training
course. It is worth asking why, when the performance of the experienced man has been
described, one would not simply get the novice to attempt it, on the view that practice
makes perfect? The answer to this question has traditionally been that there is a danger
that, by practising the whole task, the novice will make a great many errors and that
these too may be perfected by practice. Hence part-task training has been advocated for
this reason and for motivational reasons as well (King 1964, Seymour 1966), i.e. it can
be effectively combined with goal setting and maintenance of positive "attainment
discrepancy " (Lewin, Dembo, Festinger and Sears 1944).

3.2. Task Taxonomies

In the last decade a further argument for part-task training has been developed,
namely, that a task may consist of components which should be learned separately because
their optimum learning conditions differ. It has been argued that there exists a limited
number of types or categories of behaviour requiring different learning conditions and
that determining which are present in a given task is the real business of task analysis.
Unfortunately there has been a spectacular number of different behaviour classification
schemes or "taxonomies".[1]

This proliferation of behaviour classification schemes has given rise to some concern
as to what criteria should be met by a taxonomy worthy of the name. That the categories
of such a taxonomy should have demonstrably different optimum learning conditions is
clearly the major criterion. Less important, though desirable, are the two main
systematic criteria which should be met by any taxonomy namely, that the categories
should be *mutually exclusive* and *exhaustive*.

An explicit attempt to meet the major criterion is the "taxonomy of learning " by
Stolurow (1964). Two of the dimensions in Stolurow's taxonomy do indeed rest on interactions with learning conditions as demonstrated in a survey of laboratory studies.
These are (1) the "*variant-invariant sequence*" dimension which is justified by the
experimental evidence that massed practice favours learning serial tasks but not paired
associates: and (2) the "*meaningfulness*" dimension which rests on the classical
evidence that "meaningful " material is best learned by the *whole method*. However the
argument is not entirely consistent in that these dimensions are also justified on the
grounds that they affect task *difficulty*, indeed, this appears to be the only argument
for Stolurow's third main dimension of stimulus and response "*limits*". (Variations in
task difficulty are important features to be identified but, as such, only indicate the
need for more or less practice – not for different *conditions* of practice).

---

[1] Miller 1953 a, b, and c, 1954 a and b, 1956 a, b and c, 1960, 1962 a and b, 1966, Bloom 1956,
Cotterman 1959, Gagné & Bolles 1959, Jones & Fairman 1960, Lumsdaine 1960, Snyder 1960,
Demaree 1961, Parker & Downes 1961, Stolurow 1961 and 1964, Willis 1961, Fitts 1962 and 1964,
Gagné 1962 b, 1965 a and b, Gilbert 1962, Kidd 1962, Miller 1963, Folley 1964 a and b, Melton
1964, Underwood 1964, Wickens 1964, Crossman 1965, Folley & Chenzoff 1965, Mechner 1965.

Prominent in the task analysis literature are the writings of R.B. Miller who, over the years, has proposed several slightly varying schemes for codefying the processes which may intervene between environmental events and the responses of skilled men, e.g. scanning, search, and detection of cues; identification of cues; short and long term retention of task information; interpretation, decision making and problem solving.

Miller avowedly adopts utility over other criteria for his categories. He is not concerned if the training implications are the same for more than one category provided they are *identified*. Thus, the valuable notion of *time sharing* is one with a training implication which cuts across his categories. Only procedure following and "automatized" components of tasks will not suffer interference when time shared; and he argues, probably rightly, that task components which do suffer, e.g. scanning and searching, short term recall and decision making should all be proceduralized when time shared with other activities. Again, much of Miller's discussion of the training implications of his categories amounts to illustrating the difficulties rather than pointing to category-specific learning conditions. (In passing we would note that unlike other writers in this field, Miller's points are extensively exemplified: the impression, again unlike that gained from other writers, is that here is a man who has actually carried out task analyses.) Miller's system, as he has annotated it, is more a useful aide-memoire, than one in which training recommendations distinguish sharply or systematically between behaviour categories, e.g. the main point of his discussion of "search for job relevant cues" and "short term recall" (1962 a) is in both cases simply to *practise* on those materials and in those situations peculiar to the job in question.

Perhaps the most ambitious attempt to meet the major criterion for a task taxonomy is the hierarchical scheme proposed by Gagné (1965 a & b). Doubtless it will be the subject of validation studies in the near future, but perhaps we may anticipate these with a criticism based on our own observation of industrial tasks. First of all we accept that the organized behaviour which we describe as "experienced", "expert", or "skilled" is probably a hierarchy of sub-routines in something like the sense used by Miller, Galanter and Pribram (1960) and Fitts (1964) elsewhere. We doubt however whether the organization of cues and responses called *chains* (i.e. invariant order of cue-response units) and the organization of cues and responses called class *concepts* or *generalization* (i.e. the same response to a *set* of cues) will necessarily be found in that order in the structure of any and every task – i.e. Gagné's fourth and fifth levels (Gagné 1965 a). Indeed we have observed a task in which the relative positions of these two categories was the reverse of that given by Gagné (1965 a & b). The task in question was "starting-up" a distillation column, primarily following a procedure in which order is important, i.e. a chain. The subordinate steps in this chain involve identifying many "by-pass" and "isolating" valves, plant components whose appearance and position in the configuration of feed lines vary widely, but whose *function* is the same. Thus, they constitute a set of cues requiring the same response i.e. a *concept* or *generalization*.

We would therefore suggest that the value of the hierarchical notion would be considerably extended if the superordinate/subordinate relations between the categories, i.e. chains, multiple discrimination, concepts etc., were *not* fixed – the important notion to retain being that these will be in *a* hierarchy, but their relative positions will vary from task to task. Thus the major value of the hierarchical scheme, i.e. the indication of sequencing of instruction, may be retained.

4. EVALUATION OF TASK ANALYSIS

4.1. A Provisional Approach

Our position, then, is to accept flexibility in the hierarchical ordering of behaviour categories, and to include tentatively any category i.e. distinctive organizations or combinations of cue-response units, if there is evidence of associated specific optimum learning conditions, or if empirically testable propositions about such conditions have been or can be made, e.g. recent writings about "multiple discriminations ", "chains " and "generalizations" establish these as worthwhile provisional categories. The case for "chains " may serve to illustrate this increasing concern for category-specific learning conditions.

4.2. Chains

Gilbert's recommendation to learn chains retrogressively is well known though not well supported by experimental evidence, e.g. whilst supporting evidence was found in one study, (Slack 1964), two others have found a progressive condition as good or better, (Johnson and Senter 1965, Cox and Boren 1965).

In the chemical industry (as in the armed forces) procedures may be very lengthy, e.g. 30–50 steps in starting-up a distillation column is not unusual. Whether procedures of this length are learned, or their execution is supported by a job aid, check list, etc., some fragmentation into manageable units seems inevitable. Gilbert's suggestion is the "operant span " i.e. "all the performance a student could carry out if he were following a set of instructions ". If a procedural guide is to be used, the number of steps grouped together as a unit, should ideally be well within short term memory capacity: indeed one training research worker (Whitmore 1963), would accept G.A. Miller's "magic number 7 plus or minus 2 " as a rule of thumb (Miller 1956).

Our own approach has been influenced by the series of studies of long procedural tasks by Sheffield and his associates (Sheffield 1961, Sheffield and Maccoby 1961). Rather than form groups of a *fixed number* of steps, we have looked for groups of steps which " go together " i.e. which the experienced worker groups under a common name. Thus, "heat the still " and "begin reflux" are names given to groups of steps by the experienced stillman. For him the lengthy procedure of starting-up a distillation column consists of ten or so such "headings " with their associated sub-routines. It turns out that these headings would be very similar for starting-up any distillation column, i.e. they form a "perceptual blueprint " of some generality, (Sheffield 1961).

Some procedures however may have no inherent organization and it may thus be desirable to impose one. The potential usefulness of mnemonics for this purpose has lacked systematic study by psychologists, possibly because the stock-in-trade of popular texts on memorizing lacks scientific respectability. Nevertheless an objective appraisal of some popularized memorizing systems is probably overdue, (Senter 1965).

4.3. Validity

Quite the most striking feature of the literature on task analysis is the lack of reported applications of the numerous schemes to the design of real training courses. Surely what is now needed to further training technology is rigorous evaluation, rather than the invention of further taxonomies in the manner of the early personality typologists. We would argue that a valid task analytic scheme will only be built up by designing training courses which test the value of providing the learning conditions ascribed to particular categories, or which attempt to determine such conditions. In particular, experimental training courses need to be set up to test the value of analyzing tasks into hierarchies of operations. One such test would rest on the effects of ignoring or reversing the sequencing of training implied by different levels revealed in the hierarchical analysis. Another test would be the *diagnostic* value of hierarchical analysis, i.e. the extent to which locating and correcting lack of mastery of sub-operations at various levels facilitates overall mastery of the task.

A method which, in the hands of any analyst, will derive from a given job an identical specification of the training course needed, is not going to be developed overnight. The beginnings of such a method lie in the formulation and testing of category-specific training techniques of the kind we have discussed for chains. The urgent need is to see whether these categories stand up to the test of producing uniquely defined training procedures in real situations.

4.4. Reliability

Good agreement between independent analysts specifying training for the same job is the issue on which considerations of validity and reliability meet. To some extent the careful definition of behaviour categories (Cotterman, 1959, Gagné 1965 a & b), should help to reduce variations from analyst to analyst. Though it is for serious consideration whether the language used in such definitions will make them unambiguous to, say, an industrial or military training officer. If, in the event, behaviour categories cannot be defined in such a way that no more psychological judgement is needed than might be acquired in a short course, then thorough-going task analysis is going to remain for ever the province of the occupational psychologist.

Of the many writers on task analysis only Stolurow (1964), as far as we are aware, has made an attempt, to assess the reliability of his scheme. Stolurow had 8 psychologists, all distinguished in the training research field, analyze independently descriptions of tasks taken from the " method " sections of journal articles. Their agreement was less than perfect! More studies of this kind, using descriptions of industrial tasks are badly needed, since no method however valid on logical grounds or in the light of research, will be *empirically* valid unless it is reliable.

5. CONCLUSION

In conclusion, we may ask what, in general terms, does task analysis contribute to the economic and efficient utilization of manpower? Its primary contribution, clearly, will be training courses which, because they are job-oriented, produce improved performance on the job. We would also expect rigorous application of task analysis to result in shorter formal training courses (even occasionally in their abolition – Stainer 1967). This would follow, on the one hand from basing training content on observed job performance rather than on a priori syllabus and, on the other hand, from the simplifying or proceduralizing of the complex decision components of tasks which analysis may frequently make possible (Shriver, Fink and Trexler 1964, Wason and Jones 1965, Horabin, Gane and Lewis 1966). There is also the fascinating possibility that the learning of a task is usually slow only because several levels of its hierarchy of sub-operations are typically being trained at the same time – a procedure which must be inefficient if optimum learning conditions differ between levels and if mastery at each level depends on *prior* mastery at subordinate levels. It will hardly be necessary to remind this audience of the notorious cost of formal training courses, not least in manpower which, in the special case of the armed services, will often include instructional personnel whose primary capability and experience is operational.

This work was supported by a research grant from the Ministry of Labour Training Department.

REFERENCES

Annett, J., & Duncan, K.D., (1967). Task analysis techniques – a critique. *B.B.C. Working Conference on Learning Resources in Industrial and Commercial Education.* University of Aston in Birmingham, July 1967.

Bloom, B.S., (Ed.) (1956). *Taxonomy of Educational Objectives.* New York: Longmans, Green.

Cotterman, T.E., (1959). *Task classification: an approach to partially ordering information on human learning.* Dayton, Ohio: Wright Air Development Centre. WADC TN 58-374.

Cox, J.A., & Boren, L.M., (1965). A study of backward chaining. *J. Educ. Psychol.* 56, 270-274.

Crossman, E.R.F.W., (1965). *Taxonomy of Automation: State of Arts and Prospects.* Unpublished O.E.C.D. paper.

Demaree, R.C., (1961). *Development of training equipment planning information.* Lackland Air Force Base, Texas: Aeronautical Systems Division. ASD-TR-61-533.

Fitts, P.M., (1962). Factors in Complex Skill Training. *Training Research and Education,* edited by R. Glaser. New York: Wiley.

Fitts, P.M., (1964). Perceptual motor skills learning. *Categories of Human Learning,* edited by A.W. Melton, New York: Academic Press.

Folley J.D., (1964 a). *Development of an improved method of task analysis and beginnings of a theory of training.* New York: U.S. Naval Training Device Centre. NAVTRADEVCEN 1218-1.

Folley, J.D., (1964 b). *Guidelines for task analysis.* New York: U.S. Naval Training Device Centre. NAVTRADEVCEN 1218-2.

Folley, J.D., & Chenzoff, A.P., (1965). *Guidelines for Training Situation Analysis.* New York: U.S. Naval Training Device Centre. NAVTRADEVCEN 1218-4.

Gagné, R.M., (1962 a). The acquisition of knowledge. *Psychol. Review, 69,* 355-365.

Gagné, R.M., (1962 b). Human Functions in Systems. *Psychological Principles in System Development,* edited by R.M. Gagné. New York: Holt, Rinehart and Winston.

Gagné, R.M., (1965 a). The analysis of instructional objectives for the design of instruction. *Teaching Machines and Programmed Learning II,* edited by R. Glaser. Washington. National Education Association.

Gagné, R.M., (1965 b). *The Conditions of Learning.* New York: Holt, Rinehart and Winston.

Gagné, R.M., & Bolles, R.C., (1959). A review of factors in learning efficiency. *Automatic Teaching: The State of the Art.* edited by E. Galanter, New York: Wiley.

Gilbert, R.F., (1962). Mathetics: the technology of education. *J. Mathetics,* 1, 7-74.

Horabin, I.S., Gane, C.P., & Lewis, B.N., (1966). *Algorithms and the Prevention of Instruction.* Cambridge: Cambridge Consultants (Training) Ltd.

Johnson, K.A., & Senter, R.J., (1965). *A comparison of forward and backward chaining techniques for the teaching of verbal sequential tasks.* Wright-Patterson Air Force Base, Ohio: AMRL-TR-65-203.

Jones, E.M., & Fairman, J.B., (1960). Identification and analysis of human performance requirements. *Human Factors Methods for System Design,* edited by J.D. Folley. Pittsburgh: American Institute for Research.

Kidd, J.S., (1962). Human Tasks and Equipment Design. *Psychological Principles in System Development* edited by R.M. Gagné. New York: Holt, Rinehart and Winston.

King, S.D.M., (1964). *Training within the organization.* London: Tavistock Publications.

Lewin, K., Dembo, T., Festinger, L., & Sears, P.S., (1944). Level of Aspiration. *Personality and the Behaviour Disorders,* edited by J. McV. Hunt. New York: Ronald.

Lumsdaine, A.A., (1960). Design of training aids and devices. *Human factors methods for system design,* edited by J.D. Folley, Pittsburgh: American Institute for Research.

Mechner, F., (1965). Science Education and Behaviour Technology. *Teaching Machines and Programmed Learning II,* Edited by R. Glaser, Washington: National Education Association.

Melton, A.W., (1964). The Taxonomy of Human Learning: Overview. *Categories of Human Learning,* edited by A.W. Melton. New York: Academic Press.

Miller, E.E., (1963). *A classification of learning tasks in conventional language.* Dayton, Ohio: Wright Air Development Centre. AMRL-TDR-63-74.

Miller, G.A., Galanter, E., & Pribram, K.H., (1960). *Plans and the Structure of Behaviour.* New York: Holt.

Miller, G.A., (1956). The magical number seven, plus or minus two. *Psychol. Review.* 63, 81-97.

Miller, R.B., (1953 a). *A Method for Determining Human Engineering Design Requirements for Training Equipment.* Dayton, Ohio: Wright Air Development Centre. WADC TR 53-135.

Miller, R.B., (1953 b). *A Method for Man-Machine Task Analysis.* Dayton, Ohio: Wright Air Development Centre. WADC TR 53-137.

Miller, R.B., (1953 c). *Hand Book on Training and Training Equipment Design.* Dayton, Ohio: Wright Air Development Centre. WADC TR 53-136.

Miller, R.B., (1954 a). *Suggestions for Short Cuts in Task Analysis Procedures.* Pittsburg: American Institute for Research. AIR-A77-54-SR-42.

Miller, R.B., (1954 b). *Psychological Considerations in the Design of Training Equipment.* Dayton, Ohio: Wright Air Development Centre. WADC TR 54-563.

Miller, R.B., (1956 a). *A Suggested Guide to Position-Task Description.* Lowry Air Force Base, Colorado: Air Research and Development Command. ASPRL TM 56-6.

Miller, R.B., (1956 b). *A Suggested Guide to Position Structure.* Lowry Air Force Base, Colorado: Air Research and Development Command. ML TM 56-13.

Miller, R.B., (1956 c). *A Suggested Guide to Functional Characteristics of Training and Training Equipment.* Lowry Air Force Base, Colorado: Air Research and Development Command, ML TM 56-14.

Miller, R.B., (1960). *Task and Part-Task Trainers and Training.* Dayton, Ohio: Wright Air Development Centre. WADC TR 604-469.

Miller, R.B., (1962 a). Task Description and Analysis. *Psychological Principles in System Development,* edited by R.M. Gagné. New York: Holt, Rinehart and Winston.

Miller, R.B., (1962 b). Analysis and Specification of Behaviour for Training. *Training Research and Education,* edited by R. Glaser. New York: Wiley.

Miller, R.B., (1966). *Task Taxonomy: Science or Technology.* Conference on the human operator in complex systems. University of Aston: 1966.

Parker, J.F., & Downes, J.E., (1961). *Selection of training media.* Lackland Air Force Base, Texas: Aeronautical Systems Division. ASD-TR-61-473.

Senter, R.J., (1965). *Review of mnemonics and mnemonotechnics for improved memory.* Wright-Patterson Air Force Base, Ohio: AMRL-TR-65-180.

Seymour, W.D., (1966). *Industrial Skills*. London: Pitman.

Sheffield, F.D., (1961). Theoretical considerations in the learning of complex sequential tasks from demonstration and practice. *Student Response in Programmed Instruction*, edited by A.A. Lumsdaine. Washington: National Research Council.

Sheffield, F.D. & Maccoby, N., (1961). Summary and interpretation of research on organizational principles in constructing filmed demonstrations. *Student Response in Programmed Instruction*, edited by A.A. Lumsdaine. Washington: National Research Council.

Shriver, E.L., Fink, C.D., & Trexler, R.C., (1964). *Forecast systems analysis and training methods for electronics maintenance training*. Alexandria, Virginia: Human Resources Research Office. Res. Rep. 13.

Slack, C.W., (1964). *Lesson writing for teaching verbal chains*. Chicago: T.O.R. Education, Inc.

Snyder, M.B., (1960). Methods of Recording and Reporting Task Analysis Information. *Use of Task Analysis in Deriving Training and Training Equipment Requirements*. Dayton, Ohio: Wright Air Development Division. WADD-TR-60-593.

Stainer, F.W., (1967). Task analysis – a case study. *Programmed Learning and Educational Technology*, 4, 52-55.

Stolurow, L.M., (1961). *Teaching by Machine*. Washington: U.S. Government Printing Office.

Stolurow, L.M., (1964). *A taxonomy of learning task characteristics*. Dayton, Ohio: Wright Air Development Centre. AMRL-TDR-64-2.

Underwood, B.J., (1964). The Representativeness of Rote Verbal Learning. *Categories of Human Learning*, edited by A.W. Melton. New York: Academic Press.

Wallis, D., (1965). The technology of military training. *Manpower Planning* (proceedings of NATO Conference on Operational and Personnel Research, Brussels, 1965). London: English Universities Press.

Wason, P.C., & Jones, S., (1965). *The Logical Tree Project*. London: Department of Psychology, University College.

Whitmore, P.G., (1963). *Studies of Fixed Procedures Training*. Alexandria, Virginia: Human Resources Research Office.

Wickens, D.D., (1964). The Centrality of Verbal Learning. *Categories of Human Learning*, edited by A.W. Melton. New York: Academic Press.

Willis, M.P., (1961). *Deriving training device implications from learning theory principles*. New York: U.S. Naval Training Device Centre. NAVTRADEVCEN 784-1.

347

Studying the Cost-Effectiveness of Training

K.W. TILLEY

R.A.F. TECHNICAL TRAINING COMMAND

I. INTRODUCTION

Systems analysis and cost/effectiveness studies have come to play an increasingly important part in military decisions about such matters as weapon development and force composition. They have figured less prominently in discussions about training policy. I have been asked to talk about the relevance and limitations of cost/effectiveness studies for training and to discuss some of the problems one meets in making use of the technique. Before I get into my main brief, however, perhaps I should just mention the distinction which is usefully made between systems analysis and cost/effectiveness analysis.

Quade (1) argues that systems analysis characteristically attempts to look at all aspects of a problem and to look at the problem as a whole. It involves a systematic examination of objectives and acceptable criteria for measuring their realization; a comparison of the effectiveness, costs and risks of different ways of achieving the objectives, and an attempt to develop new methods if those examined are found wanting. In other words systems analysis attempts to tackle the problem of defining what ought to be done and not simply the best way of doing it. Cost/effectiveness analysis is more restricted in what it sets out to achieve. It is most useful in examining alternative ways of achieving some specified objective or objectives, rather than in comparing the value of different objectives.

There are many instances where the real difficulty in framing policy is less a matter of deciding between alternative ways of achieving objectives than in deciding what the objectives ought to be and in agreeing on ways to measure whether or not they have been achieved. The current debate about 'comprehensive' education illustrates this difficulty. Durkheim (2) defined education as " a process of systematic socialization of the younger generation ". Some accept this emphasis on moulding the values of young people and encouraging their social participation. Others attach more importance to raising standards of academic attainment and skill. It is obviously extremely difficult to decide what gains in achieving one of these objectives could be said to compensate for losses incurred in achieving the other, because basically the two objectives are not commensurable. This is not to say however, that there is nothing at all to be done. It is at least feasible to choose relevant criteria and then to draw up a balance sheet showing what the achievements of alternative educational systems really are. This will not necessarily resolve the dilemma, although conceivably it might, but it will clarify the issues involved and structure discussion of the problem. Far from removing the need for judgement it provides a framework in which judgement can be exercised more precisely. It is from this point of view that I wish to consider the contribution which cost/effectiveness analysis has to make to improvements in training.

I would like first of all to outline the various steps one has to go through in attempting to analyze the cost/effectiveness of training and then go on to try to give an example of its application.

2. THE ELEMENTS OF COST/EFFECTIVENESS ANALYSIS

Cost/effectiveness analysis normally goes through three distinguishable although overlapping stages. The first is concerned with formulating the problem and setting limits to the extent of the enquiry. The second stage is concerned with identifying alternative methods for dealing with the problem and collecting information about them. The third stage deals with the evaluation of the selected alternatives. The emphasis in any particular study is likely to be more on one of these stages than others. It is also true that although the stages are shown as sequential, in practice there is likely to be quite a bit of looping back as the study progresses. For example, attempts to derive cost estimates will often reveal the need for additional information and may indicate the need to reconsider alternatives. In most cases however, analysis will involve five basic steps. These are:

(i) Defining the objective or objectives.

(ii) Measuring the extent to which objectives are realized by alternative methods.

(iii) Estimating and comparing costs.

(iv) Developing a model of the relationships between cost and effectiveness variables.

(v) Selecting a criterion for choosing between alternatives.

Let me try to illustrate some of the issues involved in analyzing training in this way.

2.1. Defining Training Objectives

Measuring the effectiveness of training presupposes that we have a clear and unambiguous statement of its objectives. Without such a statement a critical appraisal of training methods is virtually impossible. The interest which is currently being shown in developing taxonomies of educational and training objectives is testimony to the need.

Bloom (3) has attempted to produce a hierarchy of educational objectives. He distinguishes six categories:

(i) Knowledge: i.e. remembering facts, terms and principles in the form in which they were learned.

(ii) Comprehension: i.e. translating information into some other symbolic form without relating it to other material.

(iii) Application: i.e. selecting appropriate concepts and principles to solve novel problems.

(iv) Analysis: i.e. breaking down material into its constituent parts, detecting the relationships between parts and the way in which they are organized.

(v) Synthesis: i.e. combining the elements of a communication with new material to produce a new structure.

(vi) Evaluation: i.e. judging the value of material for some specified purpose.

This attempt to provide an operational definition of the various categories, whilst not the complete answer, has important implications for testing. It at least indicates the sort of behaviour which would be acceptable as evidence of competency at the different levels.

Another important contribution is Gagné's work on task taxonomy (4). Here again the attempt is to describe complex behaviour in terms of its constituent stimulus-response elements, and to indicate the training conditions necessary for the acquisition of various categories of behaviour. As other speakers will be dealing with this whole subject in some detail there is little need for me to elaborate. I would only say that all too frequently objectives are still described in such terms as "must have a thorough understanding of _____", "must be familiar with _____".

2.2. Measuring the Effectiveness of Training

Partly because of the difficulty of specifying what jobs students may eventually be required to tackle, educational objectives tend to emphasize the ability of students to transfer or apply what has been learnt to novel situations. Training objectives on the other hand tend to stress proficiency in those skills which task analysis has revealed as key elements in the job they are required to do.

Differences in the objectives of education and training partly explain the emphasis in educational examinations on normative measurement. They are generally concerned with ranking students in a class rather than with assessing their attainment of specified objectives. The need for educational testing to concern itself more with assessing attainment of specified objectives is well ilustrated in a study recently conducted by the Systems Development Corporation in cooperation with the California State Department of Education (Newmark and Sweigert (5)).

The study attempted to assess the effectiveness of three one-year language courses in elementary Spanish; a conventional course, a programmed learning course and a televised course. The researchers rejected any suggestion that one course should be compared directly with another, because of the extreme difficulty of interpreting the results of comparisons of this kind. What exactly is being compared with what? Their aim was simply to discover to what extent each course achieved its own specified objectives in the four basic language skills, listening comprehension, speaking, reading comprehension and writing.

For each of these four basic skills a separate test was developed in which the influence on performance of any of the other skills was entirely eliminated or at least greatly reduced. For each skill also there were separate tests for vocabulary and grammar in which one aspect was held constant while the other was tested. All of these various tests were based on an absolute criterion rather than a relative measure of performance and different versions were used for each of the three language courses.

One finding of interest was that the three ostensibly similar language courses differed quite remarkably in their objectives. Only about 50 vocabulary items out of a total of over 900 were common to all three courses. There was similar variation in the grammatical structures which each course set out to teach. No less significant was the fact that all three of the courses failed, and in the case of some of the basic skills, failed conspicuously to achieve their own stated objectives. It is not pretended that developing adequate criterion-referenced tests is an easy matter. This study demonstrated however, that it can be done. It also showed that the traditional method of evaluating only a small sample of the linguistic objectives of a language course may obscure serious deficiencies in materials and/or the conditions under which learning is expected to take place.

Measuring the effectiveness of training in terms of the performance of students in a terminal examination, of whatever kind, takes no account of their level of pre-knowledge of the subject. High scores can as readily reflect the initial attainment of the students as it can the effectiveness of the training they have received. In some cases the assumption that students know nothing about a subject before they start training may be justified. More often however, such an assumption is questionable and whenever this is the case other measures are likely to be more appropriate.

(i) Gain Scores

Measure the difference between a student's initial and final knowledge of the subject. Gain scores may be appropriate where one is prepared to define the effectiveness of training in terms of the mean gain in performance. Their disadvantage is that they tend to penalize individuals who knew something about the subject when they started.

(ii) Ratio Scores

Express the amount learnt as a proportion of the amount which could have been learnt. Such scores would be appropriate where gains in knowledge by students with high pre-test scores are considered more valuable than equal gains in knowledge by students with low pre-test scores.

350

(iii) Residual Gain Scores

Measure tne difference between a student's actual achievement in the final examination and the achievement predicted by his pre-test score. Such scores identify under and over achievers and by definition are independent of initial knowledge of the subject.

The relevance of any one of these measures has to be considered in terms of the objectives which a particular training course is designed to achieve.

2.3. Estimating and Comparing Training Costs

A valid comparison of the costs of two systems of training presupposes that one can answer two questions. What cost items may legitimately be included in the analysis and what is the best estimate available of each relevant cost element? There is no general set of procedures which will inevitably produce reliable answers to these questions. Cases have to be treated on their merits.

Let me try to illustrate the first problem. A major element of cost of any formal training course is the cost of running the training school e.g. providing and maintaining classrooms and accommodation, providing various administrative services etc. If it were possible to give training on-the-job rather than in the school it might be possible to save some proportion of these overheads. Exactly how much would depend on the scale of the exercise. Simply replacing a single course by on-the-job training would do little or nothing to reduce overheads, whereas if enough courses could be given on operational stations to make it possible to close the school substantial savings would result. In the first case it would be quite inappropriate to include any element of station overheads in the cost comparison, in the other their inclusion would be quite legitimate. Similar considerations apply to other elements of cost.

Even when one has decided what cost elements to include in the study, there remains the problem of estimating their values. In cost/effectiveness analysis, unlike the preparation of budgets, the emphasis is on comparative costs rather than on absolute accuracy of costing. Providing assumptions about cost elements apply equally to the two systems being compared, particularly where the elements represent a small proportion of total cost, inaccuracy is not likely to invalidate the whole study. The real difficulties arise when, as often happens, this is not the case. Probably all one can do then is to test the sensitivity of a conclusion to a range of assumptions about the cost of a particular item.

2.4. Developing a Model of the System

A model is a simplified representation of the cause and effect relationships which operate in the real world. Ways of representing these relationships range from a set of mathematical equations or a computer program at one end of the "sophistication" scale, to a purely verbal description of the situation with intuitive predictions of the consequences of various choices at the other. The usefulness of any model will clearly depend very much on the precision with which it reflects the realities of the situation being examined. I think it is also clear that at the present time most of the training models which we can build leave much to be desired in the way of precision. This is not to say, however, that they have no value. Even at their simplest, models have the advantage of making explicit what features of a situation are being taken into account and what relationships are assumed to exist between them. They also impose the discipline of clarifying the concepts which are being used. These are very real advantages.

One form of cost/effectiveness analysis is referred to as "fixed budget" analysis where the aim is to maximize effectiveness for a given cost. An alternative approach which is possibly more relevant for training, has the aim of achieving a prescribed level of effectiveness at minimum cost. Building a model of the system involves identifying various elements of cost which are associated with achieving this level of effectiveness and examining the sensitivity of cost to variations in the training requirement.

A feature of most cost/effectiveness models is the attempt which is made to separate out different categories of cost. In many cases the primary consideration in deciding upon a particular course of action is the total cost over time rather than the expenditure involved in a particular period of time. Emphasis on total life cycle costs makes it necessary to distinguish between three different categories of cost:

(i) Research and Development Costs

i.e. costs associated with developing a system of training up to the point where it is ready for operational use.

(ii) Initial Investment Costs

i.e. costs of putting an already developed system of training into service.

(iii) Annual Operating Costs

i.e. recurring costs of operating, supporting and maintaining a system of training.

These cost categories reflect significant distinctions in the allocation of resources. Research and development costs create new opportunities but do not in themselves provide any additional training capability. Investment costs do add new capability. Operating costs simply sustain existing capability but do not add to it.

Possibly even more important however, is the fact that different categories of cost have different characteristics and implications. Research and development costs are one-time costs and are independent of the number of students it proves necessary to train. Investment and operating costs on the other hand, although they differ in other ways, are both very much affected by the size of the trainee population. Sometimes the relationship between number to be trained and cost is a linear one, in other instances the relationship takes the form of a step function. The cost in terms of student's time is directly related to the number of students to be trained, the cost in terms of instructor's time rises in steps depending on the class size which each instructor is capable of teaching.

Knowing something about the relationships between these different categories of cost is essential in comparing alternative systems of training. For example, a system with high development and investment costs but low operating costs could still be cheapest overall, provided the number of students to be trained was large.

A frequently occurring problem in military training is uncertainty about the size of future training commitments. Here again in comparing one system of training with another it may be very important to know which is more tolerant of possible fluctuations in the size of the commitment. This sort of approach attempts to highlight the implications of adopting a particular course of action, the circumstances in which it is likely to prove most successful and what possibilities exist for trading-off one set of advantages against another.

2.5. Selecting a Criterion for Choosing Between Alternatives

Sometimes, although unfortunately not very often, training will have but a single objective. In this case cost/effectiveness ratios can be calculated to indicate which system of training is to be preferred. More frequently training will have several objectives, some of which may even conflict e.g. speed and accuracy in copy typing. Even where there are multiple objectives it may still be possible to use cost/effectiveness ratios as the choice criterion, provided the objectives are themselves commensurable or could be made so. For instance, it might be possible to translate both speed and accuracy in copy typing into the time taken to produce perfect typescript.

Where objectives are not commensurable all that can be done is to draw up a pay-off matrix for the various systems of training being compared. This will not indicate an unambiguously "best" choice, but it will reveal whether gains under one criterion are accompanied by losses under another and what the magnitude of these gains and losses is. It will in fact make explicit the full implications of any decision which is taken.

3. AN EXAMPLE OF A COST/EFFECTIVENESS STUDY OF TRAINING

Having talked in general terms about the relevance of cost/effectiveness analysis for training, perhaps I could conclude by mentioning our own faltering first steps into this field.

The study to which I would like to refer sought to compare the cost/effectiveness of a conventional one week course on transistor theory with that of a programmed course which men read on their own operational stations. In addition to this main aim the study also attempted to compare the cost/effectiveness of using scrambled books or machines to present the program and examined the effects of varying the administrative backing which was provided on operational stations. In Phase 1 of the study programmed materials were simply made available on units and airmen encouraged to make use of them as and when they felt inclined and could be spared from their normal work. In Phase 2 there was more administrative control. An NCO was made responsible for seeing that men turned up for instruction and spurring on those who tended to fall by the wayside. Although the sections in which men worked had the final say in whether individuals could study the program at particular times, they were under somewhat greater pressure to allow time off than in Phase 1 of the study.

In both phases of the study trainees were asked whether they wished to take part in the experiment. There were indications however, that some of those who actually did start work on the program were "volunteers" in the Service sense of that word. Not all of the experimental trainees would have been eligible to go on the conventional transistor course and none were offered anything in the way of special incentives.

The choice of the test given at the end of the conventional course as the criterion for comparing the effectiveness of the two methods was dictated by circumstances. We had hoped however, to be able to measure gains in performance and not simply final proficiency. As trainees doing the conventional course were not given a pre-test it was decided to use an additional multiple-choice test to get over this difficulty.

3.1. Effectiveness

The results achieved pointed to three main conclusions:

(i) Whilst both groups of trainees were comparable in terms of their initial knowledge of the subject, conventional trainees did better on the conventional test than experimental trainees but less well on the multiple-choice test. This brings out a very real difficulty in studies of this kind, namely developing a test which is equally fair to two quite different forms of instruction. The general conclusion was that there was little difference between the groups in terms of overall performance.

(ii) The real difference between conventional and programmed instruction was in the number of people who completed the course. Whilst those who got through the program, irrespective of whether they were working on machines or scrambled books, performed creditably, many failed to stay the course. On average, only 14% of the trainees in Phase 1 of the experiment, where the onus on getting through the program was on themselves, managed to do so. In the more tightly controlled second phase, 54% of the trainees worked through the whole program. These figures compare with the 97% of conventional trainees who completed the course.

(iii) Although pressure of work may have made it difficult for some trainees to complete the program, it was clear that individual motivation was an important factor in determining who would persevere to the end. This was particularly true in the first phase of the study.

3.2. Costs

The transistor theory course did not attempt to teach specific equipments, nor, as a single course, was its removal from the training school likely to result in any savings in station overheads. These items of cost were therefore ignored. I will not trouble you with the detailed arguments about the legitimacy of including other items in the cost comparison. These are set out in *Table 1*, together with the various assumptions which had to be made and some of the major factors which could affect the cost of either method. The aim of this part of the exercise was to explore the sensitivity of costs to varying assumptions about the nature of possible training commitments.

3.3. Discussion

This analysis is not yet complete but perhaps I may be permitted to comment on some of the features which seem to be emerging (Table 2).

   (i) Individuals who are prepared to persevere with programmed courses achieve satisfactory standards of performance. Many are not. Assuming that men are studying programs at times when they would otherwise have been employed on their normal duties, the high fall out rate means that programmed instruction compares unfavourably with conventional instruction. One advantage of running courses on operational units is that use can be made of otherwise nonproductive time. On the assumption that men were keen to learn and would study at times when they were not otherwise gainfully employed, programmed courses become highly competitive. These assumptions would probably be justified in the case of candidates for promotion examinations for instance.

   (ii) The high fall out rate with programmed courses can be greatly reduced by proper administrative control. Assuming that the majority of men (95%) can be made to read the program in its entirety, this form of instruction becomes very much more competitive. Using commercially produced scrambled books is particularly advantageous with small numbers of students although it retains an advantage across the board. Writing one's own program is more expensive than conventional instruction if the prospective number of students to be trained is less than 300 *(see Diagrams 1a – 1d)*. Beyond this point self-written programs become progressively more viable. With a training population of 1800 men, writing one's own program is only slightly more expensive than buying one off the shelf. If task analysis is used to determine the necessary content of a program and if care is taken in selecting suitable subject matter the useful life of the program is likely to be increased. This will improve the chances that the program will be economically competitive.

   (iii) Although bought programs may have an economic advantage, particularly with small numbers of trainees, the possibility of using them depends on suitable programs being both available and acceptable. People tend to be reluctant to change their existing syllabus to take advantage of a commercially available alternative, partly no doubt, because of the NIH factor (Not Invented Here).

   (iv) Trainees studying programs on machines take somewhat less time to get through the material. This advantage of machines over books is not sufficiently great to offset the present high rental charges for machines and films. It could become important however, if rental charges were reduced or if time to complete the course were to assume greater significance. This could happen if the course was concerned with teaching expensive equipments.

4. SUMMARY

I have attempted to outline what contribution cost/effectiveness analysis has to make to training and to indicate some of the problems one meets in trying to apply it. Its promise, if not as yet its full achievement, is that it represents a systematic approach to decision making, where assumptions are made explicit, objectives and criteria are clearly defined and alternative courses of action compared in terms of their likely consequences.

TABLE 1

TABLE OF COST ELEMENTS

Cost Items	Elements Included	Assumptions Made in the Study
R & D Costs		
Task Analysis	P C	Scale of task assumed to be 300 successful students p.a. for 6 years, and the syllabus unchanged over this period.
Syllabus Preparation	P C	
Construction of pre-test	[P]	
Construction of post-test	[P] C	
Programmer Training	[P]	
Program Writing	[P]	Programs are assumed to have a life of 20 readings.
Program Validation	[P]	
Initial Investment		
Provision of Classrooms	P C	
Provision of Labs.	P C	
Provision of Equipment	P C	
Provision of Training Aids	P C	
Training Instructors	[C]	
Purchase of teaching machines/ programs	P	
Purchase of programmed books	[P]	
Operating Costs		
Instructor time	[C]	
Student time	[PC]	Students assumed available when required.
Training Administration	[P] C	Cost of NCO administrators for P.I. on operational units included – training administration for conventional instruction excluded because barely affected by removal of one course.
Station Administration	P C	
Consumable Stores	P C	
Travelling Time and Fare	[C]	Class size in conventional instruction was 14 students. (Costs also calculated on the assumption of 5 students per class.) Student time costed at capitation rates. Travelling time takes half a day of productive time.
Hire of teaching machines	[P]	
Purchase or printing of programs	[P]	
Printing of class hand-outs	[C]	

KEY: P = Programmed Instruction C = Conventional Instruction ☐ = Taken Into Account in This Study

Factors Affecting Costs

1. Success rate.
2. Length of course
3. Total number of students:
   (a) Size of trade
   (b) Stability of syllabus
4. Rate of throughput of students

TABLE 2

COMPARISON OF COSTS OF PROGRAMMED AND CONVENTIONAL INSTRUCTION FOR EQUAL EFFECTIVENESS

Cost Element	Class-room Instruc-tion	Phase I		Phase II		Assumed Tight Control		
		Books	Machines	Books	Machines	Service Written Books	Bought Books	Hired Machines
Percent completing course	97	20	4	31	66	95	95	95
Av. hours taken by successful students	26	21	17	22	19	23	23	21
Av. hours spent by un-successful students	25	6	5	11	9	18	18	18
Cost per programmed book or month of hire of machine and film	–	–	67	–	67	–	2	67
Cost of writing program	–	2200	–	2200	–	2200	–	–
R & D Costs Per Successful Student								
Course notes and Black-board summaries	0.1	–	–	–	–	–	–	–
Program writing, typing, drawing	–	1.2	–	1.2	–	1.2	–	–
Programmer Training	–	0.1	–	0.1	–	0.1	–	–
Total Capital Costs	0.1	1.3	–	1.3	–	1.3	–	–

Investment Costs Per Successful Student

Class hand-outs	0.3	-	-	-	-	-	-	-
Training Instructors	0.1	-	-	-	-	-	-	-
Programmed book printing or purchase	-	0.3	-	0.2	-	0.1	0.1	-
Total Investment Costs	0.4	0.3	-	0.2	-	0.1	0.1	-

Running Costs Per Successful Student

Cost of Instructor/Supervisor Time	2.5	0.2	0.5	1.2	1.3	2.0	2.0	2.0
Cost of successful student training time	18.2	14.7	11.9	15.4	13.3	16.1	16.1	14.7
Cost of training unsuccessful students (per successful student)	0.6	16.8	84.0	17.1	4.7	1.0	1.0	1.0
Machine and film hire	-	-	45.9	-	7.7	-	-	7.4
Travelling time and fare	5.5	-	-	-	-	-	-	-
Total Running Costs	26.8	31.7	142.3	33.7	27.0	19.1	19.1	25.1
Total Costs	27.3	33.3	142.3	35.2	27.0	20.5	19.2	25.1

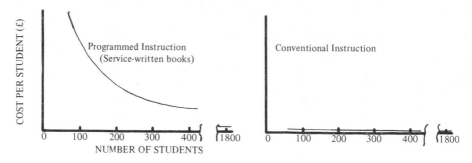

Fig. 1(a) – R. & D. COSTS

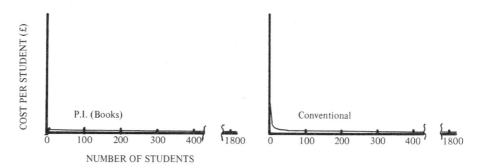

Fig. 1(b) – INVESTMENT COSTS

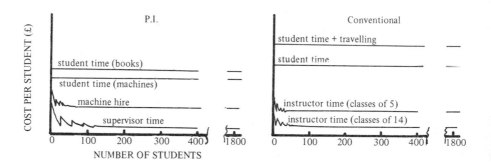

Fig. 1(c) – RUNNING COSTS

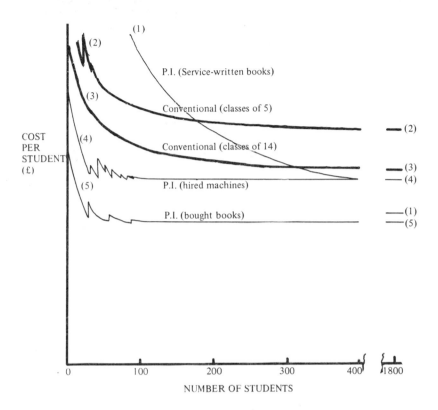

Fig. 1(d) – TOTAL COSTS

By attempting to arrive at conclusions by processes which are open to critical examination it provides a framework in which judgement can operate more precisely; it also offers an opportunity for refining judgement.

REFERENCES

1. Quade E.S. (1965) *"Cost Effectiveness: An Introduction And An Overview"* Rand Corporation, Santa Monica.
2. Durkheim E. (1956) *"Education and Sociology"* The Free Press, Glencoe.
3. Bloom B.S. (ed) (1956) *"Taxonomy Of Educational Objectives"* Longmans Green, NY.
4. Gagné R. (1956) *"*The Analysis Of Instructional Objectives For The Design Of Instruction *"* *Teaching Machines and Programmed Learning II* (Ed. R. Glaser) National Education Association of the U.S.A.
5. Newmark G. & Sweigert R.L. (1966) *"A Field Test Of Three Approaches To The Teaching Of Spanish In Elementary Schools"* California State Department of Education.

The Cost of Training Aircrew

J.B. PARRY

MINISTRY OF DEFENCE (R.A.F.)

The training of service aircrew, and especially of pilots, is long and expensive, while training wastage, even with an up-to-date selection system, is higher than in most other trades. It is not possible to get a realistic grasp of this situation from bare acquaintance with wastage and costings figures, and the purpose of this paper is to indicate the main factors that underlie it, and so provide a perspective within which objective appraisal becomes possible.

The production of an operational pilot entails three main phases. There is first a primary phase where the emphasis is on service indoctrination and a grounding in basic mathematical and scientific subjects, a grasp of which is found necessary in subsequent training. This stage contains little or no air experience and its objectives do not include the acquisition of flying skill. Its normal length is from four to six months; where aircrew have been selected for permanent commissions, this academic phase lasts very much longer, usually at least a year, in the case of the United States Air Force Academy no less than four years.

The second training phase covers basic and secondary flying instruction. This will generally take about eighteen months. The broad purpose of this long period is to teach the pupil full control of the plane; the business of using the aircraft as distinct from flying it is regarded as the function of the last phase. Inability to learn the elements of flying skill is the main cause of wastage in pilot training and it is to be expected that suspensions at the Basic stage will be higher than elsewhere.

The third phase, known as Operational Conversion, lasts some six months. Here the pupil becomes a unit with a specific role in a team with which he flies regularly. In other words the objective is crew rather than individual training. As the name implies this type of training is under the auspices of an operational command, the two previous phases coming under a command devoted entirely to training.

The cost of training varies considerably from phase to phase. Without quoting precise figures, we can say that the cost of bringing a trainee through the first phase should be thought of in terms of four figures, that of the second phase in five figure terms, while with the third phase present day costs can be even higher. This makes it obvious that a bare wastage figure (say 30%) conveys little idea of the economic cost of training failure unless we can give some idea where the wastage has been distributed. With two qualifications it is important to place failure as early as possible in the training sequence. The qualifications are, first, that it is impossible, except in the grossest cases, to anticipate flying failure at the primary stage; secondly, that while there is strong objection to delaying suspension too long, it is also possible to make the decision too soon. For this reason it is sometimes laid down that no trainee shall be suspended from air work during the first fifteen or twenty hours; this is some guarantee that the slow starter will be given time for his latent abilities to show themselves.

Apart from flying failure, a certain amount of suspension is caused by failure to master ground subjects, for medical reasons, for lack of the needed personal qualities, and finally, in training as long and exacting as this, there are always a few who exercise their right to withdraw. This variety of reasons is largely responsible for the comparatively high wastage rates and they are found in every air force. It is

believed that no peace time air force has managed to bring its pilot wastage below 20%
and it has even been suggested that it would be mistaken to aim at doing so. The R.A.F.
figure at the moment is slightly above this percentage.

It is clear that failure at the operational conversion stage is going to be
enormously costly, and in fact very little is met at this phase. And it should be noted
that some failed pilots are salvaged as navigators so that the cost of attempting to
train them as pilots will not have been completely thrown away.

The expenses of flying training fall under four main heads: the cost of maintaining
flying units, the cost of equipment (mainly aircraft), the numbers of personnel employed
and the number of hours flown. While all of these influence the figures quoted as the
cost of training or failing to train the individual pupil, some of the influences can be
demonstrated more tangibly than others. Instructor's wasted time and fuel used to no
purpose are among the more easily recognized losses; wear and tear to aircraft cannot be
evaluated for the pupil except where specific damage has been caused. Estimated course
capacity affects the number of maintenance and administrative personnel required by a
unit as well of course as the number of instructors; this is an important budgeting
feature as the personnel/pupil ratio at a flying school is several times greater than
in most other kinds of training.

The term aircraft costs covers more than basic purchase price; at the time of
purchase there is usually some doubt about a given type's reliability and a training
aircraft that is found to give rise to undue servicing problems puts a strain on all
aspects of the system.

In all training situations there are likely to be many ways of reaching a prescribed
goal, and inevitably some will be more effective than others. Responsibility for
devising an adequate training plan usually falls on the chief instructors who inevitably
vary in their ability to identify the major factors in the situation and to find a
solution that does justice to all of them. In flying training there are an unusual
number of these factors, due partly to the fact that air work is based on a one-to-one
instructor-pupil ratio (a point which is bound to make for inflexibility), the need to
relate instruction in two different media (air and ground) and the fact that unpredictable conditions such as prolonged bad weather can make heavy inroads into any flying
plan. This is an area where operational research can sometimes assist in identifying the
best kind of program, while management training can instil some important planning
principles.

Since the cost of flying training is so high it is natural to ask what can be done
to reduce it by the use of synthetic aids such as flight simulators. Very considerable
use is made of these pieces of equipment at the operational conversion stage and there
can be no doubt that the training bill would be substantially larger without them. Some
ideas of the economies brought about by the use of simulators can be given by comparing
the capital cost ratios and the hourly running cost ratios of simulator and aircraft
simulated. The cost of a simulator naturally depends on its degree of sophistication,
i.e. the number of sub-systems within the total aircraft system it can reproduce. The
flying elements which offer the greatest obstacles to simulation are representation of
the pilot's visual field – the difficulties of this are in the process of being mastered
– and "g" effects. The cost of the most advanced simulators so far produced are rather
more than half the cost of a single corresponding aircraft. The hourly cost ratio is
seldom less than 1 in 10 in the simulator's favour and in some cases nearly 1 in 50. So
far then as simulator time can be regarded as a substitute for flying time considerable
economies are effected. But although flying time is undoubtedly saved by the use of
simulators, there are many reasons why the relationship cannot be expressed in a neat
equation. The situation is less complicated in the training of navigators and air
traffic controllers, and in these areas even greater savings are anticipated through the
development of simulator techniques.

Costing analyses are concerned ultimately to establish some sort of ratio between
an input and an output, the first term covering the price and maintenance of training
equipment and the human effort of instructors and pupils, while output refers to the
proficiency attained and the value to the organization or community of the trained

product. If the analysis is pushed to the limits of mathematical expression, the assumption has to be made that money is a medium in terms of which all the foregoing factors can be evaluated. It is clear that such an assumption is far more convincing in some areas of flying training than others and I will end by citing three aspects of this situation where conviction is less than perfect.

First, it is customary to recruit aircrew by asking for volunteers; the idea of drafting people into this kind of task has never found favour. If we ask what causes people to volunteer for aircrew, we find this can only partly be explained in terms of the job's material rewards. To a considerable extent the attraction of flying overrides the volunteer's desire to sell his services to the highest bidder. This attraction must be satisfied by the form of training offered, otherwise the supply of volunteers will dry up. There is no reason why economical training methods should not prove attractive, but extreme stringency might have an adverse effect, in other words the cheapest form of training might fail to satisfy the pupil because it offered him too little of the experience he was looking for.

Secondly, training offers certain benefits that almost certainly reduce expenditure but it is not possible to measure their contribution. One instance of this are the emergency situations which can be staged and restaged in a flight simulator, and which almost certainly lead to a reduction in flying accidents. But it is not possible to establish experimentally how many accidents are avoided in this way.

Finally it is difficult, to say the least, to express the value of a trained pilot or navigator in money terms. This is largely because, in peace time conditions, they are not called on to perform the full duties they have been trained for, so that in a sense their whole career is a kind of continuation training. To some extent this is true for all servicemen, but the gap between peace time and war time activity is bound to be greatest for key personnel. There is then a particular anomaly in giving a cash value to those whose efforts might in an emergency decide the nation's fate including that of its economy.

New Outlooks in Training Research:
A Discussion

CHAIRMAN
BRIGADIER J.F.M. MELLOR
DIRECTOR OF ARMY TECHNICAL TRAINING
MINISTRY OF DEFENCE, LONDON

DISCUSSANTS

DR. GLENN L. BRYAN
OFFICE OF NAVAL RESEARCH, WASHINGTON

DR. JAMES J. REGAN
U.S. NAVAL TRAINING DEVICES CENTRE

DR. ED. L. SHRIVER
HUMAN RESOURCES RESEARCH OFFICE
GEORGE WASHINGTON UNIVERSITY

BRYAN: Our topic will be the evolution of training research and we have elected to do
something that I trust will meet with your favour, which is to conduct an informal
discussion and involve you in it to the maximum. Our general plan will be as follows.
Each of the three discussants will take something of the order of 3–5 minutes to
give you an over-view of the kinds of things that we feel competent to talk about.
Then you will be called upon by number on the handout that you have received, in a
random access way, to ask us questions. Because we have this very flexible format I
sincerely trust that we can focus on matters of your concern that fall within our
domain.

SHRIVER: I would like first to talk about the active and the passive side of
psychological research. Early on, perhaps World War I time, psychological research
was exclusively passive; it made studies of what exists, e.g. people's attitudes or
measurements of intelligence. There is no arguing about them, you just collect. As
time has gone on those studies have remained part of the psychologist's repertoire,
but additional things have come into being. These additional things I characterize
as primarily active.

   Training is active, it's doing something about something, so is the fact that we
went from the testing program into validity studies, from putting the calliper to
the man's mind on to validating things, especially during World War II. We got out
on ships, we got out on aeroplanes. In the Air Force program there was a great deal
of prediction of pilot performance and there was great effort to follow this up and
find out how well these tests were predicting. Once you've got out and described how
he performs for validity purposes, you say, "Well look we just found out what he
does, let's take a look at the training". Some of the early training research was
methods research, I think that's how psychologists came to it from the theory of
learning and they felt, "Well, our job is how to get the information over to the
student". But having worked in validity also and then out in the field, they began
asking the question, "Is this the right content to get over to the student?", "Has
the conventional course the right content?".

   So, with a subtle shift away from techniques for getting it over, a new area
developed – of analysis: how shall we analyze the job to find out what should go

364

into the training program? We used conventional courses to put these things over. We also got into simulators of various types, any kind of tools we wanted seemed to be developing to use in getting whatever content it was we wanted over to the student. A good example of this analytic phase concerns training for firing a rifle. The conventional way might be to fire at a bull's-eye target with a nice flat trajectory for a thousand yards. Analysis of the situation indicated that targets don't frequently appear at a thousand yards – 200 yards might be about as far as you would ever see a target – and furthermore the trick is not only firing at the target once you see it but a big part of it is can you see it, can you recognize likely target locations? This is analysis of the job to determine the content for the training course. It changes the content of the course; instead of firing at bull's-eye targets you might want to put targets out there that can barely be seen, and a portion of the training might go towards that end.

Also, this active role is a role of "changing", through training we *change* human performance. There are some other things that we started changing. In human engineering we started changing the way the hardware is arranged. That is we were beginning to be activists – we'd go in and say no don't do it that way, do it this way. We changed not only the hardware but we've also built machines, program-type instruction, computerized instruction, new ways of using hardware to change the individual.

We have changed over the years, the old things in our kit bag have gone on, but new things have developed. And this change goes even beyond training research, it seems that we're now more interested in cost effectiveness, more interested in how training fits in to still larger systems. Not only are we taking a systems approach to training but looking at even bigger systems and saying what is worth putting our money into training for, what things shall we train for. Also, if we can train better, say in an electronic radar battery, perhaps we should put more of the spare parts down at a lower echelon because we can now train people better, they have a greater capability, therefore this affects the spare parts stockage. Further, if we can train so simply, why train a man in the first enlistment in a school, why not train him on the job with programmed instruction? Then, if we have the capability through training of changing a man perhaps we can change him in such a way that a person who is considered only capable in selection tests of being an operator, perhaps he can also be a maintenance man. Maybe we have simplified maintenance to the point where we can combine jobs. This has big cost potential. Anyway we are taking a look at logistics, MOS's, changing MOS's, changing to multi-level training. We are doing lots of different things that had not been anticipated when we were in the passive stage. We are activists today in training research.

REGAN: Dr. Shriver has outlined for you a transition, a change which he described as evolutionary from some 15 years ago with respect to training research up to today. I guess we all agree that change is taking place, some of it may be somewhat more revolutionary, however, and it would be my intention to flesh out, if you will excuse that figure, three or four items that were briefly referred to by Dr. Shriver.

I would like first of all during the course of the time we have available to say something about training research itself, to characterize it with respect to some of the issues, areas and trends it represents; to say something about simulation for training, since that's an area in which I do have a particular interest; something about the trends in simulation from the technological point of view particularly, and to include this now famous phrase, systems approach, which does in fact have some rather important technological implications for training equipment design. Finally, I hope to have an opportunity to glance at some possibilities for the future in training research and the implications of these futures for the manpower issue in general. And all this, of course, in the context of trained manpower in a defence system.

BRYAN: I have the privilege of being a member of an organization that tries, in various ways, to foresee what is going to happen and to take some appropriate action to bring it about more smoothly and to foresee things which ought to happen and to do something about calling them to other people's attention so that they can get the necessary support.

In general we attempt to do things which will increase the alternatives which are available to systems managers, be they manpower managers or otherwise. As a result my comments will be in the general area of things that are about to take place, and things which clearly could take place; and some things that I am sure are very far away but deserve at this time your serious consideration, particularly those of you who have any manpower management or manpower management policy responsibilities.

I shall speak, if you ask the right questions, on three things. One, in the general area of the individualized adaptive instruction, sometimes spoken of as computer assisted instruction or computer based instruction, but I prefer to think of it in much more general terms. I shall, secondly, be prepared to talk about a rather radical scheme where there would be a very strong inter-action and inter-dependence between computerized assignment techniques in assigning individuals to jobs and the impact of such techniques upon training of the future, specifically upon the content of the curricula. And finally, we are very enthusiastic and excited about a new effort we are modelling that we call the "World of Work". The last is at present just in the germ stage I suppose, but it will bring together and is bringing together on a multi-disciplinary basis people who will seriously and are seriously considering the changing nature of work, the changing meaning of work, in the modern world. It is trying to think how this ought properly to be taken into account and how it perhaps will lead to a reformulation or a re-conceptualization of work that can be taken into account in some rigorous way by modern military personnel systems.

Having said that, now it's your turn. Your handout contains eight statements which we on the platform are prepared to discuss or defend.

Some Ways Training Research is Evolving Toward an Accord with Manpower Research and Planning

1. People are beginning to worry more about inter-relating variables throughout their ranges.

2. There is a trend toward more multivariate experiments.

3. There is a new willingness to leave the laboratory and its sterile environment for the dirty real world environment.

4. There is a tendency for training research efforts to become "job-validation" oriented as against "hypothesis testing" oriented.

5. More research is being devoted to the seeking of principles which are "true within stated limits" at the expense of the search for "universal" principles.

6. Future personnel systems seem destined to be more oriented toward dealing with individuals as against dealing with classes of individuals.

7. Concurrent changes in both manpower research and training research threaten to upset the *status quo*.

8. The successful development of adaptive personnel systems and sub-systems is the key to the future.

Each handout is numbered and I'd greatly appreciate it if you would respond if your number is called, choosing *one* of the questions on the handout and putting it in whatever terms you choose.

TOLCOTT: One of the ways of viewing the distinction between manpower management research and personnel research is that manpower studies must deal with aggregates

or classes of people and try to find the level of classes or the level of detail
into which manpower can be categorized or needs to be categorized for a better
understanding of attributes, performance, costs and so on. Personnel research on the
other hand tends to start with individuals and begins to identify certain common
features which perhaps puts them into categories. With reference to item number 6 on
your handout I would like to ask one of you: if this is true, can you point to the
value or the relationship that you would foresee between this kind of personnel
research and its value to the manpower planner?

BRYAN: It seems to me that while personnel research has always espoused the case of the
individual, it has in general been incapable of dealing with the individual; and a
current emphasis on individualized instruction I think is a clear case in point. We
have always talked about training individuals and indeed if you go into a classroom
you will find individuals there, but they will be treated in a lock-step way where
they are grouped and treated in batches. It now appears feasible, and perhaps in the
long run even cost effective, to adopt other strategies for teaching individuals and
to do research about individuals in a rigorous and systematic way. It is my belief
that we will not have a satisfactory meeting of personnel research and manpower
research until we can find some real meeting ground. It is difficult to know how
these two will articulate but I anticipate that it will be at the level of the
individual.

I will try to give you a case in point. If we are to develop adaptive personnel
systems, then such systems should be able to take into account many characteristics
of the individual as an individual. I would like to give you an example of what
might happen to your training curriculum if in fact individualized personnel assignments were made.

In adapting instructions to people we have talked a great deal about doing things
which would have the effect of maximizing the slope of each individual's learning.
The typical or hypothetical learning curve, since at the bottom it is not a straight
line, suggests that early on the learning was inefficient, perhaps the material was
too difficult. Later on the learning was again inefficient, perhaps the material
there had already been learned and at best is being over-learned at this point, or
perhaps the material is just too easy. There have been a number of noteworthy
beginnings, particularly in the field of manual tracking, that suggest that it would
be possible with appropriate adaptive devices to straighten out that learning curve
and maximize its slope. One way of doing this is to control the difficulty of the
stimulus material that is presented to the individual. For example, if you are
trying to teach him a tracking task you might think that you could cause the target
that he was attempting to superimpose a dot on, a moving target, you might have the
sensitivity of that target such that if he came some place close to the target early
on in the learning then he was given feedback that he was on target. But as he
developed the requisite skills and was getting better at the task, then you would
make the task itself more difficult by having the effective size of the target
reduced so that he was always working at an accomplishable but challenging level.

You might say, what does that have to do with manpower research? I think that
the next points will lock it down. Suppose that, when you accepted a man in, say,
the Navy it is already decided that at some future time there will be a job suitable
for him, and suppose that then and there you decided exactly what that job would be.
Now with computerized assignment techniques of the sort that have been used in the
U.S. Marine Corps it seems quite feasible that we shall be able to arrive at an
optimum assignment technique. Such a technique would allow you, with a very large
model, taking into account your inventory of jobs to be done, the kinds of people
that you are introducing as raw material into the system and the channel capacity of
your processing capability, to work out a system so that you could assign a man
exactly to a job. I mean exactly that you would assign Joe Bloggs so that he is
going to be an Electronics Technician on the good ship Nuts and Bolts come the 27th
of next January. These assignments would automatically be reviewed and they would

be changed. The first day of the man's enlistment it wouldn't make much difference what that assignment happened to be. You would still try to teach him to stand up straight and to speak when spoken to, to get his hair cut and so on. You would still tell him how to send his laundry and how to collect his pay. But later on the curricula that you would expose him to would be very heavily dependent upon a specific assignment. As he came closer and closer to the date of that assignment, in a kind of funnelling down, you would tailor his training to the particular assignment so that the last two or three weeks of his training would be a kind of on-the-job training. He would learn specifically the details of the job that he was about to take.

In order to capitalize maximally upon this individualization, you would also want to take full advantage of the opportunity that you had to learn even more about the man so that you might continuously diagnose his capability, including his changing capabilities, so that you could teach him those things which he needed to know and didn't already know. You would take all the things that are necessary for him to be able to do on his specific assignment and you would subtract out from that all the things that he now knew how to do and the remainder would be the contents of the curriculum.

GERHARDT: I am not sure whether I understand the game you set here but I'll try to do it my way. The statements you have here are in three classes, I think. First are the ones I agree with, second are the ones I disagree with, the third are the ones I don't understand. Fortunately, I think the most frequent is the first group. At any rate at their face value I agree.

It might be interesting to have some comments upon the number three of the statements. A laboratory is "sterile" and the real world is "dirty". I wonder if that is just a longing to get out of the laboratory and into the dirty world, or if there are specific problems that people are going to investigate when they get out into the dirty real world? In other words are there specific problems that can best be solved in the real world environment and other problems they could better do in the laboratory environment?

REGAN: There are several points that might clear up this third item that I'd like to address myself to. One is to do with the nature of the laboratory task which I do, in fact, think is changing. I think we're moving away from viewing this task, that is the experimental task, as a vehicle simply to explore other important independent variables, for example we used to study the complex tactical command control decision problems by giving college sophomores anagrams to work on or some variant of monopoly or other sorts of game-like activities. We are attempting I think to look more seriously at the nature of the tasks that we are concerned about, in the case of my example tactical decision making, we are seeing if we can deal with them in more realistic ways, possibly in the laboratory, but possibly in other somewhat non-laboratory or quasi-laboratory situations, such as operational training situations. These tasks can, I think, be treated as independent variables in and of themselves and they become a consideration. We have, in fact, done that on several occasions and it begins to appear that one can seriously affect the outcome of experiments by varying not only the nature of the task, that is its complexity, but its difficulty. It is necessary therefore to consider a number of points along some dimension of difficulty in order to get any appreciation for the kinds of effects that it's going to have on such training methods for example as part/whole or massed/distributed practice.

SHRIVER: As you mentioned part/whole I had a very simple notion that you might conduct a study and find out that spaced practice on firing a rifle is indeed better. That if you go out to the training range four times and fire 25 rounds each time you go, using 100 rounds that way, that is just as effective as firing 110 rounds all at once.

Now, that's a good laboratory-study straight answer. In terms of cost-effectiveness, in terms of the "dirty" world, it might cost a great deal of money to take the man out to the training range on four separate occasions, so in fact even though the theoretical answer that you might get in the laboratory is that spaced practice is better, in the dirty world it doesn't work out that way and massed practice is better.

BRYAN: I'd like to add that it's really a two-way street, although the item number 3 doesn't really indicate that. We have been increasingly concerned about trying to couple what happens in the laboratory with what happens subsequently in the real world. It has been our experience that our most successful laboratory researchers are among those people who spend enough time dealing with the field units — the problem in the real dirty world — and that when they go back to do their laboratory experiments, those experiments change in subtle but very important ways. Perhaps the least noticeable but one of the very important ways is in terms of what it is they choose to control or allow to vary in their subsequent experimentation.

LEESE: One of the speakers spoke of training aids and I note in your question 3 you speak of field experiments rather than the laboratory experiments. Take the case of the training aid such as a flight simulator. Everybody wants to know from operational research people what is the benefit to be obtained from a flight simulator; for example in our squadrons if something goes wrong with the mechanics of the aircraft and aircraft are grounded and flying hours are sharply reduced, operational research people are immediately asked what's the effectiveness of the squadron, how little hours of flying training can people get by with? Can they use simulation instead? I would have imagined as an amateur that you could design a large field experiment in which you had various classes of pilots who had various proportions of hours on a flight simulator as against on an actual aircraft. Could the speakers tell me if such experiments have been carried out or if not whether it would be possible to design such a trial?

REGAN: I can't cite specific experiments that have been done under exactly the circumstances you describe, which is not to suggest that there haven't been any — I simply don't know of any. The problem in general of this sort of proof-of-the-pudding issue with respect to flight simulators and other kinds of simulators has to do with measuring the operational performance. It's quite clear that pilots in transition states, which is the use to which most present-day flight simulators are put, are already pilots. That is to say they probably will not fall out of the air if they have had their trainer experience. It then becomes necessary to consider a whole host of somewhat more subtle measures of their performance. I think that there should be opportunities for much more of this sort of reliably measured evaluative work to determine what happens to behaviour in a trainer. We tend not to know about that.

Evaluation of training systems in my experience has been historically confined to a whole host of non-training issues concerning is it fungus proof and will it break if you drop it, and can you get it through the door and will the power go on when you turn it on, etc.? All important considerations, but perhaps not the central issue, which is, I suggest, "Does it in fact train someone?", which further asks the question, "Will a man's behaviour be noticeably different and presumably better as a result of this experience?". There is a lot of indication that much is true, but the further questions concerning how much better would it be under condition X than it would be under Y, particularly in your example, I think is a very difficult question to answer for reasons of the criterion problem I mentioned.

SHRIVER: Just a brief comment. At Fort Rucker in Alabama there are a number of devices which are called Whirleymites. These are for training young men to fly helicopters. They amount to an almost functioning helicopter that is tethered to the ground and runs around on a base. It will go around but it will not go up very far in the air. HumRRO is engaged on research on this. I believe it is a fair statement to say, however, that the gadget was purchased on the basis of the relatively simple notion that something that did things like this was desirable. It was not broken up into part tasks, it was not analyzed in a way that I described earlier in my thesis statement, namely, if one analyzes the situation one finds ways of breaking the job up perhaps into different analyses, into different training packages and so on. My only point is, even though this is recent and HumRRO is now engaged on it, it was still purchased on the basis of a gadget that seemed to do the right things. It's not on the basis of a thorough analysis. There is some distance to go.

BRYAN: I would like to say two things quickly and then ask a question. One is that I had intended to include in my preamble a disclaimer indicating that we were presenting our personal views and not necessarily making policy statements for the organizations to which we belong. I suspect I need to put that in at this point because I am about to go on to say as another part of the statement that you get on very thin ice in this one because things like flight pay and the like get to be involved. You tread on into the ground of the training authorities who feel quite competent to do this job sometimes without further assistance. We did try to find a case where you actually could find a trade-off function between hours of flying a simulator and hours of flying the aircraft for the Federal Aviation Agency a while back and I was unable to locate such studies in the published literature. That includes the informal governmental soft back. For one reason or another such studies don't exist. I think techniques would allow such studies to be done but it's politically inexpedient. The question is, is there anyone in the room who knows of such studies and might give an appropriate citation?

CASSIE: I don't know of any such studies. All I can do is to add to what you have said – what we have found here is that it is extremely difficult to do any work in this field of the kind that Mr. Leese has suggested for more or less the same reasons that you have outlined. There is a firm belief held by the trainers – and most sincerely held – that their syllabus of training, their syllabus of flying, is what is necessary and that if you interfere with this in any way, by giving some people less real flying in order to do simulator flying, then they might in fact suffer as a result. We feel very strongly that this is the case and we have felt as a result of this we couldn't press any further our desire and our wish to do experiments in this field.

SHRIVER: I'd like to elucidate, to give an example of what I mean by analyzing the job to break it up into part tasks which you can simulate in a cost-effective manner. My example concerns an electronics trainer. In the situation I am thinking of high fidelity simulation is thought by many to be desirable. What you want to do is have a hi-fi simulation of the real world but you want to take the risk out of it, just as this Whirleymite takes the risk out. But in electronics a simulator which was high fidelity meant that 80% of the time was spent on unbuttoning it, reaching around inside, getting the probe to the right place. Now it turns out that that aspect of the task is relatively simple to learn. The difficult part of the task is how to make the diagnosis, and this simulator, because of its high fidelity, only gave about 20% of the time for diagnosing a problem. In that case through four successive simulators we reduced the fidelity of it at each step and each time we reduced the requirements for the part task of moving around through the equipment – the easy part of it – to the point where only 10% of the time was spent on that and 90% on diagnosis. It's just a simple obvious example where the conventional wisdom of making it hi-fi is not appropriate at all, the diagnosis is the critical thing that makes a difference between individuals on a test. On that test the man will perform at a higher level if he's getting most of his training on the diagnostic work.

BRYAN: I might add a further comment. In a navy I know about we gave people some field training in firing missiles. It turns out that missiles are quite expensive and often in short supply. As a result every quarter each ship would fire a very small number of missiles. This was challenged on cost grounds and it was suggested that simulators be introduced instead of the live firing. We were brought in to assist in giving some justification of the training benefits of these live firings. It surprised me greatly that there was no information as to the training benefit of firing live missiles and there seemed to be a lack of willingness to gather together on one ship a number of missiles and to let the men on that ship fire the missiles until they were all expended, keeping track of what had happened to the men as a consequence of doing that. It would seem to me that this would give one the kind of information that one would love to have in order to determine how many missiles a man or a team should expend in order to develop his proficiency or the team's proficiency to a given level. However, despite the gloomy remarks that I have made with regard to your question, I think that the situation is improving markedly and there is a great deal more willingness to try this sort of thing, so I am looking forward to a time when we might work together much more successfully than we have over the last few years.

MELLOR: I wonder if I might make a comment? If you give men long training at which they have to struggle before eventually they can take a pride in their skills, they expect to be used and to have their skills exercised. There is experience to show that the men who have been so expensive to train take a great pride in firing the live missiles costing a great deal of money each, particularly if Senior Officers are watching these periodical firings. What is more they re-engage and remain in the Service. But if, after long training, the acme of their experience, year by year, is only to practise on simulators, you will find they don't re-engage.

BRYAN: Thank you for that comment. It would seem to be a sufficient justification for the live firings, whereas the improvements, the training benefits *per se*, might not be realizable.

WRIGHT: I'm puzzled by Item 7. The use of the word "threaten" implies to me that you see the long continuance of the *status quo* as desirable in itself? Can it ever be so and what does this item really mean?

BRYAN: I'm responsible for the word threaten. I think that there should be changes and that changes are occurring but we're in for some very turbulent times. People who have lived in their own separate worlds and who could neatly and conveniently dissect problems into their own separate responsibilities now find, as we achieve the capabilities that are inherent in electronic computers and as we become more enamoured of systems approaches, that there are other people working on the same problems who have rather different backgrounds, who are willing to make rather different assumptions and who will constrain themselves by rather different techniques. I think that in the manpower research, planning and management areas and the personnel and training research areas, that this contact is such that they are not intermixing smoothly. There is a certain amount of crashing of gears that is beginning to occur and the word threaten was used to indicate that it is to be expected that the *status quo* will change. I at least have some concern that the more powerful of these contenders might dismiss the weaker - that's me - from the field.

SHRIVER: Secretary Ferraro, in his address earlier this week, gave a list of characteristics of research that made implementation more likely and which, when you took the obverse made it less likely. I would like to refresh your memory on some of these points. Research was more likely to be implemented if it was a neat package, if it would fit into the system without changing anything else, if it was timely, if it received the attention of some senior level officer when he happened to be interested, etc. I would draw your attention to this thesis that I am introducing that we've gone from passive to active modes in research. The passive things are neat packages, attitudinal, selection, those are neat packages that can fit into the existing system, relatively speaking, without changing the system. As we get into active things training, training systems, changing MOS's, and combining operator and maintenance duties, having programmed instruction used on the job with the effect that the man would not enter school in his first enlistment but would go on the job, get programmed instructions then go to school in his second enlistment - those are the studies that I think we are headed toward and are now able to do; and they are the things that make implementation less likely.

Now, I would point out that we have jumped an echelon of management in that

Secretary Ferraro was speaking at a relatively high level saying that at managerial level you have our support to go into these new areas. At my level we want you to do that, but research isn't so implemented, so I can only say that there's some kind of clash or threatening or something. There's someone at his level saying yea, and there is someone in the research community saying we've got the methods and techniques and models, but there's someone in between and perhaps the word threaten applies to him.

CORMACK: I think it's summed up in the statement — I don't reflect the views of my Government — that emotion will only give way to logic if logic wears more rings or pips.

BROWN: Having two more rings than Lt. Cdr. Cormack, perhaps I can give you something logical. I'd like to refer back to one or two points in the earlier conversation. One quick comment on the simulator problem. I'm aware of one report from the United States recently which was a plea for the scientists or psychologists to get more actively involved in the design and implementation of the training that is done on simulators. I think it is true in most cases that many hundreds of thousands of dollars are spent on each simulator; the purpose of the simulator and the support for it is given by the scientists, but in most cases it is then turned over to the trainer for him to implement into the training program. I'm convinced that maximum training value is not received from the use of that simulator from a learning point of view without the involvement of the psychologist.

The main point I wanted to make I think relates to the question of individual differences and in my view this is the most critical point, or rather the recognition of individual differences is the most critical point, in many of our training programs. Almost all of our training programs tend (at least in my country) to be given at too fast a rate. This might be prompted to reduce costs, of course, but if your wastage rates are too high or this affects the quality of the training, the costs are going to be more in the long term. Because of this I would take a little exception to the one comment of Dr. Bryan (although I'm sure this is not what he meant) when he said that we should maximize the rate of each individual's learning. I think it's a semantic question I'm bringing up but I would hesitate to tell that to our trainers because they are maximizing rates all the time! I would much rather have it read something like maximize the learning for the rate of each individual and I'm sure this is what he means.

I was very interested in Dr. Taylor's paper which pointed out very clearly the importance of recognizing individual differences but I think it must be recognized that these effects apply within very restricted groups; and pilot training, I think, is a good example of one of these. Within the very highly select group which enters training — and you have an individualized instruction in terms of one instructor to one student — there are certain fixed limits within which you have to operate and it is very clear to us that the individual differences within that very select group have a great impact on the training which these people receive. I think it is this lack of recognition of individual differences by training staff which leads to certain inefficiencies in training. I think that if we could assist them to recognize and take these into account more, in training programs, we would all benefit.

Just one final comment — in most of the laboratory work in the past, individual differences have been denied. We need much more work which would deal directly with the effects of individual differences in training.

BRYAN: I suppose I will not disagree with your comments. It does show that we know rather less about the individual than we pretend to know. In a meeting at the University of Pittsburg — and which resulted in a book edited by Gagné called "Learning and Individual Differences" — we gathered together a group of people who were highly competent in the area and tried to identify from the other's literature what we knew about individual differences that we could say for sure ought to be taken into account with respect to learning. We hoped to get guidance from this as to how to take individual differences into account and when to take them into account. It was a very discouraging exercise. It's a very good book, I commend it to you, but if you want to use it as a way of getting good guidance from many years of laboratory research, I think you will find that we are rather less far along than some people think when they glibly speak of branching in programs on the basis of the characteristics of the individual.

NELSON: I suppose this should be addressed to Glenn Bryan. You mentioned that you're initiating project work and I know just a little bit about this but not an awful lot. It seems terribly relevant to the general topic of manpower research. I wonder if you're in a position to elaborate in any detail on this?

BRYAN: About a year ago we brought together a small group of individuals who represented some of the disciplines that had separately specialized but which were related to each other in the sense that they were all concerned about some aspect of "work". Our reason for doing this was that we believe now and believed then that the nature of work has changed so radically, that the meaning of work has changed so radically, that the need for work has changed so radically and that the rate of these changes is itself changing so very radically that it might be entirely wise to get some people thinking about the necessity for re-conceptionalizing the concept of work in the modern world. We have had, since that time, an additional meeting and we have formed a group of eminents who have agreed to meet twice yearly. They will meet each other and hopefully they will develop a study and research program which will be significant in this area. In an effort to keep the group small, we have one each of the following: Industrial Psychologist, Industrial Engineer, Social Psychologist, Industrial Psychiatrist, Business Administrator, Personnel and Training Researcher, Management Science Specialist, a Human Engineer and an Industrial Anthropologist. We will, as it becomes necessary, reluctantly increase the size of the Group and will probably include some Labour Lawyers and some Industrial Economists, for example. It has been most enlightening and stimulating to sit with this Group and to have them learn of each other's interests.

I think it would be helpful to give an example of the sort of thing that seems to be coming to the surface so far. Let's consider, if you will, the fact that an organization – such as the United States Navy and its task force on retention – is particularly interested in the job that a man gets done and it, in some sense, is trying to develop new arrangements and policies that will lead to these jobs being done more effectively and at a reduced cost. That's entirely legitimate of course but it does appear that there are at least three other jobs that the man himself – the job incumbent – may be concerned about and that perhaps the formal system should take into account in some more explicit way. For example, there is the job that the man's wife holds. Most military officers are paid at a rate where it is attractive for the wife to take on employment if the situation permits. For example, she may teach in the local public school. Under those circumstances, if the system decides that they should re-locate the man, since the system does those things, it may in fact create a situation within that family where the wife has to make a hard decision as to whether to give up the advancement opportunities that she clearly recognizes in the job that she holds. If you're interested in retaining effective personnel you may find that there are some circumstances where you fail to retain a man because his wife also has a profession, particularly if she has an interest in that and maybe is also contributing substantially towards the finances of the family.

Consider a second job that a technician may have after hours, it's called "moonlighting" in most places and it's done by radio mechanics who find employment in the local television shop and engine mechanics who work in the local garage. In many cases, this supplements their income substantially, it helps them to develop a skill which will have quick transitional value once they return to civilian life and, as a matter of fact, is referred to by some of them as a way of getting started back at being a civilian. When a system fails to acknowledge this job, it can find itself making blind personnel assignments that deprive the man of the opportunity to continue moonlighting quite unnecessarily and quite unknowingly.

Third and finally, in many instances the people in the career service are looking forward to a second career and they're very concerned about lining themselves up so that they may get into the best possible second career. Many of their own career choices, such as whether or not to re-enlist will hinge upon the value of the next assignment to their second career. I have been told by one of the members of the Group who is associated with the Tavistock Institute, that in one of the Scandinavian countries, where the young men have characteristically gone to sea, they are now having difficulty getting the young men to do so, not because the conditions of employment at sea have worsened, they haven't, but because the second career of being a small land owner and farmer has become so unproductive. If they do go to sea, many of the young men anticipate being washed up on the beach, so to speak, at an early age with limited opportunities for further employment.

This Group is looking into things like that and I think hopefully they will lead us in the direction of being able to cast our personnel systems in much larger terms of taking into account a greater proportion of a man's further life and not just those duty hours that he spends with us.

EDELMAN: I'm a bit puzzled, or perhaps the confusion is more general than mine, by the frequent use of the idea of systems thinking or systems approach. So far, I think Tolcott's presentation was the one which gave us a broad overall systems approach and within it there were a number of sub-systems, some of which pertain to manpower analysis, training and personnel management alike. A great deal of the more recent sessions have concentrated on sub-systems and I guess the problem is that you can use the term systems approach at any scale whether it's atomic or universal. I think this creates some of the confusion. I believe that much of the talk about a systems approach to training research is misleading — at least to me — because we're thinking on a rather modest scale of doing a particular part of the training job by using systems thinking. This can be done but all of the research effort eventually has to have some kind of an end result. There is another dirty real world which is not just a place where the work is done but where the decisions are made to use the results of research. As Secretary Ferraro passed on to us, people at his level are having to deal with larger system problems, say, the whole Defence Establishment or a whole Military Force. These are systems that have to be employed to discharge a particular task or mission, but there is a whole series of sub-systems that require the combination of material and human resources in the best fashion. Now the contributions that most of our colleagues here are making are directed to showing how to make those best decisions and each bit of information which is relayed to us here, hopefully, helps us make a better decision according to some criterion that we've agreed on. I don't sense enough concern, though, on the part of the community engaged in research to see that what it does has an eventual effect. I think this tends to create a very long interval between the research which we report and the utilization which can be made of it in actual forces.

I noticed in Dr. Bryan's remarks about the world of work, that he indicated that he would accept the economist with some reluctance. Maybe that was just casual, but I think that this is the key, perhaps, because as in the case of the civilian educational community, they have struggled for many years to try to get support and recognition for the jobs they're trying to do; but they hadn't, until recent years, succeeded in showing what the impact of education was in the total society. Now they've had a chance to experiment in developing societies to show that the rate of growth could be affected by the kind of educational and training job that you do and this is immediately giving them new stature and new support. I'm just wondering if there isn't a need for the research community to find a linkage for its work to be more effectively reflected at the highest possible management level so that, instead of having to argue for the value of what you're doing, it would be eagerly sought because you could show where the effect could be anticipated. I think the closest approach we have come to this, in this meeting, has been Tolcott's overall presentation as he says, hopefully, this may be accepted and we'll begin to move in that direction. I think we have a startling model to look at in the field of civilian education and how it has failed to arouse the larger part of our society, the governing part of our society, to the need for greater support for what it is doing. I think the economist is the first of the many disciplines that have to be allied with you in order to gain recognition and greater support.

BRYAN: One of the problems of doing something *ad lib* is that one ends up saying something that would have been edited out of written remarks! I certainly did not mean to imply that my reluctance at expanding the size of the Group was directed toward adding an economist. We are trying to keep the Group at a small workable size — it's already got a dozen people in it — but the Group itself has now decided which additional people we are to add to it. The Group has already indicated its recognition of a need for an appropriate economist and are actively seeking someone who has the right qualifications to be invited to join the Group.

I concur heartedly with the rest of Edelman's statement. I would like to say that there is a linkage that perhaps we haven't pointed out adequately, but, for example, in one of the large American computer companies they estimate that 15% of their technical field service manpower is devoted to having the technicians chase the training, i.e. 15% of the technicians, at any given time, are in transit or in a waiting status for the purpose of receiving training. If the research community can develop effective rules of channelling the training — so that it may be transmitted to the man without re-locating him — it would result in an effective increase of their manpower pool by 15% in this category, so cost considerations can, among other things, emphasize where the research needs are and where the pay-off might be.

EDELMAN: Your own example amplifies my point. What I'm looking for is a sensitivity measure index so that each research effort can be used to predict the possible impact on the end result. In an industrial concern you have your profit and loss statement and if you have a very effective management system, hopefully, you could determine that the failure you just mentioned in the computer field was costing money and that some alert researcher or engineer would have sensed this and said. " If you'll let me repackage this instruction, I can cut out a great deal of the field service which is merely taking the place of an adequate instruction ". There is a need on the part of this community which is concerned with research to find a mechanism and I urge you again to look at Tolcott's analysis as being the grand plan, very difficult to implement but necessarily sound in its theory, as to how to make yourselves felt in this higher echelon which feeds you and enables you to develop.

SHRIVER: I do have a thought on that, not operating from a grand plan perhaps but doing something that we can do right now. I'd like to describe the activities of my Group who previously worked on electronic maintenance and came from that into the study of what spare parts should be stocked at what echelon. What we are doing now is simulating the logistic system of the Army on an IBM 360 computer. Our reason for doing this is that we have some idea of how we can change human capabilities through training, that is, in our minds we don't have to go through the drill of finding out what capabilities we can achieve, we've reached the point where we can make guesses about it. Instead, what we have is a simulation; and what we're going to put in as parameters of the simulation are: what if we could change the person's capabilities so that he would process things in this way? We would then run that through on the simulator and the read-out would be in terms of cost-effectiveness — what it costs the logistic system and the number of Army units which are operating at 80% of their equipment, 90%, or whatever. We are doing a sensitivity study in that sense, making our guesses about what we might be able to achieve in human capabilities, running them through the computer, seeing whether it would make any difference in the long run in cost or effectiveness. When we find out from this what pays off we'll see whether we can actually achieve our aims through training.

It's just a simple example, without a grand scale design, of what we can do with simulation. In the RAND studies they were only able to simulate 25 items in inventory but with the larger computers, well, we're up to the thousands.

Leadership Style and Organizational Performance[1]

FRED E. FIEDLER
DEPARTMENT OF PSYCHOLOGY
UNIVERSITY OF ILLINOIS

I. INTRODUCTION

We generally take it for granted that the success of a group or an organization depends primarily upon the quality of its leadership. We ascribe the success of business organizations to the managerial abilities of the top men and we credit the outcome of military campaigns to the generalship of the commander. Business and industry, as well as military organizations, have, therefore, devoted a great deal of time and energy to the task of identifying and developing good leaders.

In particular, there have been two major questions in the area of leadership. The first of these is how one can identify and select the men who will rise to a position of leadership. The second question concerns the factors that determine how a man becomes an effective leader.

I.I. Major Problems in Leadership Theory

As yet, we have not been able to find any personality traits or attributes which can be utilized to differentiate effectively the potential leader from the follower. All folklore and isolated anecdotes to the contrary, there seem to be no distinct leadership traits although such attributes as higher intelligence, greater physical size, etc., are somewhat more characteristic of leaders than non-leaders. As a result, there are also no effective or practical leadership selection tests. Who becomes a leader depends in part on personality factors, such as intelligence and ability to get along with people. However, in large part, it also depends on economic, political, and social factors, and on the academic background and experience which a man happens to have and the skills a job happens to require. As Warner and Abegglen's (1955) work suggests, the most effective way to become a business executive is to come from a family which owns 51 per cent of the stock. Likewise, illiterates do not become officers, and army doctors do not work as construction labourers, no matter what people think of their leadership ability.

Let us then talk about the second question. Can we predict who will become an effective leader? Given a number of men who are assigned to positions of leadership in comparable groups or organizations, can we predict whose department, combat crew, or task force is most likely to succeed or to fail? It is to this second problem of leadership that we shall address ourselves here.

I.2. Definitions of Leadership

What, first of all, do we mean by leadership? Leadership is a problem of influencing and controlling others. By *effective* leadership we mean that the leader's group has performed well, or that it has succeeded, in comparison to other groups which performed less well or which failed. In other words, leadership effectiveness, as we define the

[1] Research conducted under Office of Naval Research Contract N6-ori-07135, and ARPA Order No. 454 under, Office of Naval Research Contract 177-472, Nonr 1834(36) and Contract DA-49-193-MD-2060 with the Office of the Surgeon General.

term here, is measured on the basis of group performance. An orchestra conductor has to be evaluated on how well his orchestra plays; a general is effective to the extent to which his troops win battles.

Yet, it has been extremely difficult to identify the leaders who are consistently successful. The successful junior staff officer does not necessarily succeed as a field commander, nor is the best field commander always the best staff officer. As a study by Flanagan (1949) showed, the performance of a naval officer on shore duty is completely unrelated to his performance aboard ship. And investigations of air force crews, open hearth shops, and similar groups have shown that the crew which performs well on one task may not perform well on a different task. For example, the performance of bomber crews in visual bombing was unrelated to the performance of these same bomber crews in radar bombing missions (Fiedler, 1967).

What I am saying is not great news. Different situations require different leadership. This means that the same type of leadership style or the same leadership behaviour will not be effective in all situations. The question is, what kinds of situations require what kinds of leadership? If we want to predict leadership performance, we must learn how to match a man's leadership style with his leadership situation.

2. MEASURING LEADERSHIP STYLE

Leadership research has identified two major modes in which leaders interact with their group members. One of these has been identified as a human relations-oriented, considerate, permissive, or nondirective type of leadership. The other is the directive, task-oriented, and structuring type of leadership which we associate more commonly with orthodox supervisory and military training. This latter is characterized by the attitude that " I'll do the thinking and you carry out the orders ". Both of these modes of leadership have been effective in some situations and not in others, neither of them works in all situations.

This is quite clear from the research program which we have conducted at the University of Illinois since 1951 under contract with the Office of Naval Research and since 1954 with the Office of the Surgeon General of the Army. Our work has utilized a measure of relationship-oriented versus task-oriented leadership styles. The score is obtained by asking the individual to think of all people with whom he has ever worked. He then describes his Least Preferred Coworker, (or LPC), that is the person in his life with whom he has been least able to work well. This may be someone with whom he works at the time or someone he knew a long time ago. The items follow the form of Osgood's Semantic Differential, for example:

Intelligent : 8 : 7 : 6 : 5 : 4 : 3 : 2 : 1 : Not Intelligent

Friendly[1] : 8 : 7 : 6 : 5 : 4 : 3 : 2 : 1 : Not Friendly

A favourable description of the Least Preferred Coworker indicates a relationship-oriented style; an unfavourable description indicates a task-oriented style of leadership. Since this Least Preferred Coworker does not need to be a member of his task group, the LPC score can be obtained before the leader is assigned to his group.

We have used this leadership style measure, or variants of it, in a wide variety of interacting groups, ranging from high school basketball teams and surveying parties to military combat crews, research and management teams, and boards of directors. We found that relationship-oriented leaders tend to be more effective in harmonious creative groups, in research organizations, and policy and decision-making groups while task-oriented leaders have been more effective in harmonious combat crew situations, in management teams, and in basketball and surveying teams. The opposite results were found in groups which were not harmonious or in which the leader did not get along with his

---

[1] Other items were confident-not confident; impatient-patient; hardworking-not hardworking; close-distant; lazy-ambitious; warm-cold; productive-not productive; sociable-not sociable; casual-formal; considerate-not considerate; dependable-not dependable; agreeable-not agreeable; creative-not creative; and sympathetic-not sympathetic.

men. These are extremely complex relations. How can we account for these findings and how can we use them?

3. SITUATIONAL FACTORS AFFECTING LEADERSHIP INFLUENCE

We define leadership as a relationship in which one person tries to influence others in the performance of a common task. It is obvious that some men are better than others in influencing their subordinates. It is equally obvious, however, that some leadership situations make it relatively easy for the leader to influence his men, while other situations make it very difficult. It was undoubtedly easier for the captain of a galley to influence his galley slaves than it is for the disliked chairman of a volunteer group to influence his members. But the influential leader is not necessarily an effective leader. By way of analogy, if you take your physician's advice, he is influencing you. But whether or not his advice will cure you is another question. Since leadership is an influence relationship, it seemed reasonable that we would need to classify situations on the basis of how much influence the situation provides the leader. Let us then look at some major situational factors which determine whether a leader will find it easy or difficult to influence his group.

3.1. Factors Determining Situational Favourableness

The first and seemingly most important factor is the degree to which the group accepts and trusts its leader, the degree to which the men have confidence in the leader and want to do what he tells them. The leader who is accepted and liked will have less difficulty in exerting influence than the leader who is disliked and distrusted. While the ability to be accepted and trusted is in part a personality attribute, it is also situational since a large proportion of groups accept their legitimate leaders.

The second important factor which determines leader influence is the leader's position power, the power that the organization vests in the leadership position. Can the leader hire and fire, can he reprimand or punish, or is he confined to mild remonstrations and silent rebukes? Is he appointed by higher authority or does he serve at the pleasure of the group? Most military leaders, and almost all managers and supervisors in industry have high position power, most committee chairmen tend to have low position power.

A third important factor is defined by the degree to which the task of the group is structured or unstructured, the degree to which the job can be spelled out and programmed in detail, or to which it must be left vague and nebulous. The typical military task or production job is highly structured, the typical policy and decision-making tasks, committee assignments and research problems are unstructured. If the job is spelled out in standard operating instructions, or if it can be performed according to certain rules and routines, the leader has correspondingly more influence because he can tell his men what to do and how to do it. But a leader cannot tell his men to be creative, or how to develop a policy or decide an issue.

These are at least three major factors which determine leader influence. These three dimensions lead to a classification of group situations shown on *Figure 1*. Just as there is no one style of leadership which is effective for all groups, so there is no one type of situation that makes a group effective. Liked leaders do not on the average perform more effectively than do disliked leaders; similarly, powerful leaders do not perform better than leaders with low position power.

Please note that this says nothing about how intrinsically difficult the task itself may be. A structured task, say building an electronic computer, may be much more difficult than an unstructured job of preparing an entertainment program. But the leader's problem of influencing the group will be greater in the volunteer committee than in the task of building a computer. It will obviously be easier to lead if you are the liked and trusted sergeant of a rifle squad (Cell 1) than if you are the informal leader of a recreational basketball team (Cell 2), and it will be very difficult indeed to be the disliked and distrusted leader of a volunteer group which is asked to plan the program of an annual meeting or the disliked chairman of a board of inquiry (Cell 8). In other words, we can order the cells on the basis of how favourable or unfavourable the situation will be for the leader.

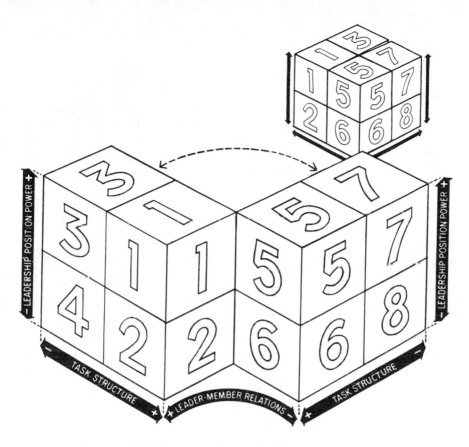

Fig. 1 A MODEL FOR THE CLASSIFICATION OF GROUP-TASK SITUATIONS.
(SOURCE: THE HARVARD BUSINESS REVIEW, SEPTEMBER-OCTOBER, 1965,
p. 117. REPRODUCED BY PERMISSION.)

4. THE CONTINGENCY MODEL

We are now able to ask what kind of leadership style various situations require. To answer this question we have correlated the leadership style score with the performance of the leader's group in each of the situations on which we had data (*Figure 2*).

The correlation between the leadership style score, and group performance is shown on the vertical axis of this graph. The difficulty of the situation is shown on the horizontal axis. There are over 800 different groups represented on this plot.

What does this figure show? Positive correlations, that is, points falling above the midline of the graph, tell us that the relationship-oriented leaders performed better than did task-oriented leaders. Negative correlations, represented by points falling below the midline of the graph, tell us that the task-oriented leaders performed better than did the relationship-oriented leaders.

Taken as a whole, the plot shows that the task-oriented leaders are most effective in two types of situations: those in which the leader has very much influence as well as those in which he has relatively little influence. The relationship-oriented person is

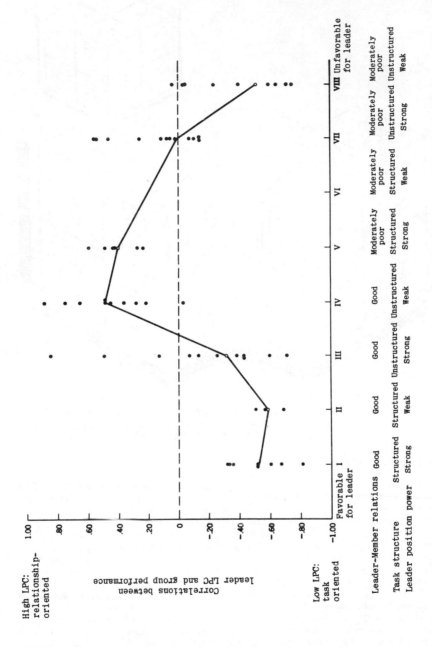

Fig. 2 CORRELATIONS BETWEEN LEADERS' LPC SCORES AND GROUP EFFECTIVENESS PLOTTED FOR EACH CELL.

most effective in situations which are only moderately favourable for the leader. In effect, these data reconcile the two major viewpoints in leadership theory.

These findings fit our everyday experience. In a situation in which the leader is well respected, liked and accepted, in which the leader has power, and in which the job is clear-cut, the leader knows what should be done and how it should be done, and the members are ready and willing to do what the leader tells them. In this case, a committee approach of participative, democratic leadership would be a waste of time. Consider the leader who is in charge of counting down a space shot. You would hardly expect him to say, "Fellows, it's twenty minutes to blastoff. What do you think we ought to do next?" Or consider the company commander whose unit is under attack. This is not the time to call a committee meeting.

In a moderately favourable situation when the leader is accepted but the task is vague and unstructured, the leader must rely on the cooperation of his subordinates. Such groups are committees, boards, panels, creative groups with tasks involving policy and decision making, or solving problems. This requires a concern with good interpersonal relations, a considerate attitude, respect for the opinions and recommendations of others. The man who pushes his committee into premature decisions, or who manipulates his group into approving his own ideas is a poor committee chairman, and he does not really make use of the resources at his disposal.

In the very unfavourable situation, the task-oriented leader again performs best. This follows the old army adage that any decision is better than no decision under conditions of crisis. The disliked committee chairman who asks his members what to do next might get the answer of "Let's all go home".

5. VALIDATION OF THE CONTINGENCY MODEL

To what extent is this model of leadership effectiveness predictive rather than just heuristic? Let me briefly describe three validation studies. One was conducted in cooperation with the Belgian Navy, a second in industrial and business settings, and a third with the cooperation of volunteer medical teams in Honduras.

5.1. The Belgian Navy Study

This investigation (Fiedler, 1966) involved 96 groups which were experimentally assembled. We had 48 groups with recruit leaders who had low position power and 48 groups with petty officers who had high position power. Forty-eight groups consisted of either Flemish men or of French-speaking Walloons, and the other 48 groups were culturally heterogeneous, that is, they had a leader from one language group while the members were from the other. The group tasks involved routing a ship through various ports by the shortest way; and writing a recruiting letter to young men urging them to make the navy their career.

The group situations were classified according to the favourableness of the group for the leader. We assumed that the leadership situation would be easier in homogeneous groups than in heterogeneous groups, that it would be easier for a petty officer than for a recruit, and for a leader who felt liked and accepted than for one who did not.

We predicted that the task-oriented leaders would perform best in the very favourable and the very unfavourable situations, but that the relationship-oriented leaders would perform best in the intermediate situations. *Figure 3* shows that the hypothesis was supported.

5.2. Industrial Work Groups

A second validation study by Hunt (1967), investigated three business and industrial concerns. The sets of groups consisted of meat markets and grocery departments of a supermarket chain, of research chemists and radiation physicists from a large research organization, and of general foremen and their departments in a heavy machinery manufacturing plant.

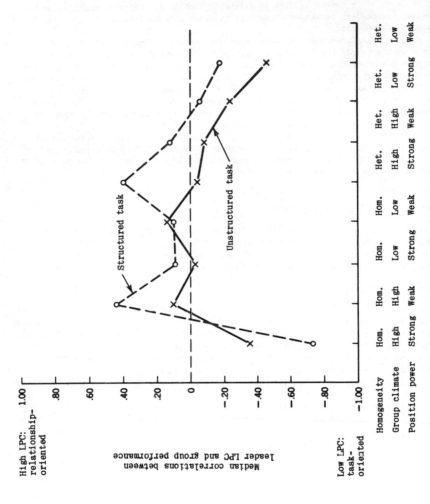

Fig. 3 MEDIAN CORRELATIONS BETWEEN LEADER LPC AND GROUP PERFORMANCE IN UNSTRUCTURED AND STRUCTURED TASKS OF THE BELGIAN NAVY STUDY

Hunt classified these groups on the basis of the three dimensions, and then correlated the leadership style score describing the least preferred coworker (LPC) with the effectiveness ratings and performance data of these groups. The points indicating the correlations have been plotted on *Figure 4*. These points have been superimposed on the curve based on the original data we had obtained in our studies. As can be seen, the obtained relations are quite similar to those which were predicted.

5.3. Medical Volunteer Teams

A third validation study (Fiedler, O'Brien, and Ilgen, 1967) was conducted in cooperation with an organization which sends teenagers to Honduras in summer to establish and operate public health clinics giving inoculations and vaccinations, and to perform community development work. The study was conducted in the summer of 1966 and involved 62 teams. Most of the teams consisted of two to three persons. Each of the teams was assigned to a village for a term of three weeks duration. There were three terms or sets of teams in Honduras during the summer. Leadership style scores were obtained before the group members left the United States. Performance scores were based on ratings of the project director and his staff members who had the opportunity to observe a large number of the teams in the course of the summer.

The difficulty of the situation for the leader was based on two measures: (a) the group atmosphere scores from the leader, that is, ratings of the extent to which his team seemed to accept him, and (b) village stressfulness ratings which were provided by the project director who considered, in his rating, the isolation of the village, the degree to which the living and working conditions were primitive, and the degree to which the teams were isolated from the other teams and the main body of the project.

We can now order teams on the basis of the situational favourableness and correlate the leader's LPC score and the group's performance for each of the steps on the favourableness scale (Figure 5). As can be seen, the results clearly support the hypothesis of the Contingency Model. This study shows that the model can be generalized to situations in which a team operates in a stressful foreign environment. We have conducted additional studies, most recently with the U.S. Post Office Department, which provide further validation of the Contingency Model hypothesis.

To recapitulate, the Contingency Model predicts the performance of all kinds of interacting task groups including various work teams in business and industry and in heterocultural situations. It shows that the effectiveness of a group is contingent upon the favourableness of the situation as well as upon the leadership style. It is obvious that our data reflect lawful and fairly general phenomena in organizational behaviour.

6. IMPLICATIONS FOR IMPROVING LEADERSHIP PERFORMANCE

What are the major implications of the model for understanding leadership and supervision, and what does the model tell us about leadership selection and training, and the more general problem of improving group performance?

The major implication is, of course, that the effectiveness of the leader depends on the favourableness of the group situation as well as on his own particular style of leadership. If we want to predict leadership performance, we have to go beyond the personal attributes of the leader, and beyond the personality variables which we can obtain with psychological tests or interviews. In fact, we cannot really speak of a good leader or a poor leader but only of a leader who is effective in Situation A and ineffective in Situation B.

We cannot predict performance much better than chance by knowing only a man's leadership style or knowing only the situation. Leaders with strong position power do not perform more effectively than leaders with weak position power. The petty officers in the Belgian Navy did not have better performing groups than did the recruit leaders who had low position power. Homogeneous groups typically do not perform better than heterogeneous groups. And liked and accepted leaders do not perform more effectively than leaders who are not liked or accepted.

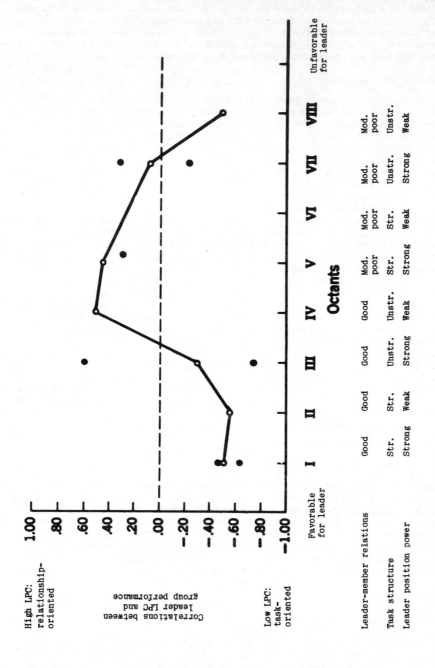

Fig. 4 CORRELATIONS BETWEEN SUPERVISOR LPC AND TEAM PERFORMANCE IN VARIOUS WORK SITUATIONS OBTAINED BY HUNT (1967).

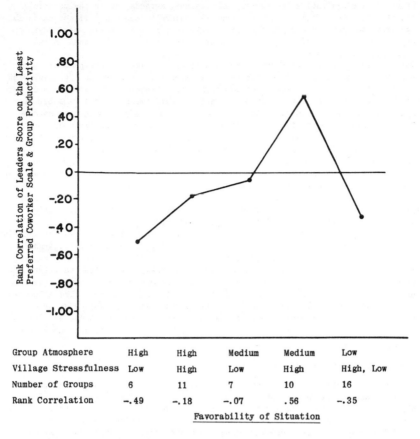

Group Atmosphere	High	High	Medium	Medium	Low
Village Stressfulness	Low	High	Low	High	High, Low
Number of Groups	6	11	7	10	16
Rank Correlation	−.49	−.18	−.07	.56	−.35

Favorability of Situation

Fig. 5. CORRELATIONS BETWEEN LEADER LPC SCORES AND TEAM PERFORMANCE UNDER DIFFERENT CONDITIONS OF GROUP ATMOSPHERE AND SITUATIONAL STRESS IN HONDURAN VILLAGES

6.1. Leader Selection

The implications of our data for leadership recruitment and selection are quite clear. If we wish to improve organizational performance by selecting leaders we must first classify the favourableness of the situation in which the prospective leaders are going to work. And if we want executives who perform effectively as leaders, we must place them into situations which fit their particular leadership style. One likely reason why our leadership selection methods have failed is that we have tried to select without taking into account the situation in which the man is going to work.

6.2. Leadership Training

A second method for improving leadership performance has been through leadership training. In fact, when we talk about improving leadership, we immediately think of training. And yet, after all these years we have no convincing evidence that leadership training improves organizational performance.

Let me stress that I am not speaking here of training military leaders or business executives in administrative procedures, in personnel methods, or in the technical aspects of their jobs. Training of this type is obviously important, if not essential, to organizational performance. My present remarks concern the training of leadership ability or leadership behavior *per se,* and my criterion of effectiveness is the organizational performance.

This is clearly a crucial problem. Yet according to Gilmer (1966, p. 245) " A rigorously controlled study of the value of executive training has ... never been conducted ". And in a recent survey of business firms, Newport (1963) found no evidence that leadership training pays off in organizational performance in any tangible manner.

Let me add one more finding to this meagre list. Our study in Belgium compared nineteen year old raw recruits with petty officers who had received two years of leadership training, and who had an average of ten years of navy leadership experience. In none of these tasks did the groups of the trained and experienced petty officers perform more effectively on the average than did the groups of the recruit leaders. Moreover, the number of years of navy experience – which is itself on-the-job training – was not correlated with the leadership performance of the petty officers.

If ten years of leadership experience and two years of leadership training produced no marked effects on performance, it is highly doubtful that a few lectures or even a few weeks of intensive training will accomplish much more.

If our theory is correct, training can be effective only if it teaches the individual first to diagnose the situation correctly and then either to modify his leadership style to fit the situation, or to modify the situation to fit his leadership style.

I submit that it is very difficult to change leadership style. When we talk about leadership styles we are not dealing with surface behaviors but with deeply ingrained patterns of relating to others. It seems doubtful that these patterns of relating can be switched on and off at will. The other possibility, teaching the individual or his superior to modify the favourableness of the situation, should be considered more seriously. I should like to discuss this in the light of my final remarks about upgrading leadership performance.

6.3. Organizational Engineering

We have considered leadership recruitment and selection, and leadership training. Let me now advance a third possibility, that of " organizational engineering " (Fiedler, 1965), for improving organizational effectiveness. We have always implicitly assumed that the executive's job is fixed but that the executive's personality is plastic and malleable. However, there are few things more difficult to change than personality. A course of psychotherapy takes years at best, and our success with changing the personality of drug addicts, criminals, and, for that matter, husbands and wives, has been less than a resounding success. Would it not be easier, therefore, to fit the executive's job to his leadership style, than to change his personality to fit each of his successive jobs?

Let me just give a few examples of how this might be done. We can change the power of a man's position by giving him final authority over his department or by requiring that all decisions be cleared by his superiors or by others in his department. We can give a man subordinates who are equal to him in rank and prestige or we can assign him men who are two or three ranks below him. We can change his title, or the flow of information, or his authority to hire and fire, to promote and give raises.

We can change the leader-member relations by changing the homogeneity of the group. Interdisciplinary groups are notoriously difficult to handle, as are groups in which members have different cultural and language background, or technical training. We can give one man subordinates who are easy-going and amiable and we can give another all the troublemakers of the organization. And we can improve a man's relations with group members by training him to be more expert on the job.

We can sometimes modify task structure. We can spell out the tasks for one man and give him detailed operating instructions while we give the very broadly defined tasks and assignments to other men.

In fact, organizations frequently do modify the jobs they assign to executives, and almost all jobs are amenable to some organizational modifications, either by the leader himself or by his own superiors. We frequently say that one supervisor can, while another one cannot, handle difficult personnel problems, that one man has to be given considerable leeway while another one can operate only if his authority is limited, and that some men are good problem solvers and others good in structured production jobs. The changes in supervisory jobs which we are discussing are quite small and do not require reorganizing the entire unit. Our research does not suggest something brand new but rather it provides a rationale and a better basis for making these organizational engineering decisions.

There can be no question that new approaches to leadership are required. We are facing increasing shortages of highly trained, highly intelligent executive manpower. We can no longer afford to discard a highly qualified specialist just because he may not perform effectively in a particular leadership position, nor should we expect that a man will be an outstanding leader no matter what the situation. Rather, we need to learn how to engineer the organization to make the leader effective.

REFERENCES

Fiedler, F.E. (1965), " Engineer the job to fit the manager ", *Harvard Business Review, 43,* 115-122.

Fiedler, F.E. (1966), " The effect of leadership and cultural heterogeneity on group performance: A test of the contingency model ", *Journal of Experimental Social Psychology, 2,* 237-264.

Fiedler, F.E. (1967), *A theory of leadership effectiveness,* New York: McGraw-Hill.

Fiedler, F.E., O'Brien, G.E., and Ilgen, D. (1967), " The effect of leadership style upon performance and adjustment in volunteer teams operating in a stressful foreign environment ", Urbana, Ill.: *Group Effectiveness Research Laboratory, University of Illinois.*

Flanagan, J.C. (1949), " Critical requirements: A new approach to employee evaluation ", *Personnel Psychology, 2,* 419-425.

Gilmer, B. von H. (1966), *Industrial Psychology: Second edition,* New York: McGraw-Hill.

Hunt, J.G. (1967), " A test of the leadership contingency model in three organizations ", Urbana, Ill.: *Group Effectiveness Research Laboratory, University of Illinois.*

Newport, M.G. (1963), " Middle management development in industrial organizations ", *Ph.D. dissertation, University of Illinois.*

Warner, W.L., and Abegglen, J.C. (1955), *Big business leaders in America,* New York: Harper.

Comments and a Reply

PIETER DRENTH

FREE UNIVERSITY OF AMSTERDAM

EDWIN FLEISHMAN

AMERICAN INSTITUTES FOR RESEARCH

DRENTH

In my opinion the work of Dr. Fiedler has made a very substantial contribution to the understanding of leadership behaviour and its effects on group performance. Once again it was shown to be a fallacy to try to find and to prescribe a " one best style of leadership ". However, Fiedler did not stop at repeating the well known opinion that leadership behaviour should depend on both structural task aspects and the social context in order to be optimally effective, but he actually isolated and operationalized three important variables in this context; and on top of that he was able to integrate this seemingly complex set of variables in a convincing and useful model. Theory and practice can turn these results to good account; the work has important implications for selection and placement, for training and especially for modifying the task structure and job-design as has been formulated at the end of the presented paper.

As is well known, much research on leadership is correlational in nature and accordingly subject to the traditional difficulties associated with this method: one gets no evidence of the direction of causality, and even a third variable might be responsible for the interrelation of the two variables. Therefore we can call ourselves happy to find in Fiedler's work a great deal of experimental data and to find quite some agreement between results based on laboratory groups and real life situations. This is something that would not necessarily be immediately expected. After all in an experimental design we nearly always deal with short-term criteria, whereas an empirical study usually works with long-range criteria.

Mainly in order to give Dr. Fiedler a chance to elaborate a little further some of his interesting lines of thought and to clarify one or two points in his paper I will make a few comments. In doing so I will not restrict myself completely to the present paper but also refer once in a while to Fiedler's earlier work, and also try to draw upon some findings from our own research on leadership.

To start off with a minor point: to our surprise we found in a study on a small Dutch sample of 13 groups of engineers a considerable variation in the usually constant MPC score (Most Preferred Co-worker). Since we found a significant correlation of this MPC measure with considerate leadership – as judged by the Ohio State Leadership Scales – it was not merely error-variance.

Now, it may very well be that this is a typical sample-factor, but I would say:

i. it might be worth checking, especially in doing research in another culture with different appraisal habits;

ii. in case one finds this variance the ASO and LPC measure are not to be used interchangeably. (The ASO – Assumed Similarity between Opposites – score indicates the distance between the most and least preferred co-worker.)

May I now make some remarks regarding the most appropriate leadership style in terms of Fiedler's concepts.

The description of the high and low LPC-leader suggests that Fiedler classifies these extremes as approximating the employee oriented and the task oriented style, or as it has been called by the Ohio State Leadership studies the distinction between consideration and initiating of structure. However, in several studies evidence has been presented that these latter two styles of leadership (consideration and initiating structure) do not represent a polar contrast like the high and low poles of the LPC (or ASO) dimension. For example in factor-analytic studies these two factors have turned out to be clearly distinct. Therefore in my opinion it is not permissible to draw a direct parallel between the one LPC dimension of Fiedler and the two different styles: task and employee orientation. As Fiedler has already noted, if a connection has to be made I am inclined to underscore the close relationship between the LPC score and the one factor " High-low on Consideration ".

Again we have some data from our own research that we would like to use for a further exploration of the ASO measure. We found a positive correlation between ASO and the satisfaction of the worker with social relations and with esteem; and a negative correlation with the satisfaction with self-actualization. It seems likely that indeed the high ASo leader creates a climate of warmth and good relations, but indiscriminately so! This experience can be shared by any group member whether he will be a good or a poor worker, for there is no way to actualize and to prove oneself.

Drawing this line further one might say that the low ASO (or LPC) leader would be comparable with the supervisor who shows consideration as a response to effort and accomplishment rather than as an undiscriminating supervisory style. According to Vroom (1964, p. 217) this " conditional consideration" is more effective in motivating subordinates than the " unconditional consideration ".

Now, as said before, one of the most significant conclusions from Fiedler's work is that there is not one absolute kind of leadership behaviour that can be advised at any time and for any situation. Generally when we think of leadership training we think of how a leader should modify his style in order to cope optimally with a particular situation. The best style of leadership is an adaptive style; Fiedler operationalizes this modification as up and down the LPC/ASO dimension. At this point I find it difficult to reconcile the two points of view.

I would think this adaptive leadership behaviour can be seen as

i. a relative emphasis on employee needs and group performance at the same time. This would be in accordance with the recent literature on leadership (Likert, Argyris, Blake, Fleishman);

ii. the above mentioned " conditional consideration " depending on the effectiveness of the subordinate.

However, neither of these two possibilities seems to coincide with the variation on the LPC dimension. Not the first possibility because here we deal with independent factors, not the second because in our foregoing remarks we developed the idea that this adaptive behaviour would just fall to the one pole – low ASO. Somewhere along these lines of thought I possibly made a mistake, or started from a wrong assumption, but maybe Dr. Fiedler can help us to clarify this obscurity.

In any case it is true that in order to obtain a real understanding of what is meant by this adaptive leadership style the essential meaning of the LPC/ASO dimension should be explored. It is also true that the original idea about this score – as indicating a personality factor or even a rather stable attitude pattern that shows consistency between situations and groups – would force us to abandon the hope of training people to be able to modify their leadership style at all.

As the next point I would like to comment on the three intervening variables: Leader-member Relations, Task Structure and Position Power.

In the first place their *sequence*. It is apparent that the sequence of importance of these three factors has a substantial influence on the path of the curve. Although the proposed sequence L-M, TS and PP has been made plausible, I believe its correctness has not yet been demonstrated empirically.

Secondly their *interrelationship*, a problem that also has been mentioned by Fiedler himself (Fiedler, 1964, p. 183). In the contingency model use is made of some sort of weighted composite procedure in which L-M receives the highest weight and PP the lowest. It seems to me that this is only applicable within certain limits. As soon as one of the variables exceeds positively or negatively a certain margin a multiple-cutoff model might apply better.

In the third place the *choice* of the three variables. Here again Fiedler has already mentioned this issue by saying that these three are not the only ones. In my opinion the need-structure of the group members is a highly important variable.

The work of Vroom has already demonstrated the importance of the need for democratic leadership as an intervening variable between on the one hand democratic leadership behaviour and on the other hand satisfaction and performance of the worker. Likewise in our own research we sometimes found the needs of the group-members to be clearly significant moderator variables. For instance – and this is to my mind highly relevant for

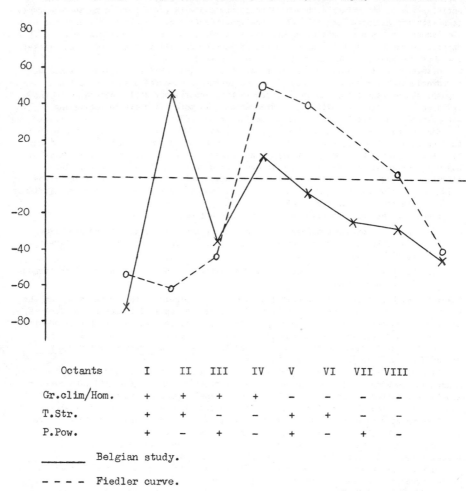

Octants	I	II	III	IV	V	VI	VII	VIII
Gr.clim/Hom.	+	+	+	+	–	–	–	–
T.Str.	+	+	–	–	+	+	–	–
P.Pow.	+	–	+	–	+	–	+	–

———— Belgian study.

- - - - Fiedler curve.

Fig. 1

Fiedler's factor " Leader-group relations " as related to the LPC dimension – the need for consideration turned out to be a significant moderator in the relationship between Social Leadership and satisfaction with the leader. Especially should this be considered in cross-cultural research where needs and expectations on this point might differ considerably.

Finally a question on the Belgian study. Maybe I did not fully understand the variables as operationalized in this study, but it seems to me that this triplet of variables has not been used consequently and comparably with the former research. On the one hand a fourth factor " group climate " has been introduced and on the other the variable " task structure " has been made an independent condition on the basis of which two separate curves have been drawn.

I have used the data to draw a curve in my opinion more comparable with the original curve of Fiedler. In order to tap the particular dimension of leader-member relations Fiedler has used either sociometric acceptance of the leader or a rating of the group's atmosphere (both seeming to reflect relatively similar relations). In accordance with this idea I have used as an index for this particular dimension in the Belgian study the two contrasts: high group climate and homogeneity versus low group climate and hetero-geneity. In doing so I obtained a curve that differed rather extensively from Fiedler's original curvelinear curve. Especially octants II, IV and V diverged rather sharply. Only the two extremes turned out to be exactly similar (see Fig.1). My question is this: Is there any reason why the data from the Belgian study have been arranged in a certain different way, and – if my rearrangement is correct – is there any explanation for the differences in results?

REFERENCES

Fiedler, F. Contingency model of leadership effectiveness in: *" Advances in experimental social psychology "*, New York, 1964, pp. 149-190.
Fiedler, F. Leadership and leadership effectiveness traits: A reconceptualization of the leader-ship trait problem. In: Petrullo, L. & Bass, B.M. *" Leadership and interpersonal behaviour "*. New York, 1961, pp. 179-186.
Vroom, V. *Work and Motivation.* Pittsburgh, 1964.

FIEDLER

Dr. Drenth makes three points. The first deals with the relationship between LPC and ASO, namely, the degree to which the two measures, the least preferred coworker scores and the older scores, the Assumed Similarity between Opposites, might be comparable. We have generally found correlations in the 90's between LPC and ASO with large samples. Dr. Drenth said that his study was based on thirteen cases. There are, therefore, possibilities of some variation due to sample size. This is not to say that these measures may not differ to some extent, but I do not feel that the measures differ markedly. The much more important point which Dr. Drenth raised concerns the problem of the different styles of task and employee relations and their relation with LPC.

Now if I may just take a few moments I would like to clarify a problem which has bothered us for some time, namely the apparent confusion between leadership behavior and leadership style. Perhaps the very best measures of leadership behavior I can name offhand are consideration and initiation of structure, the measures which the Ohio State Group introduced. We have not found any consistent relations between our measure of leadership style, LPC, and leadership behavior. We have conceptualized LPC, our leader-ship style score, as a motivational measure, that is, you don't usually act in a task-oriented or a relationship-oriented way unless the situation triggers you to act that way. I happen to have two extra graphs which indicate what I have in mind.

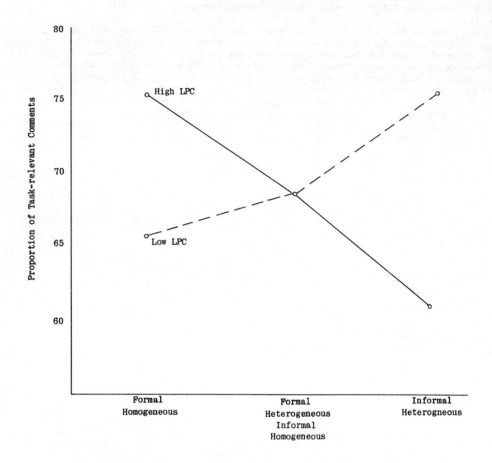

Fig. 2 PROPORTION OF TASK-RELEVANT COMMENTS BY HIGH LPC AND LOW LPC GROUPS
UNDER THREE DIFFERENT CONDITIONS OF FAVOURABLENESS IN THE DUTCH STUDY.

392

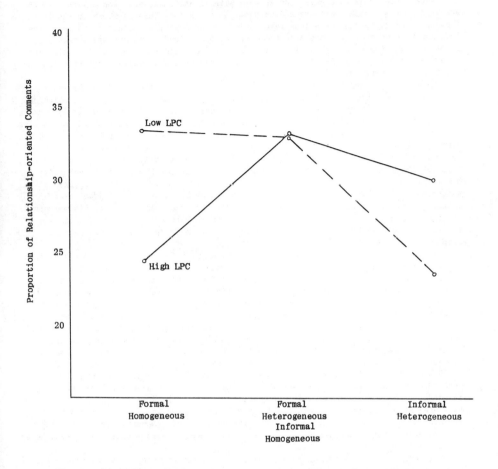

Fig. 3 PROPORTION OF RELATIONSHIP-ORIENTED COMMENTS BY HIGH LPC AND LOW LPC
GROUPS UNDER THREE DIFFERENT CONDITIONS OF FAVOURABLENESS IN THE DUTCH STUDY.

On the vertical axis of Figure 2 is the rate at which leaders make task-relevant comments. On the horizontal axis – this happens to come from a study in Holland on groups homogeneous and heterogeneous in religion – is the difficulty of the situation for the leader. Notice that the high LPC leader makes fewer and fewer task-relevant comments as the difficulty increases. The low LPC leader whom we have called task-oriented makes more and more task-oriented comments.

Exactly the opposite occurs when we work with relationship-oriented comments which are very similar to the Ohio State consideration dimension. This is shown on the third figure. As the situation gets less favourable for the leader, in other words as he has less and less control over the situations the high LPC leader makes increasingly more relationship-oriented comments. It is somewhat like a child whose mother is not paying enough attention to him. As the situation gets tough he starts asking for attention and makes more and more demands.

The low LPC leader, or task-oriented leader, in effect withdraws from the inter-personal relationship and concerns himself with the task. Now I would like to point out, therefore, that LPC and, as a matter of fact the correlation between consideration and initiation of structure, will differ markedly depending upon the slice of the situational difficulty dimension you are in. It seems to me this is perhaps one of the most important findings in our studies. The situational difficulty dimension determines the degree to which a person will concern himself with the interpersonal relationship. It also, by the way, determines the degree to which a high LPC leader or low LPC leader is adjustive for his members or maladjustive for his members. When everything goes well, when the situation is not threatening, that is when the leader has a lot of influence over his group, the low LPC person is the successful leader who can relate well to his members and can give them satisfaction. When the situation is very stressful and threatening, then it is the high LPC relationship-oriented leader who gives his members personal support and satisfaction, but he isn't successful.

Dr. Drenth's second point concerned the problem of " Can we modify leadership style ", and here again I would like to refer to these graphs; we can change leadership behavior and I suppose we can change leadership style too, but leadership behavior will differ as the situational difficulty differs. Leadership style, obviously, will remain the same.

One further comment on this problem – there have been a large number of studies which have attempted to show that considerate leaders or leaders who initiate structure are the more successful. I think if our data are correct, and this by the way is repre-sentative of similar data which we have got from other studies, then we cannot predict leadership performance by initiation of structure, consideration, or similar behaviors, because these behaviors are going to change as the situation becomes more threatening.

Dr. Drenth also suggested, quite correctly, that leader-member relations, task-structure and position power are not the only variables which affect situational favour-ableness for a leader. And with this I completely agree. In fact some of our studies have used stressfulness, e.g., in the Honduras study, where we used the stress of the village. Stress is one variable, as is the variable Dr. Drenth mentioned, namely the members' reactions to the leader. And there must be many others – cultural heterogeneity is certainly another.

This brings me to the final point, namely the degree to which cultural heterogeneity should or should not be treated separately in the Belgian study. I think the whole problem of how to develop a good metric for this situational favourableness dimension – the degree to which the situation is favourable for the leader – is a wide-open question. We badly need a metric for this, we do not have it yet. You can of course manipulate these variables in many different ways. Dr. Drenth has chosen to combine cultural hetero-geneity and group climate. I would not agree with this because group climate has been shown to be a very important factor in determining situational favourableness. The last figure shows this.

Figure 4 summarizes a series of studies on bomber crews, anti-aircraft units, and management of consumer cooperatives. All of these groups have highly structured tasks and high position power. As you can see, where the leader is sociometrically highly chosen and where the leader is sociometrically rejected, it is the task-oriented,

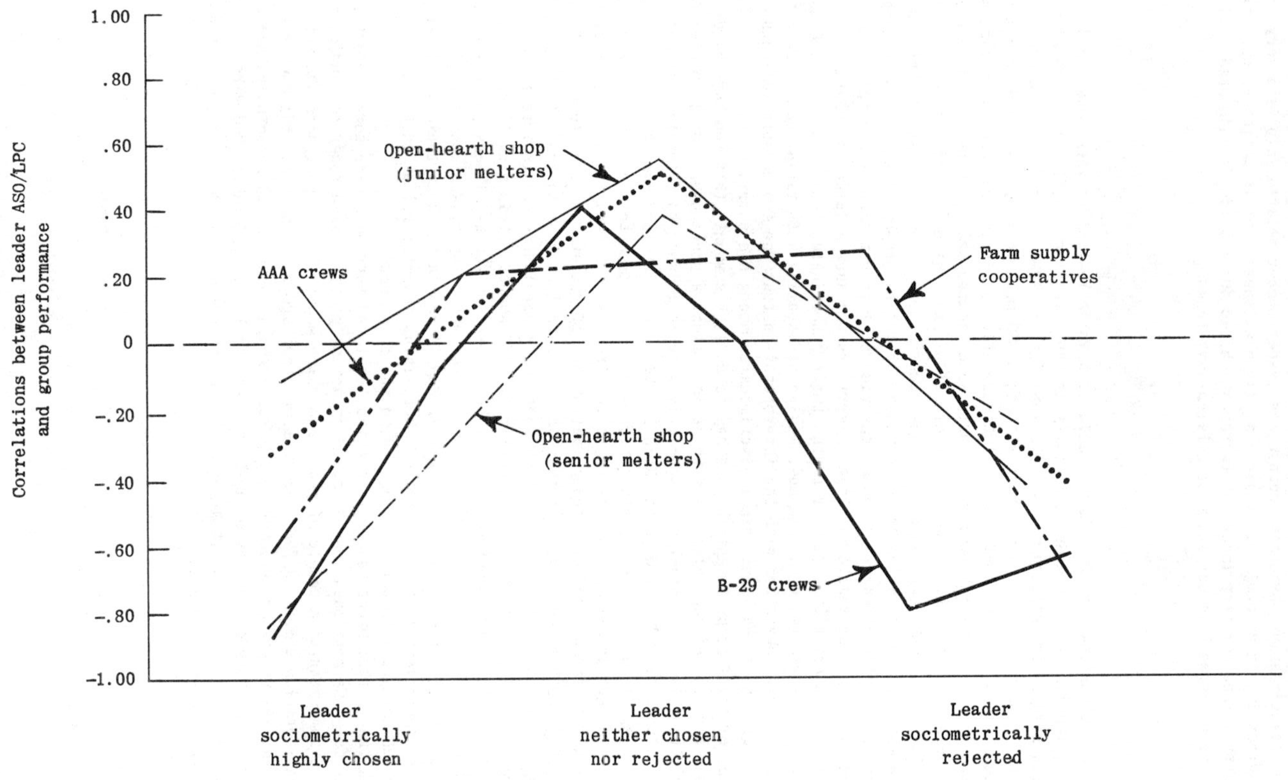

Fig. 4 CORRELATIONS BETWEEN LEADER LPC OR ASO SCORES AND GROUP PERFORMANCE UNDER THREE CONDITIONS OF LEADER ACCEPTANCE BY THE GROUP IN STUDIES OF BOMBER CREWS, ANTI-AIRCRAFT-ARTILLERY CREWS, AND CONSUMER COOPERATIVES.

low LPC leader who performs best, while in the intermediate situation it is the relationship-oriented leader who performs best. What I am saying is that we again get this curvilinear relationship, obviously because the leader-member relationship is a very important dimension in determining situational favourableness. But in addition, cultural heterogeneity is another very important factor which, as our Belgian friends predicted, made a lot of difference in our study of Belgian Navy teams.

FLEISHMAN

It is very clear that Dr. Fiedler has hold of a variable that is very potent and that a major contribution has been made in identifying the situational difficulty dimension as a moderator variable enclosing these relationships. It seems to me that a major effort now needs to be made to understand better what this ASO measure really is. And at present it seems to me that the most conservative interpretation of it is that some supervisors tend to make larger discriminations among their subordinates than do others. Apparently the supervisors that make these large discriminations have influence under certain conditions and those that don't have influence under others. There is a study that was published a year or two ago which investigated merit-rating propensities of supervisors in relation to the effectiveness of these supervisors. I forget exactly who the author of the study was, but the result was that supervisors who show a larger standard deviation among the merit-ratings they assign their subordinates tend to be regarded as more effective supervisors in the company. Now we are dealing with rating data here but at least these data are consistent with the interpretation that the ASO measure reflects, mainly, the degree to which a supervisor discriminates among his subordinates.

Now another brief point I want to make has to do with comments that you have hard-nosed versus soft-headed supervisors and these fall along a continuum. I would prefer to lay to rest this kind of terminology, especially when it is used to refer to consideration or structure, two dimensions with which I have been identified over the years. With respect to these two dimensions, consideration – as I have come to use these instruments more and get insight into what is involved in the items – consideration seems to reflect not a soft-headed approach to one's subordinates; but if you examine the items you find that we are talking here about a supervisor who tends to listen or he tends to tolerate two-way communication, he tends to seek out ideas of subordinates, he is more accepting of a subordinate's ideas. This is not necessarily soft-headed, it is a pattern. In respect to structure, this is not necessarily hard-nosed in the usual sense of the term. If you look at the items there, it reflects a task-oriented supervisor, one with set standards, one that keeps his eye on the girls. Now if you think about these two dimensions defined operationally in these terms, there is no incompatibility in the kind of supervisor emphasizing both patterns, as indeed the data show.

I think that Pieter Drenth's comments which I enjoyed very much have some support in some recent data. He mentioned consideration as acting possibly as a moderator variable. We published some results a couple of years ago which showed that supervisors who were high in consideration could, in fact, exert more structure with their subordinates without increasing grievances or turnover in the work groups, whereas supervisors who showed a great deal of structure in behavior and moderate to low consideration had very high turnover and high grievances. So it might be useful to think about consideration, as was suggested, as a moderator variable.

FIEDLER

I would agree.

The Effect of Leadership Training on Attitudes and Behaviour of Non-Commissioned Officers.

P.M. BAGCHUS

ROYAL NETHERLANDS NAVY

1. INTRODUCTION

This paper reports on an investigation that was made to evaluate the effects of a special kind of leadership training on attitudes and behaviour of non-commissioned officers of the Royal Netherlands Navy.

There seem to be three reasons why this investigation may be considered relevant.

(a) In the Netherlands Navy much attention is being given to the leadership training of non-commissioned and commissioned officers.

This sort of training can be considered valuable only if a favourable influence is being exerted by it on attitudes and/or behaviour of the trainees. A program for the evaluation of trade courses is relatively easy to carry out. By means of task analysis the requirements for the course can be laid down and by objective exams it can be decided whether the trainees meet these requirements.

Much time and effort is spent on leadership training. The evaluation of leadership training however, is much more difficult and has rarely been undertaken.

The investigation reported here is an attempt in this direction.

(b) In social psychology most research and development of theory bears on the dynamics of leadership behaviour. Much less attention is being paid to the theoretically equally interesting question of whether and to what extent people can be trained in leadership.

(c) The training evaluated in this study is of a special type. Trainees are put in a situation in which leadership and group processes develop. In feedback sessions the behaviour of the group and of its members is reflected. This is not a normative model of leadership training like the former human relations training, but the trainees learn to see that different ways of leadership are needed in different situations.

2. DESIGN OF THE STUDY*

2.1. Method

The field experiment was chosen as the method for this investigation. Two carefully matched groups were composed, one of which went to the three week training and the other not.

Campbell[1] mentions several objections to the most commonly used " Pretest-Posttest Control group design " in field experiments. The most serious drawback of this design is, that no interaction effect of pretesting can be isolated. For this reason the " Solomon Four-Group design "[1] was chosen. In this design both the experimental and the control group are randomly divided in two subgroups one of which is pretested and the other not.

---

* The investigation reported in this paper was made by Allegro, J.T., Bagchus, P.M. and de Ronde, G.F.

TABLE 1.   THE SOLOMON FOUR-GROUP DESIGN:

Sample	Treatment			
A	O_1	X	O_2	X refers to experimental variable
B	O_3		O_4	O refers to observation
C		X	O_5	
D			O_6	

In this design, referred to by Campbell as " The new ideal design for social scientists ", the effects of the experimental variable (i.e. the training) and of pretesting can be isolated by analysis of variance.

TABLE 2.   SCHEME FOR ANALYSIS OF VARIANCE IN THE SOLOMON FOUR-GROUP DESIGN.

	No X	X
pretested	O_4	O_2
unpretested	O_6	O_5

The combined main effects of non-experimental variables " maturation " and " history " can be tested through comparing O_6 with O_1 and O_3.

2.2. Theoretical Model

The theoretical model of the study was derived from a study by Miles.[2] It was hypothesized that possible changes in attitude and behaviour after the training would be mediated primarily by personality variables. Further it was hypothesized that possible effects of the training would depend on the degree of participation of the trainees in the training. Personality and participation variables were presupposed to correlate.

About three months after the training the experimental and control group were compared on a number of behavioural characteristics. An interaction between training effects and situational variables was hypothesized. The theoretical model of the study is illustrated in Fig. 1.

2.3. Main Hypotheses

(i) There will be a change in leadership attitudes of people who have followed the course compared to the matched control group of people who have not followed the training.

(ii) Leadership attitudes of the experimental group will be more differentiated after the training. Members of both the experimental and the control group fill out a Leadership Opinion Questionnaire (LOQ) in which they indicate how, in their opinion, an ideal leader behaves in normal and in crisis situations. The difference between " normal " and " crisis " scores will be larger in the experimental group than in the control group.

Fig. 1 THEORETICAL MODEL OF THE STUDY

PERSONALITY VARIABLES	PARTICIPATION VARIABLES	TRAINING CRITERION	SITUATION VARIABLES	BEHAVIOUR CRITERION
RIGIDITY	DESIRE FOR CHANGE INVOLVEMENT UNFREEZING PERCEIVED FEEDBACK	LEADERSHIP ATTITUDES		LEADERSHIP BEHAVIOUR

THREE WEEKS (TRAINING PERIOD)

THREE MONTHS

(iii) *People with a high leadership status* (as rated by two officer-trainers) *will change more* during and after the training than people with a low leadership status. This hypothesis is derived from a study by Klubeck and Bass.[3]

(iv) *Younger people will change more* than older people.

(v) *People who are less rigid will change more* than people who are more rigid.

(vi) *People who show a high degree of participation in the training will change more* than people who show a low degree of participation. All participation variables are self-reported measures, with the exception of the variable " involvement " which is rated by the trainers.

(vii) *Non-commissioned officers who score high on general satisfaction will change more* than non-commissioned officers with a low score on general satisfaction.

(viii) *Trainees who report a small social distance toward officers will change more* than trainees with a large social distance.

(ix) *Possible changes in leadership attitudes of the trainees will be in the direction of the leadership attitudes of the officer-trainers* (defined as " Training climate ").

(x) *Subordinates will be more satisfied with direct superiors who followed the training* than with direct superiors who did not.

(xi) *Non-commissioned officers who followed the training will get higher ratings from their direct superiors* (about three months after the training) than non-commissioned officers who did not follow the training.

2.4. Outline of the Investigation

The outline of the investigation is illustrated in Figure 2.

2.5. Subjects

81 non-commissioned officers of the Royal Netherlands Navy took part in the study; 42 of them followed the leadership training course; 39 served as control subjects. All of them were regular non-commissioned naval officers belonging to several trades. Their mean age was 33.7 years. On an average they had served about 12.1 months as non-commissioned officers.

3. THE CONSTRUCTION OF SCALES FOR THE MEASUREMENT OF LEADERSHIP BEHAVIOUR AND LEADERSHIP ATTITUDES

Crucial variables in the experiment are the leadership attitudes of trainers and trainees and the leadership behaviour of the direct superiors of the trainees as described by the trainees themselves.

An instrument was needed to measure both leadership attitudes and behaviour. In earlier investigations[4, 5] the well-known leadership scales from the Ohio State University Leadership studies failed to meet some essential requirements, particularly in studies where attitudes before and after a training or between different hierarchical levels were being compared. Probably because of the high " favourability value " of the items people tend to score so highly both on the Consideration scale and on the Initiating of Structure scale that there is practically no " space " left to score any higher (for instance in the study by Bagchus and Allegro[5] M before training 4.27 and 4.40 respectively on a five-point scale). Other investigators (Carter[6], Mulder[7]) stress the importance of another leadership factor, called by them Individual Prominence. This factor is supposed to refer to the strong personality of a leader, his self-confidence, his preparedness to take risks, etc.

TIME / GROUP	BEFORE TRAINING	AFTER ONE WEEK OF TRAINING	AT THE END OF TRAINING	ABOUT THREE MONTHS AFTER TRAINING
EXPERIMENTAL GROUP WITH PRETESTING	O_1 I.R.T. (RIGIDITY-SCALE) LOQ LDQ TRAINING CLIMATE GENERAL SATISFACTION SOCIAL DISTANCE TOWARD OFFICERS	DESIRE FOR CHANGE LEADERSHIP STATUS	O_2 LOQ (NORMAL AND CRISIS) UNFREEZING FEEDBACK PERCEPTION INVOLVEMENT GENERAL SATISFACTION SOCIAL DISTANCE TOWARD OFFICERS	O_2^1 LOQ LDQ* GENERAL SATISFACTION SOCIAL DISTANCE TOWARD OFFICERS SATISFACTION WITH TRAINEE (SUBORDINATES) BEHAVIOUR RATING) (SUPERIOR) LOQ)
CONTROL GROUP WITH PRETESTING	O_3 I.R.T. LOQ LDQ GENERAL SATISFACTION SOCIAL DISTANCE TOWARD OFFICERS		O_4 LOQ (NORMAL AND CRISIS) SATISFACTION SOCIAL DISTANCE TOWARD OFFICERS	O_4^1 SEE O_2^1
EXPERIMENTAL GROUP WITHOUT PRETESTING		LEADERSHIP STATUS	O_5 SEE O_2	O_5^1 SEE O_2^1
CONTROL GROUP WITHOUT PRETESTING			O_6 SEE O_4	O_6^1 SEE O_2^1

* Description of leadership behaviour of direct superior by trainee.

Fig. 2   OUTLINE OF THE INVESTIGATION

To avoid the above mentioned drawback of the Likert-type scales, an attempt was made to construct scales consisting of forced-choice items. Besides, a number of Individual Prominence items was included in the construction. The construction of the forced-choice scales started with a number of 54 single items.

Consideration   :   18 items
Individual Prominence :   18 items
Initiating Structure   :   18 items.

Each group of 18 items was randomly divided in two groups of 9 items:

CONSIDERATION	INDIVIDUAL PROMINENCE	INITIATING STRUCTURES
I	III	V
II	IV	VI

Each Roman numeral represents 9 single items. Between these 6 blocks twelve pair combinations are possible. Within each block not all possible combinations were made. But each item from one block was matched with one item from each other block on the ground of *a priori* considerations. Furthermore, four lists were composed each consisting of 27 forced-choice items in which all possible pair combinations of single items were included without overlap.

The composition of the four lists is illustrated in Table 3.

LIST NO.	CONSIDERATION + INDIVIDUAL PROMINENCE	CONSIDERATION + INITIATING STRUCTURE	INDIVIDUAL PROMINENCE + INITIATING STRUCTURE
1	I + IV	II + V	III + VI
2	II + III	I + V	IV + VI
3	I + III	II + VI	IV + V
4	II + IV	I + VI	III + V

TABLE 3.   COMPOSITION OF FOUR LISTS OF FORCED-CHOICE ITEMS

These four lists (108 items in all) were filled out by a sample of 171 non-commissioned officers in training — randomly divided into four groups. The lists were filled out by them on four different days in a counterbalancing design (see Table 4).

Group	List Number			
	first day	second day	third day	fourth day
A	1	2	3	4
B	2	1	4	3
C	3	4	1	2
D	4	3	2	1

TABLE 4. DESIGN FOR FILLING OUT THE FOUR LISTS OF FORCED CHOICE ITEMS.

The 108 items were factor analyzed (principal axes, varimax rotation). 6 Factors were rotated. However, the factor-matrix did not yield any interpretable results. It proved impossible to draw any inferences from it. For that reason, then, two sets of three criterion rotations were carried out in each of which 17 selected variables served as criterion variable.

These criterion rotations yielded two factors which could be readily interpreted. *Factor I* is characterized by items consisting of a Consideration item paired with either an Initiating Structure item or an Individual Prominence item. This factor is interpreted as a bipolar factor: " Soft " vs. " Hard " leadership. *Factor II* consists of Initiating Structure items paired with Individual Prominence items.

From the original 108 items 19 items were selected. These 19 items had a perfectly or nearly perfectly balanced frequency distribution. An item is perfectly balanced if exactly half of the subjects choose the one single item of a pair and the other half of the subjects choose the other item of the two. All items exceeding the limits of a 40% – 60% distribution were eliminated.

From these 19 items two scales were constructed:

Scale I : Soft vs. hard leadership consisting of 13 items

Scale II : Individual Prominence vs. Initiating Structure:
           6 items.

On a new sample of 55 prospective non-commissioned officers the internal consistency reliability (Spearman Brown formula) was assessed.

Scale I : r_{tt} = 0,68

Scale II : r_{tt} = 0,35

Because of its low reliability coefficient scale II was rejected. Only scale I was used as Leadership Opinion Questionnaire (LOQ) to measure leadership attitudes and as Leadership Description Questionnaire (LDQ) to measure leadership behaviour in the present investigation.

4. RESULTS

At the time of writing the analysis of the data has not yet been completed. For this reason only the seemingly most relevant findings of the study can be mentioned here.

4.1. Matching

Of course, a crucial requirement for any (field) experiment is a correct matching of experimental group and control group. By comparing the pretested experimental group to the pretested control group on all measured variables, it was possible to have a check on the matching of these two groups. On the variables age and time since appointment the *whole* experimental group and the *whole* control group could be compared to each other.

variable	experimental group	control group	test of difference
age*	33.79	33.68	n.s.
number of months* since appointment	11.69	12.43	n.s.
Rigidity Scale	92.05	98.37	$F = 3.74$ n.s.
General Satisfaction	10.14	9.16	n.s.
Social distance toward officers	12.52	11.79	n.s.
LOQ	7.52	6.37	$z = 1.53$ n.s.

* computed over *whole* experimental group and *whole* control group

TABLE 5.   MATCHING EXPERIMENTAL GROUP AND CONTROL GROUP

From Table 5 it may be concluded that there are no significant differences between the experimental group and the control group.

variable	pretested experimental group	unpretested experimental group	test of difference
age	34.14	33.43	n.s.
number of months since appointment	11.76	11.62	n.s.

TABLE 6.   MATCHING PRETESTED EXPERIMENTAL GROUP AND UNPRETESTED EXPERIMENTAL GROUP

variable	pretested control group	unpretested control group	test of difference
age	34.16	33.17	n.s.
number of months since appointment	12.05	12.73	n.s.

TABLE 7.   MATCHING PRETESTED CONTROL GROUP AND UNPRETESTED CONTROL GROUP

From Table 6 and Table 7 it may be concluded that there are no significant differences in age and time since appointment between the pretested and the unpretested groups.

4.2. Experimental Results

4.2.1. Leadership Attitudes After Three Weeks

Analysis of variance was carried out on the data of the Leadership Opinion Questionnaire.

source of variance	sum of squares	df.	estimate of variance	F-ratio	signifi-cance
experimental-control	70.11	1	70.11	15.28	**
pretest-no pretest	.90	1	.90	.20	n.s.
interaction	51.69	1	51.69	11.49	**
residual	347.19	75	4.50		
total	469.89	78			

* significant at 5% level of significance
** significant at 1% level of significance

TABLE 8. ANALYSIS OF VARIANCE ON DATA LOQ AFTER THREE WEEKS

	X	no X	M
pretest	7.10	6.16	6.65
no pretest	7.76	4.89	6.43
M	7.43	5.54	6.54

TABLE 9. MEAN LOQ SCORE (AFTER THREE WEEKS) OF PRETESTED
AND UNPRETESTED EXPERIMENTAL GROUP AND CONTROL GROUP

From Table 8, Table 9 and Figure 3 it may be concluded that there is a significant difference between the experimental group and the control group. Subjects of the experimental group have acquired " softer " opinions on leadership than subjects of the control group. However, there is a rather large interaction effect. Unpretested subjects of the control group score lower than the pretested subjects of the control group, while unpretested subjects of the experimental group score higher than the pretested subjects of the experimental group. It is rather difficult to find an explanation of this finding. Probably in spite of the correct matching on age and time since appointment there has been a bias in assigning subjects either to the pretested or the unpretested groups.

4.2.2. Differentiation in Leadership Attitudes

An analysis of variance was carried out on the opinions of the subjects as to how an ideal leader should behave in normal and in crisis situations.

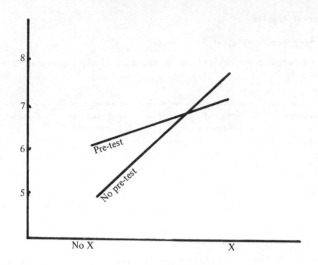

Fig. 3 INTERACTION PRETESTING AND EXPERIMENTAL
GROUP — CONTROL GROUP

source of variance	sum of squares	df.	estimate of variance	F-ratio	signifi-cance
LOQ normal — LOQ crisis	383.43	1	383.43	167.44	**
experimental-control	89.56	1	89.56	39.11	**
subjects	697.97	76	9.18	4.01	**
interaction LOQ normal-experimental	4.93	1	4.93	2.15	n.s.
residual	169.58	74	2.29		
total	1,345.47	153			

** significant at 1% level of significance

TABLE 10. ANALYSIS OF VARIANCE LOQ (NORMAL SITUATIONS) —
LOQ (CRISIS SITUATION)

From Table 10 it may be concluded that there is a significant difference between
LOQ normal and LOQ crisis. Under the " crisis-instruction" people show significantly
" harder" opinions on leadership. Further, there is a significant difference between
the experimental and the control group. Subjects of the experimental group differentiate
more between normal and crisis situations.

4.2.3. *Proficiency Ratings by Direct Superiors after Three Months*

About three months after the training each subject was rated by his direct superior on a rating scale consisting of 26 behaviour characteristics. On these proficiency ratings an analysis of variance was carried out.

source of variance	sum of squares	df.	estimate of variance	F-ratio	significance
rating categories	1,696.91	25	67.88	10.52	**
experimental-control	348.65	1	348.65	54.05	**
subjects	10,416.57	46	226.45	35.11	**
interaction categories-experimental	55.98	25	2.24	.35	n.s.
residual	7,196.13	1,115	6.45		
total	19,714.24	1,212			

** significant at 1% level of significance

TABLE 11   ANALYSIS OF VARIANCE PROFICIENCY RATING BY
DIRECT SUPERIORS

From Table 11 it may be concluded that there is a significant difference between the experimental and the control group. In fact, on all 26 rating categories the experimental group is rated higher than the control group.

4.2.4. *Satisfaction of the Subordinates of the Non-commissioned Officers (Subjects) with their Superiors*

Two randomly chosen subordinates of each subject filled out a questionnaire, part of which was an 8-item scale called " satisfaction with direct superior ". This scale is one of the subscales of an earlier constructed morale scale.

source of variance	sum of squares	df.	estimate of variance	F-ratio	significance
experimental-control	42.01	1	42.01	120.03	**
items	118.63	7	16.95	48.43	**
subjects	350.11	45	7.78	22.03	**
interaction items-experimental	21.57	7	3.08	8.80	**
residual	107.83	307	.35		
total	640.15	367			

** significant at 1% level of significance

TABLE 12   ANALYSIS OF VARIANCE ON DATA " SATISFACTION WITH DIRECT SUPERIOR "

From Table 12 it may be concluded that the subordinates of the non-commissioned officers who followed the training are more satisfied with these superiors (N.C.O.'s) than the subordinates of the non-commissioned officers who did not follow the training.

5. DISCUSSION

Only some of the findings of this investigation have been presented. In the first place because – as has been said already – not all analyses have as yet been completed. In the second place this investigation and the analysis of its data is so complex that it would be impossible to present all analyses and findings within the scope of this paper. The findings presented here are certainly remarkable enough. It could be concluded that people who have followed a three week training in leadership do change in leadership attitudes, get higher ratings from their superiors, while their subordinates are more satisfied with them. Probably it would not be unwise to feel some doubt of the validity of these conclusions.

There is a significant difference in leadership attitudes, but it is caused largely by a difficultly interpretable interaction effect.

As for the ratings by the direct superiors, it cannot be known how much of the total variance is accounted for by the raters. Besides, there are rank differences between the raters. The effect of these differences should still be analyzed. It could be possible that, despite careful matching, the experimental group was already rated higher *before* they went to the training. For several reasons this possibility could not be checked.

As for the satisfaction of the subordinates with their superiors: although two subordinates of each subject were selected at random it remains possible that there has still been some bias in the selection. For instance, possibly the selected subordinates of the subjects of the experimental group were more satisfied with them before the training. This possibility, too, could not be checked.

It is to be expected that further analysis of the data of this study will raise more questions. Nevertheless, it is to be hoped that this study is judged interesting enough to stimulate further research in this area.

REFERENCES

1. Campbell, D.T. (1957), Factors relevant to the validity of experiments in social settings, *Psych. Bull.* Vol. 54, No. 4, pp. 297-312.
2. Miles, M.B. (1961), Changes during and following laboratory training. A clinical-experimental study, *The Journal of Applied Behavioural Science*, Vol. 1, No. 3. pp. 215-243.
3. Klubeck, S. and Bass, B.M. (1954). Differential effects of training on persons of different leadership status, *Hum. Relat.* Vol. VII, pp. 59-72.
4. Dijkstra, L. and Meuwese, W. (1966). De invloed van praktisch werken in fabrieken op opinies van eerstejaars over leiderschap, arbeiders en het bedrijf, *rapport nr. 10 Groep Onderwijsresearch, Technische Hogeschool Eindhoven*.
5. Bagchus, P.M. and Allegro, J.T. (1966), *Onderzoek Kaderschool, Bureau Sociaal Psychologische Zaken, Departement van Defensie (marine)*.
6. Carter, L.F. (1954), Evaluating the performance of individuals as members of small groups, *Personnel Psychology*, Vol. 7, pp. 477-484.
7. Mulder, M. (Ed.) (1963) *Mensen, groepen, organisaties. Speurwerk in de sociale psychologie*, van Gorcum and Comp, Assen.

A Program for Developing Potential Non-Commissioned Officers[1]

MORRIS SHOWEL

HUMAN RESOURCES RESEARCH OFFICE

THE GEORGE WASHINGTON UNIVERSITY

I. INTRODUCTION

Until recently the U.S. Army had no system for identifying and developing potential noncommissioned officers. In order to meet this need the Army requested the Human Resources Research Office of The George Washington University to conduct research in this area. Dr. Paul Hood and I acted as the principal researchers on this project.

The Army's requirement specified that whatever system was developed take place as early as possible in the man's Army career. I believe it would help at this point if I briefly describe the early phases of a man's Army career as it bears on the problem of developing potential leaders.

Regardless of how a man comes into the Army, either by enlistment or via the draft, he is first sent to a Reception Station (RS) for three to five days of processing (Figure 1). It is here that he is given a thorough physical examination, is interviewed to determine his interests, and takes a battery of tests to determine his aptitude for different kinds of training. Scores on these tests are used to guide his future assignment.

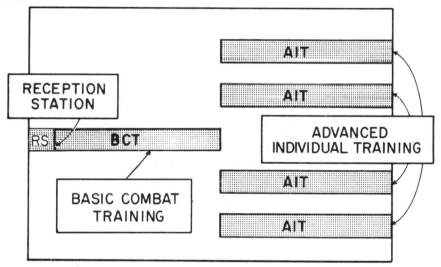

Fig. 1

[1] The research reported in this paper was performed by HumRRO Division No. 3 (Recruit Training), Presidio of Monterey, California, under Department of the Army contract with The George Washington University. The contents of this paper do not necessarily represent the official opinion of the Department of the Army.

After completing his processing, he is assigned to a training company for eight weeks of Basic Combat Training (BCT). Here he is taught the fundamentals of soldiering. Every man takes the same Basic Combat Training.

Upon completion of BCT the man moves into Advanced Individual Training (AIT), and it is here that he begins to specialize. The type of Advanced Individual Training a man receives depends on his interests, his aptitudes and, of course, the Army's needs at that particular time. Most men receive Advanced Individual Training in one of the combat arms — infantry, artillery, armour, or combat engineers. Advanced Individual Training in the combat arms lasts eight weeks. When a man completes AIT, he normally moves on and joins an operational unit.

During BCT and AIT there are opportunities to select and develop potential leaders; these opportunities, however, were not being used effectively. There were insufficient numbers of noncommissioned officers to supervise the trainees. This situation has not changed. At best, there are only two cadremen for each 50-man trainee platoon and, more often than not, a trainee platoon has only one cadreman.

In order to meet the problem of supervision, six trainees in the platoon are appointed to leadership positions — four to be squad leaders, one to be the platoon guide and the other to be the assistant platoon sergeant (Figure 2). The platoon guide and assistant platoon sergeant assist the cadremen in supervising the entire platoon. Each squad leader is responsible for one of the four ten-man squads which comprise the training platoon.

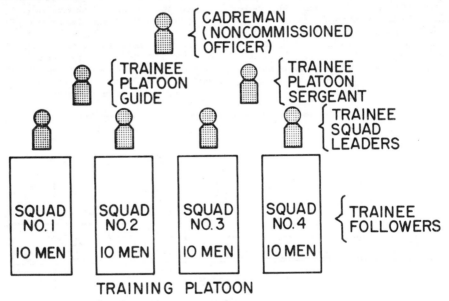

Fig. 2

In the past, these trainee leaders were appointed by the cadreman and served at his pleasure. Turnover among these leaders was high, at times there being two complete changes during the course of an eight week training cycle. Such a high attrition was to be expected when you consider that the cadreman had to make his selection during the first few days of the training cycle and had little information upon which to make a valid decision. Among the criteria used for selection were prior military experience, a college education and physical appearance or prowess.

The high turnover in trainee leaders also reflected their lack of preparation for the job. They had been given no leadership training or experience and were no more knowledgeable in the technical aspects of their job than the men they were expected to lead. They received few privileges for assuming the additional responsibilities of leadership. An additional problem was the fact that the cadreman received little guidance in how to use his trainee leaders.

In spite of these difficulties, some trainees performed effectively as leaders for the full eight week BCT or AIT cycle. Yet this fact was not noted on their Army records. In effect, they were lost to the Army. The then existing system was primarily aimed at providing assistance for the cadre. There was no provision for developing a pool of potential leaders from which the Army could select its future noncommissioned officers. This was our research mission. This meant that if possible, the system should function within and be compatible with the training sequence I have just described, BCT and AIT.

We began working on the project in 1957. The bulk of the work was carried out at Fort Ord, California, a training centre which conducts BCT and *infantry* AIT. Our intention was to design a system for infantry personnel which would readily adapt to other branches of the Army.

Over a five year period, research was conducted into a number of problem areas. Let me describe but a few. One problem was to determine those duties which characterize the junior NCO's role. To get this information, we examined the literature, visited NCO Academies, conducted a critical incident study in the United States and in Europe, and observed the day to day performance of junior NCOs both in garrison and field settings *(1, 2)*. Information resulting from this effort provided the basis for developing course content, lesson plans, and a special leadership textbook, *A Guide for the Potential Noncommissioned Officer (3)*.

Another problem was identifying those men with leadership potential *(4)*. In addition to experimenting with standard Army aptitude measures, we worked in conjunction with the Army's Personnel Research Office in developing and evaluating some measures of our own, including ratings by subordinates, peers and superiors.

There also was the problem of determining the criteria – ways to measure the validity of our selection instruments and the effectiveness of our training programs. While the Army had some tests to measure technical proficiency, there were no suitable tests for measuring leadership skill. Among the criteria we developed and evaluated were written tests of leader and follower technical proficiency, written tests of leadership knowledge and performance tests of leadership skill, and measures of leader and follower morale *(5)*.

We also were concerned with training methods and training aids and experimented with both live and automated instruction *(6)*. We tried out both school and on-the-job training and various combinations of each.

Finally, there was the problem of the duration and timing of leadership training. We experimented with two-week courses, four-week courses, and zero-week courses, and compared them with different kinds of control groups. At one time an entire Battle Group (five training companies with a total of over 1,000 men) was involved in experiments. Reports on the results of these experiments are in preparation *(7, 8)*.

Before the final results of our experiments were in, the Berlin crisis of 1961 precipitated the Army's decision to implement the most promising and feasible of the programs being studied. I will now describe the system that was adopted and that now is known as the Leader Preparation Program.

2. THE LEADERSHIP PREPARATION PROGRAM

The Program has two objectives: *First*, to provide trainees who can assist the cadre in the AIT training companies. *Second*, to provide a pool of men with both leadership training and leadership experience from which the Army can select its junior noncommissioned officers. I want to emphasize that graduates of the program are not automatically promoted or given leadership responsibility when they join their operational units.

The Leader Preparation Program has two components – a selection component and a training component.

2.1. Selection

Four criteria are used to select men for leadership training.

First, the man must demonstrate that he has the aptitude to learn the *technical* material covered in the branch to which he will be assigned. Aptitude is measured by written tests given in the Reception Station before the man starts Basic Combat Training.

Second, the man must demonstrate to his peers that he has *leadership potential.* Leadership potential is measured by " buddy ratings " secured during the fifth week of the BCT cycle. This allows five weeks in which a man can demonstrate to his peers that he has or does not have what it takes to become a leader. Incidentally, men who earn a passing score on the Leader Potential Rating have this fact noted on their official Army record, along with their other aptitude scores.

Third, the man must be acceptable to his BCT company commander. A man meeting the first two criteria may be declared ineligible for leadership training if his company commander feels there is good reason to believe he will not work out. In some cases a strong recommendation from the commander can be used to waive a rather poor showing on the aptitude area tests or buddy rating.

Fourth, and probably the one most likely to be ignored, the man must indicate a willingness to undergo leadership training. To assist him in his decision, an orientation film on the Leader Preparation Program is shown to all trainees early in the BCT cycle. All trainees meeting other eligibility requirements are given a pamphlet titled " What Did I Do? Why Me? " which explains why they have been selected for leadership training. In addition, these men are counselled by their BCT company commander. The intent of both the pamphlet and the counselling is to motivate the man to willingly accept leadership training.

In summary then, the selection component of the Leader Preparation Program takes place during Basic Combat Training – during the man's first eight weeks in the Army.

2.2. Training

The training component of the Leader Preparation Program has two phases, a school phase lasting two weeks and an on-the-job phase lasting the eight weeks of the AIT cycle.

2.2.1. Leadership School

The school phase begins after the man has completed his Basic Combat Training but before he enters Advanced Individual Training (Figure 3). The school itself has its own faculty and its own living and training facilities. Its exclusive job is to prepare the students for leadership responsibility.

Twenty-seven hours, or 23% of the scheduled instruction time is devoted to leadership. The emphasis in this block of instruction is on the duties and problems of the junior leader in the garrison training situation irrespective of his branch of service. In other words, this material is as appropriate for infantry as it is for armour or engineers. Some of the classes take the *functional* approach, covering such topics as " getting information ", " planning and organizing ", " handling problems and complaints ", and " coordinating with other leaders ". Other classes take the *situational* approach – " a leader's duties in the morning, while in garrison ", and " a leader's duties when preparing for inspection ". In addition to detailed lesson plans, a tape recording and film strip version of this material was prepared to reduce instructor requirements and to standardize the instruction. At present this material is being adapted for presentation on motion picture film and video tape.

Thirty hours, or 26% of the scheduled instruction time, is devoted to *general* subjects which are also *common* to all branches of the service. Included here are drill, physical training and housekeeping. These periods are also used to give the students practical experience in leadership.

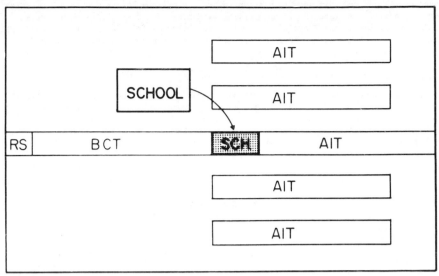

Fig. 3

The other 51% of the time, about 60 hours, is devoted to *technical* subjects *specific*
to a particular branch of the service. Included here are such things as the care and
use of weapons and equipment, and tactics. The particular content depends upon the
branch of service. Whenever possible, material dealing with the duties and problems of
the junior leader are integrated into this technical instruction.

Additional experience in leadership is provided when moving to and from classes and
in performing the customary garrison duties of maintaining self and living quarters up
to military standards. The standards of the school are very high. Students are organized
into squads and platoons and rotated daily into leadership positions. Their performance
is observed and critiqued by the faculty of the school.

During the scheduled study periods in the evening, the students can refer to the
Guide for the Potential Noncommissioned Officer, his leadership text, and to his set of
specially prepared pamphlets dealing with the technical material appropriate to his
branch of the service. The student retains both the text and the pamphlet when he
completes the two-week course. These constitute his reference materials when he moves on
to AIT.

2.2.2. On-the-job Leadership Training

The on-the-job phase of the leadership training lasts eight weeks and is conducted
within the context of Advanced Individual Training. It is here, while learning the
technical skills appropriate to his branch of the Army, that the trainee leader gets his
most intensive practical leadership experience. As in the past, he is assigned to the
position of trainee squad leader, trainee assistant platoon sergeant, or trainee platoon
sergeant and works under the supervision of the one or two cadremen assigned to his
platoon. His responsibilities are somewhat greater than in previous systems. For the
most part they involve supervision of housekeeping activities, but some remedial teaching of slow learners also may be required. He is given more privileges than in previous
systems. In addition to being excused from work details, he is quartered in a room away
from his men and he eats his meals in a section of the mess hall reserved for leaders.

The trainee leader is fairly well-prepared for his new responsibilities. In addition
to having leadership training and experience in the two-week school, he has been
exposed to some of the important technical knowledges and skills now being covered in
AIT, the use and care of weapons and equipment for example. In effect, he is two weeks

413

ahead of his men and this adds to his confidence, to his competence and to his prestige. Perhaps equally important, he is *not* serving with his BCT peers. They are two weeks farther along in their AIT cycle. This means that bonds of friendship will be less likely to interfere with his willingness to give orders or with his followers' willingness to comply.

2.2.3. *The Importance of the Cadremen*

The AIT phase of the Leader Preparation Program has always been the most difficult part to implement because so much of its success depends on the attitudes and skills of the cadremen who supervise the work of the trainee leaders. A number of problems were encountered in this area. Cadremen frequently resented the fact that they no longer had full freedom to select their trainee leaders. In the past, they alone decided who would be their squad leaders, platoon guides, and assistant platoon sergeant. Now they had to appoint graduates of the leaders' school to these leadership positions. A related difficulty was the ease with which a cadreman was once able to depose a trainee leader and appoint a new man in his position. If a trainee leader did not perform to the cadreman's satisfaction, he was removed; emphasis was primarily upon getting the *immediate* job done and not on the *long range* job of attempting to develop potential leaders. Now cadremen were encouraged to work with the poor leaders in order to improve their performance.

Another problem was the amount of latitude allowed the trainee leader and the amount of supervision and guidance given him. Some cadremen took the position that since the trainee was a graduate of the leader school, he should be able to handle his job with a minimum of supervision and guidance. Therefore, these cadremen withdrew and as was to be expected, many of the trainee leaders floundered. Other cadremen were unable to reconcile themselves to the need to give trainee leaders opportunities to lead and continued to completely dominate the leadership role in the platoon. Consequently, the trainee leaders did not get the practical experience that they needed.

In summary, the AIT cadreman was expected to fill a new role, and some of them were unwilling or unable to make the change. Complicating the problem was the fact that the leadership and technical doctrine taught in the school was not always in agreement with that practised in AIT. A frequent complaint on the part of the trainee leaders was " This isn't the way we were taught to do it in the school ".

We have tried to solve these problems by encouraging close liaison between the leader school faculty and AIT cadre and by preparing a film designed to orient the AIT cadreman to the nature and importance of his new role; that is, helping to develop trainee leaders into potential, noncommissioned officers *as well* as insuring that they get the immediate job done. We have dramatized this new role through the mnemonic word, **BROCAS**. Interestingly enough, speech is the main medium through which leadership is exercised and the **BROCAS** area of the brain is the section which controls speech.

BROCAS, as used here, stands for the following:
    " **B**rief your leaders, tell them what you want done.
    Release your leaders, let them do their job.
    Observe your leaders as they work.
    Critique your leaders on the quality of their work.
    Advise your leaders on how to do a better job.
    Support and encourage your leaders ".

2.3. After Training

Trainee leaders who survive the eight-week on-the-job phase of the Leader Preparation Program are not automatically promoted in rank or given leadership responsibilities when they join their operational units. What is done, however, is to note on their official Army record that they have completed the ten-week Program. This is designed to call their accomplishments to the attention of the new unit commander and thus facilitate their being given an opportunity to demonstrate leadership ability. Promotion in rank or to leadership responsibility is still determined by the unit commander.

3. EXTENDING THE USE OF THE LEADERSHIP PREPARATION PROGRAM

While the Program's original intent was to provide a pool from which the Army could select junior noncommissioned officers, it also is frequently used as a prep school for officer candidates. Trainees who have qualified and applied for officer training are frequently sent through the Program as a prelude to Officer Candidate School.

The program I have described was developed for light and heavy weapons infantry. Since that time, it has been adapted for all of the combat arms – artillery, combat engineers, and armour. It currently is being phased into the combat support schools – clerks, mechanics, cooks, and so forth. A version of the program is even being used by the Women's Army Corp and by the Boy Scouts in their White Stag leader development program. The Canadian Army has incorporated much of our leadership text into their own training program.

I would like to mention two vertical extensions of the Leader Preparation Program. The success of the program in AIT prompted requests to extend the program down into BCT, the first eight weeks in the Army. Two serious problems have been encountered in attempting to do this. First is the difficulty in getting valid measures of leader potential as a basis for assignment to the program. Second is the Army's natural reluctance to set aside additional time for leadership training. At present, a few Army posts are experimenting with a three-day Leader Orientation Course given prior to the start of BCT (Figure 4). Assignment to the course is based on aptitude scores and cadremen recommendations but not on "buddy ratings", since these are not available. The leadership material used in the course was developed from the Leader Preparation Program.

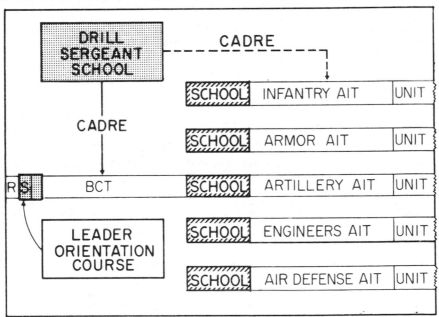

Fig. 4

The critical importance of the cadreman in the training centre has prompted the Army to initiate a training program to prepare noncommissioned officers for this training responsibility. The result is the Drill Sergeant School now in operation at all training centres. At present, graduates of the Drill Sergeant School are assigned to BCT, but there are plans to extend the program into AIT (Figure 4). Our research personnel worked closely with military personnel in building the Drill Sergeant School and some of the material used in the School was originally developed for the Leader Preparation Program.

Before closing, I would like to point out that our work was not limited to research and development. We also have been concerned with aiding the Army in implementation of the Program. Following development of the pilot version of the Program, representatives from other training centres and from other branches of the service came to Fort Ord to attend a six week training course on implementing the Leader Preparation Program. During this period, they observed the Fort Ord operation, consulted with experienced civilian and research personnel and were assisted in developing their particular versions of the Leader Preparation Program. Each group of representatives was given a kit of the material needed to implement the Program, including training schedules, lesson plans and student references. After completing the six week course, they returned to their home posts to implement the Program. During the first year of operation we visited all of these posts to observe their operation, to make suggestions and to help solve problems. We also assisted in the preparation of the Army directive which governs all Leader Preparation Programs.

4. CONCLUSION

In closing, I would like to say that we are proud of the Program, but we don't feel that it has solved all of the Army's junior leadership problems. Six years have gone by since the initial adoption and it is likely that some changes have been made in the Program ... both in its concept and its implementation. While anecdotal evidence indicates that the Program is effective and is accepted, we have no hard data in substantiation. Perhaps our most important contribution has been to gain acceptance for the idea that *some* system must be used to identify and develop potential noncommissioned officers.

REFERENCES

1. Kern, Richard P., Observations on a Number of Noncommissioned Officer Academies. Alexandria, Va.: *Human Resources Research Office Staff Memorandum*, May 1958, AD-486 297.
2. Showel, Morris, and Peterson, Christian W., A Critical Incident Study of Infantry, Airborne, and Armoured Junior Noncommissioned Officers. Alexandria, Va.: *Human Resources Research Office Staff Memorandum*, July 1958, AD-480 232.
3. Dept. of Army, A Guide for the Potential Noncommissioned Officer, December 1961, 4th edition published as *USCONARC Pamphlet No. 350-24*, June 1963.
4. Showel, Morris (1960), " Interpersonal Knowledge and Rated Leader Potential ", *J. Abnorm. Soc. Psychol.*, vol. 61, no. 1, 87-92.
5. Hood, Paul D., Kern, Richard P., and Showel, Morris, Research on the Training of Noncommissioned Officers, A Summary Report of Pilot Studies. Alexandria, Va.: *Human Resources Research Office Technical Report 65 17*, December 1965, AD-631 2-8.
6. Showel, Morris, Taylor, Elaine, and Hood, Paul D., Automation of an Instructional Block of NCO Leadership Preparation Training. Alexandria, Va.: *Human Resources Research Office Technical Report 66-21*, December 1966.
7. Hood, Paul D., Showel, Morris, Taylor, John E., Stewart, Edward C., and Boyd, Jacklyn, Preliminary Assessment of Three NCO Leadership Preparation Training Systems. Alexandria, Va.: *Human Resources Research Office Technical Report* in preparation.
8. Hood, Paul D., Showel, Morris, and Stewart, Edward C., Evaluation of Three Experimental Systems for Noncommissioned Officer Training. Alexandria, Va.: *Human Resources Research Office Technical Report* in preparation.

PART III INTERACTION OF THE CIVIL AND MILITARY OCCUPATIONAL SYSTEMS

Leonard S. Cottrell, Jr.
Albert D. Biderman
Roger W. Little

Civilian Vocational Competence as a Military Responsibility

LEONARD S. COTTRELL, JR.

RUSSELL SAGE FOUNDATION,

NEW YORK CITY.

I. INTRODUCTION

Long and firmly established doctrine holds that the military establishment must not be burdened with non-military functions and in no respect is the doctrine more vigorously asserted than in the case of what are commonly regarded as social welfare functions. To be sure, the modern military system includes an extensive and complex system of institutions and practices specifically addressed to the whole gamut of welfare functions: health, education, housing, community organizations, recreation, corrections, personal and family counselling, relief of economic hardship, retirement and so on. But these are directed to the problems of persons within the system and regarded as necessary to the health and effectiveness of the military establishment itself. The doctrine of course is directed against using the military institutions to solve or ameliorate welfare problems of the larger society. Even here however, actual practice has deviated in important respects from doctrine sometimes, be it admitted, to the detriment of the Armed Services, but sometimes to the advantage of both military and host society. Thus, in the United States prior to World War I and between World Wars, especially during the Great Depression, enlistment was a frequent solution to school drop-out, incorrigible and wayward behaviour and simple unemployment. The practice, while not officially recognized or sanctioned by civil or military authority, was sufficiently extensive to cause professional military concern over the public image of "the Army as a place for bums", notwithstanding the fact that there was also the public concept that the military "would make a man out of" a problem youth. Happily this latter was in fact a frequent outcome.

It will not be necessary to detail here the various ways in which officially and unofficially the military arm has been utilized to deal with problems of civil society. I simply wish to point out as background to my remarks that the doctrine is firm and clear, but that it is not infrequently breached under pressure of various needs and exigencies. My reason for calling attention to this state of affairs is that what I have to say suggests not only further departure from traditional doctrine, but that such departure be formally recognized and instituted as official policy and practice. Indeed a modification in the basic doctrine itself is implied and though I shall try to offer at least plausible arguments that such a change would strengthen rather than weaken military effectiveness, it is nevertheless a substantial deviation.

The basic argument of this paper can be stated briefly as follows:

Proposition I. The military establishment should assume responsibility for insuring that all personnel passing through it come out with, at minimum, sufficient civilian vocational training to enable them to meet entry requirements in some economically viable occupation.

Proposition II. Technological and social institutional changes have brought the relations between the Armed Services and the larger social system to a point where the requirement proposed above is not only a reasonable one, but necessary as well.

Proposition III. Adequate discharge of this responsibility will not only contribute indirectly to military effectiveness through general societal strengthening, but will also directly enhance military resources.

2. DISCUSSION OF PROPOSITION I

To those with administrative and planning responsibility for education and training in the Armed Services, or even to those ordinary citizens who may have read the illuminating little book *Education in the Armed Forces* by Shelburne and Groves,[1] my Proposition I will seem redundant indeed. The United States military establishment operates what is probably the largest single educational and vocational training enterprise in the world, which offers educational opportunities ranging from literacy training to advanced levels of graduate work and from simple manual skills to large, corporate management.

As a matter of fact, the Armed Services are providing far more than minimal civilian vocational preparation for many hundreds of thousands every year. This calls not only for high praise, but more tangible recognition of its contributions to the economy and human satisfaction when analyzing the defence budget. But the very extensiveness and efficacy of the effort lends support to my claim that the responsibility be more clearly recognized, more fully implemented and its implications more fully realized. For the magnitude and diversity of what is being done leads one to suspect that relatively minor modifications and extensions could go far toward greatly enhancing the contributions of the educational and training functions of the military system to the general societal welfare as well as to military effectiveness.

Among the several problem areas for which this discussion could be relevant there are three that invite special and immediate attention, both from the societal and specific military point of view.

First there is the problem of more effective bridging of the gap between the military specialty training and its relevance for civilian vocations. A great deal of specialty training is directly relevant to civilian occupations; much of it can be productively related by introducing limited amounts of bridging material. Some areas need more substantial transitional training and some have little or no relevance. The point here is that with more systematic attention and effort, a great deal of military training can in the person's own skill acquisition be made more explicitly related to potential civilian jobs. This is true all up and down the skill hierarchy.

A second related problem to be addressed in measuring up to responsibility under Proposition I is that of the obsolescence of skills. This of course is a problem peculiar to periods of rapid technological change that plagues all skill ranks in all occupations, civil and military. In seeking to deal with the problems in specific military occupations it will be found that some updating in related civilian skills will occur automatically. However, in watching for signs of obsolescence in its own skill specialities and taking corrective measures, the training branches of the services must also take necessary steps to guard against obsolescence in their own efforts to relate military training to civilian vocational potentials.

While the third problem area shares certain features in common with the first two, it has special characteristics that make it in some ways more difficult and demanding of more radical departures from current doctrine and practice. I refer here to the lower ranking skill and non-skill group. Beginning with selective processes at voluntary enlistment or draft call and continuing through various early training selective procedures, there is shaken out a population in which a high proportion is characterized by low educational achievement and identified by tests as having low aptitudes for acquiring complex mechanical or symbolic skills. These people come predominantly from low socio-economic and culturally impoverished backgrounds. In the United States they are also frequently members of disadvantaged ethnic or racial minorities. Very similar to this population in social characteristics and a cut below it in educational and aptitude level is a pool of those rejected for service in times of low demand for manpower but dipped into when conditions require increased military recruitment and/or conscription. Under present systems of selection, training and assignments to duty, the bulk of these populations find their way into the combat branches of the ground forces and in a shooting war become the muscle by which ground is won and held. Properly trained, disciplined and led, they can and do become superb soldiers.

But in the nature of things civil and military, this population in civilian life has the greatest vulnerability to unemployment and in military life, the lowest probability of exposure to training and experience in skills that will increase their chances in the job market after they complete their service. It is necessary, of course, immediately to qualify this statement. Not all performance skills for example in an infantry unit are limited to physical endurance and the care and use of weapons. Some specialities indeed do have relevance for some civilian occupations. Then too, most members of combat branches have some opportunity to compete for assignment to special training schools where at least some of the skills acquired will be useful after discharge. There is also the duty time schooling in the three R's for those who lack these elementary tools. Finally, there is the wealth of opportunity for off duty courses from elementary grades to PhD level studies. To these we can even add the military virtues so valuable to good citizenship, including one's vocational roles. The total sum would appear to be an impressive counter argument to the claim that the lowly combat soldier is disadvantaged in the securing of competitive job skills for use after discharge.

While precise data on post service careers are extremely limited,[2] it is clear that the most optimistic weighting of the plus factors still leaves a substantial need for a more adequate and systematic provision of civilian relevant vocational skills that will upgrade the employment chances of the population in question. Our claim here is that the responsibility can and should be assumed by the Armed Services, even though such an effort requires an increase in terms of service and an apparent increase in the defence budget. Can such a claim be rationally supported?

3. DISCUSSION OF PROPOSITION II

Running counter to the historic tendency of the military establishment to become isolated from the host society is the fact of vast and rapid technological changes that make such insularity progressively less possible and less desirable. The processes by which the military institutions become enmeshed with the civilian political, economic and cultural systems have been ably presented by Professor Morris Janowitz and need not detain us here.[3] We need simply to note that one important implication of this involvement is the greater mutual impingement of the military institution and its containing society upon the decisions and actions of each other.

Modern technology has created social systems in which all the major institutional components are closely interdependent and impinge intimately and immediately upon one another. The military system is not alone in feeling the effects of this complex involvement. Given this condition, it is not hard to understand why major problems are not isolated and solutions cannot be unilateral. Thus the problems of education, employment and updating of skills in order to counter obsolescence are shared problems and each major institution must not only have its needs met by joint endeavour but must assume some share of the burden in solving the common problems. Business and industry cannot dump their obsolescent personnel and expect the other institutions of society to furnish a new supply. They must participate in the work of updating skills and even in taking part of the skill deficient population and providing training and experience enough to give it a foothold on the occupational ladder. This kind of public responsibility is increasingly recognized by business and industrial leaders. Thus Mr. John D. Harper, president of Aluminium Company of America, admonished his colleagues in the National Association of Manufacturers that "... we have very little choice in the matter today. Business is involved right up to the neckline in hundreds of public problems and the public ... expects us to accept the responsibility of helping solve those problems ... Whatever justification there may have been for ignoring such problems in the past, we cannot justify apathy or inaction today".[4]

This shared effort is not a moral obligation merely, but a highly realistic necessity which the military institution cannot avoid any more than any other part of the complex social system in which they are involved. This general point has been succinctly put by Col. Samuel H. Hays, Director, Office of Military Psychology and Leadership, United States Military Academy.

"The changes wrought in society by the technological revolution play an important part in our consideration of the relative position our Armed Forces should occupy. Military institutions are a reflection of the value system of the societies which produce them. In a technological world of growing interdependence on local, national and international levels, the interrelationship between economic, political social and military institutions grows continually closer. Factors which affect one affect them all". [5]

One way that the problem of absorbing and upgrading the marginal skill and educational group by the military might be avoided could be by adopting the rational model of the completely professionalized Armed Force. This would be a rigorously selected, highly trained, more-or-less self contained system. Given present technology and ignoring for the moment political and cultural factors, such a model is no doubt realistically possible and is perhaps the most rational pattern of military forces in the modern world. However, such a structure would hardly be viable in our present social political system. To quote again from Col. Hays:

"It does not take extensive research to discover what has happened when the military forces of a society become estranged or isolated from the society which supported them. When citizens no longer feel responsible to perform military service, it is difficult for them to develop much interest in the military forces or their duties and responsibilities. In return, when soldiers no longer consider themselves understood by the community and not full citizens in the true sense of the word, the ensuing gap between military and society becomes difficult to bridge. Whatever solution might be chosen to solve the problem of manning military forces, it should include measures which would maintain the close relationship between the civilian society and the military institution which has been achieved during the past twenty-five years". [6]

Not the least of the elements contained in the mutual involvement specified by Col. Hays is the concept of an equitable distribution of the duties and rights of military service among all segments of the society. This means that the inadequately educated and low skilled groups may not be excused because of their deficiencies, but must be taken in and trained to adequate performing levels. But by the basic principle of reciprocity, service must be rewarded. The most important reward for the disadvantaged and one which has time honoured usage, is to make military service a basis for more secure membership and participation in the social system. Today the most important means to this end is equipment for economic adequacy. Aside from the argument of specific military effectiveness (which will be dealt with in the next section of this paper) this is the most conclusive argument for the reasonableness of the requirement that the military be responsible for equipping the lower skilled soldier with minimal training in a viable occupational field.

There are additional considerations which make the requirement reasonable. One is that for the particular group concerned, education and vocational training under conditions of discipline, regularity and group pressure from peers and authorities that symbolize masculinity, makes serious application to the task of achieving vocational competence a compelling one. Furthermore, when such preparation is defined as and perceived as honoured adult citizenship responsibility, it becomes more effectively motivated. A second compelling consideration is that the military services, in their efforts to develop rapid and efficient methods of training in military specialities, have probably developed methods and assembled facilities for vocational skill training that far exceed those found in civilian institutions. To be sure, these methods and facilities would require substantial supplementation to meet the more general requirements contemplated here, but this does not seem an impossible hurdle.

A telling counter argument against the reasonableness of the proposed extension of military responsibility is the budgetary one. A central desideratum upon which both military and public are highly sensitive is maximal military effectiveness at minimal cost. The extra training requirement will certainly add to the already colossal defence budget. However, let us again be realistic. The groups we are primarily concerned with here will require public expenditures in one form or another until they become economically competent. The added costs in question can be charged to welfare and anti-poverty budgets and still be used in the vocational training programs of the military. The faith that the military institutions will use these funds more efficiently than civilian agencies may appear naive. We cannot go into this argument here, but let it be noted that the record of what passed for vocational education in the public school systems over the past decades is not inspiring to put it mildly.

That the departures from doctrine suggested in this paper are not entirely out of line with thinking in the Pentagon is seen in the experimentations now being initiated under directives of the Secretary for Defence. One pilot effort is known as "Project 100,000", in which the recruiting and induction offices will admit and distribute among the services 100,000 recruits who fail to meet minimum requirements on the Armed Forces Qualification Tests and/or have disqualifying but remedial medical conditions. Among other things this is regarded as part of the contribution the military services can make to the anti-poverty effort to render the low skilled groups in American society more capable of finding and holding jobs. The implications here are obvious. Even more directly in line with our argument is "Project Transition" recently announced. The object here is specifically to offer opportunities for vocational training to military personnel before they return to civilian status.

These are tentative and experimental efforts and it is hoped that they will be studied and evaluated with great care and skill. As far as they bear on the central concern here of vocational equipment of the discharged soldier, they are designed to offer opportunities to get training but do not require such training. It is the contention here that the acquisition of vocational competence be a part of the military duty of the soldier and therefore become a compulsory part of his military training.

4. DISCUSSION OF PROPOSITION III

The claim is made here that the proposed extension of military responsibility for developing civilian vocational competence not only is justified on general grounds of strengthening the society and thus indirectly enhancing military effectiveness. It is also claimed that such an extension directly strengthens military potential. Time does not permit an extensive discussion of this proposition, but the following points should be briefly noted.

(i) *In modern warfare, the strength and productivity of the society is a critical strategic element.* The extent to which the unskilled and deficient segments of the population are rendered competent and productive, constitutes an incre-ment in strategic reserve. This is measured not only by the additions made to economic productivity and general social stability and coherence, but by the amount of drag on the social and economic system eliminated by the transfor-mation of unproductive, disorganized and alienated elements into productive, participant members of the system.

(ii) *The youths who serve and are discharged continue to be a significant military reserve.* Such reserves will represent a higher specific military potential if they can be called back not as marginal, drifting and economically inadequate persons, but as competent citizens with a stake in their society. Even by taking the substandard enlistments and putting them through vocational as well as military training, the Services will be strengthening themselves against the possible necessity for dipping into the marginal groups to meet heavy military requirements.

(iii) *It should be noted that no suggestion has been made here or elsewhere that the military services undertake to deal with the whole population of the under-educated and vocationally inadequate.* We are limiting our claims to those who are accepted for service plus some to be determined portion of the reclaimable, slightly substandard population who would be dipped into anyway if military commitments required it. Corporate business and industry, the correctional and welfare systems, as well as a more flexible and imaginative public education system, and other relevant parts of society must assume their appropriate shares of the burden of reducing to a minimum the unproductive and alienated segments of the social system.

(iv) *Except under blind impulse, men's actions always have reference to some perception and structuring of the future.* Sustained action that must overcome difficulties and endure deprivations and hardship requires some supporting anticipation. Morale is a frequently abused and little understood term, but there is no doubt that strong convictions as to future rewards is frequently an important element in good morale. A soldier who can entertain reasonably solid anticipations that he will be able to command a respected and rewarding place in the economy of his community is probably a better soldier than one who has no such base for his perceptions of his future role.

5. CONCLUSION

It is clear that my discussion is based largely on the situation in the United States. However, I would claim that it is relevant for the military establishment in any free society, whether characterized by universal service or selective service conscription or even by a completely voluntary system. It is claimed here that under any system of recruitment a more adequate program for the enhancement of civilian competence will aid recruitment, strengthen military potential and reduce the isolation of the military establishment from the parent society. In realizing these obviously desirable military values, the Armed Services will also be preparing their personnel for more competent civilian life and contributing to a stronger society.

An added consideration favouring the general position adopted here is suggested by Professor Morris Janowitz. It is especially important that in the assistance being given by NATO countries to the military forces of new nations, emphasis be placed on preparing soldiers for constructive civilian roles. We can be effective in implementing this emphasis only if we practise it more fully ourselves.[7]

It is hardly necessary to remind the reader of the pressing need for research relevant to the problems implied in this paper from the perspectives of the military as well as civilian society. To implement the goals implicit in this discussion we shall need to develop much more reliable information and understanding of the following:

(i) How to develop motivation and other general personal skills needed to achieve entry into the job market and to hold a job.

(ii) The families of core skills represented in the occupational spectrum.

(iii) The most efficient transmission of basic skills.
(Contrary to prevailing belief, we have far to go in this.)

(iv) The development of skill in learning new skills and in updating skill repertoires.

(v) Projection of anticipated skill requirements.

Other areas of research needs will become evident upon reflection, but those I have mentioned appear to me to have fairly high priority and are relevant to the problem of developing vocational competence whether done by the Armed Services or civilian agencies.

REFERENCES

1. Shelburne, J.C. and K.J. Groves. *Education in the armed forces.* New York: Centre for Applied Research in Education, Inc., 1965.
2. Katenbrink, I.G., Jr. "Military service and occupational mobility". In R.W. Little (Ed.), *Selective service and American society.* New York: Russell Sage Foundation (in press), 1968.
   See also:
   Phillips, C. *A pilot study of factors in economic success or failure:* based on selective service and social security records. Washington: U.S. Department of Health, Education and Welfare Social Security Administration, 1964.
3. Janowitz, M. *The professional soldier.* Glencoe, New York: The Free Press, 1960.
   See also:
   Janowitz, M. and R. Little. *Sociology and the military establishment.* New York: Russell Sage Foundation, 1965.
4. Harper, J.D. "Responsibilities of private enterprise". *Looking ahead,* Vol. 15, no. 3.
5. Hays, S.H. "*A military view of selective service* ". Unpublished paper: page 5. Quoted by permission of the author.
6. *IBID.* page 6. Quoted by permission of the author.
7. Janowitz, M. In a personal communication with the author.

Relationships Between Active Duty and Post-Retirement Careers*

ALBERT D. BIDERMAN

BUREAU OF SOCIAL SCIENCE RESEARCH,

WASHINGTON, D.C.

I. INTRODUCTION

The present organization of the military system in the United States depends for its functioning on its ability to move members out of the system shortly after they have spent 20 years in active service. Only through some such mechanism can a pyramidic structure such as the military maintain its essential "open opportunity" features, as well as satisfy its changing technical needs. Unlike traditional military systems whose professionals were recruited largely from gentry who could retire with some independent means or assume managerial duties in a simple agrarian economy, the present pattern almost universally entails a post-military "second career". Thus, the system rests on a rather remarkable assumption: that each year, many thousands of individuals, more or less middle aged, whose training and experience in work was largely or exclusively gained in the military, will be able to find civilian jobs of at least roughly comparable economic and status value. It assumes employment opportunities in the civilian world which are not unlike those in the military and, also, a large reservoir of them. Under sponsorship of the U.S. Department of Labour, the Bureau of Social Science Research undertook an investigation in 1964 of how the "second career" system was operating.

2. COHORT AND SAMPLE

The data on which this study is based were obtained from two sources:

(i) A three-phase panel survey of selected members of the cohort of officers and enlisted men who retired in May 1964 ("BSSR Study").

(ii) Selected items from the September 1963 Department of Defence Survey of Retired Military Personnel ("DOD Study").

The BSSR study, based on the selection of a single monthly cohort, presented certain advantages as well as drawbacks. The principal advantage was ease and economy of procedure. It was possible to collect pre-retirement data at one given time from a group of men known to be leaving the service and since corrections for different dates of retirement were unnecessary, the development of retirement data was facilitated. But, by the same token, caution must be used in generalizing from a single monthly (or even yearly) cohort to the total retired population, or using the experience of the May 1964 group as a reliable predictor for the employment experiences of future cohorts. The decision to adopt this design relied on the availability of the DOD data to provide information on the over-all success of retirees in the job market, as well as on the differential experience of various components of the retiree population. Some possibilities for longitudinal analysis were also present in the large sample of DOD data.

---

* This paper is based on the following reports by Laura M. Sharp and the present writer, *The Employment of Retired Military Personnel*, Washington, D.C.; Bureau of Social Science Research, Inc., July 1966; "Out of Uniform", *Monthly Labour Review*, January 1967, pp. 15–21; February, 1967, pp. 39–47.

2.1. The BSSR Study

Data collection for the three-phase BSSR study took place over a 1-year span, from early March 1964 until the end of February 1965.

Phase I consisted of the administration of a pre-retirement questionnaire to all career personnel retiring in May 1964. Excluded from the study population were various groups whose second career patterns might be anticipated to be atypical and who were not sufficiently large to warrant separate analysis: those with a high degree of disability (over 30%); those over a given age limit; women and those with less than 19 years of active service.

Between March and May 1964, 3,350 questionnaires were distributed to career military personnel retiring at the end of May 1964. Of this total, 2,878 individuals (86%) replied by the cutoff date. A total of 2,638 questionnaires were processed for further analysis.

In addition, 116 respondents indicated that no paid employment would be sought after retirement. In Phase II, these individuals were sent post-retirement questionnaires to determine if any of them had changed their minds about getting a job. Nonetheless, the known refusal rate for Phase I was exceedingly small (1%).

The pre-retirement questionnaire was a far more extensive and demanding instrument than is usually considered appropriate for mail surveys of a randomly selected population. Personal and educational background information, military career details and plans for retirement were among the main topics covered in the questionnaire.

Phase II participants were asked to submit weekly and monthly reports on their job-seeking activities. Furthermore, every time a participant had a job counselling interview or an employment interview he was requested to complete and send in a report on the interview. A questionnaire was then sent to the job counsellor or potential employer who had interviewed the retired military man. These counsellor and employer questionnaires tried to tap the interviewer's opinions on such items as the retiree's chances for getting the type of job he was looking for, training needs, realistic salary expectations and so forth. Each time a retiree received an actual job offer, whether or not he accepted it, he was asked to send in a special Job Offer Form. When an individual accepted a job his case was closed for the intensive survey.

Phase III involved post-retirement questionnaires which were sent to all men (2,755) who had answered the pre-retirement questionnaire, as well as to those who had sent in cards indicating that they did not plan to look for work. This questionnaire focused on the job-seeking, job-finding and job-changing processes during the first 5 months following retirement, but it also repeated some of the expectation and attitude items contained in the pre-retirement questionnaire to enable us to study the attitudinal changes which might have taken place over this period.

2.2. The DOD Sample

In September 1963, the Department of Defence conducted a Survey of Retired Military Personnel, using a sample of 19,000 drawn from lists of all currently retired uniformed personnel. This study was primarily concerned with matters other than post-retirement employment (its focus was on medical care for retired personnel and their families) but it included several items — dealing with personal employment characteristics — pertinent to our interests. The DOD questionnaires also incorporated items on military and civilian background that were of high relevance to our study. In effect then, the DOD study — in those areas covered by its questionnaire — extends the coverage span of the study to the years 1960–63.

3. PREFERENCES AND EXPECTATIONS

The overwhelming majority of the retirees — 83 per cent — planned to enter the job market immediately upon retirement; another 13 per cent planned to join the job hunt after a period of relaxation. No doubt because they expected to be gainfully employed shortly following separation, only 42 per cent of the officers and 25 per cent of the enlisted men anticipated a decline in their economic well-being in the first year after retirement. At the same time, their initial salary expectations were modest: the median salaries expected by officers and enlisted men were respectively $6,260 and $4,735. Obviously, many of the men felt that in conjunction with their retired pay and their use of military facilities, these relatively low salaries would not lead to a drop in their living standard. And they were exceedingly optimistic about the future. Hardly any of these men (3%) thought that they would have lower incomes 5 years after retirement than they had had in the service and 46 per cent of both officers and enlisted men expected to be "much better off".

To a large extent, this "optimism" was based on the men's conviction that they had valuable occupational skills to offer and that the civilian world would make at least as good a use of their talents as the military had done. Prior to retirement, most men were convinced that their service training would be of help in their post-retirement work. Further, most felt that they brought to the job market qualifications at least equal and often superior to those of civilians doing the same kind of work. Only 13 per cent of all retirees considered themselves less qualified than the civilians with whom they were about to compete. Their main concern was that their age might present a problem. When asked to rate eight factors which might affect their chances of finding a suitable job, over three-fourths of the respondents selected age. A sizeable proportion (50–60%) chose "company hiring and employment practices". Conversely, status as a retired military careerist was more often seen as an advantage than as a drawback.

The majority were generally optimistic in their expectations as to the length of time needed to locate a suitable job once they had started active job-seeking efforts. Seventy per cent of the enlisted men and 64 per cent of the officers expected to find a suitable job within 3 months.

This does not mean that they saw no difficulties before them. When asked how easy or difficult it would be to locate a civilian job equal to their service job in terms of pay, satisfaction, benefits, interest and challenge, the job-seekers were less sanguine. Sixty-two per cent of the officers and 42 per cent of the enlisted men thought it would be difficult. But, once the initial difficulties of locating a job had been overcome, they looked forward to a rosy future.

Furthermore, most men expected to be able to accomplish the transition to a civilian job without extensive retraining – only 45 per cent of the officers and 27 per cent of the enlisted men had made any plans for further training, education, or retraining at the time they were about to retire. While about two-thirds of the officers and half of the enlisted men thought that they might need some additional training to qualify for the civilian jobs they hoped to get, this was largely visualized as training that could be acquired on the job. Many officers, however, either intended to complete the requirements for a college degree or to acquire a graduate degree (Table 1).

TABLE 1

Officers, plans to obtain an academic degree (BSSR sample)

	Number	Per Cent
Total	256	100
No plans for academic degree	97	38
Plan to obtain academic degree	159	62
Bachelor's	92	35
Master's	45	18
Ph. D.	17	7
Other (law, medical, divinity)	5	2

428

4. QUALIFICATIONS AND ASPIRATIONS

In the BSSR sample, the retirees were asked to indicate their qualifications in the broad skill areas listed in the questionnaire. These encompassed most of the skills needed in the civilian job market. From the list, they were asked to pick the three skill areas in which they were best qualified. Table 2 lists those skill areas which were checked by at least 5 per cent of the officers or enlisted men.

TABLE 2

PERCENT OF BROAD CIVILIAN SKILL AREAS IN WHICH
RETIREES CONSIDER THEMSELVES BEST QUALIFIED[1] (BSSR SAMPLE)

Skill area	Officers (N=556)	Skill area	Enlisted men (N=1506)
Total[2].........	237	Total[2].........	245
Administration	48	Mechanical work	25
Aviation	31	Administration	23
Personnel administration .	21	Supply and procurement .	19
Organization and methods .	19	Security	18
Teaching	18	Personnel administration	17
Supply and procurement ...	18	Transportation and commerce	15
Public relations	12	Aviation	15
Security	10	Club and food	15
Electronics..............	9	General clerical	12
Mechanical work (all types)	8	Electronics	11
Communications	8	Construction	11
Sales	8	Communications	9
Research development	7	Ordnance	9
Engineering	5	Sales	8
Construction	5	Teaching	8
Production	5	Organization and methods	8
Writing..................	5	Public relations	6
		Agriculture	6
		Production	5
		Medicine and hospital ..	5

[1]   Proportion naming skill area as 1 of 3 in which they are best qualified.
[2]   Because of multiple choice of skill, percents add to more than 100.

Most officers aspired predominantly to jobs at the business-managerial level. Many enlisted men shared this aspiration, but the skilled trades were also frequently selected. The low interest in technical jobs is noteworthy, reflecting a limited perception of competence for all but the small group of men qualified in electronics. Conversely, it is also clear that, among both officers and enlisted personnel, men with administrative and quasi-administrative experience and aspirations dominate. This somewhat lopsided skill distribution is undoubtedly a factor in the employment difficulties experienced by some of these men.

The pre-retirement questionnaires listed types of employing institutions and asked the respondents to state for each one whether it was preferred, was acceptable, or was unacceptable. Among enlisted men and officers, the Federal Government was the institution most frequently checked as preferred. A much higher proportion of enlisted men than officers preferred Federal employment, however; about one fifth of the officers, in fact, listed the Federal Government unacceptable as an employer. The difference presumably is affected by the dual compensation and dual employment statutes in 1964 (modified since then by legislation). Regular officers in the sample were still largely barred from civil service. Large business (over 1,000 employees), medium-sized business (50 to 1,000 employees) and State and local government were the other types of institution most commonly designated as preferred.

These preferences for affiliation with large bureaucratic organizations are clearly related to the civilian job roles for which most of these men see themselves qualified. The great majority of the men apparently do not visualize a second career which would involve a radical departure from their military work pattern. Most of them rather plan to replicate their service working life in a civilian setting. There are exceptions, of course, with an occasional preference for self-employment, part-time employment, or "unusual" occupations which would satisfy a hobby. But, for most of the officers and enlisted men, aspirations were for orderly careers with a large organization.

This preference probably has its roots in the men's job value system. When asked prior to retirement to rate 19 job attributes, 94 per cent of the officers and 88 per cent of the enlisted men rated "chance for advancement" as a very important or somewhat important factor in judging a job. A job that is respected in the community was considered important by 85 per cent of the officers, whereas 80 per cent of the officers rated as important the job location in a specific geographic area. Salary considerations, albeit modest ones, were the second most preponderant type among the enlisted men: 84 per cent thought it important to earn at least $5,000 on the post-retirement job. Not at all surprising, given the potentially long and irregular hours on military duty, is the fact that 91 per cent of the enlisted and 78 per cent of the officers rated regular hours as important. On the other hand, freedom from supervision – which one might have assumed to be of interest to men who had worked for 20 years or more in a highly hierarchical context – was seldom rated important.

Long-run salary expectations were generally modest. To earn at least $15,000 or even $10,000 was not among the most frequent stipulations for a job, not even among officers. As was previously shown, they expected to earn only modest salaries in their first post-retirement job.

Interest in fringe benefits – notably, a claim to second pension – was considerable, however. It was greatest among the enlisted men, 77 per cent of whom thought it important to hold a job covered by social security and 59 per cent, a job covered by pension. While only 32 per cent of the officers stressed pensions, half of them wanted their job to be covered by social security. The superior financial resources of the officers and their significantly greater military retirement pay undoubtedly explain their lesser concern, but the responses of both groups clearly indicate that military retirement pay alone is considered inadequate protection for one's old age.

In summary, the retiree's "ideal" job as it emerges from the data is one with opportunity for recognition and advancement, but not necessarily much "executive" leeway (for officers) or independence (for enlisted men). Regular hours, retirement benefits and a congenial environment are more important than high salaries, freedom from supervision, opportunity to travel, or a chance to make important decisions and exert leadership. In this too, the preferences of the military retired appear to be quite similar to those of his civilian counterparts.

5. IN THE JOB MARKET

The great majority of the retirees in the BSSR sample of May 1964 had been able to locate a job of some kind by the time they were contacted 6 to 8 months after their retirement. At the time they completed the post-retirement questionnaire, 71 per cent of the officers and 76 per cent of the enlisted men reported that they were employed. Sixteen per cent of the officers and 21 per cent of the enlisted men were actively looking for work at that time. The others – 13 per cent of the officers and 3 per cent of the enlisted men – were full-time students, those unable to work due to physical reasons, those now permanently retired with no plans for future employment and those who were not active seekers at the time of the survey but who said they would be looking for work in the future.

In the main, placement took place rapidly. Among the job-holders, over one-half had started to work within 2 months of their retirement date – 54 per cent of the officers and 50 per cent of the enlisted men – and an additional 32 per cent of the officers and 33 per cent of the enlisted men found their first jobs during the third and fourth month after retirement.

The proportion of men actively looking for work at the time of the survey is quite high compared with the male civilian population in the same age group. This no doubt resulted partially from late job-seeking starts. Those who had not located a job within 6 to 8 months after retirement had waited longer than their job-holding colleagues to undertake active job-seeking efforts. Probably the job-seekers also included a few men who had found a job since retirement, but who were again in the job market at the time they received the post-retirement questionnaire. Many of the unemployed doubtless succeeded in locating jobs after they were surveyed. The DOD data, indeed, show a lower unemployment rate among the men who retired earlier. For both officers and enlisted men who were retired between 1958 and 1959, only 4 per cent were looking for work at the time of the survey in 1963. An additional 1–2 per cent had despaired of finding a job and had given up looking and another 1 per cent were about to begin looking for work.

Although the percentages are small, there is a disturbing uptrend in the DOD survey unemployment figures each year between 1960 and 1962 so that, for officers, 5 per cent of the 1961 retirees were looking for work and 7 per cent of the 1962 retirees. For enlisted men, the figures are 4 per cent of the 1960, 6 per cent of the 1961, and 8 per cent of the 1962 cohorts. This trend may indicate either a fairly slow adjustment to the job market by some retirees or slightly increasing difficulty in getting placed. There has been some speculation that a large number of openings in the economy for these second careers, especially for enlisted men, are in interstices of limited capacity and that, consequently, progressively greater difficulties can be expected as the number of retirees seeking employment climbs.

5.1. Variations in Employment Rates

Data from both the BSSR and DOD surveys suggest that job-seekers and job-holders differ with respect to several important personal, behavioural, and attitudinal dimensions. Thus, the DOD data show there are variations in employment status between men who served in the various branches of the service (see Table 3). Naval and Marine Corps retirees, both officers and enlisted, have a higher rate of employment than Army and Air Force retirees. The inter-service differences in employment are more pronounced in the BSSR sample of more recent retirees. Again, Air Force and Army men – and especially Army enlisted men – are most frequently in the job-seeker categories. Twenty-five per cent of the Army and 21 per cent of the Air Force were unemployed, compared with 15 per cent of the Navy men and 11 per cent of Marines.

Perhaps these differences are due partially to the slightly higher educational levels in the Navy and Marine Corps. Education and age are generally believed to be of crucial importance in their effect on employability. We examined the relationship between educational achievement of three groups of retirees: " Early job-holders " (those who had lined up a firm civilian job offer prior to retirement), "middle job-holders " (those who found a job during the 6–8 month period following retirement), and job-seekers (those who reported themselves looking for 6–8 months after retirement). The findings are summarized in Table 4. In general, the higher educated usually experienced earlier job placement and less unemployment. Only the small group of officers who were commissioned despite the lack of a high school education deviated from this pattern.

TABLE 3

EMPLOYMENT STATUS AND BRANCH OF SERVICE (DOD SAMPLE)

(Per cent)

Employment status	Branch of service				
	Army	Navy	Marine Corps	Air Force	Total
OFFICERS	(N=460)	(N=192)	(N=50)	(N=228)	[1]N=930)
Total..............	100	100	100	100	100
Full-time employed	75	79	76	73	75
Part-time employed	4	5	6	5	6
Looking for employment	7	6	4	8	7
Will look for employment	3	3	....	2	2
Retired	5	4	6	4	4
Full-time student	6	3	8	8	6
ENLISTED MEN	(N=535)	(N=946)	(N=122)	(N=540)	[2](N=2143)
Total	100	100	100	100	100
Full-time employed	73	86	85	81	81
Part-time employed	4	3	3	6	4
Looking for employment	14	5	6	6	8
Will look for employment	2	1	3	2	2
Retired	5	3	2	3	3
Full-time student	2	2	1	2	2

[1] Excludes 7 no answers.
[2] Excludes 18 no answers.

    The presumed importance of age in getting a job – and especially the supposed dis-advantages of the older job-seeker – is not clearly demonstrated by the data for the entire BSSR sample. Although, as was shown earlier, the men themselves were quite apprehensive on this score, only the fears of the enlisted men appear justified. Among the enlisted retirees, there are indeed significant differences in the unemployment rate by age group, with the older groups at a distinct disadvantage.
    Religion and race affect job status among enlisted men. (The officer sample is too homogeneous in race and religion for a sensitive test of differences.) Negroes and members of other minority groups had relatively greater difficulty in obtaining employ-ment. Thirty-three per cent of the Negroes and 27 per cent of the members of other minorities (Orientals, Spanish Americans, American Indians) were still unemployed 6–8 months after retirement, whereas only 17 per cent of the white Protestants and 19 per cent of the Catholics were still looking for work.

TABLE 4

EDUCATIONAL LEVEL AND JOB STATUS (BSSR SAMPLE)

(Per cent)

Educational level	Total		Job status			
	Number	Per cent	Early job holders	Middle job holders	Job-seekers	Others
OFFICERS						
Total	571	100	26	45	16	13
Not high school graduate	29	100	35	48	7	10
High school graduate	65	100	14	55	20	11
Some college	289	100	20	45	21	14
College graduate	188	100	38	40	10	12
ENLISTED MEN						
Total	1,614	100	15	61	20	4
Not high school graduate	529	100	11	62	24	3
High school graduate	803	100	15	62	20	3
Some college	264	100	19	55	19	7
College graduate	18	100	33	50	....	17

5.2. Type of Employer

Although prior to retirement, the men who participated in the BSSR survey expressed a strong interest in Government employment, actually among job-holders the proportion of Government employees was the same for officers and enlisted men and it was smaller than the proportion who would have liked to find Government employment. In the case of officers, this is partly due to regulations governing dual employment, dual compensation and conflict of interest. More important may be the long delays many applicants encounter in the Government hiring process, leading some to accept other work initially. Over time, the number of retired military men who work for Government agencies apparently increases. When the DOD sample is compared with the BSSR cohort, there seems to be a shift away from business employment and toward the Federal Government.

The types of employers for whom the May 1964 retirees were working 6 months after their retirement are varied. There is no decided concentration in any one sector, although substantial numbers of officers are found in the insurance and real estate businesses (19%). For enlisted men, the Federal Government (primarily the Defence and Post Office Departments) ranks high. What is most interesting is the wide scattering of these men throughout the civilian economy. The dominant pattern, especially for enlisted men, is in medium and small business establishments in a variety of plants and retail stores.

Educational level accounts for the sharpest differences in employment. Among officers who are college graduates, over half work either for large business establishments or for the Federal Government. Government employment is relatively more frequent than business among those with fewer years of education. For enlisted men the opposite holds true: Government employment is more frequently reported by those who have more than a high school education. These findings suggest that the well-educated officer (usually also of a high rank) can choose between desirable alternatives, including affiliation with educational institutions, which is desired by many but for which few have the necessary qualifications. For the enlisted man who has gone beyond high school, the opportunities are more often in Government than in the business or educational sectors, where his former rank may be a handicap.

Education differences, as well as the skill requirements of various occupations, account for the obvious differences in the kinds of jobs retirees took with various types of employers. This is shown in Table 5, which is based on the DOD data. While most of the findings are in the expected direction, some merit special comment.

A high proportion of the officers in the Federal Government are doing clerical or technical rather than administrative or professional work – no doubt a reflection of the selection of Federal employment by those less well qualified educationally. One-fourth of the officers working as salesmen are self-employed – these, no doubt, are predominantly men working on commission, as are those who regard themselves as employees of real estate, insurance, or financial agencies. Those engaged in managerial administrative work – the largest single category – are more likely to be found in large business establishments.

Enlisted men working in Federal agencies frequently hold clerical and technical positions; in State and local agencies, they are much more likely to be working in protective services as policemen and guards. When enlisted men work as salesmen (and quite a few of them do), it is often for small business establishments, particularly retail stores. Compared with officers doing sales work, they are less often self-employed or connected with large manufacturing, real estate, or insurance establishments.

5.3. Type of Job

Officers as well as enlisted men find work in a wide variety of fields. The diversity of jobs attests the broad range of "transferable skills" (or perhaps, more realistically, the generalized skill structure) which characterizes the military establishment. Yet certain areas of concentration stand out. And these, as we will show, are closely related to specific military career patterns.

Among the men in the BSSR sample, 29 per cent of the officers held business and managerial jobs, 24 per cent had professional jobs and another 24 per cent were salesmen. Among the enlisted men, 29 per cent were doing skilled or semiskilled work, 23 per cent were in service-type jobs, and 16 per cent were in clerical jobs.

Among earlier retirees represented in the DOD sample, 31 per cent of the officers were in businesses other than sales, 23 per cent in professional jobs and only 14 per cent in sales work. Among the DOD enlisted men, the largest group (36%) were service workers and only 22 per cent were in skilled and semiskilled occupations. When data from the surveys are compared there appears to be a tendency for officers as well as enlisted men to accept sales or clerical jobs initially upon retirement, but to shift gradually to other fields. Highly competitive sales jobs, with remuneration depending only on commissions, are often easy to get, but many men find it quite difficult to make a sufficient income in this kind of work.

Rank at retirement and educational level differentiate men in various categories of civilian employment. Age bears little relationship to the type of job held. Among officers, the degree holders are much more likely to work as professionals and much less frequently in sales or clerical positions. The men who have some college, but no degree, have a profile quite similar to those who have no more than a high school diploma. This finding is consistent in this survey: for officers, the college degree is crucial in qualifying men for professional and upper level business jobs; the job value of courses not part of a degree program is apparently minimal.

Among enlisted men, the comparable dividing line is the high school diploma. High school graduates are likely to find white-collar work; those who do not have a high school diploma are much more likely to be employed as skilled workers or in service

TABLE 5

OCCUPATION AND TYPE OF EMPLOYER OF JOB HOLDERS IN DOD SAMPLE

(Per cent distribution)

Occupation	Total Number	Total Per cent	Self-employed	Business¹ Large	Business¹ Medium	Business¹ Small	Educational institution	Medical institution	Government Federal	Government State & local	All other
Officers:² Number	832	....	85	188	110	93	78	6	162	66	44
Per cent	....	100	10	23	13	11	9	1	20	8	5
Engineering	74	100	1	60	14	1	5	......	9	6	3
Teaching	52	100	.....	.....	.....	.....	100	......	.....	.....	.....
Other professions	56	100	12	14	5	2	4	4	23	14	21
Business and managerial	265	100	5	25	20	11	4	1	21	8	5
Sales	116	100	24	30	17	23	1	......	1	1	3
Clerical	30	100	......	13	10	10	10	......	43	7	7
Technical	64	100	3	22	11	12	3	2	37	3	2
Skilled and semiskilled	24	100	29	25	11	25	......	......	8	4	......
Service	50	100	12	12	8	6	4	......	18	30	8
Other	101	100	21	4	8	14	2	......	37	9	5
Enlisted men:³ Number	1,900	....	156	337	299	275	66	33	495	150	89
Per cent	....	100	8	18	16	14	3	2	26	8	5
Professional	90	100	3	28	9	7	12	......	24	11	6
Business and managerial	207	100	14	16	18	15	3	2	17	9	6
Sales	136	100	21	21	18	32	......	......	2	......	5
Clerical	126	100	......	14	18	12	2	......	45	6	2
Electronic technician	78	100	5	31	13	6	1	6	45	1	1
Medical, laboratory, engineering technician	65	100	......	34	9	1	5	15	28	6	......
Other technical	97	100	4	31	11	5	3	1	38	9	......
Skilled craftsman	302	100	9	19	15	18	3	(⁴)	29	5	2
Skilled and semiskilled factory worker	107	100	2	29	41	15	......	......	12	......	1
Protective service	177	100	......	21	14	7	(⁴)	1	23	28	6
Other service	177	100	13	11	10	23	8	3	14	7	11
Other	338	100	11	6	13	14	6	1	35	7	7

1 Large business – over 2,500 employees; medium business – 50 to 2,500 employees; small business – fewer than 50 employees.

2 Excludes 1 "no answer".

3 Excludes 2 "no answer".

4 Less than 1.0 per cent.

Note: Percentage distributions may not add to 100, because of rounding.

jobs. College courses, however, make a greater marginal contribution to occupational upgrading for enlisted men than for officers. Enlisted men who have done some college work are more likely to find employment in technical, sales, and clerical work than those who have no more than a high school diploma.

Rank and education are highly correlated. Higher ranking officers are most likely to be college graduates. This explains the concentration of retirees in professional occupations (engineers, teachers, and doctors) among the top ranked officers. High-ranking officers also are much more likely than junior officers to find jobs as business excutives. Among enlisted men, rank and education operate in strictly parallel fashion: the men in the lower grades are much more likely to end up in service occupations than their higher ranked fellow servicemen. Better education may have a multiplier effect leading to promotions within the service, with rank, in turn, contributing to superior civilian job status. A higher level of education is a major attribute both in successfully negotiating the military career ladder and in a successful civilian career.

5.4. Military Skills and Civilian Jobs

The relation of military skills to civilian jobs is difficult to assess in the absence of detailed job descriptions. It is particularly difficult to determine the precise nature of the civilian jobs obtained by our subjects. Judging from job titles, close relationships obtain between a civilian job and military occupational specialty only in a minority of cases. The relationships are more pronounced among enlisted men than officers, probably because the military duties of many officers are of an administrative-managerial rather than technical-skilled nature. But, even among enlisted men, close correspondence between military specialty and civilian job is far from universal. Even in the military specialties where transfer appears most likely (such as medical and dental specialists; electronic, electrical and mechanical repairmen; crafts-men) it would appear, from the broad job categories, that no more than one-third to one-half had moved into directly comparable civilian jobs.

Most officers, regardless of their experience in the military, tended to get jobs in the professions or in the business and commercial fields. The exception was the small group of those who retired as officers and who had specialized in ordnance or in some fields usually the province of enlisted men. This group had correspondingly high place-ments in technical, clerical, sales, or skilled and service jobs.

Of 81 officers whose major specialty was aircraft pilot or crew member, 25 held executive-managerial type jobs, 26 were salesmen, 7 were engineers, 9 were teachers or school officials, 4 were mechanics and only 3 were aviators. This very low employment of pilots in their specialty — combined with the relative high unemployment rate of men with this specialty — is noteworthy in view of the complaint by the air transportation industry of a severe shortage of air crew. The age of the retirees presumably is a primary factor, not only because some are now too old to qualify as pilots in commercial aviation, but also because the seniority systems of the industry would require the retiree to say too long in semiapprentice roles at very low pay.

5.5. Job Slippage

Over-all, the findings seem to indicate that officers whose military job specialties were in high-demand fields where there are currently shortages found themselves placed most easily in their own fields. But the relationships are not always as automatic and clearcut as one might expect. Some of the slippage may be voluntary — conceivably for some men a second career is the opportunity for a long-desired switch, for example, from engineering or law to the real estate business. However, our data suggest that the acceptance of non-professional work may have resulted from job-finding difficulties as much as from voluntary decisions. The finding is most clear for officers in the DOD sample who accepted a clerical job; 37 per cent of them reported "great difficulty" in finding a first job, whereas, over-all, only about 14 per cent of the officers chose this answer. Our consistent finding was that the same military specialty groups in which relatively large numbers of men were unemployed 6 months after retirement also turned out to have the largest proportion of unrelated placements and members who reported difficulties in job-finding. Consequently, we conclude there are very real transfer problems in some specialties, including those which were believed to have high civilian transferability, such as aircraft and engineering. Furthermore, not only in air transportation but in other areas as well, non-transferability of seniority status is probably a greater employment barrier than non-transferability of skill.

This does not mean the men feel that their military experience was not helpful in obtaining the jobs they held. Well over half of the retired officers and enlisted men in the DOD sample selected the most positive answer ("helped a great deal ") when asked if their military background helped qualify them for the work they are doing in civilian life.

What the findings suggest, perhaps, is that while specific skills acquired in the military are unquestionably an asset, especially in fields where there are acute personnel shortages, this is only one part of the picture and not necessarily the most significant one. From the detailed data collected in the employer and counsellor surveys conducted as part of our intensive study, it appears that the retired serviceman is evaluated in common denominator civilian terms rather than on the basis of his specific military-acquired skills. This means primarily education, plus personality-type qualifications, for which rank achieved is one indicator. [1] There is also more indirect evidence in our survey material that in the majority of cases specific job matching probably was not attempted by employers either at the time these men were hired or when they were assigned. The retirees' own perceptions point to a feeling of relatively low utilization of their military skills in their civilian occupations, contrary to their expectations.

5.6. Income

Considering the job qualifications of the military retired population, the civilian incomes they earned in 1963 and 1964 appear to be distinctly low. The median income of officers from the DOD sample was $6,130 in 1963 – after 1 to 3 years in the civilian job market. Their colleagues who retired later in 1964 and who were surveyed 6 months after retirement did somewhat better: their median income was $7,785. Enlisted men's incomes were also lower for the earlier cohort: $4,690 for those surveyed in 1963, $4,730 for the more recent retirees.

The importance of rank and education as they affect the retirees chances in the job market is dramatically illustrated by income differences. The highest ranking officers commanded about $4,000 more annually than the lowest ranking officers ($9,500 and $5,135 respectively). The low-ranking officers, in fact, averaged less than warrant officers. Among the top three grades of enlisted men, the differences in median income were small, ranging from $5,120 to $4,970. There is, however, a substantial drop at the next lower level to $4,280 and a further sharp drop to $3,030 for lowest level of enlisted retiree.

In the 1964 group, officers who were college graduates had a median income of $9,490; for those who did not graduate from high school it was $5,830. The median income for enlisted men without a high school diploma was $4,185 compared with $4,815 for high school graduates and $6,250 for college graduates. The findings for the DOD group are similar.

---

[1] The only instance in which specific military experiences are probably an important asset is employment in government and defence industries, where certain technical or bureaucratic know-how or personal connections might be an asset. It should be noted, however, that these surveys show fewer than 30% (20% in the DOD survey and 28% in the BSSR study) of all officer respondents working for large business establishments, of which defence industries are only one subgroup. For enlisted men, the proportion is even lower.

Age and income are inversely related, with the negative effect of age most marked among enlisted men. Among officers, the relationship is more complex and the effect of age is less clear and less important than the effect of rank and education. Age at retirement, rank and education are interdependent variables because of promotion and retention policies.

Officers with military backgrounds in research and development and in the professions (law and medicine) tended to have the best paying jobs. These men, of course, are college graduates and many have a graduate or professional degree. Among enlisted men, those with an electronic background had the highest median salary. The lowest paid were those with a background in combat arms and services.

Table 6 shows the 1965 median incomes for officers and enlisted men in the various civilian occupational groupings. In professional and managerial occupations, the median incomes of enlisted men are substantially less than those for officers, but not in technical and skilled jobs. Among electronics and other technicians, skilled craftsmen, and service workers, former enlisted men tend to earn more than ex-officers.

TABLE 6

OCCUPATION AND MEDIAN INCOME OF JOB-HOLDERS IN DOD SAMPLE

Occupation	Officers		Enlisted men	
	Number	Median income	Number	Median income
Engineering	72	$9,695	42	$6,815
Teaching	51	4,900	......	......
Other professional	54	7,460	45	6,120
Personnel work	32	5,365	32	4,830
Financial	36	5,915	21	4,750
Business and administration	94	8,585	29	6,750
Other business	100	7,260	120	5,730
Sales	108	5,275	132	4,430
Clerical	28	4,625	121	3,965
Electronic technician	13	5,750	77	6,170
Medical, laboratory, or engineering technician	13	5,665	65	5,960
Other technical	34	6,710	96	5,925
Skilled craftsman	22	4,635	284	4,995
Skilled and semiskilled factory work .	......	......	100	4,220
Protective services	31	4,750	171	4,150
Other service	15	3,430	171	3,630
Other	98	4,965	324	4,235

Examination of the data indicates that the low-median incomes for the retired population as a whole are due chiefly to the placement of many men — both officers and enlisted men — in relatively unskilled jobs: clerical work, sales and protective and other services for officers; clerical and service jobs for enlisted men. In business, professional and technical occupations, it would appear that former militarymen are relatively well paid. Thus, there seems to be little evidence that these men tend to settle for low-paying jobs because of the availability of retirement income; rather, the pay problems that are in evidence are due to retirees, especially those with low levels of education, being unable to enter better paying occupations and settling, therefore, for unskilled occupations in which low rates prevail.

5.7. Job Stability

For most of the retirees, the first job accepted following retirement turned out to be a permanent one. It would not be unreasonable to assume that, given the variety of tasks with which they had experience during military life, these men might try several different jobs before settling on some kind of second career employment. But for the majority this was not the case. Among officers and enlisted men, age seems to have very little relationship to the total number of jobs held. However, there is a relationship between retirement rank and the proportion of men who had held more than one job: those who held higher military ranks were more stable. In all cases, the higher ranking officers were clearly the most stable employees – perhaps because they had had the least difficulty in locating appropriate and well-paid jobs.

Employment stability is much more prevalent in certain civilian occupations than in others. Among the DOD officers who had been on retired status from 1 to 3 years, 85 per cent of the engineers and 80 per cent of the teachers had had only one job since retirement. But 54 per cent of the medical, laboratory and engineering technicians, 53 per cent of the clerical workers and 48 per cent of the craftsmen had had two or more jobs since retirement. There are no occupations held by enlisted men which match the stability of ex-officers who are teachers or engineers. The very highest proportions of stable employees were found in finance, managerial and related occupations and sales.

In general, job stability patterns accord with expectations: those in professional, managerial and white-collar occupations experience less turn-over than those in blue-collar occupations – in part because white-collar and professional workers are less likely to be laid off in slack periods. The data also suggest that officers who have settled for occupations incongruent with their former high status (skilled craftsman, medical or laboratory technician, or other miscellaneous occupations) are most likely to undergo frequent job changes.

6. UTILIZATION OF SKILL

Prior to retirement, men in the May 1964 sample were asked their opinions about how much their military training and experience would help in civilian jobs, how the utilization of their skills in military and civilian jobs would compare and how their skills would compare with those of civilians doing the same jobs. All job-holders were asked the same questions again in the post-retirement questionnaire.

Sixty-eight per cent of the officers, but only 57 per cent of the enlisted men, who had thought their military background would be of great help in their civilian jobs indicated that this was in fact true in their present jobs. Among those who thought their military background would be of some help in their civilian jobs, over two-thirds said it was of some or a great deal of help in their present jobs. More surprising is the finding that 64 per cent of the officers and 43 per cent of the enlisted men who, prior to retirement, thought their military background would be of little help changed their minds once they were working.

The area in which the retirees tended to experience the most serious disappointment was the actual utilization of their skills in civilian jobs. Thirty-nine per cent of the officers and 47 per cent of the enlisted men perceived less utilization, whereas less than half as many – only 17 per cent of the officers and 20 per cent of the enlisted men – had anticipated this. Conversely, prior to retirement, 47 per cent of the officers and 49 per cent of the enlisted men thought they would experience greater skill utilization in their civilian jobs, but, 6 to 8 months later, only 32 per cent of the officers and 31 per cent of the enlisted men thought they were actually using their skills and abilities to a greater degree than they had in the military establishment.

This perception of low skill utilization is not due to these men's re-evaluation of the skills they had to offer. For the most part, the retired military man continued to give the same high opinion of his qualifications compared with those of civilians doing identical jobs. In fact, the proportion of those who considered themselves better qualified than civilians goes up a little bit after a few months on the job.

6.1. Assessment of Underutilization

There is little reason to assume that these men have an unrealistic view of themselves and their qualifications: their job aspirations, job behaviour, salary requirements and rating of work values all point to generally realistic self-assessments. Perceived low levels of skill utilization can therefore be assumed to reflect the reality of many job situations in which the retirees found themselves. This is one area – perhaps the outstanding one – where the military/civilian transition was unsatisfactory from the point of view of the individual. At the time they left the service, lack of skill utilization was not a major grievance among this group: 71 per cent of the officers and 67 per cent of the enlisted men indicated that the service had utilized their skills and abilities a great deal (the most positive response). The hopes for high skill use in civilian life were frustrated, especially for men with relatively low educational achievement (less than a college degree for officers, no college at all for enlisted men). The data suggest that it is those officers and enlisted men who are able to make the grade in the service on the strength of their demonstrated abilities, rather than formal education, who are least able to match this status in civilian jobs. [1] In the civilian world, formal educational attainment ranks higher than skill as a measure of acceptance and placement.

Educational differences largely seem to account for these feelings of skill under-utilization, yet age as well as military specialty and specific occupation play some part. In fact, the latter probably is the crucial factor, but it is, in turn, so strongly influenced by education that it is difficult to isolate their respective effects. Younger men more often indicated greater skill use in the civilian job than did the older men. Among officers, only those in the professional specialities and those who had specialized in communications, electronics and research and development reported more skill utilization in their civilian job. A half or more of the men in each of the other officer military occupational groups reported less skill utilization after retirement. Among the enlisted military, all occupational groups reported less skill utilization in their civilian jobs. Even among electronics technicians, mechanics and craftsmen, whose skill transference is high, many more individuals said there was less rather than more use of their skills in the civilian job.

As could be expected, those with low skill utilization are disproportionately concentrated in the civilian jobs which have been previously identified here as marginal for both officers and enlisted men – clerical work, craftsmen (for ex-officers), some types of sales work, service jobs, and factory work. More unexpected is the finding that even in related occupations, perceived skill utilization is quite low. Only in the professions, including teaching and engineering, personnel work and the executive, administrative and managerial areas, do at least 35 per cent of the officers indicate more skill utilization in their civilian job than in their previous military assignment. But even here relatively low skill utilization is reported by many.

---

[1]   See Mayer N. Zald and William Simon, "Opportunities and Commitments Among Officers", *The New Military*, Morris Janowitz, ed. (New York, Russell Sage Foundation, 1964), pp. 257–285, for a related discussion of perceived skill utilization by officers with different educational backgrounds.

Among the enlisted men, occupational outcomes differentiate more sharply between skill utilizers and nonskill utilizers. The over-all low levels of utilization are attributable to the relatively large groups in unskilled jobs (clerical, factory work, and services). Among those former enlisted men who were able to find higher level jobs such as in business, as technicians and even as salesmen, over half saw themselves working at higher skill levels in civilian life. For these men, the second career appears to offer greater intrinsic rewards than the military.

5. TRAINING NEEDS

Prior to retirement, relatively few officers and enlisted men visualized the need for training in order to qualify for the civilian jobs they hoped to find. In particular, few of the enlisted men were conscious of this need: only 27 per cent (compared with 45 per cent of the officers). Furthermore, on-the-job training, rather than formal schooling, was seen as the major need.

Following retirement and early experience in a civilian job, quite a few of the retirees revised their views. This was especially true of men who had not yet located a job: almost half of them, officers as well as enlisted men, answered "yes " to the question, "Do you think you might need additional training to qualify for the kind of work you have in mind?"

But, even among job-holders, the number was greater than it had been prior to retirement (36% of the enlisted men and 48% of the officers). Both job-seekers and job-holders continued to see the need primarily as one to be met by on-the-job training. In the DOD sample, similar responses were obtained from men who had had longer experience in the job market.

It is not paradoxical that the better educated men are more likely to see the need for further formal education than those who have never been to college? Better educated men and women are the main consumers of adult education. [1] Furthermore, the job aspirations of the better educated retirees are more likely to require additional instruction or updating of knowledge. Younger men were somewhat more willing to accept the idea of undergoing further training than were their older colleagues.

---

[1] See John W. C. Johnstone and Ramon Rivera. *Volunteers for Learning – A Study of the Education Pursuits of American Adults,* (Chicago, Aldine Publishing Co., 1965).

Convergence of the Civilian and Military Occupational Structures

ROGER W. LITTLE
THE UNIVERSITY OF ILLINOIS
AT CHICAGO CIRCLE

I. INTRODUCTION

Since the end of World War II, military manpower policy has proceeded on the assumption that the trend toward convergence of the civilian and military occupational structures would continue, with an increasing similarity between military and civilian skills. Such a policy legitimises the demands of military organization for the same range of aptitudes and raw skills as needed by civilian institutions. Recent events in the United States now suggest, however, that the limits of the civilianization of the armed forces have now been reached and military organization must henceforth, to a much greater degree, meet its manpower needs by organizational adaptation rather than competition in the labour market.

Certainly there has been a remarkable transfer of skills from the larger society to military organization.[1] However, our position is that continued emphasis on the convergence of the military and civilian occupational structures tends to promote emulation of the civilian structure while deflecting attention from the limiting factors and distinctive attributes of the military structure. This has resulted in excessive concern for qualitative selection and competition with the civilian sector for scarce aptitudes, thus increasing the tension between armed forces and society. It also ignores the unique training and educational capability of the armed forces as a functional imperative emerging from the necessity for rapid assimilation of successive classes of recruits while remaining effective as an organization. Military institutions are unique as occupational structures because they are capable of utilizing large numbers of men with general aptitudes and raw skills for relatively brief periods of time.

Perhaps the most dramatic change in military manpower research is the progressive decline in the assumed validity of entry criteria. This regretfully has not come about on the basis of an accumulation of scientific findings, but rather because of a political decision that some manpower problems had to be solved by adjusting organizational criteria to social reality. The continuous upward revision of entry requirements had finally reached a point at which the armed forces were in conflict with civilian institutions for men with scarce aptitudes and raw skills.

The demands of military organization for these scarce recruits have been sustained since the Korean Conflict by assumptions about the increasingly complex skill structure of the armed forces. Without legal compulsion in the form of conscription, the armed forces are in the position of an industry with a chronic manpower shortage. Conscription has delayed recognition of this competitive position. Industry – without such a crutch – has found that high educational and experience requirements are often based on past experience that is no longer relevant, or on assumptions that have never been tested. However, when such requirements were adjusted to the conditions of the labour market, it was often found that the previously excluded categories could perform the required tasks effectively, thus alleviating the apparent manpower shortage.[2]

With PROJECT 100,000 and its sequel, TRANSITION, the American defence establishment has embarked on an enormous test of the assumption that entry criteria must increase with the technological complexity of the armed forces. Research which a few years ago was devoted to developing criteria that would exclude with certainty the 20 per cent who might be ineffective is now interpreted more realistically to expand the 80 per cent who would be effective. Performance evaluations are often found to be more valid instruments for prediction of job effectiveness than are tests of general intelligence. [3] The implication for manpower procurement is obvious: the erosion of highly selective entry criteria expands the size of the available manpower pool by including those for whom there is little competition by non-military institutions.

Two other implications follow. First, the image of technological complexity of the armed forces may have been greatly exaggerated and entry criteria unduly inflated. By demanding an unnecessarily large share of scarce aptitudes, their productive employment in the larger society has been delayed. Second, the amount of time now spent in training rather than operational tasks may be excessive. Thus, if new criterion men are now able to complete their training with the same degree of proficiency as old (higher) criterion men have in the past, there is a basis for questioning the assumed complexity and length of the learning process required for basic training. Thus, the benefits we derive from the success of low aptitude men in the present basic training period may be at the cost of the operational time that high aptitude men could contribute if they were able to complete basic training in a shorter period of time.

Two trends in the larger society affect military manpower procurement but also require an adaptive response by military personnel policy agencies. The first is the increasing numbers of youths in the manpower pool and available for service. In contrast, the demands for manpower by military organization have either remained stable or declined. From the viewpoint of procurement this phenomenon enables recruitment agencies to be increasingly selective for qualitative factors, up to the limits with which we are now confronted. But it poses a far more serious problem for the relationship between armed forces and society in the form of the declining rate of participation in military organization and a corresponding deterioration in the conception of military service as a universal civic obligation.

The second trend is the vast increase in the educational level of the manpower pool, such that now the "average worker" is a high school graduate. Consequently, the educational level of all recruits is higher and their skill potential correspondingly greater. The urban environment is also more likely to provide opportunities for developing raw aptitudes into skills of some value to military organization, especially mechanical. The superior performance of high school graduates, despite their aptitude scores, also suggests that educational level is an indicator of effective socialization in organizational skills that are readily adaptable to military life.

2. FACTORS ACCOUNTING FOR THE ASSUMED CONVERGENCE OF THE CIVILIAN AND MILITARY OCCUPATIONAL STRUCTURES.

2.1. The Historical origin of the Classification System

The military occupational classification originated as a device for matching civilian skills obtained in total mobilization with the specific needs of military organization. [4] Consequently, the civilian occupational structure was the model for the military occupational structure developed during World War II. Simple occupational roles which had been traditionally defined within the organization as requiring skills learned "on the job" were transformed into elaborate descriptions to appropriately match civilian skills, and to establish training sequences for personnel with only aptitude for learning the required skills. However, it was not descriptive of the existing military occupational structure.

2.2. Equilibration of Entry Requirements and Labour Force Quality

In military organization, as in industry, the entry requirements for new occupations, as well as new entry requirements for old occupations, tend to be defined in terms of the *current* quality of the labour force. Since the military manpower pool, like the labour force, includes a relatively larger number of high school graduates, that level is increasingly specified as an essential entry requirement. However, earlier entrants with lower attained educational levels continue to perform the same tasks as effectively as those with higher educational levels. Consequently, the escalation of entry requirements is more likely to reflect the rising levels of education in the labour force generally than increasing technical requirements for specific tasks.

2.3. Intra-service Competition for Image Improvement

The image of a highly technical force, requiring scarce aptitudes and providing complex technical training, tends to enhance the prestige of the armed forces in relation to the larger society. The persistent quest for prestige is expressed in competition among the services for higher levels of education without regard for the specific occupational requirements. The belief that the image is reality inhibits change in organizational manpower policies. Thus, spokesmen for the defence establishment use the electronics technician as the standard for public explanations of high entry requirements and a longer term of service, not because the occupation is so common but because it is such an effective symbol for relating military organization to the larger society.

2.4. Recruiting inducement

Several studies have indicated that recruitment is stimulated by the image of the armed forces as an educational institution providing opportunities for learning advanced technical skills combined with an apprenticeship experience in a context of highly valuable service. The educational criterion is also used for differentiating among the services. For example, a sample of high school seniors were asked the most important factors in choosing a military program. "Opportunities for training " was the most frequent choice, followed by "choice of career field " and "opportunity for advancement ".[5] A comparison of high school seniors and Navy recruits, using PROJECT TALENT data in 1962 indicated that the prospect of training was the prime inducement for 43 per cent of the recruits, five times as great as the next most popular reason, "travel and adventure ".[6] A sample survey of Air Force enlisted men in April 1964 yielded similar results. A 5 per cent sample of men with one year of service indicated that the most favourable feature of an Air Force career was first, "Opportunities for more training and education " (57 per cent); second, "Adventure, travel and new experience " (28.5 per cent). Among officers with only one year of service, "Opportunities for training and education " also ranked first.[7]

We have suggested that although there has been a long-term trend toward a convergence of the military and civilian occupational structures, a limiting point has now been reached which cannot be passed without increasing the tension between armed forces and society in issues related to manpower procurement.

3. FACTORS DETERMINING THE LIMITS OF CIVILIANIZATION OF THE ARMED FORCES

3.1. The inherent uniqueness of the military mission

Not only are requirements for unique jobs created, but the role requirements of jobs with civilian equivalents are so modified that they retain only a slight similarity to the original model. Wool indicates that 80 per cent of all enlisted jobs are in occupations which account for only slightly more than 10 per cent of the total civilian male labour force. A ranking of civilian occupational groups with high frequencies which accounted for 43 per cent of the male civilian labour force included only 7.6 per cent of the identifiable enlisted positions. Wool adds that even these comparisons exaggerate the degree of convergence because many of the apparent matchings are actually only in terms of a broad functional similarity.[8]

3.2. Relative proportions receiving advanced technical training

Actually relatively few new entrants attend schools providing advanced technical training. A sample of Army enlisted men in 1962 indicated that only 49.5 per cent had completed any service school course. Since many such courses are very short in duration, a better criterion is attendance at complex service schools with a duration of twenty weeks or more. Only 6.8 per cent of enlisted men in grade 4, and 5 per cent of men in grade 3 had attended such courses. In the second enlistment career grades of 5, 6 and 7, completion of such service schools increased to 13.8 per cent, 18.6 per cent, and 20.4 per cent respectively.[9] Thus contrary to the expectations initial entrants appear to have had prior to enlistment and during the first year of service, relatively few received advanced technical training in the first enlistment. Nor was it achieved by career personnel with sufficient frequency to establish aptitude for such courses as a requirement for the career force.

3.3. Under-utilization of skills

Even when service schools are attended, the skills obtained are not fully utilized. In the sample referred to above, more than a third of the men in enlisted grades 3 and 4 (initial entrants) were not utilized at all in the duties they were performing at that time.[10] In a sample of officers (1961) only 21 per cent of all second lieutenants felt that the Army had utilized their skills and abilities "a great deal ", 51.7 per cent "somewhat ", 20.9 per cent "very little ", and 5.8 per cent "not at all ".[11] Wool also cites three studies, of missile crew personnel, fire control system repairmen and Navy electronics technicians, which indicate that men in these specialties spent at most only half of their time in the technical duties for which they had been trained.[12] Thus the role requirements of many complex jobs in military organization require the performance of many low skill tasks of such little importance that they are not regularly provided for in the tables of organization. Under-utilization increases the demand for high skill personnel and the apparent complexity of the occupational structure by precisely that amount of time and men diverted to low skill tasks while assigned to high skill occupational roles.

3.4. Discrepancies between job titles and skill requirements

Many new job titles in administrative and mechanical areas may actually require less aptitude for learning and performing complex skills than the older ground combat occupations that they have replaced. Studies in civilian industry suggest that job titles may be up-graded while actual skill levels are reduced. This also occurs in the military organization because operator skills are often built into the design of complex weaponry and communications devices. Requirements for operator skills are thus transferred to the repair and maintenance level. Even there, however, the required skill level may be reduced by designing the equipment so that defective components can be replaced on the site rather than removing the entire equipment for repair in a shop.

4. IMPLICATIONS FOR MANPOWER RESEARCH

These factors suggest that the limits of civilianization have been reached and further efforts by military organization to emulate the civilian occupational structure would be wasteful of skilled manpower. If we accepted the end of convergence as a fact of life rather than a problem to be solved, some very different approaches to manpower research would be indicated, changes in direction of effort as profound as those now observed in research on entry criteria. The primary effect of exaggerating the degree of convergence of the civilian and military occupational structures has been to obscure the limiting point at which the structures are factually unique. To ignore the limits of civilianization is to ignore also the distinctive contributions of military service to

the larger society. This often leads to a misunderstanding of the roles of military
institutions in the social order. Since military occupational skills can be (apparently)
very quickly learned, organizational continuity must depend on a relatively small cadre
who are distinguished by career commitment rather than a superior degree of occupational
proficiency acquired through long experience. Therefore the most important process
occurring in the training experience is one of socialization or acculturation in
military life, through intense interpersonal activity, rather than technical training
in the conventional academic sense.

4.1. The total socialization experience

The total socialization experience is a contribution that no other institution in
modern society can provide. Margaret Mead has pointed out that many of the problems of
American boys originate in the discontinuity between the heroic, unresponsible roles
that they are encouraged to play in childhood, and the subordinate, organizationally-
constraining roles of early adulthood. [13] In military service, however, youths have
opportunities to play transitional roles containing many of the elements of childhood
fantasy, combined with adult responsibilities. Adolescent fantasies of power and
aggression are socialized in the primitive rite of the bayonet course and in
identification with the vast technology of warfare in which they are continuously
involved. This experience is combined with the fact that in military organization, all
roles carry operational responsibilities. The recruit performing guard duty is
functionally as crucial to the organization's mission as is the commander. There is no
" second team " in military organization, no category of participants who are ineligible
to participate in the central drama of the organization's life.

However, this unique contribution has been subordinated to the presumed superior
value of technical training, cast in the format of a conventional classroom situation
requiring all of the ornaments of the academic tradition. The tutorial relationship
between the master and apprentice (in the form of " on the job training ") has been
discarded in preference for the lecturer and note-taking student. Much of this
distortion of emphasis might be attributed to the fact that classroom achievement can
be intricately measured in relatively brief experimental intervals and correlated
directly with tests of general intelligence and aptitudes, but measures of social
adjustment require more ambiguous and long range techniques, usually extending over
the entire term of service. Thus a suitable task for manpower research might be an
appraisal of the extent to which the classroom method is wasteful of operational service
time. It might begin with the question: Must there be a school for everything?

The emphasis on technical training may have the actual effect of initially attract-
ing (but not retaining) a larger proportion of men with very little commitment to
military life as a career. It appears that once advanced skills have been acquired in
technical schools, levels of aspiration are raised beyond the capacity of military roles
to fulfill them. Expectations that the effort expended in the acquisition of specialized
training will lead to opportunities for developing proficiency, increased responsibility,
pay, and personal freedom, do not materialize. Such values are sought elsewhere and
consequently their developed skills are lost to the armed forces. However, occupations
that do not promise technical training are apparently more likely to fall within the
range of realistic expectations of men assigned to them. It is interesting to note that
the highest re-enlistment rates in the American Army last year was of " infantry, gun
crews, and allied specialists (35 per cent of all first term regulars eligible for re-
enlistment, compared to 28 per cent for all occupational groups). [14]

4.2. Length of the initial term of service

Finally, a new perspective on the relation between the civilian and military
occupational structures might well lead to a reconsideration of the problem of the
length of the initial term of service. The economic factor of training " pay-off "
must be balanced against the extent to which the initial term operates as a selection

criterion by discriminating among men with varying degrees of commitment to military service. As Wilson has pointed out, long enlistments are most likely to result in re-enlistments.[15] However, the longer the initial term of service the smaller the number of men who are willing to commit themselves to such a period, and consequently, the smaller is the recruitment universe. Correspondingly, the number of commitments tends to increase with decreasing terms of service.

Many youths are now deterred from enlisting by the length of the required initial term, despite the promise of technical training. In the study comparing male high school students with Navy recruits, high school seniors were asked "What is the longest period of active duty time for which you would consider enlisting in each branch of service?" For all five services (including the Coast Guard) the two year term of service was preferred by a wide margin over alternative periods of 6 months, 3, 4 and 6 years.[16]

The preference for the 2 year term may reflect a realistic conception of the maximum acceptable occupational commitment for this age group. It is well established in industrial sociology that younger workers have extremely high job instability in what has been called the "trial work period".[17] Job obligations during this period are likely to be viewed as contingent upon lack of a "better deal", and thought of as exploratory rather than contractual in nature. Consequently, long term commitments are either rejected outright, violated recklessly, or endured with greatly reduced efficiency. At least one study of delinquency in military service indicated a disproportionate incidence among enlistees as compared to draftees.[18] Another study, comparing draftees and enlistees matched for general intelligence indicated that draftees (with the shorter, two year term) performed better and were less likely to be discharged prior to the end of their contractual term than were voluntary enlistees (with the longer, three year term).[19] These studies did not control for length of service, but they suggest that the initially more highly-motivated enlistee becomes increasingly cynical when his enlistment expectations are not fulfilled and he is yet compelled to serve a longer term than the draftee and beyond the time limits of an occupational commitment for his age group.

The basic argument sustaining the longer terms of service for initial entrants is economic, balancing the cost of training against the man-year utilization. It is contended that a shorter term of service would require a corresponding enlargement of the training establishment in order to accommodate the higher turnover of successive classes of recruits, especially highly-trained technicians. We have already indicated the small proportion of initial entrants who ever receive such specialized training so the economic argument is only of limited applicability. But a more fundamental criticism is the empirical basis for determining the optimum length of the initial term. Such terms have never been tested and are founded on purely economic considerations without regard for the behavioural factors involved. The required period of initial commitment has steadily declined in all armed forces (with more rapid transportation of replacements to remote areas and colonial stations) without any remarkable effect on organizational effectiveness. Indeed, if we consider modern armies more effective than those of history, the shorter term of service has enhanced unit effectiveness.

The longer term assumes a cumulative increase in proficiency and consequently a greater aggregate skill inventory in the forces. However, there might also be a proficiency plateau which once achieved, marks the beginning of a decline in proficiency associated with loss of motivation rather than a progressive increase until the day of discharge. Such a conception of declining motivation was administratively recognized in the nine month combat tour rotation policy in the Korean Conflict and to a much lesser extent in the present twelve month tour for all troops in Viet Nam regardless of the degree of risk to which they are exposed. But there is no behavioural science basis for these intervals either. The determination of such periods of optimum proficiency and commitment are crucial tasks for future manpower research.

5. CONCLUSIONS

We would conclude that military manpower research must be adjusted to the new reality that the convergence of the civilian and military occupational structures has reached a limiting point. Further emulation of the civilian sector by military organization will be disruptive of relations with the larger society by demanding scarce aptitudes which cannot be fully utilized in military service. But more important, it will delay essential internal changes in military organization. Military skills appear to be more limited in scope, depth, and stability than their apparent civilian equivalents. A brief term of service, consistent with the minimum training required, may capture the peak motivation of a succession of new entrants, thus enhancing the aggregate motivation and proficiency. A high rate of turnover increases the capability of military organization to respond to new skill requirements by changes in training sequences with each new class of highly-trainable recruits rather than retraining technicians with obsolete skills. The subsidiary benefits of a larger training establishment are not accurately reflected by per-capital cost benefit analyses, but include opportunities for research in new technology and doctrines, rotational billets for career personnel and the return of valuable technical and social skills to the larger society. These organizational values are more important than persisting in the search for criteria which will enlarge the proportion of new entrants with the aptitude and motivation for long-term careers. For the major contribution that military service makes to the civilian occupational structure is not technical skill but socialization and participation in a phase of the nation's cultural tradition. It is in a real sense, an introduction to life in modern society.

REFERENCES

1. Lang, Kurt, "Technology and Career Management in the Military Establishment", in Morris Janowitz, Editor, (1964) *The New Military*, Russell Sage Foundation, New York.
2. Ross, Arthur M. (1966), *"Theory and Measurement of Labour Shortages"*, Manpower Symposium, Princeton, University. Mimeographed publication, U.S. Department of Labour, Washington.
3. See for example, Goffard, S. James, Morris Showel, and Hilton M. Bialek (1964), *A Study of Category IV Personnel in Basic Training*, Technical Report 66–2, Human Resources Research Office, The George Washington University, Washington.
4. Wool, Harold M. (1965), *The Military Specialist*, Author's Printing, Washington, p.170.
5. Dear, Robert E., and Ledyard, R. Tucker (1961), *The Measurement of The Relative Appeal of Military Service Programs*. Educational Testing Service, Princeton, p.37.
6. *The United States Air Force Personnel Report*: "Characteristics and Attitudes from Sample Surveys" (1964), Vol. 8, No. 3, p.28 (Officers), p.59 (Enlisted Men).
7. Shaycroft, Marion F., Clinton A. Neyman, Jr., and John T. Dailey (1962), *Comparison of Navy Recruits with Male High School Students on the Basis of PROJECT TALENT Data*. American Institutes for Research, Pittsburgh, pp.51–53.
8. Wool, Harold M., *op. cit.*, p.232.
9. *Sample Survey of Military Personnel* (1962), "Survey Estimate of Knowledge and Opinions of Army Enlisted Men Concerning the Army's Service School and Educational Opportunities". Department of the Army, Washington.
10. *Ibidem*.
11. *Sample Survey of Military Personnel* 1961, Survey Estimate of Utilization of Skills and Abilities by the Army of Male Officers by Grade and Component, Department of the Army, Washington.
12. Wool, Harold M., *op. cit.*, p.236.
13. Mead, Margaret (1955), *Male and Female*, The New American Library, New York, p.230.
14. *Selected Manpower Statistics* (1967), Office of the Secretary of Defense, Directorate for Statistical Services, Washington, p.54.
15. Wilson, N.A.B. (1966), Psychology and Military Proficiency. *Advancement of Science*, November, pp.355–365.
16. Shaycroft, Marion F., *et al*, *op. cit.*, p.D-23.
17. Miller, Delbert C., and William H. Form (1963), *Industrial Sociology*, Harper and Row, New York, pages 563-579.
18. Klieger, Walter A., A.U. Dubuisson, and Bryan B. Sargent, III (1962), Correlates of Disciplinary Record in a Wide Range Sample, *Technical Research Note 125*, U.S. Army Personnel Research Office, Washington.
19. Helme, William H. and Alan A. Anderson (1964), Job Performance of Enlisted Men Scoring Low on AFQT, *Technical Research Note 146*, U.S. Army Personnel Research Office, Washington.

PART IV THE FUTURE OF THE MILITARY SYSTEM

J. A. A. van Doorn

A. B. Cherns

The Military Profession in Transition

J.A.A. VAN DOORN

NETHERLANDS SCHOOL OF ECONOMICS, ROTTERDAM

AND ROYAL MILITARY ACADEMY, BREDEN

I. INTRODUCTION

Sociologists have made rather few contributions to the field of manpower policy and research, where the discussion is dominated by economists, statisticians, demographic experts and, more recently, by a number of psychologists.

The fact that sociology is not represented is not in the interests of a deeper understanding of the manpower problems typical of occupational groups, which are more than statistical or administrative categories. Manpower research in the professions, for instance, is confronted with strong historical roots, a traditional identity and a set of values and norms which have a considerable impact on the market preferences and mobility of the people in question.

A sociological analysis of the professions could reveal the connections between the institutional and individual factors and practical insight would be gained into the extent that manipulation of the labour force requires a complementary policy of structural transformation. In more concrete terms, this would mean a reconstruction of training programs and a revaluation of professional standards, or even replacement of the occupational ideology by a more realistic view of social reality.

The officers corps stands first among the professions with a historical tradition and a clear identity of its own. However, the military officer and his profession are now without doubt among that part of national manpower which is in need of an institutional analysis.

As an aid to such an approach, this article discusses various aspects of the state and evolution of the military profession. The presentation is restricted to a number of Western countries, the exceptions being used as a means of comparison with tendencies identified in it.

After a short description of the rise of military professionalism, four actual processes of change are discussed:

   (i) the change in professional orientation

   (ii) in skill structure

   (iii) in social composition and

   (iv) in political affiliations.

The concluding chapter is devoted to some of the consequences for manpower policy.

2. THE RISE OF MILITARY PROFESSIONALISM

Despite the universal phenomenon of war, the military *profession* only dates from the nineteenth century.[1] Starting from the Napoleonic wars, officers began to acquire a special technique in warfare and to develop special standards and organizations in the art of collective conflicts.

451

The keynote of professionalization was the emergence of a specialized, full-time occupation; amateurs become rare. As a next step military academies were established and legal protection of the monopoly of skill was obtained. A code of professional ethics rooted in the ethos of the feudal nobility completed the process of professionalization. As a fully-fledged profession, the officer corps is characterized by:

(i) specificity of expertness, based on a body of knowledge and skill and handed on by means of formal training programs;

(ii) a life-long career commitment and a closed community with strong feelings of loyalty;

(iii) free access for all, whereby recruitment, selection and training are carried out in accordance with the standards set by the professional community;

(iv) a formal code of ethics, maintained and controlled by the profession;

(v) political neutrality (or rather passivity) and complete subordination to legal government.

The completion of military professionalization by definition largely depends on the absence of those social and cultural forces which are incompatible with the fundamental characteristics outlined above. The process was begun at various times in the course of history,[2] but by the 19th century three barriers still remained: aristocratic origin, national militias and political revolutions.

The European aristocracy has proved to be the most persistent stumbling-block on the road to professionalism, in spite of a notable exception like nineteenth-century Germany. Resistance to formal specialized training was especially strong.

This statement finds some support in the observation that countries with a predominantly aristocratic establishment, such as pre-revolutionary Russia, Poland and Great Britain, failed to achieve full military professionalization.[3] Property and status, rather than education and experience, were what guaranteed an officer's commission. Where Western-type feudal institutions have never existed, the professional soldier is recruited from middle-class groups, as is the case in the majority of new nations where, no struggle against aristocratic conservatism being necessary, the officer corps developed from the outset into a professional institution.[4]

Another indication of the aristocratic *Bildungsfeindschaft* is the absence of the nobility from the newer " technical " units resulting from the technological revolution. Artillery and engineering units are commanded by bourgeois officers, trained at technological schools; the aristocratic officer was expected to command by virtue of inherited qualities.

A second bar to professionalization has proved to be the existence of *national militias*. The resistance offered to a professional officer corps arises in that case not from the monopolistic claims of a social elite, but from the distrustful attitude of the whole population to the rise of such a monopolist.

The strength of the citizen tradition is especially evident in young democratic nations like Australia and Israel,[5] which combine a strong emphasis on the military virtues with a hostile attitude to the professional soldier and his organization. Much the same picture is to be observed in the early history of other European settlements (Canada, U.S.A.).

Thirdly, professionalization is sometimes hindered by *political revolutions*, which are unable or unwilling to use the military apparatus of the old regime.

On the one hand the new armed forces are built out of heterogeneous elements like disloyal parts of the old regular army, partisan groups and militiamen, e.g. in Soviet Russia, Indonesia, Israel, People's Republic of China. On the other hand there is sometimes a heavy emphasis on political reliability and a tendency towards indoctrination and rigid control by political agents, as in communist states. In cases of this sort the new forces often lack not only a sufficient degree of functional integration, but also professional expertness, having been selected on political rather than on training criteria.[6] Nevertheless, professionalism is characteristic of the military establishment in most countries. Over a period of barely two decades, that establishment has been

confronted with a number of radical changes in its technology, organization, social
composition and political relations which may be called the second military revolution.[7]
The impact on the military profession is the subject of the next part of this article.

3. CHANGES IN PROFESSIONAL ORIENTATION

If we accept Lasswell's definition of the peculiar skill and distinct sphere of
officership as the management and application of violence,[8] we shall have to begin by
considering changes in the pattern of violence.

Since 1945 this pattern has moved from a situation of peace, interrupted from time
to time by interstate wars, toward a situation combining a cold war between the great
powers with frequent insurrectionary violence and domestic wars in the non-Western world.
Though intergovernmental war – the conventional type of armed conflict – has become
exceptional (Korea, Israel), the armed forces have never before so obviously dominated
the political scene. Many countries exist in what one might term a state of continuous
semi-mobilization.[9]

This is true of the major powers and some of their allies. Even more so of the
Western countries which were involved for a long period in the painful process of
decolonization. The burden borne by the British and Dutch forces in this respect was a
fairly light one in comparison with that of the French, who had to fight long "dirty
wars" in Indochina and Algeria. Moreover, for years guerrilla warfare has dominated the
domestic scene in many countries from Cuba to Greece, and from Cyprus and the Congo to China.

The Cold War and the internal struggles in many countries have completely blurred
the traditional difference between war and peace. The protracted politics of deterrence,
the colonial wars of independence and other prolonged conflicts, as in Vietnam, have led
to the emergence of a new type of violence, one balanced between total involvement of
the population and peaceful coexistence between the nations. The conflict situation is
permanent and supported by military means, but the conflicts remain restricted in scope.

It is primarily this new state of affairs that has changed the politico-military
doctrines. On the one hand the strategy of massive atomic deterrence has come into being,
while on the other a fusion of military and ideological goals and techniques has been
developed, the French doctrine of "la guerre révolutionnaire" being the most remarkable
specimen of the latter.

The technological revolution and its consequences for strategic thinking have
evidently shaped the professional orientation of the military. Both the leading powers,
the USA and the USSR, have markedly stressed the development from conventional to atomic
warfare and, as a consequence of this, the evolution from traditional military thought
to a technocratic and managerial philosophy.[10]

Though the second trend has received less emphasis, guerrilla warfare in connection
with revolutionary war has been equally characteristic of the international scene during
the last twenty-five years, and has reached its dramatic culmination in Vietnam. It is
not by accident that French publications especially devote attention to this aspect of
today's widespread violence, a fact which can be explained by the military history of
France since 1945. In the articles and books concerned, the impressive reality of the
thermonuclear weapons and their dynamic impact on politics and strategy is fully
accepted, but the frequency and scope of revolutionary warfare are considered to be an
equally important challenge to the military.[11]

If a government is called upon to take the initiative in both fields, it is faced
with the difficult task of weighing priorities, as happened in France between 1945 and
1962 and in Holland from 1945-1949. This is also the case in the United States,
especially since the escalation in Vietnam. In Britain, it has been so since World
War II.[12] The enforced choice, however, causes a dilemma not only in politics and
strategy, but also in the role orientation of the professional military.

In the past the officer was a "generalist", skilled as a commander of combat units.
But this standard professional type does not seem to be the most effective one in coping
with either the atomic age or guerrilla warfare. He lacks both the special skills of the

military technician and manager, and, sometimes, the "fighter" attitude and style of the "para". Confronted with the necessity to make a choice between these extreme models of the technician and the "hero", the careerist is more likely to be attracted to the former. Technocracy and scientific management have proved to be, as is indeed the case in society as a whole, the mainstream in motivation and opportunity. A new elite or would-be elite is rising in the military establishment, the technocrats of the new weapon systems supplanting the commanders of armed men.

Yet the ideal of the "heroic leader" still persists as an attractive military self-image. To mention some research conclusions: the professional orientation of cadets both in the United States and France reflects the coexistence of the technician and the warrior-role.[13] This means, however, that the traditional uniformity of the population of the great military academies has disappeared.

This cleavage is, in a way, an adequate answer to the changed pattern of violence in the world of today. It indicates the ambiguous status of the traditional officer and the need for mental and technical specialization in accordance with the most prevalent forms of violence and warfare. The main problem is how to find a new orientation for the military of the future, since the standard model seems to be outmoded and the emerging role orientations are incompatible.

4. CHANGES IN SKILL STRUCTURE

In consequence of the changes in warfare and of the growth of the armed forces as such, the military apparatus has undergone a radical transformation.

First, there is the transition from military professionalism to professional management. The increased complexity of the task structure and the multiplication of the channels of communication have resulted in a call for managerial expertise at all hierarchical levels. The managerial orientation can primarily be observed in the field of logistics, from which it has spread to permeate the entire military establishment.[14]

The tendency has been strengthened by the introduction of highly sophisticated weapons systems, which require complicated control devices and a heavy load of maintenance work.[15] The air force is far ahead here, but the navy and army are gradually adopting a similar type of technocracy.

Both trends are stimulating an increasing input of scientific knowledge and specialized technical skill into the armed forces. The traditional resistance to change has turned into a continuous search for technological innovation. In some parts of the organization the process of change as such has become routinized by institutionalization.

The whole development has produced a marked shift in the skill structure, the most conspicuous part of which is the steady increase of the ratio of technologists and technicians at the different hierarchical levels and especially in the middle ranks.[16] As a result, the majority of the tasks in army, navy and air force are nowadays only indirectly related to combat. Nor is it only a question of changed quantities: the status and influence of the engineer in the armed forces have also grown rapidly. The technical specialist, in former times with a marginal role and low status, has penetrated the key positions in the military establishment.

This is to be seen most clearly in the highly "technical" air force, where the special knowledge of the staff officer is making itself evident at even the lower levels of command, since the commander cannot himself master all the skills required to make sound decisions.[17]

Despite the lower status of the engineer in the informal status hierarchy, the official policy in some countries makes the highest military appointments accessible to technical officers. Up till now the facts have been somewhat different, although the opportunities for officers in support and technical activities are no longer poor and are gradually becoming better.[18]

A negative consequence, however, is the danger of "civilianization" of the military establishment. The technicians are less willing to identify themselves with soldiers and to be treated as such, while at the same time the internal cohesion of the profession is affected by the orientation of the specialists to the outside world. The technical skills are much more transferable than the purely military capacities and many of the specifically trained technicians can anticipate extremely well-paid jobs.[19] In the American forces military service is even becoming more and more the first phase in a two-phase career in which the officer leaves military service for civilian employment.[20]

This tendency, together with the " civilianization" of the armed forces, constitutes a direct attack on the hard core of the professional concept. The homogeneity of the profession and the life-time commitment are seriously endangered and even the institutional identity is facing the most serious challenge in military history.

The dilemma is generally recognized.[21] As Janowitz stated, an engineering philosophy cannot suffice as the organizational basis of the armed forces, but neither does the martial spirit of the traditional profession seem to be adequate if the military establishment is intended to prevent hostilities.[22]

5. CHANGES IN SOCIAL COMPOSITION

In most of the Western countries the social basis of recruitment of military leaders has broadened immensely since the turn of the century. Social research has provided us with a mass of material on this transformation, making it sufficiently clear that the military profession has developed from an elitist vocation into a middle-class occupation – except in countries like Ireland and Australia, where the military was never considered to be an elite.[23]

The causes of this "democratization" are not the same in all countries. The gradual displacement of the aristocracy from public life, the quantitative expansion of the armed forces and the increasing demand for technical knowledge are universal factors. In addition, major wars and revolutions have very much accelerated the process and in some cases have even abruptly up-ended the social pyramid. The highly elitist character of the Polish officer corps of the thirties changed in the fifties into a corps with half of its members drawn from the industrial working class and one third from the land. The *Volksarmee* of the German Democratic Republic – heir of the aristocracy-centred Prussian army – recruits 80% of its officers from the class of workers and office employees.[24]

Sometimes the old elite is found concentrated in elite regiments and services. The traditional controversy between nobles and commoners has resolved itself into a difference between the commanding officers and the technical and support officers, the former having been educated in the great academies and the latter having a mixture of academy and non-academy, regular and reserve backgrounds.[25] The widespread pattern of self-recruitment in the officer corps is probably connected with the hard core of the profession, being most typical of the older " generalist " services and of the old academies.[26]

The broader recruitment basis means first of all a change in the relations between the armed forces and society. The officer corps is becoming more socially representative, since it reflects to a much greater extent the social stratification of society. The officer is no longer the armed part of the social elite, but the functional elite of the armed forces.

In addition, a stream of new values and norms is penetrating the military establishment. The officer of middle-, or lower-class origin is inclined to consider his job as a career, as a channel for upward social mobility. His appreciation of the military profession is not automatically derived from his class, but is part of his personal opportunity to earn a living and to climb the social ladder. Consequently, his identification with the profession is weakened.

Another factor influencing the professional attachment is the increased heterogeneity of the officers' social backgrounds. The cohesion of the traditional officer corps used to be a double one: functional integration and social-cultural consensus. Now that cohesion has to be maintained by functional and instrumental relations only, professional socialization has assumed the heavy task of creating both an institutional and a social identity.

Numerous new ties with the social environment have finally emerged. They imply a change in the self-image and the self-esteem of the military. As long as the military establishment was small and isolated, self-esteem was judged by internal criteria. Today's more frequent contacts and the broader recruitment basis make the military more sensitive to public opinion. [27]

An additional complication is found in the shift in military authority, which is changing from the rigid enforcement of discipline to the manipulation of groups and the stimulation of personal initiative. The old officer corps was able to apply techniques of social control derived from its social class to military situations. The officer of today, with his different background and having to measure up to quite different expectations on the part of the rank-and-file, can base his authority only on personal achievement and procedures based on formal training.

6. CHANGES IN POLITICAL AFFILIATIONS

Political neutrality is an essential element of military professionalism. This does not mean a lack of interest in public affairs, but an acknowledgement of civilian supremacy in politics and of the existence of the dominant political system, without explicit preferences for special doctrines or parties.

Nevertheless, the traditional officer corps can be described as conservative rather than liberal, not only in the United States, but also in a socialist country like Sweden. [28] In France, the typical officer attitude toward politics since the nineteenth century shows a pervasive distrust of republicanism and even of parliamentary government as such, without relinquishing the role of *la grande muette*. [29]

In recent times, however, the military has been developing a more explicit political ethos. The changed pattern of war – both the Cold War and the counter-guerrilla wars – have strong ideological correlates, causing the military to be more conscious and critical of political affairs.

Generally speaking, this trend relates primarily to top service personnel. Through the arms race and the policy of arms control the inter-connections between political and military leaders have become both permanent and much more highly intensified. The military establishment may be considered a part of the politico-military establishment.

The challenge of the totalitarian systems has also helped to promote a political consciousness among officers of all echelons. If a direct confrontation ensues – the USA in Korea, France in Indochina and Algeria – there is a tendency to adopt the dogmatism of the enemy. [30]

Another cause of political involvement is participation in permanent military alliances like NATO. The integration of national forces in a coalition requires the development of a common political outlook related to a common strategy.

Up till now the profession seems to have been able to withstand full political involvement. A recent exception – France in 1958 and 1961 – does not prove the opposite. The French army crisis of the forties and fifties only demonstrates that even in a modern state with a long tradition of military loyalty, professionalism alone is inadequate to ensure civilian control under exceptional circumstances.

Elsewhere, even in communist countries, the military establishment is not fully politicized. The gradual increase in party-membership among the officers in new communist states [31] is counterbalanced by the growth of critical attitudes among the younger generation of Soviet officers. It proves the possibility of reprofessionalization even after half a century of intensive indoctrination. [32]

Yet the balance between political consciousness and commitment, and between political information and indoctrination, is not easy to formulate. Even if one agrees with the results of social science, showing that military motivation and morale are not primarily dependent on ideological conviction, one may ask whether it is not necessary to create more stable and purposeful civil-military relations.

7. PROFESSIONAL CHANGE AND MANPOWER POLICY

Summarizing the results of the analysis, the process of professional change may be regarded as a process of growing differentiation and heterogeneity, as diversified orientation along the lines of different and often ambiguous institutional goals; specialization of skills; heterogeneous basis of recruitment; more explicit political orientation.

In the wake of these structural changes the progressive penetration of the outside world has modified the civilian-military relations. The military establishment is no longer an isolated community but part of the social network.

The increasing similarity between this pattern and that of other institutions in our society cannot be denied. The problems of the military are tending more and more to become the already classic problems of management and professionalism in modern society.

An effective manpower policy is one of these problems. Applying a somewhat modified definition from the field of industrial management,[33] one may accept the proposition that the capacity of a nation to shape an effective defence policy is dependent upon its ability to find, develop, commit and motivate the high-level human resources required by modern armed forces. In industrialized countries these human resources are available, but their recruitment and commitment demand, as we have seen, high costs, both in psychological and institutional terms.

The *recruitment policy* is confronted with a change from " promotion from within " to demands for manpower straight from the labour market. There is a change from non-monetary to monetary incentives, and a transfer of selection from the traditional milieu to the competitive schoolroom.

The *promotion policy* shows a tendency to prefer technical knowledge and skill to military rank and status and specialization instead of seniority. There is, in addition, the innovation of shorter military careers in the regular forces, sometimes in favour of a second career in civilian life.

Training programs are becoming more and more specialized, often requiring additional graduate training at civilian centres. The distance between technological and managerial knowledge and the commander's training is increasing. The military academies and civilian institutions of higher learning are becoming more similar in their curricula and value patterns.[34]

The *professional socialization* reflects the inherent ambivalence of the modern military establishment. The old uniform self-concept of the soldier has not been transformed into a new formula, but has become diffuse and ambiguous.

All these tendencies are in a way incompatible with the identity and homogeneity of the traditional military profession and with the process of professionalization. In conclusion, and very briefly a few possible implications will be listed, without discussion of their numerous positive and negative aspects.

(i) The first way out may be the full acceptance of the division between the orientations and skills of the technical-managerial complex and of the combat-commander complex. This solution – if it is a solution at all – provides for a fully separate recruitment policy, selection, training and career planning for both categories and would result in a " two cultures " structure of the military institution. The traditional commander model would have to make way for the elitist model of the " para " or marine-corps.

(ii) The second formula goes one step further by " civilianizing " most of the technical, administrative and other support personnel. The short-service officers with a second career and the reservists could perhaps provide a sort of intermediate formula between this and the first one.

(iii) Quite the opposite remedy would be to re-establish the broken institutional unity either by general military training as the professional basis followed by specialized education or, conversely, more scientific training for members of all services.[35]

The choice between these alternatives – and of the many solutions in between – will depend on many circumstances and first of all on the international role of the nation. The retreat of the former colonial empires from their colonial bases – Great Britain, France, the Netherlands, Belgium on the one hand – and the emergence of a world-wide *Pax Americana* on the other hand, seem to be moves in opposite directions.

REFERENCES

1. Huntington, S.P. *The Soldier and the State. The theory and politics of civil-military relations*. Cambridge, Mass.: Harvard University Press, 1957, 19 ff.
2. Van Doorn, J. " The Officer Corps: a fusion of profession and organization ", in *Archives Européennes de Sociologie*, VI, 1965, 268 f.
3. Garthoff, R.L. " The Military in Russia, 1861-1965 ". *Paper* presented to the Sixth World Congress of Sociology, Evian, Sept., 1966, 4 ff.; Wiatr, J.J.. " Military Professionalism and Transformations of Class Structure in Poland ". *Paper* presented to the Sixth World Congress of Sociology, Evian, Sept., 1966, 4, 7; For the " amateur conception " of British officership see Abrams, Ph. " The Late Profession of Arms: ambiguous goals and deteriorating means in Britain ", in: *Archives Européennes de Sociologie*, VI, 1965, 242 ff.
4. Janowitz, M. *The Military in the Political Development of New Nations*. Chicago and London: University of Chicago Press, 1964, 49-57.
5. Encel, S. " Militarism and the Citizen Tradition in Australia ". *Paper* presented to the Sixth World Congress of Sociology, Evian, Sept., 1966; Halpern, B. " The Role of the Military in Israel ", in J.J. Johnson (Ed.), *The Role of the Military in Underdeveloped Countries*. Princeton, N.J.: Princeton University Press, 1962, 246 ff.
6. In 1956 only 0.2% of all officers in the German Democratic Republic had attended a military college. In 1965, 77% of all regimental and divisional commanders had completed a degree course. Stuber, E. and K.H. Schulze, " The Problem of Militarism and the Armies of the Two German States ". *Paper* presented to the Sixth World Congress of Sociology, Evian, Sept., 1966, 33.
7. The first military revolution took place around 1600. See Roberts, M. *The Military Revolution 1560-1660* Inaugural Lecture, Queen's University of Belfast, 1956.
8. Quoted by Huntington, *op. cit.*, 11.
9. Huntington, S.P. " Patterns of Violence in World Politics ", in S.P. Huntington (Ed.) *Changing Patterns of Military Politics*. New York: The Free Press of Glencoe, 1962, 17 ff; Girardet, R. " Problèmes moraux et idéologiques ", in R. Girardet (Ed.), *La crise militaire francaise 1945-1962*. Paris: Armand Colin, 1964, 221 ff.
10. Several chapters in Janowitz, M. (Ed.) *The New Military: changing patterns of organization*. New York: Russell Sage Foundation, 1964; As regards Russia see Kolkowicz, R. " The Impact of Modern Technology on the Soviet Officer Corps ". *Paper* presented to the Sixth World Congress of Sociology, Evian, Sept., 1966.
11. Girardet, *op. cit.* 224.
12. Abrams, *op. cit.*, 258 ff.
13. Lovell, J.P. " The Professional Socialization of the West Point Cadet ", in M. Janowitz (Ed.), *The New Military: changing patterns of organization*. New York: Russell Sage Foundation, 1964, 122 ff.; " Attitudes et motivation des candidats aux grandes écoles militaires ", in *Revue Francaise de Sociologie*, II, 1961, 149 ff.
14. Eccles, H.E. *Military Concepts and Philosophy*. New Brunswick, N.J.: Rutgers University Press, 1965, 67 ff.
15. It is estimated that the American Air Force averaged 51.2 maintenance hours for each hour of flying time of the B-47 bomber. This increased to 115.6 hours for the B-52, and was judged to be even higher for the B-58 in 1959. Cf. Lang, K. " Technology and Career Management in the Military Establishment ", in M. Janowitz (Ed.), *The New Military: changing patterns of organization*. New York: Russell Sage Foundation, 1964, 42.
16. Lang, *op. cit.*, 67 ff.
17. Lang, K. " Military Organizations ", in J.C. March (Ed.), *Handbook of Organizations*, Chicago: Rand McNally, 1965, 853.
18. Abrams, *op. cit.*, 248 ff.: Kolkowicz, *op. cit.*, 5 ff., 16; Van Riper, P.P. and D.B. Unwalla " Military Careers at the Executive Level ", in *Administrative Science Quarterly*, IX, 1965, 435.
19. Biderman, A.D. " Sequels to a Military Career: the retired military professional ", in M. Janowitz (Ed.), *The New Military: changing patterns of organization*. New York: Russell Sage Foundation, 1964, 316 f., 330 ff.; Harries-Jenkins, G. *Paper* presented to the Working Group on Armed Forces and Society, International Sociological Association, London, 1967, 10 ff.

20. Biderman, *op. cit.*, 295 ff. In Britain the second career of the top-level military man in a comparable civilian job is based much more on the use of social relations. Abrams, Ph. "Democracy, Technology, and the Retired British Officer", in S.P. Huntington (Ed.), *Changing Patterns of Military Politics*. New York: The Free Press of Glencoe, 1962, 183 ff.
21. Janowitz, M. *The Professional Soldier*. Illinois: The Free Press of Glencoe, 1960, 33-36; Abrams, "Late Profession of Arms", *op. cit.*, 249 ff.; Planchais, J. "Crise de modernisme dans l'armée", in *Revue Francaise de Sociologie*, II, 1961, 118 ff.: Kolkowicz, *op. cit.*, 4 ff.: "A conflict between traditionalism and modernity".
22. Janowitz, *Professional Soldier*, op. cit., 34 f.
23. USA: Janowitz, *Professional Soldier, op. cit.*, 89-97; Britain: Abrams, *Retired Officer, op. cit.*, 178 ff.: Otley, C.B. "Militarism and the Social Affiliations of the British Army Elite". *Paper* presented to the Sixth World Congress of Sociology, Evian, Sept., 1966; France: Girardet, R. and J.-P.H. Thomas, "Problèmes de recrutement", in R. Girardet (Ed.) *La crise militaire francaise 1945-1962*. Paris: Armand Colin, 1964, 38 ff.; The Netherlands: Van Doorn, *op. cit.*, 275-279; Germany: Demeter, K. *Das Deutsche Offizierkorps in Gesellschaft und Staat 1650-1945*. Frankfurt am Main: Bernard & Graefe, 1962, 22 ff; Norway: Kjellberg, F. "Some Cultural Aspects of the Military Profession", in *Archives Européennes de Sociologie*, VI, 1965, 283 f.; Sweden: Abrahamsson, B. "The Ideology of an Elite: conservatism and national insecurity", *Paper* presented to the Sixth World Congress of Sociology, Evian, Sept. 1966, 10 f.; Italy: Janowitz, *Professional Soldier*, op. cit., 94; Spain: Bragulet, J. Busquets. "Social Origin of the Spanish Army Officer". *Paper* presented to the Sixth World Congress of Sociology, Evian, Sept., 1966; Ireland: Jackson, J.A. "The Irish Army and the Development of the Constabulary Concept". *Paper* presented to the Sixth World Congress of Sociology, Evian, Sept., 1966; Australia: Encel, *op. cit.*, 21 ff.
24. Wiatr, *op. cit.*, 9; Stuber and Schulze, *op. cit.*, 30 ff.
25. Van Riper and Unwalla, *op. cit.*, 435; Abrams, Retired Officer, *op. cit.*, 155 ff.
26. Otley, *op. cit.*, 14 ff.; Girardet and Thomas, *op. cit.*, 38 ff.; Demeter, *op. cit.*, 20 ff., 53.
27. Janowitz, *Professional Soldier*, op. cit., 225 ff.
28. Janowitz, *Professional Soldier*, op. cit., 236 ff.; Abrahamsson, *op. cit.*, 7 ff.
29. Ambler, J.S. *The French Army in Politics 1945-1962*. Ohio State University Press, 1966, 24 ff.
30. Janowitz, *Professional Soldier*, op. cit., 411 ff.; Ambler, *op. cit.*, 308 ff.; Girardet, *op. cit.*, 157 ff.
31. Stuber and Schulze, *op. cit.*, 30 ff.; Wiatr, *op. cit.*, 13.
32. Kolkowicz, *op. cit.*, 7 ff., 18.
33. Harbison, F. and Ch.A. Myers. *Management in the Industrial World: an international analysis*. New York, Toronto, London: McGraw-Hill, 1959, 87.
34. Lovell, *op. cit.*, 142; Van Doorn, *op. cit.*, 280 f.
35. Harries-Jenkins, *op. cit.*, 18 f.; Ginsburgh, R.N. "The Challenge to Military Professionalism", in *Foreign Affairs*, XLII, 1964, 265.

Organisation for Change

A.B. CHERNS

LOUGHBOROUGH UNIVERSITY OF TECHNOLOGY

This is a wide enough title and the gloss that was put upon it for me is wider still. I was asked to discuss how flexibility may be built into service structure so that the Services are in a position to respond to present and future technological changes and what the effect must be on communications, upon weapon systems and other operational structures, upon trade groupings and other occupational structures and upon the system of hierarchical ranking and other authority structures. In considering a field as wide as this, I can do little more than pose a few problems against the background in an attempt to identify the factors affecting the choice of organization open to the Services.

DEFINITIONS

Some of the most useful insights into the operation of organizations have come from viewing them as open sociotechnical systems. These and associated terms need defining, if they are to be operationally useful and I am taking my first from a recent paper by Charles Perrow[1]:

" Organizations are seen primarily as systems for getting work done, for applying techniques to the problem of altering raw materials – whether the materials be people, symbols or things. This is in contrast to other perspectives which see organizations as, for example, co-operative systems, institutions, or decision-making systems ".

" ..... this perspective treats *technology* as an *independent* variable, and *structure* – the arrangements among people for getting work done – as a dependent variable ", and

" By technology is meant the action that an individual performs upon an object, with or without the aid of tools or mechanical devices, in order to make some change in that object. The object or 'raw material' may be a living being, human or otherwise, a symbol of an inanimate object. People are raw materials in people-changing or people-processing organizations; symbols are materials in banks, advertising agencies and some research organizations; the interactions of people are raw materials to be manipulated by administrators in organizations .... "

" In the course of changing this material in an organisational setting, the individual must interact with others. The form that this interaction takes we will call the structure of the organization. It involves the arrangements or relationships that permit the co-ordination and control of work. Some work is actually concerned with changing or maintaining the structure of an organization. Most administrators have this as a key role and there is a variety of technologies for it ".

For the remaining definitions I need, I am turning to a less recent paper on socio-technical systems by Emery and Trist[2] in which they define the primary task of an

---

[1]   Charles Perrow, " A Framework for the Comparative Analysis of Organizations " American Sociological Review, 1967: pp. 194-208.
[2]   F.E. Emery & E.L. Trist, " Socio-Technical Systems ", Management Sciences, Models and Techniques, Vol. 2, Pergamon Press, London, 1960.

organization as its strategic objective or overriding mission; for example, to place
the enterprise in a position in its environment where it has some assured conditions
for growth. They go on to point out that,

" the enterprise is in constant communication with its environment and that this
may vary with (a) the productive efforts of the enterprise in meeting environmental
requirements; (b) changes in the environment that may be induced by the enterprise
and (c) changes independently taking place in the environment. Managerial control
will usually be greatest if the primary task can be based on productive activity.
If this is not possible as in commerce, the primary task will give more control if
it is based on marketing, than simply foreknowledge of the independent and environmental changes ".

THE INTERNAL AND EXTERNAL ENVIRONMENT

This extra control that the enterprise obtains through manipulating rather than
simply responding to the environment is, of course, one of the factors influencing the
military's preference for pre-emptive strikes.

Arising from the fact that any enterprise is an open system, management is concerned
with managing both an internal system and an external environment. In peace time the
management of the external environment becomes, for Services, both difficult and
delicate, exposing the people in these " boundary roles " to grave suspicion, both from
within and without the organization. But the main impact of attention from the managers
falls upon the maintenance of and control of the internal environment and the attempt
to maintain internal equilibrium. For this to be done effectively the technology of
control is concerned with the avoidance of exceptional and unprogrammed situations and,
traditionally, flexibility of a kind is obtained by acquiring a large number of interchangeable parts, rather than a large variety of programmes. In order to make the
" parts ", i.e., the Service men, interchangeable, they have to be de-individualized:
the technology becomes the technology of internal control.

ORGANIZATIONAL CHOICE

Does this give the Services a choice of organizational structures? As I have said,
the maximum control of internal environment is obtained when the parts are de-
individualized and interchangeable and the decision-making procedures specified. Such
control can be provided by a hierarchical structure of almost arbitrary shape with high
role specificity and low task definition, i.e., the powers and responsibilities of each
management position are laid down, but the task content is low. This enables a position
to be filled by virtually anyone of the appropriate rank. The shape is arbitrary because
the number of levels of authority is set by the book of rules for the exercise of
authority, rather than by the emergent levels of responsibility deriving from the
demands of the technology. Now, if your book of rules allocates certain types of
decisions to certain hierarchical levels, it follows that if all these decisions are to
be taken – and taken in the specified way – you must provide that number of authority
levels, virtually independent of the size of the organization and its other characteristics. This explains something which has puzzled me for a very long time. I could see
that the ranks, in say the Royal Air Force, were one-to-one transformations from Army
ranks and that the Army ranks had remained unchanged since they emerged from their
origins[1] through the technological requirements of warfare in the seventeenth and
eighteenth centuries. I could see also why there would be resistance to changing them,

[1] The basic rank structure of the Army originated with the requirement to maintain effective
internal equilibrium. The men provided their own equipment and basic skills and the primary
need was to keep them in order. The organization required for this was virtually independent of
the demands of the task to which the unit would be put.

but I could not understand how they had been successful in resisting the scrutiny of suspicious-minded establishment review teams.

Now what influence has all this on flexibility? An organization of the kind we have described confers considerable flexibility in the choice of primary task, providing it is of comparable technology. Thus a well-trained Army unit can guard a camp, garrison a town, repair roads (using simple technology), replace striking dock-workers, (again using simple technology), among other functions, but a change in technology becomes very hard to achieve. As soon as military units approach an operating role exercising a distinctive technology, the inappropriateness of the organizational structure becomes clear. Observation shows that whenever operational tasks become uppermost, the organization behaves much more like the organismic structure of Burns and Stalker[1], than the mechanistic picture I have just described and " task forces " of highly unorthodox structures take their place.

FLEXIBILITY

What kind of flexibility are we looking for? In the armed services a unit may be faced with three kinds of change:

(i) a change of task[2];

(ii) a change of technology, i.e., undertaking the same task using different procedures, or

(iii) a change in manpower, i.e., undertaking the same task but with different categories of people.

In this case there will almost inevitably be a consequent change in procedure, i.e., in the technology.

However, it would seem that the Services which cover a very wide range of technologies, would require different kinds of organizational structures – some flat, some tall. But the book of rules provides a stumbling block concerning the kind of decision that can be taken by people in different ranks and the identification of rank with organizational role. Examples of the inappropriateness of the authority structures of some service units are not hard to find. In a youth school, whose size justified its command by an Air Commodore, every rank below his was established to correspond with some sub-unit organization. Thus levels of authority existed without any reference to the actual number of levels of responsibility that could be discerned. In such a situation the struggle for something to do between officers of successive rank levels is pitiful to observe. In this situation it is only if an officer in one of these levels, preferably a high one, is sufficiently detached to be able to sit back and leave things to his subordinates, does anything resembling a true match of authority and responsibility emerge at the lower levels.

This gives rise to the question: Can we devise a system which would enable us to adopt a rational structure of a more flexible nature which is consistent with the career expectations of officers and men? This is bound to be very difficult. Any organizational structure is not only a channel of communication and decision making, it is also a power system and a career ladder. Every change is bound to be weighed by the people concerned in terms of its effects on their careers and their positions. Since career expectations are set by the existing structure, any change is bound to upset these expectations. So no-one advocating organizational changes of this kind need anticipate a quiet life.

---

[1] T. Burns & G.H. Stalker, " The Management of Innovation ", Tavistock, 1961.

[2] Each new task involves new role relationships with associated stresses on those already existing. The classic response to these stresses is the attempt to encapsulate the role relationships into the particular situation where they are appropriate. This is summed up in the recipe, " On parade, on parade: off parade, off parade ". The snag is that the rank relationships which embody all the formal sanctions are congruent only with the most formal and least task related situations.

Compared with other organizations, then, service units have considerable task
flexibility with the associated problems for organizational structure. They are also like
other organizations faced with the demands set by changing technology. This offers a
special set of opportunities for organizational change. Not only does a change in technology generally need to be accompanied by such change; it also makes other changes
possible. We all know that the way to get our own pet change adopted is to tack it on to
a more far-reaching one. The compensatory snag is that if we initiate a change we must
expect that what actually happens will be not what we originally conceived, but our
concept modified by the favourite reforms of everyone else through whose hands and minds
the change has to pass.

The fact that changes in task and changes in technology are in fact quite frequent
makes rigid manpower specifications not only impossible but also short-sighted.

OCCUPATIONAL CLASSIFICATION

I was involved, nearly 20 years ago, in assisting in the development of the system
of trade groups adopted during the post-war period of universal conscription in the
Royal Air Force and, like my colleagues, I could not help but be aware of the arbitrary
elements in our operation. In order to make clear distinctions, particularly for selection and classification, we were obliged to exaggerate the differences between the
various types of fitters and mechanics – electrical, mechanical, instruments, radar and
so on. If an instrument fitter could be regarded, as a result of his training in
instrument work, as equipped to service any kind of instrument he might meet in practice
to the Service, you have considerable flexibility of a kind, based on the interchangeability of people of a generic label.

New and more complex equipment, cutting across the traditional divisions meant that
you had to call on a number of people in order to service a single piece of equipment and
led to the adoption of a new system cutting across the old; a system of equipment, rather
than subject, specialities. However, this produced people who are far too task specific
and who could not be cross posted in nearly so free a way. It became necessary then to
try to replace the lost flexibility by increasing the number of equipments on which they
were trained, i.e., by building in to the individual a range of programmes. This
illustrates on a micro scale the problem I was trying to describe on a macro scale, of
the organization of a unit. Whenever you introduce one kind of flexibility by specialization you tend to become rigid in another dimension. In the case of the unit you can
go for task flexibility and flexibility of technology; the penalty you pay is a rigidity
of organizational structure.